PEARSON CUSTOM PUBLISHING

SAM Core Reading
VOLUME ONE

Compiled from:

Business: A Practical Introduction
Brian K. Williams, Stacey C. Sawyer and Susan Berston

Marketing: An Introduction
Gary Armstrong, Philip Kotler, Michael Harker and Ross Brennan

Essentials of Operations Management
Nigel Slack, Alistair Brandon-Jones and Robert Johnston

Accounting and Finance for Non-Specialists
Peter Atrill and Eddie McLaney

E-Business and E-Commerce Management:
Strategy, Implementation and Practice
Dave Chaffey

PEARSON

Harlow, England • London • New York • Boston • San Francisco • Toronto • Sydney • Auckland • Singapore • Hong Kong
Tokyo • Seoul • Taipei • New Delhi • Cape Town • Sao Paulo • Mexico City • Madrid • Amsterdam • Munich • Paris • Milan

Pearson Education Limited
Edinburgh Gate
Harlow
Essex CM20 2JE

And associated companies throughout the world

Visit us on the World Wide Web at:
www.pearsoned.co.uk

This Custom Book Edition © Pearson Education Limited 2013

Compiled from:

Business: A Practical Introduction
Brian K. Williams, Stacey C. Sawyer and Susan Berston
ISBN 978 0 13 233429 7
© 2013 by Pearson Education, Inc., Prentice Hall

Marketing: An Introduction
Gary Armstrong, Philip Kotler, Michael Harker and Ross Brennan
ISBN 978 0 273 71395 1
© Pearson Education Limited 2009

Essentials of Operations Management
Nigel Slack, Alistair Brandon-Jones and Robert Johnston
ISBN 978 0 273 75242 4
© Nigel Slack, Alistair Brandon-Jones and Robert Johnston 2011

Accounting and Finance for Non-Specialists
Peter Atrill and Eddie McLaney
ISBN 978 0 273 74588 4
© Prentice Hall Europe 1995
© Pearson Education Limited 2001, 2011

E-Business and E-Commerce Management: Strategy, Implementation and Practice
Dave Chaffey
ISBN 978 0 273 75201 1
© Dave Chaffey 2002
© Marketing Insights Limited 2002, 2009, 2011

ISBN 978 1 78236 588 4

Printed and bound in Great Britain by CPI.

SAM Core Reading

VOLUME ONE

Modules 113SAM & 115SAM
Strategy & Applied Management Department
Coventry Business School

Coventry
University

Contents

Integrated Business Practice 113SAM
Integrated Business Management 115SAM
Compiled by Brenda Mae Hollyoak

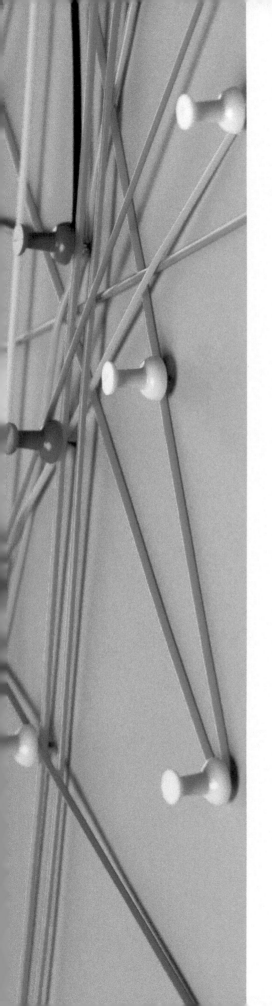

Integrated Business Practice 113SAM

Integrated Business Management 115SAM

Compiled by Brenda Mae Hollyoak

Business:
A Practical
Introduction

Brian K. Williams
Stacey C. Sawyer
Susan Berston

2

Ethics & Social Responsibility

Business as a Positive Force

After reading and studying this chapter, you will be able to answer the following essential questions:

MyBizLab

Where you see MyBizLab in this chapter, go to www.mybizlab.com for additional activities on the topic being discussed.

FORECAST: ▶
What's Ahead in This Chapter

This chapter explains the ethical and social responsibilities of businesspeople and how organizations can promote ethical behavior. It also explains the concept of corporate social responsibility, as well as the concepts of blended value and social auditing. Finally, it describes the negative effects of bad business behavior and the benefits to stakeholders of good business behavior.

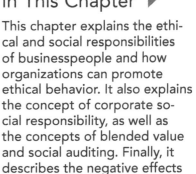

MyBizLab

Gain hands-on experience through an interactive, real-world scenario. This chapter's simulation entitled Navigating Murky Ethical Waters is located at **www.mybizlab.com**.

WINNERS & LOSERS
ETHICAL BEHAVIOR—COURAGE VERSUS CHEATING

WINNER: Doing Right When It's Difficult

What's a true test of moral character? Could you meet it?

After 20 years as a pharmaceutical salesman for Merck & Co., in 1995 Doug Durand joined TAP Pharmaceutical Products in Lake Forest, Illinois, at a salary of $140,000, with the promise of a $50,000 bonus. As a new vice president of sales, Durand was shocked to hear his sales staff in a conference call openly discussing how to bribe urologists (with a 2% "administration fee") for prescribing TAP's prostate cancer drug, Lupron. He also learned that for years TAP reps had encouraged physicians to charge government medical programs (taxpayer funded) full price for Lupron they received free or at a discount, a tactic designed to help establish Lupron as the prostate treatment of choice.

Gradually, Durand learned that TAP, instead of using science to promote its products, relied on kickbacks and freebies—giving big-screen TVs, computers, and golf vacations to cooperating urologists. He also discovered that, though required by federal law, reps could not account for half of their Lupron samples. Terrified he might be scapegoated for the illegalities, he tried applying to other companies that had offered him jobs before TAP but found them already filled.

Eventually, Durand began to secretly document TAP's abuses and finally mailed the evidence to a friend with close ties to an assistant U.S. attorney specializing in medical fraud. The friend urged him to sue TAP for fraud against the government under the federal whistleblower program. (A whistleblower is an employee who reports organizational misconduct to the public.) It wasn't easy for him to do so. "The idea of suing as a whistleblower intimidated me," Durand said. "Nobody likes a whistleblower. I thought it could end my career."

In the end, however, he found himself believing it was the right thing to do.

Eventually he left TAP for AstraMerck and later testified against his former employees and colleagues. The result: The government went after TAP and fined it heavily.[1]

LOSER: Taking Credit Where None Is Deserved

Is lying acceptable? If so, how much is allowable before it reflects poorly on your character?

William H. Swanson, chief executive officer of Raytheon, a military contractor, became known as a management sage for his *Swanson's Unwritten Rules of Management,* a folksy collection of 33 rules of business survival. Examples:

#1. *Learn to say "I don't know." If used when appropriate, it will be used often.*

#2. *Never be afraid to try something new. Remember, an amateur built an ark that survived a flood while a large group of professionals built the Titanic!*

Raytheon promoted the book on the company's website and gave away more than 300,000 copies. The magazine *Business 2.0* featured the book on its cover, and *USA Today* did a story about it.

Then came an e-mail from a San Diego chemical engineer named Carl Durrenberger, who pointed out that "nearly all of these 'unwritten rules' have indeed been written—by another author in fact, 60 years ago. Mr. Swanson has plagiarized from the little-known [1944] book *The Unwritten Laws of Engineering* by W. J. King."

It was also revealed that Swanson had pirated rules 1 through 4 from a collection known as "Rumsfeld's Rules" by U.S. Secretary of Defense Donald Rumsfeld, which were published in the *Wall Street Journal* in 2001. Rule 32, drawing a life lesson about rude treatment of waiters, was similar to something written by humor columnist Dave Barry.

Ultimately, Swanson had to issue statements of regret and apology. "I did not properly check source material," he said. "I apologize to those whose material I wish I had treated with greater care."[2]

For his failure to give credit for plagiarized material, the Raytheon directors took away almost $1 million in Swanson's 2006 compensation. The punishment might have been harsher had the board not decided that the ethical breach was "unintentional and not negligent. It was just poor judgment."[3]

YOUR CALL The problem of plagiarism—presenting others' work as your own—clearly isn't limited to college students writing term papers (for which they can be flunked). What would you have done in Swanson's case? Do you think the punishment fit the crime? What signals does Swanson's behavior send to Raytheon's stakeholders? Could you do the right but difficult thing that Durand did? Would it affect your opinion to know that Durand received a $77 million reward under the federal whistleblower statute? Still, you should know that when he made the decision to report TAP's behavior he was not aware that he could benefit so well financially.

MyBizLab

2.1 The Ethical & Social Responsibilities of Businesspeople: The Way You Live Matters

THE BIG IDEA: This section describes the global corporate social responsibility pyramid, which suggests a guide for thinking about moral matters. We also describe values, ethics, laws, and corporate social responsibility. We define ethical dilemmas and discuss the "holier-than-thou" effect.

THE ESSENTIAL QUESTION: What is the order of priorities for a businessperson?

MyBizLab: Check your understanding of these concepts at www.mybizlab.com.

■ **PANEL 2.1 Illegal, unethical, both, or neither?** These categories show how different actions can vary in being legal and ethical.

1. **Both illegal and unethical**
   Embezzlement
   Consumer fraud
   Sexual harassment
   Cash payments to avoid taxes

2. **Legal but unethical**
   Making sleazy, short-lived products
   Canceling company retirement plan
   Avoiding taxes on U.S. revenues using offshore banks

3. **Ethical but illegal**
   Paying more despite union contract limits
   Selling raw milk for human consumption

4. **Both legal and ethical**
   Green businesses
   Consumer-friendly behavior
   Employee fringe benefits
   Community contributions

Hard economic times, such as those of the recent Great Recession, can force people to take desperate measures to find or keep a job or to attract and keep customers. How far would you go to bend the rules—to push the ethical boundaries—if your job was on the line?

Prior to deciding whether a contemplated action is appropriate, suggests Hewlett-Packard's code of business conduct, an employee should pose a simple test: "Before I make a decision, I consider how it would look in a news story."[4] Certainly in the foregoing "Winners & Losers" accounts, Doug Durand looked good in the headlines and William Swanson looked bad.

So, as you contemplate making a questionable move that might make you (or your company) amazingly rich, what kind of imagined televised news images would make you think twice? You in handcuffs and an orange prison jumpsuit? You in court as defendant in an ugly civil lawsuit? You facing shouting reporters who want to know how you feel about depleting the life savings of innocent victims—even though what you did was entirely legal?

Maybe you would be more troubled by the idea of going to jail than of looking sleazy. Not all unethical actions are illegal, after all; there are lots of nuances, as the panel at left makes clear. (*See* ■ *Panel 2.1.*) But it should be your goal to be *both* legal and ethical.

Carroll's Social Responsibility Pyramid: Profit, Law, Ethics, & Citizenship

What's a way of framing my moral priorities?

University of Georgia business-ethics scholar **Archie B. Carroll** provides a guide for thinking about such practical and moral matters. His ***global corporate social responsibility pyramid* suggests the obligations of an organization in the global economy are to make a profit, to obey the law, to be ethical, and to be a good global corporate citizen.** Some people hold that a company's first and only duty is to make a profit. However, Carroll suggests an organization's global responsibilities should have the following priorities, with profit being the most fundamental (base of the pyramid) and corporate citizenship at the top:[5]

- *Make a profit* consistent with expectations for international business. (This is called economic responsibility.)

- *Obey the law of host* countries as well as international law. (This is legal responsibility.)
- *Be ethical in its practices,* taking host-country and global standards into consideration. (This is ethical responsibility.)
- *Be a good global corporate citizen,* as defined by the host country's expectations. (This is philanthropic responsibility.)

These priorities—profit, law, ethics, and citizenship—could apply to the corporation's and its employees' business behavior in its home country as well.

Values, Ethics & Laws, & Corporate Social Responsibility

How should I distinguish among values, ethics, laws, and corporate social responsibility?

We may think we know what *values, ethics, laws,* and *social responsibility* mean, but do we? Let's take a closer look.

Values: Underlying Beliefs That Help Determine Behavior

Underlying ethical and legal systems are *values,* **the relatively permanent and deeply held underlying beliefs and attitudes that help determine people's behavior.** An example of a value is humility—the opposite of overbearing pride (hubris)—as in St. Paul's advice, "In humility count others as better than yourself."[6] Values are the underpinnings for ethical systems, as in the oath physicians take to "First do no harm" to a patient (Hippocratic oath), and legal systems, as in lawyers' pledges to uphold the law and the U.S. Constitution.

Ethics & Laws: Standards of Right & Wrong

Ethics **are principles of right and wrong that influence behavior.** *Laws* **are rules of conduct or action formally recognized as binding or enforced by a controlling authority.**

Some standards are nearly universal, such as the belief that killing is never justified except for the most important of reasons (such as self-defense). Other standards are culturally based, varying according to what a particular culture considers right or wrong. This is particularly true in international business, where what one culture considers wrong both ethically and legally is considered perfectly acceptable in another culture.

■ **Example of Acts That Vary Ethically or Legally According to Culture: "Is That a Gratuity or a Bribe?"** In many Latin American and Asian countries, tipping a public official is considered a gratuity, a gift, a donation, a commission, or even a consulting fee intended to reward someone for providing you with a competitive advantage or better service.

In the United States, Canada, and many parts of Europe, however, the same act is considered a kickback, grease money, a bribe, which is certainly unethical and usually illegal. An American businessperson performing such an act with a foreign official is considered to be in violation of U.S. law—specifically, the Foreign Corrupt Practices Act—although it may be perfectly legal in the host country. ■

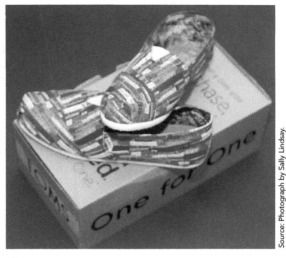

Source: Photograph by Sally Lindsay.

 Good corporate citizen. In 2006, American Blake Mycoskie was traveling in Argentina, where he observed that many children had no shoes to protect their feet. On returning home, he founded TOMS Shoes as a company that would—"One for One"—give a new pair of shoes to a child in need for every pair purchased. Later that year he returned to Argentina with family, friends, and staff members with 10,000 pairs of shoes made possible by TOMS customers.

> ℹ️ **Want to Know More? 2-1**
> **Key Terms & Definitions in Sequential Order to Study as You Go Along**
> Go to www.mybizlab.com.

> ℹ️ **Want to Know More? 2-2**
> **What Else Can Be Learned about Carroll's Pyramid?**
> Go to www.mybizlab.com.

Corporate Social Responsibility: Benefiting Society as Well as the Organization

Corporate social responsibility (CSR), **also called** *corporate citizenship,* **is a concern for taking actions that will benefit the interests of society as well as of the organization.** That is, CSR seeks to maximize a firm's positive impact on society and minimize its negative impact.

■ **Example of Corporate Social Responsibility: Pepsi Stops Selling Sugary Drinks in Schools.** In 2006, responding to complaints about products linked to childhood obesity, both Coke and Pepsi agreed to stop selling sugary soft drinks in U.S. schools. In March 2010, Pepsi went on to voluntarily agree to remove high-calorie sweetened soft drinks from schools for children up to the age of 18 in more than 200 other countries.

The company received compliments from the Center for Science in the Public Interest. "We applaud Pepsi for its global commitment," a spokesperson said. "But shame on Coca-Cola for insisting on targeting high school students in most countries around the world."[7] ■

Corporate social responsibility, or being a good corporate citizen, rests at the top of Carroll's pyramid. This reflects global society's expectations, says Carroll, "that business will engage in social activities that are not mandated by law nor generally expected of business in an ethical sense."[8]

We discuss corporate social responsibility further in Section 2.3. First, however, let us give more consideration to ethical behavior.

Defining Ethical Dilemmas

How would I recognize when I'm in an "ethical dilemma"?

An *ethical dilemma* **is a situation in which people have to decide whether to pursue a certain action that may benefit them or their organization but that is unethical or even illegal.** In business, a frequent source of ethical dilemmas is the conflict between the competing demands to make money yet also be fair and honest in business relationships.

② Ethical conflict? Painter Thomas Kinkade's company was ordered to pay damages to former gallery owners. They accused his company of exploiting their faith to force them into a business in which they competed unfairly with the Kinkade company itself. Do you think it's acceptable for a company to put hardball (if legal) money-making practices ahead of other considerations?

BRIEFING / LEGAL & ETHICAL PRACTICES

Ethical Dilemma for the Thomas Kinkade Company: Was It "Just Business" to Exploit Gallery Owners' Faith? Self-described "painter of light" Thomas Kinkade is a born-again Christian who uses religious themes in his art. But his company also used sharp-edged marketing and business tactics to make money from that art. Could Kinkade have found himself in an ethical dilemma between following his religious values and ways of selling his products?

At a presentation for prospective Kinkade Signature Gallery owners, said the former proprietors of a Virginia gallery, Kinkade and his representatives used words such as *Christian, God, partner,* and *trust* to create "a certain religious environment designed to instill a special relationship of trust."[9] What the couple was not told, their attorney said, was that they would have to sell Kinkade artworks at set retail prices even while the Thomas Kinkade Co. simultaneously undercut them with its own discount sales. ②

The result was they were forced to close their gallery and lost the life savings they had invested. An appeals court ruled

Source: s70/ZUMA Press/Newscom.

that the Kinkade company had to pay the couple $860,000 in damages plus $1.2 million in other fees and expenses, which ultimately led to the firm's bankruptcy.

Regardless of your religious beliefs, do you think hardball business practices are "just business" or "just part of the game" and therefore allowable? Or do some tactics pose an ethical dilemma for you? ■

Behaving Badly, Behaving Well

Why might I attribute purer motives to myself than to others?

Sam Waksal, MD, founder and CEO of ImClone, a biotechnology company, learned—before the news was made public—that the U.S. government would refuse to approve ImClone's new cancer drug, a decision certain to drive down the company's stock price. Waksal quickly tried to sell $5 million of his ImClone stock, an act of insider trading for which he ultimately was sentenced to 87 months in prison and fined $3 million. ***Insider trading* is the illegal use of private company information to further one's own fortunes or those of family or friends.** (This was the case that affected home-décor and lifestyle guru Martha Stewart as well.)

Behaving Badly: The "Holier-than-Thou" Effect Excuses Our Own Behavior but Not Others'

What makes some businesspeople think it's acceptable to engage in such moral sleaziness—insider trading, deceptive advertising, shady banking practices, and the like? Perhaps people have a self-inflated bias about themselves, a condition known as the *holier-than-thou effect*.[10] Many of us overestimate our willingness to do what's morally right, and it can greatly influence how we judge other people's actions, such as cheating on tests. ❸

Research shows people will make generous forecasts about their own moral behavior and less generous predictions about their peers'. But the negative predictions about others turn out to apply not only to others but to themselves as well.[11]

The holier-than-thou effect diminishes quickly when people become involved in the actual experience they are judging. As one writer says, "Dubious accounting practices will appear less shady to the person who has had to put a good face on a failing company."[12] In other words, is it really the situation, not moral character, that guides behavior?

Behaving Well: Treat Others as You Would Yourself

Why be ethical? Why be good? Maybe, suggests a brain study, people perform selfless acts not just for an emotional reward but because they're acutely tuned in to the needs and actions of others.[13] "And therefore," says one of the study authors, "I might want to treat them like I might want them to treat myself."[14]

When you graduate into the business world, will you do the right thing? Earning money is certainly acceptable, but many students have decided it's equally important to be ethical and socially responsible. For example, a high percentage of the 2009 Harvard Business School class graduating with master's degrees in business administration (MBA) signed the ***MBA oath*, a voluntary student-led pledge of intention to serve the greater good. They promised to act responsibly and ethically and refrain from advancing their "own narrow ambitions" at the expense of others.** "No one wants to have their future criticized as a place filled with unethical behaviors," said Max Anderson, a pledge organizer. He and his classmates want to learn from the ethical failures of the past, "do things differently, and accept our duty to lead responsibly."[15] Is this the way you would like to be as well?

Want to Know More? 2-3
The Inside Story on Insider Trading with ImClone, Sam Waksal, & Martha Stewart
Go to www.mybizlab.com.

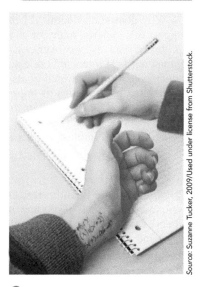
Source: Suzanne Tucker, 2009/Used under license from Shutterstock.

❸ **Cheating.** Obviously, students who don't do the work themselves are not learning and, research shows, they slip behind in knowledge and grades. How do you judge other students' cheating on tests? How do you judge yourself?

Want to Know More? 2-4
What Are Some Tests to Use to Determine If an Act Is Ethical?
Go to www.mybizlab.com.

Want to Know More? 2-5
What Are Some Important Details of the Harvard MBA Oath?
Go to www.mybizlab.com.

PRACTICAL ACTION
How Well Do You Deal with the "Cheating Culture"?

Are we a nation of cheats and liars?

David Callahan, author of *The Cheating Culture,* worries about "ordinary people's willingness to deceive others and cut corners purely to make more money or win some prize."[16] James Stewart, who wrote *Tangled Webs,* thinks there is so much high-level lying that it is "threatening to swamp the legal system, stymie the courts, and sow cynicism nationwide."[17]

Why does such unethical behavior happen? Perhaps, suggest two experts, many of us are guided by *motivated blindness.* That is, we overlook information that works against our best interests. For example, when we are busy focusing on organizational goals such as sales, they say, "the ethical implications of important decisions can fade from our minds. . . . We end up engaging in or condoning the behavior we would condemn."[18]

Motivated blindness *begins in school* and is carried into business.

School Cheating: Design for Failure
Cheating, getting unauthorized help in fulfilling graded assignments such as tests, and *plagiarism,* representing others' work as your own, are major concerns to educators—and to employers.[19]

Cheating is widespread among high school students, with 64% in one survey admitting to it, often aided by cellphones and the Internet.[20] Cheating is also an alarming problem in college, with 87% of undergraduates saying their peers at least "sometimes" plagiarize from the Web, for example.[21] It even occurs in graduate school—56% of graduate business students were found to have cheated.[22]

How do students attempt to justify this? Some may cheat on an exam and say, "I don't usually do this, but I really have to do it." They would rather cheat, that is, than show their families they got an F.[23] Whatever the motive,

research shows, students who cheated and thus didn't actually do the assigned work were more likely to fail.[24]

Workplace Cheating & Lying: Will It Come Back & Wreck Your Career?
"Students don't just say 'OK I cheated in school, but now I'm in the workplace and it ends here,'" says an Arizona professor. "They are forming bad habits that carry over into the market."[25]

Slipping into major cheating and lying begins with "small infractions—illegally downloading a few songs, skimming small amounts from the register, lies of omission on taxes—and grows by increments," suggests science writer Benedict Carey. These "small infractions" can become a way of life that grows into a deliberate strategy of deception or fraud.[26]

Why do people engage in theft and fraud in the workplace? The reasons are mainly emotional:

- **Corner cutting:** People subconsciously seek shortcuts—as by cheating—more than they realize, says Carey. We constantly make choices "between short- and long-term gains, . . . between the more virtuous choice and the less virtuous one."

- **Resentment:** We justify cheating and lying because we have resentments of an authority or of a specific rule.

- **Unfairness:** "Perhaps the most powerful urge to cheat," says Carey, "stems from a deep sense of unfairness"—such as the fact that other people had advantages you did not. Still, does that give you an excuse to, say, take credit for other people's work?

- **Fear of being a chump:** The biggest fear might be of "not being smart" and "finishing out of the money." So strong is this fear that many people cheat to avoid having to deal with feeling like chumps.

Doing the Right Thing: How Organizations Can Promote Ethical Behavior

2.2

THE BIG IDEA: To foster high ethical standards, a company needs to have support from top management for a strong ethical climate, hire ethical employees, and institute a code of ethics and training programs in ethics. An indicator that a firm has ethical problems is a history of whistleblowers. Public corporations must now comply with the Sarbanes–Oxley Act.

THE ESSENTIAL QUESTION: What are four ways organizations can foster high ethical standards?

MyBizLab: Check your understanding of these concepts at www.mybizlab.com.

My BizLab

Here's a collector's item, if you can find it—the 64-page "Enron Code of Ethics." The Houston-based energy company was once the seventh largest company in the United States, but it plunged into bankruptcy after disclosure of highly irregular financial dealings, bringing tremendous losses to stockholders and employees, and prison terms to some of its highest-ranking executives.

Clearly, any company can work up some sort of code of ethics to post in the employee lunchroom. But how can we know if it is working actively to foster high ethical standards? We suggest there are three signs to look for.

1 Top Managers Strongly Support an Ethical Climate: "We're Not Just Giving Lip Service"

Is top management support really necessary?

It may be that lower-level employees will act ethically and honorably. But if top executives wink at ethical problems, look the other way, dodge them with legal loopholes, or generate public relations smokescreens, they are clearly failing to lead by example. This will make employees cynical about the loose ethical climate. Why should a clerk not steal from the office supply cabinet when the people at the top are using the company jet for personal vacation travel?[27] ④

Source: Tayhutch/Shutterstock.

BRIEFING / SOCIALLY RESPONSIBLE BUSINESS
An Ethical Top Manager at CitiMortgage Keeps People in Their Homes. A big story in the 2007–2009 recession was how the government came forward to inject billions of dollars into banks to keep them from failing. Many people complained, however, that the banks mostly used the money to shore up their reserves or pay executive bonuses rather than to rescue depositors or mortgage holders whose homes were in danger of foreclosure. Antibank feeling brought the morale of employees of financial institutions to all-time lows.

One such institution was CitiMortgage, the nation's fourth-largest mortgage lender, part of Citigroup, which received $45 billion in U.S. financial rescue

④ **Top-level example.** In June 2009, executives from four banks receiving bailout money from U.S. taxpayers were reported to have taken corporate jets for their "personal use"—code for vacation—as in flying one's family to a luxury resort in West Virginia. Knowing this, if you were a low-level bank employee, would you feel at all guilty if you phoned in "sick" to go to a ball game?

⑤ An ethical mortgage lender. CitiMortgage, headquartered in St. Louis, became a leader in doing everything possible to avert foreclosures. CEO Sanjiv Das exemplifies the kind of executive we could all hope to see more of. His dedication to keeping mortgage holders in their homes during hard times represents an ethical model that many other bankers failed to live up to. Do you know any businesspeople whose ethics are exceptional?

funds. Gloom among employees was augmented by the wave of foreclosure filings crippling the housing market.

Fighting these problems became the job of CitiMortgage's new CEO Sanjiv Das, appointed in 2008 to head the St. Louis–headquartered company. The India-born Das, then 47, said one of his goals was to bolster employee morale and another was to avert foreclosures. To those ends, he helped pioneer a first-of-a-kind program at the bank to help homeowners who lost their jobs by allowing them to lower mortgage payments for three months while they looked for new jobs. He also promoted loan modifications, finding a way to keep six delinquent borrowers in their homes for every one foreclosed upon. ⑤

"Our mantra to [employees] is very clear," Das said. "It's about keeping people in their homes." He drew upon his value system as the son of an Indian army officer to nurture morale by expressing purpose and integrity. "The No. 1 thing I talk about are the customers. Each day, my business is to keep them in their homes, no matter what." ∎

2 The Firm Tries to Hire the Right Employees: "We Want Honest, Responsible People Working Here"

What can companies do to screen job applicants?

Few companies deliberately try to hire dishonest, irresponsible employees, but how do you screen them out? One common method is to have personality tests, but people have found ways to cheat on these.[28] Another is to run applicants through E-Verify, the federal program that allows employers to quickly check out the legal status of potential employees and remove illegal immigrants.[29] Finally, of course, they must check—really check—applicants' résumés and references. (We discuss applicant screening in considerable detail in Chapter 11.)

BRIEFING / BUSINESS CULTURE & ETIQUETTE
Who Will You Ask to Write You a Reference? (And Don't Forget to Thank Them.) Getting ready to apply for that first job? Hope you're one of those great people that companies are always looking for? The application effort can't begin too early, as you need to think about the people you will ask to write personal recommendations for you. For most students, it will be their instructors, who are frequently valued by employers for their insight into students' work habits. (And, by the way, good class attendance and participation definitely work in your favor in getting a reference.)

But here's something important to know: *Whenever people do you a favor, you need to write a note or e-mail to thank them.* Think that's obvious? Actually, many people think that "politeness and manners seem to have gone the way of the dinosaurs."[30] One woman high up in a large cosmetics company decided to refuse to help fellow alumni from her prestigious university. The reason: Over an 18-month period, she had gone out of her way to help six alumni network into new jobs. In response to all her efforts, not a single one took the time to thank her.[31]

Thus, when instructors write you references, be sure to *thank* them. By sending them a note. It's clearly the right thing to do. (And, from a purely selfish standpoint, you need to realize you may need their help again someday.) ∎

3 There Are Ethics Codes & Training Programs: "We Need to Tell Employees What We Expect of Them"

What are two kinds of ethics codes?

A *code of ethics* consists of a written set of ethical standards to help guide an organization's actions. Most codes state top management's expectations for employees, offering guidance on how to treat customers, suppliers, and competitors and prohibiting conflicts of interest, bribery, and making false accounting statements. JCPenney, for instance, is well known for its code of ethics and customer service called "Penney Principles."

ℹ️
Want to Know More? 2-6
What Are "Penney Principles"?
Go to www.mybizlab.com.

Two Kinds of Ethics Codes: Compliance-Based & Integrity-Based

Ethics codes may be either *compliance-based* or *integrity-based*.

Compliance-Based Ethics Codes. *Compliance-based ethics codes* attempt to prevent criminal misconduct by increasing control and by punishing violators. For instance, many companies ask employees to sign nondisclosure agreements in which they acknowledge that if they leak confidential information about products under development they can be fired and even sued.

■ **Example of Compliance-Based Ethics Code: Apple, Maker of Computers and iPods.** Few companies "are more secretive than Apple," according to a *New York Times* story, "or as punitive to those who dare violate the company's rules."[32] Employees are fired for leaking news to outsiders. Everyone must sign nondisclosure agreements. Those working on priority projects must pass through a maze of security doors. When then-CEO Steve Jobs had a liver transplant in 2009, the news was kept secret until he was safely back at work.[33] ■

Integrity-Based Ethics Codes. *Integrity-based ethics codes* attempt to enable responsible employee conduct by creating an environment that supports ethically desirable behavior. This approach stresses a culture of fair play, honesty, and diversity and emphasizes shared accountability among employees.

■ **Example of Integrity-Based Ethics Code: Innocent, Maker of Little Tasty Drinks.** British smoothie maker Innocent—"We call them innocent because our drinks are always completely pure, fresh, and unadulterated," says the company's website—has become known not only for healthy ingredients but also for its social commitment. By giving 10% of its profits to charity, providing help to the homeless, and using recycled bottles, Innocent strives to create a culture of ethical and socially responsible behavior. In 2009, Coca-Cola acquired a minority stake in the company.[34] ■

Ethics Training & Ethics Officers

To reinforce the ethics codes, many companies provide ethics training, often presenting employees with possible ethical dilemmas they may eventually encounter. Large companies frequently have an ethics office, headed by an ethics officer. **The job of the *ethics officer* is to integrate the organization's ethics and values initiatives, compliance activities, and business conduct practices into the company's decision-making processes.** Companies with ethics officers include the Chase Corporation, Microsoft, and Yahoo. ⑥

⑥ **Yahoo and ethics in China.** In 2007, the Internet-services company hired its first chief compliance and ethics officer. This followed a board meeting in which Yahoo was criticized for cooperating with the Chinese government on censorship as well as providing information about a Yahoo Mail user, a Chinese journalist, who was arrested and sentenced to 10 years. Do you think getting an ethics officer could sometimes be a company's way of whitewashing a problem?

Source: Lou Linwei/Alamy.

Key Takeaway 2-1
To foster high ethical standards, a company's managers must strongly support an ethical climate, hire the right kind of employees, and have ethics codes and training programs.

Want to Know More? 2-7

Whistleblowers: Heroes of the System

Go to www.mybizlab.com.

Sign of Major Ethical Problems: When Insiders Blow the Whistle

Do I think of a whistleblower as being a "snitch"?

Sometimes a company develops an ethical climate the hard way—by having its dirty laundry exposed by a *whistleblower,* **an employee who reports organizational misconduct to the government or the public,** such as corruption, fraud, overcharging, waste, or health and safety problems. Doug Durand, in "Winners & Losers" at the start of this chapter, is one such example. Another is John Kopchinski, a former pharmaceutical salesman who earned more than $51.5 million for a whistleblower lawsuit against Pfizer, the world's largest drugmaker, found guilty of promoting drugs for unapproved uses and doses.[35]

Although employers have been prohibited by health and safety laws from firing employees who report workplace hazards, in earlier years about two-thirds were fired anyway.[36] Then, in 2002, the Sarbanes-Oxley Act (discussed below) became law, giving whistleblowers protection from retaliation. Still, taking the brave step of exposing corporate wrongdoing usually comes at a cost. Although the public rightfully regards whistleblowers as heroes, employers and fellow employees may consider them "snitches."

White-Collar Fraud & the Sarbanes-Oxley Reform Act

What is Sarbanes-Oxley?

Bernard Madoff was considered one of the world's most successful investors, founder of the Wall Street firm Bernard L. Madoff Investment Securities LLC. Then in December 2008, as the U.S. economy spiraled downward, Madoff confessed to his sons that his investments were all "one big lie"—not investments at all, but rather a $50 billion *Ponzi scheme,* **using cash from newer investors to pay off older ones.** (Ponzi scheme was named for Charles Ponzi, an Italian immigrant who practiced the fraud in the early 1900s, although the scheme itself is far older.) Madoff's "offenses only came to light," says one report, "because he could no longer raise the money [a consequence of the Great Recession] to keep his scheme going."[37] A few months later, the perpetrator of possibly the world's biggest fraud, then age 71, was sentenced to 150 years in prison.[38] ⑦

Madoff joins a long list of business scoundrels whose names came to light in the early 21st century. Earlier there were Tyco International CEO Dennis Kozlowski (now serving prison time for grand larceny, securities fraud, and other crimes), WorldCom head Bernard Ebbers (doing 25 years for fraud), Adelphia CEO John Rigas (15 years for conspiracy and bank fraud), and former Enron chief Jeffrey Skilling (24 years for similar white-collar crimes). The various forms of deceit practiced by Skilling, Rigas, and other top-level managers generated a great deal of public outrage that ultimately led to reform legislation known as Sarbanes-Oxley.

Source: Mug Shot/Alamy.

⑦ **Bernard Madoff.** Perpetrator of possibly the greatest fraud in history, Madoff was sentenced to 150 years in prison. Over a period of 25 years, he defrauded investors of between $12 billion and $20 billion. He is scheduled to be released from prison on November 14, 2159.

The *Sarbanes-Oxley Act of 2002*, often known simply as *SOX* or *SarbOx*, established protections for whistleblowers and requirements for proper financial record keeping for public companies and penalties for noncompliance. Besides protecting whistleblowers from company retaliation (providing for reinstatement and back pay for those who have been punished by their employers), the law requires a firm's chief executive officer and chief financial officer to personally certify the organization's financial reports, along with various other provisions and requirements. (*See* ■ *Panel 2.2.*)

Want to Know More? 2-8

More about White-Collar Criminals

Go to www.mybizlab.com.

■ PANEL 2.2 **Sarbanes-Oxley: Principal provisions.**

1. Protects whistleblowers (people who report company fraud to the government) from employer retaliation.

2. Provides for job reinstatement and back pay to whistleblowers who are punished by their employers.

3. Requires public corporations to institute systems for employees to anonymously report auditing and accounting issues.

4. Prohibits alteration or destruction of key audit documents under pain of severe criminal penalties.

5. Requires a firm's chief executive officer (CEO) and chief financial officer (CFO) to personally certify the organization's financial reports.

6. Prohibits CEO, CFO, and company directors from taking personal loans or lines of credit from the company.

7. Requires CEO and CFO to reimburse the company for bonuses and stock options when required by restatement of corporate profits.

8. Requires the company to have established procedures and guidelines for audit committees.

9. Establishes the Public Company Accounting Oversight Board, a five-member committee under the Securities and Exchange Commission charged with overseeing the accounting industry.

2.3 Corporate Social Responsibility: Concern for the Welfare of Society

THE BIG IDEA: Corporate social responsibility is concern for taking actions that will benefit society. This section also considers blended value, measuring results in both economic and social areas, and social auditing to evaluate corporate social responsibility.

THE ESSENTIAL QUESTION: What are corporate social responsibility, blended value, and social auditing?

MyBizLab: Check your understanding of these concepts at www.mybizlab.com.

I f ethical responsibility is about being a good individual citizen, *corporate social responsibility (CSR)* is about being a good organizational citizen. As we said, CSR is a concern for taking actions that will benefit the interests of society as well as the organization. These may range from sponsorship of Little League sports teams to sending supplies to earthquake victims.

Is Corporate Social Responsibility a Good Idea? Two Views

What are the arguments for and against corporate social responsibility?

It used to be that a company's most important goal was to make money pretty much any way it wanted, regardless of the consequences. Today, however, many for-profit enterprises make a point of contributing to society as well as deriving profit from it.[39]

The Case for CSR: "Companies Aren't Separate from Society"

There are three primary arguments for corporate social responsibility:

First, since businesses create some problems (such as environmental pollution), they should help to solve them; after all, companies aren't separate from the rest of society. For example, as one writer put it, "the prices people pay for gasoline, electric power, and other energy products don't reflect their true costs, among them the impact of greenhouse gases."[40] ⑧

Second, business firms often have the resources to solve problems that the nonprofit sector does not. Thus, while they have no obligation to do so, they can make a big difference if they choose to commit to major support.

Finally, being socially responsible gives companies a positive public image that can help head off government regulation.

Thus, in the opinion of economist Paul Samuelson, who recently passed away, a company should be concerned with society's welfare as well as corporate profits. "A large corporation these days not only may engage in social responsibility," he said, "it had damned well better try to do so."[41] The same, of course, could be said about small corporations and even mom-and-pop businesses.

⑧ **Whose problem?** If fossil fuels contribute to climate change, including such effects as melting ice caps, should energy companies be held accountable? What should they do by way of making amends, if anything?

Source: siloto/Shutterstock.

The Case against CSR: "Companies Should Just Make Profits"

"The social responsibility of business is to make profits," wrote the late economist Milton Friedman in a famous 1970 article.[42] "There is one and only one social responsibility of business—to use its resources and engage in activities designed to increase its profits so long as it stays within the rules of the game, which is to say, engages in open and free competition without deception or fraud." (Note the stress on "without deception"—deception, unfortunately, often being considered within fair bounds by some businesspeople.)

Friedman argued that if a firm was distracted from its mission of maximizing profits, it would fail to provide goods and services and benefit its stockholders, thereby also failing to create jobs and expand economic growth—the real social justification for the company's existence.

More and more, however, companies are finding that being socially responsible can actually enhance profits (a point we take up again in Section 2.4).

Want to Know More? 2-9

Paul Samuelson's Famous Article

Go to www.mybizlab.com.

Want to Know More? 2-10

Milton Friedman's Famous Article

Go to www.mybizlab.com.

BRIEFING / EARNING GREEN BY GOING GREEN
Subaru Proves Going Green Can Lower, Not Increase, Costs.
The conventional wisdom is that adopting environmentally friendly processes adds to the cost of doing business. But companies can do well by doing good. "No one disputes that it's expensive to cap smokestacks and process hazardous waste," observe two management scholars. "But . . . the focus shouldn't be on cleaning up and its costs—the focus should be on creating less mess to begin with."[43]

For 20 years, the Lafayette plant of Subaru of Indiana Automotive pursued green initiatives during the course of manufacturing 800 vehicles a day. "With employees at every level of the plant looking for ways to save energy, reduce waste, and generally make processes more efficient," report the scholars, "one measure of its success is a 14% reduction in electricity consumption . . . since 2000. An even bigger achievement: It has not shipped any waste to a landfill [since 2004]." ⑨

Source: Photo Courtesy of Subaru of Indiana Automotive, Inc.

⑨ **Subaru of Indiana Automotive.** In a state that lost 46,000 auto jobs in the last decade, Subaru has never resorted to layoffs and in fact has given workers a wage increase every year. One of the major ways the company has achieved this is through a relentless focus on recycling, reducing water use by 50%, and composting 98% of the plant's waste—paper, plastic, glass, metals, and so on. Could this approach be applied to all American industry?

Some lessons to be drawn: (1) Profits come by increasing efficiency and reducing waste, although they don't always come immediately. (2) Management leadership is vital in setting goals and getting departments to cooperate. (3) Frontline workers have to be engaged in finding ways to reduce, reuse, and recycle. (4) Suppliers must be similarly involved, as in steel suppliers providing rolls of steel of exact dimensions. (5) All wastes must be considered potential products, as in cafeteria waste being sent to a waste-to-energy power plant. (6) Green initiatives give a company competitive advantages, as in reducing costs and conserving energy. [44] ■

Blended Value: Measuring Results in Both Economic & Social Areas

Can business success be judged by other ways than profit?

"We tend to categorize value as economic or social," says Jed Emerson, a managing director of Uhuru Capital Management. "You either work for a nonprofit that creates social value or you work for a for-profit that creates economic value."[45]

In reality, however, nonprofits (which represent 7% of the U.S. gross domestic product—the total dollar value of all goods and services produced) contribute economic value too, because they create jobs and consume goods and services. Conversely, for-profits create social value, as well: They pay taxes that support local communities, produce products that better people's lives, and create jobs that keep family units stable. Emerson has proposed the yardstick of ***blended value, in which the outcome of all business investments should be measured in both economic and social realms.*** "There is no 'trade off' between the two," he states, "but rather a concurrent pursuit of value—both social and financial. The two operate together, in concert, at all times."[46]

⑩ Triple bottom line. Judy Wicks, who founded the White Dog Café in Philadelphia, believes that "Profit is a tool. The major purpose of business is to serve." More specifically, she adheres to the concept that profits are only one goal of local business; the other elements of the "triple bottom line" are the fostering of social and environmental consciousness. Do you agree with this?

 BRIEFING / SMALL BUSINESS & ENTREPRENEURS
The White Dog Café Expresses Blended Value in the "Triple Bottom Line." Judy Wicks, who founded the White Dog Café in Philadelphia 28 years ago, has her own view of what business should do. "Profit is a tool," she says. "The major purpose of business is to serve."[47]

After opening her restaurant, Wicks realized she was spending so much time making it work that the only way to be socially active was through her business. Thus, the White Dog became known for buying its electricity from wind power, obtaining produce from organic farmers, and getting meat, poultry, and fish from producers practicing humane treatment of animals. Wicks also opened up the restaurant as an educational forum with guest speakers and to share ideas with competitors.

"Our customers and employees share our values," she says, "and come here for a sense of community, for a chance to be aligned with something greater than themselves." ⑩

Wicks is also cofounder of the Business Alliance for Local Living Economies, a nonprofit network established in 2001 to promote the "triple bottom line," the concept that local business should not only be profitable but also foster social and environmental consciousness. ■

Social Auditing: Evaluating Corporate Social Responsibility

How can I evaluate a company's social performance?

The obvious problem with the blended-value idea is that it is fairly easy to measure progress in financial performance but not so easy to measure social performance (such as environmental value). It has been only in the last few years that society has been grappling with environmental impacts, for example. Thus, Emerson believes, it may well take several years to learn how to adequately track and report social value.

Fortunately, there is already a tool for evaluating socially responsible business activities, and it is called *social auditing*. **A *social audit* is a systematic assessment of a company's performance in implementing socially responsible programs, often based on predefined goals.**

Some examples of the goals are as follows.

1 Corporate Policy: Positions on Political & Social Issues

Corporate policy **describes the positions a company takes on political and social issues.** Many companies take positions on environmental matters. Example: Owners of the New Belgium Brewery decided at the outset that the Fort Collins, Colorado, beer maker would be kind to the environment, and it became the first U.S. brewery to be powered entirely by wind.[48]

2 Community Activities: Sponsorship, Fund-Raising, Donations, & Other Support

Many companies contribute to the United Way, sponsor sports teams, buy ads in school newspapers, donate to museums, enable employees to volunteer time to charities, and support similar community activities. Example: Comet Skateboards of Oakland, California, is a backer of the Hood Games in East Oakland and South Central Los Angeles, community events featuring skateboarding, music, and fashion.[49] Hood Games events provide a way for youths, skateboarders, musicians, and others to perform, with events and merchandise being used to enrich the community. ⓫

3 Cause-Related Marketing: Supporting Worthy Causes

Cause-related marketing, **or simply *cause marketing,* is a commercial activity in which a business forms a partnership with a charity or nonprofit to support a worthy cause, product, or service.** Example: If you subscribe to cell-phone company CREDO Mobile, every time you make a phone call the company will make a donation to nonprofit groups like the Alliance for Climate Protection or Human Rights Watch.

4 Social Entrepreneurship: Leveraging Business for Social Change

Social entrepreneurship **is defined as innovative, social value–creating activity that can occur within or across for-profit or nonprofit sectors.** The focus is generally on creating social value rather than shareholder wealth. The activity is also characterized by innovation, or the creation of something new, rather than simply repeating existing business practices.[50]

■ **Example of Social Entrepreneurship: Acción Makes Small Loans to the Poor.** When *Fast Company* magazine named 43 entrepreneurial organizations for its 2007 Social Capitalist Award, it singled out firms working in areas such as antipoverty, literacy, and the environment that were trying to make a difference by applying free-market solutions to some of the world's oldest problems. Examples are microlending institutions such as Acción International, which provides poor clients with loans for as little as $100 with which to start businesses.[51] Another such microcredit organization is Wokai, founded by two 25-year-old San Francisco–area women to aid small entrepreneurs in China.[52] ■

Source: Warren Goldswain/Shutterstock.

⓫ **Comet Skateboards supports Hood Games.** Many companies support various community activities—at least during economic good times. Comet Skateboards is a bit unusual in supporting street competitions in minority neighborhoods, such as this one in East Oakland, California. What would be another cool thing for a company to sponsor?

Want to Know More? 2-11

What Companies Rank High for Social Responsibility?

Go to www.mybizlab.com.

Source: Christopher Crane.

⑫ **Sustainability.** Founded in 2001 by Tom Szaky, then a 20-year-old Princeton University freshman, TerraCycle is an eco-friendly innovator that converts non-recyclable or hard-to-recycle waste into over 1,500 different products, such as those shown here. People and organizations who join one of its "brigades" are paid to collect and send waste to them, such as used snack bags and drink pouches.

5 Sustainability: "Green Is Good"

Sustainability **is defined as economic development that meets the needs of the present without compromising the ability of future generations to meet their own needs.**[53] Companies large and small have launched green marketing campaigns promoting environmentally friendly causes, products, or stores.[54] ⑫ Example: By using recycled textiles in his products, Rob Anderson transformed Interface, a Georgia carpet manufacturer he founded, into the world's first billion-dollar sustainable company—"taking nothing from the earth that is not rapidly and naturally renewable, and doing no harm to the biosphere."[55]

6 Philanthropy: "Not Dying Rich"

"He who dies rich dies thus disgraced." So said 1880s steel manufacturer Andrew Carnegie, after he turned from making money to *philanthropy,* **making charitable donations to benefit humankind.** Carnegie became well known as a supporter of free public libraries, among other good works.

More recently, Microsoft's Bill Gates, one of the richest persons in the world, announced he would focus on spending billions from his foundation on health, education, and overcoming poverty.[56] In 2010, Gates and fellow philanthropist Warren Buffett were joined by director George Lucas, Oracle database billionaire Larry Ellison, and 38 other megawealthy people who pledged to donate the majority of their riches to charity.[57]

Not only individuals, but also companies practice philanthropy.

■ **Example of Philanthropy: Mary Kay Contributes to Organizations Working to Stem Violence against Women.** The Mary Kay Foundation, created by the late cosmetics company founder Mary Kay Ash, has made donations to organizations that work to stem violence against women, awarding more than $11 million in grants to shelters for women and children in all 50 states. In 2005, it also lobbied Congress to commit more than $500 million in federal funds to combat domestic violence, sexual assault, and stalking.[58] ■

Key Takeaway 2-2
A social audit may assess a firm's corporate policy, community activities, cause-related marketing, social entrepreneurship, sustainability, and philanthropy.

The Payoffs from Doing Good: The Benefits to Stakeholders

2.4

THE BIG IDEA: It might be expected that customers and the community should benefit from ethical behavior and corporate social responsibility, but this section also shows how owners, employees, and suppliers benefit as well.

THE ESSENTIAL QUESTION: In what ways do customers, owners, employees, suppliers, and the community benefit from ethics and corporate social responsibility (CSR)?

MyBizLab: Check your understanding of these concepts at www.mybizlab.com.

My BizLab

When all is said and done, why *should* a company be ethical and socially responsible? A close look suggests there are practical reasons for doing good—reasons important to any hardheaded businessperson.

The Negative Effects of Being Bad

What are ways that illegal behavior can hurt a company?

"It takes 10 years to build up your company's reputation," says legendary investor Warren Buffett, "but 10 seconds for you to lose it."[59] Indeed, Buffett found his own reputation diminished overnight after one of his executives pocketed $3 million from trading in the stock of a chemical company Buffett's firm was acquiring.[60]

Illegal behavior can result in whopping jail sentences and fines, as we have seen. Unethical or illegal behavior can also damage not only a company's reputation but its finances as well, as follows.

High Costs of Employee Fraud

Employee fraud, which can occur because of workers' perceptions of employer unfairness, mistreatment, or management hypocrisy, costs employers about 5% of every dollar earned. Frauds by executives are particularly costly, resulting in a median loss of $723,000.[61] ⑬

Diminished Stock Price

In one survey, 74% of people polled said their perception of a company's honesty affected their decision about whether to buy its stock.[62] The announcement of certain kinds of illegalities—tax evasion, bribery, or violations of government contracts—can hurt a company's stock price, according to some research.[63] Other research shows that investments in unethical firms earn abnormally negative returns for long periods of time.[64]

Diminished Sales Growth

A company convicted of illegal activity may suffer from diminished sales growth that lasts far longer than the damage to the stock price—indeed, it may last for several years.[65]

⑬ **Fraud.** Dell Computer confessed that for four years it improperly inflated reports of financial results. The two most common fraud schemes are corruption, which the Association of Certified Fraud Examiners says occurs in 27% of all cases, and fraudulent billing schemes, which occur in 24%. Financial statement fraud is the most costly type, with a median loss of $2 million in 2008. Have you heard or read about any employee fraud happening with a firm located near you?

Source: iDesign/Shutterstock.

Want to Know More? 2-12
More about the Effects of Lawsuits
Go to www.mybizlab.com.

Damaging Lawsuits

Lawsuits resulting from a company's illegal behavior can clearly hurt its profitability. The executives and directors of former energy company Enron were sued for inflating earnings to drive up the stock price (and collect $1.1 billion in profits on the stock they personally owned).

The Positive Effects of Being Good

How do stakeholders benefit from a firm's good behavior?

There are positive—and proven—reasons for a firm to observe sound ethical and socially responsible practices.

Benefiting Customers

Ethical and socially conscious businesses may actually enjoy a competitive edge with customers. The evidence: In one survey, 80% of the people polled said they decide to buy a firm's goods or services partly on their perception of its ethics.[66] In another survey, 72% of adults said they would rather buy products and services from a company with ethical business practices and higher prices than from a company with questionable business practices and lower prices.[67] In a third survey, 76% of the people polled said they would switch from their current brand to one associated with a good cause if price and quality were equal.[68] Finally, 88% of respondents in a fourth survey said they were more apt to buy from companies that are socially responsible than from companies that are not.[69]

Benefiting Owners

In general, studies show, profitability is enhanced by a company's reputation for honesty and corporate citizenship.[70] In addition, companies that made a public commitment to ethics have been found to have a higher market value than companies that merely adopted an ethics code or those that didn't have an ethics code at all.[71]

⑭ **Ending child hunger.** ConAgra's campaign to end child hunger benefits everyone: hungry children, the company's brands, and of course ConAgra's owners—the stockholders.

Source: Courtesy of ConAgra Foods.

BRIEFING / LEGAL & ETHICAL PRACTICES

A Food Giant Benefits Its Owners by Feeding Hungry Children. American food companies have come under attack for designing foods that cause obesity, a matter that threatens sales and profitability and the owners' investments.[72] The industry responds that it has modified more than 10,000 recipes to reduce calories and changed children's TV ads to showcase healthy choices such as 100% fruit juice.[73]

Omaha-based ConAgra Foods has gone beyond these moves in backing a campaign called "Child Hunger Ends Here," using TV specials and social media and providing 250 million pounds of food to Feeding America, a group that supplies food banks. ConAgra is also donating one meal for each eight-digit package code—up to 2.5 million meals—on specially marked ConAgra brands, such as Chef Boyardee, Healthy Choice, and Marie Callender's. ⑭

Many consumers think marketing campaigns that link a company to a social cause are done "only for publicity and marketing purposes, not because they truly care about the issue," says one account.[74] However, some firms have risen above that bar—Pepsi, Tide, Nike, and Newman's Own being identified as those that "place as much importance on supporting a social cause as they place on profit." ∎

Benefiting Employees

A National Business Ethics Survey found that 79% of employees said their firms' concern for ethics was a key reason they continued to work at their respective companies.[75] This is particularly true for members of the younger generation, who, points out *BusinessWeek,* are "demanding more attention to stakeholders and seeking more from their jobs than just 9-to-5 work hours and a steady paycheck." As a result, companies such as Home Depot (which committed to building 100,000 affordable green homes and planting 3 million trees) are trying to become more socially responsible to help attract these and other workers.[76]

In addition, responsible behavior can improve the quality of a company's job applicants. In one study of 1,020 people surveyed online, 83% rated a company's record of business ethics as "very important" when deciding whether to accept a job offer (only 2% rated it "unimportant").[77]

Benefiting Suppliers

One way in which CSR-conscious companies can be beneficial is in insisting on the elimination of *sweatshop* working conditions among suppliers. **A *sweatshop* is a shop, factory, or farm in which employees work long hours at low wages— or no wages, in the case of prison or slave and some child labor—usually under environmentally, physically, or mentally abusive conditions.**

Although we may tend to think that sweatshops exist mainly in developing countries, they can also be found in the United States in some garment factories and upholstery shops and on some farms employing illegal immigrants.[78] When suppliers' standards are raised, not only do their employees benefit but so do the vendors themselves, who may attract a better client base.

Benefiting the Local & National Community

When a socially responsible company gives its employees time off for voluntary activities, supports social causes, or donates money, goods, and services, it clearly benefits the community.

■ **Example of Benefiting the Community: Hurricane Katrina Victims Benefit from Corporate Goodwill—and So Do the Donors.** After Hurricane Katrina destroyed much of New Orleans and the Gulf Coast, corporations responded generously.

Papa John's employees handed out thousands of pizzas. Emigrant Savings Bank deposited $1,000 into the account of each customer in the areas hardest hit. General Electric donated millions of dollars of cash and equipment, including a mobile power plant. Biotechnology company Amgen donated $2.5 million. Georgia Pacific sent 65 truckloads of consumer goods. Walmart donated 18 vacant buildings to relief agencies. Pfizer sent a steady stream of drugs.

While such measures certainly generate goodwill, they also serve to publicize the firms' business or products.[79] ■

Benefiting the International Community

Should a firm buy goods produced by a country employing slave labor? Should it pay bribes to get its imports through another country's borders? Should it be concerned about global climate change? By the actions it pursues, a corporation can make an important difference in such matters.

It can also benefit itself by helping to shape the laws and regulations emerging that govern corporate behavior at regional or international levels. The thinking goes: If regulation is coming anyway, "let's play a part in shaping the rules of the game and leveling the playing field."[80]

 **BRIEFING / GLOBAL BUSINESS**
Unilever Benefits the International Community by Addressing Important World Problems. Unilever, a $40 billion Dutch-British rival to Procter & Gamble, isn't concerned just with selling consumer

tissue, soap, and detergent. It also wants to help fight poverty, water scarcity, and the effects of climate change. For instance, the company helps women in remote Indian villages start microenterprises, finances eco-friendly "drip" irrigation for farmers, recycles waste at a toothpaste factory, operates a free community laundry in a Brazilian slum, and is reducing carbon dioxide emissions at its factories.

The reasons are not just for public relations. "Some 40% of the company's sales and most of its growth now take place in developing nations," according to *BusinessWeek*. Moreover, "as environmental regulations grow tighter around the world, Unilever must invest in green technologies or its leadership in packaged foods, soaps, and other goods could be imperiled."[81] ∎

One important consequence of the focus on good global corporate citizenship is the ***Global Compact,*** **a voluntary agreement established in 2000 by the United Nations that promotes human rights, good labor practices, environmental protection, and anticorruption standards for businesses.** (See ∎ *Panel 2.3.*) About 3,000 businesses (including Nike, Levi Strauss, and Hewlett-Packard) from more than 100 countries have signed the compact.[82]

∎ **PANEL 2.3 The 10 principles of the U.N. Global Compact.** These are intended to promote social and environmental principles for businesses. Why would any company refuse to sign on to and abide by these principles?

Principles	Business should . . .
Human Rights	1. support and respect the protection of internationally proclaimed human rights; and
	2. make sure that they are not complicit in human rights abuses.
Labor Standards	3. uphold the freedom of association and the effective recognition of the right to collective bargaining;
	4. uphold the elimination of all forms of forced and compulsory labor;
	5. uphold the abolition of child labor; and
	6. uphold the elimination of discrimination in employment and occupation.
Environment	7. support a precautionary approach to environmental challenges;
	8. undertake initiatives to promote environmental responsibility; and
	9. encourage the development and diffusion of environmentally friendly technologies.
Anti-corruption	10. work against corruption in all its forms, including extortion and bribery.

Source: United Nations Global Compact, www.unglobalcompact.org/AboutTheGC/TheTenPrinciples/ index.html (accessed April 25, 2011).

Interdependency in Solving Common Problems: The Threat of Global Climate Change

Is climate change forcing closer cooperation among the countries and companies of the world?

"There is really no such thing as nature untainted by people," an article in *Science* points out. Indeed, as of 1995, only 17% of the world's land area remained directly uninfluenced by humans, and the amount is surely less by now.[83]

That human footprint, most scientists believe, has contributed to what has been called "the most compelling issue of our time": *global warming,* or *global climate change,* **an increase in the average temperature of the earth's atmosphere.**[84] Scientists generally agree global warming is caused by the emission of carbon dioxide produced by the burning of fossil fuels and industrial pollutants. The foreseeable effects are nothing short of the greatest calamity: more severe hurricanes and tornadoes, more lightning and wildfires, melting glaciers, rising sea levels, crop devastation, and changing animal migrations. A 2006 report by economist Nicholas Stern found that if no action is taken to control greenhouse gas emissions, the costs and risks of climate change "will be equivalent to losing at least 5% of global GDP [gross domestic product] each year, now and forever."[85]

Can Climate Change Be Reversed?

Is it possible to reverse the serious environmental consequences from the changing climate? Irreversible effects on plants, animals, farming, and weather are already apparent. The glaciers in Glacier National Park have decreased in number from 150 to 26 since 1850. The snows of Mt. Kilimanjaro are soon to be history. Shrinking sea ice may reduce the number of polar bears by two-thirds by 2050.[86] Many scientists take the gloomy view that there may be no return.[87]

To be sure, there are some aggressive attempts to rein in energy use. For example, environment ministers in Europe, citing their moral duty to future generations, have agreed to cut greenhouse gas emissions 20% below 1990 levels by 2020.[88] As for the two largest greenhouse gas–producing countries (40% of the world's total), the United States pledged in 2009 to cut emissions 17% from 2005 levels by 2020, and China announced it would cut emissions 40% to 45% by that year.[89] Left unanswered are questions of how both nations will achieve such cuts.

BRIEFING / EARNING GREEN BY GOING GREEN

What Can Business Do to Fight Climate Change? In the United States, the U.S. Chamber of Commerce, which is supposed to represent the views of business, has been most resistant to climate change legislation.[90] However, a number of companies, including Apple and Pacific Gas & Electric, resigned from the Chamber in protest.[91] Perhaps, then, business can begin to take the lead. After years of being slow to address climate change, major corporations—including industrial giants that make products ranging from electricity to chemicals to bulldozers—have begun to call for limits on global warming emissions.[92] Five reasons for this change are shown at right. (*See* ■ *Panel 2.4.*)

One way that has been proposed to reduce emission of greenhouse gases is for the world's nations to level a global carbon tax on anyone who drives a car or uses electricity produced by fossil fuels, with some tax revenues being used to help the poor and the middle class.[93] A second system is "cap and trade," in which governments mandate limits (caps) on carbon emissions and give companies emission-reduction allowances (credits) to emit specific amounts. If a company doesn't reach its cap, it can trade its credits to other firms that need to increase their emission allowances.[94] ■

■ **PANEL 2.4 Five reasons why business has become interested in climate change.**

1. **More awareness of social responsibility.** There is a growing awareness that climate change could ruin corporate leaders who continue to deny it. Corporations have become aware that their existence, like the rest of the world, is connected to the environment.

2. **Desire to influence regulation.** Some companies believe government regulation of carbon dioxide emissions is inevitable, and they want to have a say in policy making, so as to reduce the burden on themselves.

3. **Saving on energy use.** High fuel prices punish inefficiency. Making transportation, manufacturing, and workplace heating and cooling more efficient reduces energy use and saves money—as well as reduces carbon emissions.

4. **Finding new markets.** Some companies see lucrative new markets in clean-energy technologies, such as materials used in solar cells, wind turbines, fuel cells, and lightweight automobiles, which will all become more desirable in a world in which carbon emissions carry a cost.

5. **Desire to crush competition.** Being first to market with an environmentally friendly product—as Toyota has been with its hybrid Prius, which runs on both gasoline and electricity—is a way of beating competitors.

What You Can Do: The "Civic Generation" Can Be a Force for Change

What are two ways I could be an "activist doer"?

If you're a young adult born between 1982 and 2000—part of the so-called Millennial Generation—you are an "activist doer," a member of the most civic-minded generation since those of the 1930s and 1940s, according to experts.[95]

Is there a way you can take this impulse to serve and exercise it in the business world? Let's consider how you might go about it.

Working with Companies as an Intern to Advise on Saving Energy

An *intern* **is a student or a recent graduate who undergoes supervised practical training in a business setting.** (We discuss interning further in Chapter 11.) Recently, some companies have been bringing in student interns during the summer to help them analyze their energy use under a program called the Climate Corps fellowship supported by the Environmental Defense Fund.[96]

Companies that included eBay, Hewlett-Packard, and Sony Pictures used the research and recommendations of several interns to save a total of $35 million over five years. Student John Joseph, for instance, helped Intuit, a Mountain View, California, software company, find how it could cut $500,000 a year from its energy bill through such steps as setting lights in the restrooms to turn off automatically when not in use.

Volunteering Your Services for Free

There's nothing to stop you from giving away your services. It's a good way to create goodwill that may lead to a paying job later.[97] Katherine Yaros, for instance, spent her freshman spring break from the University of Michigan–Dearborn building a wheelchair ramp so a paralyzed Detroit man could leave his home. The second year, she spent spring vacation working at a residential treatment center for troubled girls. "Volunteering is not such a casual thing anymore," says Yaros, 19. "Giving back is part of our own way of being empowered to create a positive change within the community."[98]

(i)

Want to Know More? 2-13

Explore the Environmental Defense Fund's Climate Corps

Go to www.mybizlab.com.

LEARNING & SKILLS PORTFOLIO

Summary

2.1 The Ethical & Social Responsibilities of Businesspeople: The Way You Live Matters

THE ESSENTIAL QUESTION: *What is the order of priorities for a businessperson?*

What's a way of framing my moral priorities? Archie Carroll's pyramid suggests a company or an individual should be profitable, obey the law, be ethical, and be a good corporate citizen—in that order.

How should I distinguish among values, ethics, laws, and corporate social responsibility? Values are the relatively permanent and deeply held underlying beliefs and attitudes that help determine people's behavior. Ethics are the standards of right and wrong that influence behavior. Laws are rules of conduct or action formally recognized as binding or enforced by a controlling authority. Corporate social responsibility (CSR) is a concern for taking actions that will benefit the interests of society as well as of the organization.

How would I recognize when I'm in an "ethical dilemma"? An ethical dilemma is a situation in which people have to decide whether to pursue a course of action that may benefit them or their organization but that is unethical or even illegal.

Why might I attribute purer motives to myself than to others? Illegal trading is the illegal use of private company information to further one's own fortunes or those of family or friends. People indulge in such practices perhaps because of the holier-than-thou effect: a self-inflated bias in which people make generous predictions about their own moral behavior and less generous predictions about their peers'. Some students at Harvard Business School signed an MBA oath, a voluntary student-led pledge of intention to serve the greater good rather than advance their own narrow interests.

2.2 Doing the Right Thing: How Organizations Can Promote Ethical Behavior

THE ESSENTIAL QUESTION: *What are four ways organizations can foster high ethical standards?*

Is top management support really necessary? If top managers wink at ethical problems, they fail to lead by example and make employees cynical.

What can companies do to screen job applicants? Managers check applicants by giving them personality tests, running them through E-Verify, and above all checking their résumés and references.

What are two kinds of ethics codes? A code of ethics consists of a formal written set of ethical standards guiding an organization's actions. There are two kinds of ethics codes: (1) Compliance-based codes attempt to prevent criminal misconduct by increasing control and by punishing violators.

(2) Integrity-based ethics codes attempt to enable responsible employee conduct by creating an environment that supports ethically desirable behavior. Some companies hire an ethics officer to integrate the organization's ethics and values initiatives, compliance activities, and business conduct practices into the company's decision-making practices.

Do I think of a whistleblower as being a "snitch"? A whistleblower is an employee who reports organizational misconduct to the government or the public.

What is Sarbanes-Oxley? Various kinds of business fraud inspired the Sarbanes-Oxley Act of 2002 (SOX or SarbOx), which establishes protections for whistleblowers and requirements for proper financial record keeping for public companies and penalties for noncompliance.

2.3 Corporate Social Responsibility: Concern for the Welfare of Society

THE ESSENTIAL QUESTION: *What are corporate social responsibility, blended value, and social auditing?*

What are the arguments for and against corporate social responsibility? The case for CSR is that (1) since businesses create some problems, they should help solve them; (2) business often has the resources to solve problems in ways that the nonprofit sector does not; and (3) being socially responsible gives businesses a favorable public image that can help head off government regulation. The case against CSR is that business has only one responsibility—to engage in activities designed to increase its profits so long as it engages in open and free competition without deception or fraud.

Can business success be judged by other ways than profit? The yardstick of blended value has been proposed, in which the outcome of all business investments should be measured in *both* economic and social realms.

How can I evaluate a company's social performance? One tool for evaluating socially responsible business activities is the social audit, a systematic assessment of a company's performance in implementing socially responsible programs, often based on predefined goals. Six examples of the goals are (1) corporate policy, which is the positions a company takes on political and social issues; (2) community activities a company contributes to; (3) cause-related marketing, a commercial activity in which a business forms a partnership with a charity or nonprofit to support a worthy cause, product, or service; (4) a company's social entrepreneurship, the innovative, social value–creating activity that can occur within or across for-profit or nonprofit sectors; (5) sustainability, economic development that meets the needs of the present without compromising the ability of future generations to meet their own needs; and (6) philanthropy, making charitable donations to benefit humankind.

2.4 The Payoffs from Doing Good: The Benefits to Stakeholders

THE ESSENTIAL QUESTION: *In what ways do customers, owners, employees, suppliers, and the community benefit from ethics and corporate social responsibility (CSR)?*

What are ways that illegal behavior can hurt a company? Ethical or illegal misbehavior can harm not only a company's reputation but also its finances, as in losses from employee fraud, diminished stock price, diminished sales growth, and damaging lawsuits.

How do stakeholders benefit from a firm's good behavior? Positive reasons for a firm's observing sound ethical and socially responsible practices are that it will benefit customers, owners, employees, suppliers, the local and national community, and the international community. Good corporate citizenship has resulted in the Global Compact, a voluntary agreement by the United Nations that promotes human rights, good labor practices, environmental protection, and anticorruption standards for businesses.

Is climate change forcing closer cooperation among the countries and companies of the world? Global climate change, the increase in the average temperature of the earth's atmosphere, is caused by the emission of carbon dioxide produced by the burning of fossil fuels and industrial pollutants. Irreversible effects on plants, animals, farming, and weather are already apparent. To rein in energy use, European governments have agreed to cut greenhouse gas emissions 20% below 1990 levels by 2020. The United States has pledged to cut emissions 17% and China has pledged to cut emissions 40% to 45% by that year.

What are two ways I could be an "activist doer"? One way is to become an intern—one who undergoes supervised training in a business setting—in a company where you might advise on saving energy, for instance. Another way is to volunteer your services for free as a way to create goodwill that may lead to a paying job later.

Key Terms

MyBizLab

- blended value
- cause-related marketing
- code of ethics
- compliance-based ethics codes
- corporate policy
- corporate social responsibility (CSR)
- ethical dilemma
- ethics
- ethics officer

- global climate change
- Global Compact
- global corporate social responsibility pyramid
- global warming
- insider trading
- integrity-based ethics codes
- intern
- laws
- MBA oath

- philanthropy
- Ponzi scheme
- Sarbanes-Oxley Act of 2002
- social audit
- social entrepreneurship
- sustainability
- sweatshop
- values
- whistleblower

Pop Quiz Prep

1. According to the global corporate social responsibility pyramid, what priority is at the top of the pyramid?
2. What is the definition of *ethics*?
3. How do companies use E-Verify with regard to job applicants?
4. What is the nature of a compliance-based ethics code?
5. What is a common argument against corporate social responsibility?
6. What is a problem with the blended-value idea?
7. What is the Global Compact?
8. What are the potential consequences to a company for ignoring unethical or illegal behavior?

Critical Thinking Questions

1. Do you think it's ethical to surf the Web for personal use on the company's dime? What, if any, do you believe is an adequate amount of time employees should be allowed to use the Internet for nonwork-related purposes?
2. Can you give examples of companies that, in your experience, are responsible corporate citizens? How did you learn of their efforts, and specifically what are these efforts? Are you more inclined to purchase things from these types of companies?
3. In the past, were you ever motivated to purchase a product related to cause marketing, such as the Pink Ribbon Campaign or Product Red Campaign? What was the product, and was the "cause" a major decision-making factor in your purchase? If you have not purchased such a product, what types of company advertisements, if any, have you seen? Explain.
4. Do you agree that the stakeholders of a company (customers, investors, employees, banks, suppliers, and people in the community) need to know immediately when an offer of interest to purchase is made to a company? If you were an employee of a company, how soon would you want to know if the company might be sold or if there were financial troubles?
5. If you decided to donate the majority of your future riches to charity, as Bill and Melinda Gates and Warren Buffett have, what would your causes or charities be? (Bill Gates is founder and former CEO of Microsoft; Buffett is CEO of Berkshire Hathaway, which owns subsidiaries engaged in numerous business activities.)

Cases

Go to MyBizLab

VIDEO CASE
Patagonia: Social Responsibility & Managing Ethics

(Video running time 4:01 minutes; activity time 30 minutes)

"Would you report your company if it were illegally dumping waste on public land, even if it cost you your job?" That's the question with which this video about Patagonia begins. Headquartered in Ventura, California, Patagonia takes great pains to make sure it is not this kind of company.

Founded by Yvon Chouinard in 1972, Patagonia—named for the southernmost region of South America—designs and makes apparel and equipment for outdoor types who bike, hike, ski, fish, or surf. (You may have seen fellow students wearing Patagonia rain jackets and fleece-lined coats.) A customer's decision to buy from this company usually has to do with not only purchasing quality products but also doing business with a socially responsible and ethical global citizen, one named "Coolest Company on the Planet" by *Fortune* in 2007.

As part of its focus, Patagonia is involved in a number of environmental and wildlife campaigns, including prevention of oil drilling that may endanger animal life. Its devotion to environmental causes is demonstrated in the construction of its Reno, Nevada, distribution center, which features green design and technologies. In 2008, Patagonia won the Eco-Friendly Company of the Year award at a trade show in Munich, Germany.

In addition, Patagonia has an environmental internship program, which provides employees with up to two months' paid leave with full benefits so that they can do volunteer work with a nonprofit organization of their choice. It also belongs to the "1% for the Planet" alliance, a program in which businesses donate 1% of their sales to the preservation and restoration of the natural environment.

Finally, Patagonia is a great believer in corporate transparency. In the past, points out CEO Casey Sheahan, some executives might have considered it acceptable for a company to hide some of its less desirable activities. Now, he says, "you have to become transparent with everything you do because eventually, with the power of the Web and social media, customers are going to find out what you're doing anyway, so why not tell

them?" With this thought in mind, the company stays focused on its social responsibilities along with the quality of its products and its economic performance.

What's Your Take?

1. Discuss what is meant by the application of "transparency" in Patagonia's business practices. How is the company trying to accomplish this? Provide examples.
2. In what ways is Patagonia committed to producing products under legal, fair, safe, and humane working conditions?
3. In the video, Jill Dumain, Patagonia's Director of Environmental Analysis, states that "we started realizing as a company that what we make pollutes, and we had been known as an environmental company." What are ways the company pollutes, and what alternatives is it implementing?

BUSINESS DECISION CASE
Oprah Winfrey Not Forgotten: The Importance of Giving Back

The chapter discusses the case for and against corporate social responsibility—and the positive effects of "being good" and trying to make the world a better place. Many times, social responsibility and philanthropy are associated with companies and nonprofit organizations, but have you ever stopped to think about the difference a single individual can make? While some companies and nonprofits have tirelessly contributed to bettering society, employees, customers, and the local communities in which they operate, have you ever thought about an individual like Oprah Winfrey and the power

she possesses as a philanthropist? What is it that inspires some people to give in such profound and immense ways?

Oprah's childhood reveals much about her philanthropic roots. She has long believed that education is the door to freedom, offering a chance at a brighter future.[99] She was raised in rural Mississippi by her grandmother, who read books to her and instilled in her a love of reading, learning, and going to the library. Oprah began memorizing Bible verses and performing for her grandmother's friends at the age of three. At the age of five, she began kindergarten—already knowing how to read and write.[100] In middle school a teacher suggested that Oprah attend Nicolet High School in Glendale, Wisconsin. At Nicolet, Oprah was the only African American student, but she was later quoted as saying, "In 1968 it was real hip to know a black person, so I was very popular."[101] She went on to graduate from Tennessee State, where she earned a degree in speech and drama.[102]

Oprah is the most powerful African American woman of all time. *Forbes* magazine has calculated her net worth at $2.7 billion.[103] In 2005, she became the first African American person listed by *BusinessWeek* magazine in its top 50 philanthropists list—reportedly giving away over $300 million of her own money.[104] She is commonly touted with top billing of those celebrities who give away the largest percentage of their own money. What has propelled her to these heights and why has she given back so generously?

According to a *BusinessWeek* interview, Oprah's inspiration as a philanthropist came one Christmas at around the age of 12, when she knew there would be no gifts under the tree—or even a tree. When a trio of nuns showed up at her family's home with food and gifts (and a doll of her very own), she says, "I remember feeling that I mattered enough to these nuns—who I had never met and to this day still do not know their names—and what it meant that they had remembered me. I wasn't forgotten."[105]

Oprah's causes are related to education and empowerment. Her Angel Network, which began in 1998, has given over $80 million to various causes and nonprofits. Oprah personally donated $11 million of her own money to Hurricane Katrina victims.[106] In 2007, she spent $40 million to build the Oprah Winfrey Leadership Academy for girls in Johannesburg, South Africa. The project is meant to empower young girls to become leaders of their communities.[107] On her success, Oprah says, "What material success does is provide you with the ability to concentrate on other things that really matter. And that is being able to make a difference, not only in your own life, but in other people's lives."[108]

What's Your Take?

1. Are you aware of other celebrities who have made significant contributions as philanthropists, and if so, what are their causes?

2. It is stated that companies are not separate from society. Are celebrities separate from society? Do you think celebrities with exorbitant earnings have an obligation to society? Explain.

3. Oprah is quoted as saying, "to whom much is given, much is expected." How do you interpret this? Explain.

4. Do you think Oprah's childhood contributed to her philanthropic generosity? Had she come from different means, do you think she'd still be as generous?

Briefings   My BizLab Activities & Cases

Go to www.mybizlab.com for online activities and exercises related to the timely topics discussed in this chapter's Briefings, as well as additional theme-related Briefing *Spotlights* highlighting how these concepts apply in today's business environment.

In-chapter Briefing:
- Who Will You Ask to Write You a Reference? (And Don't Forget to Thank Them.)

Activity:
- Developing Marketable Business Skills – Volunteering

Briefing Spotlight:
- How Much Is Too Much?

In-chapter Briefing:
- Subaru Proves Going Green Can Lower, Not Increase, Costs
- What Can Business Do to Fight Climate Change?

Activity:
- Going to the Net! – McDonald's Potato Energy & Other Best Global Practices

Briefing Spotlight:
- Rolling Out the Green Carpet

In-chapter Briefing:
- Unilever Benefits the International Community by Addressing Important World Problems

Activity:
- Going to the Net! – The Gap's Social Responsibility Report

Briefing Spotlight:
- Hot Steam to Cold Cash

In-chapter Briefing:
- Ethical Dilemma for the Thomas Kinkade Company: Was It "Just Business" to Exploit Gallery Owners' Faith?
- A Food Giant Benefits Its Owners by Feeding Hungry Children

Activity:
- Developing Marketable Business Skills – Technology's Impact on Ethics
- Ethical Dilemma Case – Going Mainstream & Downstream?
- Going to the Net! – National Whistleblowers Center Website

Briefing Spotlight:
- GMAC – Robo Cops or Crooks?

In-chapter Briefing:
- The White Dog Café Expresses Blended Value in the "Triple Bottom Line"

Activity:
- Going to the Net! – Social Entrepreneurs: A Hybrid of Nonprofit with For-Profit

Briefing Spotlight:
- A Guy Who Works for Peanuts

In-chapter Briefing:
- An Ethical Top Manager at CitiMortgage Keeps People in Their Homes

Activity:
- Developing Marketable Business Skills – The Toyota Recall
- Developing Marketable Business Skills – Activism or Slacktivism?
- Developing Marketable Business Skills – Two Views of Corporate Social Responsibility
- Going to the Net! – The Philanthrocapitalism of the Gates Foundation
- Going to the Net! – The 100 Best Corporate Citizens: What Makes Them the Best?

Briefing Spotlight:
- Just Good Corporate Citizens

Additional Briefing Spotlights available at MyBizLab:
- A WORLD OF CONSTANT CHANGE
- BUSINESS SKILLS & CAREER DEVELOPMENT
- CUSTOMER FOCUS
- INFO TECH & SOCIAL MEDIA
- PERSONAL FINANCE

7

Management & Leadership

Realizing Exceptional Results

After reading and studying this chapter, you will be able to answer the following essential questions:

7.1 Management: What It Is, How You Do It— The Four Essential Functions

THE ESSENTIAL QUESTION: *Why are managers needed, what do they do, what are their levels, and how do they make decisions?*

7.2 Planning: You Set Goals & Decide How to Achieve Them

THE ESSENTIAL QUESTION: *What are the benefits of planning, and what is the planning process?*

7.3 Organizing: You Arrange Tasks, People, & Other Resources to Get Things Done

THE ESSENTIAL QUESTION: *What do organization charts show, and what three skills do managers need?*

7.4 Leading: You Motivate People to Work to Achieve Important Goals

THE ESSENTIAL QUESTION: *How do leaders and managers differ, and what are the different types of leaders?*

7.5 Controlling: You Monitor Performance, Compare It with Goals, & Take Corrective Action

THE ESSENTIAL QUESTION: *How does control work, and how should I use it to be an effective manager?*

MyBizLab

Where you see MyBizLab in this chapter, go to www.mybizlab.com for additional activities on the topic being discussed.

FORECAST: What's Ahead in This Chapter

We consider the four functions of management: (1) planning, (2) organizing, (3) leading, and (4) controlling. We discuss the hierarchy of top, middle, and supervisory managers and how managers make decisions. We then consider planning, its benefits, vision and mission statements, and strategic, tactical, and operational planning. Finally, we discuss organizing, leading, and controlling.

MyBizLab

Gain hands-on experience through an interactive, real-world scenario. This chapter's simulation entitled Plan for Success is located at **www.mybizlab.com**.

WINNERS & LOSERS

LEADERSHIP QUALITIES

WINNER: Apple's Steve Jobs

In November 2009, Steve Jobs appeared on the cover of *Fortune* magazine as the "CEO of the Decade." Why him? An article blurb explained: "Apple's imperious, brilliant CEO transformed American business."[1]

Jobs, who died in 2011, had been identified with Apple since he cofounded it in 1976. He was fired in the 1980s (over differences with a new CEO he himself had hired), was invited to return in 1997, and became permanent CEO in January 2000. The company, worth about $5 billion in 2000, jumped in value to about $317 billion in 2011, exceeding that of ExxonMobil.

What was the secret to Jobs's success? Said Oracle CEO Larry Ellison, "He's really in pursuit of . . . technical and aesthetic perfection."[2] Added *Fortune* writer Adam Lishinsky: "He may not pay attention to customer research, but he works slavishly to make products customers will buy. He's a visionary, but he's grounded in reality too, closely monitoring Apple's various operational and market metrics. . . . The rare pairing of micromanagement with big-picture vision is a Jobs hallmark."[3]

Jobs recognized that gorgeous design could differentiate Apple's computers from rivals' bland products, and he was intensely involved in those details. He also controlled the details of the message about a product, rehearsing "over and over every line he and others utter in public about Apple," said Lishinsky. He was careful to guard against overexposure, usually speaking only when he had products to announce. This had the effect of building a frenzy of suspense and speculation in the media that paid off in a lot of free advertising.

Equally important, Jobs had a knack for innovation and "pouncing at the right moment," as when he used his years in exile from Apple to found the computer animation studio Pixar, later sold to Disney. After his return to Apple, he launched the breakthrough iMac followed by the iTunes music software, the Mac OS X operating system, the first Apple retail stores, the first iPod, and the first iPad.

Over this period, then, Jobs reshaped not only personal computers but also movies, telecommunications, and music—as well as the worlds of retail and design. And he and Apple created billions in shareholder wealth.

Source: Kimihiro Hoshino/AFP/Getty Images/Newscom.

LOSER: Microsoft's Steve Ballmer

For Microsoft, the same 12 years was a different story. Founder Bill Gates stepped aside in 2000 and handed over the job of CEO to his longtime second in command, Steve Ballmer. At that time, says observer Daniel Lyons, "Microsoft was still the meanest, mightiest tech company in the world, a juggernaut that bullied friends and foes alike and which possessed an operating-system franchise [Windows] that was practically a license to print money."[4]

Twelve years later, Windows was still running on 90% of personal computers, Microsoft Office dominated desktop applications, and revenue had nearly tripled, from $23 billion to $62 billion. But Microsoft's stock had dropped from $120 to $24 a share, while Apple's had increased 750%. And the company was being overtaken in new markets.

Apple created the iPod, the iTunes store, and the iPhone; Microsoft responded with the Zune music player and its own new stores, but they have not caught on. Google came out of nowhere to dominate Internet search and e-mail (with Gmail) and created its own operating system, Android, for mobile devices; Microsoft brought out its Bing search engine and then its mobile-devices software platform, Windows Mobile, both of which have been overshadowed by others. Amazon.com grew to dominate online retail, started a cloud computing business, and launched the Kindle e-reader; Microsoft brought out its own cloud-computing service four years later.

How did Microsoft lose its edge? Lyons thinks that Ballmer is smart about business but is a nontechie and also was distracted by battles with antitrust regulators. The Vista operating system was released with so many problems that it took engineers three years to undo the mess. Finally, Ballmer allowed Microsoft to "become bureaucratic and lumbering," Lyons says, so that it was unable to respond quickly and catch up with new rivals. Meanwhile a new generation of Internet startups—Facebook, YouTube, Twitter—have taken root.

Ballmer hopes that the 2009 Windows 7 operating system will be a "once-in-a-lifetime reset." But in 2011, Windows' market share was starting to slip.

Source: Courtesy of Microsoft®.

YOUR CALL Management, said one pioneer of management ideas, is "the art of getting things done through people."[5] Do you think there can be many styles of effective management that can get things done through people? What if during the last 10 years, Ballmer had headed Apple and Jobs had headed Microsoft? In the end, do you think management and leadership styles really affect results?

MyBizLab

7.1 Management: What It Is, How You Do It—The Four Essential Functions

THE BIG IDEA: Managers are needed to make an organization more effective and more efficient. Management has four functions: *planning, organizing, leading*, and *controlling*. It has three levels: *top, middle*, and *supervisory*. Managers make decisions by identifying problems, thinking up alternative solutions, evaluating alternatives, selecting a solution, and implementing and evaluating the solution chosen.

THE ESSENTIAL QUESTION: Why are managers needed, what do they do, what are their levels, and how do they make decisions?

MyBizLab: Check your understanding of these concepts at www.mybizlab.com.

■ **PANEL 7.1 The four functions of management.** As a manager, you need to do *planning, organizing, leading,* and *controlling* to accomplish the firm's goals. Although shown here in sequential order, all four functions should happen *concurrently.*

As a manager, you need to do . . .

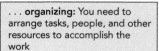

. . . **planning:** You need to set goals and decide how to achieve them

↓

. . . **organizing:** You need to arrange tasks, people, and other resources to accomplish the work

↓

. . . **leading:** You need to motivate people to work hard to achieve the organization's goals

↓

. . . **controlling:** You need to monitor performance, compare it with goals, and take corrective action as needed

↓

. . . **so as to accomplish the firm's goals.** You need to do these tasks to achieve the organization's goals *effectively* and *efficiently*

Could you run a business organization without managers? Couldn't you and your friends establish a democratically run enterprise in which everyone just pitches in, all members contribute their own specialized talents toward creating and selling a product, and all members vote on every decision?

The Need for Management: To Achieve Effectiveness & Efficiency

Are managers really necessary? Why?

Certainly democratic ways of running companies have been tried. (Contractor South Mountain Company of Martha's Vineyard, Massachusetts, is managed by 17 worker-owner employees.)[6] But imagine how long it could take to get major decisions made. An organization might stumble along for a while without managers, but eventually it will find it needs them if it is to deliver a quality product on time—that is, to achieve its goals *effectively* and *efficiently*.

- **Effectiveness—realizing goals:** Effectiveness is about the ends. **To be *effective* means to achieve results, to realize the firm's goals by making the right decisions and executing them successfully.**
- **Efficiency—the means of realizing goals:** Efficiency is about the means. **To be *efficient* means to use people, money, raw materials, and other resources wisely and cost-effectively.**

The Four Things Managers Must Do

What are the four functions I'm supposed to perform as a manager?

We defined *management* briefly in Chapter 1, but let's expand it here. ***Management* is the pursuit of organizational goals effectively and efficiently through (1) planning, (2) organization, (3) leading, and (4) controlling the organization's resources.** (*See* ■ *Panel 7.1.*)

Let's consider each of these four functions, using the example of Jeff Bezos and Amazon.com.

1 Planning: "What Are My Goals & How Do I Achieve Them?"

Planning **is defined as setting goals and deciding how to achieve them.** In a for-profit organization, one of these goals is to satisfy customers. Thus, top executives must plan the right strategy to achieve this goal.

■ **Example** of Planning: Internet Retailer Amazon.com. In 1994, Jeff Bezos left a successful career on Wall Street with a plan to use the World Wide Web to launch an online retail bookseller. Based in Seattle, his company, Amazon.com, has the goal of being "earth's most customer-centric company, where people can come to find and discover anything they may want to buy online." The entrepreneur made two important decisions early on: (1) He decided to specialize in selling books first (and move on to other products later). ❶ (2) He decided to forgo early opportunities to turn a profit in order to build a "customer-centric" company—that is, develop a base of satisfied customers. ■

❶ **Box of books?** Amazon.com started out with a very deliberate plan: specialize in selling books first, then move on to other products. It also decided to work on building a base of satisfied customers. How well do you think the plan has worked so far? What major online competitors for Amazon can you name?

2 Organizing: "How Do I Arrange Tasks, People, & Other Resources to Get Things Done?"

Organizing **is defined as arranging tasks, people, and other resources to accomplish the work.** Thus, the company must design a structure and establish conditions for achieving the goal of satisfying customers.

■ **Example** of Organizing: Amazon.com. As part of the strategy of concentrating on customers first, Bezos believes in "conserving money for things that matter," as in saving on office furniture by making desks out of cheap wooden doors atop sawed-off two-by-fours. He has also tried to create, in one description, "a decentralized, disentangled company where small groups can innovate and test their visions independently of everyone else."[7]

A great deal of effort has been put into boosting sales by making the website as customer centered as possible. For instance, beginning in 1995, Amazon pioneered letting customers post reviews about products on its site, playing "a central role in the change in consumer behavior by being the first successful Web retailer to embrace customers' views," says one account.[8] In 1999 it unveiled Wish Lists, allowing people to share their favorite products, and in 2006 it created discussion hubs that enable consumers to talk about a wider range of topics, such as yoga or *Harry Potter.* By assembling one of the world's largest collections of customer opinions, Amazon has built a website with a leading source of product reviews, which lure even more viewers to the site. ■

ⓘ

Want to Know More? 7-1
Key Terms & Definitions in Sequential Order to Study as You Go Along
Go to www.mybizlab.com.

3 Leading: "How Do I Motivate People to Work to Achieve Important Goals?"

Leading **is defined as motivating, directing, and otherwise influencing people to work hard to achieve the organization's goals.** Leading means establishing a vision and a mission for the company and then communicating and guiding others to realize the organizational goals.

■ **Example** of Leading: Amazon.com's Jeff Bezos. Bezos's public image is as a quirky, goofy geek with a famous booming laugh. But he is the founder of Amazon, of course, and companies tend to do well when founders remain with the firms they created. The reasons: their personal fortunes are tied to the company stock, they don't usually risk long-term performance for the short, they

Key Takeaway 7-1
Managers pursue organizational goals through planning, organization, leading, and controlling.

Source: Feature Photo Service/Newscom.

❷ Jeff Bezos of Amazon.com. Bezos is known for his quirky personality, resourcefulness, numbers orientation, and willingness to take big chances. Do these qualities contribute to superior leadership abilities? How essential do you think these characteristics were to Bezos's and Amazon's survival and ultimate success?

know their industries, and they have learned to fight in the early years.[9] Bezos's focus on growing market share over profits has made Wall Street uneasy, and indeed Amazon continued to post net losses in the early years. But Bezos has been blessed not only with great good luck but also with boundless optimism. ❷

He also combines a contradictory decision-making style that shows a focus on numbers and spreadsheets where quantitative data really matter yet also a willingness to take nervy gambles. For decisions that can be backed by facts, "the most junior person in the company can win an argument with the most senior person," says Bezos.[10] For other decisions, those that can't be backed by data—such as whether to allow third parties to compete with Amazon by selling products on Amazon's website—Bezos relies on his senior executives, whom he often recruits from larger companies. ■

4 Controlling: "How Do I Monitor Performance, Compare It with Goals, & Take Corrective Action?"

***Controlling* is defined as monitoring performance, comparing it with goals, and taking corrective action as needed.** That is, controlling means determining what actually occurs while trying to meet the organization's goals.

■ **Example of Controlling: Amazon.com.** The business is always watching its numbers and tinkering with procedures to continue to keep costs down and extend market share. For instance, when the company's stock price declined, Amazon took corrective action by cutting costs, laying off employees, and closing a distribution center. The company posted its first full-year profit in 2003. Over a five-year period, the company's shares zoomed 245%. ■

We expand on the four functions of planning, organizing, leading, and controlling in the rest of this chapter.

■ **PANEL 7.2 The three levels of management: top, middle, and supervisory.**

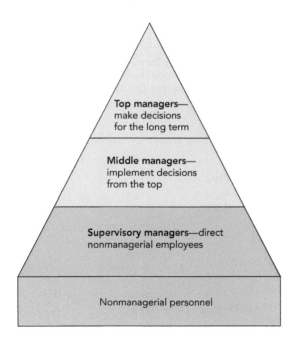

Top managers— make decisions for the long term

Middle managers— implement decisions from the top

Supervisory managers—direct nonmanagerial employees

Nonmanagerial personnel

Pyramid Power: The Three Levels of Management

What are the three levels of management?

In the traditional view of management, managers are arranged in a pyramid-like organization, with one layer sitting at the top and two or more layers of managers beneath. In this model, managers fall into three levels: *top, middle,* and *supervisory.* (*See* ■ *Panel 7.2.*) The pyramid is the classic model of management organization, but it is only one of many management models. We discuss others in Chapter 8.

1 Top Managers: Those Who Make Decisions for the Long Term

***Top managers,* the highest level of management, make long-term decisions about the overall direction of the organization and establish the objectives, strategies, and policies for it.** These are key executives with titles such as *chief executive officer (CEO), chief operating officer (COO), president,* and *senior vice president.* In 2007, the national median salary for a CEO with 500 to 5,000 employees was $500,000, and $849,375 for those at companies with more than 5,000 employees.[11] In 2010, median compensation for CEOs at 200 major companies was $9.6 million.[12]

2 Middle Managers: Those Who Implement Decisions from the Top

***Middle managers* implement the policies and plans of the top managers above them and supervise and coordinate the activities of the supervisory managers below them.** Middle managers have titles like *general manager, division manager, plant manager,* and *branch sales manager.* Depending on industry and company size, annual salaries may be $42,000 to $212,000.

3 Supervisory Managers: Those Who Direct Nonmanagerial Employees

***Supervisory managers* make short-term operating decisions, directing the daily tasks of nonmanagerial personnel.** The job titles in this group are on the order of *department head, foreman* or *forewoman, team leader,* or *supervisor.* Their salaries run around $40,000 a year or more.

What Managers Do: Practical Decision Making

What steps should I take as a manager to reach a decision?

Regardless of level, all managers *make decisions.* **A *decision* is a choice made from among available alternatives.** ***Decision making* is the process of identifying and choosing alternative courses of action.** Typically there are four phases involved in making a practical decision. (*See* ■ *Panel 7.3.*)

1 Identify the Problem or Opportunity: What's Wrong? What's Possible?

Managers find no shortage of ***problems,* or difficulties that impede the achievement of goals.** Technology glitches. Staff turnover. Customer complaints. And so on.

Creative managers also often find ***opportunities*—favorable circumstances that present possibilities for progress beyond existing goals.** You need to look past the parade of daily problems and try to actually do *better* than the goals your boss expects you to achieve. When a competitor's top software engineer unexpectedly quits, that creates an opportunity for your company to hire that person.

2 Think Up Possible Solutions: Brainstorming Ideas

Bright ideas are a firm's greatest competitive resource. After you've identified the problem or opportunity and determined its causes, you need to come up with possible solutions. The more creative and innovative the alternatives, the better. One way to achieve this is through ***brainstorming,* in which individuals or members of a group generate multiple ideas and alternatives for solving problems.**

3 Weigh Alternative Solutions & Select One: Are They Effective, Feasible, & Ethical?

Each alternative needs to be evaluated not only according to cost and quality but also according to whether it is effective, feasible, and ethical.

Is It Effective? A proposed solution needs to be evaluated to be sure it is effective—that is, not just "good enough" but the best under the circumstances.

Is It Feasible? A proposed solution may not be feasible for a variety of reasons: The top decision makers or customers won't accept it. Time is short. Costs are high. Technology isn't available. Company policies don't allow it. The action can't be reversed if there's trouble.

Want to Know More? 7-2
Why Would Anyone Want to Be a Middle Manager?
Go to www.mybizlab.com.

■ PANEL 7.3 **The four phases of practical decision making.**

Phase 1: Identify the problem or opportunity.
Phase 2: Dream up possible solutions.
Phase 3: Weigh alternative solutions and select one.
Phase 4: Implement the solution, then evaluate it.

Want to Know More? 7-3
Are Today's Teens & Young Adults More Apt to Believe in Lying & Cheating?
Go to www.mybizlab.com.

Source: Feverpitch/Shutterstock.

❸ **Ethical considerations.** When making a decision about whether to go with a proposed alternative, ethics should certainly be a consideration. How often do you think businesspeople really consider ethics in day-to-day decision making?

❹ **More customer friendly?** Based on your book-buying habits, Amazon's website will recommend similar titles of interest, a traditional service of independent booksellers. But over the last 13 years, little stores were undermined by superstores like Borders, which now has been flattened by Amazon. These events have "made people long for a little bookstore," says Anne Patchet, a novelist and bookseller. The Annapolis Bookstore & Café, located near the U.S. Naval Academy, specializes in maritime and sailing books. In the era of Amazon and e-books, is this strategy realistic?

Source: Photograph by Sally Lindsay.

Is It Ethical? At times a proposed alternative will seem to be right on nearly all counts. However, if it isn't ethical, you shouldn't give it a second look. ❸

Billionaire investor Warren Buffett is reported to have said, "When you hire someone, you look for brains, energy, and integrity, and if they don't have the third, integrity, you better watch out, because the first two will kill you."[13]

4 Implement & Evaluate the Solution Chosen

With some decisions, implementation can be quite difficult. When one company acquires another, for instance, it may take months to consolidate the departments, accounting systems, inventories, and so on.

Successful Implementation. For implementation to be successful, you need to do careful planning (especially if reversing an action will be difficult) and you need to consider how the people affected will feel about the change (inconvenienced, insecure, or even fearful, all of which can trigger resistance).

This is why it helps to give employees and customers some leeway during a changeover in business practices.

Evaluation. You need to follow up and evaluate the results of the decision. If the action is not working, you need to consider whether to give the new action more time, change it slightly, try another alternative, or start over.

We show how this process works in the following Briefing.

BRIEFING / SMALL BUSINESS & ENTREPRENEURS
Jeff Bezos's Major Decision: What Kind of Company Should Amazon Be? In Chapter 6, we emphasized that the initial decisions you make can be crucial, as Jeff Bezos demonstrated when creating and launching Amazon.[14]

(1) *Determining the problem or opportunity:* After reading a report that projected annual growth of e-commerce at 2,300%, Bezos made a list of 20 products that he thought could be sold on the Internet.

(2) *Thinking up alternative solutions:* Bezos then narrowed the list of products to those five he felt were most promising: CDs, computer hardware, computer software, videos, and books.

(3) *Evaluating alternatives and selecting a solution:* Bezos settled on selling books as his initial product, owing to the large market for reading material, the low price that could be offered, and the large number of titles available. He chose Seattle as the company headquarters for its high-tech workforce and closeness to a large book distributor.

(4) *Implementing and evaluating the solution:* Amazon's website debuted in July 1995 with a searchable database of over 1 million titles. After customers found the desired title, they were given the option of ordering the book with a credit card and having it delivered in a few days. It quickly became clear, however, that books could be shipped directly from wholesalers and publishers to Amazon and then immediately forwarded to customers, so that investing in a large warehouse was unnecessary. Within a month, Amazon had filled orders from all 50 states and 45 other countries.

With the basic concept of Amazon deemed a success, Bezos and his staff then began to focus on making the website as customer-friendly as possible. ❹ ■

Do you think smart people, experienced people, people in authority usually make rational decisions? A peek at reality:

- **Smart people:** Doctors and nurses who attended seminars via videoconference were more likely to be influenced by the charisma (personal magnetism) of the presenter than were people who were face to face with the presenter.[15] Maybe, then, dealing with people in the real world rather than the online world leads to better judgments.

- **Experienced people:** Project managers with more than 10 years of experience were found to miss more deadlines, create more errors, and generate higher costs than less-experienced colleagues—probably, says one scholar, because "the more experience we have, the more overconfident we get."[16]

- **People in authority:** Board members from gender and racial minorities might be expected to reduce corporate "group think" (uncritical thinking), but they often don't—perhaps because they are usually from the same educational and class background as white male directors. In any case, says one writer, diversity can't always overcome the "enormous pressure to agree with those sitting around the table with you."[17]

Education, sophistication, and experience don't disqualify people from doing things that are against their best interests. So, how can you make better decisions? Some tips:

- **How can I know when it's time to make a decision?** Should you decide now or should you wait? How do you know when you're keeping an open mind or just procrastinating ("analysis paralysis")? One expert on decision making suggests the time to decide is *now* if you can answer "yes" to the following questions:[18] *Do I have a reasonable grasp of the problem? Would I be satisfied if I chose one of the existing alternatives? Would it be unlikely that I could come up with a better alternative if I had more time? Could the best alternatives disappear if I wait?*

- **How can I know if my decision might be biased?** Some biases to look out for:

    Am I considering actual evidence or hanging on to my prior beliefs? This is called the *prior-hypothesis bias.* You need to be tough-minded and weigh the evidence, not look for data to support your prior beliefs.

    Am I being too cocky? This is the *overconfidence bias.* As we said, this could be a problem for decision makers with lots of experience.

    Are events connected or are they just chance? This is the *ignoring randomness bias.* Don't attribute trends to a single random event—a one-time spike in sales, for example.

- **How can I make tough choices?** Most daily decisions are small, says a management consultant, but the larger ones, where more is at stake, can be truly painful. Some ways to make decision making easier:[19]

    Gather facts, but not all possible facts, and don't delay decision making. You need to get enough data on which to make a decision but not overdo the fact gathering. Postponing decisions about small problems may simply make them large ones. Waiting rarely improves the quality of even big decisions and, in fact, can result in losing money, time, and peace of mind or missing opportunities.

    When overwhelmed, narrow your choices. Sometimes there are many good alternatives, and you can simplify decision making by eliminating some options.

    Realize you can't always have a positive outcome. Going through a well-reasoned process of choosing among alternatives increases the chances of success, even if you can't be assured of a positive outcome.

7.2 Planning: You Set Goals & Decide How to Achieve Them

THE BIG IDEA: Planning helps you (1) cope with uncertainty, (2) think ahead, (3) coordinate activities, and (4) check on your progress. Managers shape their plans on the basis of vision statements (what the company wants to become) and mission statements (what the company's fundamental purposes are). Top managers develop strategic plans, middle managers develop tactical plans, and supervisory managers develop operational plans. All these plans specify goals (broad, long-range targets) and objectives (specific, short-term targets). Performing a SWOT analysis—identifying a company's strengths, weaknesses, opportunities, and threats—can help establish strategic planning. Managers should also do contingency planning.

THE ESSENTIAL QUESTION: What are the benefits of planning, and what is the planning process?

MyBizLab

MyBizLab: Check your understanding of these concepts at www.mybizlab.com.

All companies must find ways to respond to rapidly changing markets, and sticking with one business strategy may be a sure path to failure. As a manager, how should you meet this challenge? You could copy competitors or find unexplored niches to exploit. You could produce standardized offerings at low cost (as in fast-food restaurants). You could connect clients to other people (as with eBay). You could apply customized expertise to clients' problems (as law firms do).[20]

Whatever approach you take, all involve planning. We describe . . .

- Four benefits of planning
- Vision and mission statements
- Strategic, tactical, and operational planning
- Goals and objectives
- Assessing your competitive position with SWOT analysis
- Contingency planning

5 Planning. It's often hard to take the time to do, say, a five-year plan when your job is to meet the weekly and monthly objectives. But what could happen if you don't devote time to planning?

Source: Yuri Arcurs/Shutterstock.

Why Plan? Four Benefits

How does planning help a manager?

As we stated earlier, *planning* is defined as setting goals and deciding how to achieve them. When you make a plan, you make a blueprint for action that describes what you need to do to realize your goals. **5**

You can always hope you'll muddle through the next time a natural disaster strikes, or you could try to plan for it (stock up on flashlight batteries and nonperishable food, for instance). Managers face similar choices. Should you wing it through every crisis or have a plan in place?

The benefits of planning are . . .

1 Planning Helps You Cope with Uncertainty

Don't like unpleasant surprises? Most of us don't. That's why planning for various (including unpleasant) possible events is necessary.

2 Planning Helps You Think Ahead

The product you are offering at some point may well achieve maturity, and sales will begin to drop. Thus, you need to plan beyond your present work circumstances, so that you can quickly move to the next stage.

3 Planning Helps You Coordinate Activities

A plan defines the responsibilities of various departments and coordinates their activities for the achievement of common goals—so that the right hand knows what the left hand is doing.

4 Planning Helps You Check on Your Progress

How well is your work going in an organization? You won't know unless you have some way of checking your progress. You need to have some expectations of what you're supposed to do—in other words, a plan.

The Basis for Planning: Vision & Mission Statements

How do vision and mission statements differ?

"Everyone wants a clear reason to get up in the morning," says journalist Dick Leider. "As humans we hunger for meaning and purpose in our lives."[21] An organization has a purpose, too—a vision. And the vision should suggest the direction in which the organization should go—the mission. From these are derived the organization's goals and objectives. (*See* ■ *Panel 7.4.*)

The Vision: "This Is What We Want to Become"

A *vision statement* **describes the company's vision, the long-term goal of what the organization wants to become.** A vision "should describe what's happening to the world you compete in and what you want to do about it," says one *Fortune* article. "It should guide your decisions."[22]

An example of a vision statement, from Ford Motor Company, is:

To become the world's leading consumer company for automotive products and services.

Other examples of vision statements are shown at right. (*See* ■ *Panel 7.5.*)

The Mission Statement: "These Are Our Fundamental Purposes"

A *mission statement* **is a statement of the organization's fundamental purposes.** The mission statement identifies the goods or services the organization provides and will provide and the reasons for providing them.

■ **PANEL 7.4 Making plans.** What an organization wishes to become is expressed in a *vision statement*. Its fundamental purposes are expressed in a *mission statement*. From these are derived *strategic planning*, then *tactical planning*, and finally *operational planning*. The purpose of each kind of planning is to specify *goals* and *objectives*.

> Vision statement: "What do we want to become?"
>
> Mission statement: "What are our fundamental purposes?"
>
> Strategic planning: Done by top managers for the next 1–5 years
> Goals, objectives
>
> Tactical planning: Done by middle managers for the next 6–24 months
> Goals, objectives
>
> Operational planning: Done by supervisory managers for the next 1–52 weeks
> Goals, objectives

■ **PANEL 7.5 Vision and mission statements.**

Vision statements

- **Amazon:** "Our vision is to be earth's most customer centric company."
- **Clothing maker Patagonia:** "We prefer the human scale to the corporate, vagabonding to tourism, and the quirky and lively to the toned-down and flattened out."
- **Marriott Hotels:** "Our vision is to be the world's leading provider of hospitality services."
- **Handicrafters website Etsy:** "Our vision is to build a new economy and present a better choice."

Mission statements

- **Amazon:** "To build a place where people can come to find and discover anything they might want to buy online."
- **Clothing maker Patagonia:** "Build the best product, cause no unnecessary harm, use business to inspire and implement solutions to the environmental crisis."
- **Marriott Hotels:** "Our commitment is that every guest leaves satisfied."
- **Handicrafters website Etsy:** "To enable people to make a living making things, and to reconnect makers with buyers."

An example of a mission statement, also from Ford, is:

We are a global, diverse family with a proud heritage, passionately committed to providing outstanding products and services.

Other mission statements are shown on p. 199. *(See ■ Panel 7.5.)*

Three Types of Planning for Three Levels of Management: Strategic, Tactical, & Operational

What are the three levels of planning, and who does it?

Clear, inspirational vision statements and mission statements mark the start of the planning process. Once these are developed, it is top management's job to do *strategic planning*. The strategic priorities and policies are then passed down the organizational pyramid to middle management, which needs to do *tactical planning*. Middle managers then pass these plans along to supervisory management to do *operational planning*. Each type of planning has different time horizons, although the times overlap, since the plans are somewhat elastic.

Strategic Planning by Top Managers: 1 to 5 Years

Top managers make long-term decisions about the overall direction of the organization. The CEO, the vice presidents, and the division heads need to pay attention to the competitive environment outside the organization, being alert for long-run opportunities and problems. These executives must be future oriented, dealing with uncertain, highly competitive conditions.

Using their mission and vision statements, top managers do **strategic planning**—**determining the organization's long-term goals for the next 1 to 5 years with the resources they anticipate having.** "Strategic planning requires visionary and directional thinking," says one authority.[23] It should communicate not only general goals about growth and profits but also ways to achieve them.

■ **Example of Strategic Planning: Ford Motor Company Gets Ready for a New Era in Truck Engines.** To continue dominating the market for large pickup trucks, which generates much of its overall profit, and still meet new federal environmental regulations, Ford's top management decided on the major goal of bringing out a new Super Duty pickup, to go on sale in spring 2010. Its most prominent feature was to be a new diesel engine with state-of-the-art antipollution technology, superior fuel economy, and no significant maintenance required before 300,000 miles.

Bob Fascetti, Ford's chief engineer of big engines, was handed a nearly impossible schedule: 30 months, a year faster than usual. He gave the assignment to Adam Gryglak, chief diesel engineer.[24] ■

Tactical Planning by Middle Managers: 6 to 24 Months

Middle managers implement the policies and plans of the top managers above them and supervise and coordinate the activities of the supervisory managers below them. In for-profit organizations, middle managers are the functional managers and department managers. Their decisions often must be made without a base of clearly defined informational procedures, perhaps requiring detailed analysis and computations.

Middle managers do **tactical planning, determining what contributions their work units can make with their existing resources during the next 6 months to 2 years.** Often the top and supervisory managers will have a hand in developing the tactical plans.

ⓘ
Want to Know More? 7-4

If You Become a Supervisor, What Will Your Responsibilities & Activities Involve?

Go to www.mybizlab.com.

Source: Roy Ritchie.

⑥ The new engine guy. Middle manager Adam Gryglak, Ford's chief diesel engineer, and his Project Scorpion team, drew up a tactical plan to develop a new truck engine in only 30 months. This was accomplished in part by having a "skunkworks" away from Ford's main tech center and outside the usual reporting arrangements.

■ **Example of Tactical Planning: Ford's "Project Scorpion" to Develop a New Engine.** Ford normally has a strict product-development hierarchy, but diesel engineer Adam Gryglak realized he'd never meet his deadline following the usual process. So in October 2006 he put together a team of engineers and, with his boss's permission, moved them out of Ford's tech center in Dearborn, Michigan, to get away from the close scrutiny and second-guessing of top management. (This is the arrangement known as a "skunkworks," with reporting outside of usual channels, that we mentioned in Chapter 6.) He called the project Scorpion, after the heavy metal band the Scorpions. ⑥

Away from the atmosphere of rigidity, Gryglak's team felt free to experiment. For instance, Ford usually forces suppliers to adapt their technology in hundreds of small ways to Ford's specifications, which means lots of reworking. But with time short, the engineers learned to trust their suppliers more, as in letting the German company Bosch work on the engine's antipollution device with minimal reengineering. ■

Operational Planning by Supervisory Managers: 1 to 52 Weeks

The supervisory managers are the managers at the bottom of the pyramid who direct the daily tasks of nonmanagerial personnel. Some of their decisions may be predictable ones that follow well-defined procedures, but others require using independent judgment.

Following the plans of middle and top managers, supervisory managers do ***operational planning,* determining how to accomplish specific tasks with existing resources within the next 1-week to 1-year period.**

Employees may take part in formulating operational plans, as may middle managers.

■ **Example of Operational Planning: Ford's Project Scorpion.** Some of Gryglak's engineers acted in supervisory capacities, responsible for different details of the truck engine's development. For instance, some working on the goal of increasing fuel efficiency finally led Team Scorpion to decide to build the engine out of a lighter material.

Key Takeaway 7-2
Three types of planning are strategic, tactical, and operational.

Scorpion's approach (the team approach, discussed in Chapter 8) also had another payoff: Specialists used to working only with fellow specialists became more familiar with what other engineers were up to. "We saved months by knowing hourly what the other guys were thinking and what their problems were," said a veteran engineer. "The result was that the engine fit into the truck perfectly the first time, and that almost never happens." ■

Goals & Objectives

What's the difference between a goal and an objective?

Whatever its type—strategic, tactical, or operational—the purpose of planning is to achieve a goal. A *goal* **is a broad, long-range target that an organization wishes to attain.** An *objective* **is a specific, short-term target designed to achieve the organization's goals.**

■ **Example of Goals and Objectives: Construction Contractors and Subcontractors.** In construction, a company called a prime contractor wins the work, such as building an office complex, which would be considered the *goal*. The prime contractor then contracts out to subcontractors the individual building activities, which could be considered the *objectives*—grading the site, pouring the foundation, erecting the steel frame, performing the electrical work, and so on. ❼ ■

Source: John Korpics.

❼ **Higher goals.** Completed in 1931, New York City's famous Empire State Building has 102 floors, representing enormous energy costs. In 2008, the building's owners began a five-year green refurbishing, with the *goal* of reducing energy use by 38% and saving $4.4 million a year. An important *objective* toward that goal: replace the existing windows, all 6,500 of them, with solar-efficient panes, as this worker is doing on the 61st floor.

Assessing Your Competitive Position for Strategic Planning: SWOT Analysis

How would SWOT help me figure out a strategic plan?

Strategic planning often starts with a *SWOT analysis,* **which is a description of the strengths (S), weaknesses (W), opportunities (O), and threats (T) affecting the organization.** A SWOT analysis should provide senior management with a realistic picture of their organization in relation to its internal and external environments so they can better establish strategy in pursuit of its mission.

The SWOT analysis has two parts: inside matters and outside matters—that is, a picture of *internal strengths and weaknesses* and a picture of *external opportunities and threats.* (See ■ *Panel 7.6.*)

■ **PANEL 7.6 A SWOT analysis.** Examples of strengths, weaknesses, opportunities, and threats for a hypothetical company.

Internal Strengths—S
Examples: Technology leader, seasoned management, cost advantages, energy-reduction technology, etc.

Internal Weaknesses—W
Examples: Outdated facilities, weak implementation strategy, missing key skills, etc.

External Opportunities—O
Examples: Diversify into related services, compete in new markets, capitalize on complacency of competitors, etc.

External Threats—T
Examples: Growing consumer power, government regulatory pressure, changing buyer tastes, spike in fuel costs, etc.

BRIEFING / GLOBAL BUSINESS

Toyota Takes a Look at Itself—A Hypothetical SWOT Analysis. If in 2011, Toyota Motor Corp. were to do a SWOT, it might find the following:[25]

Internal strengths: World's biggest carmaker. Manufacturing system known for quality and efficiency. Cars enjoy reputation for quality and reliability. Toyota RAV4 top pick 4 out of 5 years by *Consumer Reports.* Toyotas perform well in dependability.

Internal weaknesses: Recalls of 12 million vehicles worldwide for problems involving floor mats and sticky accelerators drive down market share. Rust problems on frames of older Tundra pickups. Underused plants in Japan. Weak earnings forcing various cuts, as in company's famed research-and-development budget.

External opportunities: Loyal customers. Many GM, Chrysler, and European cars are not as reliable. Chance to make smaller cars for young urbanites with cramped parking spaces. Chance to be cutting edge with gas-electric hybrids.

External threats: Currency-exchange rates (yen versus dollar) reduce Toyota profits. Combined, more Honda and Nissan cars sold in the United States than Toyotas sold in the United States. Toyota buyers are getting older. Volkswagen passes Toyota in global sales. Honda and Subaru still strong. Ford brands just about caught up with Toyota in Power quality survey. Reliability of European cars improving. ■

Other Plans: Contingency

What's a contingency plan?

Contingency planning is the creation of alternative hypothetical courses of action that a company can use if its original plans don't prove workable. The scenarios present alternative combinations of different factors—economic, competitive, budgetary, and so on—to anticipate changes in the environment. Because the scenarios look anywhere from two to five years into the future, they are usually written in rather general terms. Contingency planning not only equips a firm to prepare for uncertainty and even emergencies, it also gets managers thinking *strategically.*

BRIEFING / A WORLD OF CONSTANT CHANGE

AlixPartners Creates Doomsday Contingency Plans for (Currently) Profitable Companies. For more than two decades, AlixPartners made money by leading turnarounds of companies in trouble, some of them near bankruptcy. But in early 2009, as the United States and the world sank further into recession and credit dried up, chief executive Fred Crawford started hearing from a different set of potential clients: healthy firms suddenly worried about the future. "They're not used to dramatic slowdowns in demand, to customers going bankrupt or not paying them," he said. "Some well-run companies are being snuck up on."[26]

AlixPartners is now in the business of creating doomsday contingency plans for still-profitable companies to help them cope with possible economic reversals. ⑧

Managers who used to be focused on growth may be ill-prepared for dealing with flagging sales, leaning on clients to pay bills, laying off employees, and canceling product lines. But Crawford suggests that if clients have projected a 5% drop in revenues in their next-year budget, they should refigure it for a 15% drop. "Every company should be ready to pull the trigger on a plan that imagines a scenario worse than they could ever predict," he says. ■

⑧ **What are the odds?** In a defining picture from the March 2011 Japanese tsunami disaster, this 100-foot pleasure boat wound up on the roof of a two-story building in Otsuchi. Crisis planning is a special type of contingency planning. In a world in which nearly anything can happen, how much "what if" should be realistically put into a crisis or contingency plan?

Source: Hideo Kurihara/Alamy.

7.3

Organizing: You Arrange Tasks, People, & Other Resources to Get Things Done

THE BIG IDEA: Organization charts represent traditional hierarchical management arrangements and show both authority (vertically) and specialization (horizontally). To be successful, managers need to develop their skills in three areas: technical, conceptual, and human.

THE ESSENTIAL QUESTION: What do organization charts show, and what three skills do managers need?

MyBizLab: Check your understanding of these concepts at www.mybizlab.com.

MyBizLab

Prior to its merger with Southern Pacific, the Union Pacific railroad had so many fatal accidents that in 1997 the Federal Railroad Administration (FRA) sent inspectors to UP's Omaha headquarters, where they learned UP's structure seemed to discourage teamwork and communication. In fact, the top-down, military-style organization had its roots in the post–Civil War era, when executive ranks were staffed with former combat-hardened officers. "When something happened," said a UP vice president explaining the attitude of leading by fear, "you pulled out your gun and shot the guy in charge of the territory." Said the head of the FRA of UP's dysfunctional working arrangements, "They were separated from each other in a way that almost guaranteed problems."[27] That culture began to change after the UP-SP merger in 1999.

The Organization Chart

What does an organization chart show?

Though traditional, a pyramid-style hierarchy of top, middle, and supervisory managers need not be unworkable, as Union Pacific's was, and many companies are based on this arrangement. Hierarchical organizations are frequently represented in an ***organization chart, a box-and-lines illustration of the formal lines of authority and the official positions or work specializations.*** (*See* ■ *Panel 7.7.*)

■ **PANEL 7.7 An organization chart.** This basic type of chart shows both the formal lines of authority and the work specialization. (Other kinds of charts are described later.)

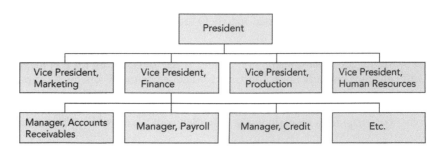

The organization chart provides two kinds of information about the company's structure: (1) the vertical hierarchy of authority, and (2) the horizontal specialization.

Vertical Hierarchy of Authority: Who Reports to Whom

A top-to-bottom scan of an organization chart shows the *vertical hierarchy,* the chain of command, who officially communicates with whom. In a simple two-person organization, the owner might communicate with just an assistant. In a complex organization, the president might talk principally to the vice presidents, who talk to the assistant vice presidents, and so on.

Horizontal Specialization: Who Specializes in What Work

A side-to-side scan of the organization chart shows *horizontal specialization,* the different jobs or work specialization. The husband-and-wife partners in a two-person advertising firm might agree that one is the "inside person," handling production and research, and the other is the "outside person," handling sales, client relations, and finances. A large firm might have vice presidents for each task—production, marketing, finance, and so on.

The Skills That Star Managers Need

To be a top-notch manager, what skills should I develop?

One researcher found that through education and experience managers acquire three principal skills: *technical, human,* and *conceptual.*[28]

1 Technical Skills: The Ability to Perform a Specific Job

Technical skills **consist of the job-specific knowledge needed to perform well in a specialized field.** Having the requisite technical skills seems to be the most important for supervisory managers.

▪ **Example** of Technical Skills: Judy McGrath of MTV Networks. Judy McGrath was 26 when she arrived in New York with an English degree. After a period of writing articles for women's magazines, she was hired to create promotional material for MTV, eventually rising to CEO, a position from which she retired in May 2011. ❾ MTV, which was launched as a music video channel in 1981, now comprises TV channels, websites, and wireless services. In her climb up the management ladder, McGrath clearly acquired the specific knowledge needed to function in the world of TV and digital entertainment. But technical expertise is more important at lower levels, and when she rose to the top she could rely on others for this. ▪

2 Human Skills: The Ability to Interact Well with People

Perhaps the hardest set of skills to master, *human skills* **consist of the ability to work well in cooperation with other people to get things done.** These skills—the ability to motivate, to inspire trust, and to communicate with others—are necessary for managers at all levels.

▪ **Example** of Human Skills: Judy McGrath. McGrath "is known for her skillful management of talent and the chaos that comes with a creative enterprise," reports a business magazine article. "Judy's ability to concentrate on people" is intense, says an MTV executive. Even as a busy top executive, she tried to listen to everyone, from interns to vice presidents, then offer advice. This approach helped foster a company culture of inclusiveness, creativity, and risk taking.[29] ▪

❾ **Judy McGrath.** As chair and CEO of MTV Networks, McGrath mastered the three principal skills—technical, human, and conceptual—that all managers need. Which of these skills do you think you've developed the most so far?

Source: Frances M. Roberts/Newscom.

Want to Know More? 7-5

What Are Some Examples of Conceptual Skills & Why Are They Important for Managers?

Go to www.mybizlab.com.

Key Takeaway 7-3
Managers need technical, human, and conceptual skills.

3 Conceptual Skills: The Ability to Think Analytically

***Conceptual skills* consist of the ability to think analytically, to visualize an organization as a whole and understand how the parts work together.** Conceptual skills are particularly important for top managers, who must deal with problems that are ambiguous but that could have far-reaching consequences.

■ **Example of Conceptual Skills: Judy McGrath.** During McGrath's career at MTV, she showed she had the "big picture" ability to stay on top of her job. Most nights she lugged a bagful of scripts and tapes home and exchanged Blackberry messages with executives well past midnight. She networked constantly with entertainment industry executives and stars, but also read widely—everything from *U.S. Weekly* to the Samuel Beckett novel *Malone Dies.* "Judy was the only person I ever worked with who knew as much about great literature as what was going on between East Coast and West Coast rappers," a former MTV executive said. "I always thought her intuitive appreciation of storytelling and characters was an enormous secret weapon."[30] ■

How the Mix of Skills Changes as One Rises to the Top

It's important to know that *the required mix of skills changes as one rises through the organization, from supervisory manager to middle manager to top manager—* generally from *less technical* to *more conceptual.* ❿ Thus . . .

- A supervisor needs more technical skills, a fair amount of human skills, and fewer conceptual skills.
- A middle manager needs roughly an even distribution of each skill.
- A top manager needs more conceptual skills, a fair amount of human skills, and fewer technical skills.

Source: Sally Ryan/The New York Times/Redux.

❿ **Upward bound.** The mix of management skills changes the higher one rises in the organization. In the informal environs of Silicon Valley technology companies, it's often hard to tell managers from subordinates, as in these offices at Groupon, the online coupon firm that promotes entertainment, food, and shopping deals through its popularity with consumers. Do you have the right mix of skills to rise to the top?

Leading: You Motivate People to Work to Achieve Important Goals

7.4

THE BIG IDEA: Leaders cope with change, whereas managers cope with complexity. Three styles of leadership, ranging from boss centered to employee centered, are autocratic, participative, and free-rein. Transactional leaders are concerned with getting people to do ordinary things; transformational leaders are concerned with getting them to do exceptional things. There are four key things that transformational leaders do.

THE ESSENTIAL QUESTION: How do leaders and managers differ, and what are the different types of leaders?

MyBizLab: Check your understanding of these concepts at www.mybizlab.com.

My BizLab

W hen you as a manager *direct* or *order* someone to do something, is that the same as *leading?* Certainly that has been a time-honored way by which managers got employees to do things. And it's still the preferred way of managing low-skill workers, such as those in farming, fast-food restaurants, and dry cleaning.

But, as the heading above suggests, leadership is really about *motivating* people. Nowadays, therefore, particularly with so-called **knowledge workers—people who work primarily with information or who develop and use knowledge in the workplace,** such as scientists, engineers, and database administrators—managers strive to empower employees. *Empowerment* **means employees share management responsibilities, including decision making.** This means that leading has become a much more subtle process than it was in the days when a manager could simply say "Do this!" ⑪

Leader versus Manager: Dealing with Change versus Dealing with Complexity

What's the difference between leaders and managers?

Although we see the words *leader* and *manager* seemingly used interchangeably, management scholar John Kotter suggests they are different: *Leaders* cope with *change*, he says, whereas *managers* cope with *complexity*.[31]

How Leaders Cope with Change

Business has become so volatile and competitive that it's no longer enough for a company to get by on just making minor improvements. What's required are leaders who can deal with great changes by creating a vision and strategic plan and inspiring others to rally around common goals.

Leaders cope with change in three ways: (1) by determining what needs to be done and setting a direction through planning and budgeting; (2) by communicating the new direction so that people can align behind it; and (3) by motivating and inspiring people by appealing to human needs, values, and emotions to keep them moving ahead in spite of obstacles.

Source: Photo by Brian Ach.

⑪ **Management sharing.** Danny Meyer, shown here with partners Paul Bolles-Beaven *(left)* and chef Michael Romano *(center)*, is founder of Union Square Hospitality Group in New York, which owns several restaurants, including the flagship Union Square Café shown here. Considered to be one of the best restaurateurs in the United States, Meyer frequently brings his chefs into ownership positions and empowers each staff member to do whatever is required to achieve a positive experience for all patrons. How would it change your job motivation if you became part owner?

How Managers Cope with Complexity

Today's organizations, especially multinationals, can be incredibly complex. Good management is essential, therefore, to keep them from slipping into chaos.

Managers cope with complexity in three ways: (1) by *planning and budgeting*, setting targets and specifying the resources and means for achieving them; (2) by *organizing*, creating the necessary structure and hiring the people to fulfill the jobs; and (3) by *controlling and problem solving*, monitoring results and solving problems as they arise.

You Need Not Be a Manager to Be a Leader

Key Takeaway 7-4
Managers cope with complexity, leaders cope with change.

While it's possible to be a manager without being a leader, it's also true that you can be a leader without being a manager—that is, showing the way through your own example and motivating others to do their best. Indeed, any employee can lead. In today's business most efforts are *team* efforts (as we discuss in Chapter 8): everyone has to work together to achieve common goals.

Want to Know More? 7-6
What Are Some Other Leadership Styles?
Go to www.mybizlab.com.

Leadership Styles: From Boss-Centered to Employee-Centered Leadership

What are three common styles of leadership?

Researchers have looked at all kinds of leaders to see what kind of *traits,* or characteristics, they have in common, but most results do not seem to be reliable.[32] Some leaders are kind and empathetic, and some are unkind and arrogant, and both types may get results.

Similarly, there are different *styles,* or ways authority is used, that characterize leaders, although no single type works best for any given set of circumstances. Three common leadership styles are (1) *autocratic,* (2) *participative (democratic),* and (3) *free-rein (laissez-faire).*[33] They range along a continuum from boss-centered leadership to employee-centered leadership.

Autocratic Leadership: "Do This Because I Said So!"

***Autocratic leaders* make decisions without consulting others.** This "my way or the highway" style tends to work in hierarchical organizations with a militaristic orientation, such as the U.S. Army or some branches of law enforcement, but it can also be effective in less formal kinds of organizations where focus and determination are important.

■ **Example of Autocratic Leadership: Martha Stewart.** Autocratic leadership is sometimes quite successful, as with style guru Martha Stewart, who built Martha Stewart Living Omnimedia with personal attention to every detail. "Whether you liked her or not," says one account, "she was meticulous and demanding."[34] It could be argued that this style allowed her to flourish in a competitive environment such as the entertainment industry. ⑫ ■

Participative (Democratic) Leadership: "Let Me Get Your Thoughts on What to Do"

***Participative leaders,* also called *democratic leaders,* delegate authority and involve employees in their decisions.** This style involves a good deal of communication—requiring the leader to have good listening skills and empathy—between the leader and the led. Although it may not increase effectiveness, it usually enhances job satisfaction.

⑫ **Two autocratic leaders.** Television personalities Martha Stewart *(The Martha Stewart Show)* and Donald Trump *(The Apprentice)* also built business empires partly by exercising an autocratic leadership style. Martha Stewart Living Omnimedia is devoted to media-lifestyle products. The Trump Organization is mainly concerned with real estate and Trump Entertainment Resorts operates casinos and hotels. Do you think autocratic managers typically set and demand higher performance standards?

■ **Example of Participative Leadership: Herman Miller Furniture's D. J. Pree.** The Herman Miller office furniture company, headed by the late D. J. Pree (and his sons Hugh and Max, who succeeded him), was a pioneer in participative leadership (or participative management), allowing employees to share in decision making and profits. In 1950, employees were given opportunities to structure their workloads and comment on corporate decision making. In 1983, the company introduced an employee stock-ownership program.[35] ■

Free-Rein Leadership Style: "Here's the Goal, Do What You Want to Achieve It"

The opposite of autocratic leaders, **free-rein leaders, also known as laissez-faire leaders, set objectives, and employees are relatively free to choose how to achieve them.** This style of leadership is often successful with professionals such as research scientists, doctors, and computer engineers.

■ **Example of Free-Rein Leadership: Intuit's Steve Bennett.** Steve Bennett, former CEO of Intuit, the Mountain View, California, maker of Quicken and TurboTax software, seems to be an example of a free-rein leader. "We want everyone to aim for what we call True North objectives—or better short-term as well as long-term results—and we want everyone to feel enthused and connected at work," he said.[36] Thus, he told his managers to create a "psychological contract" with their subordinates, describing what is expected, how well they are performing, and what they must do to get ahead. ■

What Style Works Best?

How well a particular style works depends on the people and the situation, as well as the company's mission and strategy. For instance, autocratic leadership works well in many newspaper newsrooms—it helped the *New York Times* win several

Source: Courtesy of United Scrap Metal.

⑬ **Successful leadership.** CEO Marsha Serlin and her son Brad, chief operating officer, who head up United Scrap Metal near Chicago, practice a kind of participative leadership. For instance, before they are interviewed by the Serlins, job applicants are screened by rank-and-file employees sorting scrap metal in the yard to see whether they will fit into the family atmosphere. Brad takes his subordinates' opinions seriously and is willing to scuttle an application on their say-so. We learn more about United Scrap Metal in Chapter 10.

journalism awards.[37] Participative leadership doesn't work well with low-skill or low-motivated employees, but it does with others, especially educated professionals in small groups. Free-rein leadership works well with highly skilled and motivated employees. ⑬

Some leaders will vary the styles depending on who they're dealing with—whether it's a new employee, for example, or an old hand who knows more about a process than they do. "Some people think you either have a demanding, command-and-control style or you have a nurturing, encouraging style," says Jim McNerney, former chairman and CEO of 3M. "I believe you can't have one without the other."[38]

Transactional versus Transformational Leaders

What leader would I be, transactional or transformational?

Two positive traits of a good leader are what are called *transactional* and *transformational* leadership behaviors. One is concerned with getting people to do *ordinary* things, the other with getting people to do *exceptional* things.

Transactional Leadership: Promoting a Well-Run Organization

***Transactional leadership* focuses on creating a smooth-running organization, motivating employees to meet performance goals.** Transactional leaders are concerned with setting goals, clarifying employee roles, providing rewards and punishments related to performance, and monitoring progress.[39] If the transactional leader's steady pursuit of order, stability, and performance goals sounds dull, it is nevertheless essential to a well-run organization. Several studies have found that self-effacing, diligent, conscientious types who have good execution and organizational skills make the best managers.[40]

■ **Example of Transactional Leadership: Jacqueline Kosecoff of Prescription Solutions.** The CEO of Prescription Solutions, which manages prescription drug benefits of commercial, Medicare, and government health plans, Jacqueline Kosecoff has a three-pronged approach to leadership.

The first is "coming up with the concept for a product or service to offer," she says. "And then you have to make sure that the entire team believes in that concept and understands it." The second prong is execution. "You often hear people say, 'The devil's in the details,'" says Kosecoff. "I think it's the divine." The third prong is measurement. "We measure when we're succeeding," she says. "And we also measure where we're not succeeding" and then try to fix it.[41]

Nothing about Kosecoff's leadership style or philosophy seems particularly flashy. But it has produced solid results. ■

Transformational Leadership: Promoting Vision, Creativity, & Exceptional Performance

***Transformational leadership* focuses on inspiring long-term vision, creativity, and exceptional performance in employees.** It strives to promote high levels of commitment and loyalty that can produce significant organizational change. Transactional leaders appeal to followers to put the interests of the organization ahead of their own self-interests.

Four Key Things That Transformational Leaders Do

Transformational leaders act in four ways to create changes in followers' goals, values, and beliefs.[42]

1. **They Inspire Motivation by Promoting a Grand Design: "Let Me Present an Overarching Vision for the Future."** Transformational leaders offer a grand design or ultimate goal for the organization that serves as a beacon of hope and common purpose. The vision attracts commitment and energizes employees by promoting high ideals and creating meaning in employees' lives.

   ■ **Example of Inspirational Motivation: Tero Ojanperä of Nokia.** Tero Ojanperä, executive vice president of Finnish phone maker Nokia, has a magnetism described in a 2009 *Fast Company* article as "a cross between Andy Warhol mystic and James Bond villain."[43]

   Ojanperä likes to point out that the company used to make "great car tires and also great rubber boots." Now, he says, Nokia "will quickly be the world's biggest entertainment media network." When his audience snickers, Ojanperä says, "That's okay. Laugh. That's what people did when we said we were going to be the biggest cellphone company in the world—back when we were making car tires and rubber boots."

   Is magnetic and enthusiastic leadership enough to carry a company through perilous times? When the *Fast Company* article appeared, Nokia still held first place in world market share for cellphones. The following year, however, it fell to third place behind Apple and Samsung.[44] The company is now working furiously to switch its phones from its own Symbian software and run Microsoft Windows Phone software to avoid being left behind in the fast-moving mobile phone industry. ■

ⓘ

Want to Know More? 7-7

Who Are Some of History's Most Transformational Business Figures?

Go to www.mybizlab.com.

⑭ Transformational. Tero Ojanperä, executive vice president of services and developer experience for Finnish smartphone maker Nokia, is considered a transformational figure. But even a company led by powerful, enthusiastic executives can find itself lagging if its business strategy is outmoded. Once number 1 in mobile phone market share, Nokia is now scrambling to climb back from number 3 (behind Apple and Samsung). What transformational leaders can you think of?

Source: Jo Yong hak/Reuters.

Want to Know More? 7-8

What Is Your Leadership Style? Take This Online Quiz

Go to www.mybizlab.com.

Want to Know More? 7-9

What Are Some of the Top-Ranked Undergraduate Management Programs?

Go to www.mybizlab.com.

2. **They Inspire Trust by Expressing Their Integrity: "We All Want to Do What's Right."** Transformational leaders model desirable values by displaying high ethical standards, even making personal sacrifices for the good of the organization, thus inspiring trust in their employees.

   ■ **Example of Expressing Integrity: Anna Roddick of the Body Shop.** The late Anna Roddick, founder of eco-friendly grooming-and-cosmetics firm the Body Shop, opposed animal testing and encouraged fair trade, environmental awareness, and respect for human rights. ■

3. **They Actively Encourage Employee Development: "You Have the Opportunity to Excel Here."** These leaders encourage their followers to grow and excel by empowering them, giving them more responsibility and challenging work, and providing individualized mentoring.

   ■ **Example of Encouraging Individual Growth: Kim Jordan of New Belgium Brewing Company.** Based in Fort Collins, Colorado, New Belgium Brewing Company gives every employee who has worked there five years a free trip to Belgium, the country whose beer tradition the U.S. company strives to follow. New Belgium also encourages employee ownership and staff participation in strategic planning and budgeting. "People are engaged and committed," Jordan says.[45] ■

4. **They Communicate a Strong Sense of Purpose: "There Are Great Challenges That We Can Conquer Together."** Transformational leaders communicate the organization's strengths, weaknesses, opportunities, and threats so that employees develop a strong sense of purpose and learn to view problems as personal challenges to be overcome.

BRIEFING / EARNING GREEN BY GOING GREEN
Nike's Mark Porter Communicates a Strong Sense of Purpose. CEO Mark Porter of Nike, who started with the athletic equipment and apparel company 30 years earlier as a footwear designer, demonstrates that "designing with both technology and sustainability in mind can transform everyone's performance," according to one report.[46] The technology—specifically Nike Flywire superlightweight shoes "stitched cable-style with threads stronger than steel"—proved itself at the Olympics.

Nike also announced its Considered initiative, which has the goal of making every pair of sneakers meet green standards (reduced waste and toxins, designed for easy recycling) by 2011. ⑮ "To us, this is a long-term commitment that will put us in a better, more competitive position," says Porter. "For example, to reduce waste, we've created this new modular design, with component parts that can be interchanged not only for aesthetic purposes but for functional purposes as well." ■

⑮ **Green purpose.** Nike CEO Mark Porter strongly communicated his desire to have every pair of sneakers meet green standards. The Air Generate MSL Men's Training Shoe follows this direction, with scrap waste from the cutting operation used for components of the shoe.

Source: Photograph by Sally Lindsay.

Controlling: You Monitor Performance, Compare It with Goals, & Take Corrective Action

7.5

THE BIG IDEA: Control is needed for at least six reasons: it can help you deal with changes and uncertainties, become aware of opportunities, detect errors and irregularities, increase productivity or add value, deal with complexity, and decentralize decision making and facilitate teamwork. Four control process steps are (1) establish standards, (2) monitor performance, (3) compare performance against standards, and (4) take corrective action, if needed.

THE ESSENTIAL QUESTION: How does control work, and how should I use it to be an effective manager?

MyBizLab: Check your understanding of these concepts at www.mybizlab.com.

My BizLab

ontrol is monitoring performance, comparing it with goals, and taking corrective action as needed. Thus, control—answering the question, "Are we on track?" or making sure that performance meets goals—is concerned with achieving productivity and realizing results.

Why Control Is Needed: Six Reasons

Is control really a necessary management function? Why?

There are six reasons why control is important. Control can help you . . .

1 Deal with Changes & Uncertainties

All businesses must deal with changes and uncertainties: New competitors. Changing customer tastes. New technologies. Altered laws and regulations. Control systems can help you anticipate, monitor, and react to these shifting circumstances.[47]

■ **Example of Dealing with Changes: Starbucks Changes Its Growth Strategy.** Before the recent recession, Starbucks tried to grow by expanding the number of stores (coffeehouses) in the United States. Falling short of its goals, the company decided in early 2011 to alter its strategy and try to achieve growth by selling consumer products in grocery stores, tripling the number of Starbucks stores in China (to 1,500 by 2015), and expanding further in digital media.[48] ⓰ ■

2 Become Aware of Opportunities

Controls can help alert you to opportunities you might otherwise not have noticed. Some examples: New overseas markets. Hot-selling product lines. Competitive prices on materials. Changing population trends.

⓰ Tea or coffee? Starbucks is betting on being able to alter the drinking habits of some Chinese by tripling the number of its stores in China by 2015. What role do you think the control function plays in the company's China strategy?

Source: Zhang Yang/TAO Images Limited/Alamy.

Authentic American Dining

⑰ Opportunity. If restaurants are among the most wasteful energy users in the world, isn't there an opportunity here for a "people, planet, profit" approach? That is, you serve people good food. You recycle everything and employ strong energy-control measures. You make a reasonable profit. That's the approach taken by media mogul Ted Turner and his partner with Ted's Montana Grill, whose motto is "Eat great. Do good." Is this a reasonable strategy for mom 'n' pop restaurants?

BRIEFING / EARNING GREEN BY GOING GREEN

Becoming Aware of Opportunities—Ted Turner's Montana Grills Offer Green Grub. Restaurants are the retail world's largest energy users, with a restaurant using five times more energy per square foot than any other commercial building.[49] Moreover, nearly 80% of commercial food service energy dollars are in inefficient cooking, holding, and storage, and a typical restaurant also generates 100,000 pounds of garbage per year, more than almost any other retail business.

Media entrepreneur Ted Turner and restaurateur George McKerrow Jr. saw an opportunity in such numbers. Their casual dining chain of Ted's Montana Grill, founded in 2002, is designed to leave a smaller impact on the environment. In these places, "you won't find a plastic straw or cup," says one account. "The straws are made from biodegradable paper. The menus are printed on 100% recycled paper. Even the cups are cornstarch."[50]

The chain now consists of 46 restaurants in 16 states, and Turner hopes the effort will inspire other restaurant owners to think about energy use and waste. "Imagine the implications for global warming if we get the whole restaurant industry to go green," he says. ⑰ ▪

3 Detect Errors & Irregularities

Customer dissatisfaction. Employee turnover. Cost overruns. Manufacturing defects. Accounting errors. All such matters may be tolerable in the short term, but if left to fester they can bring down an organization.

▪ **Example of Detecting Errors and Irregularities: Discovering Computer Crime.** "Cybercriminals are actively probing corporate networks for weaknesses," says a 2011 account, and "businesses face unprecedented pressure to let everyone know when they've been hacked."[51] As of midyear, there were 251 publicly acknowledged data breaches, according to the nonprofit Privacy Rights Clearinghouse.

Internet hackers invade the accounts of thousands of credit card holders and steal only a few pennies from each—amounts not usually missed by the consumers but worth thousands of dollars to the hackers. Thus, security software that monitors charge accounts for small, unexplained deductions can be a worthwhile control strategy. ▪

4 Increase Productivity, Eliminate Waste, Reduce Costs, or Add Value

Control systems can increase productivity, eliminate waste, reduce labor costs, and decrease materials costs. In addition, they can add value to products or services, making them more attractive to customers.

▪ **Example of Increasing Productivity and Adding Value: Electronic Stability Control Lowers SUV Deaths.** Death rates for drivers of sport-utility vehicles used to be high (82 per million vehicles for 1999–2002 models), a significant source of concern to insurance companies. But the rates have dropped an amazing 66% for recent models (28 per million vehicles for 2005–2008 models). These numbers come from a study by the Insurance Institute for Highway Safety, which found that installing stability control—which uses brakes and engine power to keep SUVs on the road—made a tremendous difference.[52] ▪

5 Deal with Complexity

Different product lines, different customer bases, different company cultures—all are complexities that must be dealt with. When one company merges with another, these differences may suddenly become important. Controls help managers integrate and coordinate these disparate elements.

> ■ **Example of Dealing with Complexity: Macy's Reads the Numbers and Goes from a Nationwide Merchandising Approach to a Local Approach.** Macy's has had to deal with two incidents of massive complexity. The first occurred in 2006, when it acquired and pulled together several retail chains—Marshall Field's, Robinsons-May, Kaufmann's, and other local stores. It then tried to meld them into one chain under the name of Macy's and to harness them with a single national strategy.
>
> But when control numbers showed the new organization losing money, CEO Terry Lundgren altered the strategy. In 2007, he changed course from a one-size-fits-all national approach to a "going local" approach, tailoring merchandise in local stores to suit local tastes.[53] ■

6 Decentralize Decision Making & Facilitate Teamwork

Managers can use controls to decentralize decision making at the company's lower levels and encourage employees to work as a team.

> ■ **Example of Decentralizing Decision Making and Facilitating Teamwork: Whole Foods Market.** In contrast to most retail companies, where ordering decisions are made high up, employees are hired by supervisors rather than fellow employees, and everyone's paycheck is secret, at Whole Foods each store organizes itself into eight teams, compensation is tied to team rather than individual performance, and performance reports and pay are open to all. Each team is tasked with improving the food for which it is responsible and is given great responsibility in hiring, firing, shelf stocking, and responding to consumers. The success of this approach is seen in the stock price—up from $2.13 in 1991 to $37.07 in 2010.[54] ⑱ ■

⑱ **Teamwork.** Whole Foods employees are organized into eight teams per store, with each team given great responsibility for performance and each individual compensated for the team's performance. If you're an ambitious go-go type of person, do you think this arrangement would hamper your individual chances of recognition and success?

Source: o44/Zuma Press/Newscom.

Taking Control: Four Steps in the Control Process

What are the control process steps I need to be aware of?

Generally control systems follow the same steps, although they may be modified to fit individual situations. The four ***control process* steps are (1) establish standards; (2) monitor performance; (3) compare performance against standards; and (4) take corrective action, if needed.** These steps are illustrated at right. (*See* ■ *Panel 7.8.*)

1 Establish Standards: "What Is the Desired Outcome?"

A ***control standard* is the desired performance level for a given goal.** Standards can be set for almost anything, although they are more easily measured when they are made quantifiable. For-profit organizations might have standards of financial performance, employee hiring, manufacturing defects, percentage increase in market share, percentage reduction in costs, number of customer complaints, and return on investment. More subjective standards, such as level of employee morale, can also be set, although they may have to be expressed more quantifiably, using measurements such as reduced absenteeism and fewer sick days.

■ **PANEL 7.8 Steps in the control process.**

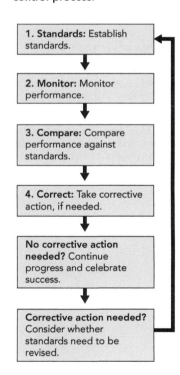

1. **Standards:** Establish standards.

2. **Monitor:** Monitor performance.

3. **Compare:** Compare performance against standards.

4. **Correct:** Take corrective action, if needed.

No corrective action needed? Continue progress and celebrate success.

Corrective action needed? Consider whether standards need to be revised.

⑲ **Performance monitoring.** As a boss you could sit in your office and keep tabs on the work by receiving reports by e-mail and phone. Or you could go out into the workplace and observe and ask questions—"management by walking around (MBWA)," as this manager is doing. Do you think some employees would consider the MBWA approach confrontational and the equivalent of "looking over their shoulder"?

Source: Marcin Balcerzak/Shutterstock.

Source: Andresr/Shutterstock.

⑳ **Range of variation.** Short for *magnetic resonance imaging,* an MRI machine uses a magnetic field and radio waves to create detailed three-dimensional image "slices" of the human body, such as the nervous system from the spine to the brain. Manufacturing an expensive machine that performs such a critical function means it's not possible to have a great range of variation.

2 Monitor Performance: "What Is the Actual Outcome?"

The next step in the control process is to measure performance—for example, by number of products sold or units produced. Less quantifiable activities, such as new patents applied for by a research scientist, may be measured by opinions expressed in peer reports.

Performance measures draw on three sources: (1) written reports, such as computerized printouts; (2) oral reports, such as subordinates' weekly verbal statements of accomplishments; and (3) personal observations, such as those made by a manager walking around the factory floor ("management by walking around"). ⑲

3 Compare Performance against Standards: "How Does the Actual Differ from the Desired?"

The next step compares measured performance against the standards established. Performance that exceeds standards becomes an occasion for handing out bonuses, promotions, and other rewards. When performance is below standards, managers need to ask whether the deviation from performance is significant. The greater the deviation, the greater the need for action.

How acceptable the deviation is depends on the *range of variation* built in to the standards set in step 1. For instance, a range of 3% to 4% error is considered acceptable in political polling, but only 0% error is supposed to be acceptable in actual voting, where there is supposed to be no range of variation—where, as the expression goes, "every vote counts." In machining parts for a high-end automobile such as a Bentley, the range of variation is less tolerant than when machining parts for a motorbike. ⑳

4 Take Corrective Action, If Needed: "What Changes Are Necessary to Obtain Desirable Outcomes?"

There are three possible scenarios:

- Make no changes.
- Recognize and celebrate positive performance that meets or exceeds the standards set by bestowing rewards—whether it's a verbal "job well done" or more substantial payoffs such as raises, bonuses, and promotions in order to reinforce good behavior.
- Correct negative performance by examining the reasons why and taking appropriate action. Sometimes the standards are unrealistic and need to be altered. Sometimes employees haven't been given the resources for achieving the standards. And sometimes employees may need more attention and direction from management.

LEARNING & SKILLS PORTFOLIO

Summary

7.1 Management: What It Is, How You Do It— The Four Essential Functions

THE ESSENTIAL QUESTION: *Why are managers needed, what do they do, what are their levels, and how do they make decisions?*

Are managers really necessary? Why? Managers help an organization achieve its goals effectively and efficiently. To be effective means to achieve results, to realize the firm's goals by making the right decisions and executing them successfully. To be efficient means to use people, money, raw materials, and other resources wisely and cost-effectively.

What are the four functions I'm supposed to perform as a manager? Management is defined as the pursuit of organizational goals effectively and efficiently through (1) planning, (2) organization, (3) leading, and (4) controlling the organization's resources. Planning is defined as setting goals and deciding how to achieve them. Organizing is defined as arranging tasks, people, and other resources to accomplish the work. Leading is defined as motivating, directing, and otherwise influencing people to work hard to achieve the organization's goals. Controlling is defined as monitoring performance, comparing it with goals, and taking corrective action as needed.

What are the three levels of management? The three levels of management are top, middle, and supervisory. Top managers, the highest level of management, make long-term decisions about the overall direction of the organization and establish the objectives, strategies, and policies for it. Middle managers implement the policies and plans of the top managers above them and supervise and coordinate the activities of the supervisory managers below them. Supervisory managers make short-term operating decisions, directing the daily tasks of nonmanagerial personnel.

What steps should I take as a manager to reach a decision? A decision is a choice made from among available alternatives. Decision making is the process of identifying and choosing alternative courses of action. Typically there are four phases associated with making a practical decision. Phase 1 is to identify the problem or opportunity. Problems are difficulties that inhibit the achievement of goals. Opportunities are situations that present possibilities for exceeding existing goals. Phase 2 is to dream up possible solutions, using brainstorming, in which individuals generate multiple ideas and alternatives for solving problems. Phase 3 is to weigh alternative solutions and select one, weighing each alternative not only according to cost and quality but also according to whether one is effective, feasible, and ethical. Phase 4 is to implement the solution, then evaluate it.

7.2 Planning: You Set Goals & Decide How to Achieve Them

THE ESSENTIAL QUESTION: *What are the benefits of planning, and what is the planning process?*

How does planning help a manager? Planning helps you cope with uncertainty, think ahead, coordinate activities, and check on your progress.

How do vision and mission statements differ? A vision statement describes the long-term goal of what the organization wants to become. A mission statement is a statement of the organization's fundamental purposes.

What are the three levels of planning, and who does it? Using mission and vision statements, top managers do strategic planning—they determine what the organization's long-term goals should be for the next 1 to 5 years with the resources they expect to have available. Middle managers do tactical planning—they determine what contributions their departments or similar work units can make with their given resources during the next 6 months to 2 years. Supervisory managers do operational planning—they determine how to accomplish specific tasks with available resources within the next 21-week to 1-year period.

What's the difference between a goal and an objective? Whatever its type, the purpose of planning is to achieve a goal. A goal is a broad, long-range target that an organization wishes to attain. An objective is a specific, short-term target designed to achieve the organization's goals.

How would SWOT help me figure out a strategic plan? The starting point for establishing strategic planning is often a SWOT analysis, which is a search for the strengths (S), weaknesses (W), opportunities (O), and threats (T) affecting the organization. A SWOT analysis should provide senior management with a realistic understanding of their organization in relation to its internal and external environments so they can better formulate strategy in pursuit of its mission.

What's a contingency plan? Contingency planning is the creation of alternative hypothetical courses of action that a company can use if its original plans don't prove workable.

7.3 Organizing: You Arrange Tasks, People, & Other Resources to Get Things Done

THE ESSENTIAL QUESTION: *What do organization charts show, and what three skills do managers need?*

What does an organization chart show? Hierarchical organizations are frequently represented in an organization chart, a box-and-lines illustration showing the formal lines of authority and the organization's official positions or work specializations. The organization provides two kinds of information about the company's structure: the vertical hierarchy of authority and the horizontal specialization.

To be a top-notch manager, what skills should I develop? Managers acquire three principal skills. Technical skills consist of the job-specific knowledge needed to perform well in a specialized field. Human skills consist of the ability to work well in cooperation with other people to get things done. Conceptual skills consist of the ability to think analytically—to visualize an organization as a whole and understand how the parts work together.

7.4 Leading: You Motivate People to Work to Achieve Important Goals

THE ESSENTIAL QUESTION: *How do leaders and managers differ, and what are the different types of leaders?*

What's the difference between leaders and managers? Leadership is really about motivating people, particularly with so-called knowledge workers—people who work primarily with information or who develop and use knowledge in the workplace. Managers strive to empower such employees; empowerment means employees share management responsibilities, including decision making. The difference between managers and leaders is that leaders cope with change, whereas managers cope with complexity.

What are three common styles of leadership? Three styles are autocratic, participative, and free-rein. Autocratic leaders make decisions without consulting others. Participative leaders delegate authority and involve employees in their decisions. Free-rein leaders set objectives, and employees are relatively free to choose how to achieve them.

What leader would I be, transactional or transformational? Two kinds of leadership behavior are transactional and transformational. Transactional leadership focuses on creating a smooth-running organization, motivating employees to meet performance goals. Transformational leadership focuses on inspiring long-term vision, creativity, and exceptional performance in employees. Transformational leaders inspire motivation by promoting a grand design for the organization, inspire trust by expressing their integrity, actively encourage employee development, and communicate a strong sense of purpose.

7.5 Controlling: You Monitor Performance, Compare It with Goals, & Take Corrective Action

THE ESSENTIAL QUESTION: *How does control work, and how should I use it to be an effective manager?*

Is control really a necessary management function? Why? There are six reasons why control is important. Control can help you (1) deal with changes and uncertainties; (2) become aware of opportunities; (3) detect errors and irregularities; (4) increase productivity, eliminate waste, reduce costs, or add value; (5) deal with complexity; and (6) decentralize decision making and facilitate teamwork.

What are the control process steps I need to be aware of? The four control process steps are (1) establish control standards, the desired performance level for a given goal; (2) monitor performance; (3) compare performance against standards; and (4) take corrective action, if needed.

Key Terms

MyBizLab

autocratic leaders
brainstorming
conceptual skills
contingency planning
control process
control standard
controlling
decision
decision making
effective
efficient
empowerment
free-rein leaders

goal
human skills
knowledge workers
leading
management
middle managers
mission statement
objective
operational planning
opportunities
organization chart
organizing

participative leaders
planning
problems
strategic planning
supervisory managers
SWOT analysis
tactical planning
technical skills
top managers
transactional leadership
transformational leadership
vision statement

Pop Quiz Prep

1. How is the *controlling function of management* defined?
2. Someone with the title "department head" falls under which category of employee?
3. What does a mission statement do?
4. What is the time frame for strategic planning?

5. What does a glance up and down an organization chart show?
6. Star managers need technical, human, and conceptual skills. Generally speaking, how do these needs vary with management level?

7. What is the relationship between leading and managing?

8. What kind of behavior would you expect from autocratic leaders?

9. Can a control standard be subjective?

10. What is the final step of the control process?

Critical Thinking Questions

1. The most frequently asked question about leadership is whether leaders are born or made. It turns out that maybe it's a little of both. Based upon what you know to be the qualities of a leader, what do you think? Please explain.

2. A micromanager is someone who closely observes or controls the work of his or her subordinates or employees. Micromanagement is a result of impatience and the desire for more expediency. The most common reason for micromanagement has to do with the manager's focus on detail, emotional insecurity, and doubts about employee competence. Discuss the impact that micromanagement can have on employees in a professional work environment and what possible solutions you could suggest for employees subjected to this type of management.

3. You may have heard it before—companies evaluate prospective employees, in addition to required skills and résumé, upon personality and "fit." A culture is basically the personality of an organization, and while it's hard to express, it's easy to sense whether you might fit in. Based upon your personality, what do you think would be the right organizational culture for you? Discuss.

4. The control function of management allows a company to become aware of opportunities it might not have otherwise noticed, such as new overseas markets, hot-selling product lines, competitive prices on materials, and changing population trends. For each of these opportunities, give a "real life" example of how the control function has created opportunities for a company.

5. The graduate school you've wanted to attend since before you started college has wait-listed you. As the time draws near for you to notify the other schools to which you have been accepted, you realize that your wait-list status and chances of acceptance to your first-choice school appear to be slim. What is your contingency plan, and how would you deal with this situation using some of the functions of a manager?

Cases

Triple Rock Brewing Company Management Insist on a Relaxed Work Setting

Triple Rock Brewing Company is located in Berkeley, California, adjacent to the University of California campus. The video features short interviews with the restaurant's general manager, chef, and bartender, depicting what can result from an environment of collaborative teamwork, employee empowerment, and an obsessive focus on quality and the customer experience. Each relays the importance of their part in the planning and organizing that goes into running an efficient operation resulting in happy employees and even sometimes, happier customers.

Jesse Sarañina, general manager of Triple Rock Brewing Company, insists on a relaxed work setting. This laid-back environment is what keeps the customers coming back, and it is equally important that the employees feel relaxed while performing their work. "I give everybody the responsibility and room to relax and be themselves, and to have fun doing what they're doing," he says. His goal is for every customer walking through the door to enjoy themselves, and he feels that it starts with a relaxed environment, an outgrowth of confident and well-trained employees. From the "front of house" management, to servers, to bartenders, to the chef—the teamwork and value of the employee and customer is part of the culture. "We operate on mutual respect," he adds. His overall responsibilities involve not just managing day-to-day operations, but being acutely aware of conceptual thinking, which helps when brainstorming ideas to continuously grow the business.

Jim Humberd is the chef at Triple Rock, and he emphatically believes that planning and organizing is the key to success of the customer and employee experience. For the kitchen to operate correctly, he emphasizes, "it takes planning ahead—anticipating level of volume, how busy or slow it is going to be." On Tuesday, Humberd likes to begin planning some of the food items for the busiest day of the week, Thursday. "You must be ready ahead of time," he continues, "so it's understanding how long it takes to complete the work and have the right people in place to execute 'the service' for the day." He believes that planning ahead not only serves the customer well, but instills more faith in the staff about the decision-making process. He believes the management function of planning allows his staff (servers) to accomplish their work by having the food and tools they need.

Humberd also emphasizes the importance of the leading function of management. "A manager should have the ability to understand people and all different types of people and different types of scenarios. The challenge is to tap into each person every day." He is passionate when it comes to understanding his employees and providing them with tools to motivate.

As a manager, Sarañina expresses the uncertainty the job can bring, "with all of the many variables that come into play each day," and the skills needed to "script the scenario in my head beforehand so that I can use my experience to deal with it appropriately." This type of decision making allows Triple Rock to be proactive when dealing with the many uncertainties of running a production facility (brewery) and providing a quality service and product. The importance of making good decisions using timely information is evidenced in the video.

In conclusion, Sarañina states that "an [employee] must possess an unwavering dedication to the job." "Complacency," he states, "is the biggest killer in management. If you slide into a point of complacency, and you're there just to get a paycheck, then you're not looking out for the business and growing the business." To learn more about this company, and see their real-time "Beer Board Cam" and what their product line consists of, go to www.triplerock.com.

What's Your Take?

1. What type of management style does Glenn Pitman, the bartender, employ? Would you want to work for a manager like him?

2. What type of culture do you think exists in this work environment, and is this a culture you could see yourself a part of? What are the positives or negatives of this type of culture? Discuss.

3. Which of the three employees interviewed (general manager, chef, or bartender) has the most difficult job? Why?

4. What emphasis does Sarañina, the general manager, place on the control function and defining a standard?

5. Discuss how the video conveys employee empowerment. Can you give an example?

Is Middle Management as We Know It Becoming Extinct? Or Does It Need a Revival?

Is the middle-level manager becoming obsolete or extinct? This case explores the rise of instant communication technologies and questions whether the new technology has become a replacement for the general manager. Or is this just an oversimplification of the functions of a manager?

Lynda Gratton is a professor of management practice at the London Business School and author of a number of influential management books. In an article for the *Harvard Business Review* entitled "The End of the Middle Manager," she states, "new technology has itself become the great general manager." She goes on to say, "Moreover, skilled teams are increasingly self-managed. . . . There is little competitive advantage left in being a jack-of-all-trades when your main competitor might be Wikipedia." In her work, she is leading an international business consortium focused on the future of the workplace. Gratton believes that the old-school middle manager is an endangered species. So, you might ask, "What does the middle-manager of the future look like?"[55]

The case for the obsolescence of the middle-level manager has to do with the current generation of workers called Millennials or Generation Y—those born between the mid-1970s and 1999. Gen Y workers prefer not to be closely supervised. Many grew up as "latchkey kids" and, as children of the current Baby Boom Generation, they are used to making decisions on their own. (A latchkey kid is a child who returns from school to an empty home because his or her parent or parents are away at work.) This generation sees little value in reporting to a middle manager who simply tracks what they do—particularly when they feel that much of what the middle manager accomplishes can be done by themselves, by their peers, or by using technology. In the midst of automated corporate systems and controls, some come to question the value of a middle-level manager. The rise of instant communication technologies made possible through use of the Internet, such as e-mail, texting, and instant messaging and new media used through websites like YouTube and social networking sites like Facebook and Twitter, may explain the Millennials' reputation for being somewhat peer-oriented due to easier facilitation of communication through technology.[56] Millennials' preference to interact with peers and technology is not surprising when you consider they came of age during the computer and Internet revolution.

It is not only with Millennials that technology has affected the role of the middle manager. Because the technology revolution has allowed companies to interact with their customers and employees very differently, the role of the middle manager has changed with this trend. Technology allows virtual teams around the globe to work and collaborate, thus changing the nature of human interaction and communication. But does this trend suggest that the functions of managers no longer are needed?

The idea that technology can allow those doing the "real" work to connect in ways a manager has yet to do can be seen by the middle management cuts that have been ongoing over the last decade. Cutting out middle management has larger cost savings than one might think. The savings are not only in the salaries of those individuals but also in the time and energy expended by their subordinates and upper management to interact with them.[57] It is not surprising then, that middle managers are being let go and replaced by either technology or a less expensive employee. Could that less expensive employee be a Gen Y by chance?

What's Your Take?

1. Do you agree that Millennials want more personal leadership and mentoring and less "middle management"? If you're unsure of the answer, discuss what type of leadership you would prefer in the workplace.

2. Does Gratton's research suggest that managers could be replaced with a tweet? (A tweet is a post or status update using Twitter.) Do you think this seems like an oversimplistic view of the responsibilities of a middle manager?

3. What should a middle-level manager do to deal with this perceived obsolescence? Discuss your ideas.

4. What types of technology exist to manage remote employees? In what ways can a manager use technology to be a better manager for Millennials?

Briefings

My BizLab Activities & Cases

Go to www.mybizlab.com for online activities and exercises related to the timely topics discussed in this chapter's Briefings, as well as additional theme-related Briefing *Spotlights* highlighting how these concepts apply in today's business environment.

In-chapter Briefing:
- AlixPartners Creates Doomsday Contingency Plans for (Currently) Profitable Companies

Activity:
- Developing Marketable Business Skills – Climate Change & Individual Energy Use
- Going to the Net! – Cash in Your Border's Gift Cards!
- Going to the Net! – Larry Page, Google Co-founder, Is Promoted from within to CEO

Briefing Spotlight:
- Big Change, Big Risk

In-chapter Briefing:
- Nike's Mike Porter Communicates a Strong Sense of Purpose
- Becoming Aware of Opportunities—Ted Turner's Montana Grills Offer Green Grub

Activity:
- Developing Marketable Business Skills – Losing Sight of a Firm's Main Focus

Briefing Spotlight:
- Four for 2011

In-chapter Briefing:
- Toyota Takes a Look at Itself—A Hypothetical SWOT Analysis

Activity:
- Developing Marketable Business Skills – Discuss Robert Nardelli's Leadership Style at Home Depot, a Global Home Improvement Specialty Retailer

Briefing Spotlight:
- A Taste for Success

In-chapter Briefing:
- Jeff Bezos's Major Decision: What Kind of Company Should Amazon Be?

Activity:
- Developing Marketable Business Skills – Interview a Small Business Owner to Learn More about Management Styles in a Small Business Environment

Briefing Spotlight:
- Managing Entrepreneurial Prosperity

Additional Briefing Spotlights available at MyBizLab:

- BUSINESS CULTURE & ETIQUETTE
- BUSINESS SKILLS & CAREER DEVELOPMENT
- CUSTOMER FOCUS
- INFO TECH & SOCIAL MEDIA
- LEGAL & ETHICAL PRACTICES
- PERSONAL FINANCE
- SOCIALLY RESPONSIBLE BUSINESS

Marketing: An Introduction

Gary Armstrong
Philip Kotler
Michael Harker
Ross Brennan

CHAPTER 1
Marketing: Managing profitable customer relationships

AFTER STUDYING THIS CHAPTER, YOU SHOULD BE ABLE TO

- define marketing and outline the steps in the marketing process
- explain the importance of understanding customers and the marketplace and identify the five core marketplace concepts
- identify the key elements of a customer-driven marketing strategy and discuss the marketing management orientations that guide marketing strategy
- discuss customer relationship management and identify strategies for creating value *for* customers and capturing value *from* customers in return
- describe the major trends and forces that are changing the marketing landscape in this age of relationships

THE WAY AHEAD Previewing the concepts

We'll start with a simple question: What *is* marketing? Simply put, marketing is managing profitable customer relationships. The aim of marketing is to create value for customers and to capture value in return. Chapter 1 is organised around five steps in the marketing process – from understanding customer needs, to designing customer-driven marketing strategies and programmes, to building customer relationships and capturing value for the firm. Understanding these basic concepts, and forming your own ideas about what they really mean to you, will give you a solid foundation for all that follows.

Our first stop is to look at an organisation that you might not think of as having much need for marketing ideas and concepts – UEFA, the governing body of European football.

CHAPTER CONTENTS

Marketing European football

What are the biggest sporting events in the world? Everyone has their own opinion, but if you weigh a number of factors like television audience size, number of countries or teams involved, revenues and expenditure – not to mention the ability to bring much of the world to a halt – then the top five probably include the World Cup, the summer Olympic Games, the European football Championship, the Superbowl and the European Champions League.

Source: Getty Images.

Of these five, two are overseen by UEFA – the Union of European Football Associations.[1] There is a lot at stake here: regional and national pride, global TV audiences in the billions and lots and lots of money. UEFA defines its core purpose as being to promote, protect and develop European football at every level of the game, to promote the principles of unity and solidarity, and to deal with all questions relating to European football.[2] It does this by taking the excitement, the attention and the cash that big tournaments generate and using it to support its other activities.

Because of this, a lot of what UEFA does is marketing-related – whether sponsorship of an event or tournament by a commercial enterprise, a social programme to use the power of sport to alleviate problems like racism, the buying and selling of broadcasting and merchandising rights, public relations and managing relationships with governments, teams and an almost infinite number of journalists – not to mention the fans!

The marketing function of UEFA – people, resources and responsibilities for marketing affairs – is split across four divisions, each with its own focus.[3]

The **Marketing and Media Rights Division** develops marketing and media strategies for all UEFA competitions – the Champions League, the UEFA Cup, the European Football Championships and less prominent competitions like women's football, junior level tournaments and various 'futsal' events (the name is an abbreviation of the Portuguese term **fut**ebol de **sal**ão and the game is an indoor version of the standard sport). It has the responsibility to find the best price for broadcasting rights and agreeing terms and conditions with broadcasting partners and then maintaining relationships with these key partners.

UEFA Marketing and Media Management (UMMM) is the commercial division of UEFA responsible for generating revenue from sponsorship and licensing for competitions, and managing the relationships with all associated commercial partners. In essence, this division sells the rights to be associated with prestigious and exciting international events. It maintains high prices by strictly limiting the number of companies that are given these licences. Euro2008 in Austria and Switzerland had a core sponsorship panel of just ten companies – big global names like Adidas, Coke and Carlsberg. In the 2007–2008 Champions League season, the competition had just five sponsors – Heineken, Mastercard, Vodafone, Ford and Sony. Any number of merchandise items are produced for major tournaments – replica team strips, footballs, and even items for the desk-oriented like mouse mats and coffee mugs.[4]

UEFA Media Technologies SA (UMT) is the service company created by UEFA to support broadcast and sponsorship partners with multimedia content.[5] It links with the TV companies to try to ensure the best possible coverage of games. Untypically, during Euro 2008 the broadcasting of one game – an exciting match between Germany and Turkey – was interrupted by a severe electrical storm which disrupted power supplies. Many national broadcasters and sponsors were very unhappy at the failure of the systems at a critical time.[6] Other than TV, this division is increasingly involved with supporting UEFA's online operations – whether providing and maintaining statistical databases or selling downloadable recordings of games in order to maintain and develop relationships with fans and journalists.

The **Communications and Public Affairs Division** (CPAD) is responsible for public relations activity – such as briefing and supporting the activities of journalists. The division also has the responsibility of managing the work UEFA does with various charity and social groups. For example, CPAD works with the International Red Cross – the 'official charity partner of Euro2008' – among other projects with other organisations that have charitable or social causes to advance through the money and publicity generated by the sport.

That UEFA expends so much effort on marketing activity may surprise you – but think about it – it has brands, it provides services, it has connections and relationships with various publics and it generates significant revenue. One UEFA marketing manager – Philippe Le Floc'h – comments on the Champions League, a competition that alone generated €750m in 2007:

It is the best club competition in the world. It is a competition of champions, the best clubs, and the best players in the world. We have to make sure that whoever comes to the stadium, or watches on television, can fully experience it. We've thought about changing the music, but it is the second most recognised feature after the star ball and we get requests from all over the world for it to be used at weddings.[7]

Is everyone happy at the marketing activities of UEFA? Not quite. Some people aren't convinced that UEFA is sticking to its core mission of supporting football – they worry that it is moving too far towards becoming fully commercialised and that the sport is being used to make some people rich whilst traditional fans are being sidelined.

For Yves Stemmle, Switzerland's opening match against the Czech Republic in the 2008 European soccer championship won't be just about advancing to the next round. It will be about his civil rights.

'They want me to drink only Carlsberg beer and wear things with this,' said Stemmle, 36, pointing to the Euro 2008 logo on his hat as he sat in a Lugano café before a warm-up game with Slovakia. 'They can't tell me what to wear.'

Some fans say UEFA, European soccer's governing body, has put profits ahead of their interests and plans to turn them away from stadiums and 'fan zones' if they wear clothes bearing the logos of companies that aren't tournament sponsors. UEFA estimates the 23-day championship, which begins June 7 in Basel, will generate 2 billion Swiss francs ($1.9 billion) in revenue from media rights, tickets and sponsors. After expenses, it expects to retain 330 million francs to cover administrative costs and fund other tournaments.

A Swiss tabloid, SonntagsBlick, published a caricature showing UEFA President Michel Platini as Moses holding up 11 commandments to heed during the event. The first: Drink only Carlsberg beer. Lamp posts around Zurich are sprouting stickers saying, 'UEFA: We Care About Money,' a play on the group's slogan, 'We Care About Football.'

Organizers of previous events have protected sponsors' rights inside stadiums by refusing entry to groups of fans paid to wear corporate logos. UEFA is extending its campaign against ambush marketers into fan zones, areas in each of the host cities where supporters gather to watch games on giant TV screens. That has aroused the ire of some fans.

'Fan zones are paid for and run by the city and access is free,' says Patrick Cotting, who lectures on marketing and sponsorships at the University of Lugano and consults for the Euro 2008 organizers in Basel. 'There's no legal precedent that would forbid individuals from entering a public space because they're wearing the wrong T-shirt.'

Copenhagen-based Carlsberg is paying at least 100 million kroner ($21 million) for the sponsorship, its biggest ever, giving it the right to exclusive sales in the eight biggest fan zones in each host city.

'There are plenty of other places in the local cities where fans can drink other beers and we totally respect that,' said Keld Strudahl, head of international marketing for the company.

In Austria, beermaker Ottakringer Brauerei AG is taking advantage of the popular backlash by selling its beer with a red-white-red logo, the colours of Austria's flag, and calling it the 'unofficial fan beer' drunk by 'real fans who want to show their support in whatever way they want'.

'Soccer used to belong to the people,' said Carlo Kuemin, 70, as he huddled under an umbrella in the standing-only curve of Lugano's Cornaredo Stadium during the Switzerland–Slovakia match. 'Not any more. The sponsors *govern the events now. It's all about the money.'*

Stemmle, the fan in the café, isn't taking UEFA's actions lying down.

'I have a ticket to the opening match between Switzerland and the Czech Republic,' he said. 'I'm only going to wear things they don't allow.'[8]

UEFA then is an organisation that recognises the need to build and maintain relationships with its stake-holders – including customers. Our example shows, however, that marketing actions can have unintended consequences – care and attention is needed!

Sources: See notes 1–8 at the end of this chapter.

Today's successful organisations have one thing in common: they are strongly customer-focused and heavily committed to marketing. These organisations share a passion for satisfying customer needs in well-defined target markets. They motivate everyone in the organisation to help build lasting customer relationships through superior customer value and satisfaction. As Wal-Mart founder Sam Walton asserted: 'There is only one boss. The customer. And he can fire everybody in the company from the chairman on down, simply by spending his money somewhere else.'

WHAT IS MARKETING?

Marketing, more than any other business function, deals with customers. Although we will soon explore more detailed definitions of marketing, perhaps the simplest definition is this one: marketing is managing profitable customer relationships. The twofold goal of marketing is to attract new customers by promising superior value and to keep and grow current customers by delivering satisfaction.

Tesco states its core purpose as being 'to create value for customers to earn their life-time loyalty', and that 'no one tries harder for customers'. IKEA's vision is to 'create a better everyday life for the many people'. Dell leads the personal computer industry by consistently making good on its promise to 'be direct'. Dell makes it easy for customers to custom-design their own computers and have them delivered quickly to their home or office. These and other highly successful companies know that if they take care of their customers, market share and profits will follow.

Sound marketing is critical to the success of every organisation. Large for-profit firms such as Procter & Gamble, Toyota and Zara use marketing. But so do not-for-profit organisations such as universities, museums, symphony orchestras and even churches – as seen in Marketing at Work 1.2 (page 27).

You already know a lot about marketing – it's all around you. You see the results of marketing in the abundance of products in your nearby department store. You see marketing in the advertisements on your TV screen, that spice up your magazines, stuff your mailbox or border your Web pages. At home, where you work, and where you study, you see marketing in almost everything you do. Yet, there is much more to marketing than meets the consumer's casual eye. Behind it all is a massive network of people and activities competing for your attention and purchases. Marketing is a set of extremely varied practices, and Europe is a diverse and exciting continent. In this book we will look at Russian beer brands being launched in the UK, French cars being advertised in Germany, Danish foods being sold in Arab supermarkets and European aircraft being sold round the world – and many other examples of marketing in, to and from Europe.

This book will give you a complete and formal introduction to the basic concepts and practices of today's marketing. In this chapter, we begin by defining *marketing* and the marketing process.

Marketing defined

What *is* marketing? Many people think of marketing only as selling and advertising. Even if you have chosen to study marketing deliberately and with forethought, you might think the same. And no wonder – every day we are bombarded with television commercials, direct-mail offers and Internet pop-up ads. However, selling and advertising are only the tip of the marketing iceberg.

Today, marketing must be understood not in the old sense of making a sale – 'telling and selling' – but in the new sense of *satisfying customer needs*. If the marketer does a good job of understanding consumer needs, develops products and services that provide superior customer value, and prices, distributes and promotes them effectively, these products will sell very easily. Thus, selling and advertising are only part of a larger 'marketing mix' – a set of marketing tools that work together to satisfy customer needs and build customer relationships. Marketing is as much attitude as action, as much perspective as planning.

Broadly defined, marketing is a social and managerial process by which individuals and organisations obtain what they need and want through creating and exchanging value with others. In a narrower business context, marketing involves building profitable, value-laden exchange relationships with customers. Hence, we define **marketing** as the process by which companies create value for customers and build strong customer relationships in order to capture value from customers in return.[9]

The marketing process

Figure 1.1 presents a simple five-step model of the marketing process. In the first four steps, companies work to understand consumers, create customer value and build strong customer relationships. In the final step, companies reap the rewards of creating superior customer value. By creating value *for* consumers, they in turn capture value *from* consumers in the form of sales, profits and long-term customer equity.

In this and the next chapter we will examine the steps of this simple model of marketing. In this chapter, we will review each step but focus more on the customer relationship steps – understanding customers, building customer relationships and capturing value from customers. In Chapter 2, we'll look more deeply into the second and third steps – designing marketing strategies and constructing marketing programmes.

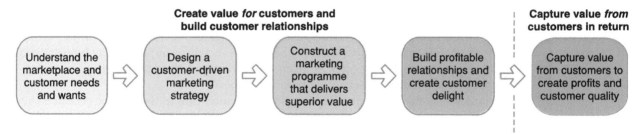

FIGURE 1.1

A simple model of the marketing process

UNDERSTANDING THE MARKETPLACE AND CUSTOMER NEEDS

As a first step, marketers need to understand customer needs and wants and the marketplace within which they operate. We now examine five core customer and marketplace concepts:

1   needs, wants and demands;

2   marketing offers (products, services and experiences);

3   value and satisfaction;

4   exchanges and relationships; and

5   markets.

Customer needs, wants and demands

The most basic concept underlying marketing is that of human needs. Human **needs** are states of felt deprivation. They include basic *physical* needs for food, clothing, warmth and safety; *social* needs for belonging and affection; and *individual* needs for knowledge and self-expression. These needs were not created by marketers; they are a basic part of the human make-up.

Wants are the form human needs take as they are shaped by culture and individual personality. A hungry person *needs* food but *wants* a Big Mac, fries and a soft drink. A person in Mauritius *needs* food but *wants* a mango, rice, lentils and beans. Wants are shaped by one's society and are described in terms of objects that will satisfy needs. When backed by buying power, wants become **demands**. Given their wants and resources, people demand products with benefits that add up to the most value and satisfaction.

Outstanding marketing companies go to great lengths to learn about and understand their customers' needs, wants and demands. They conduct consumer research and analyse mountains of customer data – Tesco collect gigabytes per day through their Clubcards. Marketing people at all levels – including top management – stay close to customers. For example, at Richer Sounds Hi-Fi (**www.richersounds.com**) every after-sales questionnaire filled in and returned by a customer passes across the desk of the founder, Julian Richer, and Harley-Davidson's chairman regularly mounts his Harley and rides with customers to get feedback and ideas.

Market offerings – products, services and experiences

Consumers' needs and wants are fulfilled through a **market offering** – some combination of products, services, information or experiences offered to a market to satisfy a need or want. Market offerings are not limited to physical *products*. They also include *services*, activities or benefits offered for sale that are essentially intangible and do not result in the ownership of anything. Examples include banking, airlines, hotels, accountancy and home repair services. More broadly, market offerings also include other entities, such as *persons*, *places*, *organisations*, *information* and *ideas*. For example, for the International Red Cross, the 'marketing offer' is health education and charitable workplace giving – not to mention efforts in recruiting blood donors.

Many sellers make the mistake of paying more attention to the specific products they offer than to the benefits and experiences produced by these products. These sellers suffer from **marketing myopia**. They are so taken with their products that they focus only on existing wants and lose sight of underlying customer needs.[10] They forget that a product is only a tool to solve a consumer problem. A manufacturer of quarter-inch drill bits may think that the customer needs a drill bit. But what the customer *really* needs is a quarter-inch hole. These sellers will have trouble if a new product comes along that serves the customer's need better or less expensively. The customer will have the same *need* but will *want* the new product.

Smart marketers look beyond the attributes of the products and services they sell. By orchestrating several services and products, they create *brand experiences* for consumers. For example, Europe's biggest theme park is Parque Warner, just outside Madrid. Visiting this is certainly an experience; so is a ride on a Harley-Davidson motorcycle. Your Nikes are more than just shoes: they are an empowering experience that makes you think you can 'just do it'. And you don't just watch AC Milan play: you immerse yourself in the San Siro experience.[11] 'What consumers really want [are offers] that dazzle their senses, touch their hearts, and stimulate their minds', declares one expert. 'They want [offers] that deliver an experience.'[12]

Customer value and satisfaction

Consumers usually face a broad array of products and services that might satisfy a given need. How do they choose among these many market offerings? Customers form expectations about the value and satisfaction that various market offerings will deliver and buy accordingly. Satisfied customers buy again and tell others about their good experiences. Dissatisfied customers often switch to competitors and disparage the product to others.

Marketers must be careful to set the right level of expectations. If they set expectations too low, they may satisfy those who buy but fail to attract enough buyers. If they raise expectations too high, buyers will be disappointed. Customer value and customer satisfaction are key building blocks for developing and managing customer relationships. We will revisit these core concepts later in the chapter.

Exchanges and relationships

Marketing occurs when people decide to satisfy needs and wants through exchange relationships. **Exchange** is the act of obtaining a desired object from someone by offering something in return. In the broadest sense, the marketer tries to bring about a response to some market offering. The response may be more than simply buying or trading products and services. For instance, a political candidate wants votes, a church wants a bigger congregation, an orchestra wants an audience, and a social action group wants to change government policy and public opinion.

Marketing consists of actions taken to build and maintain desirable exchange *relationships* with target audiences involving a product, service, idea or other object. Beyond simply attracting new customers and creating transactions, the goal is to retain customers and grow their business with the company. Marketers want to build strong relationships by consistently delivering superior customer value. We will expand on the important concept of managing customer relationships later in the chapter.

Markets

The concepts of exchange and relationships lead to the concept of a market. A **market** is the set of actual and potential buyers of a product. These buyers share a particular need or want that can be satisfied through exchange relationships.

Marketing means managing markets to bring about profitable customer relationships. However, creating these relationships takes work. Sellers must search for buyers, identify their needs, design good market offerings, set prices for them, promote them, and store and deliver them. Activities such as product development, research, communication, distribution, pricing and service are core marketing activities.

Although we normally think of marketing as being carried on by sellers, buyers also carry on marketing. Consumers do marketing when they search for the goods they need at prices they can afford. Company purchasing agents do marketing when they track down sellers and bargain for good terms.

Figure 1.2 shows the main elements in a modern marketing system. In the usual situation, marketing involves serving a market of final consumers in the face of competitors. The company and their competitors send their respective offers and messages to consumers, either directly or through marketing intermediaries. All the actors in the system are affected by major environmental forces (demographic, economic, physical, technological, political/legal, social/cultural) and we'll discuss these environmental forces in Chapter 3.

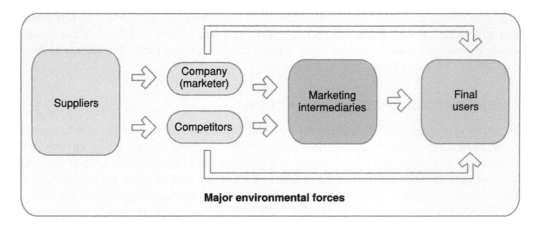

FIGURE 1.2

Elements of a modern marketing system

Each party in the system adds value for the next level. All of the arrows represent relationships that must be developed and managed. Thus, a company's success at building profitable relationships depends not only on its own actions but also on how well the entire system serves the needs of final consumers. Aldi cannot fulfil its promise of low prices unless its suppliers provide merchandise at low costs. And BMW cannot deliver high quality to car buyers unless its dealers provide outstanding sales and service.

DESIGNING A CUSTOMER-DRIVEN MARKETING STRATEGY

Once it fully understands consumers and the marketplace, marketing management can design a customer-driven marketing strategy. We define **marketing management** as the art and science of choosing target markets and building profitable relationships with them. The marketing manager's aim is to find, attract, keep and grow target customers by creating, delivering and communicating superior customer value.

To design a winning marketing strategy, the marketing manager must answer two important questions: What customers will we serve (what's our target market)? and How can we serve these customers best (what's our value proposition)? We will discuss these marketing strategy concepts briefly here, and then look at them in more detail in the next chapter.

Selecting customers to serve

The company must first decide *who* it will serve. It does this by dividing the market into segments of customers (*market segmentation*) and selecting which segments it will go after (*target marketing*). Some people think of marketing management as finding as many customers as possible and increasing demand. But marketing managers know that they cannot serve all customers in every way. By trying to serve all customers, they may not serve any customers well. Instead, the company wants to select only customers that it can serve well and profitably. For example, Marks & Spencer profitably targets the affluent; Lidl profitably targets families with modest means.

Some marketers may even seek *fewer* customers and reduced demand. For example, some public transport systems have trouble meeting demand during peak usage periods. In these and other cases of excess demand, organisations may practice *demarketing* to reduce the number of customers or to shift their demand temporarily or permanently. In order to reduce demand for seats on trains, for example, the London Underground has a price structure to persuade tourists and other leisure travellers to take their trips after the morning rush hour, and many public healthcare organisations across Europe use demarketing to persuade people to use services only when they need them, and not simply when it is convenient.[13]

Thus, marketing managers must decide which customers they want to target, and on the level, timing and nature of their demand. Simply put, marketing management is *customer management* and *demand management*.

Choosing a value proposition

The company must also decide how it will serve targeted customers – how it will *differentiate and position* itself in the marketplace. A company's *value proposition* is the set of benefits or values it promises to deliver to consumers to satisfy their needs. Porsche promises driving performance and excitement: 'What a dog feels like when its leash breaks'. Red Bull energy drink, on the other hand, captures a large part of the energy drink market by promising 'It gives you w-i-i-i-ngs!'

Such value propositions differentiate one brand from another. They answer the customer's question 'Why should I buy your brand rather than a competitor's?' Companies must design strong value propositions that give them the greatest advantage in their target markets.

Marketing management orientations

Marketing management wants to design strategies that will build profitable relationships with target consumers. But what *philosophy* should guide these marketing strategies? What weight should be given to the interests of customers, the organisation and society? Very often, these interests conflict.

There are five alternative concepts under which organisations design and carry out their marketing strategies: the *production, product, selling, marketing* and *societal marketing concepts*.

The production concept

The **production concept** holds that consumers will favour products that are available and highly affordable. Therefore, management should focus on improving production and distribution efficiency. This concept is one of the oldest orientations that guides sellers.

The production concept is still a useful philosophy in some situations. For example, Asian computer maker Legend dominates the highly competitive, price-sensitive Chinese PC market through low labour costs, high production efficiency and mass distribution. However, although useful in some situations, the production concept can lead to marketing myopia. Companies adopting this orientation run a major risk of focusing too narrowly on their own operations and losing sight of the real objective – satisfying customer needs and building customer relationships.

The product concept

The **product concept** holds that consumers will favour products that offer the most in quality, performance and innovative features. Under this concept, marketing strategy focuses on making continuous product improvements.

Product quality and improvement are important parts of most marketing strategies. However, focusing *only* on the company's products can also lead to marketing myopia. For example, some manufacturers believe that if they can 'build a better mousetrap, the world will beat a path to their door'. But they are often rudely shocked. Buyers may well be looking for a better solution to a mouse problem but not necessarily for a better mousetrap. The better solution might be a chemical spray, an exterminating service, or something that works better than a mousetrap. Furthermore, a better mousetrap will not sell unless the manufacturer designs, packages and prices it attractively, places it in convenient distribution channels, brings it to the attention of people who need it, and convinces buyers that it is a better product.

The selling concept

Many companies follow the **selling concept,** which holds that consumers will not buy enough of the firm's products unless it undertakes a large-scale selling and promotion effort. The concept is typically practised with unsought goods – those that buyers do not normally think of buying or contributing to, such as insurance policies or donating blood. These industries must be good at tracking down prospects and selling them on product benefits.

Such aggressive selling, however, carries high risks. It focuses on creating sales transactions rather than on building long-term, profitable customer relationships. The aim often is to sell what the company makes rather than making what the market wants. It assumes that customers who are coaxed into buying the product will like it. Or, if they don't like it, they will possibly forget their disappointment and buy it again later. These are usually poor assumptions.

The marketing concept

The **marketing concept** holds that achieving organisational goals depends on knowing the needs and wants of target markets and delivering the desired satisfactions better than competitors do. Under the marketing concept, customer focus and value are the *paths* to sales and profits. Instead of a product-centered 'make and sell' philosophy, the marketing concept is a customer-centered 'sense and respond' philosophy. It views marketing not as 'hunting' but as 'gardening'. The job is not to find the right customers for your product, but to find the right products for your customers.

Figure 1.3 contrasts the selling concept and the marketing concept. The selling concept takes an *inside-out* perspective. It starts with the factory, focuses on the company's existing products, and calls for heavy selling and promotion to obtain profitable sales. It focuses primarily on customer conquest – getting short-term sales with little concern about who buys or why.

In contrast, the marketing concept takes an *outside-in* perspective. In the words of one Ford executive, 'If we're not customer driven, our cars won't be either'.[14] The marketing concept starts with a well-defined market, focuses on customer needs and integrates all the marketing activities that affect customers. In turn, it leads to profits by creating lasting relationships with the right customers based on customer value and satisfaction.

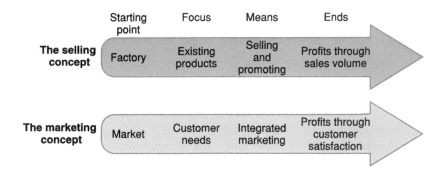

FIGURE 1.3

The selling and marketing concepts contrasted

Implementing the marketing concept often means more than simply responding to customers' stated desires and obvious needs. *Customer-driven* companies research current customers in detail to learn about their desires, gather new product and service ideas and test proposed product improvements. Such customer-driven marketing usually works well when a clear need exists and when customers know what they want.

In many cases, however, customers *don't* know what they want or even what is possible. For example, even 20 years ago, how many consumers would have thought to ask for now commonplace products such as mobile phones, notebook computers, 24-hour online buying and satellite navigation systems in their cars? Such situations call for *customer-driving* marketing – understanding customer needs even better than customers themselves do and creating products and services that meet existing and latent needs, now and in the future. As an executive at 3M puts it: 'Our goal is to lead customers where they want to go before *they* know where they want to go.' In Marketing at Work 1.1 several managers from a variety of firms give their perspectives on what marketing is and how their companies implement it.

MARKETING AT WORK 1.1

Managers on marketing

So how and why do businesses take marketing so seriously? Let's look at the personal perspectives from some current managers working in business today.

Electrolux – the Swedish manufacturer of household appliances – has been in business for nearly a hundred years and currently sells more than 40 million products globally for about €11 billion annually. The corporate motto is '*Thinking of you*' – but is their embracing of the marketing concept more than skin-deep? Richard Sells, the chief innovation officer at Electrolux, gives his take as a designer on the importance of marketing:

I think marketing ultimately is the bringing together of a consumer offer that is relevant and attractive to consumers, so whether you talk about that from the point of view of brand marketing, product marketing, marketing services, the offer in store – ultimately it's about bringing together an offer that is relevant and understanding the

consumer well enough to know that that offer is relevant. Most of the home appliance markets are saturated, and therefore consumers are looking for more sophisticated appliances. They're looking for better designed appliances, things that add some value to their home. They're no longer simply saying, 'OK, I'll have a dishwasher because I've never had one before', and so in that respect it's important that we understand what their needs are. You know, does a product that we are offering give some unique feature. The feeling can be sort of, you know, 'Wow, how did Electrolux know I needed that, because it really does solve my problem.'

Land Rover is a familiar name. For 60 years they have been producing high quality utility vehicles. Colin Green is their director of Global Marketing:

I think marketing at its essence is understanding consumer needs, understanding whether you can satisfy those consumer needs and then presenting

yourself in the marketplace through the principles of the four Ps – Price, Product, Promotion and Place – and getting those activities entirely focused on what the consumer is demanding and how you can meet those needs.

You'd expect a marketing manager to be onside with the idea of the importance of marketing, but what about at the very top level? Philip Popham, the managing director of Land Rover, comments:

For me, marketing is all about positioning your brand and your product correctly. It's about developing and building desirability which really does take away the need for the selling process, it builds desirability of the product so people want it and it builds loyalty. It's about handling the customer in the right way, making him or her proud to be associated with the brand, proud to be associated with the product which he or she has purchased and wanting more of that in the future, that's what good marketing is.

Land Rover and Electrolux are huge companies employing thousands of people and marketing their products globally. What about smaller businesses, is marketing relevant there as well? Acme Whistles has been in business for more than 130 years, with its 100 employees making and selling 6 million whistles per year. Quite simply, they think they make the world's best whistles. Acme products are used by police forces and animal trainers around the globe, by referees in most professional football leagues and in the early 1900s they supplied the whistles for use on the Titanic! Simon Topman, the MD at Acme, explains his take on how marketing is relevant to his business:

> Our marketing is undoubtedly affected by the way that we make things. A very good example of that is a tradition that was laid down by Joseph Hudson, our founder, who like any founder of a business was perhaps a little eccentric and a very determined individual. One of the things he used to do was personally blow every whistle before it left the factory. The production now is about 6 million a year so, of course, that isn't possible anymore – but we still do test every single one. Everything that leaves this factory is as we say in our marketing literature: 'Individually tested and guaranteed.' There are rejects, but we find them, not the customers.
>
> Successful marketing for me is linking together all resources of the company with the demand of the customer. So that everybody within this place right down to the cleaners knows what the customer wants and understands that keeping the machinery clean and the floor space around it clean is yet another way of making sure that the plating isn't contaminated, or the solder isn't contaminated, so the whistle looks better and lasts longer. And when you have all that lined up properly, then I think you have a great story to tell, great marketing and a business that's truly tuned in to its customers.
>
> Our ultimate aim is to make sure that that very famous brand name Acme, and our product link with it, is obligatory for the buyers of whistles. That such is the demand by the customer that retailers can't afford to not carry that product. To that extent we educate our entire workforce from the cleaners all the way through to those who are dealing with sales calls on what the customer wants, why the customer wants it, how they want it so that we're filling up that chain all the way from the very bottom right through to the customer. The whole company is focused on that customer – making our product the best they can possibly get, the one they've got to have.

Sources: Corporate websites for Acme Whistles (www.acmewhistles.co.uk), Electrolux (www.electrolux.com/), Land Rover (www.landrover.com/), and interviews with managers conducted by Pearson Education Ltd.

How firms market their products varies from industry to industry, as these images from Electrolux, Acme Whistles and Land Rover show – but there are commonalities as well. *Photos sources*: Electrolux (bottom left); Getty Images/Frank Greenaway (top right); The Advertising Archives (bottom right). All with permission.

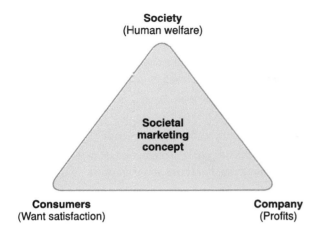

Society
(Human welfare)

Societal
marketing
concept

Consumers
(Want satisfaction)

Company
(Profits)

FIGURE 1.4

Three considerations underlying
the societal marketing concept

The societal marketing concept

The **societal marketing concept** questions whether the pure marketing concept overlooks possible conflicts between consumer *short-term wants* and consumer *long-term
welfare*. Is a firm that satisfies the immediate needs and wants of target markets always
doing what's best for consumers in the long run? The societal marketing concept holds
that marketing strategy should deliver value to customers in a way that maintains or
improves both the consumer's *and the society's* well-being.

Consider the fast-food industry. You may view today's giant fast-food chains as offering tasty and convenient food at reasonable prices. Yet many consumer nutritionists and
environmental groups have voiced concerns. They point to increasing levels of obesity
in adults and in children at ever earlier ages – leading to healthy life expectancy figures in
cities like Glasgow being the lowest in Europe at about 60 years for a man.[15] What's more,
these products are wrapped in convenient packaging, leading to waste and pollution. Thus,
in satisfying short-term consumer wants, the highly successful fast-food chains may be
harming consumer health and causing environmental problems in the long run.[16]

As Figure 1.4 shows, companies should balance three considerations in setting their
marketing strategies: company profits, consumer wants *and* society's interests. Cadbury
had a problem in 2007 when warnings for nut-allergy sufferers were missed off the packaging of its Creme Eggs. Despite this happening at Easter, when sales are at their absolute
peak, and such allergies affecting only a tiny proportion of the population, Cadbury felt
it had no choice but to recall the products.[17]

PREPARING A MARKETING PLAN AND PROGRAMME

The company's marketing strategy outlines which customers the company will serve and
how it will create value for these customers. Next, the marketer develops a marketing
programme that will actually deliver the intended value to target customers. The marketing programme builds customer relationships by transforming the marketing strategy
into action. It consists of the firm's *marketing mix*, the set of marketing tools the firm
uses to implement its marketing strategy.

The major marketing mix tools are classified into four broad groups, called the *four Ps*
of marketing: product, price, place and promotion. To deliver on its value proposition,
the firm must first create a need-satisfying market offering (product). It must decide
how much it will charge for the offer (price) and how it will make the offer available to
target consumers (place). Finally, it must communicate with target customers about the
offer and persuade them of its merits (promotion). We will explore marketing programmes
and the marketing mix in much more detail in later chapters.

BUILDING CUSTOMER RELATIONSHIPS

The first three steps in the marketing process – understanding the marketplace and customer needs, designing a customer-driven marketing strategy and constructing marketing programmes – all lead up to the fourth and most important step: building profitable customer relationships.

Managing marketing relationships

The necessity of managing the organisation's relationships, sometimes called *relationship marketing* or, popularly, *customer relationship management (CRM)*, is perhaps the most important new idea in modern marketing. Until recently, CRM has been defined narrowly as a customer data management activity. By this definition, it involves managing detailed information about individual customers and carefully managing customer 'touch points' in order to maximise customer loyalty – that is, the company uses its data about past transactions and interactions as a corporate memory, to help it more effectively engage with its customers in the present. We will discuss this narrower CRM activity in Chapter 4, which deals with managing marketing information.

More recently, however, customer relationship management has taken on a broader meaning. In this broader sense, **customer relationship management** is the overall process of building and maintaining profitable customer relationships by delivering superior customer value and satisfaction. It deals with all aspects of acquiring, keeping and growing customers – the opening case of UEFA showed how complex this can be.

Relationship building blocks: customer value and satisfaction

The key to building lasting customer relationships is to create superior customer value and satisfaction. Satisfied customers are more likely to be loyal customers and to give the company a larger share of their business for longer.

Customer value Attracting and retaining customers can be a difficult task. Customers often face a bewildering array of products and services from which to choose. A customer buys from the firm that offers the highest **customer perceived value** – the customer's evaluation of the difference between all the benefits and all the costs of a market offering relative to those of competing offers.

For example, Toyota Prius hybrid car owners gain a number of benefits. The most obvious benefit is fuel efficiency and hence reduced running costs. However, by purchasing a Prius the owners may also receive some status and image values. Driving a Prius makes owners feel and appear more environmentally responsible. When deciding whether to purchase a Prius, customers will weigh these and other perceived values of owning the car against the money, effort and psychic costs of acquiring it. Moreover, they will compare the value of owning a Prius against that of owning another hybrid or non-hybrid car. They will select the brand that gives them the greatest perceived value. Other drivers may prioritise other factors rather than efficiency and environmental impact – such as performance and social status reinforcement. These people would be more likely to buy a Ferrari or a Mercedes.

Customers often do not judge product values and costs accurately or objectively. They act on *perceived* value. For example, is the Prius really the most economical choice? Running costs may be significantly cheaper, but an alternative like a Skoda might be much cheaper to buy. In reality, it might take years to save enough in reduced fuel costs to offset the car's higher price. However, Prius buyers perceive that they are getting real value. A recent survey of the ownership experiences of 69,000 new car buyers showed that Prius owners *perceived* more overall value for their money than buyers of any other new car.[18] How many of them are likely to have considered it objectively – even to the extent of some calculations on the back of an envelope?

Customer satisfaction Customer satisfaction depends on the product's perceived performance relative to a buyer's expectations. If the product's performance falls short of expectations, the customer is dissatisfied. If performance matches expectations, the customer is satisfied. If performance exceeds expectations, the customer is highly satisfied or delighted.

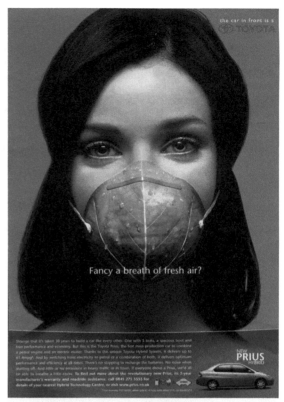

Perceived customer value: when deciding to purchase a Prius, customers will weigh its benefits against the benefits of owning another hybrid or non-hybrid brand.

Outstanding marketing companies go out of their way to keep important customers satisfied. Highly satisfied customers make repeat purchases and tell others about their good experiences with the product. Most studies show that higher levels of customer satisfaction lead to greater customer loyalty, which in turn results in better company performance.[19] The key is to match customer expectations with company performance. Smart companies aim to *delight* customers by promising only what they can deliver, then delivering *more* than they promise.

However, although the customer-centred firm seeks to deliver high customer satisfaction relative to competitors, it does not attempt to *maximise* customer satisfaction. A company can always increase customer satisfaction by lowering its price or increasing its services. But this may result in lower profits. Thus, the purpose of marketing is to generate customer value profitably. This requires a very delicate balance: The marketer must continue to generate more customer value and satisfaction but not 'give away the house'.

Customer relationship levels and tools

Companies can build customer relationships at many levels, depending on the nature of the target market. At one extreme, a company with many low-margin customers may seek to develop *basic relationships* with them. For example, Tesco has handed out millions of Clubcard loyalty cards which it uses to collect and analyse data on the shopping habits of a good proportion of the UK population. At the other extreme, in markets with few customers and high margins, sellers want to create *full partnerships* with key customers. This is often the case where one business is selling to another – P&G customer teams work closely with Sainsbury's, Asda, Carrefour and other major supermarkets – but also where the product is customised or tailored to the specific needs of a specific customer – such as a bespoke suit. In between these two extreme situations, other levels of customer relationships are appropriate.

Beyond offering consistently high value and satisfaction, marketers can use specific marketing tools to develop stronger bonds with consumers. For example, many companies now offer *frequency marketing programmes* that reward customers who buy frequently or in large amounts. Airlines offer frequent-flyer programmes and hotels give room upgrades to their frequent guests.

Source: http://www.porscheclubgb.com/. With permission: Porsche.

Building customer relationships. Porsche helps to maintain the community spirit of Porsche owners by sponsoring and endorsing owners' clubs across Europe.

Other companies sponsor *club marketing programmes* that offer members special discounts and create member communities. For example, Porsche, the German sports car manufacturer, sponsors owners' clubs in many countries around the world. As well as organising purely social events like dinners, track days and charity fund-raising events, the clubs also run trips to the Porsche manufacturing and development centres in Stuttgart, Leipzig and Weissach. Porsche as a commercial enterprise has a brand and human presence at all of these events and makes sure that the relationships with current owners are maintained and developed over time.[20]

To build customer relationships, companies can add structural ties as well as financial and social benefits. A business marketer might supply customers with special equipment or online linkages that help them manage their orders, payroll or inventory. As we'll discuss in detail in Chapter 11, Smiths – an offshoot of the well-known high street newsagent WHSmith – uses web-based software with its thousands of customers to manage the inventory and logistical difficulties in distributing millions of newspapers and magazines daily.

The changing nature of customer relationships

Dramatic changes are occurring in the ways in which companies are relating to their customers. Yesterday's companies focused on mass marketing to all customers at arm's length. Today's companies are building more direct and lasting relationships with more carefully selected customers. Here are some important trends in the way companies are relating to their customers.

Relating with more carefully selected customers

Few firms today still practise true mass marketing – selling in a standardised way to any customer who comes along. Today, most marketers realise that they don't want relationships with every customer. Instead, companies now are targeting fewer, more profitable customers. Called *selective relationship management*, many companies now use customer profitability analysis to weed out customers that cost them money and to target ones that are profitable for pampering. Once they identify profitable customers, firms can create attractive offers and special handling to capture these customers and earn their loyalty.

But what should the company do with unprofitable customers? If it can't turn them into profitable ones, it may even want to 'fire' customers that are too unreasonable or that cost more to serve than they are worth. For example, banks now routinely assess customer profitability based on such factors as an account's average balances, account activity, services usage, branch visits and other variables. For most banks, profitable customers with large balances are pampered with premium services, whereas unprofitable, low-balance ones get the cold shoulder. The Dutch bank ING Direct selects accounts differently. It seeks relationships with customers who don't need or want expensive pampering while firing those who do.

> ING Direct is the fast-food chain of financial services. With a handful of offerings including savings accounts, mortgages and CDs and home equity loans, the bank is about as no-frills as it gets. Yet its profits are downright gaudy. ING Direct's secret? Selective relationship management. The bank lures low-maintenance customers with high interest rates. Then, to offset that generosity, the bank does 91 per cent of its transactions online and offers bare-bones service. In fact, ING Direct USA routinely 'fires' overly demanding customers. By ditching clients who need the direction, hand-holding and personalised service of a branch bank, the company has driven its cost per account to a third of the industry average.
>
> ING Direct USA CEO Arkadi Kuhlmann explains: 'We need to keep expenses down, which doesn't work when customers want a lot of [hand-holding]. If the average customer phone call costs us $5.25 and the average account revenue is $12 per month, all it takes is 100,000 misbehaving customers for costs to go through the roof. So when a customer calls too many times or wants too many exceptions to the rule, our sales associate can basically say: Look, this doesn't fit you. You need to go back to your community bank and get the kind of contact you're comfortable with . . . It's all about finding customers who are comfortable with a self-serve business; we try to get you in and out fast . . . Even though our touch is light and short, it's all about how you feel in the end. The smile at a take-out window can be just as satisfying as good service at a sit-down restaurant. While this makes for some unhappy customers, [those are the] ones you want out the door anyway.'[21]

Great Rates

No Fees

No Minimums

No Bull

ING DIRECT
Save "our Money"

ingdirect.com
1-800-ING-DIRECT

Selective relationship management: ING Direct seeks relationships with customers who don't need or want expensive pampering, routinely 'firing' overly demanding customers. The bank lures low-maintenance customers with high interest rates and no fees or minimums. 'No bull!'

Source: ING Direct. With permission.

Of course, marketing strategies and tactics like this can cause significant issues for society as a whole – as we saw with the dissatisfied football fans in the UEFA case – and we'll discuss these in Chapter 16.

Relating for the long term

Just as companies are being more selective about which customers they choose to serve, they are serving chosen customers in a deeper, more lasting way. Today's companies are going beyond designing strategies to *attract* new customers and create *transactions* with them. They are using customer relationship management to *retain* current customers and build profitable, long-term *relationships* with them. The new view is that marketing is the science and art of creating, developing and sustaining interactive relationships with profitable customers.[22]

Why the new emphasis on retaining and developing/growing customers? In the past, growing markets and an upbeat economy meant a plentiful supply of new customers. However, companies today face some new marketing realities. Changing demographics, more sophisticated competitors, and overcapacity in many industries mean that there are fewer customers to go around. Many companies are now fighting for shares of flat or fading markets.

As a result, the costs of attracting new consumers are rising. In fact, on average, it can cost a lot more to attract a new customer than it does to keep a current customer satisfied – meaning that some investment in keeping current customers can save a lot further down the line.

Relating directly

Beyond connecting more deeply with their customers, many companies are also connecting more *directly*. In fact, direct marketing is booming. Consumers can now buy virtually any product without going to a shop – by telephone, mail-order catalogues, kiosks and online. Businesses routinely shop on the Web for items ranging from standard office supplies to high-priced, high-tech computer equipment.

Some companies sell *only* via direct channels – firms such as Dell, Expedia and Amazon.com, to name only a few. Other companies use direct connections to supplement their other communications and distribution channels. For example, XBox 360 consoles and games are available from many high-street retailers, but once set up and connected to the Web customers can buy new games, add-ons for games they already own, music and films through the online marketplace – as well as being able to purchase trailers and demos of new games.

Some marketers have hailed direct marketing as the 'marketing model of the next century'. They envision a day when all buying and selling will involve direct connections between companies and their customers. Others, although agreeing that direct marketing will play a growing and important role, see it as just one more way to approach the marketplace. We will take a closer look at the world of direct marketing in Chapters 13 and 14.

Partner relationship management

When it comes to creating customer value and building strong customer relationships, today's marketers know that they can't go it alone. They must work closely with a variety of marketing partners. In addition to being good at *customer relationship management*, marketers must also be good at **partner relationship management**. Major changes are occurring in how marketers partner with others inside and outside the company jointly to bring more value to customers.

Partners inside the company

Traditionally, marketers have been charged with understanding customers and representing customer needs to different company departments. The old thinking was that marketing is done only by marketing, sales, and customer support people. However, in today's more connected world, marketing no longer has sole ownership of customer interactions. Every functional area can interact with customers, especially electronically. The new *thinking is* that every employee must be customer-focused. David Packard, late co-founder of Hewlett-Packard, wisely said, 'Marketing is far too important to be left only to the marketing department'.[23] This has led to the idea of 'the part-time marketer' – someone who works for the organisation but not in the marketing department who has, nevertheless, the opportunity to impact positively or negatively upon how customers think about the firm. Technicians can make a good or bad impression, as can shop-floor staff and anyone who answers the phone when a customer calls.[24]

Today, rather than letting each department go its own way, firms are linking all departments in the cause of creating customer value. Rather than assigning only sales and marketing people to customers, they are forming cross-functional customer teams. Marketing at Work 1.1 gave the perspectives of those not employed as marketers but who nevertheless understood the importance of marketing in their roles as senior managers or product designers. As an example of this culture, P&G assigns 'customer development teams' to each of its major retailer accounts. These teams – consisting of sales and marketing people, operations specialists, market and financial analysts and others – coordinate the efforts of many P&G departments towards helping the retailer be more successful.

Marketing partners outside the firm

Changes are also occurring in how marketers connect with their suppliers, channel partners and even competitors. Most companies today are networked companies, relying heavily on partnerships with other firms.

Marketing channels consist of distributors, retailers and others who connect the company to its buyers. The *supply chain* describes a longer channel, stretching from raw materials to components to final products that are carried to final buyers. For example, the supply chain for personal computers consists of suppliers of computer chips and other components, the computer manufacturer, and the distributors, retailers and others who sell the computers.

Through *supply chain management*, many companies today are strengthening their connections with partners all along the supply chain. They know that their fortunes rest not just on how well they perform. Success at building customer relationships also rests on how well their entire supply chain performs against competitors' supply chains. These companies don't just treat suppliers as vendors and distributors as customers. They treat both as partners in delivering customer value. On the one hand, for example, Mercedes works closely with carefully selected suppliers to improve quality and operations efficiency. On the other hand, it works with its franchise dealers to provide top-grade sales and service support that will bring customers in the door and keep them coming back.

Beyond managing the supply chain, today's companies are also discovering that they need *strategic* partners if they hope to be effective. In the new, more competitive global environment, going it alone is going out of style. *Strategic alliances* are booming across almost all industries and services. For example, Dell joins forces with software creators such as Oracle and Microsoft to help boost business sales of its servers and their software. And Volkswagen is working jointly with agricultural processing firm Archer Daniels Midland further to develop and utilise biodiesel fuel.

Sometimes even competitors work together for mutual benefit. For example oral-care competitors Procter & Gamble and Philips joined forces to create the innovative IntelliClean system, a combination power toothbrush and toothpaste dispensing system. And Sony has partnered with Ericsson to produce mobile phone handsets – the Japanese electronics giant brings decades of experience in manufacturing high quality handheld gadgets and the Swedish telecoms giant brings detailed knowledge of mobile phones in respect of design and use by customers.[25]

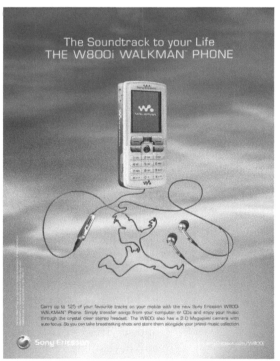

Source: http://www.livingroom.org.au/cameraphone/sony-ericsson-w550.jpg. Permission from The Advertising Archives.

Partnership relationship management: both Sony and Ericsson benefit from working together. Sony brings manufacturing excellence and Ericsson understands the markets and customers.

CAPTURING VALUE FROM CUSTOMERS

The first four steps in the marketing process involve building customer relationships by creating and delivering superior customer value. The final step involves capturing value in return, in the form of current and future sales, market share and profits. By creating superior customer value, the firm creates highly satisfied customers who stay loyal and buy more. This, in turn, means greater long-run returns for the firm. Here, we discuss the outcomes of creating customer value: customer loyalty and retention, share of market and share of customer, and customer equity.

Creating customer loyalty and retention

Good customer relationship management creates customer delight. In turn, delighted customers remain loyal and talk favourably to others about the company and its products. Studies show big differences in the loyalty of customers who are less satisfied, somewhat satisfied and completely satisfied. Even a slight drop from complete satisfaction can create an enormous drop in loyalty. Thus, the aim of customer relationship management is to create not just customer satisfaction, but customer delight.[26]

Companies are realising that losing a customer means losing more than a single sale. It means losing the entire stream of purchases that the customer would make over a lifetime of patronage. For example, Porsche believe that someone who buys a new Porsche will typically replace it with a new car after seven years. Five years after purchase, the company starts to target these owners with letters and other communications to make sure their next car is a Porsche as well – if this works, that is another £70,000 in revenue. Indeed, Lexus estimates that a single satisfied and loyal customer is worth $600,000 in lifetime sales. You almost certainly visit a supermarket once a week or more – you may not spend much per visit, but consider how this sum adds up over a year or two. Thus, working to retain and grow customers makes good economic sense. In fact, a company can lose money on a specific transaction but still benefit greatly from a long-term relationship. Banks recognise this when putting together account packages for students. While at university, it is likely they will cost rather than make their bank money – because of reduced rate loans and overdrafts, low-level balances and often free gifts for account opening. When the student becomes a full-time worker four or five years later that is the point at which that customer will begin to become profitable – statistics tell us that you are more likely to get divorced than change your bank.[27]

This means that companies must aim high in building customer relationships. Customer delight creates an emotional relationship with a product or service, not just a rational preference.

Growing share of customer

Beyond simply retaining good customers to capture customer lifetime value, good customer relationship management can help marketers to increase their **share of customer** – the share they get of the customer's purchasing in their product categories. Thus, banks want to increase 'share of wallet'. Supermarkets and restaurants want to get more 'share of stomach'. Car companies want to increase 'share of garage' and airlines want greater 'share of travel'.

To increase share of customer, firms can offer greater variety to current customers. Or they can train employees to cross-sell and up-sell in order to market more products and services to existing customers. For example, Amazon is highly skilled at managing and developing relationships with its customers to increase its share of each customer's purchases. Originally an online bookseller, Amazon now offers customers music, DVDs, gifts, toys, consumer electronics, office products and home improvement items. In addition, based on each customer's purchase history, the company recommends related products that might be of interest – and the more you buy the better they become at predicting what else will interest you. In this way, Amazon captures a greater share of each customer's spending budget.

Building customer equity

We can now see the importance of not just acquiring customers, but of keeping and growing them as well. Customer relationship management takes a long-term view. Companies want not only to create profitable customers, but to 'own' them for life, capture their **customer lifetime value**, and earn a greater share of their purchases.

What is customer equity?

The ultimate aim of customer relationship management is to produce high *customer equity*.[28] **Customer equity** is the combined discounted customer lifetime values of all of the company's current and potential customers. Clearly, the more loyal the firm's profitable customers, the higher the firm's customer equity. Customer equity may be a better measure of a firm's performance than current sales or market share. Whereas sales and market share reflect the past, customer equity suggests the future. Consider the US car manufacturer Cadillac:

> In the 1970s and 1980s Cadillac had some of the most loyal customers in the industry. To an entire generation of car buyers, the name 'Cadillac' defined American luxury. Cadillac's share of the luxury car market reached a whopping 51 per cent in 1976. Based on market share and sales, the brand's future looked rosy. However, measures of customer equity would have painted a bleaker picture. Cadillac customers were getting older (average age 60) and average customer lifetime value was falling. Many Cadillac buyers were on their last car. Thus, although Cadillac's market share was good, its customer equity was not. Compare this with BMW. Its more youthful and vigorous image didn't win BMW the early market share war. However, it did win BMW younger customers with higher customer lifetime values. The result? In the years that followed, BMW's market share and profits soared while Cadillac's fortunes eroded badly. Thus, market share is not the answer. We should care not just about current sales but also about future sales. Customer lifetime value and customer equity are the name of the game. Recognising this, Cadillac is now making the Caddy cool again by targeting a younger generation of consumers with new high-performance models and its highly successful Break Through advertising campaign.[29]

Building the right relationships with the right customers

Companies should manage customer equity carefully. They should view customers as assets that need to be managed and maximised. But not all customers, not even all loyal customers, are good investments. Surprisingly, some loyal customers can be unprofitable, and some disloyal customers can be profitable. Which customers should the company acquire and retain? 'Up to a point, the choice is obvious: Keep the consistent big spenders and lose the erratic small spenders,' says one expert. 'But what about the erratic big spenders and the consistent small spenders? It's often unclear whether they should be acquired or retained, and at what cost.'[30]

The company can classify customers according to their potential profitability and manage its relationships with them accordingly. Figure 1.5 classifies customers into one of four relationship groups, according to their profitability and projected loyalty.[31] Each group requires a different relationship management strategy. 'Strangers' show low profitability and little projected loyalty. There is little fit between the company's offerings and their needs. The relationship management strategy for these customers is simple: don't invest anything in them.

'Butterflies' are profitable but not loyal. There is a good fit between the company's offerings and their needs. However, as with real butterflies, we can enjoy them for only a short while and then they're gone. Efforts to convert butterflies into loyal customers are rarely successful. Instead, the company should enjoy the butterflies for the moment.

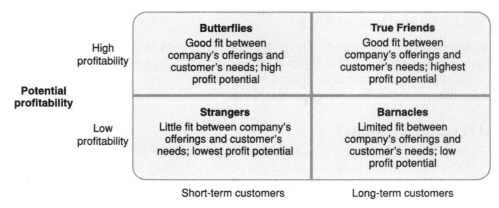

It should use promotional blitzes to attract them, create satisfying and profitable transactions with them, and then cease investing in them until the next time around.

'True friends' are both profitable and loyal. There is a strong fit between their needs and the company's offerings. The firm wants to make continuous relationship investments to delight these customers and nurture, retain and grow them. It wants to turn true friends into 'true believers', who come back regularly and tell others about their good experiences with the company.

'Barnacles' are highly loyal but not very profitable. There is a limited fit between their needs and the company's offerings. An example is smaller bank customers who bank regularly but do not generate enough returns to cover the costs of maintaining their accounts. Like barnacles on the hull of a ship, they create drag. Barnacles are perhaps the most problematic customers. The company might be able to improve their profitability by selling them more, raising their fees, or reducing service to them. However, if they cannot be made profitable, they should be 'fired'.

The point here is an important one: different types of customer require different relationship management strategies. The goal is to build the *right relationships* with the *right customers*.

MAKING CONNECTIONS Linking the concepts

We've covered a lot of territory. Again, slow down for a moment and develop *your own* thoughts about marketing.

■ In *your own words*, what *is* marketing and what does it seek to accomplish?

■ How well does Renault manage its relationships with customers? What customer relationship management strategy does it use? Compare the relationship management strategies of Tesco and Asda.

■ Think of a company for which you are a 'true friend'. What strategy does this company use to manage its relationship with you?

THE NEW MARKETING LANDSCAPE

As the world spins on, dramatic changes are occurring in the marketplace. Richard Love of Hewlett-Packard observes, 'The pace of change is so rapid that the ability to change has now become a competitive advantage.' As the marketplace changes, so must those who serve it.

In this section, we examine the major trends and forces that are changing the marketing landscape and challenging marketing strategy. We look at four major developments: the new digital age, rapid globalisation, the call for more ethics and social responsibility, and the growth in not-for-profit marketing.

The new digital age

The Internet has and is continuing to revolutionise how companies create value for customers and build and maintain customer relationships. The digital age has fundamentally changed customers' notions of convenience, speed, price, product information and service. Thus, today's marketing requires new thinking and action. Companies need to retain most of the skills and practices that have worked in the past. But they will also need to add major new competencies and practices if they hope to grow and prosper in the changing digital environment. Now, more than ever before, we are all connected to each other and to things near and far in the world around us. Where it once took weeks or months to travel across Europe, we can now travel around the globe in only hours or days. Where it once took days or weeks to receive news about important world events, we now see them as they are occurring through live satellite broadcasts. Where it once took weeks to correspond with others in distant places, they are now only moments away by phone or email.

The technology boom has created exciting new ways to learn about and track customers, and to create products and services tailored to individual customer needs. Technology is also helping companies to distribute products more efficiently and effectively. And it's helping them to communicate with customers in large groups or one-to-one.

Through video conferencing, marketing researchers at a company's headquarters in Paris can look in on focus groups in Prague without ever stepping onto a plane. With only a few clicks of a mouse button, a direct marketer can tap into online data services to learn anything from what car you drive to what you read to what flavour of ice cream you prefer. Or, using today's powerful computers, marketers can create their own detailed customer databases and use them to target individual customers with offers designed to meet their specific needs.

Technology has also brought a new wave of communication and advertising tools – on mobile phones, podcasts, and even in virtual online worlds like Second Life. Marketers can use these tools to zero in on selected customers with carefully targeted messages. Through e-commerce, customers can learn about, design, order and pay for products and services, without ever leaving home. Then, through the marvels of express delivery, they can receive their purchases in less than 24 hours. From virtual reality displays that test new products to online virtual stores that sell them, the technology boom is affecting every aspect of marketing.

The Internet

Today, the **Internet** links individuals and businesses of all types to each other and to information all around the world. It allows anytime, anywhere connections to information, entertainment and communication. Companies are using the Internet to build closer relationships with customers and marketing partners. Beyond competing in traditional market*places*, they now have access to exciting new market*spaces*.

These days, it's hard to find a company that doesn't use the Web in a significant way – or one that doesn't have new opportunities and challenges for marketers. We will explore the impact of the new digital age in more detail in Chapter 14.

Rapid globalisation

As they are redefining their relationships with customers and partners, marketers are also taking a fresh look at the ways in which they connect with the broader world around them. In a rapidly shrinking world, many marketers are now connected *globally* with their customers and marketing partners.

Today, almost every company, large or small, is touched in some way by global competition. Your local florist might buy its flowers from the Netherlands, while BMW and Mercedes compete in their home market of Germany with giant Japanese rivals like Toyota and Nissan. A fledgling Internet retailer finds itself receiving orders from all over the world at the same time as an Italian consumer goods producer introduces new products into emerging markets abroad.

Coca-Cola offers a mind-boggling 400 different brands in more than 200 countries. MTV has joined the elite of global brands, delivering localised versions of its music channels in 30 languages to 161 countries.[32]

Today, companies are not only trying to sell more of their locally produced goods in international markets, they also are buying more supplies and components abroad. For example, Isaac Mizrahi, one of America's top fashion designers, may choose cloth woven from Australian wool with designs printed in Italy. He will design a dress and email the drawing to a Hong Kong agent, who will place the order with a Chinese factory. Finished dresses will be flown to New York, where they will be redistributed to department and speciality stores around the country.

Thus, managers in countries around the world are increasingly taking a global, not just local, view of the company's industry, competitors and opportunities. They are asking: What is global marketing? How does it differ from domestic marketing? How do global competitors and forces affect our business? To what extent should we 'go global'? We will discuss the global marketplace in more detail in Chapter 15.

The call for more ethics and social responsibility

Marketers are re-examining their relationships with social values and responsibilities and with the very Earth that sustains us. As the worldwide consumerism and environmentalism movements mature, today's marketers are being called on to take greater responsibility for the social and environmental impact of their actions – whether it be the place of manufacture, the packaging surrounding the product or how far the finished item travels before being sold. Corporate ethics and social responsibility have become hot topics for almost every business and few companies can ignore the renewed and very demanding environmental movement.

The social responsibility and environmental movements will place even stricter demands on companies in the future. Some companies resist these movements, budging only when forced by legislation or organised consumer outcries. More forward-looking companies, however, readily accept their responsibilities to the world around them. They view socially responsible actions as an opportunity to do well by doing good. They seek ways to profit by serving the best long-term interests of their customers and communities.

Some companies – such as Ben & Jerry's, Bodyshop, the Co-op and others – are practising 'caring capitalism', setting themselves apart by being civic-minded and responsible. They are building social responsibility and action into their company value and mission statements. For example, the financial services division of the Co-op – the Co-operative Bank – is a leader in respect of investing the money of its clients. Armaments manufacturers, industries which pollute heavily and companies that provide poor conditions for their staff are all on the Co-op's investment blacklist. In turn, the supermarket portion of the business has been a pioneer on many consumer rights issues – genetically modified foods, sourcing from sustainable resources and clear labelling on all foods. We will revisit the relationship between marketing and social responsibility in greater detail in Chapter 16.

The growth of not-for-profit sector marketing

In the past, marketing has been most widely applied in the for-profit business sector. In recent years, however, marketing also has become a major part of the strategies of many not-for-profit organisations, such as universities, hospitals, museums, orchestras and even churches. Many performing arts groups – even Russia's famous Mariinsky company, which usually performs opera and ballet to packed houses – face huge operating deficits that they must cover by more aggressive donor marketing from businesses like Gazprom, BP and Total, for example.[33] Finally, many long-standing not-for-profit organisations – the YMCA, the Salvation Army, the Scouts and, of course, the organisations we see in Marketing at Work 1.2 – are now modernising their missions and 'products' to attract more members, visitors or donors.[34]

The Mariinsky theatre in St Petersburg, Russia, uses marketing to raise money from sponsors.

Source: Photo by Maria Smirnova.

MARKETING AT WORK 1.2

The marketing domain

That commercial organisations use marketing techniques and ideas to support branded manufactured goods like motorcycles, cars or electronic items is probably something you expected. That being said, do marketing ideas have validity and value in other contexts? Neil Rami, managing director of Marketing Birmingham is someone who thinks they do:

> I think like any city we're in a global competitive environment and because of the size and the scale of this city we do operate globally. You know, we have the largest event and conference sector per head of population in Western Europe, that means that we're competing for business

Cities, charities and cathedrals can put marketing concepts and ideas to good use as profit-making enterprises.
Source: Photos from Corbis/Peter Adams (left); Getty Images (right).

not only with Paris, Detroit, Barcelona – the conventional conference centres – but also with Johannesburg, Dubai and increasingly China and the Asian subcontinent.

Ultimately for me marketing is about informing people's views, it's about increasing their propensity to buy, and it's about doing that in a profitable way. That's no different when it comes to the marketing of cities, whether you're in Liverpool, Newcastle, London or Birmingham, we're all in the same business. My job is to increase people's propensity to visit Birmingham and to do it cost-effectively. We're not a profit-making business but we very much require resources, both financial and human capital to promote the city and marketing effectively is a requirement.

Taking it further, do the benefits of being marketing-oriented apply to organisations that have priorities other than the bottom line? Lucy Caldicott, head of fundraising at VSO, thinks that they do:

Fund-raising is what in a corporate environment you'd call sales and its exactly the same in that it's about generating revenue for your organisation. In my past I've worked for American Express in direct marketing so I came from a very strong brand organisation with quite a history of using sophisticated direct marketing techniques and that is exactly the sort of way a lot of charities raise money. The skills that you develop in a marketing function in a company are completely transferable to charity work. For example, the [VSO] communications team is responsible for the brand and what the brand means and how we live the brand and the kind of words we use to describe ourselves. Also, fund-raising is a

hugely competitive environment so there are hundreds and hundreds of charities competing for funds.

Vicky Starnes, head of marketing at VSO, adds:

Here at VSO we're marketing the opportunity for people to make a difference first hand, and also to have the experience of a lifetime. We're looking for professionals to volunteer overseas, for anything up to two years, working with a partner organisation in a developing country. And together with the local community they're working to change people's lives and really tackle poverty in the country where they're working. I think marketing for volunteer recruitment is quite a special kind of marketing. Really what we're asking people to do is give up up to two years' worth of their lives, and commit that to us at VSO, and the communities that they're trying to help. We need to be very targeted in reaching the right kind of professionals, because if we don't have the right kind of opportunities for somebody to actually do their work and make a difference with it, there's no point us sending them out there. I think in a more conventional charitable organisation people would be really looking to attract funds from the general public, they'll be calling on emotive motivations and topics, and trying to show people how their money could be used and why they should be giving money. The marketing we're doing here at VSO to recruit volunteers is totally different from that, because we're appealing to people for their professional skills.

Commercial enterprises like Electrolux and Land Rover obviously have a need for marketing, and we've just seen how charities and cities can benefit as well. How about a cathedral – surely they don't need to know anything about marketing? Mark McVey, head of marketing and PR for St Paul's Cathedral in London, disagrees:

Previously I've worked at Hampton Court and the Tower of London and the basic product we have is very similar in terms of we are trying to attract the same audience, the same market. Tourists are typically coming to London for short breaks. They might set aside one day to do attractions and they'll most probably want to have two or three visits within that day. And we need to make sure that we are actually within their radar to be able to ensure that they come to us on that particular day. One of our greatest competitors is our exterior image, and we need to ensure that they know about what there is to do and see inside. My role as marketing manager is to try to ensure that we get as many people inside the building as possible. It's clearly important for income generation because we need to be able to have enough money to keep this great building going – and we only do that by getting them inside. We don't have a huge marketing budget and therefore we need to be rather clever with the resources we've got. We don't advertise in the conventional sense – we're adopting a much more subtle approach in talking to the tour operators, people that are putting on educational visits, so that we can then influence them, tell them of the benefits of St Paul's, how we can work with them and how we can enhance the packages that they're putting together.

We've developed our website, and that is now becoming an effective marketing tool. We have our marketing leaflets that we produce in the sort of hundreds of thousands that are distributed round all of the tourist information centres and hotels. We attend a number of trade fairs to get our message out to the wider market.

I think marketing has become more relevant since London became a much more competitive place. Up until seven or eight years ago we could just open our doors, and people would flock in, even though we were charging.

Now that we've got the free museums, it's become a much more crowded marketplace and therefore we have got to make sure that we hold on to our market share.

Canon Lucy Wingate – who holds a more traditional position at St Paul's – also recognises the importance of marketing:

We're such an iconic building, we've got a relationship with people all over the world. We're one of the 'Top 20 most recognised buildings' in the world along with the White House and the Taj Mahal, so we've got those kinds of constituencies to think about when we're thinking about how the building relates to other people. We can't pick one group, and just target that market if I can use that kind of

language, we can't just say 'We're going to describe ourselves or even sell ourselves to one particular type of person'. It just doesn't work like that. We're very conscious of our history, and I suppose what we would say is that we're part of the cultural memory of the UK, and of Christianity in particular. Our core activity is the services that we hold and providing what we might call 'sacred space' within a 24/7 modern city like London. All of our visitors who come and pay, and all of our marketing, will be to support that core business.

Sources: Organisational websites for VSO (www.vso.org.uk), Marketing Birmingham (www.marketingbirmingham.com) and St Paul's Cathedral (www.stpauls.co.uk), and interviews with representatives by Pearson Education Ltd.

Government agencies have also shown an increased interest in marketing. For example, the national defence forces of most European countries – who rely on volunteers rather than conscripts – have a marketing plan to attract recruits, and various government agencies across the Continent are now designing *social marketing campaigns* to encourage energy conservation and concern for the environment or to discourage smoking, excessive drinking and drug use.

SO, WHAT IS MARKETING? PULLING IT ALL TOGETHER

At the start of this chapter, Figure 1.1 presented a simple model of the marketing process. Now that we've discussed all of the steps in the process, Figure 1.6 presents an expanded model that will help you pull it all together. What is marketing? Simply put, marketing is the process of building profitable customer relationships by creating value for customers and capturing value in return.

The first four steps of the marketing process focus on creating value for customers. The company first gains a full understanding of the marketplace by researching customer needs and managing marketing information. It then designs a customer-driven marketing strategy based on the answers to two simple questions. The first question is: What consumers will we serve? (market segmentation and targeting). Good marketing companies know that they cannot serve all customers in every way. Instead, they need to focus their resources on the customers they can serve best and most profitably. The second marketing strategy question is: How can we best serve targeted customers?

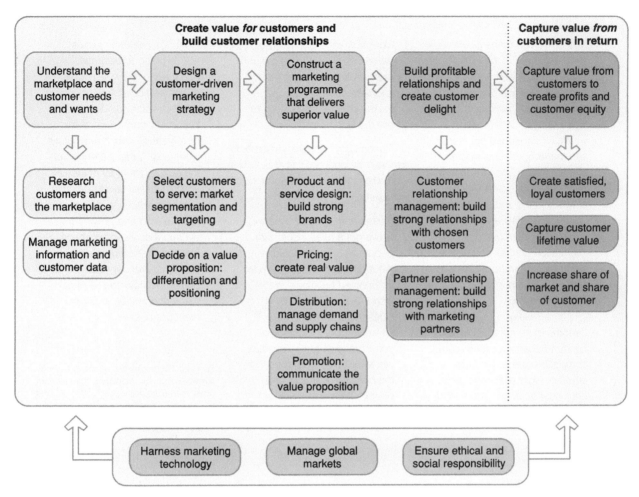

FIGURE 1.6

An expanded model of the marketing process

(differentiation and positioning). Here, the marketer outlines a value proposition that spells out what values the company will deliver in order to win target customers.

With its marketing strategy decided, the company now constructs a marketing programme – consisting of the four marketing mix elements, or the four Ps – that transforms the marketing strategy into real value for customers. The company develops product offers and creates strong brand identities for them. It prices these offers to create real customer value and distributes the offers to make them available to target customers. Finally, the company designs promotional programmes that communicate the value proposition to target customers and persuade them to act on the market offering.

Perhaps the most important step in the marketing process involves building value-laden, profitable relationships with target customers. Throughout the process, marketers practise customer relationship management to create customer satisfaction and delight. In creating customer value and relationships, however, the company cannot go it alone. It must work closely with marketing partners both inside the company and throughout the marketing system. Thus, beyond practising good customer relationship management, firms must also practise good partner relationship management.

The first four steps in the marketing process create value *for* customers. In the final step, the company reaps the rewards of its strong customer relationships by capturing value *from* customers. Delivering superior customer value creates highly satisfied customers who will buy more and will buy again. This helps the company to capture customer lifetime value and greater share of customer. The result is increased long-term customer equity for the firm.

Finally, in the face of today's changing marketing landscape, companies must take into account three additional factors. In building customer and partner relationships, they must harness marketing technology, take advantage of global opportunities, and ensure that they act in an ethical and socially responsible way.

Figure 1.6 provides a good road map to future chapters of the text. Chapters 1 and 2 introduce the marketing process, with a focus on building customer relationships and capturing value from customers. Chapters 3, 4, and 5 address the first step of the marketing process – understanding the marketing environment, managing marketing information, and understanding consumer behaviour. In Chapter 6, we look more deeply into the two major marketing strategy decisions: selecting which customers to serve (segmentation and targeting) and deciding on a value proposition (differentiation and positioning). Chapters 7 to 13 discuss the marketing mix variables, one by one. Then, the final three chapters examine the special marketing factors: marketing technology in the digital age, global marketing, and marketing ethics and social responsibility.

So, here we go, down the road to learning marketing. We hope you'll enjoy the journey!

THE JOURNEY YOU'VE TAKEN Reviewing the concepts

Today's successful companies – whether large or small, for-profit or not-for-profit, domestic or global – share a strong customer focus and a heavy commitment to marketing. The goal of marketing is to build and manage profitable customer relationships. Marketing seeks to attract new customers by promising superior value and to keep and grow current customers by delivering satisfaction. Marketing operates within a dynamic global environment, which can quickly make yesterday's winning strategies obsolete. To be successful, companies will have to be strongly market-focused.

1 Define marketing and outline the steps in the marketing process.

Marketing is the process by which companies create value for customers and build strong customer relationships in order to capture value from customers in return.

The marketing process involves five steps. The first four steps create value for customers. First, marketers need to understand the marketplace and customer needs and wants. Next, marketers design a customer-driven marketing strategy with the goal of getting, keeping and growing target customers. In the third step, marketers construct a marketing programme that actually delivers superior value. All of these steps form the basis for the fourth step, building profitable customer relationships and creating customer delight. In the final step, the company reaps the rewards of strong customer relationships by capturing value from customers.

2 Explain the importance of understanding customers and the marketplace, and identify the five core marketplace concepts.

Outstanding marketing companies go to great lengths to learn about and understand their customers' needs, wants and demands. This understanding helps them to design want-satisfying market offerings and build value-laden customer relationships by which they can capture customer lifetime value and greater share of customer. The result is increased long-term customer equity for the firm.

The core marketplace concepts are needs, wants and demands; market offerings (products, services and experiences); value and satisfaction; exchange and relationships; and markets. Wants are the form taken by human needs when shaped by culture and individual personality. When backed by buying power, wants become demands. Companies address needs by putting forth a value proposition, a set of benefits that they promise to consumers to satisfy their needs. The value proposition is fulfilled through a market offering, which delivers customer value and satisfaction, resulting in long-term exchange relationships with customers.

3 Identify the key elements of a customer-driven marketing strategy and discuss marketing management orientations that guide marketing strategy.

To design a winning marketing strategy, the company must first decide *whom* it will serve. It does this by dividing the market into segments of customers (*market segmentation*) and selecting which segments it will cultivate (*target marketing*). Next, the company must decide *how* it will serve targeted customers (how it will *differentiate and position* itself in the marketplace).

Marketing management can adopt one of five competing market orientations. The *production concept* holds that management's task is to improve production efficiency and bring down prices. The *product concept* holds that consumers favour products that offer the most in quality, performance and innovative features; thus, little promotional effort is required. The *selling concept* holds that consumers will not buy enough of the organisation's products unless it undertakes a large-scale selling and promotion effort. The *marketing concept* holds that achieving organisational goals depends on determining the needs and wants of target markets and delivering the desired satisfactions more effectively and efficiently than competitors do. The *societal marketing concept* holds that generating customer satisfaction *and* long-term societal well-being are the keys to both achieving the company's goals and fulfilling its responsibilities.

4 Discuss customer relationship management, and identify strategies for creating value *for* customers and capturing value *from* customers in return.

Broadly defined, *customer relationship management* is the process of building and maintaining profitable customer relationships by delivering superior customer value and satisfaction. The aim of customer relationship management is to produce high *customer equity*, the total combined customer lifetime values of all of the company's customers. The key to building lasting relationships is the creation of superior *customer value* and *satisfaction*.

Companies want not only to acquire profitable customers, but to build relationships that will keep them and grow 'share of customer'. Different types of customer require different customer relationship management strategies. The marketer's aim is to build the *right relationships* with the *right customers*. In return for creating value *for* targeted customers, the company captures value *from* customers in the form of profits and customer equity.

In building customer relationships, good marketers realise that they cannot go it alone. They must work closely with marketing partners inside and outside the company. In addition to being good at customer relationship management, they must also be good at *partner relationship management*.

5 Describe the major trends and forces that are changing the marketing landscape in this new age of relationships.

As the world spins on, dramatic changes are occurring in the marketing arena. The boom in computer, telecommunications, information, transportation and other technologies has created exciting new ways to learn about and track customers, and to create products and services tailored to individual customer needs.

In a rapidly shrinking world, many marketers are now connected *globally* with their customers and marketing partners. Today, almost every company, large or small, is touched in some way by global competition. Today's marketers are also re-examining their ethical and societal responsibilities. Marketers are being called upon to take greater responsibility for the social and environmental impact of their actions. In the past, marketing has been most widely applied in the for-profit business sector. In recent years, however, marketing has also become a major part of the strategies of many not-for-profit organisations, such as colleges, hospitals, museums, symphony orchestras and even churches.

Pulling it all together, as discussed throughout the chapter the major new developments in marketing can be summed up in a single word: *relationships*. Today, marketers of all kinds are taking advantage of new opportunities for building relationships with their customers, their marketing partners, and the world around them.

NAVIGATING THE KEY TERMS

Customer equity
Customer lifetime value
Customer perceived value
Customer relationship
   management
Customer satisfaction
Demands
Exchange

Internet
Market
Marketing
Marketing concept
Marketing management
Marketing myopia
Market offering
Needs

Partner relationship
   management
Product concept
Selling concept
Share of customer
Societal marketing concept
Wants

NOTES AND REFERENCES

1 http://www.uefa.com/.

2 http://www.uefa.com/uefa/aboutuefa/index.html.

3 http://www.uefa.com/uefa/keytopics/kind=131072/index.html.

4 http://www.euro2008.uefa.com/countries/cities/city=1191/news/
newsid=726502.html#euro+merchandise+proving.

5 http://www.sportandtechnology.com/features/0532.html.

6 http://www.sportbusiness.com/news/167372/storms-knock-out-euro-2008-global-television-feed.

7 http://www.guardian.co.uk/football/2007/feb/15/newsstory.sport.

8 http://www.bloomberg.com/apps/news?pid=20670001&refer=europe&sid=aAgM1tkB5W.
© 2008 Bloomberg L.P. All rights reserved. Used with permission.

9 The American Marketing Association offers this definition: 'Marketing is an organizational
function and a set of processes for creating, communicating, and delivering value to
customers and for managing customer relationships in ways that benefit the organization
and its stakeholders.' Accessed at http://www.marketingpower.com/mg-dictionary-
view1862.php?, September 2005. See also Lisa M. Keefe, 'What Is the Meaning of
"Marketing"', *Marketing News*, 15 September 2004, pp. 17–18; and Chekitan S. Dev and
Don E. Schultz, 'A Customer-Focused Approach Can Bring the Current Marketing Mix
into the 21st Century', *Marketing Management*, January–February 2005, pp. 18–24.

10 See Theodore Levitt's classic article, 'Marketing Myopia', *Harvard Business Review*,
July–August 1960, pp. 45–56. For more recent discussions, see James R. Stock, 'Marketing
Myopia Revisited: Lessons for Logistics', *International Journal of Physical Distribution &
Logistics Management*, 2(1/2), 2002, pp. 12–21; and Yves Doz, Jose Santos and Peter J.
Williamson, 'Marketing Myopia Re-Visited: Why Every Company Needs to Learn from
the World', *Ivey Business Journal*, January–February 2004, p. 1.

11 http://www.parquewarner.com/; http://www.acmilan.com/InfoPage.aspx?id=42776.

12 See Erika Rasmusson, 'Marketing More than a Product', *Sales & Marketing Management*,
February 2000, p. 99; and Lawrence A. Crosby and Sheree L. Johnson, 'Managing
Experiences', *Marketing Management*, January–February 2005, pp. 12–14.

13 See F. Lega, 'Developing a marketing function in public healthcare systems: A framework
for action', *Health Policy*, October 2006, 78(2/3), pp. 340–52.

14 See David Lewis, 'Southwest Staff Go Nuts (for Customers!)', Sales & Marketing Institute,
accessed at www.salesmarketing.org.nz/article623.html, May 2005. For more on market
orientation and firm performance, see Ahmet H. Kirca, Satish Jayachandran and William O.
Bearden, 'Marketing Orientation: A Meta-Analytic Review and Assessment of Its
Antecedents and Impact on Performance', *Journal of Marketing*, April 2005, pp. 24–41.

15 See 'Healthy Life Expectancy in Scotland', available from http://www.scotland.gov.uk/ Topics/Statistics/Browse/Health/TrendLifeExpectancy/LinkLifeExpectancySummary.

16 See 'Deep Fried Mars Mar Myth is Dispelled', BBC: http://news.bbc.co.uk/1/hi/scotland/ 4103415.stm or 'America's Most Fattening Burger', *Time*, 3 January 2005, p. 186; and 'For the Health-Unconscious, Era of Mammoth Burger Is Here', *Wall Street Journal*, 27 January 2005, p. B.1.

17 'How Effective are Product Recalls?', BBC: http://news.bbc.co.uk/1/hi/magazine/6379389.stm.

18 'The 2004 Total Value Awards: Incentives Don't Correlate to Value Says Strategic Vision', *Strategic Vision*, 4 October 2004, accessed at www.strategicvision.com, February 2005; Chad Lawhorn, 'Gas Costs Steer Study into Hybrids', *Knight Ridder Tribune Business News*, 29 April 2005, p. 1; and Ronald D. White, 'Car Buyers Think Hard and Long Distance about Mileage', *Los Angeles Times*, 30 April 2005, p. C.1.

19 Catherine Arnold, 'Satisfaction's the Name of the Game', *Marketing News*, 15 October 2004, pp. 39, 45; Eugene W. Anderson, Claes Fornell and Sanal K. Mazvancheryl, 'Customer Satisfaction and Shareholder Value', *Journal of Marketing*, October 2004, pp. 172–85; and Christian Homburg, Nicole Koschate and Wayne D. Hoyer, 'Do Satisfied Customers Really Pay More? A Study Between Customer Satisfaction and Willingness to Pay', *Journal of Marketing*, April 2005, pp. 84–96.

20 See for example http://www.porscheclubgb.com/Default.aspx.

21 ING Web page at: www.ingdirect.co.uk, accessed Augst 2008. Other information adapted from Elizabeth Esfahani, 'How to Get Tough with Bad Customers', *Business 2.0*, October 2004, p. 52. See also Amey Stone, 'Bare Bones, Plump Profits', *BusinessWeek*, 14 March, 2005, p. 88.

22 See E. Gummesson, *Total Relationship Marketing* (Oxford: Butterworth-Heinemann, 1999); C. Grönroos, *Service Management and Marketing: Customer Management in Service Competition* (London: Wiley, 1990); and M.J. Harker, 'Relationship Marketing Defined', *Marketing Intelligence and Planning*, 17(1), 1999, pp. 13–21.

23 Philip Kotler and Kevin Lane Keller, *Marketing Management*, 12th edn (Upper Saddle River, NJ: Prentice Hall, 2006), p. 27.

24 See E. Gummesson, 'Marketing Orientation Revisited: The Crucial Role of the Part-Time Marketer', *European Journal of Marketing*, 25(2), 1991, pp. 60–75.

25 http://www.sonyericsson.com/cws/corporate/company/aboutus/profile.

26 For more discussion of customer loyalty, see Fred Reichheld and Christine Detrick, 'Loyalty: A Prescription for Cutting Costs', *Marketing Management*, September–October 2003, pp. 24–5; Jacquelyn S. Thomas, Robert C. Blattberg and Edward J. Fox, 'Recapturing Lost Customers', *Journal of Marketing Research*, February 2004, pp. 31–45, and Clara Agustin and Jagdip Singh, 'Curvilinear Effects of Consumer Loyalty Determinants in Relational Exchanges', *Journal of Marketing Research*, February 2005, pp. 96–108.

27 http://business.timesonline.co.uk/tol/business/money/savings/article1302837.ece; http://www.guardian.co.uk/money/2008/jun/14/banks.currentaccounts.

28 See Roland T. Rust, Valerie A. Zeithaml and Katherine A. Lemon, *Driving Customer Equity* (New York Free Press 2000); Robert C. Blattberg, Gary Getz and Jacquelyn S. Thomas, *Customer Equity* (Boston, MA: Harvard business School Press, 2001); Rust, Lemon and Zeithaml, 'Return on Marketing: Using Customer Equity to Focus Marketing Strategy', *Journal of Marketing*, January 2004, pp. 109–27; James D. Lenskold, 'Customer-Centered Marketing ROI', *Marketing Management*, January/February 2004, pp. 26–32; and Rust, Zeithaml and Lemon, 'Customer-Centered Brand Management', *Harvard Business Review*, September 2004, p. 110.

29 This example is adapted from information in Rust, Lemon and Zeithaml, 'Where Should the Next Marketing Dollar Go?', *Marketing Management*, September–October 2001, pp. 24–8. Also see David Welch and David Kiley, 'Can Caddy's Driver Make GM Cool?', *BusinessWeek*, 20 September 2004, pp. 105–6; John K. Teahen Jr, 'Cadillac Kid: "Gotta Compete"', *Knight Ridder Tribune Business News*, 7 May 2005, p. 1.

30 Ravi Dhar and Rashi Glazer, 'Hedging Customers', *Harvard Business Review*, May 2003, pp. 86–92.

31 Werner Reinartz and V. Kumar, 'The Mismanagement of Customer Loyalty', *Harvard Business Review*, July 2002, pp. 86–94. For more on customer equity management, see Sunil Gupta, Donald R. Lehman and Jennifer Ames Stuart, 'Valuing Customers', *Journal of Marketing Research*, February 2004, pp. 7–18; Michael D. Johnson and Fred Selnes, 'Customer Portfolio Management: Toward a Dynamic Theory of Exchange Relationships', *Journal of Marketing*, April 2004, pp. 1–17; Sunil Gupta and Donald R. Lehman, *Managing Customers as Investments* (Philadelphia: Wharton School Publishing, 2005); and Roland T. Rust, Katherine N. Lemon and Das Narayandas, *Customer Equity Management* (Upper Saddle River, NJ: Prentice Hall, 2005).

32 'MTV's Search for Global Harmony', *Financial Times*: http://www.ft.com/cms/s/0/ f52e958c-3631-11dd-8bb8-0000779fd2ac.html.

33 http://www.mariinsky.ru/en/about/sponsors/.

34 For other examples, and for a good review of non-profit marketing, see Philip Kotler and Alan R. Andreasen, *Strategic Marketing for Nonprofit Organizations*, 6th edn (Upper Saddle River, NJ: Prentice Hall, 2003); Philip Kotler and Karen Fox, *Strategic Marketing for Educational Institutions* (Upper Saddle River, NJ: Prentice Hall, 1995); Norman Shawchuck, Philip Kotler, Bruce Wren and Gustave Rath, *Marketing for Congregations: Choosing to Serve People More Effectively* (Nashville, TN: Abingdon Press, 1993); Philip Kotler, John Bowen and James Makens, *Marketing for Hospitality and Tourism*, 3rd edn (Upper Saddle River, NJ: Prentice Hall, 2003); and 'The Nonprofit Marketing Landscape', special section, *Journal of Business Research*, June 2005, pp. 797–862.

CHAPTER 3
The marketing environment

AFTER STUDYING THIS CHAPTER, YOU SHOULD BE ABLE TO

- describe the environmental forces that affect the company's ability to serve its customers
- explain how changes in the demographic and economic environments affect marketing decisions
- identify the major trends in the firm's natural and technological environments
- explain the key changes in the political and cultural environments
- discuss how companies can react to the marketing environment

THE WAY AHEAD Previewing the concepts

In Part One (Chapters 1 and 2), you learned about the basic concepts of marketing and the steps in the marketing process for building profitable relationships with targeted consumers. In Part Two, as you continue your journey towards learning about marketing, we'll look deeper into the first step of the marketing process – understanding the marketplace and customer needs and wants. In this chapter, you'll discover that marketing does not operate in a vacuum but rather in a complex and changing environment. Other *actors* in this environment – suppliers, intermediaries, customers, competitors, publics and others – may work with or against the company. Major environmental *forces* – demographic, economic, natural, technological, political and cultural – shape marketing opportunities, pose threats, and affect the company's ability to serve customers and develop lasting relationships with them. To understand marketing, and to develop effective marketing strategies, you must first understand the context in which marketing operates.

To illustrate just how swiftly and how unexpectedly serious damage can be inflicted on a company by something entirely outside its control, we start off by looking at the Danish company Arla Foods, and the damage that it suffered in Middle Eastern markets after a Danish newspaper published cartoons that many people of the Islamic faith found offensive. Through no fault of its own, Arla found its brand reputation damaged, its relationships with customers and retailers undermined, and its sales slashed. Read on to see how they set out to put this right.

CHAPTER CONTENTS

The company's microenvironment
The company
Suppliers
Marketing intermediaries
Customers
Competitors
Publics

The company's macroenvironment
Demographic environment
Economic environment
Natural environment
Technological environment
Political environment
Cultural environment

Responding to the marketing environment

The boycott of Arla Foods in the Middle East

Dr Ibrahim Abosag, *Lecturer in Marketing, Manchester Business School, University of Manchester, UK*

The Danish company Arla Foods is a global dairy group with production facilities in 11 countries and sales offices in 24 countries, which sells its products in over 100 countries. Arla started its operation in the Middle East some 40 years ago. Soon after its entry into the Middle East market it became the market leader, mainly because of the absence of any credible local competitors. Over the years, Arla has maintained its position as market leader in the Middle East in cheese, butter and cream production. In the mid-1980s, Arla started to operate the Danya Foods dairy in Saudi Arabia's capital, Riyadh. The production facilities in Riyadh are seen to enhance and strengthen its position as market leader in the region. It employs more than 1,200 people across the Middle East, mostly in Saudi Arabia. From its early days in the Middle East until the end of 2005, Arla enjoyed excellent brand recognition, and according to the executive director of the Overseas Division, Finn Hansen (2005), 'consumer awareness of our brands is on a par with, say, Coca-Cola'.

However, in early 2006 Arla lost its market lead because of a boycott of Danish products in many parts of the Middle East. The publication in 2005 by a Danish tabloid newspaper of a series of cartoon caricatures of the Prophet Muhammad sparked uproar across the Middle East. Consumers started to boycott Danish products and a trade boycott followed shortly after; major local retailers such as Al-Othaim Holding and Azizia Panda announced the withdrawal of all Danish products from their shelves. Arla Foods' brands such as Lurpak butter, Puck cream cheese, Three Cows white cheese and Dano powdered milk, felt the double impact of both the consumer and the trade boycott. The most intense boycotting campaigns were carried out in Saudi Arabia, the biggest market in the Middle East. Arla Foods' products were withdrawn from more than 50,000 stores across the region in less than five days, losing over 60 per cent of its market. The main Saudi competitor Almarai took advantage of the cartoon crisis and took the lead in the market. In 2008, Almarai was still the market leader.

The campaigners were successful in posting the images of Danish brands on the internet calling upon consumers to boycott these brands. Also, mobile phone messages carrying boycott lists of Danish products were widely circulated. Similarly, a number of retail stores put all Danish brands, including Arlas's, in a special section on one side of the store accompanied by a large notice calling on consumers not to buy. At the same time, Western stores doing business in the region tried to limit the damage to their own reputations. For example, the French-owned supermarket chain Carrefour stopped selling Danish goods, while several firms, including the Swiss food multinational Nestlé, placed advertisements in Saudi newspapers to counter rumours that their products were made in Denmark.

Product boycotts are not new, but this one was organised, widespread and quite devastating in its impact. Demonstrations were organised and in some countries they reached riot level. Two drivers of Arla official cars and distribution lorries were attacked. The headquarters premises were stoned and threats were issued by demonstrators. The impact was such that Arla was forced to close its plant in Riyadh, lay off employees in Denmark for ten weeks and postpone its plan to double sales in the region by 2010.

Over 40 years of marketing investment and brand building had been undermined in a blink of an eye. With a large-scale boycott happening and no previous experience of anything like this, the whole situation was new to the senior managers of Arla Foods. There were no tried and tested damage limitation

Arla Foods owns leading dairy brands in the Middle East.
Photo source: Arla Foods. With permission.

strategies because the campaign was unprecedented. Faced with an unenviable task, the general manager Erik Folden and the marketing manager Torben Terp Hansen in Arla Foods' headquarters in Saudi Arabia considered ways of restoring faith in Arla Foods' brands. They realised that successful boycotts can have a short-term impact on sales and a long-term impact on a company's most precious asset, its reputation. The main intention was to protect the brand by distancing Arla Foods' brands from the trigger of the boycott.

The initial reaction from Arla was to keep silent. 'Consumer sentiments were high and we knew it was not the right time yet to address our society. "Silence is golden" and we kept it for almost 45 days' (Torben Terp Hansen). During this period, Arla Foods' executives worked on developing 'a comeback strategy' involving seven steps. The first step was to distance themselves from the cartoons, a message that was communicated by Arla managers widely through newspapers and TV stations. The second step revolved around the International Support of the Prophet Conference on 23 March 2006 in Bahrain. The conference discussed Arla Foods' statement and issued a religious recommendation to exempt the company from any boycott. The Bahrain statement cleared Arla of any responsibility and emphasised that Arla should not be punished for the action of others.

In the third step, the company made the Bahrain statement public. To serve this purpose, a statement was published in all newspapers and TV channels thanking the conference for removing Arla Foods from the boycott list. The Bahrain statement was attached alongside the company's statement. A printed version of the statement was placed on the doors of outlets. Soon after, Arla Foods organised a Press and Trade Conference in Riyadh, which was attended by the major retailers and spearheaded by Al-Othaim Holding. The aim was to persuade the retailers to make a collective decision to accept Arla Foods back onto their shelves. Although Arla Foods was successful in restarting its relationships with some of the retailers, it failed to secure the support from the big retailer Azizia Panda who continued to boycott Arla products. Nonetheless, Arla published another 'thank you statement' through the media for those retailers who accepted Arla Foods back. The statement contained the logos of the retailers who agreed to sell Arla Foods brands.

The fourth step was getting back to the stores. Now the retailers were safe in taking back Arla products because Arla had distanced itself from the cartoons. Reuters television covered the return of Arla Foods' brands to stores across the region. Despite all of the statements and coverage, some customers maintained their boycott. This meant that step five had to focus on promotion. Given the huge product stock returns from markets since the boycott started, and because customers are price sensitive, heavy consumer and trade offers were made to entice retailers and consumers to break their boycott.

In step six Arla concentrated on corporate and brand communication. Two main messages were at the heart of its communication. Firstly, it informed the public about its position on the cartoons. Secondly, it reminded consumers about the long heritage Arla Foods had in the region. The communication platform for all brands was aligned with the corporate one and phrases such as '40 years with you' and 'together for generations' were used. Brand communication was designed to show understanding of the region's values, culture and sentiments. However, this communication strategy was essentially a short-term measure. Two months later, the strategy was replaced in step seven by the long-term brand communication. This was seen as an important step to regain the hearts and minds of consumers. To achieve this, heavy investments were made into charities, social activities and social responsibility campaigns: product donations, ties with official governmental bodies, children's cancer activities, and donations of ambulances to Saudi Red Crescent. These activities, which endured for some considerable time, were designed to improve the perception of Arla Foods across the Middle East, and specifically in Saudi Arabia.

A year after the boycott started, at the end of 2006, Arla Foods had recovered most of its market share in most Middle Eastern countries with the exception of Saudi Arabia where it had only recovered 50 per cent. By early 2008 Arla Foods had managed to recover 70 per cent of its market in Saudi Arabia.

The boycott against Arla lasted a lot longer than many others. A similar boycott of American products faded quite quickly, in only a few weeks. The intensity and the scale of the boycott against the American products did not force American companies to react in the way Arla Foods had to. Even in 2008, Arla still had more work to do to repair all of the damage inflicted by the boycott.

Source: With thanks to Torben Terp Hansen, General Manager of Arla Foods, Lebanon.

Marketers need to be good at building relationships with customers, others in the company and external partners. To do this effectively, they must understand the major environmental forces that surround all of these relationships. A company's **marketing environment** consists of the actors and forces outside marketing that affect marketing management's ability to build and maintain successful relationships with target customers. Successful companies know the vital importance of constantly watching and adapting to the changing environment.

The environment continues to change rapidly, and both consumers and marketers wonder what the future will bring. More than any other group in the company, marketers must be the trend trackers and opportunity seekers. Although every manager in an organisation needs to observe the outside environment, marketers have two special aptitudes. They have disciplined methods – marketing research and marketing intelligence – for collecting information about the marketing environment. They also spend more time in the customer and competitor environments. By carefully studying the environment, marketers can adapt their strategies to meet new marketplace challenges and opportunities.

The marketing environment is made up of a *microenvironment* and a *macroenvironment*. The **microenvironment** consists of the actors close to the company that affect its ability to serve its customers – the company, suppliers, marketing intermediaries, customer markets, competitors and publics. The **macroenvironment** consists of the larger societal forces that affect the microenvironment – demographic, economic, natural, technological, political and cultural forces. We look first at the company's microenvironment.

THE COMPANY'S MICROENVIRONMENT

Marketing management's job is to build relationships with customers by creating customer value and satisfaction. However, marketing managers cannot do this alone. Figure 3.1 shows the major actors in the marketer's microenvironment. Marketing success will require building relationships with other company departments, suppliers, marketing intermediaries, customers, competitors and various publics, which combine to make up the company's value delivery network.

The company

In designing marketing plans, marketing management takes other company groups into account – groups such as top management, finance, research and development (R&D), purchasing, operations and accounting. All these interrelated groups form the internal environment. Top management sets the company's mission, objectives, broad strategies and policies. Marketing managers make decisions within the strategies and plans made by top management.

FIGURE 3.1

Actors in the microenvironment

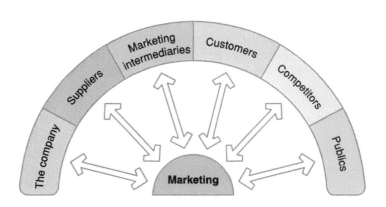

Marketing managers must also work closely with other company departments. Finance is concerned with finding and using funds to carry out the marketing plan. The R&D department focuses on designing safe and attractive products. Purchasing worries about getting supplies and materials, whereas operations is responsible for producing and distributing the desired quality and quantity of products. Accounting has to measure revenues and costs to help marketing know how well it is achieving its objectives. Together, all of these departments have an impact on the marketing department's plans and actions. Under the marketing concept, all of these functions must 'think consumer'. They should work in harmony to provide superior customer value and satisfaction.

Suppliers

Suppliers form an important link in the company's overall customer value delivery system. They provide the resources needed by the company to produce its goods and services. Supplier problems can seriously affect marketing. Marketing managers must watch supply availability – supply shortages or delays, labour strikes and other events can cost sales in the short term and damage customer satisfaction in the long term. Marketing managers also monitor the price trends of their key inputs. Rising supply costs may force price increases that can harm the company's sales volume.

Most marketers today treat their suppliers as partners in creating and delivering customer value. Tesco goes to great lengths to work with its suppliers. For example, it helps them to test new products in its stores. Tesco has signed up to the Office of Fair Trading supermarket Code of Practice on the treatment of suppliers, which means that it undertakes to treat suppliers fairly at all times and to avoid such practices as delaying payments to suppliers or insisting that suppliers contribute financially to supermarket promotional activities. In the most recent audit by the Office of Fair Trading Tesco was found to be implementing this Code effectively.

Marketing intermediaries

Marketing intermediaries help the company to promote, sell and distribute its goods to final buyers. They include resellers, physical distribution firms, marketing services agencies and financial intermediaries. *Resellers* are distribution channel firms that help the company find customers or make sales to them. These include wholesalers and retailers, who buy and resell merchandise. Selecting and partnering with resellers is not easy. No longer do manufacturers have many small, independent resellers from which to choose. They now face large and growing reseller organisations such as Tesco, Carrefour, Aldi and Fnac. These organisations frequently have enough power to dictate terms or even shut the manufacturer out of large markets.

Physical distribution firms help the company to stock and move goods from their points of origin to their destinations. Working with warehouse and transportation firms, a company must determine the best ways to store and ship goods, balancing factors such as cost, delivery, speed and safety. *Marketing services agencies* are the marketing research firms, advertising agencies, media firms and marketing consulting firms that help the company target and promote its products to the right markets. *Financial intermediaries* include banks, credit companies, insurance companies and other businesses that help finance transactions or insure against the risks associated with the buying and selling of goods.

Like suppliers, marketing intermediaries form an important component of the company's overall value delivery system. In its quest to create satisfying customer relationships, the company must do more than just optimise its own performance. It must partner effectively with marketing intermediaries to optimise the performance of the entire system.

Thus, today's marketers recognise the importance of working with their intermediaries as partners rather than simply as channels through which they sell their products. For example, when Coca-Cola signs on as the exclusive drinks provider for a fast-food chain, such as McDonald's or Subway, it provides much more than just soft drinks. It also pledges powerful marketing support.

Coke assigns cross-functional teams dedicated to understanding the finer points of each retail partner's business. It conducts a staggering amount of research on beverage consumers and shares these insights with its partners. It analyses the demographics of geographical areas and helps partners to determine which Coke brands are preferred in their areas. Coca-Cola has even studied the design of drive-through menu boards to better understand which layouts, fonts, letter sizes, colours and visuals induce consumers to order more food and drink.[1]

Customers

The company needs to study five types of customer markets closely. *Consumer markets* consist of individuals and households that buy goods and services for personal consumption. *Business markets* buy goods and services for further processing or for use in their production process, whereas *reseller markets* buy goods and services to resell at a profit. *Government markets* are made up of government agencies that buy goods and services to produce public services or transfer the goods and services to others who need them. Finally, *international markets* consist of these buyers in other countries, including consumers, producers, resellers and governments. Each market type has special characteristics that call for careful study by the seller.

Competitors

The marketing concept states that to be successful a company must provide greater customer value and satisfaction than its competitors do. Thus, marketers must do more than simply adapt to the needs of target consumers. They also must gain strategic advantage by positioning their offerings strongly against competitors' offerings in the minds of consumers.

No single competitive marketing strategy is best for all companies. Each firm should consider its own size and industry position compared to those of its competitors. Large firms with dominant positions in an industry can use certain strategies that smaller firms cannot afford. But being large is not enough. There are winning strategies for large firms, but there are also losing ones. And small firms can develop strategies that give them better rates of return than large firms enjoy.

Publics

The company's marketing environment also includes various publics. A **public** is any group that has an actual or potential interest in or impact on an organisation's ability to achieve its objectives. We can identify seven types of publics.

- *Financial publics* influence the company's ability to obtain funds. Banks, investment houses and shareholders are the major financial publics.
- *Media publics* carry news, features and editorial opinion. They include newspapers, magazines, websites, and radio and television stations.
- *Government publics*. Management must take government developments into account. Marketers must often consult the company's lawyers on issues of product safety, truth in advertising, and other matters.

- *Citizen-action publics*. A company's marketing decisions may be questioned by consumer organisations, environmental groups, minority groups and others. Its public relations department can help it stay in touch with consumer and citizen groups.

- *Local publics* include neighbourhood residents and community organisations. Large companies usually appoint a community relations officer to deal with the community, attend meetings, answer questions and contribute to worthwhile causes.

- *General public*. A company needs to be concerned about the general public's attitude toward its products and activities. The public's image of the company affects its buying.

- *Internal publics* include workers, managers, volunteers and the board of directors. Large companies use newsletters and other means to inform and motivate their internal publics. When employees feel good about their company, this positive attitude spills over to external publics.

A company can prepare marketing plans for these major publics as well as for its customer markets. Suppose the company wants a specific response from a particular public, such as goodwill, favourable word of mouth, or donations of time or money. The company would have to design an offer to this public that is attractive enough to produce the desired response.

THE COMPANY'S MACROENVIRONMENT

The company and all of the other actors operate in a larger macroenvironment of forces that shape opportunities and pose threats to the company. Figure 3.2 shows the six major forces in the company's macroenvironment. In the remaining sections of this chapter, we examine these forces and show how they affect marketing plans.

Demographic environment

Demography is the study of human populations in terms of size, density, location, age, gender, race, occupation and other statistics. The demographic environment is of major interest to marketers because it involves people, and people make up markets. The world population is growing at an explosive rate. It now totals more than 6.6 billion and will exceed 8.1 billion by the year 2030.[2] The world's large and highly diverse population poses both opportunities and challenges.

Changes in the world demographic environment have major implications for business. For example, consider China. More than a quarter of a century ago, to curb its rapidly growing population, the Chinese government passed regulations limiting families to one child each. As a result, Chinese children – known as 'little emperors and empresses' – are being showered with attention and luxuries under what's known as the 'six-pocket

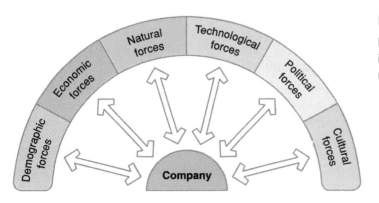

FIGURE 3.2

Major forces in the company's macroenvironment

syndrome'. As many as six adults – two parents and four doting grandparents – may be indulging the whims of each 'only child'. Parents in the average Beijing household now spend about 40 per cent of their income on their cherished only child. Among other things, this trend has created huge market opportunities for children's educational products.

In China's increasingly competitive society, parents these days are desperate to give Junior an early edge. That's creating opportunities for companies peddling educational offerings aimed at kids. Disney, for example, is moving full speed into educational products. Magic English, a €225 Disney package that includes workbooks, flash cards, and 26 videodisks, has been phenomenally successful. Disney has also launched interactive educational CD-ROMs featuring the likes of Winnie the Pooh and *101 Dalmations'* Cruella DeVille. Disney isn't alone in catering to the lucrative Chinese coddled-kiddies market. For example, Time Warner is testing the waters in Shanghai with an interactive language course called English Time. The 200-lesson, 40-CD set takes as long as four years for a child to complete. Time Warner is expecting strong sales, despite the €3,300 price tag.[3]

Demographics and business: Chinese regulations limiting families to one child have resulted in what is known as the 'six-pocket syndrome'. Chinese children are being showered with attention and luxuries, creating opportunities for marketers.

Source: Mark Leong/Redux/eyevine.

Interestingly, the one-child policy is creating another major Chinese demographic development – a rapidly ageing population. In what some deem a potential 'demographic earthquake', by 2004 58 per cent of the Chinese population was aged over 40. And because of the one-child policy, close to 75 per cent of all Chinese households will be childless, either because they chose to have no children or because their only child has left the nest. The result is an ageing society that will need to be more self-reliant, which in turn will cause a large growth in service markets such as education for older people, leisure clubs and nursing homes.[4]

Thus, marketers keep close track of demographic trends and developments in their markets, both at home and abroad. They track changing age and family structures, geographic population shifts, educational characteristics and population diversity. Here, we discuss the most important demographic trends in Europe.

Changing age structure of the population

The population of the 27 Member States of the EU stood at more than 493 million in 2007.[5] It is very difficult to forecast the EU population because of the very large inward and outward flows of migrants, and because the population of the EU depends on when, and whether, new countries such as Turkey are allowed to join. Net inward migration to the EU is expected to be the biggest factor leading to population growth, since the natural growth of the population (where births exceed deaths) is expected to decline as families across the EU choose to have fewer children. Birth rates in the richest countries of the EU, such as the UK, France and Italy, are already well below the 'replacement level' (where births and deaths are just in balance). The single most important demographic trend in the EU is the changing age structure of the population. Internationally, in Europe, North America and several other parts of the world (such as Australia and New Zealand) there are three generational groups that are considered particularly important by marketers – the baby boomers, Generation X and Generation Y.

The baby boomers This is the generation born between 1946 and 1964, a period when birth rates in countries affected by the Second World War rose sharply (hence the 'baby boom'). Since then, the **baby boomers** have become one of the most powerful forces shaping the marketing environment. The baby boomers have now grown to maturity, many of them are property owners, and they account for around a quarter of the population.

Marketers have typically paid the most attention to the smaller upper crust of the boomer generation – the more educated, mobile and wealthy segments. These segments have gone by many names. In the 1980s, they were called 'yuppies' (young urban professionals), and 'DINKs' (dual-income, no-kids couples). In the 1990s, yuppies and DINKs gave way to a new breed, with names such as 'DEWKs' (dual-earners with kids) and 'MOBYs' (mother older, baby younger). Now, to the chagrin of many in this generation, they are acquiring such titles as 'WOOFs' (well-off older folks) or even 'GRUMPIES' (just what the name suggests).

As a group, the baby boomers are the most affluent Europeans. However, although the more affluent boomers have grabbed most of the headlines, baby boomers cut across all walks of life, creating a diverse set of target segments for businesses. There are wealthy boomers but also boomers with more modest means.

The youngest boomers are now in their early forties; the oldest are entering their sixties. Thus, the boomers have evolved from the 'youthquake generation' to the 'backache generation'. The maturing boomers are rethinking the purpose and value of their work, responsibilities and relationships. They are approaching life with a new stability and reasonableness in the way they live, think, eat and spend. As they reach their peak earning and spending years, the boomers constitute a lucrative market for new housing and home remodelling, financial services, travel and entertainment, eating out, health and fitness products, and high-priced cars and other luxuries.

It would be a mistake to think of the boomers as ageing, staid retirees. In fact, the boomers are spending large amounts each year on *anti*-ageing products and services. And unlike previous generations, boomers are likely to postpone retirement. Many boomers are rediscovering the excitement of life and have the money to enjoy themselves.

Generation X The baby boom was followed by a 'birth dearth', creating another generation of people born between 1965 and 1976. The term **'Generation X'** was made famous in the book of that name by Douglas Coupland, published in 1991, although the term had been in use for several years before Coupland wrote his book.[6] They are named 'Generation X' because they lie in the shadow of the boomers and lack obvious distinguishing characteristics. Others call them the 'baby busters,' the 'yiffies' (young, individualistic, freedom-minded few), or the 'generation caught in the middle' (between the larger baby boomers and later Generation Ys).

The Generation Xers are defined as much by their shared experiences as by their age. Increasing divorce rates and higher employment for their mothers made them the first generation of latchkey kids (left to look after themselves after school). They grew up during the 1970s and 1980s, which were particularly troubled times in the world economy, with rampant inflation and high unemployment. Having grown up in times of recession when companies ceased to offer 'lifetime employment' and started to reduce their workforces ('downsizing'), they developed a more cautious economic outlook. They care about the environment and respond favourably to socially responsible companies. Although they seek success, they are less materialistic; they prize experience, not acquisition. They are cautious romantics who want a better quality of life and are more interested in job satisfaction than in sacrificing personal happiness and growth for promotion. Often, family comes first, career second.

As a result, the Gen Xers are a more sceptical bunch. 'Marketing to Gen Xers is difficult,' says one marketer, 'and it's all about word of mouth. You can't tell them you're good, and they have zero interest in a slick brochure that says so. You have to rely on somebody they know and trust to give you instant credibility. They have a lot of "filters" in place.'[7]

Once labelled as 'the MTV generation' and viewed as body-piercing slackers who whined about 'McJobs', the GenXers have now grown up and are beginning to take over. The GenXers are displacing the lifestyles, culture and materialistic values of the baby boomers. Very soon they will overtake the baby boomers as a primary market for almost every product category.[8] With so much potential, many companies are focusing on Gen Xers as an important target segment.

Generation Y Both the baby boomers and Gen Xers will one day be passing the reins to **Generation Y** (also called echo boomers). This is the generation born between 1977 and 1994, when the number of births increased as the baby boomers entered their child-bearing years. The echo boom has created a large teen and young adult market.

Older members of Generation Y have now graduated from university and are moving up in their careers. Like the trailing edge of the Generation Xers ahead of them, one distinguishing characteristic of Generation Y is their utter fluency and comfort with computer, digital and Internet technology. In the richer countries of the EU nine out of ten teens have a home computer, 73 per cent of teens surf the Internet every day, and over 80 per cent of 15–19-year-olds own a mobile phone. In all, they are an impatient, now-oriented bunch. 'Blame it on the relentless and dizzying pace of the Internet, 24-hour cable news cycles, cell phones, and TiVo for creating the on-demand, gotta-get-it-now universe in which we live,' says one observer. 'Perhaps nowhere is the trend more pronounced than among the Gen Y set.'[9]

Generation Y represents an attractive target for marketers. However, reaching this message-saturated segment effectively requires creative marketing approaches. For example, the popularity of action sports with Gen Yers has provided creative marketing opportunities for products ranging from clothes to video games, films and even beverages. Red Bull's edgy and irreverent positioning makes it a natural for the action-sport crowd. Red Bull has become a true action-sports supporter. It sponsors the Red Bull Air Race World Series and the Red Bull X-Alps adventure racing event, is endorsed by athletes from a wide range of sports including cricket, football and athletics, and sponsors top adventure sports stars such as the amazing Austrian base jumping star Felix Baumgartner (if you were unaware of Felix's exploits, you should really check them out at **www.felixbaumgartner.com**).

The motor industry is aggressively targeting this future generation of car buyers. For example, BMW offers a motor sports training programme for young drivers, some of whom are too young to have a licence. As a part of its 'Ultimate Driving Experience' tour, BMW offers go-kart drivers between the ages of 15 and 23 an array of scholarships, training and race experience to help develop their racing careers. 'We are courting teenagers,' says a BMW marketing executive. 'BMW is the premier brand for youth, so we have a reason to work harder with the next generation.'[10]

New brands and new services have emerged to deliver what the Generation Y market wants, while simultaneously providing marketers with a more effective means to communicate with them. Setanta, a provider of premium TV sports channels, is an excellent example (see Marketing at Work 3.1).

MARKETING AT WORK 3.1

Setanta: Pub channel to global sports broadcaster

Sean Ennis, *Department of Marketing, University of Strathclyde, Scotland*

Setanta Television has undergone a major transformation since its inception in 1990. Two Irishmen, living in London at the time, were very frustrated when they could not access a World Cup football game involving their home country against Holland. Given the large Irish diaspora based in London, they approached FIFA and persuaded them to sell them the rights to a feed of the game. They hired out their local pub and charged people £5 to watch it.

Over the next couple of years they expanded this initiative and acquired the rights from the Gaelic Athletic Association (GAA) to transmit broadcasts of the Irish championship games to the Irish diaspora in the United Kingdom, North America and Australia.

Fast forward to the present decade and Setanta entered into a deal with the Scottish Premier League to show a number of games. In early 2007, they had over 250,000 customers.

Perhaps of more significance was the appointment in April 2007, of a UK director of brand marketing to develop further business and take Setanta from its overdependence on the Irish diaspora and move it to a position where it could be recognised as a major holder of global sports TV rights in the UK. In the preceding months, prior to the appointment of the UK director, Setanta acquired the rights to broadcast rugby (Magners League), golf (American PGA tournaments) and various European football games from various leagues.

Perhaps its most significant move was successfully to launch a bid, in partnership with ITV, for TV rights to show the England football team's home fixtures and some FA Cup games. Setanta now reaches into over 100 million homes worldwide and operates more sports channels than any other independent broadcaster in Ireland and the UK.

The European Union, worried by the increasing dominance of Sky television, allowed a number of competitors such as Virgin Media, BT and Freeview, as well as Setanta, to bid for various packages from the English Premier League. In this case, Setanta bid £392 million for 46 live matches.

The UK director of brand marketing, Timothy Ryan, set a target of 1 million subscribers by the end of 2007, growing to 1.9 million by year end 2009. The major marketing initiative was to offer a subscription to its package of nine digital channels (including RacingUK) for £10 per month. They backed this campaign by allocating a budget of £5 million and employing the services of Desmond Lynam (a well-known TV personality) and a host of present and former sportspeople to encourage people to take out a subscription.

One of its key selling points is that it is 'platform neutral'. Although the costs to the viewer can vary, depending on which platform, it is available on Sky, Freeview, Virgin Media and BT Vision.

Sky remains the dominant platform for broadcasting sport by a very large measure. Currently over 6 million of its 8 million subscribers take out the sports package.

In summary, while Sky continues to dominate the sports broadcasting rights, Setanta has made inroads into the market. In part, this has been driven by the legislative environment, where the EU has demanded that one group should not hold exclusive rights to football in England.

The changing face of UK football

The biggest winner arising from the emergence of pay-per-view, dedicated sports channels is the Premier League in England: a body that represents the 20 clubs in arguably the richest football league in the world. In fact, the actions of the EU, ostensibly to create competition, have only succeeded in driving up the value of the broadcasting rights to very high levels. This allows clubs to pay very high – some would say too high – wages to footballers. It can be argued that this provides a very entertaining league where fans are exposed to the best players in the world on a regular basis. Many clubs, such as Arsenal, Manchester United and Manchester City, on the back of the inflow of revenue, have built new stadia or significantly improved existing ones. All-seater stadia are now the order of the day.

In tandem with these developments, most clubs have invested significantly in broadening the fan base and increasing commercial opportunities through branding, merchandising and international expansion (through developing linkages with clubs in key markets such as China and Japan). This has led to more revenue streams flowing into the clubs. By building the brand value, clubs are also able to attract more lucrative sponsorship deals across a number of different platforms: for example, shirt advertising, perimeter advertising, naming rights for stadia, stands and so on.

On the face of it, everything points to a very positive situation in English football. However, so far we have ignored one key interest group in our discussions: the fan.

Fans, by contrast, have had to face up to inexorable price increases in season tickets and admission to individual matches. Few clubs in the Premier League have ever seen fit to reduce their prices, apart from a couple of struggling clubs who perennially finish in the middle of the table. The arrival of very successful businesspeople to the domain of club ownership, has meant that, increasingly, hard-nosed business principles are employed to judge the effectiveness and efficiency of the clubs. While success is measured by the number of trophies won, it is also judged by the level of profitability and return on investment that accrues at the end of the financial year. While the attitude of Roman Abramovich, a Russian industrialist who owns Chelsea, may be viewed as fairly philanthropic, the American businessmen who own Manchester United seek a serious return on their investment and are unlikely to be swayed by misty-eyed sentimentality.

It is no longer possible to watch premier football on 'free-to-air' television due to the increasing dominance of BSkyB and more recently, Setanta. Despite the arguments about creating a more competitive market, the actions of the EU have meant that the individual viewer now has to take out an extra subscription to gain access to the televised games.

As well as having to pay to watch football on the television, fans are also facing increasing costs in terms of food and beverage at games.

While football games traditionally took place on Saturday afternoons at 3 pm, increasingly games are played on Sunday morning, Friday and Monday evenings and at other potentially inconvenient times for the fans. The sight of bleary-eyed supporters making their way from the north-east of England to London for a 12.30 kick-off has become a regular occurrence. As the TV

companies are effectively bankrolling the industry, it can be argued that they are entitled to fix the schedules in order to maximise their audiences.

Since the inception of the Premier League in 1992, attendances have risen, challenging the fears of the football administrators who felt that blanket coverage of live football would only encourage spectators to stay at home or go to the pub to watch the games. But in the last couple of years, attendances at some of the struggling Premier League clubs have shown signs of decline. Some fans and football journalists have expressed the view that the product has become predictable and 'tired'. Despite these worrying observations, revenues continue to increase and the likes of Setanta seek to spread their involvement in this league.

The future?

Over the next five years or so, it is anticipated that football fans will make increasing use of mobile technology to access games, watch clips of goal action and make greater use of PCs to view games. The powerful clubs in the UK and Europe are also looking with increasingly envious eyes at the potential revenue that can be generated from running their own subscription-based TV channel. It does not take a genius to work out the potential revenue that could be generated for Manchester United from running such a service across the globe, targeting growth markets such as China, the Gulf region and North America. If 250,000 people worldwide were prepared to pay the equivalent of £10 to view an individual league game or pay £250 for a TV season ticket to view all games in the regular season, it suddenly becomes a significant source of revenue.

In a further attempt to capitalise on the global interest in the Premier League, football administrators

recently put forward a proposal to have each of the member clubs play one regular league game in a foreign city. While this initiative received a lot of negative comments from UEFA and other European football clubs, it has not entirely disappeared off the radar. Indeed it is likely that it will emerge again over the next couple of years, albeit in a reduced format.

In summary, football in the UK has never been as strong financially as it is today. Money appears to flow into the coffers of the premier clubs, sparking off a virtuous (or vicious) circle of escalating salaries for players. The concept of the fan is also changing. The traditional fan who attends each game and buys a season ticket is joined by virtual fans from all over the world who watch the game in downtown Hong Kong, access the game via their laptop through a pirate TV channel or get the highlights of the game sent to their mobile phone. The product is showing signs of tiredness and may possibly need rejuvenation, either in the format of the league or the introduction of clubs such as Celtic and Rangers from the neighbouring Scottish league. This is possibly a longer-term prospect. The concept of a more structured European league also continues to fester in the background.

There is no doubt that the emergence of BSkyB in the 1990s and the subsequent evolution of Setanta, has had a profound impact on the structure, shape and direction of the football industry in the United Kingdom. It remains to be seen what direction this sector will take in the next decade.

Sources: 'Analysis: Setanta puts itself on the satellite map', *Marketing Week*, 30 November 2006, p. 14; Jeremy Lee, 'Setanta pushes into Sky territory', *Marketing Week*, 11 April 2007, p. 19; Raymond Snoddy, 'Fans are losers in Premiership TV fight', *Marketing*, 10 May 2006, p. 18; 'Sports Broadcasting – SETANTA: Football pitch hots up', *Marketing Week*, 2 August 2007, p. 22.

Generational marketing Do marketers have to create separate products and market-ing programmes for each generation? Some experts warn that marketers have to be careful about turning off one generation each time they craft a product or message that appeals effectively to another. Others caution that each generation spans decades of time and many socio-economic levels. For example, marketers often split the baby boomers into three smaller groups – leading boomers, core boomers and trailing boomers – each with its own beliefs and behaviours. Similarly, they split Generation Y into Gen Y adults and Gen Y teens. Thus, marketers need to form more precise age-specific segments within each group. More importantly, defining people by their birth date may be less effective than segmenting them by their lifestyle or life stage.

The changing family

The 'traditional household' consists of a husband, wife and children (and sometimes grandparents). But this stereotypical notion of a household is becoming less and less representative of the way modern society really is.

In Europe today, married couples with children now make up only about 34 per cent of households, and this percentage is falling. The average size of a household is about 2.5 people, but this varies considerably across Europe, standing, for example, at 3.1 in Ireland and 2.2 in Germany. More people are divorcing or separating, choosing not to marry, marrying later, or marrying without intending to have children. Marketers must increasingly consider the special needs of non-traditional households, because they are now growing more rapidly than traditional households. Each group has distinctive needs and buying habits. The type of household that is forecast to grow fastest across Europe for the next two decades is the single-person household. This trend will be seen all across Europe, but the proportion of people living in single-person households now and in the future varies considerably from nation to nation. For example, the proportion of the population living in single-person households in the Mediterranean countries and in Ireland is typically around 5–10 per cent, while in northern European countries like Denmark, Sweden, Finland and Germany it is typically 15–20 per cent.[11]

Women are making up an increasing proportion of the working population. In 2006 in the EU 72 per cent of men aged 15–64 were in paid employment, compared to 57 per cent of women of the same age group. Again, this figure varies considerably across Europe: for example, 73 per cent of women in Denmark were in paid employment, and only 46 per cent of women in Italy.[12] The significant number of women in the workforce has spawned the child day-care business and increased consumption of career-oriented women's clothing, financial services, and convenience foods and services.

Geographic shifts in population

This is a period of great migratory movements between and within countries. Net migration is the difference between immigration (the number of people entering a country) and emigration (the number of people leaving). In recent years the number of immigrants from the rest of the world into Europe has considerably exceeded the number of emigrants; it is estimated that net inward migration into the EU was between 1.5 million and 2 million people each year from 2002 to 2005. Within the EU countries there has been a net migration of people westwards; that is to say that Western European countries, particularly the United Kingdom and Germany, have seen large inflows of population from countries in Eastern Europe. Such population shifts interest marketers because people in different geographical regions buy differently. Tobacco consumption provides a good way of understanding this; in Finland 23 per cent of adults smoke (27 per cent of men, 20 per cent of women), in France, 27 per cent of adults smoke (33 per cent of men, 21 per cent of women), in Denmark 30 per cent of adults smoke (32 per cent of men, 29 per cent of women), while in Hungary 42 per cent of adults smoke (53 per cent of men, 30 per cent of women).[13] As workers from Eastern European countries such as

Hungary move west to find jobs, marketers have to ask themselves whether their consumption behaviour will resemble more the country where they were born, or the country where they choose to work.

The shift in where people live has also caused a shift in where they work. For example, the migration toward metropolitan and suburban areas has resulted in a rapid increase in the number of people who 'telecommute' – work at home or in a remote office and conduct their business by phone, fax, modem, or the Internet. This trend, in turn, has created a booming SOHO (small office/home office) market.

A better-educated, more white-collar, more professional population

The European population is becoming better educated, and European workers are increasingly employed in professional or 'white collar' (managerial or equivalent) jobs. This generalisation is valid more or less everywhere across the Continent. For example, in Spain the proportion of people achieving a tertiary educational qualification (that is, a qualification beyond secondary school level) increased from 37 per cent in 1991 to 67 per cent in 2006, and in Ukraine that proportion increased from 47 per cent to 73 per cent. The number of students enrolled in tertiary education in the EU has increased steadily over the last decade and is expected to continue to grow; for example, the growth in the number of students in tertiary education between 1994 and 2004 was 25 per cent in Spain, 35 per cent in the United Kingdom, 59 per cent in Ireland and 83 per cent in Sweden. Governments across Europe recognise that economic success is increasingly dependent on having a well-educated population, and are investing in education. Typically, public spending on education in European countries runs at about 5 per cent of gross domestic product (GDP, a measure of the total national income).[14] The rising number of educated people will increase the demand for good quality products, books, magazines, travel, personal computers and Internet services. Over the next decade job growth is likely to be strongest for professional workers and weakest for jobs in manufacturing.

Increasing diversity

Countries vary in their ethnic and racial make-up. For example, in Japan almost everyone is Japanese. The situation is very different in the United Kingdom, with people from virtually all nations. Roughly 20 per cent of the births in the UK are to mothers born outside the country. Taking England alone, in 2005 it was estimated that 84.7 per cent of the population was White British, and another 4.4 per cent was White but not British (including Irish people and immigrants from Eastern Europe). The largest ethnic minority group in England was Asian (very largely of Indian, Pakistani or Bangladeshi origin), who made up 5.3 per cent of the population, followed by the Black population at 2.7 per cent (fairly equally divided between people of African and of Caribbean origin).[15] Focusing in even more tightly on London alone, it is estimated that a third of Londoners were born outside the UK, but Londoners born outside the UK made up a higher proportion, around 38 per cent, of London's labour force; they are more likely to be parents than Londoners born in the UK.

Marketers in the public and private sectors often have to factor in the ethnic composition of their markets when devising marketing strategies. Lloyds TSB bank has launched an Islamic bank account (which conforms to Islamic, Shariah law) aimed at a predominantly Asian target market that practises Islam. The Mayor of London's office makes publicity and information material available in Arabic, Bengali, Chinese, Greek, Gujurati, Hindi, Punjabi, Turkish, Urdu and Vietnamese as well as English. In a multi-racial city, like London, opportunities for marketers to turn a profit by serving the specific needs of particular ethnic groups abound – just ask **www.afrotherapy.com** of London (suppliers of hair care and beauty products for those with black skin), **www.ranifashions.com** of Luton near London (suppliers of traditional Indian clothing) or the food store Polish Specialities of Hammersmith in west London.

Diversity goes beyond ethnic heritage. For example, many major companies have recently begun explicitly to target gay and lesbian consumers. Evidence from countries in which a gay lifestyle is widely accepted, such as the UK, the USA and Germany, suggests that gay men and lesbians represent a tremendous marketing opportunity – being, on average, better educated, more likely to be in a professional job, and better paid. In addition, gay men and lesbians tend to be early adopters of trends that eventually are adopted by the mainstream. For example, according to one expert, 'in the weeks following an episode of the Bravo hit show *Queer Eye for the Straight Guy* – in which five gay men, known as the Fab 5,

Multicultural marketing: an increasing number of businesses in Europe target the large, and often affluent, ethnic minority markets.

make over a low-maintenance straight man – many businesses whose products are featured have seen a significant sales boost'. Lucky Brand jeans saw a 17 per cent sales jump for the two months following a mention on *Queer Eye*.[16]

Companies in several industries are now waking up to the needs and potential of the gay and lesbian segment. For example, Gay.com, a website that attracts more than 2 million unique visitors each month from more than 100 countries, has also attracted a diverse set of well-known advertisers, such as American Express, Halo pet care products, Delta Airlines and a number of different holiday destinations. In fact, holiday companies and holiday destinations have recently demonstrated a particularly strong interest in the large amounts of money that are being spent in what is called the 'gay tourism' or 'pink tourism' market.[17] A wide range of cities around the world are vying to attract gay and lesbian tourists. Many of them provide detailed information through their websites, and other media, to prospective gay and lesbian tourists. For example, the city of Manchester in northern England claims that: 'Manchester's gay scene is famously one of Britain's friendliest, busiest and most welcoming. There's a huge range of stylish bars and clubs in the Gay Village and while here you'll find shopping heaven, an arts scene to match anywhere in Europe, and more trendy restaurants than you can shake a credit card at.'[18] The city of Melbourne, Australia says: 'Life's a party, or at least it should be, and Melbourne's gay and lesbian community certainly know how to enjoy it',[19] and gay and lesbian tourists eager to visit Germany can find out everything they need to know at the 'Gayfriendly Germany' section of the official German tourism website.[20]

MAKING CONNECTIONS Linking the concepts

Pull over here for a moment and think about how deeply these demographic factors affect all of us and, as a result, marketers' strategies.

■ Apply these demographic developments to your own life. Think of some specific examples of how the changing demographic factors affect you and your buying behaviour.

■ Identify a specific company that has done a good job of reacting to the shifting demographic environment – generational segments (baby boomers, Generation X or Generation Y), the changing family and increased diversity. Compare this company to one that's done a poor job.

Economic environment

Markets require buying power as well as people. The **economic environment** consists of factors that affect consumer purchasing power and spending patterns. Nations vary greatly in their levels and distribution of income. Some countries have *subsistence economies* – they consume most of their own agricultural and industrial output. These countries offer few market opportunities. At the other extreme are *industrial economies*, which constitute rich markets for many different kinds of goods. Marketers must pay close attention to major trends and consumer spending patterns both across and within their world markets. The following are some of the major economic trends in Europe.

Changes in income

The general trend in incomes throughout the EU over the last two decades has been upwards. This can be seen in the first four columns of Table 3.1, which show GDP per capita (a measure of how much income per head is created in the economy), for five selected EU Member States, together with an EU average. The five nations shown in Table 3.1 have been chosen to show the range of income per head to be found across the EU; Germany and the United Kingdom represent the richest group of nations, Spain represents the 'middle income' group of nations, and Lithuania and Poland represent the poorer nations of the EU, with income per head at about 50 per cent of the EU average. However, a closer inspection will show that the growth rate of income per head has been far higher in the poorer nations than in the richer nations, indicating a narrowing of the income gap between Europe's richest countries and its poorest countries. During the period from 1996 to 2005, when average EU GDP per capita rose by 43.5 per cent, GDP per capita in Lithuania rose by 114 per cent. When looking at figures like these it is important to remember that the largest economies in the EU are far larger than the smaller economies. Germany alone represents over a fifth of EU GDP, and the four largest economies combined – Germany, the UK, France and Italy – represent two-thirds of EU GDP. At the other end of the scale, there are ten EU member countries that each represent less than 1 per cent of total EU GDP – the Czech Republic, Cyprus, Latvia, Lithuania, Luxembourg, Hungary, Malta, Slovenia and Slovakia.

The growth of consumer spending in the EU was adversely affected in 2008–2009 by the so-called credit crunch. Although this problem largely originated in the USA, where banks had lent large sums of money to people who, it turned out, did not have

TABLE 3.1 Key economic indicators for the EU and five individual EU Member States

	1996	2005	Percentage of EU average 2005	2006		1996	2001	2006
	GDP per capita (in euros)			Inequality of income distribution (income quintile share ratio)	Percentage of consumer spending on food and non-alcoholic beverages			
EU	16,300	23,400	100	4.8	EU	14.3	13.1	12.7
Germany	19,200	25,700	109.8	4.1	Germany	12.1	11.6	11.0
United Kingdom	17,800	27,300	116.8	5.4	United Kingdom	11.2	9.6	9.1
Spain	14,200	23,100	98.7	5.3	Spain	16.9	14.5	13.8
Lithuania	5,700	12,200	52.1	6.3	Lithuania	38.8	29.2	25.8
Poland	6,900	11,700	49.9	5.6	Poland	26.4	22.9	20.9

the means to repay it, it was also felt throughout the EU, particularly in countries such as the UK where consumers had borrowed heavily to buy houses, cars and durable consumer goods. As a consequence the supply of funds banks had to lend to consumers diminished sharply, and a lot of consumers found themselves worse off when their short-term discounted mortgage deals came to an end and they had to refinance at a higher interest rate. These financially squeezed consumers have adjusted to their changing financial situations and are spending more carefully. *Value marketing* has become the watchword for many marketers. Rather than offering high quality at a high price, or lesser quality at very low prices, marketers are looking for ways to offer today's more financially cautious buyers greater value – just the right combination of product quality and good service at a fair price.

Marketers should pay attention to *income distribution* as well as average income. Income distribution in Europe is very skewed. At the top are *upper-class* consumers, whose spending patterns are not affected by current economic events and who are a major market for luxury goods. There is a comfortable *middle class* that is fairly careful about its spending but can still afford the good life some of the time. The *working class* must stick close to the basics of food, clothing and shelter and must try hard to save. Finally, the *underclass* (persons on welfare and many pensioners) must count their pennies when making even the most basic purchases.

While the first four columns of Table 3.1 demonstrate the inequality of incomes between European nations, the fifth column shows the 'inequality of income distribution' within selected countries. We already know that, on average, income per head in Lithuania is about a half of income per head in Germany; now we can see that the income distribution *within* Lithuania is much more unequal than the income distribution within Germany. People in the top fifth of income earners in Lithuania earn on average 6.3 times as much as those in the bottom fifth, while in Germany the ratio is only 4.1. This distribution of income creates a tiered market. Many companies – such as Rolex and Dior – aggressively target the affluent. Others – such as Aldi and Lidl – target those with more modest means. Still other companies tailor their marketing offers across a range of markets, from the affluent to the less affluent.

Changing consumer spending patterns

Table 3.1 also shows the proportion of total expenditures made by European households on food and non-alcoholic beverages – essential purchases that no one can do without. This shows that consumers at different income levels have different spending patterns. Some of these differences were noted over a century ago by Ernst Engel, who studied how people shifted their spending as their income rose. He found that as family income rises, the percentage spent on food declines, the percentage spent on housing remains about constant (except for such utilities as gas, electricity and public services, which decrease), and both the percentage spent on most other categories and that devoted to savings increase. **Engel's laws** generally have been supported by later studies. The information in the final columns of Table 3.1 shows that the proportion of European consumer expenditure going on essentials has declined as average incomes across Europe have risen; it also shows that the proportion of income spent on essentials is much higher in the poorer countries of Europe than in richer countries such as the UK and Germany. However, since incomes are rising fast in poorer countries, such as Lithuania and Poland, the proportion of income spent on essentials is declining much faster here than elsewhere in Europe.

Changes in major economic variables such as income, cost of living, interest rates, and savings and borrowing patterns have a large impact on the marketplace. Companies watch these variables by using economic forecasting. Businesses do not have to be wiped out by an economic downturn or caught short in a boom. With adequate warning, they can take advantage of changes in the economic environment.

Natural environment

The **natural environment** involves the natural resources that are needed as inputs by marketers or that are affected by marketing activities. Environmental concerns have grown steadily during the past three decades. In many cities around the world, air and water pollution have reached dangerous levels. World concern continues to mount about the possibilities of global warming, and many environmentalists fear that soon we will be buried in our own rubbish.

Marketers should be aware of several trends in the natural environment. The first involves growing *shortages of raw materials*. Once upon a time air and water may have seemed to be infinite resources, but few people believe this today. Air pollution chokes many of the world's large cities, and water shortages are already a big problem in some parts of the world. Renewable resources, such as forests and food, also have to be used wisely. Non-renewable resources, such as oil, coal and various minerals, are likely to become more difficult to find and increasingly expensive. Firms making products that require these scarce resources face large cost increases, even if the materials do remain available.

A second environmental trend is *increased pollution*. Industry will almost always damage the quality of the natural environment. Consider the disposal of chemical and nuclear wastes, the dangerous mercury levels in the oceans, the quantity of chemical pollutants in the soil and food supply, and the littering of the environment with non-biodegradable bottles, plastics and other packaging materials.

A third trend is *increased government intervention* in natural resource management. The governments of different countries vary in their concern and efforts to promote a clean environment. Some, like the German government, vigorously pursue environmental quality. Others, especially many poorer nations, do little about pollution, largely because they lack the needed funds or political will. Even the richer nations lack the vast funds and political accord needed to mount a worldwide environmental effort. The general hope is that companies around the world will accept more social responsibility, and that less expensive devices can be found to control and reduce pollution.

Concern for the natural environment has spawned the so-called green movement. Today, enlightened companies go beyond what government regulations dictate. They are developing *environmentally sustainable* strategies and practices in an effort to create a world economy that the planet can support indefinitely. They are responding to consumer demands with products that do less damage to the environment. For example, the Volkswagen 'Blue Motion' range of cars delivers far better fuel economy and causes less damage to the environment for each kilometre travelled than previous generations of vehicles. We will return to the theme of sustainability in Chapter 16.

Other companies are developing recyclable or biodegradable packaging, recycled materials and components, better pollution controls, and more energy-efficient operations. Public transport operator Stagecoach has announced plans to run the first carbon-neutral bus network in the UK, by offsetting the emissions from its fleet of buses with a huge tree-planting scheme. McDonald's has a long-standing rainforest policy and a commitment to purchasing recycled products and to energy-efficient restaurant construction techniques. Panasonic Europe is investing in technology to reduce the environmental impact of its factories, by using filtration systems for

Source: Volkswagen Group.

Responding to consumer demands for more environmentally responsible products, Volkswagen has created the Blue Motion range of cars.

waste water that go far beyond regulatory requirements, by exercising strict control over exhaust emissions, and by keeping energy consumption to a minimum.

These companies are looking to do more than just good deeds. More and more, companies are recognising the link between a healthy ecology and a healthy economy. They are learning that environmentally responsible actions can also be good business (see Marketing at Work 3.2).[21]

Technological environment

The **technological environment** is perhaps the most dramatic force now shaping our destiny. Technology has released such wonders as antibiotics, organ transplants, mobile phones, laptop computers and the Internet. It also has released such horrors as nuclear missiles, chemical weapons and assault rifles. It has created such mixed blessings as the car, television and credit cards.

Our attitude toward technology depends on whether we are more impressed with its wonders or its blunders. For example, what would you think about having a tiny little transmitter implanted in all of the products you buy that would allow tracking products from their point of production through use and disposal? On the one hand, it would provide many advantages to both buyers and sellers. On the other hand, it could be a bit scary. Either way, it's already happening:

Envision a world in which every product contains a tiny transmitter, loaded with information. As you stroll through the supermarket aisles, shelf sensors detect your selections and beam ads to your shopping cart screen, offering special deals on related products. As your cart fills, scanners detect that you might be buying for a dinner party; the screen suggests a wine to go with the meal you've planned. When you leave the store, exit scanners total up your purchases and automatically charge them to your credit card. At home, readers track what goes into and out of your pantry, updating your shopping list when stocks run low. For Sunday dinner, you pop a Butterball turkey into your 'smart oven', which follows instructions from an embedded chip and cooks the bird to perfection.

Seem far-fetched? Not really. In fact, it might soon become a reality, thanks to tiny radio-frequency identification (RFID) transmitters – or 'smart chips' – that can be embedded in the products you buy. Beyond benefits to consumers, the RFID chips also give producers and retailers an amazing new way to track their products electronically – anywhere in the world, any time, automatically – from factories, to warehouses, to retail shelves, to recycling centres.[22]

The technological environment changes rapidly. Think of all of today's common products that were not available 100 years ago, or even 30 years ago. Anyone who died 150 years ago did not know about cars, planes, radios or the electric light. Someone who died only 80 years ago did not know about television, aerosol cans, automatic dishwashers, air conditioners, antibiotics or computers. Anyone who died during the Second World War did not know about photocopying, synthetic detergents, tape recorders, birth control pills or communications satellites. Even people who died as recently as the 1960s did not know about personal computers, mobile phones, DVD players or the Internet.

New technologies create new markets and opportunities. However, every new technology replaces an older technology. Transistors damaged the vacuum tube (valve) industry, photocopying damaged the carbon-paper business, the car damaged the railway business, CDs damaged the record industry, and in turn music and video downloads are damaging the CD and DVD businesses. When old industries fought or ignored new technologies, their businesses declined. Thus, marketers should watch the technological environment closely. Companies that do not keep up will soon find their products outdated. And they will miss new product and market opportunities.

MARKETING AT WORK 3.2

Gibson: Making money *and* leaving the world a better place

If a tree falls in the rainforest and no one is there to trumpet its eco-friendliness, does it still make a sound? It might – if that wood is destined for an electric guitar. Gibson Guitar, the iconic guitar maker, has worked since the late 1980s to make its wood supply environmentally sustainable. Gibson's electric-guitar division recently switched to 100 per cent fair-trade-certified wood. Other Gibson divisions, including Baldwin Piano, plan to follow suit.

Yet unlike Starbucks, The Body Shop, and other businesses that eagerly brandish their green deeds, Gibson CEO Henry Juszkiewicz doesn't much care to flaunt his environmental credentials (the guy drives a Hummer, after all). What matters to him is ensuring that Gibson has enough exotic wood, mostly mahogany, to keep making guitars for generations.

'We're mercenaries. We're a company. We're for-profit,' Juszkiewicz says in his Nashville office, packed with so many music-industry mementos it looks like his own private Hard Rock Café. 'I'm not a conservationist.' High-end guitar enthusiasts, after all, demand that their instruments be made of exotic woods. But prices for exotics can swing wildly, governed by an unsteady supply and the threat that some species may be placed on an extinction watch list.

Juszkiewicz wanted to eliminate the guesswork by building a network of growers rather than relying on brokers scouring world markets for the best prices. He approached the Rainforest Alliance, a non-profit conservation group, to discuss buying wood from Mexican suppliers certified as sustainable. (Such growers are graded against environmental, labour, and community standards – and for responsible harvesting.)

But that hardly made a dent in Gibson's sourcing problems. So the company hired away two Rainforest Alliance employees to source wood in Costa Rica and Brazil. 'Within the first year of hiring these guys, they were able to develop significant sources,' Juszkiewicz says. 'We went from less than 1 per cent usage of certified product to something like 80 per cent.' Since then, Gibson has forged a direct relationship with growers in Guatemala. That provides both stability of supply and quality, since Gibson is able to instruct farmers on its exacting specifications.

Initially, Juszkiewicz says, Gibson paid a premium for purchasing wood this way. Now buying direct creates modest savings – and the relationships help curb traditional slash-and-burn harvesting, which threatens supplies of precious woods. 'In the short run, a slight price increase won't necessarily hurt them because a guitar is a higher-value product,' says an industry expert. 'In the long run, it helps ensure that they can tap this supply not just in 5 years but in 50 years.'

Tensie Whelan, executive director of the Rainforest Alliance, says she's seeing a critical mass of CEOs discovering that environmentally friendly practices can be good business. But she still teases Juszkiewicz, one of the first: 'He'll say he's a businessman, that he's just out to make money. But believe me, he's passionate about wanting to leave the world a better place.'

Source: Adapted from Ryan Underwood, 'In Tune with the Environment', *Fast Company*, December 19, 2007.

Gibson Guitar works to make its exotic hardwood supply environmentally sustainable. The company has learned that environmentally friendly practices can also be good business. *Photo sources*: © PNC/zefa/Corbis (background); Gibson Les Paul image © Gibson Guitar Corp. Used with express written permission of Gibson Guitar Corp.

One of the keys to developing and exploiting new technologies is spending on research and development (R&D). Total EU R&D spending reached an estimated €210 billion in 2006, just over 1.8 per cent of GDP – the EU target is to raise R&D spending to 3 per cent of GDP by 2010. The EU countries with the highest R&D intensity are Sweden (3.82 per cent of GDP) and Finland (3.45 per cent of GDP), while those countries from Eastern Europe that have joined the EU more recently tend to have lower R&D intensity – 0.48 per cent of GDP in Bulgaria, 0.49 per cent in Slovakia. Scientists today are researching a wide range of promising new products and services, ranging from practical solar energy, electric cars and cancer cures to voice-controlled computers and genetically engineered food crops.

Technological environment: technology is perhaps the most dramatic force shaping the marketing environment. Here, a herder makes a call on his mobile phone.

Source: Getty Images/Joseph Van Os.

Today's research is carried out usually by research teams rather than by lone inventors such as Louis Pasteur, George Stephenson or Karl Benz. Many companies are adding marketing people to R&D teams to try to obtain a stronger marketing orientation. Scientists also speculate on fantasy products, such as flying cars, three-dimensional televisions and space colonies. The challenge in each case is not only technical but also commercial – to make *practical, affordable* versions of these products.

As products and technology become more complex, the public needs to know that these are safe. Thus, government agencies investigate and ban potentially unsafe products. In the European Union, the European Food Safety Authority (EFSA) works with the European Commission, the European Parliament and the authorities in individual countries to assess and eliminate food safety risks. The European Commissioner for Consumer Affairs is in charge of promoting consumer interests, health and safety throughout the EU. This involves working with national consumer protection organisations and recommending regulations to protect consumer interests. Such regulations can result in much higher research costs and in longer times between new-product ideas and their introduction. Marketers should be aware of these regulations when applying new technologies and developing new products.

Political environment

Marketing decisions are strongly affected by developments in the political environment. The **political environment** consists of laws, government agencies and pressure groups that influence or limit various organisations and individuals in a given society.

The European Union

How the European Union was created By 2007 the European Union had expanded to include 27 countries with a combined population of 493 million people. The largest member states in terms of population are Germany (82.4 million), France (62.9 million), the United Kingdom (60.4 million), Italy (58.8 million), Spain (43.8 million) and Poland (38.2 million). Altogether, the EU represents the third largest population block in the world after China and India. If the three countries under consideration as candidates for EU membership – Croatia, the Former Yugoslav Republic of Macedonia, and Turkey – were to join, then the combined population would be close to 600 million. How did such a large and economically powerful international union come about?

The origins of the European Union can be traced back at least as far as the 1950s. Initially there were six members of the European Coal and Steel Community (ECSC), which was established by Belgium, France, Germany, Italy, Luxembourg and the Netherlands in 1952. Politically, the principal motivation behind greater European cooperation could be found in the aftermath of the Second World War (1939–45), during which the major countries of Europe fought each other to a standstill and largely destroyed Europe's industrial capacity. In particular, the cooperation between those great European powers, and rivals, France and Germany was symbolic of the desire to avoid further major conflicts. (Remember that, at the time, this was 'West Germany', since Germany had been partitioned into East, the German Democratic Republic, and West, the Federal Republic of Germany, after the War. German reunification was not to occur until 1990.)

The most prominent forerunner of the European Union was the European Economic Community (EEC), established by the six members of the ECSC in 1957 by the Treaty of Rome. During the next 30 years the EEC expanded periodically; Denmark, Ireland and the UK joined in 1973, Greece in 1981, Spain and Portugal in 1986. Then, in 1987, the Single European Act was passed which was designed to make real progress towards the goal of having a 'single European market'. By the beginning of 1993 the economic reforms to implement the Single European Act had been completed, establishing the free movement of goods, services, people and money within the EEC. In principle, nationals of the EEC states could work wherever they wished within the Community, and businesses could buy and sell as easily across national borders within the EEC as they could within their own countries. Around the same time, in 1992, the Treaty of Maastricht was signed, which was to lead to the creation of the single European currency (the euro) and to closer cooperation between member states on foreign and domestic policy. It was with the Maastricht Treaty that the name 'European Economic Community' was dropped in favour of the new term 'European Union' (EU).

Further major expansion of the European Union followed, with three new member states joining in 1995, ten in 2004 and a further two joining in 2007 to make up 27 in all. Here are all 27, with the year in which they joined the EU, or its predecessors (the ECSC or the EEC):

1952: Belgium, France, Germany, Italy, Luxembourg, the Netherlands

1973: Denmark, Ireland, the United Kingdom

1981: Greece

1986: Spain, Portugal

1995: Austria, Finland, Sweden

2004: Czech Republic, Estonia, Latvia, Lithuania, Hungary, Poland, Slovenia, Slovakia, Cyprus, Malta

2007: Bulgaria, Romania

The objectives of the EU Initially, the main driving force behind European cooperation was the desire to avoid further major conflicts between the member states, and to promote peace more widely within Europe. However, the two principal factors promoting closer European cooperation for the last three or four decades have been politics and economics. Politically, there have always been some within Europe who wish to promote the concept of a 'United States of Europe', that is, ever-closer political union leading eventually to the creation of a European superstate. Economically, the main argument for closer European cooperation is that, through the creation of a huge single market for goods, services, labour and capital in Europe, all of the member states will reap substantial economic benefits. For example, by eliminating the barriers to the free movement of labour, skilled workers can travel across Europe to wherever they are most needed, and employers in search of skilled labour need not restrict themselves to the local economy but can search among all of the member states. Both the political and economic goals of the EU are reflected in the formal objectives, to be found in the key treaties that are the foundation of the Union.

The following are the formal, stated objectives of the EU:

To promote economic progress and social progress and a high level of employment and to achieve balanced and sustainable development, in particular through the creation of an area without internal frontiers, through the strengthening of economic and social cohesion and through the establishment of economic and monetary union, ultimately including a single currency . . .

To assert its identity on the international scene, in particular through the implementation of a common foreign and security policy including the progressive framing of a common defence policy, which might lead to a common defence . . .

To strengthen the protection of the rights and interests of the nationals of Member States through the introduction of a citizenship of the Union,

To maintain and develop the Union as an area of freedom, security and justice, in which the free movement of persons is assured in conjunction with appropriate measures with respect to external border controls, asylum, immigration and the prevention and combating of crime,

To maintain in full the *acquis communautaire* and build on it with a view to considering to what extent the policies and forms of cooperation introduced by this Treaty may need to be revised with the aim of ensuring the effectiveness of the mechanisms and the institutions of the Community.[23]

The *acquis communautaire* refers to the accumulated body of European laws developed by the EU so far; this covers a wide range of subjects, including the free movement of people, goods, services and money within the EU, laws on free competition, intellectual property, public procurement and many other topics.

Legislation regulating business

Even the most liberal advocates of free-market economies agree that the system works best with at least some regulation. Well-conceived regulation can encourage competition and ensure fair markets for goods and services. Thus, governments develop *public policy* to guide commerce – sets of laws and regulations that limit business for the good of society as a whole. Almost every marketing activity is subject to a wide range of laws and regulations.

Increasing legislation Legislation affecting business around the world has increased steadily over the years. Europe has many laws covering issues such as competition, fair trade practices, environmental protection, product safety, truth in advertising, consumer privacy, packaging and labelling, pricing and other important areas. The European Commission has been active in establishing a new framework of laws covering competitive behaviour, product standards, product liability, and commercial transactions for the nations of the European Union.

Of course, marketers must become familiar with the relevant legislation in whichever markets they operate around the world. For example, Norway bans several forms of sales promotion – trading stamps, contests, premiums – as being inappropriate or unfair ways of promoting products. Thailand requires food processors selling national brands to market low price brands also, so that low-income consumers can find economy brands on the shelves. In India, food companies must obtain special approval to launch brands that duplicate those already existing on the market, such as ad ..ional cola drinks or new brands of rice.

Understanding the public policy implications of a particular marketing activity is not a simple matter. For example, in Europe, there are laws created at the EU and at the national levels, and these regulations often overlap – one of the goals of the EU is progressively to harmonise national laws so that the same legal system applies throughout the Union, but it will be quite a while before that goal is achieved. For example, food products sold in Athens are governed both by relevant EU and Greek national laws. Moreover, regulations are constantly changing – what was allowed last year may now be prohibited, and what was prohibited may now be allowed. Marketers must work hard to keep up with changes in regulations and their interpretations.

Business legislation has been enacted for a number of reasons. The first is to *protect companies* from each other. Although business executives may praise competition, they sometimes try to neutralise it when it threatens them. So laws are passed to define and prevent unfair competition. In Europe, such laws are enforced by the Directorate General for Competition and by national competition authorities such as the Office of Fair Trading in the UK, the Competition Authority in Ireland, the Konkurrensverket in Sweden, and the Conseil de la Concurrence in France.

The second purpose of government regulation is to *protect consumers* from unfair business practices. Some firms, if left alone, would make shoddy products, tell lies in their advertising, and deceive consumers through their packaging and pricing. Unfair business practices have been defined and sanctions are enforced by various agencies.

The third purpose of government regulation is to *protect the interests of society* against unrestrained business behaviour. Profitable business activity does not always create a better quality of life. Regulation arises to ensure that firms take responsibility for the social costs of their production or products.

Changing government agency enforcement International marketers will encounter dozens, or even hundreds, of agencies set up to enforce trade policies and regulations. We have mentioned several of those that will be found in Europe in the preceding paragraphs, while in the USA, for example, businesses have to consider the Federal Trade Commission, the Food and Drug Administration and the Federal Communications Commission, among others. Because such government agencies have some discretion in enforcing the laws, they can have a major impact on a company's marketing performance. Few of these agencies employ marketing professionals, however, so that it can be difficult to get them to understand the impact that their actions can have on company marketing strategies.

New laws and their enforcement will continue to increase. Business executives must watch these developments when planning their products and marketing programmes. Marketers need to know about the major laws protecting competition, consumers and society. They need to understand these laws at the local, state, national and international levels.

Increased emphasis on ethics and socially responsible actions

Written regulations cannot possibly cover all potential marketing abuses, and existing laws are often difficult to enforce. However, beyond written laws and regulations, business is also governed by social codes and rules of professional ethics.

Socially responsible behaviour Enlightened companies encourage their managers to look beyond what the regulatory system allows and simply 'do the right thing'. These socially responsible firms actively seek out ways to protect the long-term interests of their consumers and the environment.

The recent rash of business scandals and increased concerns about the environment have created fresh interest in the issues of ethics and social responsibility. Almost every aspect of marketing involves such issues. Unfortunately, because these issues usually involve conflicting interests, well-meaning people can honestly disagree about the right course of action in a given situation. Thus, many industrial and professional trade associations have suggested codes of ethics. And more companies are now developing policies, guidelines and other responses to complex social responsibility issues.

The boom in e-commerce and Internet marketing has created a new set of social and ethical issues. Online privacy issues are the primary concern. For example, website visitors often provide extensive personal information that might leave them open to abuse by unscrupulous marketers. Moreover, both Intel and Microsoft have been accused of covert, high-tech computer chip and software invasions of customers' personal computers to obtain information for marketing purposes. Most companies are now careful to disclose fully their Internet privacy policies.[24]

Throughout the text, we present examples that summarise the main public policy and social responsibility issues surrounding major marketing decisions. These exhibits discuss the legal issues that marketers should understand and the common ethical and societal concerns that marketers face. In Chapter 16 we discuss a broad range of societal marketing issues in greater depth.

Cause-related marketing To exercise their social responsibility and build more positive images, many companies are now linking themselves to worthwhile causes. These days, every product seems to be tied to some cause. Buy women's underwear or swimwear from a Debenhams store and support breast cancer research. Shop at Tesco and collect free vouchers that your local school can use to buy computer equipment. Purchase Habitat Coffee and help Habitat for Humanity build a house for a needy family. Pay for these purchases with the right credit or debit card and you can support a local cultural arts group or help fight heart disease.

Cause-related marketing has become a primary form of corporate giving. It lets companies 'do well by doing good' by linking purchases of the company's products or services with fund-raising for worthwhile causes or charitable organisations. Companies now sponsor dozens of cause-related marketing campaigns each year. Many are backed by large budgets and a full complement of marketing activities. Consider this example:

> In May 2004, Nike began selling simple yellow synthetic silicon rubber bracelets – stamped with the phrase 'Live Strong' – at Niketown outlets around the country. The price was $1, and proceeds were given to the Lance Armstrong Foundation, the non-profit charitable organisation associated with the champion cyclist, who is also a Nike athlete and famous cancer survivor. 'Live Strong' is the foundation's motto; yellow echoes the colour of the lead rider's jersey in the Tour de France. Nike paid for the entire first run of five million bracelets, meaning that 100 per cent of the proceeds, plus another $1 million Nike threw in, went straight to the foundation.
>
> Sales really took off when the Tour de France got under way that summer. Armstrong wore the wristband and so did his whole team. As the tour wore on, competitors and even officials started wearing them. As Armstrong cruised to his record-setting sixth consecutive Tour de France victory, celebrities started wearing them, and suddenly the bracelets were everywhere – a charitable must-have. In less than a year, the foundation had sold more than 40 million 'Live Strong' bracelets for $1 each. On one day alone, the Foundation sold an amazing 900,000 bracelets when Armstrong appeared on 'The Oprah Winfrey Show' and Winfrey challenged her viewers to break the previous single-day record of 382,000.[25]

Cause-related marketing has stirred some controversy. Critics worry that cause-related marketing is more a strategy for selling than a strategy for giving – that 'cause-related' marketing is really 'cause-exploitative' marketing. Thus, companies using cause-related marketing might find themselves walking a fine line between increased sales and an improved image, and facing charges of exploitation.

However, if handled well, cause-related marketing can greatly benefit both the company and the cause. The company gains an effective marketing tool while building a more positive public image. The charitable organisation or cause gains greater visibility and important new sources of funding.

Cultural environment

The **cultural environment** is made up of institutions and other forces that affect a society's basic values, perceptions, preferences and behaviours. People grow up in a particular society that shapes their basic beliefs and values. They absorb a worldview that defines their relationships with others. The following cultural characteristics can affect marketing decision-making.

Persistence of cultural values

People in a given society hold many beliefs and values. Their core beliefs and values have a high degree of persistence. For example, most Europeans believe in working, getting married, giving to charity and being honest. These beliefs shape more specific attitudes and behaviours found in everyday life. *Core* beliefs and values are passed on from parents to children and are reinforced by schools, churches, business and government.

Secondary beliefs and values are more open to change. Believing in marriage is a core belief; believing that people should get married early in life is a secondary belief. Marketers have some chance of changing secondary values but little chance of changing core values. For example, family-planning marketers could argue more effectively that people should get married later than that they should not get married at all.

Shifts in secondary cultural values

Although core values are fairly persistent, cultural swings do take place. Consider the impact of popular music groups, film stars and other celebrities on young people's hairstyling and clothing norms. Marketers want to predict cultural shifts in order to spot new opportunities or threats. Several firms offer 'futures' forecasts in this connection, such as the Yankelovich Monitor, Market Facts' BrainWaves Group, and the Trends Research Institute.

The Yankelovich Monitor has tracked consumer value trends for years. At the dawn of the twenty-first century, it looked back to capture lessons from the past decade that might offer insight into the 2000s.[26] Yankelovich maintains that the 'decade drivers' for the 2000s will primarily come from the baby boomers and Generation X. The baby boomers will be driven by four factors: 'adventure' (fuelled by a sense of youthfulness), 'smarts' (fuelled by a sense of empowerment and willingness to accept change), 'intergenerational support' (caring for younger and older, often in non-traditional arrangements), and 'retreading' (embracing early retirement with second career or phase of their work life). Generation X will be driven by three factors: 'redefining the good life' (being highly motivated to improve their economic well-being and remain in control), 'new rituals' (returning to traditional values but with a tolerant mindset and active lifestyle), and 'cutting and pasting' (balancing work, play, sleep, family and other aspects of their lives).

The major cultural values of a society are expressed in people's views of themselves and others, as well as in their views of organisations, society, nature and the universe.

People's views of themselves People vary in their emphasis on serving themselves versus serving others. Some people seek personal pleasure, wanting fun, change and escape. Others seek self-realisation through religion, recreation, or the avid pursuit of careers or other life goals. People use products, brands and services as a means of self-expression, and they buy products and services that match their views of themselves.

Yankelovich Monitor recently discovered a conflicted consumer segment whose purchases are motivated by self-views of both duty and fun:

Yankelovich's Monitor has identified a paradoxical consumer segment motivated equally by duty and fun. Comprising more than one-third of the population, these folks want to have their cake and rely on it, too. 'Duty and Fun' consumers agree that 'duty should always come before pleasure' *and* say that they 'try to have as much fun as they can now and let the future take care of itself'. Their split personalities indicate an internal struggle that affects everyday life and buying. To reach these conflicted consumers, marketers must give them something that makes them smile at the register, while offering sound payment options, guarantees, testimonials, and other forms of assurance. For example, PetSmart permits shoppers to bring their pets shopping, allowing duty and fun to happily coexist. And with its hybrid Prius, Toyota merges a respected company brand (duty) and leading-edge technology (fun), turning what could have been a fuddy-duddy failure into a ride for those sold on dutiful fun.[27]

People's views of others Recently, observers have noted a shift from a 'me society' to a 'we society' in which more people want to be with and serve others.

After years of serious 'nesting' – staying close to the security and creature comforts of home and hearth – people are now venturing out of their homes to hang out in the real world. The nesting instinct has gone in and out of fashion before. When the first big wave hit in the early '80s, trend watchers coined the term 'cocooning' to describe the surge of boomers buying their first homes and filling them up with oversize furniture and fancy gadgets. The dot-com boom set off another round, partly fuelled by cool home gizmos like plasma TVs and PlayStations. Though many expected 9/11 to send people even deeper into nesting mode, sociologists say it actually got people out looking for companionship. After being hunkered down through terror alerts and the war in Iraq, many people were naturally itching to get out. Marketers are beginning to address the shift.[28]

More and more, people want to get out of the house and be with others. This trend suggests a greater demand for 'social support' products and services that improve direct communication between people, such as health clubs and family vacations.

People's views of organisations People vary in their attitudes toward corporations, government agencies, trade unions, universities and other organisations. By and large, people are willing to work for major organisations and expect them, in turn, to carry out society's work.

The late 1980s saw a sharp decrease in confidence in and loyalty towards business and political organisations and institutions. In the workplace, there has been an overall decline in organisational loyalty. During the 1990s, waves of company downsizings bred cynicism and distrust. And in this decade, corporate scandals at Enron, WorldCom, Tyco International and other large companies have resulted in a further loss of confidence in big business. Many people today see work not as a source of satisfaction but as a required chore to earn money to enjoy their non-work hours. This trend suggests that organisations need to find new ways to win consumer and employee confidence.

People's views of society People vary in their attitudes toward their society; conservatives defend the status quo, liberals want to change it, malcontents want to leave it. People's orientation to their society influences their consumption patterns and attitudes toward the marketplace.

People's views of nature People vary in their attitudes toward the natural world. Some feel ruled by it, others feel in harmony with it, and still others seek to master it. A long-term trend has been people's growing mastery over nature through techno-logy and the belief that nature is bountiful. More recently, however, people have recognised that nature is finite and fragile, that it can be destroyed or spoiled by human activities.

This renewed love of things natural has created a sizeable 'lifestyles of health and sustainability' (LOHAS) market: consumers who seek out everything from natural, organic and nutritional products to fuel-efficient cars and alternative medicine. Business has responded by offering more products and services catering to such interests. The global market for organic food and drink was estimated to be worth around €25 billion in 2006; Europe is the largest organic food market in the world, followed by North America in second place. Within Europe Germany is the largest overall organic con-sumer followed by the UK, but although Germans and the British are avid consumers of organic produce, the share of the food market taken by organic products is highest in Switzerland and Austria, at 6 per cent of the market, compared with 3 per cent in Germany and 1.6 per cent in the UK. Many European companies have emerged to exploit this large and growing market opportunity – for example, Biopark Markt GmbH in Germany (organic meat suppliers), St Merryn Meat Ltd in the UK (a slaughterhouse that supplies organic meat to supermarkets), and Bodin et Fils SA in France (the largest European supplier of organic poultry).

People's views of the universe Finally, people vary in their beliefs about the origin of the universe and their place in it. It is very difficult to make generalisations about the religious faith of Europeans. Many European countries, such as France, Italy and Ireland, are predominantly Christian, while others, like Albania, are predominantly Muslim. The largest candidate for membership of the EU, Turkey, is overwhelmingly a Muslim country. However, the extent of religious observance and the significance of religion in people's lives varies considerably across the Continent. Church attendance is much higher in Ireland than elsewhere in Europe, for example. The great majority of Irish people say that they attend a formal religious ceremony regularly, but only a minority of people in the UK says the same thing. In many parts of Europe there is evidence that attendance at religious ceremonies is declining. Nevertheless, religion itself, and cultural practices associated with religion, remain important factors influenc-ing the behaviour of European consumers. For example, there is a tradition in the Roman Catholic Church of not eating meat on Fridays, but eating fish is deemed to be perfectly acceptable. Even though the religious basis for this tradition is not at all clear, the cultural tradition lives on and the Irish Sea Fisheries Board reports that 30 per cent of the wet fish sold in Ireland is sold on a Friday.[29]

MAKING CONNECTIONS Linking the concepts

Slow down and take a break. You've now read about a large number of environmental forces. How are all of these environments *linked* with each other? With company marketing strategy?

■ How are major demographic forces linked with economic changes? With major cultural trends? How are the natural and technological environments linked? Think of an example of a company that has recognised one of these links and turned it into a marketing opportunity.

■ Is the marketing environment uncontrollable – something that the company can only prepare for and react to? Or can companies be proactive in changing environmental factors? Think of a good example that makes your point, then read on.

RESPONDING TO THE MARKETING ENVIRONMENT

Someone once observed, 'There are three kinds of companies: those who make things happen, those who watch things happen, and those who wonder what's happened.'[30] Many companies view the marketing environment as an uncontrollable element to which they must react and adapt. They passively accept the marketing environment and do not try to change it. They analyse the environmental forces and design strategies that will help the company avoid the threats and take advantage of the opportunities the environment provides.

Other companies take a *proactive* stance toward the marketing environment. Rather than simply watching and reacting, these firms take aggressive actions to affect the publics and forces in their marketing environment. Such companies hire lobbyists – people whose profession is to persuade politicians of a point of view – to influence legislation affecting their industries and stage media events to gain favourable press coverage. They run advertorials (advertisements expressing editorial points of view) to shape public opinion. They pursue legal actions and make complaints to regulators to keep competitors in line, and they form contractual agreements to control their distribution channels better.

Often, companies can find positive ways to overcome seemingly uncontrollable environmental constraints. For example:

> Cathay Pacific Airlines . . . determined that many travellers were avoiding Hong Kong because of lengthy delays at immigration. Rather than assuming that this was a problem they could not solve, Cathay's senior staff asked the Hong Kong government how to avoid these immigration delays. After lengthy discussions, the airline agreed to make an annual grant-in-aid to the government to hire more immigration inspectors – but these reinforcements would service primarily the Cathay Pacific gates. The reduced waiting period increased customer value and thus strengthened [Cathay's competitive advantage].[31]

Marketing management cannot always control environmental forces. In many cases, it must settle for simply watching and reacting to the environment. For example, a company would have little success trying to influence geographic population shifts, the economic environment, or major cultural values. But whenever possible, smart marketing managers will take a *proactive* rather than *reactive* approach to the marketing environment.

THE JOURNEY YOU'VE TAKEN Reviewing the concepts

In this chapter and the next two chapters, you'll examine the environments of marketing and how companies analyse these environments to understand the marketplace and consumers better. Companies must constantly watch and manage the *marketing environment* in order to seek opportunities and ward off threats. The marketing environment comprises all the actors and forces influencing the company's ability to transact business effectively with its target market.

1 **Describe the environmental forces that affect the company's ability to serve its customers.**

The company's *microenvironment* consists of other actors close to the company that combine to form the company's value delivery network or that affect its ability to serve its customers. It includes the company's *internal environment* – its several departments and management levels – as it influences marketing decision-making. *Marketing-channel firms* – suppliers and marketing intermediaries, including resellers, physical distribution firms, marketing services agencies and financial intermediaries – cooperate to create customer value. Five types of customer *markets* include consumer, business, reseller, government and international markets. *Competitors* vie with the company in an effort to serve customers better. Finally, various *publics* have an actual or potential interest in or impact on the company's ability to meet its objectives.

The *macroenvironment* consists of larger societal forces that affect the entire microenvironment. The six forces making up the company's macro-environment include demographic, economic, natural, technological, political and cultural. These forces shape opportunities and pose threats to the company.

2 Explain how changes in the demographic and economic environments affect marketing decisions.

Demography is the study of the characteristics of human populations. Today's *demographic environment* shows a changing age structure, shifting family profiles, geographic population shifts, a better-educated and more white-collar population, and increasing diversity. The *economic environment* consists of factors that affect buying power and patterns. The economic environment is characterised by more consumer concern for value and shifting consumer spending patterns. Today's squeezed consumers are seeking greater value – just the right combination of good quality and service at a fair price. The distribution of income also is shifting. The rich have grown richer, the middle class has shrunk, and the poor have remained poor, leading to a two-tiered market. Many companies now tailor their marketing offers to two different markets – the affluent and the less affluent.

3 Identify the major trends in the firm's natural and technological environments.

The *natural environment* shows three major trends: shortages of certain raw materials, higher pollu-tion levels, and more government intervention in natural resource management. Environmental concerns create marketing opportunities for alert companies. The marketer should watch for four major trends in the *technological environment*: the rapid pace of technological change, high R&D budgets, the concentration by companies on minor product improvements, and increased govern-ment regulation. Companies that fail to keep up with technological change will miss out on new product and marketing opportunities.

4 Explain the key changes in the political and cultural environments.

The *political environment* consists of laws, agencies and groups that influence or limit marketing actions. The political environment has undergone three changes that affect marketing worldwide: increasing legislation regulating business, strong government agency enforcement, and greater emphasis on ethics and socially responsible actions. The *cultural environment* is made up of institutions and forces that affect a society's values, perceptions, preferences and behaviours. The environment shows long-term trends toward a 'we society,' a lessening trust of institutions, greater appreciation for nature, and the search for more meaningful and enduring values.

5 Discuss how companies can react to the marketing environment.

Companies can passively accept the marketing environment as an uncontrollable element to which they must adapt, avoiding threats and taking advantage of opportunities as they arise. Or they can take a *proactive* stance, working to change the environment rather than simply reacting to it. Whenever possible, companies should try to be proactive rather than reactive.

NAVIGATING THE KEY TERMS

Baby boomers	Generation X	Microenvironment
Cultural environment	Gemertion Y	Natural environment
Demography	Macroenvironment	Political environment
Economic environment	Marketing environment	Public
Engel's laws	Marketing intermediaries	Technological environment

NOTES AND REFERENCES

1 See Sarah Lorge, 'The Coke Advantage', *Sales & Marketing Management*, December 1998, p. 17; and Chad Terhune 'Coke Wins a 10-Year Contract From Subway, Ousting PepsiCo', *Wall Street Journal*, 28 November 2003, p. B.3.

2 World POPClock, US Census Bureau, accessed online at www.census.gov, July 2005. This website provides continuously updated projections of the US and world populations.

3 Adapted from Frederik Balfour, 'Educating the "Little Emperors": There's a Big Market for Products That Help China's Coddled Kids Get Ahead', *Business Week*, 10 November 2003, p. 22. See also Clay Chandler, 'Little Emperors', *Fortune*, 4 October 2004, pp. 138–50.

4 See 'China's Golden Oldies', *The Economist*, 26 February 2005, p. 74.

5 http://epp.eurostat.ec.europa.eu, accessed 16 May 2008.

6 Anushka Asthana and Vanessa Thorpe, 'Whatever happened to the original Generation X?', *The Observer*, 23 January 2005, available from http://www.guardian.co.uk/uk/2005/jan/23/britishidentity.anushkaasthana.

7 'Mixed Success: One Who Targeted Gen X and Succeeded – Sort Of', *Journal of Financial Planning*, February 2004, p. 15. Also see Neil Leslie, 'Farther Along on the X Axis', *American Demographics*, May 2004, pp. 21–4.

8 See 'Overlooked and Under X-Plointed', *American Demographics*, May 2004, p. 48; and Howard Schneider, 'Grunge Marketing', *Mortgage Banking*, November 2004, p. 106.

9 Tobi Elkin, 'Gen Y Quizzed about On-Demand', *Advertising Age*, 14 February 2003, p. 37. See also Rebecca Gardyn, 'Born to Be Wired', *American Demographics*, April 2003, pp. 14–15; Noah Rubin Brier, 'Coming of Age', *American Demographics*, November 2004, pp. 16–20; and Michael A. Belch, Kathleen A. Krentler and Laura A. Willis-Flurry, 'Teen Internet Mavens: Influence in Family Decision Making', *Journal of Business Research*, May 2005, pp. 569–75.

10 See 'Automakers Mix It up to Chase Young Buyers', *Automotive News*, 26 April 2004, p. 28B; and 'Elusive Gen Y Demand Edgier Marketing', *Automotive News*, 25 April 2005, p. 28B.

11 'Trends in Households in the European Union: 1995–2025', Eurostat, 2003, available at http://epp.eurostat.ec.europa.eu/cache/ity_offpub/ks-nk-03-024/en/ks-nk-03-024-en.pdf.

12 'The Life of Women and Men in Europe: A Statistical Portrait', Eurostat, 2008, available at http://epp.eurostat.ec.europa.eu/cache/ity_offpub/ks-80-07-135/en/ks-80-07-135-en.pdf.

13 World Health Organisation information obtained from http://www.who.int/tobacco/global_data/country_profiles/euro/en/, accessed 17 May 2008.

14 Information obtained from UNESCO, accessed at http://stats.uis.unesco.org, 18 May 2008.

15 'Social Trends 38: 2008 edition', 2008, Office for National Statistics, available at http://www.statistics.gov.uk/socialtrends38/.

16 Ellen Florian, 'Queer Eye Makes Over the Economy', *Fortune*, 9 February 2004, p. 38. See also Gillian K. Oakenfull and Timothy B. Greenlee, 'Queer Eye for a Gay Guy: Using Market-Specific Symbols in Advertising to Attract Gay Consumers Without Alienating the Mainstream', *Psychology and Marketing*, May 2005, pp. 421ff.

17 Howard L. Hughes, 'Pink Tourism: Holidays of Gay Men and Lesbians', 2006, CABI Publishing.

18 Information accessed at http://www.visitmanchester.com, May 2008.

19 Information accessed at http://www.visitvictoria.com, May 2008.

20 Information accessed at http://www.germany-tourism.co.uk/EGB/attractions_events/gaygermany.htm, May 2008.

21 Information from 'Pollution Prevention Pays', accessed at http://solutions.3m.com/wps/portal/_l/en_US/_s.155/113842/_s.155/115848, June 2005; and 'Sustainability Key to UPS's Environmental Initiatives', accessed at www.pressroom.ups.com/mediakits/factsheet/0,2305,1140,00.html, June 2005.

22 Ann Bednarz, 'IBM Has Some Tall RFID Plans', *Network World*, 2 May 2005, pp. 17–18; Jack Neff, 'P&G Products to Wear Wire', *Advertising Age*, 15 December 2004, pp. 1, 32; Tom Van Riper, 'Retailers Eye RFID Technology to Make Shopping Easier', *Knight Ridder Tribune Business News*, 23 May 2005, p. 1; and information accessed online at www.autoidlabs.org, August 2005.

23 'Consolidated Versions of the Treaty on European Union and of the Treaty Establishing the European Community', *Official Journal of the European Communities*, 2002.

24 For more on online privacy, see Eric Goldman, 'The Internet Privacy Fallacy', *Computer and Internet Lawyer*, January 2003, p. 20; 'The Spies in Your Computer', *New York Times*, 18 February 2004, p. A18; Amir M. Hormozi, 'Cookies and Privacy', *Information Systems Security*, January/February 2005, pp. 51–60; and Alan R. Peslak, 'Internet Privacy Policies: A Review and Survey of the Fortune 50', *Information Resources Management Journal*, January–March 2005, pp. 29ff.

25 Adapted from Rob Walker, 'Yellow Fever', *New York Times Magazine*, 29 August 2004, p. 23; with information from Zan Dubin Scott, 'Style & Culture; On Wrist Watch; Ribbons, Make Way for Rubber', *Los Angeles Times*, 20 March 2005, p. E.25.

26 For more on Yankelovich Monitor, see /www.yankelovich.com/y-monitor.asp.

27 Adapted from Becky Ebenkamp, 'Fun/Duty Now, for the Future', *Brandweek*, 5 January 2004, p. 16.

28 Portions of this example are adapted from information in Eileen Daspin, 'The End of Nesting', *Wall Street Journal*, 16 May 2003, p. W1. Also see 'The Cocoon Cracks Open', *Brandweek*, 28 April 2003, pp. 32–6; and Dan Lippe, 'Gimme Shelter', *Advertising Age*, special report, 5 April 2004, pp. S1–S8.

29 Information accessed at http://www.independent.ie/national-news, June 2008.

30 See Philip Kotler, *Kotler on Marketing* (New York: Free Press, 1999), p. 3; and Kotler, *Marketing Insights from A to Z* (Hoboken, NJ: John Wiley & Sons, 2003), pp. 23–4.

31 Howard E. Butz Jr and Leonard D. Goodstein, 'Measuring Customer Value: Gaining the Strategic Advantage', *Organisational Dynamics*, Winter 1996, pp. 66–7.

CHAPTER 5
Consumer and business buyer behaviour

AFTER STUDYING THIS CHAPTER, YOU SHOULD BE ABLE TO

- understand the consumer market and the major factors that influence consumer buyer behaviour
- identify and discuss the stages in the buyer decision process
- describe the adoption and diffusion process for new products
- define the business market and identify the major factors that influence business buyer behaviour
- list and define the steps in the business buying decision process

THE WAY AHEAD Previewing the concepts

In the previous chapter, you studied how marketers obtain, analyse and use information to understand the marketplace and to assess marketing programmes. In this chapter, you'll continue your marketing journey with a closer look at the most important element of the marketplace – customers. The aim of marketing is to affect how customers think about and behave towards the organisation and its marketing offers. To affect the *whats, whens* and *hows* of buying behaviour marketers must first understand the *whys*. We look first at *final consumer* buying influences and processes and then at the buying behaviour of *business customers*. You'll see that understanding buying behaviour is an essential but very difficult task.

Our first point of interest: the huge Airbus A380, a new aircraft that is designed to carry a lot of passengers, or a lot of freight, over vast distances. There's little doubt that the A380 is a brilliant conception, delivering not just massive carrying capacity and state-of-the-art technology, but also environmental benefits such as increased fuel efficiency and lower noise. But what is going to make or break the commercial success of this plane are the buying decisions made by airline executives; those buying decisions, in turn, are driven by the buying decisions of their customers. Let's take a look at what lies behind all of those important decisions.

CHAPTER CONTENTS

Airbus A380

George S. Low, *Associate Professor of Marketing, M.J. Neeley School of Business, Texas Christian University, USA*

Marketing strategy situation

Airbus is one of the leading aircraft manufacturers in the global aircraft industry. Their newest addition to their aircraft product line is the A380, an extremely large, two-floor plane that can be used as either a passenger or freight plane. Development of this project began in late 2000, with production beginning in early 2002. It was expected that the A380 would be ready for delivery by 2007; however, starting in 2005 delays began to occur because of manufacturing problems. Three delays occurred, and the delivery date was pushed back to 2010. These production delays have resulted in an expected $6 billion loss in earnings along with a struggle to keep customers onboard; FedEx has already pulled out of a deal for ten A380s and bought Boeing's 777 instead. Airbus's top salesman, John Leahy, has responded to these delays by re-negotiating contracts and attempting to keep customers from bailing out like FedEx did. His strategy is to persuade customers to take discounts on future orders as opposed to the cash compensation they were originally expecting. Airbus knew there was risk involved when they came up with the plans for the A380, but they were not prepared for the delays, the loss in earnings, or the strain on the company's reputation.

Company background

Airbus is a sub-company of the European Aeronautic Defence & Space Co., EADS. EADS decided to

Source: Alamy Images/Antony Nettle.

invest in an organisation that could rival America's aerospace giants, such as Boeing, and so created Airbus – the European equivalent. Airbus is based in France, but has offices throughout Europe and the United States, and deals with most of its costs in euros and sterling. The main mission of Airbus is to 'meet the needs of airlines and operators by producing the most modern and comprehensive aircraft family on the market, complemented by the highest standard of product support'. They remain environmentally conscious and continue to work towards building quieter and more fuel-efficient aircraft. The company has a good reputation in the minds of the public but also has the reputation of being very politically-oriented. Airbus is sometimes thought of as succeeding thanks to public subsidies, but not being a very robust commercial operation.

The global aviation industry is extremely cut-throat so introducing any new product is risky, but there is a constant attempt to develop newer planes with better technology. At the same time, both passenger and freight air traffic are expected to grow over the next ten years. The hope is that the A380, because of

its very large capacity, will enable a growth in air journeys by both people and freight while restricting growth in the total number of flights. However, there is, of course, risk involved in the launching of the Airbus A380, since it is just as likely that no change in the industry will occur and the 'A380 is a very large aircraft for a very small market'.

Customers

The main customers that Airbus is focused on are the major airlines, paying passengers and freight customers. The large planes are able to provide something for everyone since they can carry more cargo, but are also state of the art when it comes to luxury and style for high paying travellers. Some of the companies that have already ordered A380s are FedEx, UPS, Emirates, Thai Airways and Singapore Airlines. Singapore Airlines is first in line for deliveries of the plane, while FedEx was angered by the delays and pulled out of the deal.

There's a close relationship between the decisions made by operators of passenger airlines about which planes to buy, and the decisions made by the airline operators' customers about which airline they will fly with. A lot of people are involved in making the decision about which planes an airline should buy. It is a long-term decision that will affect the future of the company. Airline engineers analyse the aircraft from a number of angles: operating efficiency, safety, maintenance costs, and so on. Airline accountants focus on the lifetime costs associated with owning and operating the aircraft. The purchase price of an aircraft, despite being a very large sum of money, is only one part of the total costs involved in owning and operating an aircraft. Airline marketers are interested in how their customers will respond to the new aircraft. This, of course, involves understanding their own customers' behaviour, with a key focus on the different market segments that they serve. Passengers in first class pay top prices and expect the very best in terms of comfort and service. Business class passengers want somewhere they can get on with their work and maybe sleep in reasonable comfort to get ready for an important meeting. The rest of the passengers (that's most of us who ever fly) would like a pleasant journey, but mainly they just want to arrive safely, on time, and with their luggage intact. Before making the decision about which type of aircraft to buy, the airline operator analyses the extent to which each competing product can deliver the features and benefits that it wants to provide to its customers. Of course, different airlines themselves have different priorities: some are luxury airlines offering the best of everything, while others are budget airlines that aim to get you to your destination safely and on time but with a minimum of additional services. Consequently, different airlines, wishing to offer their customers different types of experience, will have different buying criteria when considering which aircraft to buy.

As well as passenger airlines, Airbus wants to sell the A380 to freight operators, like UPS and FedEx. These operators don't have to worry about the needs of passengers, but that doesn't make them any less demanding. The aircraft is one of the primary tools that these companies use to deliver on their promises to their customers. They sell their services to both businesses and to consumers. Although you might only want to send a package across the Atlantic once a year (to your brother in the USA every Christmas), there are plenty of business customers that are sending lots of packages across the ocean every day. So the freight operators have to deliver a reliable, secure, high-speed service to both business customers and private consumers, and they know that the right choice of aircraft is vital if they are going to make this happen.

The A380

Airbus chose a double-deck configuration because the structure required is significantly lighter than a single deck with twin tails. The design of the A380 was meant to be able to use existing airport infrastructure with minor modifications to the airports, and direct operating costs per seat 15–20 per cent less than those for the 747–400. The plane also has more floor space and more seating than the previous largest aircraft. The main cabin is about 20 inches wider than the Boeing 747's, and has economy passengers seated ten across, while the upper-deck economy class has eight seats across. Airbus wants to provide customers with wider seats and aisles for greater comfort. The name 380 was chosen because the 8 represents the cross-section of the twin decks. The wings are also quite long, almost

20 per cent longer than the 747's; even so, they are flexible and able to bend almost 4 metres during take-off and landing.

The innovative technology can be seen first by the pilots in the cockpit. The electronics include an environmental surveillance system which integrates weather radar, traffic alert and collision avoidance and a ground-proximity warning system. This allows pilots to see easily what type of weather they are flying into as well as what the weather will be in the next couple of hours. The technology also allows pilots to locate other planes easily and avoid any potential accidents, making the plane safer for both customers and cargo. The ground-proximity system provides another safety feature as it makes landing easier for the pilots. Additionally, the A380 uses new technology in an attempt to have a larger range, lower fuel burn and emissions, and less noise. Airbus says it is more fuel-efficient than a car – and it averages about 90.6 mpg per passenger.

Another luxury from the A380 is the low noise. The four huge Rolls-Royce engines emit little more than a low hum, even during take-off when engine noise is usually most noticeable. Landing is also quiet, the landing gear can barely be heard as it descends. It is easy to talk to passengers across the aisle and in adjoining rows without raising your voice. This provides the customers with a pleasant voyage as there is no annoying engine noise and conversation is not disrupted by turbulence or loud landings and take-offs. Sounds like a great product! But whether or not it succeeds depends on a whole range of buying decisions. Will airline operators believe that the A380 is the best plane to buy to serve their customers? Will freight operators be persuaded that it is the best product to meet the demands of their business and private customers? And, perhaps most important, will air passengers decide that they want to fly with operators who use the A380, because it makes their journeys that little bit more pleasant?

Sources: Doris Burke, 'Anatomy of an A380', *Fortune Magazine*, 5 March 2007, **155**(4), pp. 101–8; Nelson D. Schwartz, 'Big Plane, Big Problems', *Fortune Magazine*, 5 March 2007, **155**(4), pp. 95–8; Airbus Corporation Website, http://www.airbus.com/en/corporate/ethics/mission_values/; 'Airbus' New Flight Plan', *The Wall Street Journal*, 9 March 2007; Rod Stone, 'Airbus Parent EADS Appoints Rudiger Grube as Co-Chairman', *The Wall Street Journal*, 5 April 2007; Andrew Lee, 'The A380 is a Gamble Worth Taking', *The Engineer*, 10 February 2005; 'Airbus A380 Completes Test flight', *BBC News*, 27 April 2005; Robert Wall, 'Schedule UPSet', *Aviation Week & Space Technology*, 5 March 2007, **166**(10); 'The Airbus 380', Airliners.net, 9 April 2007, http://www.airliners.net/info/stats.main?id=29; Noelle Knox, 'A380 Makes Massive Debut', *USA Today*, 19 January 2005; 'Airbus A380: A Whale of a Plane!', *BBC News*, 10 May 2005; Carol Matlock, 'Aloft on Airbus' Giant New A380', *BusinessWeek Online*, 8 February 2007; Greg Lindsay, 'Airbust? A380 Hits Marketing Turbulence', *Advertising Age*, 2 April 2007, **78**(14); Marc Graser, 'The Nonproduct Placement that Boosts Airbus', *Advertising Age*, 9 May 2005; Barbara Peterson, 'Airbus A380: Taking the Largest Passenger Jet for a Test Drive', *Popular Mechanics*, 22 March 2007, http://www.popularmechanics.com/bolgs/science_news/4213543.html.

The Airbus A380 example shows that many different factors affect business and consumer buying behaviour. Buying behaviour is never simple, yet understanding it is the essential task of marketing management. First we explore the dynamics of the consumer market and consumer buyer behaviour. We then examine business markets and the business buying process.

CONSUMER MARKETS AND CONSUMER BUYER BEHAVIOUR

Consumer buyer behaviour refers to the buying behaviour of final consumers – individuals and households who buy goods and services for personal consumption. All of these final consumers combine to make up the **consumer market**. The European Union consumer market consists of more than 490 million people who consume many trillions of euros' worth of goods and services each year, making it one of the most attractive consumer markets in the world. The world consumer market consists of more than 6.4 *billion* people.[1]

Consumers around the world vary tremendously in age, income, education level and tastes. They also buy an incredible variety of goods and services. The ways in which these diverse consumers connect with each other and with other elements of the world around them influence their choices among various products, services and companies. Here we examine the fascinating array of factors that affect consumer behaviour.

Model of consumer behaviour

Consumers make many buying decisions every day. Most large companies research consumer buying decisions in great detail to answer questions about what consumers buy, where they buy, how and how much they buy, when they buy, and why they buy. Marketers can study actual consumer purchases to find out what they buy, where and how much. But learning about the *whys* of consumer buying behaviour is not so easy – the answers are often locked deep within the consumer's head.

Penetrating the dark recesses of the consumer's mind is no easy task. Often, consumers themselves don't know exactly what influences their purchases. 'Ninety-five per cent of the thought, emotion, and learning [that drive our purchases] occur in the unconscious mind – that is, without our awareness,' notes one consumer behaviour expert.[2]

The central question for marketers is: how do consumers respond to various marketing efforts the company might use? The starting point is the stimulus-response model

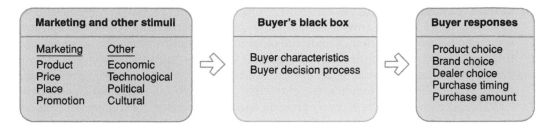

FIGURE 5.1

Model of buyer behaviour

of buyer behaviour shown in Figure 5.1. This figure shows that marketing and other stimuli enter the consumer's 'black box' and produce certain responses. Marketers must figure out what is in the buyer's black box.

At the most basic level marketing stimuli consist of the 'marketing mix': product, price, place and promotion for goods, with the addition of people, physical evidence and process for service products. Other stimuli include major forces and events in the buyer's environment: economic, technological, political and cultural. All these inputs enter the buyer's mind where they are turned into a set of observable buyer responses: product choice, brand choice, dealer choice, purchase timing and purchase amount.

The marketer wants to understand how the stimuli are changed into responses inside the consumer's mind. There are two components: first, the buyer's characteristics influence how he or she perceives and reacts to the stimuli; second, the buyer's decision process itself affects the buyer's behaviour. We look first at buyer characteristics as they affect buying behaviour and then discuss the buyer decision process.

Characteristics affecting consumer behaviour

Consumer purchases are influenced strongly by cultural, social, personal and psychological characteristics, as shown in Figure 5.2. For the most part, marketers cannot control such factors, but they must take them into account.

Cultural Factors

Cultural factors exert a broad and deep influence on consumer behaviour. The marketer needs to understand the role played by the buyer's *culture*, *subculture* and *social class*.

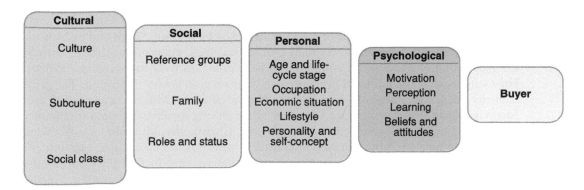

FIGURE 5.2

Factors influencing consumer behaviour

Culture Culture is the most basic cause of a person's wants and behaviour. Human behaviour is largely learned. Growing up in a society, a child learns basic values, perceptions, wants and behaviours from the family and other important institutions. For example, the former Prime Minister of the United Kingdom, Tony Blair, identified a number of core British values: creativity, tolerance, openness, adaptability, work and self-improvement, strong communities and families, fair play, rights and responsibilities, and an outward-looking approach to the world. Every group or society has a culture, and cultural influences on buying behaviour may vary greatly from country to country. Failure to adjust to these differences can result in ineffective marketing or embarrassing mistakes.

Marketers are always trying to spot *cultural shifts* in order to discover new products that might be wanted. For example, the cultural shift toward greater concern about health and fitness has created a huge industry for health and fitness services, exercise equipment and clothing, more-natural foods, and a variety of diets. The shift toward informality has resulted in more demand for casual clothing and simpler home furnishings.

Subculture Each culture contains smaller **subcultures**, or groups of people with shared value systems based on common life experiences and situations. Subcultures include nationalities, religions, racial groups and geographic regions. Many subcultures make up important market segments, and marketers often design products and marketing programmes tailored to their needs. Ethnic minorities are an example of subculture groups. It is estimated that there are 5.5 million ethnic minority consumers in Britain, and the value of the ethnic minority market as a whole is estimated to be £12 billion a year.[3] Britain has seen several waves of immigration during the last 60 years, including migrants from the Republic of Ireland, the Caribbean, the Indian subcontinent, Africa, Cyprus and Hong Kong. A new wave of immigration from Eastern Europe recently followed the expansion of the European Union in 2004 and 2005. Several ethnic minority groups tend to have more children than the white indigenous population, making them an important target market for baby products companies and for any company that is targeting younger consumers. The ethnic minority market in Britain has a younger age structure than the indigenous population. In the late 1990s only 31 per cent of white British people were aged under 24, compared with 48 per cent of the ethnic minority population.

In geographical terms, ethnic minority groups in Britain are heavily concentrated in the major cities of England, and nearly half live in Greater London. The high geographical concentration makes it easier to devise targeted marketing strategies for ethnic minority groups. However, while there are specialist ethnic minority media (such as radio stations, television stations and newspapers) in Britain, they are nowhere near as well developed as in the United States of America.

The consumer buying behaviour of ethnic minority groups in Britain is influenced by many factors, among which income levels, religion and family structure can be considered particularly important. The British Chinese community has the highest average income level among ethnic minority groups, followed by African-Asians and by Indians. While these groups have relatively high average incomes, other ethnic groups such as the Pakistani and Bangladeshi communities have comparatively low average incomes. For many members of ethnic minority groups their religion is very important. The great majority of British Pakistanis and British Bangladeshis are Muslim, most white and Afro-Caribbean British people are Christian, while among the British Indian community several religions are represented, including Islam, Christianity, Hinduism and Sikhism. Religion can play an important role in consumer decisions. For example, Muslims are forbidden to eat certain foods or to consume alcohol, and may require specifically designed financial services products that do not involve the payment of interest. Finally, family structures vary considerably between ethnic groups. Since they have more children, ethnic minority groups tend to have larger families than the indigenous white community. Additionally, among some Asian subcultures the traditional extended family, where multiple generations live together under the same roof, still exists, although this structure seems to be in decline among British Asians.

Having identified a gap in the market for financial services aimed at the large Muslim minority in Britain, Lloyds TSB launched a range of Shariah (Islamic law) approved financial services, including an Islamic current account and a Shariah-approved home finance service. Muslims signing up to any of these products could rest assured that their money would always be handled in accordance with Shariah. The money that account holders placed with the bank would not be used for any interest-based business activities. In order to reassure Muslim customers of the integrity of the service, Lloyds TSB recruited a committee of religious and legal advisers of the Islamic faith.

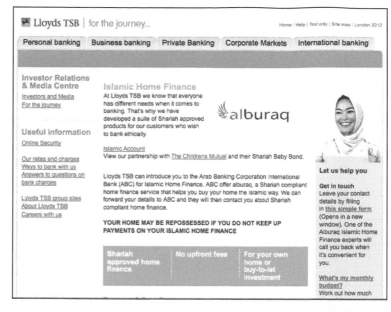

Lloyds TSB is offering services designed to meet the specific needs of people of the Islamic faith.

The worldwide population of people aged over 60 is growing faster than any other age group, and is expected to double from today's 605 million to around 1.2 billion by 2025. Although other countries are also ageing, European countries are ageing faster than those of any other continent. By 2050 it is estimated that 35 per cent of Europe's population will be aged over 60. In the longer term the ageing population represents a considerable public policy challenge, since there will be fewer workers and more retired people. Major efforts by both governments and private firms are going into the promotion of pension plans to persuade younger people that they need to start saving early for retirement. For the moment, however, mature consumers are better off financially than are younger consumer groups. Because mature consumers have more time and money, they are an ideal market for exotic travel, restaurants, high-tech home entertainment products, leisure goods and services, designer furniture and fashions, financial services and health care services.[4]

Their desire to look as young as they feel also makes more mature consumers good candidates for cosmetics and personal care products, health foods, fitness products and other items that combat the effects of ageing. The best strategy is to appeal to their active, multidimensional lives. For example, Kellogg's aired a TV spot for All-Bran cereal in which individuals ranging in age from 53 to 81 are featured playing ice hockey, water skiing, running hurdles, and playing baseball, all to the tune of 'Wild Thing'. A Pepsi ad features a young man in the middle of a mosh pit at a rock concert who turns around to see his father rocking out nearby. And an Aetna commercial portrays someone who, after retiring from a career as a lawyer, fulfils a lifelong dream of becoming an archeologist.[5]

Social class Almost every society has some form of social class structure. **Social classes** are society's relatively permanent and ordered divisions whose members share similar values, interests and behaviours. Social scientists have identified the ten European social classes shown in Table 5.1.

Social class is not determined by a single factor, such as income, but is measured as a combination of occupation, income, education, wealth and other variables. In some social systems, members of different classes are reared for certain roles and cannot

TABLE 5.1 The European socio-economic classification

	ESeC class	Common term	Employment regulation
1	Large employers, higher grade professional, administrative and managerial occupations	Higher salariat	Service relationship
2	Lower grade professional, administrative and managerial occupations and higher grade technician and supervisory occupations	Lower salariat	Service relationship (modified)
3	Intermediate occupations	Higher grade white collar workers	Mixed
4	Small employer and self-employed occupations (exc. agriculture etc.)	Petit bourgeoisie or independents	–
5	Self-employed occupations (agriculture etc.)	Petit bourgeoisie or independents	–
6	Lower supervisory and lower technician occupations	Higher grade blue collar workers	Mixed
7	Lower services, sales and clerical occupations	Lower grade white collar workers	Labour contract (modified)
8	Lower technical occupations	Skilled workers	Labour contract (modified)
9	Routine occupations	Semi- and non-skilled workers	Labour contract
10	Never worked and long-term unemployed	Unemployed	–

Source: http://www.iser.essex.ac.uk/research/esec/user-guide/the-european-socio-economic-classification.

change their social positions. In Europe, however, the lines between social classes are not fixed and rigid; people can move to a higher social class or drop into a lower one. Marketers are interested in social class because people within a given social class tend to exhibit similar buying behaviour. Social classes show distinct product and brand preferences in areas such as clothing, home furnishings, leisure activity and cars.

Social factors

A consumer's behaviour is also influenced by social factors, such as the consumer's *small groups*, *family*, and *social roles* and *status*.

Groups A person's behaviour is influenced by many small **groups**. Groups that have a direct influence and to which a person belongs are called membership groups. In contrast, reference groups serve as direct (face-to-face) or indirect points of comparison or reference in forming a person's attitudes or behaviour. People are often influenced by reference groups to which they do not belong. For example, an aspirational group is one to which the individual wishes to belong, as when a young boy hopes someday to emulate Thierry Henry and play soccer for France and for great club sides like Arsenal and Barcelona.

Marketers try to identify the reference groups of their target markets. Reference groups expose a person to new behaviours and lifestyles, influence the person's attitudes and self-concept, and create pressures to conform that may affect the person's product and brand choices. The importance of group influence varies across products and brands. It tends to be strongest when the product is visible to others whom the buyer respects.

Manufacturers of products and brands subjected to strong group influence must figure out how to reach **opinion leaders** – people within a reference group who, because of special skills, knowledge, personality, or other characteristics, exert influence on others. Some experts call this 10 per cent of Europeans *the influentials* or *leading adopters*. These consumers 'drive trends, influence mass opinion and, most importantly, sell a great many products,' says one expert. They often use their big circle of acquaintances to 'spread their knowledge on what's good and what's bad'.[6]

Many marketers try to identify opinion leaders for their products and direct marketing efforts toward them. They use *buzz marketing* by enlisting or even creating opinion leaders to spread the word about their brands.

Sneeze, a London marketing agency, uses *buzz marketing* to create successful word-of-mouth campaigns for its clients.

Two or three years ago, a Premiership football club (I'm not allowed to tell you which one) was trying to sign up fans to its text bulletin service. For 25p a message (working out at around £100 a year), fans would get a text whenever something interesting happened at the club – team selections, injury updates, half-time scores, that sort of thing.

Despite promoting the service in club literature, on its website, and with armies of attractive girls handing out leaflets on match days, the club could not get the rate of new subscriptions to rise above a disappointing 20 a week. So it hired a small marketing agency called Sneeze.

'We got a group of 14 or 16 actors, who were all football fans, but pretended to be fans [of the unnamed club],' explains Graham Goodkind, Sneeze's founder and chairman. 'And they went round bars and clubs around the ground, in groups of two, saying that one of their mates had been sacked from work because he kept on getting these text messages and talking to everyone about it, and his boss had had enough and given him the boot. So they were going round with this petition trying to get his job back – kind of a vaguely plausible story.

'And then the actors would pull out of their pocket some crumpled-up leaflet, which was for the text subscription service. They'd have a mobile phone in their pocket, and they'd show them how it worked. "What's the harm in that?" they'd say. And they could have these conversations with lots of people – that was the beauty of it. Two people could spend maybe 20 minutes or half an hour in each pub, working the whole pub. We did it at two home games and reckon we got about 4,000 people on the petition in total.'

The petition went in the bin, of course, but subscriptions to the club's texting service soared. 'The week after we had done the activity it went up to 120 sign-ups,' says Goodkind, who is also boss of the Frank PR agency. 'Then you saw that after that it was 125, and the next week was 75, and the next week was 60. That was the talkability, because obviously if you get that service you tell your mates about it. We saw a massive effectiveness.'[7]

Family Family members can strongly influence buyer behaviour. The family is the most important consumer buying organisation in society, and it has been researched extensively. Marketers are interested in the roles and influence of the husband, wife and children on the purchase of different products and services.

Husband–wife involvement varies widely by product category and by stage in the buying process. Buying roles change with evolving consumer lifestyles. For example, in many countries, the wife has traditionally been the main purchasing agent for the family in the areas of food, household products and clothing. But with a growing proportion of women holding jobs outside the home and the willingness of husbands to do more of the family's purchasing, all this is changing. The traditional division of labour between men and women in the family, with men earning the money and women running the home, is already a distant memory in many European countries and is breaking down elsewhere. The traditional buying roles of men and women are also breaking down.[8]

Such changes suggest that marketers in industries that have sold their products only to men or only to women are now courting the opposite sex. For example, consider Barbara K Enterprises:

It's no surprise that many women feel awkward using home-repair tools designed for men. Enter Barbara Kavovit, CEO of Barbara K Enterprises. A self-made woman, Barbara entered the home improvement business by starting her own construction company, passing out fliers and going door-to-door in Westchester County, New York. Seven years later, she created a lifestyle brand that offers innovative, women-friendly home repair and improvement products. On a mission to 'inspire women to become more self-reliant and confident in their own abilities', and to help them overcome the fear factor of do-it-yourself home repair, Barbara K has developed a strong market niche. More than 70 per cent of female home owners do minor home repairs themselves, and 37 per cent say they would rather work on a home improvement project than cook or shop. For these women, Barbara K Enterprises has created a line of high-quality tools and accessories, from hammers and cordless drills to putty knives and pliers. The tools are shaped for smaller hands, have spring-assisted grips, are guaranteed for life, and come in stylish blue and black designs – not pink! Last year, the company sold more than $5 million worth of tools and tool kits emblazoned with the Barbara K name, at stores such as Target, Ace Hardware, and Bed Bath & Beyond.[9]

Children may also have a strong influence on family buying decisions. For example, children as young as age 6 may influence the family car purchase decision. Recognising this fact, Vauxhall launched a new kid-focused ad campaign for its Zafira and Meriva models. Whereas most other multi-purpose vehicle (MPV) ads have focused on selling features that are important to adults, like carrying home large purchases from the DIY store, Vauxhall used George, Harry and Amir, three young boys, as the stars of their TV campaign. The light-hearted campaign portrayed the boys as the mature, thoughtful members of the family and their parents as argumentative and disorganised. Supported by newspaper advertising that drove home the features and benefits of the products, the TV campaign concentrated on getting the message across to kids, and their parents, that this car was designed with them in mind.

Source: Vauxhall General Motors.

Vauxhall got the message across to kids that the Zafira and the Meriva were designed with them in mind.

Roles and status A person belongs to many groups – family, clubs, organisations. The person's position in each group can be defined in terms of both role and status. A role consists of the activities people are expected to perform according to the persons around them. Each role carries a status reflecting the general esteem given to it by society.

People usually choose products appropriate to their roles and status. Consider the various roles a working mother plays. In her company, she plays the role of a brand manager; in her family, she plays the role of wife and mother; at her favourite sporting events, she plays the role of avid fan. As a brand manager, she will buy the kind of clothing that reflects her role and status in her company.

Personal factors

A buyer's decisions are also influenced by personal characteristics such as the buyer's *age and life-cycle stage, occupation, economic situation, lifestyle* and *personality and self-concept.*

Age and life-cycle stage People change the goods and services they buy over their life-times. Tastes in food, clothes, furniture and recreation are often age-related. Buying is also shaped by the stage of the family life cycle – the stages through which families might pass as they mature over time. Marketers often define their target markets in terms of life-cycle stage and develop appropriate products and marketing plans for each stage.

Traditional family life-cycle stages include young singles and married couples with children. Today, however, marketers are increasingly catering to a growing number of alternative, non-traditional stages such as unmarried couples, singles marrying later in life, childless couples, same-sex couples, single parents, extended parents (those with young adult children returning home), and others.

Sony recently overhauled its marketing approach in order to target products and services to consumers based on their life stages. It created a new unit called the Consumer Segment Marketing Division, which has identified seven life-stage segments. They include, among others, Gen Y (under 25), Young Professionals/DINKs (double income no kids, 25 to 34), Families (35 to 54), and Zoomers (55 and over). A recent Sony ad aimed at Zoomers, people who have just retired or are close to doing so, shows a man living his dream by going into outer space. The ad deals not just with going into retirement, but with the psychological life-stage changes that go with it. 'The goal is to get closer to consumers,' says a Sony segment marketing executive.[10]

Occupation A person's occupation affects the goods and services bought. Blue-collar workers tend to buy more rugged work clothes, whereas executives buy more business suits. Marketers try to identify the occupational groups that have an above-average interest in their products and services. A company can even specialise in making products needed by a given occupational group. For example, Goliath Footwear from West Yorkshire in the UK specialises in rugged, durable, no-nonsense safety boots – including the Furnace Masters, a line of safety boots designed for people working with molten metals, which are heat resistant up to 300 degrees centigrade, and feature quick-release fasteners so that they can be removed speedily in the event of a molten metal splash.

Economic situation A person's economic situation will affect product choice. Marketers of income-sensitive goods watch trends in personal income, savings and interest rates. If economic indicators point to a recession, marketers can take steps to redesign, reposition and reprice their products closely. Some marketers target consumers who have lots of money and resources, charging prices to match. For example, Rolex positions it luxury watches as 'a tribute to elegance, an object of passion, a symbol for all time'. Other marketers target consumers with more modest means. Timex makes more affordable watches that are renowned for their reliability and durability, epitomised by the famous Timex Ironman Triathlon model, designed to withstand the toughest sporting conditions.

Lifestyle People coming from the same subculture, social class and occupation may have quite different lifestyles. **Lifestyle** is a person's pattern of living as expressed in his or her psychographics. It involves measuring consumers' major AIO dimensions – activities (work, hobbies, shopping, sports, social events), interests (food, fashion, family, recreation) and opinions (about themselves, social issues, business, products). Lifestyle captures something more than the person's social class or personality. It profiles a person's whole pattern of acting and interacting in the world.

Several research firms have developed lifestyle classifications. The most widely used is SRI Consulting's *Values and Lifestyles (VALS)* typology. VALS classifies people according to how they spend their time and money. It divides consumers into eight groups based on two major dimensions: primary motivation and resources. *Primary motivations* include ideals, achievement and self-expression. According to SRI Consulting, consumers who are primarily motivated by ideals are guided by knowledge and principles. Consumers who are primarily motivated by *achievement* look for products and services that demonstrate success to their peers. Consumers who are primarily motivated by *self-expression* desire social or physical activity, variety and risk.

Consumers within each orientation are further classified into those with *high resources* and those with *low resources*, depending on whether they have high or low levels of income, education, health, self-confidence, energy and other factors. Consumers with either very high or very low levels of resources are classified without regard to their primary motivations (Innovators, Survivors). Innovators are people with so many resources that they exhibit all three primary motivations in varying degrees. In contrast, Survivors are people with so few resources that they do not show a strong primary motivation. They must focus on meeting needs rather than fulfilling desires.

One study identified five key food-related lifestyle segments in Croatia as follows:

- The *relaxed* segment, representing 13 per cent of the population. They have no clear buying motives and the quality of food is not particularly important to them; they are influenced by friends and by the mass media. Buying and preparing food is not a major concern of this segment.

- The *traditionalist* segment accounts for 27 per cent of the population. Cooking and eating food are considered to be important social events for this segment, and members of the family like to help out at meal times. They enjoy shopping for food and like to experiment with new recipes.

- The *modern* segment, representing 32 per cent of the population. The members of this segment do not like to spend too much time on buying, preparing and cooking food; they make detailed shopping lists and plan their food shopping trips carefully. Their main motivation is to reduce the amount of time they spend on buying and cooking food.

- The *concerned* segment makes up only around 11 per cent of the population. They are particularly interested in the safety and nutritional value of the food that they buy, and are convinced of the advantages of organic food. This segment tends to be relatively old and with above average incomes. Members of this segment pay a lot of attention to the information on food product labels.

- The *hedonist* segment, representing 17 per cent of the population. This segment tends to comprise older consumers with lower than average education and income. Their main motivation is to enjoy the food that they eat. Women who belong to this segment spend a lot of time shopping for food and take pride in their cooking abilities.[11]

Lifestyle segmentation can also be used to understand how consumers use the Internet, computers and other technology. Forrester developed its 'Technographics' scheme, which segments consumers according to motivation, desire and ability to invest in technology. The framework splits people into ten categories, including:

- *Fast Forwards*: the biggest spenders on computer technology. Fast Forwards are career-focused, time-strapped, driven, and top users of technology.

- *New Age Nurturers*: also big spenders. However, they are focused on technology for home uses, such as family education and entertainment.

- *Mouse Potatoes*: consumers who are dedicated to interactive entertainment and willing to spend for the latest in 'technotainment'.

- *Techno-Strivers*: consumers who are up-and-coming believers in technology for career advancement.

- *Traditionalists*: small-town folks, suspicious of technology beyond the basics.[12]

Delta Airlines used Technographics to target online ticket sales better. It created marketing campaigns for time-strapped Fast Forwards and New Age Nurturers, and eliminated Technology Pessimists (those sceptical of technology) from its list of targets. When used carefully, the lifestyle concept can help marketers understand changing consumer values and how they affect buying behaviour.

Personality and self-concept Each person's distinct personality influences his or her buying behaviour. **Personality** refers to the unique psychological characteristics that lead to relatively consistent and lasting responses to one's own environment. Personality is usually described in terms of traits such as self-confidence, dominance, sociability, autonomy, defensiveness, adaptability and aggressiveness. Personality can be useful in analysing consumer behaviour for certain product or brand choices. For example, coffee marketers have discovered that heavy coffee drinkers tend to be high on sociability. Thus, to attract customers, Starbucks and other coffeehouses create environments in which people can relax and socialise over a cup of steaming coffee.

The idea is that brands also have personalities, and that consumers are likely to choose brands with personalities that match their own. A *brand personality* is the specific mix of human traits that may be attributed to a particular brand. One researcher identified five brand personality traits:

1 Sincerity (down-to-earth, honest, wholesome and cheerful)

2 Excitement (daring, spirited, imaginative and up to date)

3 Competence (reliable, intelligent and successful)

4 Sophistication (upper class and charming)

5 Ruggedness (outdoorsy and tough)[13]

The researcher found that a number of well-known brands tended to be strongly associated with one particular trait: Levi's with 'ruggedness', MTV with 'excitement', CNN with 'competence', and Campbell's with 'sincerity'. Hence, these brands will attract people who are high on the same personality traits.

Many marketers use a concept related to personality – a person's *self-concept* (also called *self-image*). The basic self-concept premiss is that people's possessions contribute to and reflect their identities; that is, 'we are what we have'. Thus, in order to understand consumer behaviour, the marketer must first understand the relationship between consumer self-concept and possessions.

Brand personality: well-known brands tend to be strongly associated with one or more traits. Red Bull is associated with extreme 'excitement'.

Source: Alamy Images/Tony Lockhart.

Psychological factors

A person's buying choices are further influenced by four major psychological factors: *motivation*, *perception*, *learning* and *beliefs and attitudes*.

Motivation A person has many needs at any given time. Some are biological, arising from states of tension such as hunger, thirst or discomfort. Others are psychological, arising from the need for recognition, esteem or belonging. A need becomes a motive when it is aroused to a sufficient level of intensity. A **motive (or drive)** is a need that is sufficiently pressing to direct the person to seek satisfaction. Psychologists have developed theories of human motivation. Two of the most popular – the theories of Sigmund Freud and Abraham Maslow – have quite different meanings for consumer analysis and marketing.

Sigmund Freud assumed that people are largely unconscious about the real psychological forces shaping their behaviour. He saw the person as growing up and repressing many urges. These urges are never eliminated or under perfect control; they emerge in dreams, in slips of the tongue, in neurotic and obsessive behaviour, or ultimately in psychoses.

Freud's theory suggests that a person's buying decisions are affected by subconscious motives that even the buyer may not fully understand. Thus, an ageing baby boomer who buys a sporty BMW 330Ci convertible might explain that he simply likes the feel of the wind in his thinning hair. At a deeper level, he may be trying to impress others with his success. At a still deeper level, he may be buying the car to feel young and independent again.

The term *motivation research* refers to qualitative research designed to probe consumers' hidden, subconscious motivations. Consumers often don't know or can't describe just why they act as they do. Thus, motivation researchers use a variety of probing techniques to uncover underlying emotions and attitudes toward brands and buying situations. These sometimes bizarre techniques range from sentence completion, word association, and inkblot or cartoon interpretation tests, to having consumers form daydreams and fantasies about brands or buying situations. One writer offers the following tongue-in-cheek summary of a motivation research session:

> Good morning, ladies and gentlemen. We've called you here today for a little consumer research. Now, lie down on the couch, toss your inhibitions out the window, and let's try a little free association. First, think about brands as if they were your *friends*. Imagine you could talk to your TV dinner. What would he say? And what would you say to him? . . . Now, think of your shampoo as an animal. Go on, don't be shy. Would it be a panda or a lion? A snake or a wooly worm? For our final exercise, let's all sit up and pull out our magic markers. Draw a picture of a typical cake-mix user. Would she wear an apron or a negligee? A business suit or a can-can dress?[14]

Such projective techniques seem pretty strange, and some marketers dismiss such motivation research as mumbo-jumbo. But many marketers routinely use such touchy-feely approaches to dig deeply into consumer psyches and develop better marketing strategies.

Many companies employ teams of psychologists, anthropologists, and other social scientists to carry out motivation research. One ad agency routinely conducts one-to-one, therapy-like interviews to delve into the inner workings of consumers. Another company asks consumers to describe their favourite brands as animals or cars (say, Volkswagens versus Peugeots) in order to assess the prestige associated with various brands. Still others rely on hypnosis, dream therapy, or soft lights and mood music to plumb the murky depths of consumer psyches.

Abraham Maslow sought to explain why people are driven by particular needs at particular times. Why does one person spend much time and energy on personal safety and another on gaining the esteem of others? Maslow's answer is that human needs are arranged in a hierarchy, as shown in Figure 5.3, from the most pressing at the bottom to the least pressing at the top.[15] They include *physiological* needs, *safety* needs, *social* needs, *esteem* needs and *self-actualisation* needs.

A person tries to satisfy the most important need first. When that need is satisfied, it will stop being a motivator and the person will then try to satisfy the next most important need. For example, starving people (physiological need) will not take an interest in the latest happenings in the art world (self-actualisation needs), nor in how they are seen or esteemed by others (social or esteem needs), nor even in whether they are breathing clean air (safety needs). But as each important need is satisfied, the next most important need will come into play.

Perception   A motivated person is ready to act. How the person acts is influenced by his or her own perception of the situation. All of us learn by the flow of information through our five senses: sight, hearing, smell, touch and taste. However, each of us receives, organises and interprets this sensory information in an individual way. **Perception** is the process by which people select, organise and interpret information to form a meaningful picture of the world.

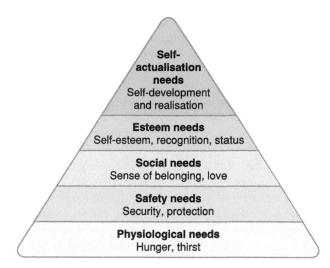

FIGURE 5.3

Maslow's hierarchy of needs

Source: Adapted from A.H. Maslow (1970) *Motivation and Personality*, 2nd edn.

People can form different perceptions of the same stimulus because of three perceptual processes: selective attention, selective distortion and selective retention. People are exposed to a great many stimuli every day. For example, one analyst estimates that people are exposed to about 5,000 ads every day.[16] It is impossible for a person to pay attention to all these stimuli. *Selective attention* – the tendency for people to screen out most of the information to which they are exposed – means that marketers have to work especially hard to attract the consumer's attention.

Even noticed stimuli do not always come across in the intended way. Each person fits incoming information into an existing mindset. *Selective distortion* describes the tendency of people to interpret information in a way that will support what they already believe. For example, if you distrust a company, you might perceive even honest ads from the company as questionable. Selective distortion means that marketers must try to understand the mindsets of consumers and how these will affect interpretations of advertising and sales information.

People will also forget much of what they learn. They tend to retain information that supports their attitudes and beliefs. Because of *selective retention*, consumers are likely to remember good points made about a brand they favour and to forget good points made about competing brands. Because of selective exposure, distortion and retention, marketers have to work hard to get their messages through. This fact explains why marketers use so much drama and repetition in sending messages to their market.

Interestingly, although most marketers worry about whether their offers will be perceived at all, some consumers worry that they will be affected by marketing messages without even knowing it – through *subliminal advertising*. In 1957, a researcher announced that he had flashed the phrases 'Eat popcorn' and 'Drink Coca-Cola' on a screen in a New Jersey movie theatre every five seconds for 1/300th of a second. He reported that although viewers did not consciously recognise these messages, they absorbed them subconsciously and bought 58 per cent more popcorn and 18 per cent more Coke. Suddenly advertisers and consumer-protection groups became intensely interested in subliminal perception. Although the researcher later admitted to making up the data, the issue has not died. Some consumers still fear that they are being manipulated by subliminal messages.

Numerous studies by psychologists and consumer researchers have found no link between subliminal messages and consumer behaviour. It appears that subliminal advertising simply doesn't have the power attributed to it by its critics. Most advertisers scoff at the notion of an industry conspiracy to manipulate consumers through 'invisible' messages. Says one industry insider: '[Some consumers believe we are] wizards who can manipulate them at will. Ha! Snort! Oh my sides! As we know, just between us, most of [us] have difficulty getting a 2 per cent increase in sales with the help of $50 million in media and extremely liminal images of sex, money, power, and other [motivators] of human emotion. The very idea of [us] as puppeteers, cruelly pulling the strings of consumer marionettes, is almost too much to bear.'[17]

Learning When people act, they learn. **Learning** describes changes in an individual's behaviour arising from experience. Learning theorists say that most human behaviour is learned. Learning occurs through the interplay of drives, stimuli, cues, responses and reinforcement.

A *drive* is a strong internal stimulus that calls for action. A drive becomes a motive when it is directed toward a particular *stimulus object*. For example, a person's drive for self-actualisation might motivate him or her to look into buying a digital camera. The consumer's response to the idea of buying a camera is conditioned by the surrounding cues. *Cues* are minor stimuli that determine when, where and how the person responds. For example, the person might spot several camera brands in a shop window, hear of a special sale price, or discuss cameras with a friend. These are all cues that might influence a consumer's *response* to his or her interest in buying the product.

Suppose the consumer buys a Pentax digital camera. If the experience is rewarding, the consumer will probably use the camera more and more, and his or her response will be *reinforced*. Then, the next time the consumer shops for a camera, or for binoculars or some similar product, the probability is greater that he or she will buy a Pentax product. The practical significance of learning theory for marketers is that they can build up demand for a product by associating it with strong drives, using motivating cues, and providing positive reinforcement.

Beliefs and attitudes Through doing and learning, people acquire beliefs and attitudes. These, in turn, influence their buying behaviour. A *belief* is a descriptive thought that a person has about something. Beliefs may be based on real knowledge, opinion or faith, and may or may not carry an emotional charge. Marketers are interested in the beliefs that people formulate about specific products and services, because these beliefs make up product and brand images that affect buying behaviour. If some of the beliefs are wrong and prevent purchase, the marketer will want to launch a campaign to correct them.

People have attitudes regarding religion, politics, clothes, music, food, and almost everything else. *Attitude* describes a person's relatively consistent evaluations, feelings and tendencies toward an object or idea. Attitudes put people into a frame of mind of liking or disliking things, of moving towards or away from them. Our digital camera buyer may hold attitudes such as 'Buy the best', 'The Japanese make the best electronics products in the world', and 'Creativity and self-expression are among the most important things in life'. If so, the Pentax camera would fit well into the consumer's existing attitudes.

Attitudes are difficult to change. A person's attitudes fit into a pattern, and to change one attitude may require difficult adjustments in many others. Thus, a company should usually try to fit its products into existing attitudes rather than attempt to change attitudes. Of course, there are exceptions in which the cost of trying to change attitudes may pay off handsomely. The traditional and dull Scottish breakfast of porridge oats has recently received a substantial boost from changes in lifestyles, greater awareness of healthy eating, and some clever marketing:

Oats have traditionally never enjoyed the sexiest image. But today even the most stylish and faddish foodie will happily admit to starting the day with a bowl of porridge.

Wheat free, low on the Glycaemic Index – which means they are slow energy releasing – and low in calories and fat, oats tick all the boxes as a nutritious and versatile food du jour.

Unlike a slice of white bread or a sugary bowl of cereal for example, the complex carbs in oats help balance blood sugar levels and leave you feeling full up for longer – an excellent way to refuel and curb hunger pangs.

Rich in fibre and protein, their nutritional benefits are also a huge plus. Studies have shown that oats can lower cholesterol, reduce high blood pressure and even improve libido. If further evidence was needed of their super-food status, Britain's longest-living man, David Henderson from Montrose, survived to the ripe old age of 109 and put his long life and good health down to his daily bowl of porridge.

In an age when we are more aware than ever that we are what we eat, it was not long before the rather plain little oat underwent a glamorous makeover. Witness the Scott's Porage Oats advert featuring a young lady ogling up a ruggedly handsome porridge-eating Scotsman's kilt. Soon after this, oatcakes appeared in deliberately more modern flavours – Nairns brought out cracked black pepper oatcakes, closely followed by stem ginger, mixed berry and fruit and spice varieties. Word spread of their appeal as a versatile, healthy snack and before long, oats were flying off shelves in all their forms. Sainsbury's reported a 60 per cent increase in oat sales in the last six months, and according to reports by market researchers TNS last year, oats are now Britain's second favourite breakfast cereal, with the oat industry bringing in £79 million per year.

Scots have long appreciated the benefits of oats. Native to Eurasia, they are the seeds of cereals belonging to the Avena genus and have been grown in Scotland for centuries. They have a lower summer heat requirement and greater tolerance of rain than cereals such as wheat, rye or barley, so are well suited to the Scottish climate. Our forefathers mixed them with a little fat to create oatcakes, one of the first convenience foods, a handy-sized and portable alternative to bread, but with the huge advantage that once baked they kept for long periods.

Scottish chieftains carried around small sacks of oatmeal when travelling by horseback and baked oatcakes on the back of their iron shields for sustenance. Today a pack of emergency oatcakes in the pocket does the same job for the you-are-what-you-eat generation, proving that a good thing will stand the test of time.[18]

We can now appreciate the many forces acting on consumer behaviour. The consumer's choice results from the complex interplay of cultural, social, personal and psychological factors.

The buyer decision process

Now that we have looked at the influences that affect buyers, we are ready to look at how consumers make buying decisions. Figure 5.4 shows that the buyer decision process consists of five stages: *need recognition, information search, evaluation of alternatives, purchase decision* and *post-purchase behaviour*. Clearly, the buying process starts long before the actual purchase and continues long after. Marketers need to focus on the entire buying process rather than on just the purchase decision.[19]

The figure suggests that consumers pass through all five stages with every purchase. But in more routine purchases, consumers often skip or reverse some of these stages. A woman buying her regular brand of toothpaste would recognise the need and go right to the purchase decision, skipping information search and evaluation. However, we use the model in Figure 5.4 because it shows all the considerations that arise when a consumer faces a new and complex purchase situation.

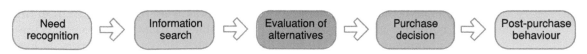

FIGURE 5.4

Buyer decision process

Need recognition

The buying process starts with *need recognition*: the buyer recognises a problem or need. The need can be triggered by *internal stimuli* when one of the person's normal needs – hunger, thirst, sex – rises to a level high enough to become a drive. A need can also be triggered by *external stimuli*. For example, an advertisement or a discussion with a friend might get you thinking about buying a new car. At this stage, the marketer should research consumers to find out what kinds of needs or problems arise, what brought them about, and how they led the consumer to this particular product.

Information search

An interested consumer may or may not search for more information. If the consumer's drive is strong and a satisfying product is near at hand, the consumer is likely to buy it then. If not, the consumer may store the need in memory or undertake an *information search* related to the need. For example, once you've decided you need a new mobile phone, you will probably pay more attention to phone advertisements, phones owned by friends and conversations about phones. Or you may actively look for reading material, email friends and gather information in other ways. The amount of searching you do will depend on the strength of your drive, the amount of information you start with, the ease of obtaining more information, the value you place on additional information and the satisfaction you get from searching.

Consumers can obtain information from any of several sources. These include *personal sources* (family, friends, neighbours, acquaintances), *commercial sources* (advertising, salespeople, 'websites' dealers, packaging, displays), *public sources* (mass media, consumer-rating organisations, Internet searches) and *experiential sources* (handling, examining, using the product). The relative influence of these information sources varies with the product and the buyer. Generally, the consumer receives the most information about a product from commercial sources – those controlled by the marketer. The most effective sources, however, tend to be personal. Commercial sources normally *inform* the buyer, but personal sources *legitimise* or *evaluate* products for the buyer. As one marketer states, 'It's rare that an advertising campaign can be as effective as a neighbor leaning over the fence and saying, "This is a wonderful product".'[20]

As more information is obtained, the consumer's awareness and knowledge of the available brands and features increases. In your phone information search, you may learn about the several brands available. This might help you to drop certain brands from consideration. A company must design its marketing mix to make prospects aware of and knowledgeable about its brand. It should carefully identify consumers' sources of information and the importance of each source.

Evaluation of alternatives

We have seen how the consumer uses information to arrive at a set of final brand choices. How does the consumer choose among the alternative brands? The marketer needs to know about *alternative evaluation*: that is, how the consumer processes information to arrive at brand choices. Unfortunately, consumers do not use a simple and single evaluation process in all buying situations. Instead, several evaluation processes are at work.

The consumer arrives at attitudes toward different brands through some evaluation procedure. How consumers go about evaluating purchase alternatives depends on the individual consumer and the specific buying situation. In some cases, consumers use careful calculations and logical thinking. At other times, the same consumers do little or no evaluating; instead they buy on impulse and rely on intuition. Sometimes consumers make buying decisions on their own; sometimes they turn to friends, consumer guides, or salespeople for buying advice.

Suppose you've narrowed your phone choices to three brands. And suppose that you are primarily interested in four attributes – style, features, guarantee and price. By this time, you've probably formed beliefs about how each brand rates on each attribute. Clearly, if one phone rated best on all the attributes, we could predict that you would choose it. However, the brands will no doubt vary in appeal. You might base your buying decision on only one attribute, and your choice would be easy to predict. If you wanted style above everything else, you would buy the phone that you think has the best styling. But most buyers consider several attributes, each with different importance. If we knew the importance that you assigned to each of the four attributes, we could predict your phone choice more reliably.

Marketers should study buyers to find out how they actually evaluate brand alternatives. If they know what evaluative processes go on, marketers can take steps to influence the buyer's decision.

Purchase decision

In the evaluation stage, the consumer ranks brands and forms purchase intentions. Generally, the consumer's *purchase decision* will be to buy the most preferred brand, but two factors can come between the purchase *intention* and the purchase *decision*. The first factor is the *attitudes of others*. If someone important to you thinks that you should buy the latest phone, then the chances of your buying an older model are reduced.

The second factor is *unexpected situational factors*. The consumer may form a purchase intention based on factors such as expected income, expected price and expected product benefits. However, unexpected events may change the purchase intention. For example, the economy might take a turn for the worse, a close competitor might drop its price, or a friend might report being disappointed in your preferred phone. Thus, preferences and even purchase intentions do not always result in actual purchase choice.

Post-purchase behaviour

The marketer's job does not end when the product is bought. After purchasing the product, the consumer will be satisfied or dissatisfied and will engage in *post-purchase behaviour* of interest to the marketer. What determines whether the buyer is satisfied or dissatisfied with a purchase? The answer lies in the relationship between the *consumer's expectations* and the product's *perceived performance*. If the product falls short of expectations, the consumer is disappointed; if it meets expectations, the consumer is satisfied; if it exceeds expectations, the consumer is delighted.

The larger the gap between expectations and performance, the greater the consumer's dissatisfaction. This suggests that sellers should promise only what their brands can deliver so that buyers are satisfied. Some sellers might even understate product performance levels to boost later consumer satisfaction. For example, Boeing's salespeople tend to be conservative when they estimate the potential benefits of their aircraft. They almost always underestimate fuel efficiency – they promise a 5 per cent savings that turns out to be 8 per cent. Customers are delighted with better than expected performance; they buy again and tell other potential customers that Boeing lives up to its promises.

Almost all major purchases result in **cognitive dissonance**, or discomfort caused by post-purchase conflict. After the purchase, consumers are satisfied with the benefits of the chosen brand and are glad to avoid the drawbacks of the brands not bought. However, every purchase involves compromise. Consumers feel uneasy about acquiring the drawbacks of the chosen brand and about losing the benefits of the brands not purchased. Thus, consumers feel at least some post-purchase dissonance for every purchase.[21]

Why is it so important to satisfy the customer? Customer satisfaction is a key to building profitable relationships with consumers – to keeping and growing consumers and reaping their customer lifetime value. Satisfied customers buy a product again, talk favourably to others about the product, pay less attention to competing brands and advertising, and buy other products from the company. Many marketers go beyond merely *meeting* the expectations of customers – they aim to *delight* the customer. Marketing at Work 5.1 illustrates the buying decision process for both consumer and business buyers of ceramic tiles, and the market research process that one company went through to try to work out how to delight its customers.

MARKETING AT WORK 5.1

The Tile Warehouse: Getting customer-focused

Caroline Tynan, *Professor of Marketing*, and **Sally McKechnie**, *Associate Professor in Marketing, Nottingham University Business School, UK*

The Tile Warehouse is a small family business based in the East Midlands of England, which sells a broad range of ceramic and natural stone floor and wall coverings and ancillary products/services to retail and commercial customers in this region. It was founded in 1980 by John and Marie Lockwood as The Tile Studio, a high street tile boutique, offering a selection of high quality ceramic tiles for the discerning retail customer. At the time the market for ceramic tiles was still in the early stages of growth and UK customer preferences were relatively underdeveloped compared to those in mainland Europe. Nevertheless company sales (by value and volume) were disappointing over the initial years of trading. Demand for ceramic floor and wall coverings was stronger in the commercial sector than the retail sector. Since most of the commercial tiling specialists were based in the South East of England, John and Marie recognised an

opportunity to reinvent and rebrand the business by establishing it as a northern front runner in selling tiles and tile-related products on a wholesale basis. So in 1985, once they had found a suitable out-of-town warehouse site, they closed down the high street boutique and began serving tradesmen (tilers and decorators), professionals (architects and interior designers) as well as retail customers, under the new trading name of The Tile Warehouse.

Clearly John and Marie had made the right move because over the next ten years the business enjoyed growing turnover and healthy profits. However, their good fortune changed in the mid-1990s as competition in the region increased significantly. This period had witnessed not only the rapid growth of DIY multiples in the UK (such as Texas Homecare, Homebase, Do It All and Great Mills) offering building materials and decorative products for homes and gardens to meet a rising level of consumer demand for home improvement products, but also consolidation as multiples repositioned themselves towards particular product groups. Many general DIY multiples offered ceramic tiles as part of their product mix because of the growth opportunity, and consequently the 'DIY sheds' entered the low priced end of the ceramic tiles marketplace. At

the same time specialist wholesalers (that is, category killers such as Topps Tiles) also moved in and began driving prices down even further. Inevitably The Tile Warehouse found itself struggling to compete as an independent specialist against the unprecedentedly low prices offered by the competition.

For the company this was a real blow. John had spent his working life 'in the business of selling tiles' and had always taken a pride in the in-depth specialist product knowledge and expertise of the company's long-serving staff. In the late 1990s the industry was becoming more cut-throat and customer needs were changing. John knew that the future survival of the company could not be taken for granted; they would now have to try to differentiate themselves from the encroaching competition and protect their margins by focusing on selling tiles in the middle to high price range instead. Over the next couple of years the company put the sales staff through various sales and customer service training courses. An immediate result was winning a national award for 'Excellence in Independent Retail' in 2003. Unfortunately this investment in training did not yield the increase in sales they had hoped for. In mid 2004 John and Marie called a family conference with their son Joe, who had carved a successful marketing career in the European film industry over the past ten years, and invited him to take his place in the family business. Joe had already been toying with the idea of taking a career break and agreed to join the business for a two-year period with the remit of bringing in his marketing expertise to develop and implement a marketing strategy for The Tile Warehouse.

When he arrived in 2005 the company had just won the national award for independent retail excellence for the second time. However, Joe knew that this was not the time for the company to become complacent. His first major task was to establish how best to differentiate The Tile Warehouse from Topps Tiles at the low-price end of the market, and from the DIY multiples in the low- to medium-price category. Furthermore, as the company sold ceramic tiles to both the retail and commercial sectors, he knew from experience that it was important to examine information on market trends and buying behaviour.

Clearly a major issue would be to obtain up-to-date and relevant information which he could then best use to differentiate and deliver The Tile Warehouse's offering for both types of customers. Joe's first step was to check with John what market information was available on file. Unlike in his previous workplace where this information was to hand and regularly updated, Joe was dismayed to find that apart from a collection of trade directories and publications from the tiling trade association, trade press clippings and regular internal sales analysis reports, much of the sales and marketing information was in John's head!

Joe proceeded to hire two marketing assistants, Gavin and Lucy, who had just graduated with business degrees from local universities. Gavin was asked to analyse the marketing environment using information gathered from secondary sources, and Lucy was hired to assist Joe with the website design and implementation of direct marketing campaigns. While marketing information was

being gathered and an electronic presence planned, Joe focused on developing a new complementary brand dedicated to serving the specific needs of all professional technical specifiers of ceramic tiles in the commercial sector (such as architects, designers and building consultants) based in the region. Recognising that commercial contracts are normally procured directly from tile manufacturers, John had for some time spotted an opening for the company to build profitable relationships with specifiers of small- to medium-sized contracts. With his parents' approval, Joe launched Prospec UK.

The Tile Warehouse brand continued to appeal to consumers and business buyers. Essentially, when it comes to interior design decisions, consumers have to decide whether to choose, purchase and fit tiles themselves or to use the services of a professional interior designer or a design specialist at a kitchen or bathroom centre. Hence the overlap in the area of interior design services in Figure 5.5.

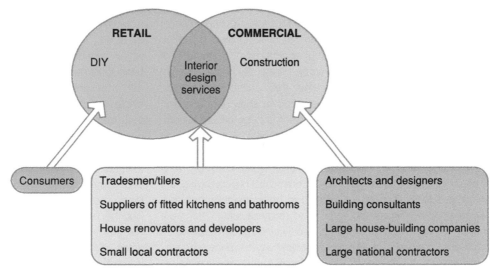

FIGURE 5.5

Ceramic tile market by market sector and customer type

Source: Internal company report.

Gavin's analysis of market trends data from industry reports and internal documents revealed that the UK ceramic tiles market was growing at an average of between 5 and 6 per cent pa and was expected to continue at this rate within the foreseeable future. While the markets for DIY and interior design services were highly fragmented, UK consumer tastes in interior design were becoming more cosmopolitan and influenced by a rise in home improvement-related television programming. As far as the tiling industry was concerned, it was important to recognise that consumer preferences for wall and floor coverings would be affected by changing fashions and an increased interest in DIY projects, making prospects good in the retail sector. Although dominated by multiples, there was still room for the independents. By comparison, in the commercial sector forecasts were somewhat mixed with growth in private and public sector building projects expected to rise, particularly in light of recent central and local government initiatives, but the area of private house-building becoming less buoyant.

Joe still needed to understand more about the buying behaviour for ceramic tiles. Apart from being able to identify the types of consumer households they ought to be targeting for advertising and direct marketing campaigns (mainly wealthy and affluent households in urban and suburban areas), he now had two brands to manage, and a wide variety of business buyers to serve on a limited budget and with a very small team. He commissioned a local market research agency to run some focus groups and in-depth interviews with a sample of consumers, trade/small commercial customers and large commercial customers to examine their perceptions of the company, explore their buying behaviour for ceramic tile-related products and services, and identify how they would prefer the company to communicate with them.

A summary of the main findings of the qualitative study with regard to buying behaviour are provided in Table 5.2.

Overall, the research revealed that purchasing decisions are made individually or jointly for consumer and trade buyers, and jointly for large business buyers. In the examples of joint decision-making described, a number of individuals were identified as participants in the buying decision-making process. Although the composition is not fixed, Joe realised that the company needed to be monitoring more closely who exactly is involved in existing and potential purchases and the roles that participants play in the buying decision.

Normally consumers shopped in couples for tiles and made several trips to outlets before making any purchase. A combination of a low level of product involvement, a high level of perceived risk and disappointment at the lack of interior design advice and expertise amongst showroom staff resulted in advice being sought from a number of sources. Many had never bought ceramic tiles before and wanted to see modern showroom displays. Some wanted to be offered a complete tiling solution that included professional installation of tiles (a 'supply and fit' service). For trade/small commercial buyers buying tiles tended to be a straight rebuy or a modified rebuy situation. They were mainly concerned about the provision of technical advice, price, convenience (location and opening hours) and stock availability. Showroom displays were also important as they helped to visualise what their customers are looking for. Finally,

each of the three buying situations applied to the large commercial buyers, many of which attached great importance to compliance with technical standards and the company's green credentials with respect to product sourcing. Technical advice and product range mattered as well.

The Tile Warehouse in its early stages had no formal marketing information system or marketing specialist expertise. Its clear market position, supported by selling and limited advertising and public relations activities, had been sufficient to make the company very successful. However, once customer expectations and the nature of competition began to change in an increasingly tough marketplace, the company had to become more customer-focused if it was going to be able successfully to differentiate itself in both market sectors from its cost-focused competitors.

When trying to introduce a marketing orientation into the company Joe was hampered by the constraints common in small firms such as the limited availability of money, time and marketing awareness. This was made more difficult by having to straddle two sectors, which exhibited different buying behaviours and buying situations, with the same staff and within a single outlet. While acknowledging that getting the family business customer-focused was much harder than expected, without being able to understand the impact of retail and commercial developments on the business, especially buying behaviour for ceramic tiles, Joe would not have been able to make progress in successfully repositioning the company. Without being able to establish the similarities and differences in the buying behaviour of consumer and business buyers of ceramic tiles, the marketing team

TABLE 5.2 Buying behaviour for ceramic tiles by customer type

Customer type	Consumer	Trade/small commercial	Large commercial
Decision-making	Individual Joint	Individual (solo operator) Joint (specialist contractors)	n/a Joint
Buying situation	New buy Modified rebuy	Straight rebuy Modified rebuy New buy	Straight rebuy Modified rebuy New buy
Buying centre members (examples given)	Spouse/partner Friends and family members Interior designer Tradesperson/tiler	Tradesperson/tiler Consumer or builder/contractor Supplier of fitted kitchens/bathrooms Interior designer	Architect/designer Purchasing manager Contract manager Builder/contractor Secretary
Choice criteria	Customer service Interior design advice and expertise Fresh and modern showroom displays Specialist product knowledge Product quality Provision of 'supply and fit' service Provision of samples	Price Location Customer service Technical advice Stock availability Product range Product quality Opening hours Fresh and modern showroom displays Provision of 'supply and fit' service Provision of samples	Product quality – conformity to international technical standards and ethical/greener product sourcing Customer service Technical advice Product range Online catalogue Provision of samples Delivery time

Source: Internal company report.

would not have been able to identify common factors in buying behaviour. As a result, while continuing to deliver excellent customer service, they have built efficiencies in developing different service elements and marketing communications for consumer and business offers, generated new sales leads and improved their approach to customer account management.

Sources: This case study has been produced as part of a Knowledge Transfer Partnership between the Tile Warehouse and Nottingham University Business School. The authors wish to thank Joe Lockwood and Gavin Llewellyn for their assistance with the preparation of the case study and Andrew Darwent for his valuable advice throughout the project partnership. Additional sources: Key Note Report (2005) *The Construction Industry*; Key Note (2006) *DIY and Home Improvements Industry*; Key Note (2006) *Ceramic Tiles and Wallcoverings*; Mintel (2006) *Carpets and Other Floorcoverings – UK*; Internal company documents; company websites: www.thetilewarehouse.com, www.propsectiles.com; The Tile Association website: www.tiles.org.uk.

A dissatisfied consumer responds differently. Bad word-of-mouth often travels farther and faster than good word of mouth. It can quickly damage consumer attitudes about a company and its products. But companies cannot simply rely on dissatisfied customers to volunteer their complaints when they are dissatisfied. Most unhappy customers never tell the company about their problem. Therefore, a company should measure customer satisfaction regularly. It should set up systems that *encourage* customers to complain. In this way, the company can learn how well it is doing and how it can improve.

But what should companies do about dissatisfied customers? At a minimum, most companies offer free telephone numbers and websites to handle complaints and enquiries.

For example, floorcare products company Vax offers extensive consumer advice to Australian consumers at **www.vax.com.au** and to British consumers at **www.vax.co.uk** but is also very conscious that consumers may have individual problems that need the assistance of a customer care adviser:

> At Vax we are dedicated to ensuring that you are happy with your floorcare appliance. Should you be unhappy for any reason, our dedicated helpline can help you. All our advisers are fully trained and will be able to help you solve any problems, quickly and easily. (**www.vax.co.uk/support/careline.php**)

Consumers in the UK can telephone the Vax Careline on 0870 606 1248, while Australian consumers have their own Vaxcare telephone number, 1300 364 040.

By studying the overall buyer decision, marketers may be able to find ways to help consumers move through it. For example, if consumers are not buying a new product because they do not perceive a need for it, marketing might launch advertising messages that trigger the need and show how the product solves consumers' problems. If consumers know about the product but are not buying because they hold unfavourable attitudes toward it, the marketer must find ways either to change the product or change consumer perceptions.

The buyer decision process for new products

We have looked at the stages buyers go through in trying to satisfy a need. Buyers may pass quickly or slowly through these stages, and some of the stages may even be reversed. Much depends on the nature of the buyer, the product and the buying situation.

We now look at how buyers approach the purchase of new products. A **new product** is a good, service or idea that is perceived by some potential customers as new. It may have been around for a while, but our interest is in how consumers learn about products for the first time and make decisions on whether to adopt them. We define the **adoption process** as 'the mental process through which an individual passes from first learning about an innovation to final adoption', and *adoption* as the decision by an individual to become a regular user of the product.[22]

Stages in the adoption process

Consumers go through five stages in the process of adopting a new product:

- *Awareness:* The consumer becomes aware of the new product, but lacks information about it.
- *Interest:* The consumer seeks information about the new product.
- *Evaluation:* The consumer considers whether trying the new product makes sense.
- *Trial:* The consumer tries the new product on a small scale to improve his or her estimate of its value.
- *Adoption:* The consumer decides to make full and regular use of the new product.

This model suggests that the new product marketer should think about how to help consumers move through these stages. A manufacturer of high-definition televisions (HDTVs) may discover that many consumers in the interest stage do not move to the trial stage because of uncertainty and the large investment. If these same consumers were willing to use HDTVs on a trial basis for a small fee, the manufacturer could consider offering a trial-use plan with an option to buy.

Individual differences in innovativeness

People differ greatly in their readiness to try new products. In each product area, there are 'consumption pioneers' and early adopters. Other individuals adopt new products

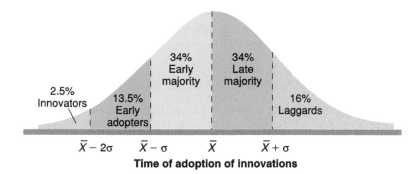

FIGURE 5.6

Adopter categorisation on the basis of relative time of adoption of innovations

Source: Reprinted with the permission of The Free Press, a Division of Simon & Schuster, Inc., from *Diffusion of Innovations*, 5th edn, by Everett M. Rogers. Copyright © 1995, 2003 by Everett M. Rogers. Copyright © 1962, 1971, 1983 by The Free Press. All rights reserved.

much later. People can be classified into the adopter categories shown in Figure 5.6. After a slow start, an increasing number of people adopt the new product. The number of adopters reaches a peak and then drops off as fewer non-adopters remain. Innovators are defined as the first 2.5 per cent of the buyers to adopt a new idea (those beyond two standard deviations from mean adoption time); the early adopters are the next 13.5 per cent (between one and two standard deviations); and so on.

The five adopter groups have differing values. *Innovators* are adventurous – they try new ideas at some risk. *Early adopters* are guided by respect – they are opinion leaders in their communities and adopt new ideas early but carefully. The *early majority* are deliberate – although they are rarely leaders, they adopt new ideas before the average person. The *late majority* are sceptical – they adopt an innovation only after a majority of people have tried it. Finally, *laggards* are tradition bound – they are suspicious of changes and adopt the innovation only when it has become something of a tradition itself.

This adopter classification suggests that an innovating firm should research the characteristics of innovators and early adopters and should direct marketing efforts toward them. In general, innovators tend to be relatively younger, better educated, and higher in income than later adopters and non-adopters. They are more receptive to unfamiliar things, rely more on their own values and judgement, and are more willing to take risks. They are less brand loyal and more likely to take advantage of special promotions such as discounts, coupons and samples.

Influence of product characteristics on rate of adoption

The characteristics of the new product affect its rate of adoption. Some products catch on almost overnight (iPod), whereas others take a long time to gain acceptance (HDTV). Five characteristics are especially important in influencing an innovation's rate of adoption. For example, consider the characteristics of HDTV in relation to the rate of adoption:

- *Relative advantage*: the degree to which the innovation appears superior to existing products. The greater the perceived relative advantage of using HDTV – say, in picture quality and ease of viewing – the sooner HDTVs will be adopted.

- *Compatibility*: the degree to which the innovation fits the values and experiences of potential consumers. HDTV, for example, is highly compatible with the lifestyles found in upper middle-class homes. However, it is not very compatible with the programming and broadcasting systems currently available to consumers.

- *Complexity*: the degree to which the innovation is difficult to understand or use. HDTVs are not very complex and, therefore, once more programming is available and prices come down, will take less time to penetrate European homes than more complex innovations.

- *Divisibility*: the degree to which the innovation may be tried on a limited basis. HDTVs are still very expensive. To the extent that people can lease them with an option to buy, their rate of adoption will increase.

- *Communicability*: the degree to which the results of using the innovation can be observed or described to others. Because HDTV lends itself to demonstration and description, its use will spread faster among consumers.

Other characteristics influence the rate of adoption, such as initial and ongoing costs, risk and uncertainty, and social approval. The new product marketer has to research all these factors when developing the new product and its marketing programme.

Consumer behaviour across international borders

Understanding consumer behaviour is difficult enough for companies marketing within the borders of a single country. For companies operating in many countries, however, understanding and serving the needs of consumers can be daunting. Although consumers in different countries may have some things in common, their values, attitudes and behaviours often vary greatly. International marketers must understand such differences and adjust their products and marketing programmes accordingly.

Sometimes the differences are obvious. For example, in the United Kingdom, where most people eat cereal regularly for breakfast, Kellogg's focuses its marketing on persuading consumers to select a Kellogg's brand rather than a competitor's brand. In France, however, where most people prefer croissants and coffee or no breakfast at all, Kellogg's advertising simply attempts to convince people that they should eat cereal for breakfast. Its packaging includes step-by-step instructions on how to prepare cereal. In India, where many consumers eat heavy, fried breakfasts and many consumers skip the meal altogether, Kellogg's advertising attempts to convince buyers to switch to a lighter, more nutritious breakfast diet.

Often, differences across international markets are more subtle. They may result from physical differences in consumers and their environments. For example, Remington makes smaller electric shavers to fit the smaller hands of Japanese consumers. Other differences result from varying customs. In Japan, for example, where humility and deference are considered great virtues, pushy, hard-hitting sales approaches are considered offensive. Failing to understand such differences in customs and behaviours from one country to another can spell disaster for a marketer's international products and programmes.

Marketers must decide on the degree to which they will adapt their products and marketing programmes to meet the unique cultures and needs of consumers in various markets. On the one hand, they want to standardise their offerings in order to simplify operations and take advantage of cost economies. On the other hand, adapting marketing efforts within each country results in products and programmes that better satisfy the needs of local consumers. The question of whether to adapt or standardise the marketing mix across international markets has created a lively debate in recent years.

MAKING CONNECTIONS Linking the concepts

Here's a good place to take some time out and apply the concepts you've examined in the first part of this chapter.

- Think about a specific major purchase you've made recently. What buying process did you follow? What major factors influenced your decision?

- Pick a company that we've discussed in a previous chapter – Setanta, Arla, Boots or another. How does the company you chose use its understanding of customers and their buying behaviour to build better customer relationships?

- Think about a company like Intel, which sells its products to computer makers and other businesses rather than to final consumers. How would Intel's marketing to business customers differ from Starbucks's marketing to final consumers? The second part of the chapter deals with this issue.

BUSINESS MARKETS AND BUSINESS BUYER BEHAVIOUR

In one way or another, most large companies sell to other organisations. Companies such as Boeing, IBM, Caterpillar, Corus and countless other firms sell *most* of their products to other businesses. Even large consumer products companies, which make products used by final consumers, must first sell their products to other businesses. For example, Procter & Gamble makes many familiar consumer brands – personal care products like Dove, Lux, Sunsilk and Signal, home care products such as Cif, Comfort, Domestos and Surf, food products like Bertolli, Knorr, Slim-Fast and Hellman's, and others. But to sell these products to consumers, Procter & Gamble must first sell them to the wholesalers and retailers that serve the consumer market.

Business buyer behaviour refers to the buying behaviour of the organisations that buy goods and services for use in the production of other products and services that are sold, rented, or supplied to others. It also includes the behaviour of retailing and wholesaling firms that acquire goods to resell or rent them to others at a profit. In the *business buying process*, business buyers determine which products and services their organisations need to purchase, and then find, evaluate and choose among alternative suppliers and brands. *Business-to-business (B-to-B) marketers* must do their best to understand business markets and business buyer behaviour.

Business markets

The business market is *huge*. In fact, business markets involve far more money and goods than do consumer markets. For example, think about the large number of business transactions involved in the production and sale of a single set of Pirelli tyres. Various suppliers sell Pirelli the rubber, steel, equipment and other goods that it needs to produce the tyres. Pirelli then sells the finished tyres to retailers, who in turn sell them to consumers. Thus, many sets of *business* purchases were made for only one set of *consumer* purchases. In addition, Pirelli sells tyres as original equipment to manufacturers who install them on new vehicles, and as replacement tyres to companies that maintain their own fleets of company cars, trucks, buses or other vehicles.

Characteristics of business markets

In some ways, business markets are similar to consumer markets. Both involve people who assume buying roles and make purchase decisions to satisfy needs. However, business markets differ in many ways from consumer markets. The main differences are in *market structure and demand*, the *nature of the buying unit*, and the *types of decisions and the decision process* involved.

Market structure and demand

The business marketer normally deals with *far fewer but far larger buyers* than the consumer marketer does. Even in large business markets, a few buyers often account for most of the purchasing. For example, when Pirelli sells replacement tyres to final consumers, its potential market includes the owners of the millions of cars currently in use in the European Union and around the world. But Pirelli's fate in the business market depends on getting orders from one of only a handful of large car makers. Similarly, Black & Decker sells its power tools and outdoor equipment to tens of millions of consumers worldwide. However, it must sell these products through DIY retail outlets – such as B&Q and Homebase in the UK and Ireland, Brico in Italy, and Bauhaus in Germany – which provide its key routes to the market.

Business markets are also *more geographically concentrated*. Further, business demand is **derived demand** – it derives ultimately from the demand for consumer goods. Hewlett-Packard and Dell buy Intel microprocessor chips because consumers buy personal computers. If consumer demand for PCs drops, so will the demand for computer chips.

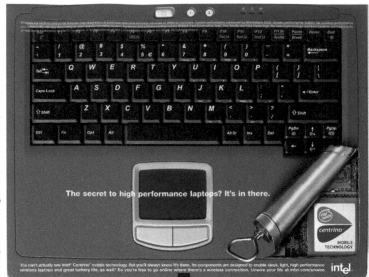

Derived demand: Intel's long-running 'Intel Inside' advertising campaign boosts demand for Intel chips and for the computers containing them.

Therefore, B-to-B marketers sometimes promote their products directly to final consumers to increase business demand. For example, Intel's long-running 'Intel Inside' advertising campaign sells personal computers to buyers on the virtues of Intel microprocessors. The increased demand for Intel chips boosts demand for the PCs containing them, and both Intel and its business partners win.

Similarly, W.L. Gore promotes Gore-Tex® directly to final consumers as a key branded ingredient in waterproof and breathable outdoor clothing – from mountaineering or sailing jackets through to winter ice-climbing boots. You see Gore-Tex® hangtags on clothing lines such as Scarpa mountaineering boots, Henri-Lloyd sailing foul-weather gear, and The North Face walking and mountaineering jackets. By making Gore-Tex® familiar and attractive to final buyers, W.L. Gore also makes the products containing it more attractive.

Nature of the buying unit

Compared with consumer purchases, a business purchase usually involves *more decision participants* and a *more professional purchasing effort*. Often, business buying is done by trained purchasing agents who spend their working lives learning how to buy better. The more complex the purchase, the more likely it is that several people will participate in the decision-making process. Buying committees made up of technical experts and top management are common in the buying of major goods.

Beyond this, many companies are now upgrading their purchasing functions to 'supply management' or 'supplier development' functions. B-to-B marketers now face a new breed of higher-level, better-trained supply managers. These supply managers sometimes seem to know more about the supplier company than it knows about itself. Therefore, business marketers must have well-trained marketers and salespeople to deal with these well-trained buyers.

Types of decisions and the decision process

Business buyers usually face *more complex* buying decisions than do consumer buyers. Purchases often involve large sums of money, complex technical and economic considerations, and interactions among many people at many levels of the buyer's organisation. Because the purchases are more complex, business buyers may take longer to make their decisions. The business buying process also tends to be *more formalised* than the consumer buying process. Large business purchases usually call for detailed product specifications, written purchase orders, careful supplier searches and formal approval.

Finally, in the business buying process, buyer and seller are often much *more dependent* on each other. Consumer marketers are often at a distance from their customers. In contrast, B-to-B marketers may roll up their sleeves and work closely with their customers during all stages of the buying process – from helping customers define problems, to finding solutions, to supporting after-sale operation. They often customise their offerings to individual customer needs.

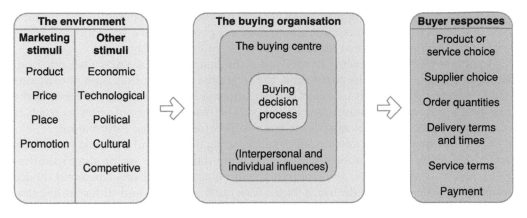

FIGURE 5.7
A model of business buyer behaviour

Business buyer behaviour

At the most basic level, marketers want to know how business buyers will respond to various marketing stimuli. Figure 5.7 shows a model of business buyer behaviour. In this model, marketing and other stimuli affect the buying organisation and produce certain buyer responses. As with consumer buying, the marketing stimuli for business buying consist of the Four Ps: product, price, place and promotion (plus people, physical evidence and service delivery process for service products). Other stimuli include major forces in the environment: economic, technological, political, cultural and competitive. These stimuli enter the organisation and are turned into buyer responses: product or service choice; supplier choice; order quantities; and delivery, service and payment terms. In order to design good marketing mix strategies, the marketer must understand what happens within the organisation to turn stimuli into purchase responses.

Within the organisation, buying activity consists of two major parts: the buying centre, made up of all the people involved in the buying decision, and the buying-decision process. The model shows that the buying centre and the buying decision process are influenced by internal organisational, interpersonal and individual factors as well as by external environmental factors.

The model in Figure 5.7 suggests four questions about business buyer behaviour. What buying decisions do business buyers make? Who participates in the buying process? What are the major influences on buyers? How do business buyers make their buying decisions?

Major types of buying situations

There are three major types of buying situations.[23] At one extreme is the *straight rebuy*, which is a fairly routine decision. At the other extreme is the *new task*, which may call for thorough research. In the middle is the *modified rebuy*, which requires some research.

In a **straight rebuy**, the buyer reorders something without any modifications. It is usually handled on a routine basis by the purchasing department. Based on past buying satisfaction, the buyer simply chooses from the various suppliers on its list. 'In' suppliers try to maintain product and service quality. They often propose automatic reordering systems so that the purchasing agent will save reordering time. 'Out' suppliers try to offer something new or exploit dissatisfaction so that the buyer will consider them.

In a **modified rebuy**, the buyer wants to modify product specifications, prices, terms or suppliers. The modified rebuy usually involves more decision participants than does the straight rebuy. The in suppliers may become nervous and feel pressured to put their best foot forward to protect an account. Out suppliers may see the modified rebuy situation as an opportunity to make a better offer and gain new business.

A company buying a product or service for the first time faces a **new task** situation. In such cases, the greater the cost or risk, the larger the number of decision participants and the greater their efforts to collect information will be. The new task situation is the marketer's greatest opportunity and challenge. The marketer not only tries to reach as many key buying influences as possible but also provides help and information.

The buyer makes the fewest decisions in the straight rebuy and the most in the new task decision. In the new task situation, the buyer must decide on product specifications, suppliers, price limits, payment terms, order quantities, delivery times and service terms. The order of these decisions varies with each situation, and different decision participants influence each choice.

Many business buyers prefer to buy a packaged solution to a problem from a single seller. Instead of buying and putting all the components together, the buyer may ask sellers to supply the components *and* assemble the package or system. The sale often goes to the firm that provides the most complete system meeting the customer's needs. Thus, **systems selling** is often a key business marketing strategy for winning and holding accounts. For example, Veolia Environnement provides a complete solution for its customers' industrial waste problems:

> Veolia Environnement is a 25 billion euro turnover company that few consumers will ever have heard of. Yet it operates all round the world, generating 48 per cent of its revenue from France, 33 per cent from elsewhere in Europe, 10 per cent from the Americas, and 9 per cent from the rest of the world. Veolia Environnement has subsidiaries in 27 European countries, from France and Portugal in the west to Russia in the east. Industrial waste management is one of Veolia's key business areas. The company can simply arrange to collect and dispose of waste products on behalf of manufacturing, commercial and public sector organisations, but promotes its 'integrated solutions and total waste management' to businesses that want their waste systems professionally managed from start to finish. For example, Veolia offers a complete range of integrated industrial site waste management services, including high pressure water jetting, tank and vessel cleaning, emergency response, chemical cleaning, on-site processing, chemical decontamination and land decontamination. Many municipal authorities across Europe also use Veolia's integrated waste management solutions to deliver their statutory obligation to provide waste and recycling services to local communities.[24]

Participants in the business buying process

Who does the buying of the trillions of euros' worth of goods and services needed by business organisations? The decision-making unit of a buying organisation is called its **buying centre**: all the individuals and units that participate in the business decision-making process. The buying centre includes all members of the organisation who play a role in the purchase decision process. This group includes the actual users of the product or service, those who make the buying decision, those who influence the buying decision, those who do the actual buying, and those who control buying information.

The buying centre is not a fixed and formally identified unit within the buying organisation. It is a set of buying roles assumed by different people for different purchases. Within the organisation, the size and make-up of the buying centre will vary for different products and for different buying situations. For some routine purchases, one person – say a buyer – may assume all the buying centre roles and serve as the only person involved in the buying decision. For more complex purchases, the buying centre may include 20 or 30 people from different levels and departments in the organisation.

The buying centre concept presents a major marketing challenge. The business marketer must learn who participates in the decision, each participant's relative influence, and what evaluation criteria each decision participant uses. For example, the Malaysian company San Miguel Woven Products sells disposable surgical gowns to hospitals. It identifies the hospital personnel involved in this buying decision as the purchasing manager, the operating room administrator and the surgeons. Each participant plays a different role. The purchasing manager analyses whether the hospital should buy disposable gowns or reusable gowns. If analysis favours disposable gowns, then the operating room administrator compares competing products and prices and makes a choice. This administrator considers the gown's absorbency, antiseptic quality, design and cost, and normally buys the brand that meets requirements at the lowest cost. Finally, surgeons affect the decision later by reporting their satisfaction or dissatisfaction with the brand.

The buying centre usually includes some obvious participants who are involved formally in the buying decision. For example, the decision to buy a corporate jet will probably involve the company's CEO, chief pilot, a purchasing agent, some legal staff, a member of top management and others formally charged with the buying decision. It may also involve less obvious, informal participants, some of whom may actually make or strongly affect the buying decision. Sometimes, even the people in the buying centre are not aware of all the buying participants. For example, the decision about which corporate jet to buy may actually be made by a corporate board member who has an interest in flying and who knows a lot about aircraft. This board member may work behind the scenes to sway the decision. Many business buying decisions result from the complex interactions of ever-changing buying centre participants.

Major influences on business buyers

Business buyers are subject to many influences when they make their buying decisions. Some marketers assume that the major influences are economic. They think buyers will favour the supplier who offers the lowest price or the best product or the most service. They concentrate on offering strong economic benefits to buyers. However, business buyers respond to both economic and personal factors. Far from being cold, calculating and impersonal, business buyers are human and social as well. They react to both reason and emotion.

Today, most business-to-business marketers recognise that emotion plays an important role in business buying decisions. For example, you might expect that an advertisement promoting large trucks to corporate fleet buyers would stress objective technical, performance and economic factors. However, a recent ad for Volvo heavy-duty trucks shows two drivers arm-wrestling and claims, 'It solves all your fleet problems. Except who gets to drive.' It turns out that, in the face of an industry-wide driver shortage, the type of truck a fleet provides can help it to attract qualified drivers. The Volvo ad stresses the raw beauty of the truck and its comfort and roominess, features that make it more appealing to drivers. The ad concludes that Volvo trucks are 'built to make fleets more profitable and drivers a lot more possessive'.

Figure 5.8 lists various groups of influences on business buyers – environmental, organisational, interpersonal and individual. *Environmental factors* play a major role. For example, buyer behaviour can be heavily influenced by factors in the current and expected economic environment, such as the level of primary demand, the economic outlook and the cost of money. Another environmental factor is shortages in key materials. Many companies now are more willing to buy and hold larger inventories of scarce materials to ensure adequate supply. Business buyers are also affected by technological, political and competitive developments in the environment. Finally, culture and customs can strongly influence business buyer reactions to the marketer's behaviour and strategies, especially in the international marketing environment (see Marketing at Work 5.2).

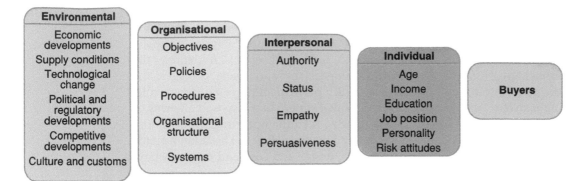

FIGURE 5.8

Major influences on business buyer behaviour

MARKETING AT WORK 5.2

International marketing manners: When in Rome, do as the Romans do

Picture this: The imaginary American firm Consolidated Amalgamation, Inc. thinks it's time that the rest of the world enjoyed the same fine products it has offered American consumers for two generations. It dispatches Vice President Harry E. Slicksmile to Europe, Africa and Asia to explore the territory. Mr Slicksmile stops first in London, where he makes short work of some bankers – he rings them up on the phone. He handles Parisians with similar ease. After securing a table at La Tour d'Argent, he greets his luncheon guest, the director of an industrial engineering firm, with the words, 'Just call me Harry, Jacques'.

In Germany, Mr Slicksmile is a powerhouse. Whisking through a lavish, state-of-the-art marketing presentation, complete with flip charts and audiovisuals, he shows 'em that this all-American boy *knows* how to make a buck. Heading on to Milan, Harry strikes up a conversation with the Japanese businessman

sitting next to him on the plane. He flips his card onto the guy's tray and, when the two say goodbye, shakes hands warmly and clasps the man's right arm. Later, for his appointment with the owner of an Italian packaging design firm, our hero wears his comfy corduroy sports coat, khaki trousers, and favourite casual shoes. Everybody knows Italians are zany and laid back.

Mr Slicksmile next swings through Saudi Arabia, where he coolly presents a potential client with a multimillion-dollar proposal in a classy pigskin binder. His final stop is Beijing, China, where he talks business over lunch with a group of Chinese executives. After completing the meal, he drops his chopsticks into his bowl of rice and presents each guest with an elegant Tiffany clock as a reminder of his visit.

A great tour, sure to generate a pile of orders, right? Wrong. Six months later, Consolidated Amalgamation has nothing to show for the trip but a stack of bills. Abroad, they weren't wild about Harry.

This hypothetical case has been exaggerated for emphasis. Americans are seldom such dolts. But experts say success in international

business has a lot to do with knowing the territory and its people.

Poor Harry tried all right, but in all the wrong ways. The British do not, as a rule, make deals over the phone as much as Americans do. It's not so much a 'cultural' difference as a difference in approach. A proper Frenchman neither likes instant familiarity – questions about family, church, or alma mater – nor refers to strangers by their first names. 'That poor fellow, Jacques, probably wouldn't show anything, but he'd recoil. He'd *not* be pleased,' explains an expert on French business practices. 'It's considered poor taste,' he continues. 'Even after months of business dealings, I'd wait for him or her to make the invitation [to use first names] . . . You are always right, in Europe, to say "Mister".'

Harry's flashy presentation would likely have been a flop with the Germans, who dislike overstatement and showiness. According to one German expert, however, German businessmen have become accustomed to dealing with Americans. Although differences in body language and customs remain, the past 20 years have softened them. 'I hugged an American woman at a business meeting last night,' he said. 'That would be normal in France, but [older] Germans still have difficulty [with the custom].' He says that calling secretaries by their first names would still be considered rude: 'They have a right to be called by the surname. You'd certainly ask – and get – permission first.' In Germany, people address each other formally and correctly – someone with two doctorates (which is fairly common) must be referred to as 'Herr Doktor Doktor'.

When Harry Slicksmile grabbed his new Japanese acquaintance by the arm, the executive probably considered him disrespectful and presumptuous. Japan, like many Asian countries, is a 'no-contact culture' in which even shaking hands is a strange experience. Harry made matters worse by tossing his business card. Japanese people revere the business card as an extension of self and as an indicator of rank. They do not *hand* it to people, they *present* it – with both hands. In addition, the Japanese are sticklers about rank. Unlike Americans, they don't heap praise on subordinates in a room; they will praise only the highest-ranking official present.

Hapless Harry also goofed when he assumed that Italians are like Hollywood's stereotypes of them. The flair for design and style that has characterised Italian culture for

centuries is embodied in the businesspeople of Milan and Rome. They dress beautifully and admire flair, but they dislike garishness or impropriety in others' attire.

To the Saudi Arabians, the pigskin binder would have been considered vile. An American salesman who really did present such a binder was unceremoniously tossed out and his company was blacklisted from working with Saudi businesses. In China, Harry casually dropping his chopsticks could have been misinterpreted as an act of aggression. Stabbing chopsticks into a bowl of rice and leaving them signifies death to the Chinese. The clocks Harry offered as gifts might have confirmed such dark intentions. To 'give a clock' in Chinese sounds the same as 'seeing someone off to his end'.

Thus, to compete successfully in global markets, or even to deal effectively with international firms in their home markets, companies must help their managers to understand the needs, customs and cultures of international business buyers. 'When doing business in a foreign country and a foreign culture – particularly a non-Western culture – assume nothing,' advises an international business specialist. 'Take nothing for granted. Turn every stone. Ask every question. Dig into every detail. Because cultures really

Companies must help their managers understand international customers and customs. For example, Japanese people revere the business card as an extension of self; they do not hand it out but present it. *Source:* BLOOMimage/Getty Images.

are different, and those differences can have a major impact.' So the old advice is still good advice: when in Rome, do as the Romans do.

Sources: Portions adapted from Susan Harte, 'When in Rome, You Should Learn to Do What the Romans Do', *The Atlanta Journal-Constitution*, 22 January 1990, pp. D1, D6. Additional examples can be found in David A. Ricks, *Blunders in International Business Around the World* (Malden, MA: Blackwell Publishing, 2000); Terri Morrison, Wayne A. Conway and Joseph J. Douress, *Dun & Bradstreet's Guide to Doing Business* (Upper Saddle River, NJ: Prentice Hall, 2000); James K. Sebenius, 'The Hidden Challenge of Cross-Border Negotiatons', *Harvard Business Review*, March 2002, pp. 76–85; Ross Thompson, 'Lost in Translation', *Medical Marketing and Media*, March 2005, p. 82; and information accessed at www.executiveplanet.com, December 2005.

Business buyer behaviour is also influenced strongly by *organisational factors*. Each buying organisation has its own objectives, policies, procedures, structure and systems, and the business marketer must understand these factors well. Questions such as these arise: How many people are involved in the buying decision? Who are they? What are their evaluative criteria? What are the company's policies and limits on its buyers?

The buying centre usually includes many participants who influence each other, so *interpersonal factors* also influence the business buying process. However, it is often difficult to assess such interpersonal factors and group dynamics. Buying centre participants do not wear tags that label them as 'key decision maker' or 'not influential'. Nor do buying centre participants with the highest rank always have the most influence. Participants may influence the buying decision because they control rewards and punishments, are well liked, have special expertise, or have a special relationship with other important participants. Interpersonal factors are often very subtle. Whenever possible, business marketers must try to understand these factors and design strategies that take them into account.

Finally, business buyers are influenced by *individual factors*. Each participant in the business buying decision process brings in personal motives, perceptions and preferences. These individual factors are affected by personal characteristics such as age, income, education, professional identification, personality and attitudes toward risk. Also, buyers have different buying styles. Some may be technical types who make in-depth analyses of competitive proposals before choosing a supplier. Other buyers may be intuitive negotiators who are adept at pitting the sellers against one another for the best deal.

The business buying process

Figure 5.9 lists the eight stages of the business buying process.[25] Buyers who face a new task buying situation usually go through all stages of the buying process. Buyers making modified or straight rebuys may skip some of the stages. We will examine these steps for the typical new task buying situation.

Problem recognition The buying process begins when someone in the company recognises a problem or need that can be met by acquiring a specific product or service. *Problem recognition* can result from internal or external stimuli. Internally, the company may decide to launch a new product that requires new production equipment and materials. Or a machine may break down and need new parts. Perhaps a purchasing manager is unhappy with a current supplier's product quality, service or prices. Externally, the buyer may get some new ideas at a trade show, see an ad, or receive a call from a salesperson who offers a better product or a lower price. In fact, in their advertising, business marketers often alert customers to potential problems and then show how their products provide solutions.

General need description Having recognised a need, the buyer next prepares a general *need description* that describes the characteristics and quantity of the needed item. For standard items, this process presents few problems. For complex items, however, the buyer may have to work with others – engineers, users, consultants – to define the item. The team may want to rank the importance of reliability, durability, price and other attributes desired in the item. In this phase, the alert business marketer can help the buyers define their needs and provide information about the value of different product characteristics.

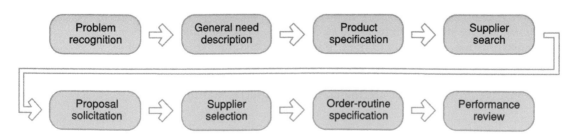

FIGURE 5.9

Stages of the business buying process

Product specification The buying organisation next develops the item's technical product specifications, often with the help of a value analysis engineering team. **Value analysis** is an approach to cost reduction in which components are studied carefully to determine if they can be redesigned, standardised, or made by less costly methods of production. The team decides on the best product characteristics and specifies them accordingly. Sellers, too, can use value analysis as a tool to help secure a new account. By showing buyers a better way to make an object, outside sellers can turn straight rebuy situations into new task situations that give them a chance to obtain new business.

Supplier search The buyer now conducts a *supplier search* to find the best vendors. The buyer can compile a small list of qualified suppliers by reviewing trade directories, doing a computer search, or phoning other companies for recommendations. Today, more and more companies are turning to the Internet to find suppliers. For marketers, this has levelled the playing field – the Internet gives smaller suppliers many of the same advantages as larger competitors.

The newer the buying task, and the more complex and costly the item, the greater the amount of time the buyer will spend searching for suppliers. The supplier's task is to get listed in major directories and build a good reputation in the marketplace. Salespeople should watch for companies in the process of searching for suppliers and make certain that their firm is considered.

Proposal solicitation In the *proposal solicitation* stage of the business buying process, the buyer invites qualified suppliers to submit proposals. In response, some suppliers will send only a catalogue or a salesperson. However, when the item is complex or expensive, the buyer will usually require detailed written proposals or formal presentations from each potential supplier.

Business marketers must be skilled in researching, writing and presenting proposals in response to buyer proposal solicitations. Proposals should be marketing documents, not just technical documents. Presentations should inspire confidence and should make the marketer's company stand out from the competition.

Supplier selection The members of the buying centre now review the proposals and select a supplier or suppliers. During *supplier selection*, the buying centre often will draw up a list of the desired supplier attributes and their relative importance. In one survey, purchasing executives listed the following attributes as most important in influencing the relationship between supplier and customer: quality products and services, on-time delivery, ethical corporate behaviour, honest communication and competitive prices. Other important factors include repair and servicing capabilities, technical aid and advice, geographic location, performance history and reputation. The members of the buying centre will rate suppliers against these attributes and identify the best suppliers.

Buyers may attempt to negotiate with preferred suppliers for better prices and terms before making the final selections. In the end, they may select a single supplier or a few suppliers. Many buyers prefer multiple sources of supplies to avoid being totally dependent on one supplier and to allow comparisons of prices and performance of several suppliers over time. Today's supplier development managers want to develop a full network of supplier partners that can help the company bring more value to its customers.

Order-routine specification The buyer now prepares an *order-routine specification*. It includes the final order with the chosen supplier or suppliers and lists items such as technical specifications, quantity needed, expected time of delivery, return policies and warranties. In the case of maintenance, repair and operating items, buyers may use blanket contracts rather than periodic purchase orders. A blanket contract creates a long-term relationship in which the supplier promises to resupply the buyer as needed at agreed prices for a set time period.

Many large buyers now practice *vendor-managed inventory*, in which they turn over ordering and inventory responsibilities to their suppliers. Under such systems, buyers share sales and inventory information directly with key suppliers. The suppliers then monitor inventories and replenish stock automatically as needed.

Performance review In this stage, the buyer reviews supplier performance. The buyer may contact users and ask them to rate their satisfaction. The *performance review* may lead the buyer to continue, modify or drop the arrangement. The seller's job is to monitor the same factors used by the buyer to make sure that the seller is giving the expected satisfaction.

The eight-stage buying process model provides a simple view of business buying as it might occur in a new task buying situation. The actual process is usually much more complex. In the modified rebuy or straight rebuy situation, some of these stages would be compressed or bypassed. Each organisation buys in its own way, and each buying situation has unique requirements.

Different buying centre participants may be involved at different stages of the process. Although certain buying process steps usually do occur, buyers do not always follow them in the same order, and they may add other steps. Often, buyers will repeat certain stages of the process. Finally, a customer relationship might involve many different types of purchases ongoing at a given time, all in different stages of the buying process. The seller must manage the total customer relationship, not just individual purchases.

E-procurement: buying electronically and on the Internet

During the past few years, advances in information technology have changed the face of the business-to-business marketing process. Electronic and online purchasing, often called *e-procurement*, has grown rapidly.

Companies can do e-procurement in any of several ways. They can set up their own *company buying sites*. For example, General Electric operates a company trading site on which it posts its buying needs and invites bids, negotiates terms and places orders. Or the company can create extranet links with key suppliers. For instance, they can create direct procurement accounts with suppliers like Dell or Staples through which company buyers can purchase equipment, materials, and supplies.

B-to-B marketers can help customers who wish to purchase online by creating well designed, easy-to-use websites. For example, *BtoB* magazine regularly rates Hewlett-Packard's B-to-B website among very best.

The HP site consists of some 1,900 site areas and 2.5 million pages. It integrates an enormous amount of product and company information, putting it within only a few mouse clicks of customers' computers. IT buying-decision makers can enter the site, click directly into their customer segment – large enterprise business; small or medium business; or government, health, or educational institution – and quickly find product overviews, detailed technical information, and purchasing solutions. The site lets customers create customized catalogs for frequently purchased products, set up automatic approval routing for orders, and conduct end-to-end transaction processing. To build deeper, more personalized online relationships with customers, HP.com features flash demos that show how to use the site, e-newsletters, live chats with sales reps, online classes, and real-time customer support. The site has really paid off. Roughly 55 per cent of the company's total sales now come from the website.[26]

E-procurement gives buyers access to new suppliers, lowers purchasing costs, and hastens order processing and delivery. In turn, business marketers can connect with customers online to share marketing information, sell products and services, provide customer support services and maintain ongoing customer relationships.

So far, most of the products bought online are MRO materials – maintenance, repair and operations. For instance, the London Borough of Barnet purchases everything from chickens to lightbulbs over the Internet. National Semiconductor has automated almost all of the company's 3,500 monthly requisitions to buy materials ranging from the sterile booties worn in its fabrication plants to state-of-the-art software. General Electric, one of the world's biggest purchasers, plans to be buying *all* of its general operating and industrial supplies online within the next few years.

The actual amount of money spent on these types of MRO materials pales in comparison with the amount spent for items such as aircraft parts, computer systems and steel tubing. Yet, MRO materials make up 80 per cent of all business orders and the transaction costs for order processing are high. Thus, companies have much to gain by streamlining the MRO buying process on the Web.

Business-to-business e-procurement yields many benefits. First, it shaves transaction costs and results in more efficient purchasing for both buyers and suppliers. A Web-powered purchasing program eliminates the paperwork associated with traditional requisition and ordering procedures. One recent study found that e-procurement cuts down requisition-to-order costs by an average of 58 per cent.[27]

E-procurement reduces the time between order and delivery. Time savings are particularly dramatic for companies with many overseas suppliers. Adaptec, a leading supplier of computer storage, used an extranet to tie all of its Taiwanese chip suppliers together in a kind of virtual family. Now messages from Adaptec flow in seconds from its headquarters to its Asian partners, and Adaptec has reduced the time between the order and delivery of its chips from as long as 16 weeks to just 55 days – the same turnaround time for companies that build their own chips.

Finally, beyond the cost and time savings, e-procurement frees purchasing people to focus on more strategic issues. For many purchasing professionals, going online means reducing drudgery and paperwork, and spending more time managing inventory and working creatively with suppliers. 'That is the key,' says the H-P executive. 'You can now focus people on value-added activities. Procurement professionals can now find different sources and work with suppliers to reduce costs and to develop new products.'[28]

The rapidly expanding use of e-purchasing, however, also presents some problems. For example, at the same time as the Web makes it possible for suppliers and customers to share business data and even collaborate on product design, it can also erode decades-old customer–supplier relationships. Many firms are using the Web to search for better suppliers.

E-purchasing can also create potential security disasters. Although email and home banking transactions can be protected through basic encryption, the secure environment that businesses need to carry out confidential interactions is often still lacking. Companies are spending millions for research on defensive strategies to keep hackers at bay. Cisco Systems, for example, specifies the types of routers, firewalls and security procedures that its partners must use to safeguard extranet connections. In fact, the company goes even further – it sends its own security engineers to examine a partner's defences and holds the partner liable for any security breach that originates from its computer.

THE JOURNEY YOU'VE TAKEN Reviewing the concepts

This chapter is the last of three chapters that address understanding the marketplace and consumers. Here, we've looked closely at consumers and their buying behaviour. The European Union consumer market consists of around 500 million people who consume many trillions of euros' worth of goods and services each year. The business market involves far more euros and items than the consumer market. Final consumers and business buyers vary greatly in their characteristics and circumstances. Understanding *consumer* and *business buyer behaviour* is one of the biggest challenges marketers face.

1 Describe the consumer market and the major factors that influence consumer buyer behaviour.

The *consumer market* consists of all the individuals and households who buy or acquire goods and services for personal consumption. A simple stimulus-response model of consumer behaviour suggests that marketing stimuli and other major forces enter the consumer's 'black box'. This black box has two parts: buyer characteristics and the buyer's decision process. Once in the black box, the inputs result in observable buyer responses, such as product choice, brand choice, dealer choice, purchase timing and purchase amount.

Consumer buyer behaviour is influenced by four key sets of buyer characteristics: cultural, social, personal and psychological. Understanding these factors can help marketers to identify interested buyers and to shape products and appeals to serve consumer needs better. *Culture* is the most basic determinant of a person's wants and behaviour. People in different cultural, sub-cultural and social class groups have different product and brand preferences. *Social factors* – such as small group and family influences – strongly affect product and brand choices, as do *personal characteristics*, such as age, life-cycle stage, occupation, economic circumstances, lifestyle and personality. Finally, consumer buying behaviour is influenced by four major sets of *psychological factors* – motivation, perception, learning, and beliefs and attitudes. Each of these factors provides a different perspective for understanding the workings of the buyer's black box.

2 Identify and discuss the stages in the buyer decision process.

When making a purchase, the buyer goes through a decision process consisting of need recognition, information search, evaluation of alternatives, purchase decision and post-purchase behaviour. During *need recognition*, the consumer recognises a problem or need that could be satisfied by a product or service. Once the need is recognised, the consumer moves into the *information search* stage. With information in hand, the consumer proceeds to *alternative evaluation* and assesses brands in the choice set. From there, the consumer makes a *purchase decision* and actually buys the product. In the final stage of the buyer decision process, *post-purchase behaviour*, the consumer takes action based on satisfaction or dissatisfaction. The marketer's job is to understand the buyer's behaviour at each stage and the influences that are operating.

3 Describe the adoption and diffusion process for new products.

The product *adoption process* comprises five stages: awareness, interest, evaluation, trial and adoption. New product marketers must think about how to help consumers move through these stages. With regard to the *diffusion process* for new products, consumers respond at different rates, depending on consumer and product characteristics. Consumers may be innovators, early adopters, early majority, late majority or laggards. Each group may require different marketing approaches. Marketers often try to bring their new products to the attention of potential early adopters, especially those who are opinion leaders.

4 Define the business market and identify the major factors that influence business buyer behaviour.

The *business market* comprises all organisations that buy goods and services for use in the production of other products and services or for the purpose of reselling or renting them to others at a profit. As compared to consumer markets, business markets usually have fewer, larger buyers who are more geographically concentrated. Business demand is derived demand, and the business buying decision usually involves more, and more professional, buyers.

Business buyers make decisions that vary with the three types of *buying situations*: straight rebuys, modified rebuys and new tasks. The decision-making unit of a buying organisation – the *buying centre* – can consist of many different persons playing many different roles. The business marketer needs to know the following: Who are the major buying centre participants? In what decisions do they exercise influence and to what degree? What evaluation criteria does each decision participant use? The business marketer also needs to understand the major environmental, organisational, interpersonal and individual influences on the buying process.

5 List and define the steps in the business buying decision process.

The *business buying decision process* itself can be quite involved, with eight basic stages: problem recognition, general need description, product specification, supplier search, proposal solicitation, supplier selection, order-routine specification and performance review. Buyers who face a new task buying situation usually go through all stages of the buying process. Buyers making modified or straight rebuys may skip some of the stages. Companies must manage the overall customer relationship, which often includes many different buying decisions in various stages of the buying decision process.

Recent advances in information technology have given birth to 'e-purchasing', by which business buyers are purchasing all kinds of products and services electronically, either through electronic data interchange links (EDI) or on the Internet. Such cyberbuying gives buyers access to new suppliers, lowers purchasing costs, and hastens order processing and delivery. However, it can also erode customer–supplier relationships and create potential security problems. Still, business marketers are increasingly connecting with customers online to share marketing information, sell products and services provide customer support services and maintain ongoing customer relationships.

NAVIGATING THE KEY TERMS

Adoption process	Groups	Perception
Business buyer behaviour	Learning	Personality
Buying centre	Lifestyle	Social classes
Cognitive dissonance	Modified rebuy	Straight rebuy
Consumer buyer behaviour	Motive (or drive)	Subculture
Consumer market	New product	Systems selling
Culture	New task	Value analysis
Derived demand	Opinion leaders	

NOTES AND REFERENCES

1 World POPClock, US Census Bureau, www.census.gov, July 2005. This website provides continuously updated projections of the US and world populations.

2 Brad Weiners, 'Getting Inside – Way Inside – Your Customer's Head', *Business 2.0*, April 2003, pp. 54–5.

3 Dawn Burton, 'Incorporating ethnicity into marketing intelligence and planning', *Marketing Intelligence and Planning*, **20**(7), 2002, pp. 442–51. Ahmad Jamal, 'Marketing in a multicultural world: The interplay of marketing, ethnicity and consumption', *European Journal of Marketing*, **37**(11/12), 2003, pp. 1599–620.

4 See Peter Francese, 'Older and Wealthier', *American Demographics*, November 2002, pp. 40–1; Alison Stein Wellner, 'The Next 25 Years', *American Demographics*, April 2003, pp. 24–7; and information accessed at www.census.gov, April 2005.

5 See D. Allen Kerr, 'Where There's Gray, There's Green', *Marketing News*, 25 May 1998, p. 2; Laura Petrecca, 'Savvy, Aging Boomers Buy into Pharma Mantra', *Advertising Age*, 8 July 2002, pp. S8–S9; Peter Francese, 'Consumers Today', *American Demographics*, April 2003, pp. 28–9; and Robin Goldwyn Blumenthal, 'Gray Is Good', *Barron's*, 22 March 2004, p. 37.

6 See Edward Keller and Jonathan Berry, *The Influentials* (New York, NY: The Free Press, 2003); John Battelle, 'The Net of Influence', *Business 2.0*, March 2004, p. 70; Alicia Clegg, 'Following the Leaders', *Marketing Week*, 30 September 2004, pp. 47–9; Ronald E. Goldsmith, 'The Influentials', *Journal of Product & Brand Management*, 2005, pp. 371–2; and Matthew Creamer, 'Study: Go Traditional to Influence Influencers', *Advertising Age*, 7 March 2005, p. 8.

7 L. Benedictus, 'Psst! Have you heard?' *The Guardian*, 30 January 2007. Copyright Guardian News and Media Ltd 2007.

8 See Sharon Goldman Edry, 'No Longer Just Fun and Games', *American Demographics*, May 2001, pp. 36–8; Hillary Chura, 'Marketing Messages for Women Fall Short', *Advertising Age*, 23 September 2002, pp. 4, 14–15; and Pallavi Gogoi, 'I Am Woman, Hear Me Shop', *BusinessWeek Online*, 14 February 2005, accessed at www.bwonline.com.

9 See Johneen Manning, 'Female Em-POWER-Ing Tools, Handywomen Rejoice!', GFKA.com, November 2003; Allen P. Roberts Jr, 'Barbara K: How I Did It. With Great Power Tools Comes Great Responsibility', *Inc.*, May 2005, pp. 112–14; and information accessed at www.barbarak.com, July 2005.

10 Tobi Elkin, 'Sony Marketing Aims at Lifestyle Segments', *Advertising Age*, 18 March 2002, pp. 3, 72; and Kenneth Hein, 'When Is Enough Enough?', *Brandweek*, 2 December 2002, pp. 26–8.

11 T. Kesic and S. Piri-Rajh, 'Market segmentation on the basis of food-related lifestyles of Croatian Families', *British Food Journal*, **105**(3), 2003, pp. 162–74.

12 Information accessed at www.forrester.com/Data/ConsumerTechno, July 2005; and Colin Chung, 'Quantitative Research Approach to Understanding How Consumers Adopt Technology-Related Products and Services', accessed at www.onetooneinteractive.com/advisor_chung.html, July 2005.

13 Jennifer Aaker, 'Dimensions of Measuring Brand Personality', *Journal of Marketing Research*, August 1997, pp. 347–56. See also Aaker, 'The Malleable Self: The Role of Self Expression in Persuasion', *Journal of Marketing Research*, May 1999, pp. 45–57; and Audrey Azoulay and Jean-Noel Kapferer, 'Do Brand Personality Scales Really Measure Brand Personality?', *Journal of Brand Management*, November 2003, p. 143.

14 Annetta Miller and Dody Tsiantar, 'Psyching Out Consumers', *Newsweek*, 27 February 1989, pp. 46–7. See also Alison Stein Wellner, 'Research on a Shoestring,' *American Demographics*, April 2001, pp. 38–9; and Leon G. Schiffman and Leslie L. Kanuk, *Consumer Behaviour*, 8th edn (Upper Saddle River, NJ: Prentice Hall, 2004), chapter 4.

15 See Abraham H. Maslow, 'A Theory of Human Motivation', *Psychological Review*, 50 (1943), pp. 370–96. See also Maslow, *Motivation and Personality*, 3rd edn (New York: HarperCollins Publishers, 1987); and Barbara Marx Hubbard, 'Seeking Our Future Potentials', *The Futurist*, May 1998, pp. 29–32.

16 Charles Pappas, 'Ad Nauseam', *Advertising Age*, 10 July 2000, pp. 16–18.

17 Bob Garfield, ' "Subliminal" Seduction and Other Urban Myths', *Advertising Age*, 18 September 2000, pp. 4, 105. See also 'We Have Ways of Making You Think', *Marketing Week*, 25 September 2003, p. 14; and Si Cantwell, 'Common Sense; Scrutiny Helps Catch Catchy Ads', *Wilmington Star-News*, 1 April 2004, p. 1B.

18 C. Sawers, 'Porridge is the new fast food', *The Scotsman*, 17 August 2005.

19 For a deeper discussion of the buyer decision process, see Philip Kotler and Kevin Lane Keller, *Marketing Management*, 12th edn (Upper Saddle River, NJ: Prentice Hall, 2006), pp. 191–203.

20 Duglas Pruden and Terry G. Vavra, 'Controlling the Grapevine', *Marketing Management*, July–August 2004, pp. 25–30.

21 See Leon Festinger, *A Theory of Cognitive Dissonance* (Stanford, CA: Stanford University Press, 1957); Schiffman and Kanuk, *Consumer Behaviour*, pp. 219–20; Patti Williams and Jennifer L. Aaker, 'Can Mixed Emotions Peacefully Coexist?', March 2002, pp. 636–49; Adam Ferrier, 'Young Are Not Marketing Savvy; They're Suckers', *B&T Weekly*, 22 October 2004, p. 13; and 'Cognitive Dissonance and the Stability of Service Quality Perceptions', *The Journal of Services Marketing*, 2004, pp. 433ff.

22 The following discussion draws from the work of Everett M. Rogers. See his *Diffusion of Innovations*, 5th edn (New York: Free Press, 2003). See also Eric Waarts, Yvonne M. van Everdingen and Jos van Hillegersberg, 'The Dynamics of Factors Affecting the Adoption of Innovations', *The Journal of Product Innovation Management*, November 2002, pp. 412–23; Chaun-Fong Shih and Alladi Venkatesh, 'Beyond Adoption: Development and Application of a Use-Diffusion Model', *Journal of Marketing*, January 2004, pp. 59–72; and Richard R. Nelson, Alexander Peterhansl and Bhaven Sampat, 'Why and How Innovations Get Adopted: A Tale of Four Models', *Industrial and Corporate Change*, October 2004, pp. 679–99.

23 Patrick J. Robinson, Charles W. Faris and Yoram Wind, *Industrial Buying Behaviour and Creative Marketing* (Boston: Allyn & Bacon, 1967). See also James C. Anderson and James A. Narus, *Business Market Management*, 2nd edn (Upper Saddle River, NJ: Prentice Hall, 2004), ch. 3.

24 Based on information from www.veoliaenvironnement.com.

25 Robinson, Faris and Wind, *Industrial Buying Behaviour*, p. 14.

26 Kate Maddox, '#1 Hewlett-Packard Co.: www.hp.com', *BtoB*, 11 August 2003, p. 1; and 'Great Web Sites: www.hp.com', *BtoB Online*, 13 September 2004, accessed at www.btobonline.com/article.cms?articleId=21878.

27 Demir Barlas, 'E-Procurement: Steady Value', *Line56.com*, 4 January 2005, accessed at www.line56.com.

28 Michael A. Verespej, 'E-Procurement Explosion', *Industry Week*, March 2002, pp. 25–8.

Essentials of Operations Management

Nigel Slack
Alistair Brandon-Jones
Robert Johnston

Chapter 1

Operations management

Key questions

➤ What is operations management?

➤ Why is operations management important in all types of organization?

➤ What is the input–transformation–output process?

➤ What is the process hierarchy?

➤ How do operations processes have different characteristics?

➤ What are the activities of operations management?

Introduction

Operations management is about how organizations design, deliver, and improve services and products for their customers. Everything you wear, eat, sit on, use, read or knock about on the sports field comes to you courtesy of the operations managers who organized its creation. Every book you borrow from the library, every treatment you receive at the hospital, every service you expect in the shops and every lecture you attend at university – all have been created. While the people who supervised their creation may not always be called operations managers, that is what they really are. And that is what this book is concerned with – the tasks, issues and decisions of those operations managers who have made the services and products on which we all depend. This is an introductory chapter, so we will examine what we mean by 'operations management', how operations processes can be found everywhere, how they are all similar yet different, and what it is that operations managers do.

Operations in practice IKEA[1]

(All chapters start with an 'Operations in practice' example that illustrates some of the issues that will be covered in the chapter.)

Love it or hate it, IKEA is the most successful furniture retailer ever. With 276 stores in 36 countries, it has managed to develop its own special way of selling furniture. The stores' layout means customers often spend two hours in the store – far longer than in rival furniture retailers. IKEA's philosophy goes back to the original business, started in the 1950s in Sweden by Ingvar Kamprad. He built a showroom on the outskirts of Stockholm where land was cheap and simply displayed suppliers' furniture as it would be in a domestic setting. Increasing sales soon allowed IKEA to start ordering its own self-designed products from local manufacturers. However, it was innovation in its operations that dramatically reduced its selling costs. These included the idea of selling furniture as self-assembly flat packs (which reduced production and transport costs) and its 'showroom–warehouse' concept which required customers to pick the furniture up themselves from the warehouse (which reduced retailing costs). Both of these operating principles are still the basis of IKEA's retail operations process today.

Stores are designed to facilitate the smooth flow of customers, from parking, moving through the store itself, to ordering and picking up products. At the entrance to each store large notice-boards provide advice to shoppers. For young children, there is a supervised children's play area, a small cinema, and a parent and baby room so parents can leave their children in the supervised play area for a time. Parents are recalled via the loudspeaker system if the child has any problems. IKEA 'allow customers to make up their minds in their own time' but 'information points' have staff who can help. All furniture carries a ticket with a code number which indicates its location in the warehouse. (For larger items, customers go to the information desks for assistance.) There is also an area where smaller items are displayed, and can be picked directly. Customers then pass through the warehouse where they pick up the items viewed in the showroom. Finally, customers pay at the checkouts, where a ramped conveyor belt moves purchases up to the checkout staff. The exit area has service points and a loading area that allows customers to bring their cars from the car park and load their purchases.

Behind the public face of IKEA's huge stores is a complex worldwide network of suppliers: 1,300 direct suppliers, about 10,000 sub-suppliers, wholesale and transport operations including 26 Distribution Centres. This supply network is vitally important to IKEA. From

Source: Alamy Images

purchasing raw materials, right through to finished products arriving in its customers' homes, IKEA relies on close partnerships with its suppliers to achieve both ongoing supply efficiency and new product development. However, IKEA closely controls all supply and development activities from IKEA's home town of Älmhult in Sweden.

However, success brings its own problems and some customers became increasingly frustrated with overcrowding and long waiting times. In response IKEA in the UK launched a £150 m programme to 'design out' the bottlenecks. The changes included:

- Clearly marked in-store short cuts allowing customers who just want to visit one area to avoid having to go through all the preceding areas.
- Express checkout tills for customers with a bag only rather than a trolley.
- Extra 'help staff' at key points to help customers.
- Redesign of the car parks, making them easier to navigate.
- Dropping the ban on taking trolleys out to the car parks for loading (originally implemented to stop vehicles being damaged).
- A new warehouse system to stop popular product lines running out during the day.
- More children's play areas.

IKEA spokeswoman Nicki Craddock said: *'We know people love our products but hate our shopping experience. We are being told that by customers every day, so we can't afford not to make changes. We realized a lot of people took offence at being herded like sheep on the long route around stores. Now if you know what you are looking for and just want to get in, grab it and get out, you can.'*

Operations management is a vital part of IKEA's success

IKEA shows how important operations management is for its own success and the success of any type of organization. Of course, IKEA understands its market and its customers. Just as important, it knows that the way it manages the network of operations that design, produce and deliver its products and services must be right for its market. No organization can survive in the long term if it cannot supply its customers effectively. This is essentially what operations management is about – designing, producing and delivering products and services that satisfy market requirements. For any business, it is a vitally important activity. Consider just some of the activities that IKEA's operations managers are involved in.

- Arranging the store's layout to give smooth and effective flow of customers (called process design).
- Designing stylish products that can be flat-packed efficiently (called product design).
- Making sure that all staff can contribute to the company's success (called job design).
- Locating stores of an appropriate size in the most effective place (called supply network design).
- Arranging for the delivery of products to stores (called supply chain management).

- Coping with fluctuations in demand (called capacity management).
- Maintaining cleanliness and safety of storage area (called failure prevention).
- Avoiding running out of products for sale (called inventory management).
- Monitoring and enhancing quality of service to customers (called quality management).
- Continually examining and improving operations practice (called operations improvement).

Importantly, these activities are only a small part of IKEA's total operations management effort. But they do give an indication, first of how operations management should contribute to the businesses success, and second, what would happen if IKEA's operations managers failed to be effective in carrying out any of its activities. Badly designed processes, inappropriate products, poor locations, disaffected staff, empty shelves, or forgetting the importance of continually improving quality, could all turn a previously successful organization into a failing one. Yet, although the relative importance of these activities will vary between different organizations, operations managers in all organizations will be making the same *type* of decision (even if *what* they actually decide is different).

What is operations management?

Operations management
Operations function

Operations management is the activity of managing the resources which create and deliver services and products. The **operations function** is the part of the organization that is responsible for this activity. Every organization has an operations function because every organization produces some type of services and/or products. However, not all types of organization will necessarily call the operations function by this name. (Note that we also use the shorter terms 'the operation' and 'operations' interchangeably with the 'operations function'.) **Operations**

Operations managers

managers are the people who have particular responsibility for managing some, or all, of the resources which comprise the operations function. Again, in some organizations the operations manager could be called by some other name. For example, he or she might be called the 'fleet manager' in a distribution company, the 'administrative manager' in a hospital or the 'store manager' in a supermarket.

Operations in the organization

Three core functions

The operations function is central to the organization because it creates the services and products which are its reason for existing, but it is not the only function. It is, however, one of the **three core functions** of any organization. These are:

- the marketing (including sales) function – which is responsible for *communicating* the organization's services and products (or more generically, offerings) to its markets in order to generate customer requests for service;

- the service/product development function – which is responsible for developing new and modified offerings in order to generate future customer requests for service;
- the operations function – which is responsible for *fulfilling* customer requests for service through the creation and delivery of services and products.

Support functions

In addition, there are the **support functions** which enable the core functions to operate effectively. These include, for example:

- the accounting and finance function – which provides the information to help economic decision-making and manages the financial resources of the organization;
- the human resources function – which recruits and develops the organization's staff as well as looking after their welfare.

Remember that different organizations will call their various functions by different names and will have a different set of support functions. Almost all organizations, however, will have the three core functions, because all organizations have a fundamental need to sell their services, satisfy their customers and create the means to satisfy customers in the future. Table 1.1 shows the activities of the three core functions for a sample of organizations.

In practice, there is not always a clear division between the three core functions or between core and support functions. This leads to some confusion over where the boundaries of the operations function should be drawn. In this book we use a relatively **broad definition of operations**. We treat much of the product/service development, technical and information systems activities and some of the human resource, marketing and accounting and finance activities as coming within the sphere of operations management. We view the operations function as comprising all the activities necessary for the day-to-day fulfilment of customer requests. This includes sourcing services and products from suppliers and transporting them to customers.

Broad definition of operations

Working effectively with the other parts of the organization is one of the most important responsibilities of operations management. It is a fundamental of modern management that functional boundaries should not hinder efficient internal processes. Figure 1.1 illustrates some of the relationships between operations and some other functions in terms of the flow of information between them. Although it is not comprehensive, it gives an idea of the nature of each relationship.

Table 1.1 The activities of core functions in some organizations

Core functional activities	Internet service provider (ISP)	Fast food chain	International aid charity	Furniture manufacturer
Marketing and sales	Promote services to users and get registrations Sell advertising space	Advertise on TV Devise promotional materials	Develop funding contracts Mail out appeals for donations	Advertise in magazines Determine pricing policy Sell to stores
Product/service development	Devise new services and commission new information content	Design hamburgers, pizzas, etc. Design décor for restaurants	Develop new appeals campaigns Design new assistance programmes	Design new furniture Coordinate with fashionable colours
Operations	Maintain hardware, software and content Implement new links and services	Make burgers, pizzas etc. Serve customers Clear away Maintain equipment	Give service to the beneficiaries of the charity	Make components Assemble furniture

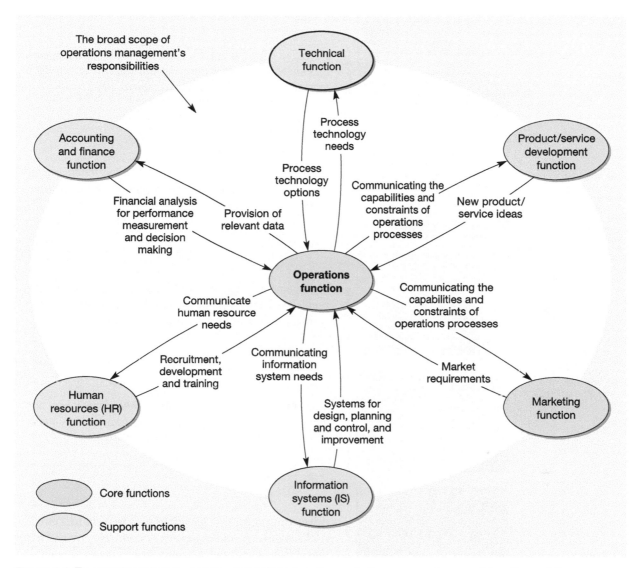

Figure 1.1 The relationship between the operations function and other core and support functions of the organization

Operations management is important in all types of organization

In some types of organization it is relatively easy to visualize the operations function and what it does, even if we have never seen it. For example, most people have seen images of automobile assembly. But what about an advertising agency? We know vaguely what they do – they produce the advertisements that we see in magazines and on television – but what is their operations function? The clue lies in the word 'produce'. Any business that produces something must use resources to do so, and so must have an operations activity. So, the advertising agency and the automobile plant have one important element in common: both have a higher objective – to make a profit from creating and delivering their services or products. Yet not-for-profit organizations also use their resources to produce services, not to make a profit, but to serve society in some way. Look at the following examples of what operations management does in five very different organizations and some common themes emerge.

Physician (general practitioner) – *Operations management uses knowledge to effectively diagnose conditions in order to treat real and perceived patient concerns*

Automobile assembly factory – *Operations management uses machines to efficiently assemble products that satisfy current customer demands*

Management consultant – *Operations management uses people to effectively create the services that will address current and potential client needs*

Disaster relief charity – *Operations management uses our and our partners' resources to speedily provide the supplies and services that relieve community suffering*

Advertising agency – *Operations management uses our staff's knowledge and experience to creatively present ideas that delight clients and address their real needs*

Whatever terminology is used there is a common theme and a common purpose to how we can visualize the operations activity in any type of organization: small or large, manufacturing or service, public or private, profit or not-for-profit. Operations management uses *resources* to *appropriately create outputs* that *fulfil defined market requirements*. See Figure 1.2. However, although the essential nature and purpose of operations management is the same in every type of organization, there are some special issues to consider, particularly in smaller organizations and those whose purpose is to maximize something other than profit.

Operations management in the smaller organization

Irrespective of their size, all companies need to produce and deliver their products and services efficiently and effectively. However, managing operations in a small or medium-size organization has its own set of problems. Large companies may have the resources to dedicate individuals to specialized tasks, but smaller companies often cannot, so people may have to do different jobs as the need arises. Such an informality may allow a quick response as opportunities present themselves. But decision-making can also become confused as **individuals' roles can overlap in small operations**. However, small operations can also have significant advantages; the short case on Acme Whistles illustrates this.

The role of operations management in smaller organizations often overlaps significantly with other functions

Operations management uses . . .

resources	to	appropriately	create produce	outputs	that	fulfil	defined	market	requirements
			change				potential	citizens'	
experience									
people		effectively	sell	ideas		match	perceived	client	dreams
machines		efficiently	assemble	products		satisfy	current	customer	demands
knowledge		creatively	move	services		exceed	emerging	society	needs
partners		etc.	cure	etc.		delight	real	etc.	concerns
etc.			shape			etc.	etc.		etc.
			etc.						

Figure 1.2 Operations management uses resources to appropriately create outputs that fulfil defined market requirements

Short case
Acme Whistles[2]

Source: Simon Topman/Acme Whistles

Acme Whistles can trace its history back to 1870 when Joseph Hudson decided he had the answer to the London Metropolitan Police's request for something to replace the wooden rattles that were used to sound the alarm. So the world's first police whistle was born. Soon Acme grew to be the premier supplier of whistles for police forces around the world. *'In many ways'*, says Simon Topman, owner and Managing Director of the company, *'the company is very much the same as it was in Joseph's day. The machinery is more modern, of course, and we have a wider variety of products, but many of our products are similar to their predecessors. For example, football referees seem to prefer the traditional snail-shaped whistle. So, although we have dramatically improved the performance of the product, our customers want it to look the same. We have also maintained the same manufacturing tradition from those early days. The original owner insisted on personally blowing every single whistle before it left the factory. We still do the same, not by personally blowing them, but by using an air line, so the same tradition of quality has endured.'*

The company's range of whistles has expanded to include sports whistles (they provide the whistles for the soccer World Cup), distress whistles, (silent) dog whistles, novelty whistles, instrumental whistles (used by all of the world's top orchestras), and many more types. *'We are always trying to improve our products'*, says Simon, *'it's a business of constant innovation. Sometimes I think that after 130 years surely there is nothing more to do, but we always find some new feature to incorporate. Of course, managing the operations in a small company is very different to working in a large one. Everyone has much broader jobs; we cannot afford the overheads of having specialist people* in specialized roles. But this relative informality has a lot of advantages. It means that we can maintain our philosophy of quality amongst everybody in the company, and it means that we can react very quickly when the market demands it.' Nor is the company's small size any barrier to its ability to innovate. *'On the contrary'*, says Simon, *'there is something about the culture of the company that is extremely important in fostering innovation. Because we are small we all know each other and we all want to contribute something to the company. It is not uncommon for employees to figure out new ideas for different types of whistle. If an idea looks promising, we will put a small and informal team together to look at it further. It is not unusual for people who have been with us only a few months to start wanting to make innovations. It's as though something happens to them when they walk through the door of the factory that encourages their natural inventiveness.'*

Operations management in not-for-profit organizations

Terms such as *competitive advantage*, *markets* and *business*, which are used in this book, are usually associated with companies in the for-profit sector. Yet operations management is also relevant to organizations whose purpose is not primarily to earn profits. Managing the operations in an animal welfare charity, hospital, research organization or government department is essentially the same as in commercial organizations. **Operations have to take the same decisions** – how to create services and products, invest in technology, contract out some of their activities, devise performance measures, and improve their operations performance and so on. However, the strategic objectives of not-for-profit organizations may be more complex and involve a mixture of political, economic, social and environmental objectives. Nevertheless, the vast majority of the topics covered in this book have relevance to all types of organization, including non-profit, even if some terms may have to be adapted.

Operations decisions are the same in commercial and not-for-profit organizations

Short case
Oxfam International[3]

Oxfam International is a confederation of 13 like-minded organizations based around the world that, together with partners and allies, work directly with communities seeking to ensure that poor people can improve their lives and livelihoods and have a say in decisions that affect them. With an annual expenditure that exceeds US$700 million, Oxfam International focuses its efforts in several areas, including development work, long-term programmes to eradicate poverty and combat injustice, emergency relief delivering immediate life-saving assistance to people affected by natural disasters or conflict, helping to build their resilience to future disasters, campaigning and raising public awareness of the causes of poverty, encouraging ordinary people to take action for a fairer world, and advocacy and research that pressures decision-makers to change policies and practices that reinforce poverty and injustice.

All of Oxfam International's activities depend on effective and professional operations management. For example, Oxfam's network of charity shops, run by volunteers, is a key source of income. The shops sell donated items and handcrafts from around the world giving small-scale producers fair prices, training, advice and funding. Supply chain management and development is just as central to the running of these shops as it is to the biggest commercial chain of stores. The operations challenges involved in Oxfam's ongoing 'Clean Water' exercise are different but certainly no less important. Around 80 per cent of diseases and over one-third of deaths in the developing world are caused by contaminated water and Oxfam has a particular expertise in providing clean water and sanitation facilities. The better their coordinated efforts of identifying potential projects, working with local communities, providing help and education and helping to provide civil engineering expertise, the more effective Oxfam is at fulfilling its objectives.

Source: Rex Features

More dramatically, Oxfam International's response to emergency situations, providing humanitarian aid where it is needed, must be fast, appropriate and efficient. Whether the disasters are natural or political, they become emergencies when the people involved can no longer cope. In such situations, Oxfam, through its network of staff in local offices, is able to advise on what and where help is needed. Indeed, local teams are often able to provide warnings of impending disasters, giving more time to assess needs and coordinate a multi-agency response. The organization's headquarters in Oxford in the UK provides advice, materials and staff, often deploying emergency support staff on short-term assignments. Shelters, blankets and clothing can be flown out at short notice from the Emergencies Warehouse. Engineers and sanitation equipment can also be provided, including water tanks, latrines, hygiene kits and containers. When an emergency is over, Oxfam continues to work with the affected communities through their local offices to help people rebuild their lives and livelihoods. In an effort to improve the timeliness, effectiveness and appropriateness of its response to emergencies, Oxfam recently adopted a more systematic approach to evaluating the successes and failures of its humanitarian work. Real-time evaluations, which seek to assess and influence emergency response programmes in their early stages, were implemented during the response to floods in Mozambique and

South Asia, the earthquake in Peru, Hurricane Felix in Nicaragua and the conflicts in Uganda. These exercises provided Oxfam's humanitarian teams with the opportunity to gauge the effectiveness of their response, and make crucial adjustments at an early stage if necessary. The evaluations highlighted several potential improvements. For example, it became evident that there was a need to improve preparation ahead of emergencies, as well as the need to develop more

effective coordination planning tools. It was also decided that adopting a common working approach with shared standards would improve the effectiveness of their response to emergencies. Oxfam also emphasizes the importance of the role played by local partners in emergencies. They are often closer to, and more in tune with, affected communities, but may require additional support and empowerment to scale up their response and comply with the international humanitarian standards.

The new operations agenda

Modern business pressures have changed the operations agenda

The business environment has a significant impact on what is expected from operations management. In recent years there have been new pressures for which the operations function has needed to develop responses. Table 1.2 lists some of these **business pressures** and the operations responses to them. These operations responses form a major part of a *new agenda* for operations. Parts of this agenda are trends which have always existed but have accelerated, such as globalization and increased cost pressures. Part of the agenda involves seeking ways to exploit new technologies, most notably the Internet. Of course, the list in Table 1.2 is not comprehensive, nor is it universal. But very few businesses will be unaffected by at least some of these concerns. When businesses have to cope with a more challenging environment, they look to their operations function to help them respond.

Table 1.2 Changes in the business environment are shaping a new operations agenda

The business environment is changing . . .	*Prompting operations responses . . .*
For example, • Increased cost-based competition • Higher quality expectations • Demands for better service • More choice and variety • Rapidly developing technologies • Frequent new product/service introduction • Increased ethical sensitivity • Environmental impacts are more transparent • More legal regulation • Greater security awareness	For example, • Globalization of operations networking • Information-based technologies • Internet-based integration of operations activities • Supply chain management • Customer relationship management • Flexible working patterns • Mass customization • Fast time-to-market methods • Lean process design • Environmentally sensitive design • Supplier 'partnership' and development • Failure analysis • Business recovery planning

The input–transformation–output process

Transformation process model

Input resources

Outputs of services and products

All operations create services and products by changing *inputs* into *outputs* using an 'input-transformation-output' process. Figure 1.3 shows this general **transformation process model**. Put simply, operations are processes that take in a set of **input resources** which are used to transform something, or are transformed themselves, into **outputs of services and products**. Although all operations conform to this general input–transformation–output

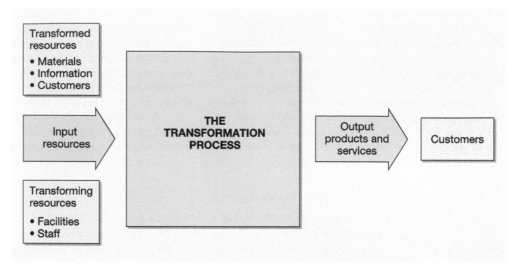

Figure 1.3 All operations are input–transformation–output processes

model, they differ in the nature of their specific inputs and outputs. For example, if you stand far enough away from a hospital or a car plant, they might look very similar, but move closer and clear differences do start to emerge. One is a service operation, creating and delivering services that change the physiological or psychological condition of patients; the other is a manufacturing operation producing products. What is inside each operation will also be different. The motor vehicle plant contains metal-forming machinery and assembly processes, whereas the hospital contains diagnostic, care and therapeutic processes. Perhaps the most important difference between the two operations, however, is the nature of their inputs. The vehicle plant transforms steel, plastic, cloth, tyres and other materials into vehicles. The hospital transforms the customers themselves. The patients form part of the input to, and the output from, the operation. This has important implications for how the operation needs to be managed.

Inputs to the process

Transformed resources   One set of inputs to any operation's processes are **transformed resources**. These are the resources that are treated, transformed or converted in the process. They are usually a mixture of the following:

- **Customers** – operations which process customers might change their *physical properties* in a similar way to materials processors: for example, hairdressers or cosmetic surgeons. Some *store* (or more politely *accommodate*) customers: hotels, for example. Airlines, mass rapid transport systems and bus companies transform the *location* of their customers, while hospitals transform their *physiological state*. Some are concerned with transforming their *psychological state*, for example most entertainment services such as music, theatre, television, radio and theme parks.
- **Materials** – operations which process materials could do so to transform their *physical properties* (shape or composition, for example). Most manufacturing operations are like this. Other operations process materials to change their *location* (parcel delivery companies, for example). Some, like retail operations, do so to change the *possession* of the materials. Finally, some operations *store* materials, such as in warehouses.
- **Information** – operations which process information could do so to transform their *informational properties* (that is the purpose or form of the information); accountants do this. Some change the *possession* of the information, for example market research

Table 1.3 Dominant transformed resource inputs of various operations

Predominantly processing inputs of customers	Predominantly processing inputs of materials	Predominantly processing inputs of information
Hairdressers	All manufacturing operations	Accountants
Hotels	Mining companies	Bank headquarters
Hospitals	Retail operations	Market research company
Mass rapid transport	Warehouses	Financial analysts
Theatres	Postal services	News service
Theme parks	Container shipping line	University research unit
Dentists	Trucking companies	Telecoms company

companies sell information. Some *store* the information, for example archives and libraries. Finally, some operations, such as telecommunication companies, change the *location* of the information.

Often one of these is dominant in an operation. For example, a bank devotes part of its energies to producing printed statements of accounts for its customers. In doing so, it is processing **inputs of material**, but no one would claim that a bank is a printer. The bank is also concerned with processing **inputs of customers**. It gives them advice regarding their financial affairs, cashes their cheques, deposits their cash and has direct contact with them. However, most of the bank's activities are concerned with processing **inputs of information** about its customers' financial affairs. As customers, we may be unhappy with badly printed statements and we may be unhappy if we are not treated appropriately in the bank. However, if the bank makes errors in our financial transactions, we suffer in a far more fundamental way. Table 1.3 gives examples of operations with their dominant transformed resources.

The other set of inputs to any operations process are **transforming resources**. These are the resources which act upon the transformed resources. There are two types which form the 'building blocks' of all operations:

- **facilities** – the buildings, equipment, plant and process technology of the operation;
- **staff** – the people who operate, maintain, plan and manage the operation. (Note that we use the term 'staff' to describe all the people in the operation, at any level.)

The exact nature of both facilities and staff will differ between operations. To a five-star hotel, its facilities consist mainly of 'low-tech' buildings, furniture and fittings. To a nuclear-powered aircraft carrier, its facilities are 'high-tech' nuclear generators and sophisticated electronic equipment. Staff will also differ between operations. Most staff employed in a factory assembling domestic refrigerators may not need a very high level of technical skill. In contrast, most staff employed by an accounting company are, hopefully, highly skilled in their own particular 'technical' skill (accounting). Yet although skills vary, all staff can make a contribution. An assembly worker who consistently misassembles refrigerators will dissatisfy customers and increase costs just as surely as an accountant who cannot add up. The balance between facilities and staff also varies. A computer chip manufacturing company, such as Intel, will have significant investment in physical facilities. A single chip fabrication plant can cost in excess of $4 billion, so operations managers will spend a lot of their time managing their facilities. Conversely, a management consultancy firm depends largely on the quality of its staff. Here operations management is largely concerned with the development and deployment of consultant skills and knowledge.

Outputs from the process

Some operations create and deliver just services and others just products, but most operations produce a mixture of the two. Figure 1.4 shows a number of operations (including some

<!-- margin notes -->
Material inputs
Customer inputs

Information inputs

Transforming resources

Facilities
Staff

'Pure' products

'Pure' service

Facilitating services

Facilitating products

described as examples in this chapter) positioned in a spectrum from **'pure' product** operations to **'pure' service** operations. Crude oil producers are concerned almost exclusively with the product which comes from their oil wells. So are aluminium smelters, but they might also produce some services such as technical advice. Services produced in these circumstances are called **facilitating services**. To an even greater extent, machine tool manufacturers produce facilitating services such as technical advice and applications engineering. The services produced by a restaurant are an essential part of what the customer is paying for. It is both a manufacturing operation which produces meals and a provider of service in the advice, ambience and service of the food. An information systems provider may produce software 'products', but primarily it is providing a service to its customers, with **facilitating products**. Certainly, a management consultancy, although it produces reports and documents, would see itself primarily as a service provider. Finally, pure services produce no products, a psychotherapy clinic, for example.

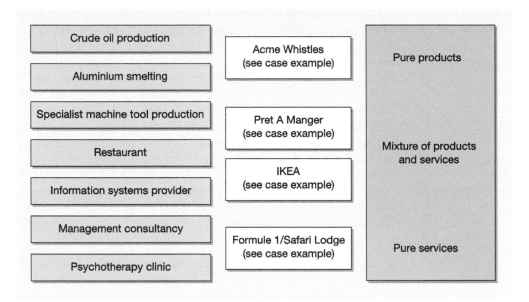

Figure 1.4 The output from most types of operation is a mixture of services and products

Services and products are merging

Increasingly, the distinction between services and products is both difficult to define and not particularly useful. Internet-based retailers, for example, are increasingly 'transporting' a larger proportion of their services into customers' homes. Even official statistics have difficulty in separating services and products. Software sold on a disc is classified as a product. The same software sold over the Internet is a service. Some authorities see the essential purpose of all operations processes as being to 'service customers'. Therefore, they argue, All operations are service providers **all operations are service providers** which may create and deliver products as a part of serving their customers.

Short case
Pret A Manger[4]

Source: Alamy Images

Described by the press as having *'revolutionized the concept of sandwich making and eating'*, Pret A Manger opened their first shop in the mid-1980s, in London. Now they have over 130 shops in UK, New York, Hong Kong and Tokyo. They say that their secret is to focus continually on quality – not just of their food, but in every aspect of their operations practice. They go to extraordinary lengths to avoid the chemicals and preservatives common in most 'fast' food, say the company. *'Many food retailers focus on extending the shelf life of their food, but that's of no interest to us. We maintain our edge by selling food that simply can't be beaten for freshness. At the end of the day, we give whatever we haven't sold to charity to help feed those who would otherwise go hungry. When we were just starting out, a big supplier tried to sell us coleslaw that lasted sixteen days. Can you imagine! Salad that lasts sixteen days? There and then we decided Pret would stick to wholesome fresh food – natural stuff. We have not changed that policy.'*

The first Pret A Manger shop had its own kitchen where fresh ingredients were delivered first thing every morning, and food was prepared throughout the day. Every Pret shop since has followed this model. The team members serving on the tills at lunchtime will have been making sandwiches in the kitchen that morning. The company rejected the idea of a huge centralized

sandwich factory even though it could significantly reduce costs. Pret also own and manage all their shops directly so that they can ensure consistently high standards in all their shops. *'We are determined never to forget that our hard-working people make all the difference. They are our heart and soul. When they care, our business is sound. If they cease to care, our business goes down the drain. In a retail sector where high staff turnover is normal, we're pleased to say our people are much more likely to stay around! We work hard at building great teams. We take our reward schemes and career opportunities very seriously. We don't work nights (generally), we wear jeans, we party!'* Customer feedback is regarded as being particularly important at Pret. Examining customers' comments for improvement ideas is a key part of weekly management meetings, and of the daily team briefs in each shop.

The processes hierarchy

Processes

Internal supplier
Internal customer

So far we have discussed operations management, and the input–transformation–output model, at the level of 'the operation'. For example, we have described 'the whistle factory', 'the sandwich shop', 'the disaster relief operation', and so on. Now look *inside* any of these operations. One will see that all operations consist of a collection of processes (though these processes may be called 'units' or 'departments') interconnecting with each other to form a network. Each process acts as a smaller version of the whole operation of which it forms a part, and transformed resources flow between them. In fact within any operation, the mechanisms that actually transform inputs into outputs are these **processes**. A process is 'an arrangement of resources that produce some mixture of products and services'. They are the 'building blocks' of all operations, and they form an 'internal network' within an operation. Each process is, at the same time, an **internal supplier** and an **internal customer** for other processes. This 'internal customer' concept provides a model to analyse the internal activities of an operation. It is also a useful reminder that, by treating internal customers with the same degree of care as external customers, the effectiveness of the whole operation can be improved. Table 1.4 illustrates how a wide range of operations can be described in this way.

Table 1.4 Some operations described in terms of their processes

Operation	Some of the operation's inputs	Some of the operation's processes	Some of the operation's outputs
Airline	Aircraft Pilots and air crew Ground crew Passengers and freight	Check passengers in Board passengers Fly passengers and freight around the world Care for passengers	Transported passengers and freight
Department store	Goods for sale Sales staff Information systems Customers	Source and store goods Display goods Give sales advice Sell goods	Customers and goods 'assembled' together
Police	Police officers Computer systems Information systems Public (law-abiding and criminals)	Crime prevention Crime detection Information gathering Detaining suspects	Lawful society, public with a feeling of security
Frozen food manufacturer	Fresh food Operators Processing technology Cold storage facilities	Source raw materials Prepare food Freeze food Pack and freeze food	Frozen food

Within each of these processes is another network of individual units of resource such as individual people and individual items of process technology (machines, computers, storage facilities, etc.). Again, transformed resources flow between each unit of transforming resource. So any business, or operation, is made up of a network of processes and any process is made up of a network of resources. In addition, any business or operation can itself be viewed as part of a greater network of businesses or operations. It will have operations that supply it with the products and services it needs and unless it deals directly with the end-consumer, it will supply customers who themselves may go on to supply their own customers. Moreover, any operation could have several suppliers and several customers and may be in competition with other operations producing similar services to those it

Supply network

Operations can be analysed at three levels

produces itself. This network of operations is called the **supply network**. In this way the input–transformation–output model can be used at a number of different 'levels of analysis'. Here we have used the idea to **analyse businesses at three levels**, the process, the operation and the supply network. One could define many different 'levels of analysis': moving upwards from small to larger processes, right up to the huge supply network that describes a whole industry.

Hierarchy of operations

This idea is called the **hierarchy of operations** and is illustrated for a business that makes television programmes and DVDs in Figure 1.5. It will have inputs of production, technical and administrative staff, cameras, lighting, sound and recording equipment, and so on. It transforms these into finished programmes, music, videos, etc. At a more macro level, the business itself is part of a whole supply network, acquiring services from creative agencies, casting agencies and studios, liaising with promotion agencies and serving its broadcasting company customers. At a more micro level, within this overall operation there are many individual processes: workshops manufacturing the sets; marketing processes that liaise with potential customers; maintenance and repair processes that care for, modify and design technical equipment; and so on. Each of these individual processes can be represented as a network of yet smaller processes, or even individual units of resource. So, the set manufacturing process could consist of four smaller processes: one that designs the sets, one that constructs them, one that acquires the props, and one that finishes (paints) the set.

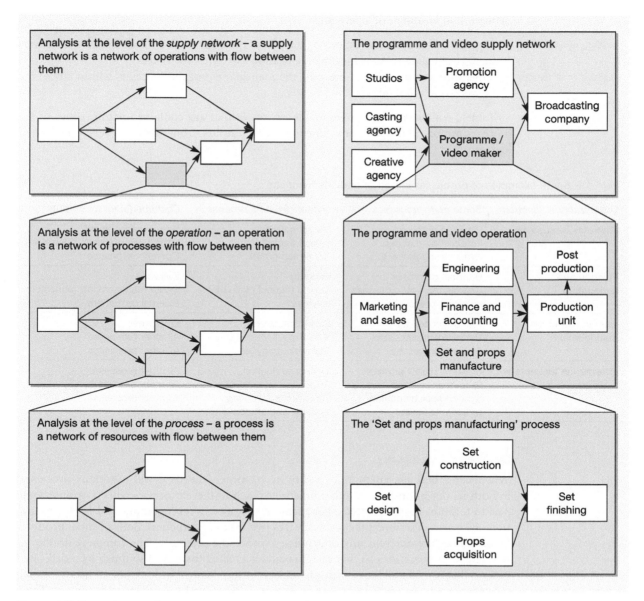

Figure 1.5 Operations and process management requires analysis at three levels: the supply network, the operation, and the process

Operations management is relevant to all parts of the business

All functions manage processes

The example in Figure 1.5 demonstrates that it is not just the operations function that manages processes; **all functions manage processes**. For example, the marketing function will have processes that create forecasts, create advertising campaigns and create marketing plans. These processes also need managing using principles similar to those within the operations function. Each function will have its 'technical' knowledge. In marketing, this is the expertise in designing and shaping marketing plans; in finance, it is the technical knowledge of financial reporting. Yet each will also have a 'process management' role of creating and delivering plans, policies, reports and services. The implications of this are very important. As all managers have some responsibility for managing processes, they are, to some extent, operations managers. They all should want to give good service to their (often internal) cus-

All managers, not just operations managers, manage processes

tomers, and they all will want to do this efficiently. So, **operations management is relevant for all functions**, and all managers should have something to learn from the principles, concepts, approaches and techniques of operations management. It also means that we must distinguish between two meanings of 'operations':

Operations as a function

- **'Operations' as a function**, meaning the part of the organization which creates and delivers the services and products for the organization's external customers;

Operations as an activity

- **'Operations' as an activity**, meaning the management of the processes within any of the organization's functions.

Table 1.5 illustrates just some of the processes that are contained within some of the more common non-operations functions, the outputs from these processes and their 'customers'.

Table 1.5 Some examples of processes in non-operations functions

Organizational function	Some of its processes	Outputs from its process	Customer(s) for its outputs
Marketing and sales	Planning process Forecasting process Order taking process	Marketing plans Sales forecasts Confirmed orders	Senior management Sales staff, planners, operations Operations, finance
Finance and accounting	Budgeting process Capital approval processes Invoicing processes	Budgets Capital request evaluations Invoices	Everyone Senior management, requesters External customers
Human resources management	Payroll processes Recruitment processes Training processes	Salary statements New hires Trained employees	Employees All other processes All other processes
Information technology	Systems review process Help desk process System implementation project processes	System evaluation Advice Implemented working systems and aftercare	All other processes All other processes All other processes

Business processes

Whenever a business attempts to satisfy its customers' needs it will use many processes, in both its operations and its other functions. Each of these processes will contribute some part to fulfilling customer needs. For example, the television programme and DVD production company, described previously, creates two types of 'product'. Both of these products involve a slightly different mix of processes within the company. The company decides to reorganize its operations so that each product is created from start to finish by a dedicated process that contains all the elements necessary for its production. So customer needs for each

'End-to-end' business processes

product are entirely fulfilled from within what is called an **'end-to-end' business process**. These often cut across conventional organizational boundaries. Reorganizing (or 're-engineering')

Business process re-engineering

process boundaries and organizational responsibilities around these business processes is the philosophy behind **business process re-engineering** (BPR).

Operations processes have different characteristics

Although all operations processes are similar in that they all transform inputs, they do differ in a number of ways, four of which, known as the four Vs, are particularly important:

Volume
Variety
Variation
Visibility

- The **volume** of their output;
- The **variety** of their output;
- The **variation** in the demand for their output;
- The degree of **visibility** which customers have of the production of their output.

The volume dimension

Repeatability
Systematization

Let us take a familiar example. The epitome of high-volume hamburger production is McDonald's, which serves millions of burgers around the world every day. Volume has important implications for the way McDonald's operations are organized. The first thing you notice is the **repeatability** of the tasks people are doing and the **systematization** of the work where standard procedures are set down specifying how each part of the job should be carried out. Also, because tasks are systematized and repeated, it is worthwhile developing specialized fryers and ovens. All this gives *low unit costs*. Now consider a small local cafeteria serving a few 'short-order' dishes. The range of items on the menu may be similar to the larger operation, but the volume will be far lower, so the repetition will also be far lower and the number of staff will be lower (possibly only one person) and therefore individual staff are likely to perform a wider range of tasks. This may be more rewarding for the staff, but less open to systematization. Also it is less feasible to invest in specialized equipment. So the cost per burger served is likely to be higher (even if the price is comparable).

The variety dimension

Standardized

A taxi company offers a high-variety service. It is prepared to pick you up from almost anywhere and drop you off almost anywhere. To offer this variety it must be relatively *flexible*. Drivers must have a good knowledge of the area, and communication between the base and the taxis must be effective. However, the cost per kilometre travelled will be higher for a taxi than for a less customized form of transport such as a bus service. Although both provide the same basic service (transportation), the taxi service has a high variety of routes and times to offer its customers, while the bus service has a few well-defined routes, with a set schedule. If all goes to schedule, little, if any, flexibility is required from the operation. All is **standardized** and regular, which results in relatively low costs compared with using a taxi for the same journey.

The variation dimension

Consider the demand pattern for a successful summer holiday resort hotel. Not surprisingly, more customers want to stay in summer vacation times than in the middle of winter. At the height of 'the season' the hotel could be full to its capacity. Off-season demand, however, could be a small fraction of its capacity. Such a marked variation in demand means that the operation must change its capacity in some way, for example, by hiring extra staff for the summer. The hotel must try to predict the likely level of demand. If it gets this wrong, it could result in too much or too little capacity. Also, recruitment costs, overtime costs and under-utilization of its rooms all have the effect of increasing the hotel's costs operation compared with a hotel of a similar standard with level demand. A hotel which has relatively level demand can plan its activities well in advance. Staff can be scheduled, food can be bought and rooms can be cleaned in a *routine* and *predictable* manner. This results in a high utilization of resources and unit costs which are likely to be lower than those in hotels with a highly variable demand pattern.

The visibility dimension

Visibility is a slightly more difficult dimension of operations to envisage. It refers to how much of the operation's activities its customers experience, or how much the operation is **exposed** to its customers. Generally, customer-processing operations are more exposed to their customers than material- or information-processing operations. But even customer-processing operations have some choice as to how visible they wish their operations to be. For example, a retailer could operate as a high-visibility 'bricks and mortar', or a lower-visibility web-based operation. In the 'bricks and mortar', high-visibility operation, customers will directly experience most of its 'value-adding' activities. Customers will have a relatively *short waiting tolerance*, and may walk out if not served in a reasonable time. Customers' perceptions, rather than objective criteria, will also be important. If they perceive that a member of the operation's staff is discourteous to them, they are likely to be dissatisfied (even if the staff member meant no discourtesy), so high-visibility operations require staff with good customer contact skills. Customers could also request goods which clearly would not be sold in such a shop, but because the customers are actually in the operation they can ask what they like! This is called **high received variety**. This makes it difficult for high-visibility operations to achieve high productivity of resources, so they tend to be relatively high-cost operations. Conversely, a web-based retailer, while not a pure low-contact operation, has far lower visibility. Behind its web site it can be more 'factory-like'. The *time lag* between the order being placed and the items ordered by the customer being retrieved and dispatched does not have to be minutes as in the shop, but can be hours or even days. This allows the tasks of finding the items, packing and dispatching them to be *standardized* by staff who need few **customer contact skills**. Also, there can be relatively *high staff utilization*. The web-based organization can also centralize its operation on one (physical) site, whereas the 'bricks and mortar' shop needs many shops close to centres of demand. Therefore, the low-visibility web-based operation will have lower costs than the shop.

Visibility means process exposure

High received variety

Customer contact skills

Short case
Two very different hotels

Formule 1

Hotels are high-contact operations – they are staff-intensive and have to cope with a range of customers, each with a variety of needs and expectations. So, how can a highly successful chain of affordable hotels avoid the costs of high customer contact? Formule 1, a subsidiary of the French Accor group, manages to offer outstanding value by adopting two principles not always associated with hotel operations – standardization and an innovative use of technology. Formule 1 hotels are usually located close to the roads, junctions and cities which make them visible and accessible to prospective customers. The hotels themselves are made from state-of-the-art volumetric prefabrications. The prefabricated units are arranged in various configurations to suit the characteristics of each individual site. All rooms are nine square metres in area, and are designed to be attractive, functional, comfortable and soundproof. Most importantly, they are designed to be easy to clean and maintain. All have the same fittings, including a double bed, an additional bunk-type bed, a wash basin, a storage area, a working table with seat, a wardrobe and a television set. The reception of a Formule 1 hotel is staffed only from

6.30 am to 10.00 am and from 5.00 pm to 10.00 pm. Outside these times an automatic machine sells rooms to credit card users, provides access to the hotel, dispenses a security code for the room and even prints a receipt. Technology is also evident in the washrooms. Showers and toilets are automatically cleaned after each use by using nozzles and heating elements to spray the room with a disinfectant solution and dry it before it is used again. To keep things even simpler, Formule 1 hotels do not include a restaurant as they are usually located near existing restaurants. However, a continental breakfast is available, usually between 6.30 am and 10.00 am, and of course on a 'self-service' basis!

Mwagusi Safari Lodge

The Mwagusi Safari Lodge lies within Tanzania's Ruaha National Park, a huge undeveloped wilderness, whose beautiful open landscape is especially good for seeing elephant, buffalo and lion. Nestled into a bank of the Mwagusi Sand River, this small exclusive tented camp overlooks a watering hole in the riverbed. Its ten tents are within thatched bandas (accommodation), each furnished comfortably in the traditional style of the camp. Each banda has an en-suite bathroom with flush toilet and a hot shower. Game viewing can be experienced even from the seclusion of the veranda. The sight of thousands of buffalo flooding the riverbed below the tents and dining room banda is not uncommon, and elephants, giraffes, and wild dogs are frequent uninvited guests to the site. There are two staff for each customer, allowing individual needs and preferences to be met quickly at all times. Guest numbers vary throughout the year, occupancy

being low in the rainy season from January to April, and full in the best game viewing period from September to November. There are game drives and walks throughout the area, each selected for customers' individual preferences. Drives are taken in specially adapted open-sided four-wheel-drive vehicles, equipped with reference books, photography equipment, medical kits and all the necessities for a day in the bush. Walking safaris, accompanied by an experienced guide can be customized for every visitor's requirements and abilities. Lunch can be taken communally, so that visitors can discuss their interests with other guides and managers. Dinner is often served under the stars in a secluded corner of the dry riverbed.

Mixed high- and low-visibility processes

Some operations have both high- and low-visibility processes within the same operation. In an airport, for example, some activities are totally 'visible' to its customers such as information desks answering people's queries. These staff operate in what is termed a **front-office** environment. Other parts of the airport have little, if any, customer 'visibility', such as the baggage handlers. These rarely-seen staff perform the vital but low-contact tasks, in the **back-office** part of the operation.

Front office

Back office

The implications of the four Vs of operations processes

All four dimensions have implications for the cost of creating services or products. Put simply, high volume, low variety, low variation and low customer contact all help to keep processing costs down. Conversely, low volume, high variety, high variation and high customer contact generally carry some kind of cost penalty for the operation. This is why the volume dimension is drawn with its 'low' end at the left, unlike the other dimensions, to keep all the 'low cost' implications on the right. To some extent the position of an operation in the **four dimensions** is determined by the demand of the market it is serving. However, most operations have some discretion in moving themselves on the dimensions. Figure 1.6 summarizes the implications of such positioning.

'Four Vs' analysis of processes

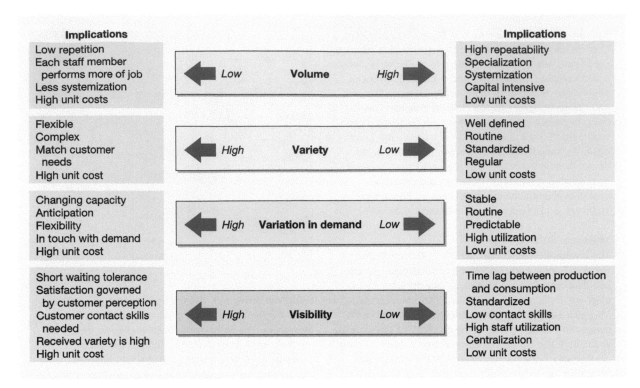

Figure 1.6 A typology of operations

> ## Worked example
>
> Figure 1.7 illustrates the different positions on the dimensions of the Formule 1 hotel chain and the Mwagusi Safari Lodge (*see* the short case on 'Two very different hotels'). Both provide the same basic service as any other hotel. However, one is of a small, intimate nature with relatively few customers. Its variety of services is almost infinite in the sense that customers can make individual requests in terms of food and entertainment. Variation is high and customer contact, and therefore visibility, is also very high (in order to ascertain customers' requirements and provide for them). All of this is very different from Formule 1, where volume is high (although not as high as in a large city-centre hotel), variety of service is strictly limited, and business and holiday customers use the hotel at different times, which limits variation. Most notably, though, customer contact is kept to a minimum. The Mwagusi Safari Lodge hotel has very high levels of service but provides them at a high cost. Conversely, Formule 1 has arranged its operation in such a way as to minimize its costs.

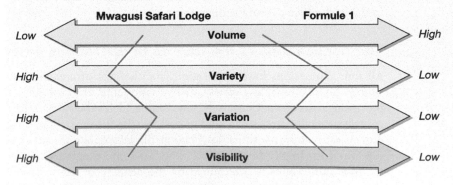

Figure 1.7 Profiles of two operations

The activities of operations management

Operations managers find themselves involved with many different activities within the organization. Many of these are cross-functional, involving managers from other parts of the organization, but other activities are seen as the prime responsibilities of operations managers specifically. These all begin with the letter D.

Directing the overall strategy of the operation. A general understanding of operations and their strategic purpose, together with an appreciation of how operations performance should be assessed is a prerequisite to managing any type of operations. This chapter, together with Chapters 2 and 3, are devoted to this set of activities.

Designing the operation's services, products and processes. Design is the activity of determining the physical form, shape and composition of operations and processes together with the products and services that they produce. Chapters 4–6 deal with these issues.

Delivering to customers. The ongoing creation of services and products must be managed, from choosing and controlling the suppliers of input resources right through to their delivery of products and services to customers. The activities involved in this ongoing delivery are examined in Chapters 7–11.

Developing process performance. Increasingly, it is recognized that for any operation or any process, managers cannot simply routinely deliver services and products in the same way that they always have done. They have a responsibility to develop the capabilities of their processes to improve process performance. These development responsibilities are looked at in Chapters 12 and 13.

The model of operations management

Operations activities define operations management and operations strategy

We can now combine two ideas to develop the model of operations management which will be used throughout this book. The first is the input–transformation–output model and the second is the categorization of operations management's activity areas. Figure 1.8 shows how these two ideas go together. The model now shows two interconnected loops of **activities**. The bottom one more or less corresponds to what is usually seen as operations management, and the top one to what is seen as operations strategy. This book concentrates on the former but tries to cover enough of the latter to allow the reader to make strategic sense of the operations manager's job.

Critical commentary

The central idea in this introductory chapter is that all organizations have operations processes which produce products and services and all these processes are essentially similar. However, some believe that by even trying to characterize processes in this way (perhaps even by calling them 'processes') one loses or distorts their nature, depersonalizes or takes the 'humanity' out of the way in which we think of the organization. This point is often raised in not-for-profit organizations, especially by 'professional' staff. For example the head of one European 'Medical Association' (a doctors' trade union) criticized hospital authorities for expecting a *'sausage factory service based on productivity targets'*.[5] No matter how similar they appear on paper, it is argued, a hospital can never be viewed in the same way as a factory. Even in commercial businesses, professionals, such as creative staff, often express discomfort at their expertise being described as a 'process'.

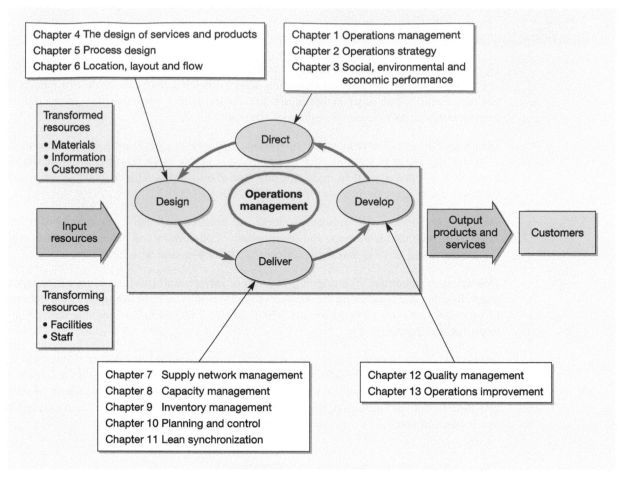

Figure 1.8 A general model of operations management

Summary answers to key questions

Check and improve your understanding of this chapter using self-assessment questions and a personalized study plan, audio and video downloads, and an eBook – all at www.myomlab.com.

➤ What is operations management?

■ Operations management is the activity of managing the resources which are devoted to the creation and delivery of services and products. It is one of the core functions of any business, although it may not be called operations management in some industries.

■ Operations management is concerned with managing processes. All processes have internal customers and suppliers. As all management functions also have processes, operations management has relevance for all managers.

➤ Why is operations management important in all types of organization?

■ Operations management uses the organization's resources to create outputs that fulfil defined market requirements. This is the fundamental activity of any type of enterprise.

- Operations management is increasingly important because today's business environment requires new thinking from operations managers.

➤ What is the input–transformation–output process?

- All operations can be modelled as input–transformation–output processes. They all have inputs of transforming resources, which are usually divided into 'facilities' and 'staff', and transformed resources, which are some mixture of customers, materials and information.
- Few operations create and deliver only services or products. Most produce some mixture of products and services.

➤ What is the process hierarchy?

- All operations are part of a larger supply network which, through the individual contributions of each operation, satisfies end-customer requirements.
- All operations are made up of processes that form a network of internal customer–supplier relationships within the operation.
- End-to-end business processes that satisfy customer needs often cut across functionally based processes.

➤ How do operations processes have different characteristics?

- Operations differ in terms of the volume of their outputs, the variety of outputs, the variation in demand for their outputs, and the degree of visibility they have.
- High volume, low variety, low variation and low customer visibility are usually associated with low cost.

➤ What are the activities of operations management?

- Responsibilities include defining an operations strategy, understanding social, environmental and economic objectives, designing the operation's services, products and processes, delivering to customers, and developing the operation over time.

Learning exercises

These problems and applications will help to improve your analysis of operations. You can find more practice problems as well as worked examples and guided solutions on MyOMLab at www.myomlab.com.

1 Read the short case on Pret A Manger and **(a)** identify the processes in a typical Pret A Manger shop together with their inputs and outputs, **(b)** Pret A Manger also supplies business lunches (of sandwiches and other take-away food). What are the implications for how it manages its processes within the shop? **(c)** What would be the advantages and disadvantages if Pret A Manger introduced 'central kitchens' that made the sandwiches for a number of shops in an area? (As far as we know, they have no plans to do so.)

2 Compare and contrast Acme Whistles and Pret A Manger in terms of the way that they will need to manage their operations.

3   Visit and observe three restaurants, cafés or somewhere that food is served. Compare them in terms of the Volume of demand that they have to cope with, the Variety of menu items they service, the Variation in demand during the day, week and year, and the Visibility you have of the preparation of the food. Think about and discuss the impact of volume, variety, variation and visibility on the day-to-day management of each of the operations and consider how each operation attempts to cope with its volume, variety, variation and visibility.

4   (Advanced) Find a copy of a financial newspaper or magazine (*Financial Times*, *Wall Street Journal*, *Economist*, etc.) and identify one company which is described in the paper that day. Using the list of issues identified in Table 1.1, what do you think would be the *new operations agenda* for that company?

Want to know more?

Chase, R.B., Jacobs, F.R. and Aquilano, N.J. (2004) *Operations Management for Competitive Advantage* (10th edn), McGraw-Hill/Irwin, Boston, MA. There are many good general textbooks on operations management. This was one of the first and is still one of the best, though written very much for an American audience.

Chopra, S., Deshmukh, S., Van Mieghem, J., Zemel, E. and Anupindi, R. (2005) *Managing Business Process Flows: Principles of Operations Management*, Prentice-Hall, Englewood Cliffs, NJ. Takes a 'process' view of operations. Mathematical but rewarding.

Heizer, J. and Render, B. (2006) *Operations Management* (8th edn), Prentice Hall, Englewood Cliffs, NJ. Another good US authored general text on the subject.

Johnston, R. and Clark, G. (2008) *Service Operations Management* (3rd edn), Financial Times-Prentice Hall, Harlow. What can we say! A great treatment of service operations from the same stable as this textbook.

Useful websites

www.opsman.org Useful materials and resources.

www.iomnet.org.uk The Institute of Operations Management site. One of the main professional bodies for the subject.

www.poms.org A US academic society for production and operations management. Academic, but some useful material, including a link to an encyclopaedia of operations management terms.

www.sussex.ac.uk/Users/dt31/TOMI/ One of the longest-established portals for the subject. Useful for academics and students alike.

www.ft.com Useful for researching topics and companies.

www.journaloperationsmanagement.org The home site for the best known operations management journal. A bit academic, but some pages are useful.

Now that you have finished reading this chapter, why not visit MyOMLab at www.myomlab.com where you'll find more learning resources to help you make the most of your studies and get a better grade.

Chapter 3 | Social, environmental and economic performance

Key questions

➤ Why is operations performance important in any organization?

➤ How should the operations function judge itself?

➤ What does top management expect from the operations function?

➤ What are the performance objectives of operations and what are the internal and external benefits which derive from excelling in each of them?

➤ How do operations performance objectives trade off against each other?

Introduction

Operations are judged by the way they perform. There are many individuals and groups doing the judging and there are many different aspects of performance on which the assessment is being made. Here, we take what is called a 'triple bottom line' approach to understand an operation's total performance. If we want to understand the strategic contribution of the operations function, it is important to understand how we can measure its performance. This chapter examines social, environmental, and economic performance before focusing on how operations can impact on the success of the whole organization. Finally, we examine how performance objectives trade off against each other. Figure 3.1 shows where this chapter fits into the overall operations model.

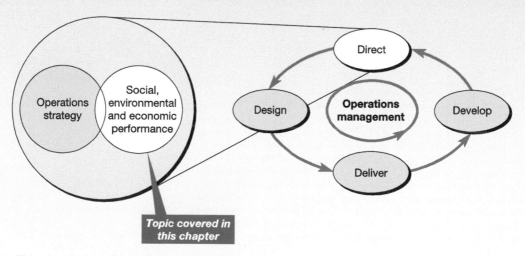

Figure 3.1 This chapter examines social, environmental and economic performance

Check and improve your understanding of this chapter using self-assessment questions and a personalized study plan, audio and video downloads, and an eBook – all at www.myomlab.com.

Operations in practice A tale of two terminals[1]

On 15 April 2008 British Airways (BA) announced that two of its most senior executives, its director of operations and its director of customer services, would leave the company. They were paying the price for the disastrous opening of British Airways' new Terminal 5 at London's Heathrow airport. The opening of the £4.3bn terminal, said BA's boss, Willie Walsh, with magnificent understatement, 'was not the company's finest hour'. The chaos at the terminal on its opening days made news around the world and was seen by many as one of the most public failures of basic operations management in the modern history of aviation. 'It's a terrible, terrible PR nightmare to have hanging over you', said David Learmount, an aviation expert. 'Somebody who may have been a faithful customer and still not have their luggage after three weeks is not good for their [BA's] image. The one thing that's worse than having a stack of 15,000 bags is adding 5,000 a day to that heap.' According to a BA spokeswoman it needed an extra 400 volunteer staff and courier companies to wade through the backlog of late baggage. So the new terminal that had opened on 27 March could not even cope with BA's full short-haul service until 8 April (two hundred flights in and out of T5 were cancelled in its first three days). This delayed moving its long-haul operations to the new building from Terminal 4 as scheduled on 30 April, which, in turn, disrupted the operations of other airlines, many of which were scheduled to move into Terminal 4 once BA had moved its long-haul flights from there. Sharing the blame with BA was the British Airports Authority (BAA) which was already suffering criticism from passenger groups, airlines and businesses for allegedly poor performance. BAA's non-executive chairman, Sir Nigel Rudd, said he was 'bitterly disappointed' about the opening of the terminal. 'It was clearly a huge embarrassment to the company, me personally, and the board. Nothing can take away that failure. We had all believed genuinely that it would be a great opening, which clearly it wasn't.'

Yet it all should have been so different. T5 took more than six years and around 60,000 workers to build, and it's an impressive building. It is Europe's largest free-standing structure. It was also keenly anticipated by travellers and BA alike. Willie Walsh has said that the terminal 'will completely change his passengers' experience'. He was right, but not in the way he imagined! So what went wrong? As is often the case with major operations failures, it was not one thing, but several interrelated problems (all of which could have been avoided). Press reports initially blamed glitches with the state-of-the-art baggage handling system that consisted

Source: Alamy Images

of 18 km of conveyor belts and was (theoretically) capable of transporting 12,000 bags per hour. Almost inevitably, the baggage handling system experienced problems which had not been exposed in testing. However, BAA, the airport operator, doubted that the main problem was the baggage system itself. The system had worked until it became clogged with bags that were overwhelming BA's handlers loading them onto the aircraft. Partly this may have been because staff were not sufficiently familiar with the new system and its operating processes, but handling staff had also suffered delays getting to their new (and unfamiliar) work areas, negotiating (new) security checks and finding (again, new) car parking spaces. Also, once staff were 'airside' they had problems logging in. The cumulative effect of these problems meant that the airline was unable to get ground handling staff to the correct locations for loading and unloading bags from the aircraft, so baggage could not be loaded onto aircraft fast enough, so baggage backed up, clogging the baggage handling system, which in turn meant closing baggage check-in and baggage drops, leading eventually to baggage check-in being halted.

However, not every airline underestimates the operational complexity of airport processes. During the same year that Terminal 5 at Heathrow was suffering queues, lost bags and bad publicity, Dubai International Airport's Terminal 3 opened quietly with little publicity and fewer problems. Like T5, it is also huge and designed to impress. Its new shimmering facilities are solely dedicated to Emirates Airline. Largely built underground (20 metres beneath the taxiway area) the multi-level environment reduces passenger walking by using 157 elevators, 97 escalators and 82 moving walkways. Its underground baggage handling system is the deepest and the largest of its kind in the world with 90 km of baggage belts handling around 15,000 items →

Source: Rex Features

per hour. Also like T5 it handles about 30 million passengers a year.

A key difference between the two terminals was that Dubai's T3 could observe and learn lessons from the botched opening of Heathrow's Terminal 5. Paul Griffiths, the former head of London's Gatwick Airport, who is now Dubai Airport's chief executive, insisted that his own new terminal should not be publicly shamed in the same way. 'There was a lot of arrogance and hubris around the opening of T5, with all the . . . publicity that BA generated', Mr Griffiths says. 'The first rule of customer service is under-promise and over-deliver because that way you get their loyalty. BA was telling people that they were getting a glimpse of the future with T5, which created expectation and increased the chances of disappointment. Having watched the development of T5, it was clear that we had to make sure that everyone was on-message. We just had to bang heads together so that people realized what was at stake. We knew the world would be watching and waiting after T5 to see whether T3 was the next big terminal fiasco. We worked very hard to make sure that didn't happen.'

Paul Griffiths was also convinced that Terminal 3 should undergo a phased programme with flights added progressively, rather than a 'big bang' approach where the terminal opened for business on one day. 'We exhaustively tested the terminal systems throughout the summer . . . We continue to make sure we're putting large loads on it, week by week, improving reliability. We put a few flights in bit by bit, in waves rather than a big bang.' Prior to the opening he also said that Dubai Airports would never reveal a single opening date for its new Terminal 3 until all pre-opening test programmes had been completed. 'T3 opened so quietly', said one journalist, 'that passengers would have known that the terminal was new only if they had touched the still-drying paint.'

Operations performance is vital for any organization

Operations management is a 'make or break' activity

It is no exaggeration to view operations management as being able to either '**make or break**' any business. This is not just because the operations function is large and, in most businesses, represents the bulk of its assets and the majority of its people, but because the operations function gives the ability to compete by providing customer responsiveness and by developing the capabilities that will keep it ahead of its competitors in the future. For example, operations management principles and the performance of its operations function proved hugely important in the Heathrow T5 and Dubai T3 launches. It was a basic failure to understand the importance of operations processes that (temporarily) damaged British Airways' reputation. It was Dubai's attention to detail and thorough operational preparation that avoided similar problems.

Operations managers face many new challenges as the economic, social, political and technological environment changes. Many of these decisions and challenges seem largely economic in nature. What will be the impact on our costs of adding a new product or service feature? Can we generate an acceptable return if we invest in new technology? Other decisions have more of a 'social' aspect. How do we make sure that all our suppliers treat their staff fairly? Finally, some have an environmental impact. Are we doing enough to reduce our carbon footprint? Furthermore, the 'economic' decisions also have an environmental aspect to them. Will a new product feature make end-of-life recycling more difficult? Will the new technology increase pollution? Similarly the 'social' decisions must be made in the context of their economic consequences. Sure, we want suppliers to treat staff well, but we also need to make a profit. And this is the great dilemma. How do operations managers try to be, simultaneously, economically viable whilst being socially and environmentally responsible?

The triple bottom line

Triple bottom line

One common term that tries to capture the idea of a broader approach to assessing an organization's performance is the '**triple bottom line**' (TBL, or 3BL), also known as 'people, planet and profit'. Essentially, it is a straightforward idea, simply that organizations should measure themselves not just on the traditional economic profit that they generate for their owners, but also on the impact their operations have on society (broadly, in the sense of communities, and individually, for example in terms of their employees) and the ecological impact on the environment. The influential initiative that has come out of this triple bottom line approach is that of 'sustainability'. A sustainable business is one that creates an acceptable profit for its owners, but minimizes the damage to the environment and enhances the existence of the people with whom it has contact. In other words, it balances economic, environmental and societal interests. This gives the organization its 'license to operate' in society. The assumption underlying the triple bottom line (which is not universally accepted) is that a sustainable business is more likely to remain successful in the long-term than one which focuses on economic goals alone. Only a company that produces a balanced TBL is really accounting for the total cost of running its operations. Figure 3.2 illustrates some of the issues involved in achieving the triple bottom line.

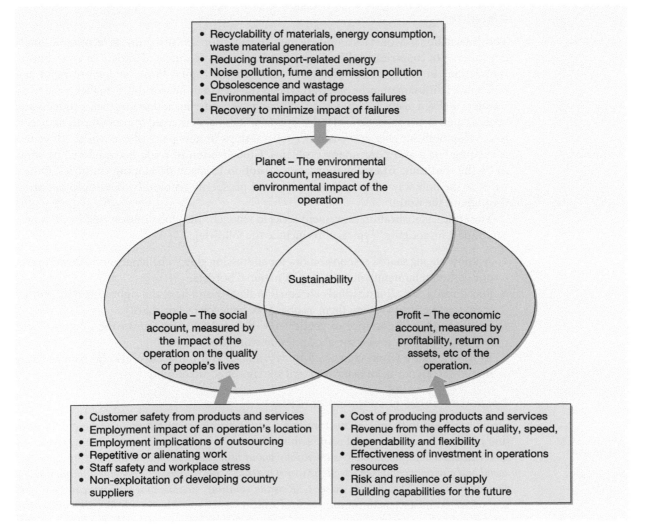

Figure 3.2 Some ways in which operations can impact each element of the triple bottom line

The social bottom line

The fundamental idea behind the social bottom line is not simply that there is a connection between businesses and the society in which they operate (defined broadly) – that is self-evident. Rather it is that businesses should accept that they bear some responsibility for the impact they have on society and balance the external 'societal' consequences of their actions with the more direct internal consequences, such as profit.

Society is made up of organizations, groups and individuals. Each is more than a simple unit of economic exchange. Organizations have responsibility for the general well-being of society beyond short-term economic self-interest. At the level of the individual, this means devising jobs and work patterns which allow individuals to contribute their talents without undue stress. At a group level, it means recognizing and dealing honestly with employee representatives. This principle also extends beyond the boundaries of the organization. Any business has a responsibility to ensure that it does not knowingly disadvantage individuals in its suppliers or trading partners. Businesses are also a part of the larger community, often integrated into the economic and social fabric of an area. Increasingly, organizations are recognizing their responsibility to local communities by helping to promote their economic and social well-being. Of the many issues that affect society at large, arguably the one that has had the most profound effect on the way business has developed over the last few decades has been the globalization of business activity.

Globalization

The International Monetary Fund defines globalization as 'the growing economic inter-dependence of countries worldwide through increasing volume and variety of cross-border transactions in goods and services, free international capital flows, and more rapid and widespread diffusion of technology'. It reflects the idea that the world is a smaller place to do business in. Even many medium-sized companies are sourcing and selling their products and services on a global basis. Considerable opportunities have emerged for operations managers to develop both supplier and customer relationships in new parts of the world. All of this is exciting but it also poses many problems. **Globalization** of trade is considered by some to be the root cause of exploitation and corruption in many developing countries. Others see it as the only way of spreading the levels of prosperity enjoyed by developed countries throughout the world.

The ethical globalization movement seeks to reconcile the globalization trend with how it can impact on societies. Typical aims include the following:

- Acknowledging shared responsibilities for addressing global challenges and affirming that our common humanity doesn't stop at national borders.
- Recognizing that all individuals are equal in dignity and have the right to certain entitlements, rather than viewing them as objects of benevolence or charity.
- Embracing the importance of gender and the need for attention to the often different impacts of economic and social policies on women and men.
- Affirming that a world connected by technology and trade must also be connected by shared values, norms of behaviour and systems of accountability.

Corporate social responsibility (CSR)

Strongly related to the social 'bottom line' (and to some extent the environmental 'bottom line') is that of **corporate social responsibility** (generally known as CSR). According to the UK government's definition, *'CSR is essentially about how business takes account of its economic, social and environmental impacts in the way it operates – maximizing the benefits and minimizing the downsides. . . . Specifically, we see CSR as the voluntary actions that business can take, over and above compliance with minimum legal requirements, to address both its own competitive interests and the interests of wider society.'* A more direct link with the stakeholder concept is

Globalization

Corporate social responsibility

to be found in the definition used by Marks and Spencer, the UK-based retailer. '*Corporate Social Responsibility . . . is listening and responding to the needs of a company's stakeholders. This includes the requirements of sustainable development. We believe that building good relationships with employees, suppliers and wider society is the best guarantee of long-term success. This is the backbone of our approach to CSR.*' The issue of how broader social performance objectives can be included in operations management's activities is of increasing importance, from both an ethical and a commercial point of view.

The environmental bottom line

Environmental sustainability (according to the World Bank) means 'ensuring that the overall productivity of accumulated human and physical capital resulting from development actions more than compensates for the direct or indirect loss or degradation of the environment', or (according to the Brundtland Report from the United Nations) it is 'meeting the needs of the present without compromising the ability of future generations to meet their own needs'. Put more directly, it is generally taken to mean the extent to which business activity negatively impacts on the natural environment. It is clearly an important issue, not only because of the obvious impact on the immediate environment of hazardous waste, air and even noise pollution, but also because of the less obvious, but potentially far more damaging issues around global warming.

From the perspective of individual organizations, the challenging issues of dealing with sustainability are connected with the scale of the problem and the general perception of 'green' issues. Firstly, the scale issue is that cause and effect in the environmental sustainability area are judged at different levels. The effects of, and arguments for, environmentally sustainable activities are felt at a global level, while those activities themselves are essentially local. It has been argued that it is difficult to use the concept at a corporate or even at the regional level. Secondly, there is a paradox with sustainability-based decisions. It is that the more the public becomes sensitized to the benefits of firms acting in an environmentally sensitive way, the more those firms are tempted to exaggerate their environmental credentials, the so-called 'greenwashing' effect.

Environmental protection

Operations managers cannot avoid responsibility for **environmental protection** generally, or their organization's environmental performance more specifically. It is often operational failures which are at the root of pollution disasters and operations decisions (such as product design) which impact on longer-term environmental issues. The pollution-causing disasters which make the headlines seem to be the result of a whole variety of causes – oil tankers run aground, nuclear waste is misclassified, chemicals leak into a river, or gas clouds drift over industrial towns. But in fact they all have something in common. They were all the result of an operational failure. Somehow operations procedures were inadequate. Less dramatic in the short term, but perhaps more important in the long term, is the environmental impact of products which cannot be recycled and processes which consume large amounts of energy – again, both issues which are part of the operations management's broader responsibilities.

Again, it is important to understand that broad issues such as environmental responsibility are intimately connected with the day-to-day decisions of operations managers. Many of these are concerned with waste. Operations management decisions in product and service design significantly affect the utilization of materials both in the short term and in long-term recyclability. Process design influences the proportion of energy and labour that is wasted as well as materials wastage. Planning and control may affect material wastage (packaging being wasted by mistakes in purchasing, for example), but also affects energy and labour wastage. Improvement, of course, is dedicated largely to reducing wastage. Here environmental responsibility and the conventional concerns of operations management coincide. Reducing waste, in all it forms, may be environmentally sound but it also saves cost for the organization. At other times, decisions can be more difficult. Process technologies may be efficient from the operations point of view but may cause pollution, the economic and social consequences of which are borne by society at large. Such conflicts are usually resolved through regulation and legislation. Not that such mechanisms are always effective – there is evidence that just-in-time principles applied in Japan may have produced significant economic gains for the companies which adopted them, but at the price of an overcrowded and polluted road system.

The economic bottom line

An organization's top management represent the interests of the owners (or trustees, or electorate, etc.) and therefore are the direct custodians of the organization's basic purpose. They also have responsibility for translating the broad objectives of the organization into a more tangible form. Broadly they should expect all their operations managers to contribute to the economic success of the organization by **using its resources effectively**. To do this it must be creative, innovative and energetic in improving its processes, products and services. In more detail, effective operations management can give five types of advantage to the business (see Figure 3.3):

Operations can have a significant impact on economic success

- It can reduce the **costs** of producing services and products.
- It can achieve customer satisfaction through good quality and service (and therefore **revenue** in a for-profit organization).
- It can reduce the **risk** of operational failure, because well designed and well-run operations should be less likely to fail, and if they do they should be able to recover faster and with less disruption (this is called *resilience*).
- It can reduce the amount of **investment** (sometimes called *capital employed*) that is necessary to produce the required type and quantity of products and services by increasing the effective capacity of the operation and by being innovative in how it uses its physical resources.
- It can provide the basis for *future* **innovation** by learning from its experience of operating its processes, so building a solid base of operations skills, knowledge and capability within the business.

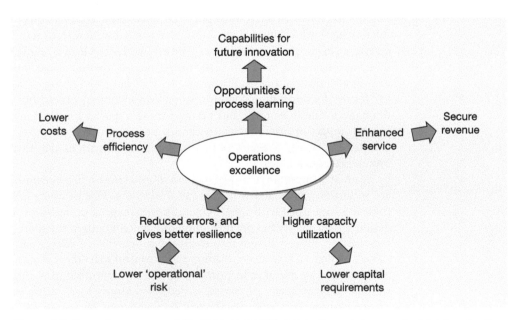

Figure 3.3 Operations can contribute to competitiveness through low costs, high levels of service (securing revenue), lower operational risk, lower capital requirements, and providing the capabilities that determine future innovation

The five operations performance objectives

Broad stakeholder objectives form the backdrop to operations decision-making, and top management's objectives provide a strategic framework, but running operations at an operational day-to-day level requires a more tightly defined set of objectives. These are the **five basic 'performance objectives'** and they apply to all types of operation. Imagine that you are an operations manager in any kind of business – a hospital administrator, for example, or a production manager at a car plant. What kind of things are you likely to want to do in order to satisfy customers and contribute to competitiveness?

- You would want to do things right; that is, you would not want to make mistakes, and would want to satisfy your customers by providing error-free services and products which are 'fit for their purpose'. This is giving a **quality** advantage.

- You would want to do things fast, minimizing the time between a customer asking for services or products and the customer receiving them in full, thus increasing the availability of your services and products and giving a **speed** advantage.

- You would want to do things on time, so as to keep the delivery promises you have made. If the operation can do this, it is giving a **dependability** advantage.

- You would want to be able to change what you do; that is, being able to vary or adapt the operation's activities to cope with unexpected circumstances or to give customers individual treatment. Being able to change far enough and fast enough to meet customer requirements gives a **flexibility** advantage.

- You would want to do things cheaply; that is, create and deliver services and products at a cost which enables them to be priced appropriately for the market while still allowing for a return to the organization; or, in a not-for-profit organization, give good value to the taxpayers or whoever is funding the operation. When the organization is managing to do this, it is giving a **cost** advantage.

The next part of this chapter examines these five performance objectives in more detail by looking at what they mean for four different operations: a general hospital, an automobile factory, a city bus company and a supermarket chain.

The quality objective

Quality is consistent conformance to customers' expectations, in other words, 'doing things right', but the things which the operation needs to do right will vary according to the kind of operation. All operations regard quality as a particularly important objective. In some ways quality is the most visible part of what an operation does. Furthermore, it is something that a customer finds relatively easy to judge about the operation. Is the service or product as it is supposed to be? Is it right or is it wrong? There is something fundamental about quality. Because of this, it is clearly **a major influence on customer satisfaction or dissatisfaction**. A customer perception of high-quality products and services means customer satisfaction and therefore the likelihood that the customer will return. Figure 3.4 illustrates how quality could be judged in four operations.

Quality inside the operation

When quality means consistently creating and delivering services and products to specification, it not only leads to external customer satisfaction, but makes life easier inside the operation as well.

Quality reduces costs. The fewer mistakes made by each process in the operation, the less time will be needed to correct the mistakes and the less confusion and irritation will be spread. For example, if a supermarket's regional warehouse sends the wrong goods to the supermarket, it will mean staff time, and therefore cost, being used to sort out the problem.

Quality could mean . . .

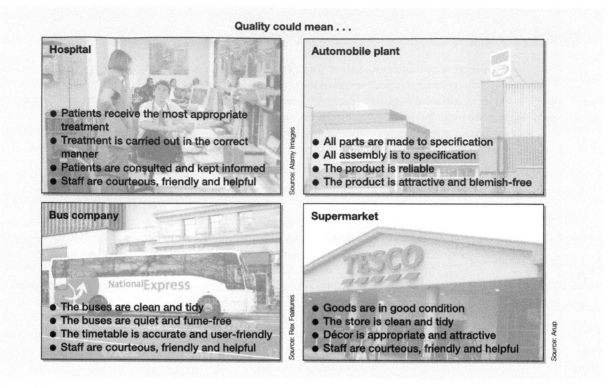

Hospital
- Patients receive the most appropriate treatment
- Treatment is carried out in the correct manner
- Patients are consulted and kept informed
- Staff are courteous, friendly and helpful

Automobile plant
- All parts are made to specification
- All assembly is to specification
- The product is reliable
- The product is attractive and blemish-free

Bus company
- The buses are clean and tidy
- The buses are quiet and fume-free
- The timetable is accurate and user-friendly
- Staff are courteous, friendly and helpful

Supermarket
- Goods are in good condition
- The store is clean and tidy
- Décor is appropriate and attractive
- Staff are courteous, friendly and helpful

Figure 3.4 Quality means different things in different operations

Quality increases dependability. Increased costs are not the only consequence of poor quality. At the supermarket, poor quality could also mean that products run out on the shelves, resulting in lost revenue to the operation. Sorting the problem out could also distract the supermarket management from giving attention to the other parts of the supermarket operation. This in turn could result in further mistakes being made. So, quality (like the other performance objectives, as we shall see) has both an external impact which influences customer satisfaction and an internal impact which leads to stable and efficient processes.

Short case
Organically good quality[2]

'*Organic farming means taking care and getting all the details right. It is about quality from start to finish. Not only the quality of the meat that we produce but also quality of life and quality of care for the countryside.*' Nick Fuge is the farm manager at Lower Hurst Farm located within the Peak District National Park of the UK. He has day-to-day responsibility for the well-being of all the livestock and the operation of the farm on strict organic principles. The 85-hectare farm has been producing high-quality beef for almost 20 years but changed to fully organic production in 1998. Organic farming is a tough regime. No artificial fertilizers, genetically modified feedstuff or growth-promoting agents are used. All beef sold from the farm is home-bred and can be traced back to the animal from which it came.

'*The quality of the herd is most important*', says Nick, '*as is animal care. Our customers trust us to ensure that the cattle are organically and humanely reared, and slaughtered in a manner that minimizes any distress. If you want to*

understand the difference between conventional and organic farming, look at the way we use veterinary help. Most conventional farmers use veterinarians like an emergency service to put things right when there is a problem with an animal. The amount we pay for veterinary assistance is lower because we try to avoid problems with the animals from the start. We use veterinarians as consultants to help us in preventing problems in the first place.'

Catherine Pyne runs the butchery and the mail-order meat business. 'After butchering, the cuts of meat are individually vacuum-packed, weighed and then blast-frozen. We worked extensively with the Department of Food and Nutrition at Oxford Brooks University to devise the best way to encapsulate the nutritional, textural and flavoursome characteristics of the meat in its prime state.

So, when you defrost and cook any of our products you will have the same tasty and succulent eating qualities associated with the best fresh meat.' After freezing, the products are packed in boxes, designed and labelled for storage in a home freezer. Customers order by phone or through the Internet for next-day delivery in a special 'mini-deep-freeze' reusable container which maintains the meat in its frozen state. 'It isn't just the quality of our product which has made us a success', says Catherine. 'We give a personal and inclusive level of service to our customers that makes them feel close to us and maintains trust in how we produce and prepare the meat. The team of people we have here is also an important aspect of our business. We are proud of our product and feel that it is vitally important to be personally identified with it.'

The speed objective

Speed means the elapsed time between customers requesting services or products and receiving them. Figure 3.5 illustrates what speed means for the four operations. The main benefit to the operation's (external) customers of speedy delivery of services or products is that the faster they can have the service or product, the more likely they are to buy it, or the more they will pay for it, or the greater the **benefit they receive** (see the short case 'When speed means life or death').

Speed increases value for some customers

Speed inside the operation

Inside the operation, speed is also important. Fast response to external customers is greatly helped by speedy decision-making and speedy movement of materials and information inside the operation. Speed brings other benefits too.

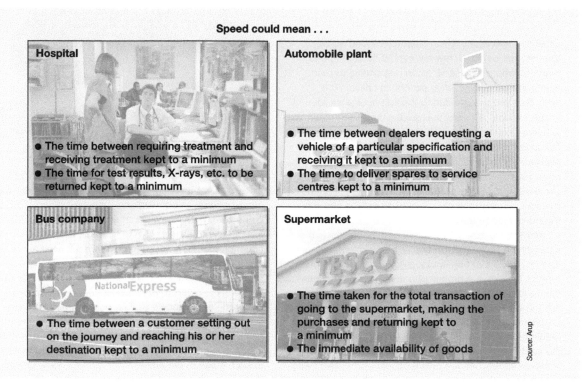

Speed could mean . . .

Hospital
- The time between requiring treatment and receiving treatment kept to a minimum
- The time for test results, X-rays, etc. to be returned kept to a minimum

Automobile plant
- The time between dealers requesting a vehicle of a particular specification and receiving it kept to a minimum
- The time to deliver spares to service centres kept to a minimum

Bus company
- The time between a customer setting out on the journey and reaching his or her destination kept to a minimum

Supermarket
- The time taken for the total transaction of going to the supermarket, making the purchases and returning kept to a minimum
- The immediate availability of goods

Source: Arup

Figure 3.5 Speed means different things in different operations

Speed reduces inventories. Take, for example, the automobile plant. Steel for the vehicle's door panels is delivered to the press shop, pressed into shape, transported to the painting area, coated for colour and protection, and moved to the assembly line where it is fitted to the automobile. This is a simple three-stage process, but in practice material does not flow smoothly from one stage to the next. Firstly, the steel is delivered as part of a far larger batch containing enough steel to make possibly several hundred products. Eventually it is taken to the press area, pressed into shape, and again waits to be transported to the paint area. It then waits to be painted, only to wait once more until it is transported to the assembly line. Yet again, it waits until it is eventually fitted to the automobile. The material's journey time is far longer than the time needed to make and fit the product. It actually spends most of its time waiting as stocks (inventories) of parts and products. The longer items take to move through a process, the more time they will be waiting and the higher inventory will be.

Speed reduces risks. Forecasting tomorrow's events is far less of a risk than forecasting next year's. The further ahead companies forecast, the more likely they are to get it wrong. The faster the throughput time of a process the later forecasting can be left. Consider the automobile plant again. If the total throughput time for the door panel is six weeks, door panels are being processed through their first operation six weeks before they reach their final destination. The quantity of door panels being processed will be determined by the forecasts for demand six weeks ahead. If instead of six weeks, they take only one week to move through the plant, the door panels being processed through their first stage are intended to meet demand only one week ahead. Under these circumstances it is far more likely that the number and type of door panels being processed are the number and type which eventually will be needed.

Short case
When speed means life or death[3]

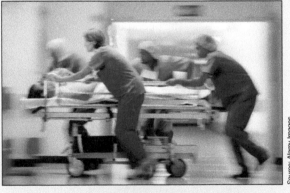

Source: Alamy Images

Of all the operations which have to respond quickly to customer demand, few have more need of speed than the emergency services. In responding to road accidents especially, every second is critical. The treatment you receive during the first hour after your accident (what is called the 'golden hour') can determine whether you survive and fully recover or not. Making full use of the golden hour means speeding up three elements of the total time to treatment – the time it takes for the emergency services to find out about the accident, the time it takes them to travel to the scene of the accident, and the time it takes to get the casualty to appropriate treatment.

Alerting the emergency services immediately is the idea behind Mercedes-Benz's TeleAid system. As soon as the vehicle's airbag is triggered, an on-board computer reports through the mobile phone network to a control centre (drivers can also trigger the system manually if not too badly hurt), satellite tracking allows the vehicle to be precisely located and the owner identified (if special medication is needed). Getting to the accident quickly is the next hurdle. Often the fastest method is by helicopter. When most rescues are only a couple of minutes' flying time back to the hospital speed can really saves lives.

However, it is not always possible to land a helicopter safely at night (because of possible overhead wires and other hazards) so conventional ambulances will always be needed, both to get paramedics quickly to accident victims and to speed them to hospital. One increasingly common method of ensuring that ambulances arrive quickly at the accident site is to position them, not at hospitals, but close to where accidents are likely to occur. Computer analysis of previous accident data helps to select the ambulance's waiting position, and global positioning systems help controllers to mobilize the nearest unit. At all times a key requirement for fast service is effective communication between all who are involved in each stage of the emergency. Modern communications technology can play an important role in this.

The dependability objective

Dependability is judged over time

Dependability means doing things in time for customers to receive their services or products exactly when they are needed, or at least when they were promised. Figure 3.6 illustrates what dependability means in the four operations. Customers might only judge the dependability of an operation after the service or product has been delivered. Initially this may not affect the likelihood that customers will select the service – they have already 'consumed' it. **Over time**, however, dependability can override all other criteria. No matter how cheap or fast a bus service is, if the service is always late (or unpredictably early) or the buses are always full, then potential passengers will be better off calling a taxi.

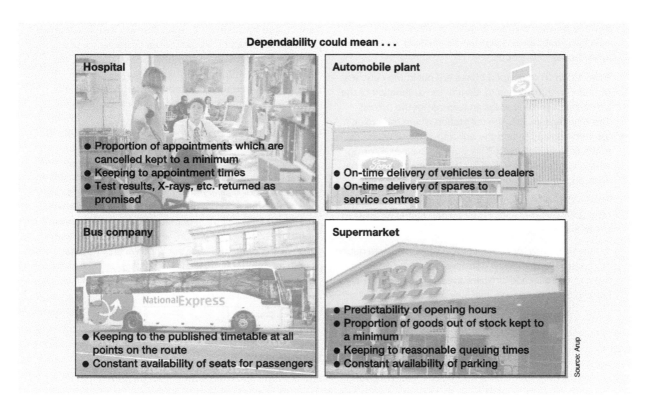

Dependability could mean . . .

Hospital
- Proportion of appointments which are cancelled kept to a minimum
- Keeping to appointment times
- Test results, X-rays, etc. returned as promised

Automobile plant
- On-time delivery of vehicles to dealers
- On-time delivery of spares to service centres

Bus company
- Keeping to the published timetable at all points on the route
- Constant availability of seats for passengers

Supermarket
- Predictability of opening hours
- Proportion of goods out of stock kept to a minimum
- Keeping to reasonable queuing times
- Constant availability of parking

Source: Anup

Figure 3.6 Dependability means different things in different operations

Short case
Dabbawalas hit 99.9999% dependability[4]

Mumbai is India's most densely populated city, and every working day its millions of commuters crowd onto packed trains for an often lengthy commute to their workplaces. Going home for lunch is not possible, so many office workers have a cooked meal sent either from their home, or from a caterer. It is Mumbai's 5,000-strong dabbawala collective that provides this service, usually for a monthly fee. The meal is cooked in the morning (by family or

Source: Getty Images

caterer), placed in regulation dabbas or tiffin (lunch) boxes and delivered to each individual worker's office at lunch time. After lunch the boxes are collected and returned so that they can be re-sent the next day. 'Dabbawala' means 'one who carries a box', or more colloquially, 'lunch box delivery man'. This is how the service works:

7am–9am The dabbas (boxes) are collected by dabbawalas on bicycles from nearly 200,000 suburban homes or from the dabba makers and taken to railway stations. The dabbas have distinguishing marks on them, using colours and symbols (necessary because many dabbawalas are barely literate). The dabbawala then takes them to a designated sorting place, where he and other collecting dabbawalas sort (and sometimes bundle) the lunch boxes into groups.

9am–11am The grouped boxes are put in the coaches of trains, with markings to identify the destination of the box (usually there is a designated car for the boxes). The markings include the rail station where the boxes are to be unloaded and the building address where the box has to be delivered. This may involve boxes being sorted at intermediary stations, with each single dabba changing hands up to four times.

10am–12midday Dabbas taken into Mumbai using the otherwise under-utilized capacity on commuter trains in the mid-morning.

11am–12midday Arrive downtown Mumbai where dabbas are handed over to **local dabbawalas**, who distribute them to more locations where there is more sorting and loading on to handcarts, bicycles and dabbawalas.

12midday–1pm Dabbas are delivered to appropriate office locations.

2pm Process moves into reverse, after lunch, when the empty boxes are collected from office locations and returned to suburban stations.

6pm Empty dabbas sent back to the respective houses.

The service has a remarkable record of almost flawlessly reliable delivery, even on the days of severe weather such as Mumbai's characteristic monsoons. Dabbawalas all receive the same pay and at both the receiving and the sending ends, are known to the customers personally, so are trusted by customers. Also, they are well accustomed to the local areas they collect from or deliver to, which reduces the chances of errors. Raghunath Medge, the president of the Bombay Tiffin Box Supply Charity Trust, which oversees the dabbawallas, highlights the importance of their hands-on operations management. *'Proper time management is our key to success. We do everything to keep the customer happy and they help in our marketing.'* There is no system of documentation. The success of the operation depends on teamwork and human ingenuity. Such is the dedication and commitment of the barefoot delivery men (there are only a few delivery women) that the complex logistics operation works with only three layers of management. Although the service remains essentially low-tech, with the barefoot delivery men as the prime movers, the dabbawalas now use some modern technology, for example they now allow booking for delivery through SMS and their web site, (www.mydabbawala.com).

Dependability inside the operation

Inside the operation, internal customers will judge each other's performance partly by how reliable the other processes are in delivering material or information on time. Operations where internal dependability is high are more effective than those which are not, for a number of reasons.

Dependability saves time. Take, for example, the maintenance and repair centre for the city bus company. If the centre runs out of some crucial spare parts, the manager of the centre will need to spend time trying to arrange a special delivery of the required parts and the resources allocated to service the buses will not be used as productively as they would have been without this disruption. More seriously, the fleet will be short of buses until they can be repaired and the fleet operations manager will have to spend time rescheduling services. So, entirely due to the one failure of dependability of supply, a significant part of the operation's time has been wasted coping with the disruption.

Dependability saves money. Ineffective use of time will translate into extra cost. The spare parts might cost more to be delivered at short notice and maintenance staff will expect to be paid even when there is not a bus to work on. Nor will the fixed costs of the operation, such as heating and rent, be reduced because the two buses are not being serviced. The rescheduling of buses will probably mean that some routes have inappropriately sized buses and some services could have to be cancelled. This will result in empty bus seats (if too large a bus has to be used) or a loss of revenue (if potential passengers are not transported).

Dependability gives stability. The disruption caused to operations by a lack of dependability goes beyond time and cost. It affects the 'quality' of the operation's time. If everything in an operation is always perfectly dependable, a level of trust will have built up between the different parts of the operation. There will be no 'surprises' and everything will be predictable. Under such circumstances, each part of the operation can concentrate on improving its own area of responsibility without having its attention continually diverted by a lack of dependable service from the other parts.

The flexibility objective

Flexibility means being able to **change** the operation in some way. This may mean changing what the operation does, how it is doing it, or when it is doing it. Specifically, customers will need the operation to change so that it can provide four types of requirement:

- **Service/product flexibility** – the operation's ability to introduce new or modified services and products;
- **mix flexibility** – the operation's ability to create a wide range or mix of services and products;
- **volume flexibility** – the operation's ability to change its level of output or activity to produce different quantities or volumes of services and products over time;
- **delivery flexibility** – the operation's ability to change the timing of the delivery of its services or products.

Figure 3.7 gives examples of what these different types of flexibility mean to the four different operations.

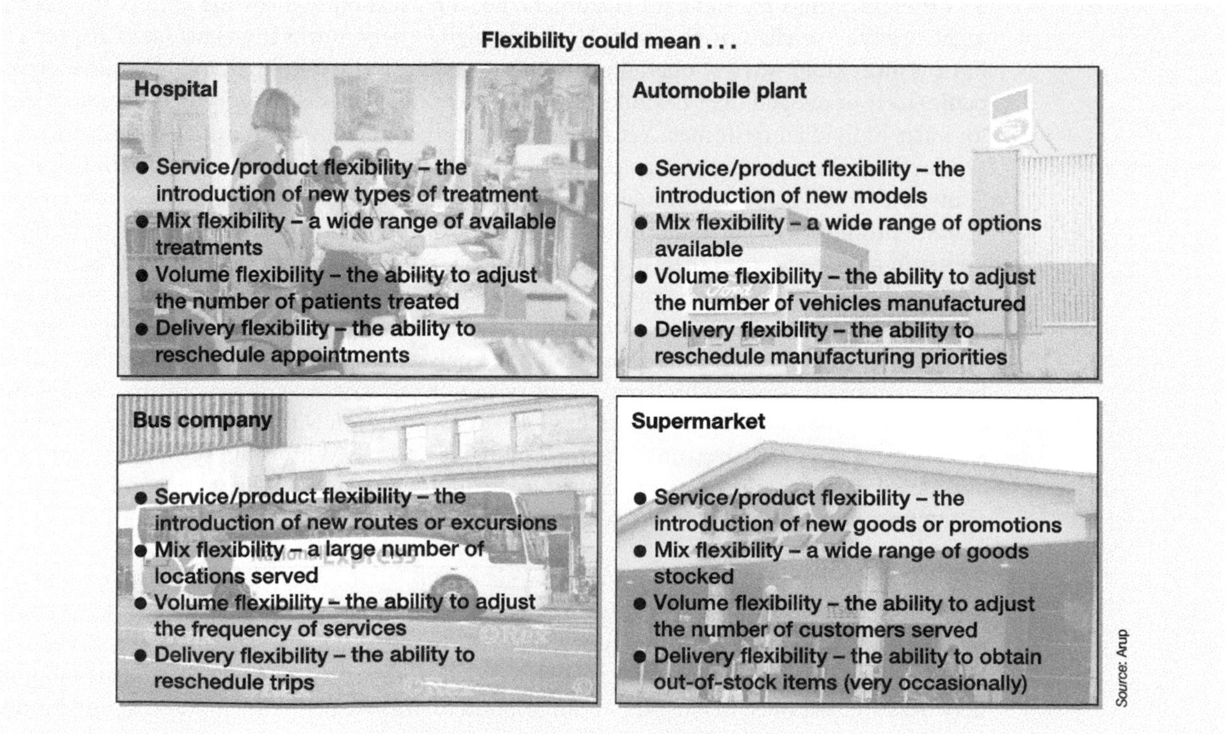

Margin notes:
Flexibility means being able to change in some way

Service/product flexibility

Mix flexibility

Volume flexibility

Delivery flexibility

Flexibility could mean . . .

Hospital
- Service/product flexibility – the introduction of new types of treatment
- Mix flexibility – a wide range of available treatments
- Volume flexibility – the ability to adjust the number of patients treated
- Delivery flexibility – the ability to reschedule appointments

Automobile plant
- Service/product flexibility – the introduction of new models
- Mix flexibility – a wide range of options available
- Volume flexibility – the ability to adjust the number of vehicles manufactured
- Delivery flexibility – the ability to reschedule manufacturing priorities

Bus company
- Service/product flexibility – the introduction of new routes or excursions
- Mix flexibility – a large number of locations served
- Volume flexibility – the ability to adjust the frequency of services
- Delivery flexibility – the ability to reschedule trips

Supermarket
- Service/product flexibility – the introduction of new goods or promotions
- Mix flexibility – a wide range of goods stocked
- Volume flexibility – the ability to adjust the number of customers served
- Delivery flexibility – the ability to obtain out-of-stock items (very occasionally)

Source: Arup

Figure 3.7 Flexibility means different things in different operations

Short case
Flexibility and dependability in the newsroom[5]

Source: BBC/Jeff Overs

Television news is big business. Satellite and cable, as well as developments in terrestrial transmission, have all helped to boost the popularity of 24-hour news services. However, news perishes fast. A daily newspaper delivered one day late is practically worthless. This is why broadcasting organizations like the BBC have to ensure that up-to-date news is delivered on time, every time. The BBC's ability to achieve high levels of dependability is made possible by the technology employed in news gathering and editing. At one time news editors would have to schedule a video-taped report to start its countdown five seconds prior to its broadcasting time. With new technology the video can be started from a freeze-frame and will broadcast the instant the command to play is given. The team have faith in the dependability of the process. In addition, technology allows them the flexibility to achieve dependability, even when news stories break just before transmission. In the hours before scheduled transmission, journalists and editors prepare an 'inventory' of news items stored electronically. The presenter will prepare his or her commentary on the autocue and each item will be timed to the second. If the team needs to make a short-term adjustment to the planned schedule, the news studio's technology allows the editors to take broadcasts live from journalists at their locations, on satellite 'takes', directly into the programme. Editors can even type news reports directly onto the autocue for the presenter to read as they are typed – nerve-racking, but it keeps the programme on time.

Mass customization

One of the beneficial external effects of flexibility is the increased ability of operations to do different things for different customers. So, high flexibility gives the ability to create a high variety of services or products. Normally high variety means high cost (see Chapter 1). Furthermore, high-variety operations do not usually produce in high volume. Some companies have developed their flexibility in such a way that products and services are customized for each individual customer. Yet they manage to produce them in a high-volume, mass-production manner which keeps costs down. This approach is called **mass customization**. Sometimes this is achieved through flexibility in design. For example, Dell is one of the largest volume producers of personal computers in the world, yet allows each customer to 'design' (albeit in a limited sense) their own configuration. Sometimes flexible technology is used to achieve the same effect. For example, Paris Miki, an up-market eyewear retailer which has the largest number of eyewear stores in the world, uses its own 'Mikissimes Design System' to capture a digital image of the customer and analyse facial characteristics. Together with a list of customers' personal preferences, the system then recommends a particular design and displays it on the image of the customer's face. In consultation with the optician the customer can adjust shapes and sizes until the final design is chosen. Within the store the frames are assembled from a range of pre-manufactured components and the lenses ground and fitted to the frames. The whole process takes around an hour.

Mass customization

Agility

Agility

Judging operations in terms of their **agility** has become popular. Agility is really a combination of all the five performance objectives, but particularly flexibility and speed. In addition, agility implies that an operation and the supply chain of which it is a part (supply networks are described in Chapter 7) can respond to uncertainty in the market. Agility means responding to market requirements by creating new and existing services and products fast and flexibly.

Flexibility inside the operation

Developing a flexible operation can also have advantages to the internal customers within the operation.

Flexibility speeds up response. Fast service often depends on the operation being flexible. For example, if the hospital has to cope with a sudden influx of patients from a road accident, it clearly needs to deal with injuries quickly. Under such circumstances a flexible hospital which can speedily transfer extra skilled staff and equipment to the Accident and Emergency department will provide the fast service which the patients need.

Flexibility saves time. In many parts of the hospital, staff have to treat a wide variety of complaints. Fractures, cuts or drug overdoses do not come in batches. Each patient is an individual with individual needs. The hospital staff cannot take time to 'get into the routine' of treating a particular complaint; they must have the flexibility to adapt quickly. They must also have sufficiently flexible facilities and equipment so that time is not wasted waiting for equipment to be brought to the patient. The time of the hospital's resources is being saved because they are flexible in 'changing over' from one task to the next.

Flexibility maintains dependability. Internal flexibility can also help to keep the operation on schedule when unexpected events disrupt the operation's plans. For example, if the sudden influx of patients to the hospital requires emergency surgical procedures, routine operations will be disrupted. This is likely to cause distress and considerable inconvenience. A flexible hospital might be able to minimize the disruption by possibly having reserved operating theatres for such an emergency, and being able to bring in medical staff quickly that are 'on call'.

The cost objective

To the companies which compete directly on price, cost will clearly be their major operations objective. The lower the cost of creating and delivering their services and products, the lower can be the price to their customers. Even those companies which do not compete on price will be interested in keeping costs low. Every euro or dollar removed from an operation's

---

Short case
Everyday low prices at Aldi[6]

Source: Alamy Images

Aldi is an international 'limited assortment' supermarket specializing in 'private label', mainly food products. It has carefully focused its service concept and delivery system to attract customers in a highly competitive market. The company believes that its unique approach to operations management make it 'virtually impossible for competitors to match our combination of price and quality'.

Aldi operations challenge the norms of retailing. They are deliberately simple, using basic facilities to keep down overheads. Most stores stock only a limited range of goods (typically around 700 compared with 25,000 to 30,000 stocked by conventional supermarket chains). The private label approach means that the products have been produced according to Aldi quality specifications and are only sold in Aldi stores. Without the high costs of brand marketing and advertising and with Aldi's formidable purchasing power, prices can be 30 per cent below their branded equivalents. Other cost-saving practices include open carton displays which eliminate the need for special shelving, no grocery bags to encourage reuse as well as saving costs, and using a 'cart rental' system which requires customers to return the cart to the store to get their coin deposit back.

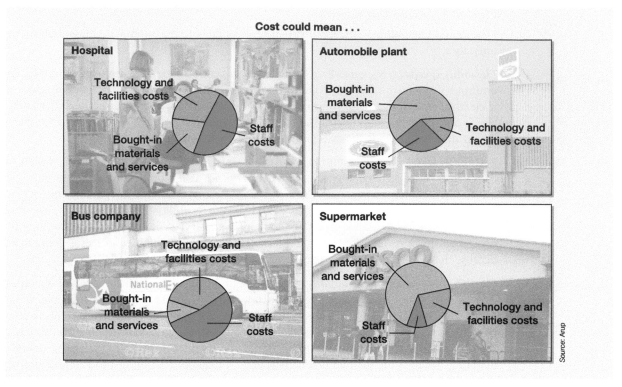

Figure 3.8 Cost means different things in different operations

Source: Arup

Low cost is a universally attractive objective

cost base is a further euro or dollar added to its profits. Not surprisingly, **low cost is a universally attractive objective**. The short-case 'Everyday low prices at Aldi' describes how one retailer keeps its costs down. The ways in which operations management can influence cost will depend largely on where the operation costs are incurred. The operation will spend its money on staff (the money spent on employing people), facilities, technology and equipment (the money spent on buying, caring for, operating and replacing the operation's 'hardware') and materials (the money spent on the 'bought-in' materials consumed or transformed in the operation). Figure 3.8 shows typical cost breakdowns for the hospital, car plant, supermarket and bus company.

Cost reduction through internal effectiveness

Our previous discussion distinguished between the benefits of each performance objective to externally and internally. Each of the various performance objectives has several internal effects, but **all of them affect cost**. So, one important way to improve cost performance is to improve the performance of the other operations objectives (see Figure 3.9).

All performance objectives affect cost

- High-quality operations do not waste time or effort having to re-do things, nor are their internal customers inconvenienced by flawed service.
- Fast operations reduce the level of in-process inventory between and within processes, as well as reducing administrative overheads.
- Dependable operations do not spring any unwelcome surprises on their internal customers. They can be relied on to deliver exactly as planned. This eliminates wasteful disruption and allows the other micro-operations to operate efficiently.
- Flexible operations adapt to changing circumstances quickly and without disrupting the rest of the operation. Flexible micro-operations can also change over between tasks quickly and without wasting time and capacity.

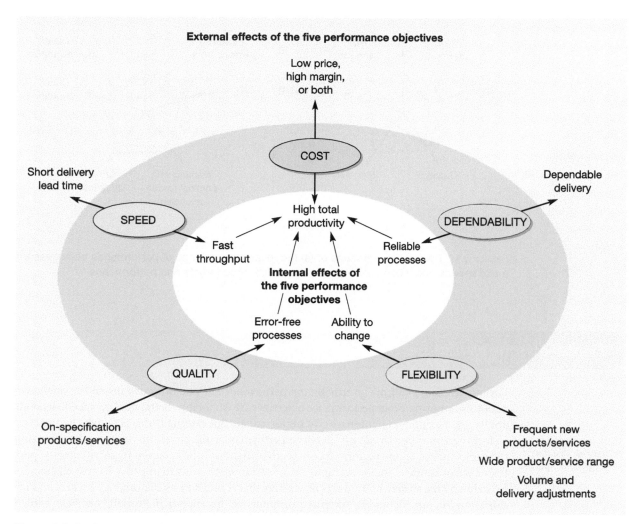

Figure 3.9 Performance objectives have both external and internal effects. Internally, cost is influenced by the other performance objectives

The polar representation of performance objectives

Polar representation

A useful way of representing the relative importance of performance objectives for a product or service is shown in Figure 3.10(a). This is called the **polar representation** because the scales which represent the importance of each performance objective have the same origin. A line describes the relative importance of each performance objective. The closer the line is to the centre, the less important is the performance objective to the operation. Two services are shown, a taxi and a bus service. Each essentially provides the same basic service, but with different objectives. The differences between the two services are clearly shown by the diagram. Of course, the polar diagram can be adapted to accommodate any number of different performance objectives. For example, Figure 3.10(b) shows a proposal for using a polar diagram to assess the relative performance of different police forces in the UK.[7] Note that this proposal uses three measures of quality (reassurance, crime reduction and crime detection), one measure of cost (economic efficiency), and one measure of how the police force develops its relationship with 'internal' customers (the criminal justice agencies). Note also that actual performance as well as required performance is marked on the diagram.

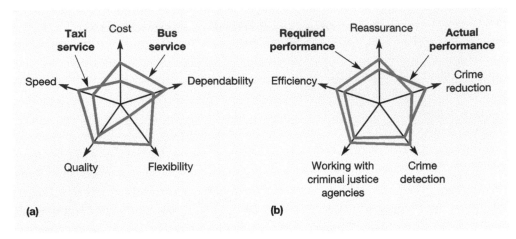

Figure 3.10 Polar representations of (a) the relative importance of performance objectives for a taxi service and a bus service, and (b) a police force targets and performance

Trade-offs between performance objectives

There can be a trade-off between an operation's performance objectives

Earlier we examined how improving the performance of one objective inside the operation could also improve other performance objectives. Most notably, better quality, speed, dependability and flexibility can improve cost performance. But externally this is not always the case. In fact there may be a *'trade-off'* **between performance objectives**. In other words improving the performance of one performance objective might only be achieved by sacrificing the performance of another. So, for example, an operation might wish to improve its cost efficiencies by reducing the variety of products or services that it offers to its customers. *'There is no such thing as a free lunch'* could be taken as a summary of this approach. Probably the best-known summary of the trade-off idea comes from Professor Wickham Skinner, who said:

> *'most managers will readily admit that there are compromises or trade-offs to be made in designing an airplane or truck. In the case of an airplane, trade-offs would involve matters such as cruising speed, take-off and landing distances, initial cost, maintenance, fuel consumption, passenger comfort and cargo or passenger capacity. For instance, no one today can design a 500-passenger plane that can land on an aircraft carrier and also break the sound barrier. Much the same thing is true in [operations]'.*[8]

The efficient frontier

But there are two views of trade-offs. The first emphasizes 'repositioning' performance objectives by trading off improvements in some objectives for a reduction in performance in others. The other emphasizes increasing the 'effectiveness' of the operation by overcoming trade-offs so that improvements in one or more aspects of performance can be achieved without any reduction in the performance of others. Most businesses at some time or other will adopt both approaches. This is best illustrated through the concept of the '**efficient frontier**' of operations performance.

Trade-offs and the efficient frontier

Figure 3.11(a) shows the relative performance of several companies in the same industry in terms of their cost efficiency and the variety of products or services that they offer to their customers. Presumably all the operations would ideally like to be able to offer very high variety while still having very high levels of cost efficiency. However, the increased complexity that a high variety of product or service offerings brings will generally reduce the operation's ability to operate efficiently. Conversely, one way of improving cost efficiency is to severely

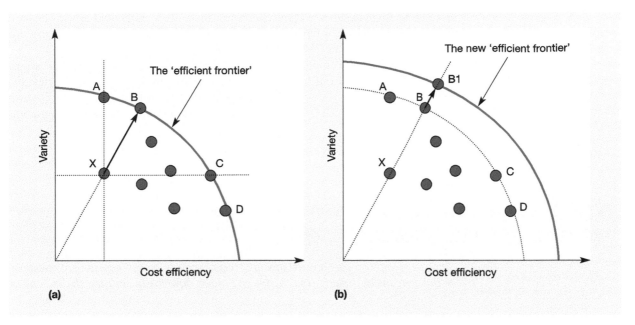

Figure 3.11 The efficient frontier identifies operations with performances that dominate other operations' performance

limit the variety on offer to customers. The spread of results in Figure 3.11(a) is typical of an exercise such as this. Operations A, B, C, D have all chosen a different balance between variety and cost efficiency. However, none is dominated by any other operation in the sense that another operation necessarily has 'superior' performance. Operation X, however, has an inferior performance because operation A is able to offer higher variety at the same level of cost efficiency and operation C offers the same variety but with better cost efficiency. The convex line on which operations A, B, C and D lie is known as the 'efficient frontier'. They may choose to position themselves differently (presumably because of different market strategies) but they cannot be criticized for being ineffective. Of course, any of these operations that lie on the efficient frontier may come to believe that the balance they have chosen between variety and cost efficiency is inappropriate. In these circumstances they may choose to reposition themselves at some other point along the efficient frontier. By contrast, operation X has also chosen to balance variety and cost efficiency in a particular way but is not doing so effectively. Operation B has the same ratio between the two performance objectives but is achieving them more effectively.

However, a strategy that emphasizes increasing effectiveness is not confined to those operations that are dominated, such as operation X. Those with a position on the efficient frontier will generally also want to improve their operations effectiveness by overcoming the trade-off that is implicit in the efficient frontier curve. For example, suppose operation B in Figure 3.11(b) wants to improve both its variety and its cost efficiency simultaneously and move to position B1. It may be able to do this, but only if it adopts operations improvements that extend the efficient frontier. For example, one of the decisions that any supermarket manager has to make is how many checkout positions to open at any time. If too many checkouts are opened then there will be times when the checkout staff do not have any customers to serve and will be idle. The customers, however, will have excellent service in terms of little or no waiting time. Conversely, if too few checkouts are opened, the staff will be working all the time but customers will have to wait in long queues. There seems to be a direct trade-off between staff utilization (and therefore cost) and customer waiting time (speed of service). Yet even the supermarket manager might, for example, allocate a number of 'core' staff to operate the checkouts but also arrange for those other staff who are performing other jobs in the supermarket to be trained and 'on call' should demand suddenly increase. If the manager on duty sees a build-up of customers at the checkouts, these other staff could quickly be used to staff checkouts. By devising a flexible system of staff allocation, the manager can both improve customer service and keep staff utilization high.

This distinction between positioning on the efficient frontier and increasing operations effectiveness by extending the frontier is an important one. Any business must make clear the extent to which it is expecting the operation to reposition itself in terms of its performance objectives and the extent to which it is expecting the operation to improve its effectiveness in several ways simultaneously.

Summary answers to key questions

Check and improve your understanding of this chapter using self-assessment questions and a personalized study plan, audio and video downloads, and an eBook – all at ***www.myomlab.com****.*

➤ Why is operations performance important in any organization?

- Operations management can either 'make or break' any business. It is large and, in most businesses, represents the bulk of its assets, but also because the operations function gives the ability to compete by providing the ability to respond to customers and by developing the capabilities that will keep it ahead of its competitors in the future.

➤ How should the operations function judge itself?

- Operations performance can be judged using the 'triple bottom line' approach. This includes social, environmental and economic performance.

➤ What does top management expect from the operations function?

- Operations can contribute to the organization as a whole by:
  - achieving customer satisfaction
  - reducing the costs
  - reducing the risk of operational failure
  - reducing the amount of investment
  - providing the basis for future innovation.

➤ What are the performance objectives of operations and what are the internal and external benefits which derive from excelling in each of them?

- By 'doing things right', operations seek to influence the quality of the company's services and products. Externally, quality is an important aspect of customer satisfaction or dissatisfaction. Internally, quality operations both reduce costs and increase dependability.
- By 'doing things fast', operations seek to influence the speed with which services and products are delivered. Externally, speed is an important aspect of customer service. Internally, speed both reduces inventories by decreasing internal throughput time and reduces risks by delaying the commitment of resources.

- By 'doing things on time', operations seek to influence the dependability of the delivery of services and products. Externally, dependability is an important aspect of customer service. Internally, dependability within operations increases operational reliability, thus saving the time and money that would otherwise be taken up in solving reliability problems and also giving stability to the operation.

- By 'changing what they do', operations seek to influence the flexibility with which the company creates its offerings. Externally, flexibility can:
  - create new offerings (service/product flexibility);
  - create a wide range or mix of offerings (mix flexibility);
  - create different quantities or volumes of offerings (volume flexibility);
  - create offerings at different times (delivery flexibility).

  Internally, flexibility can help speed up response times, save time wasted in changeovers, and maintain dependability.

- By 'doing things cheaply', operations seek to influence the cost of the company's offerings. Externally, low costs allow organizations to reduce their price in order to gain higher volumes or, alternatively, increase their profitability on existing volume levels. Internally, cost performance is helped by good performance in the other performance objectives.

➤ **How do operations performance objectives trade off against each other?**

- Trade-offs are the extent to which improvements in one performance objective can be achieved by sacrificing performance in others. The 'efficient frontier' concept is a useful approach to articulating trade-offs and distinguishes between repositioning performance on the efficient frontier and improving performance by overcoming trade-offs.

Learning exercises

These problems and applications will help to improve your analysis of operations. You can find more practice problems as well as worked examples and guided solutions on MyOMLab at www.myomlab.com.

1. The 'forensic science' service of a European country has traditionally been organized to provide separate forensic science laboratories for each police force around the country. In order to save costs, the government has decided to centralize this service in one large central facility close to the country's capital. What do you think are the external advantages and disadvantages of this to the stakeholders of the operation? What do you think are the internal implications to the new centralized operation that will provide this service?

2. *Step 1.* Look again at the figures in the chapter which illustrate the meaning of each performance objective for the four operations. Consider the bus company and the supermarket, and in particular consider their external customers.

   Step 2. Draw the relative required performance for both operations on a polar diagram.

   Step 3. Consider the internal effects of each performance objective. For both operations, identify how quality, speed, dependability and flexibility can help to reduce the cost of producing their services.

3. Visit the websites of two or three large oil companies such as Exxon, Shell, Elf, etc. Examine how they describe their policies towards their customers, suppliers, shareholders, employees and society at large. Identify areas of the company's operations where there may be conflicts between the needs of these different stakeholder groups. Discuss or reflect on how (if at all) such companies try and reconcile these conflicts.

Want to know more?

Bourne, M., Kennerley, M. and Franco, M. (2005) Managing through measures: a study of the impact on performance, *Journal of Manufacturing Technology Management*, vol. 16, issue 4, 373–95. What it says on the tin.

Kaplan, R.S. and Norton, D.P. (2005) The Balanced Scorecard: measures that drive performance, *Harvard Business Review*, Jul/Aug. The latest pronouncements on the Balanced Scorecard approach.

Pine, B.J. (1993) *Mass Customization*, Harvard Business School Press, Boston. The first substantial work on the idea of mass customization. Still a classic.

Savitz, A.W. and Weber, K. (2006) *The Triple Bottom Line: How Today's Best-Run Companies Are Achieving Economic, Social and Environmental Success – and How You Can Too*, Jossey-Bass, San Francisco, CA. An up-to-date treatment of the triple bottom line.

Waddock, S. (2003) Stakeholder performance implications of corporate responsibility, *International Journal of Business Performance Management*, vol. 5, numbers 2–3, 114–24. An introduction to stakeholder analysis.

Useful websites

www.aomonline.org General strategy site of the American Academy of Management.

www.cranfield.ac.uk/som Look for the 'Best factory awards' link. Manufacturing, but interesting.

www.opsman.org Lots of useful stuff.

www.worldbank.org Global issues. Useful for international operations strategy research.

www.weforum.org Global issues, including some operations strategy ones.

www.ft.com Great for industry and company examples.

Now that you have finished reading this chapter, why not visit MyOMLab at www.myomlab.com where you'll find more learning resources to help you make the most of your studies and get a better grade.

Chapter 5

Process design

Key questions

➤ What is process design?

➤ How do volume and variety affect process design?

➤ How are processes designed in detail?

➤ What are the human implications for process design?

Introduction

Say you are a 'designer' and most people will assume that you are someone who is concerned with how a product looks. However, the design activity is much broader than that and while there is no universally recognized definition of 'design'. We take it to mean 'the process by which some functional requirement of people is satisfied through the shaping or configuration of the resources and/or activities that compose a service, a product, or the transformation process that creates and delivers them'. All operations managers are designers. When they purchase or rearrange the position of a piece of equipment, or when they change the way of working within a process, it is a design decision because it affects the physical shape and nature of their processes. This chapter examines the design of processes. Figure 5.1 shows where this chapter fits within the overall model of operations management.

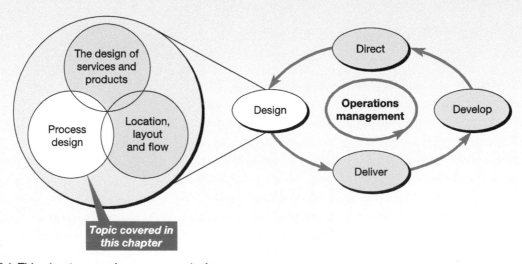

Figure 5.1 This chapter examines process design

Operations in practice Fast-food drive-throughs[1]

The quick-service restaurant (QSR) industry reckons that the very first drive-through dates back to 1928 when Royce Hailey first promoted the drive-through service at his Pig Stand restaurant in Los Angeles. Customers would simply drive by the back door of the restaurant where the chef would come out and deliver the restaurant's famous 'Barbequed Pig' sandwiches. Today, drive-through processes are slicker and faster. They are also more common. In 1975, McDonald's did not have any drive-throughs, but now more than 90 per cent of its US restaurants incorporate a drive-through process. In fact 80 per cent of recent fast-food growth has come through the growing number of drive-throughs. Says one industry specialist, *'There are a growing number of customers for whom fast-food is not fast enough. They want to cut waiting time to the very minimum without even getting out of their car. Meeting their needs depends on how smooth we can get the process.'*

The competition to design the fastest and most reliable drive-through process is fierce. Starbucks' drive-throughs have strategically placed cameras at the order boards so that servers can recognize regular customers and start making their order even before it's placed. Burger King has experimented with sophisticated sound systems, simpler menu boards and see-through food bags to ensure greater accuracy (no point in being fast if you don't deliver what the customer ordered). These details matter. McDonald's reckon that their sales increase one per cent for every six seconds saved at a drive-through, while a single Burger King restaurant calculated that its takings increased by 15,000 dollars a year each time it reduced queuing time by one second.

Source: Getty Images

Menu items must be easy to read and understand. Designing 'combo meals' (burger, fries and a cola), for example, saves time at the ordering stage. Perhaps the most remarkable experiment in making drive-through process times slicker is being carried out by McDonald's in the USA. On California's central coast 150 miles from Los Angeles, a call centre takes orders remotely from 40 McDonald's outlets around the country. The orders are then sent back to the restaurants through the Internet and the food is assembled only a few metres from where the order was placed. It may only save a few seconds on each order, but that can add up to extra sales at busy times of the day. However, not everyone is thrilled by the boom in drive-throughs. People living in the vicinity may complain of the extra traffic they attract and the unhealthy image of fast food combined with a process that does not even make customers get out of their car, is, for some, a step too far.

What is process design?

Design happens before creation

To 'design' is to conceive the looks, arrangement, and workings of something *before it is created*. In that sense it is a conceptual exercise. Yet it is one which must deliver a solution that will work in practice. Design is also an activity that can be approached at different levels of detail. One may envisage the general shape and intention of something before getting down to defining its details. This is certainly true for process design. At the start of the process design activity it is important to understand the design objectives, especially at first, when the overall shape and nature of the process is being decided. The most common way of doing this is by positioning it according to its volume and variety characteristics. Eventually the details of the process must be analysed to ensure that it fulfils its objectives effectively. Yet, it is often only through getting to grips with the detail of a design that the feasibility of its overall shape can be assessed. Don't think of this as a simple sequential process. There may be aspects concerned with the objectives or the broad positioning of the process that will need to be modified following its more detailed analysis.

What objectives should process design have?

The whole point of process design is to make sure that the performance of the process is appropriate for whatever it is trying to achieve. For example, if an operation competed primarily on its ability to respond quickly to customer requests, its processes would need to be designed to give fast throughput times. This would minimize the time between customers requesting a service or product and their receiving it. Similarly, if an operation competed on low price, cost-related objectives would dominate its process design. Some kind of logic should link what the operation as a whole is attempting to achieve and the **performance objectives** of its individual processes. This is illustrated in Table 5.1.

Process design should reflect process objectives

Operations performance objectives translate directly to process design objectives as shown in Table 5.1. As processes are managed at a very operational level, process design also needs to consider a more 'micro' and detailed set of objectives. These are largely concerned with flow through the process. When whatever are being 'processed' enter a process, they will progress through a series of activities where they are 'transformed' in some way. Between these activities they may dwell for some time in inventories, waiting to be transformed by the next activity. This means that the time that a unit spends in the process (its throughput time) will be longer than the sum of all the transforming activities that it passes through. Also the resources that perform the processes activities may not be used all the time because not all units will necessarily require the same activities and the capacity of each resource may not match the demand placed upon it. So neither the units moving through the process, nor the resources performing the activities may be fully utilized.

Table 5.1 The impact of strategic performance objectives on process design objectives and performance

Operations performance objective	Typical process design objectives	Some benefits of good process design
Quality	• Provide appropriate resources, capable of achieving the services or product specification • Error-free processing	• Products and services produced 'on-specification' • Less recycling and wasted effort within the process
Speed	• Minimum throughput time • Output rate appropriate for demand	• Short customer waiting time • Low in-process inventory
Dependability	• Provide dependable process resources • Reliable process output timing and volume	• On-time deliveries of products and services • Less disruption, confusion and rescheduling within the process
Flexibility	• Provide resources with an appropriate range of capabilities • Change easily between processing states (what, how, or how much is being processed)	• Ability to process a wide range of products and services • Low cost/fast product and service change • Low cost/fast volume and timing changes • Ability to cope with unexpected events (e.g. supply or a processing failure)

Cost	• Appropriate capacity to meet demand
	• Eliminate process waste in terms of
	  – excess capacity
	  – excess process capability
	  – in-process delays
	  – in-process errors
	  – inappropriate process inputs
		• Low processing costs
		• Low resource costs (capital costs)
		• Low delay and inventory costs (working capital costs)

Because of this the way that units leave the process is unlikely to be exactly the same as the way they arrive at the process. It is common for more 'micro' performance flow objectives to be used that describe process flow performance. For example:

Throughput rate

- **Throughput rate** (or flow rate) is the rate at which units emerge from the process, i.e. the number of units passing through the process per unit of time.

Throughput time

- **Throughput time** is the average elapsed time taken for inputs to move through the process and become outputs.

Work in process

- The number of units in the process (also called the '**work in process**' or in-process inventory), as an average over a period of time.

Utilization

- The **utilization** of process resources is the proportion of available time that the resources within the process are performing useful work.

Environmentally sensitive design

With the issues of environmental protection becoming more important, both process and service/product designers have to take account of 'green' issues. In many developed countries, legislation has already provided some basic standards which restrict the use of toxic materials, limit discharges to air and water, and protect employees and the public from immediate and long-term harm. Interest has focused on some fundamental issues:

Short case
Ecologically smart[2]

Source: Getty Images

When Daimler-Chrysler started to examine the feasibility of the Smart town car, the challenge was not just to examine the economic feasibility of the product but also to build in environmental sensitivity to the design of the product and the process that was to make it. This is why environmental protection is now a fundamental part of all production activities in its 'Smartville' plant at Hambach near France's border with Germany. The product itself is designed on environmentally compatible principles. Even before assembly starts, the product's disassembly must be considered. In fact the modular construction of the Smart car helps to guarantee economical dismantling at the end of its life. This also helps with the recycling of materials. Over 85 per cent of the Smart's components are recyclable and recycled material is used in its initial construction. For example, the Smart's instrument panel comprises 12 per cent recycled plastic material. Similarly, production processes are designed to be ecologically sustainable. The plant's environmentally friendly painting technique allows less paint to be used while maintaining a high quality of protection. It also involves no solvent emission and no hazardous waste, as well as the recycling of surplus material. It is not only the use of new technology that contributes to the plant's ecological credentials. Ensuring a smooth and efficient movement of materials within the plant also saves time, effort and, above all, energy. So, traffic flow outside and through the building has been optimized, buildings are made accessible to suppliers delivering to the plant, and conveyor systems are designed to be loaded equally in both directions so as to avoid empty runs. The company even claims that the buildings themselves are a model for ecological compatibility. No construction materials contain formaldehyde or CFCs and the outside of the buildings are lined with 'TRESPA', a raw material made from European timber that is quick to regenerate.

- *The sources of inputs* to a service or product. (Will they damage rainforests? Will they use up scarce minerals? Will they exploit the poor or use child labour?)
- *Quantities and sources of energy* consumed in the process. (Do plastic beverage bottles use more energy than glass ones? Should waste heat be recovered and used in fish farming?)
- *The amounts and type of waste material* that are created in the processes. (Can this waste be recycled efficiently, or must it be burnt or buried in landfill sites? Will the waste have a long-term impact on the environment as it decomposes and escapes?)
- *The life of the product itself.* It is argued that if a product has a useful life of, say, twenty years, it will consume fewer resources than one that only lasts five years, which must therefore be replaced four times in the same period. However, the long-life product may require more initial inputs, and may prove to be inefficient in the latter part of its use, when the latest products use less energy or maintenance to run.
- *The end-of-life of the product.* (Will the redundant product be difficult to dispose of in an environmentally friendly way? Could it be recycled or used as a source of energy? Could it still be useful in third-world conditions? Could it be used to benefit the environment, such as old cars being used to make artificial reefs for sea life?)

Designers are faced with complex trade-offs between these factors, although it is not always easy to obtain all the information that is needed to make the 'best' choices. For example, it is relatively straightforward to design a long-life product, using strong material, over-designed components, ample corrosion protection, and so on. However, its production might use more materials and energy and it could create more waste on disposal. To help make more rational decisions in the design activity, some industries are experimenting *Life cycle analysis* with **life cycle analysis**. This technique analyses all the production inputs, the life-cycle use of the product and its final disposal, in terms of total energy used (and more recently, of all the emitted wastes such as carbon dioxide, sulphurous and nitrous gases, organic solvents, solid waste, etc.). The inputs and wastes are evaluated at *every* stage in its creation, beginning with the extraction or farming of the basic raw materials. The short case 'Ecologically smart' demonstrates that it is possible to include ecological considerations in all aspects of product and process design.

Process types – the volume–variety effect on process design

In Chapter 1 we saw how processes in operations can range from creating a very high volume of products or services (for example, a food canning factory) to a very low volume (for example, major project consulting engineers). Also they can range from producing a very low variety of products or services (for example, in an electricity utility) to a very high variety (as, for example, in an architects' practice). Usually the two dimensions of volume and variety go together. Low-volume operations processes often have a high variety of services and products, and high-volume operations processes often have a narrow variety of services and products. Thus there is a continuum from low volume and high variety through to high volume and low variety, on which we can position operations. Different operations, even those in the same operation, may adopt different types of processes. In a medical service, compare the approach taken during mass medical treatments, such as large-scale immunization programmes, with that taken for a transplant operation where the treatment is designed specifically to meet the needs of one person. These differences go well beyond their differing technologies or the processing requirements of their products or services. They are explained by the fact that no one type of process design is best for all types *Volume–variety positions* of operation in all circumstances. The differences are because of the different **volume–variety positions** of the operations.

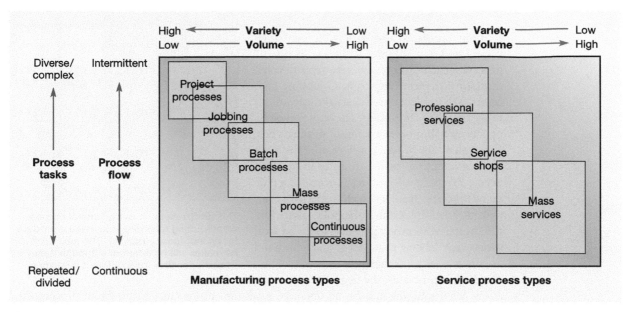

Figure 5.2 Different process types imply different volume–variety characteristics for the process

Process types

Process types

The position of a process on the volume–variety continuum shapes its overall design and the general approach to managing its activities. These 'general approaches' to designing and managing processes are called **process types**. Different terms are sometimes used to identify process types depending on whether they are predominantly manufacturing or service processes, and there is some variation in the terms used. For example, it is not uncommon to find the 'manufacturing' terms used in service industries. Figure 5.2 illustrates how these 'process types' are used to describe different positions on the volume–variety spectrum.

Project processes

Project processes

Project processes are those which deal with discrete, usually highly customized products. Often the timescale of making the product or service is relatively long, as is the interval between the completion of each product or service. So low volume and high variety are characteristics of project processes. The activities involved in making the product can be ill-defined and uncertain, sometimes changing during the production process itself. Examples of project processes include shipbuilding, most construction companies, movie production companies, large fabrication operations such as those manufacturing turbo generators, and installing a computer system. The essence of project processes is that each job has a well-defined start and finish, the time interval between starting

The major construction site shown in this picture is a project process. Each 'product' (project) is different and poses different challenges to those running the process (civil engineers).

different jobs is relatively long and the transforming resources which make the product will probably have been organized especially for each product. The process map for project processes will almost certainly be complex. This is partly because each unit of output is so large with many activities occurring at the same time and partly because the activities in such processes often involve significant discretion to act according to professional judgement.

Jobbing processes

Jobbing processes

Jobbing processes also deal with very high variety and low volumes. Whereas in project processes each product has resources devoted more or less exclusively to it, in jobbing processes each product has to share the operation's resources with many others. The resources of the operation will process a series of products but, although all the products will require the same kind of attention, each will differ in its exact needs. Examples of jobbing processes include many precision engineers such as specialist toolmakers, furniture restorers, bespoke tailors, and the printer who produces tickets for the local social event. Jobbing processes produce more and usually smaller items than project processes but, like project processes, the degree of repetition

This craftsperson is using general purpose wood-cutting technology to make a product for an individual customer. The next product he makes will be different (although it may be similar), possibly for a different customer.

is low. Many jobs will probably be 'one-offs'. Again, any process map for a jobbing process could be relatively complex for similar reasons to project processes. However, jobbing processes usually produce physically smaller products and, although sometimes involving considerable skill, such processes often involve fewer unpredictable circumstances.

Batch processes

Batch processes

Batch processes can often look like jobbing processes, but batch does not have quite the degree of variety associated with jobbing. As the name implies, each time batch processes produce a product they produce more than one. So each part of the operation has periods when it is repeating itself, at least while the 'batch' is being processed. The size of the batch could be just two or three, in which case the batch process will differ little from jobbing, especially if each batch is a totally novel product. Conversely, if the batches are large, and especially if the products are familiar to the

In this kitchen, food is being prepared in batches. All batches go through the same sequence (preparation, cooking, storing), but each batch is a different dish.

operation, batch processes can be fairly repetitive. Because of this, the batch type of process can be found over a wide range of volume and variety levels. Examples of batch processes include machine tool manufacturing, the production of some special gourmet frozen foods, and the manufacture of most of the component parts which go into mass-produced assemblies such as automobiles.

Mass processes

Mass processes

Mass processes are those which produce goods in high volume and relatively narrow variety – narrow, that is, in terms of the fundamentals of the product design. An automobile plant, for example, might produce several thousand variants of car if every option of engine size, colour, extra equipment, etc. is taken into account. Yet essentially it is a mass operation because the different variants of its product do not affect

This automobile plant is everyone's idea of a mass process. Each product is almost (but not quite) the same, and is made in large quantities.

the basic process of production. The activities in the automobile plant, like all mass operations, are essentially repetitive and largely predictable. Examples of mass processes include the automobile plant, a television factory, most food processes and DVD production. Several variants of a product could be produced on a mass process such as an assembly line, but the process itself is unaffected. The equipment used at each stage of the process can be designed to handle several different types of components loaded into the assembly equipment. So, provided the sequence of components in the equipment is synchronized with the sequence of models moving through the process, the process seems to be almost totally repetitive.

Continuous processes

Continuous processes

Continuous processes are one step beyond mass processes insomuch as they operate at even higher volume and often have even lower variety. They also usually operate for longer periods of time. Sometimes they are literally continuous in that their products are inseparable, being produced in an endless flow. Continuous processes are often associated with relatively inflexible, capital-intensive technologies with highly predictable flow. Examples of continuous processes include petrochemical refineries, electricity utilities, steel making and some paper making. There are often few elements of discretion in this type of process and although products may be stored during the process, the predominant characteristic of most continuous

This continuous water treatment process almost never stops (it only stops for maintenance) and performs a narrow range of tasks (filters impurities). Often we only notice the process if it goes wrong!

processes is of smooth flow from one part of the process to another. Inspections are likely to form part of the process, although the control applied as a consequence of those inspections is often automatic rather than requiring human discretion.

Professional services

Professional services

Professional services are defined as high-contact organizations where customers spend a considerable time in the service process. Such services provide high levels of customization, the service process being highly adaptable in order to meet individual customer needs. A great deal of staff time is spent in the front office and contact staff are given considerable discretion in servicing customers. Professional services tend to be people-based rather than equipment-based, with emphasis placed on the process (how the service is delivered) rather than the 'product' (what is delivered). Professional services include management consultants, lawyers' practices, architects, doctors' surgeries, auditors, health and safety inspectors and some computer field service operations. A typical example would be OEE, a consultancy that sells the problem-solving

Here consultants are preparing to start a consultancy assignment. They are discussing how they might approach the various stages of the assignment, from understanding the real nature of the problem through to the implementation of their recommended solutions. This is a process map, although a very high level one. It guides the nature and sequence of the consultants' activities.

expertise of its skilled staff to tackle clients' problems. Typically, the problem will first be discussed with clients and the boundaries of the project defined. Each 'product' is different, and a high proportion of work takes place at the client's premises, with frequent contact between consultants and the client.

Service shops

Service shops

Service shops are characterized by levels of customer contact, customization, volumes of customers and staff discretion, which position them between the extremes of professional and mass services (see next paragraph). Service is provided via mixes of front- and back-office activities. Service shops include banks, high-street shops, holiday tour operators, car rental companies, schools, most restaurants, hotels and travel agents. For example, an equipment hire and sales organization may have a range of products displayed in front-office outlets, while back-office operations look after purchasing and administration. The front-office staff have some technical training and can advise customers dur-

The health club shown in the picture has front-office staff who can give advice on exercise programmes and other treatments. To maintain a dependable service the staff need to follow defined processes every day.

ing the process of selling the product. Essentially the customer is buying a fairly standardized product but will be influenced by the process of the sale which is customized to the customer's individual needs.

Mass services

Mass services

Mass services have many customer transactions, involving limited contact time and little customization. Such services may be equipment-based and 'product'-oriented, with most value added in the back office and relatively little judgement applied by front-office staff. Staff are likely to have a closely defined division of labour and to follow set procedures. Mass services include supermarkets, a national rail network, an airport, telecommunications services and libraries. For example, rail services such as SNCF in France all move a large number of passengers with a variety of rolling stock on an immense infrastructure of railways.

This is an account management centre for a large retail bank. It deals with thousands of customer requests every day. Although each customer request is different, they are all of the same type – involving customers' accounts.

Passengers pick a journey from the range offered. One of the most common types of mass service is the call centres used by almost all companies that deal directly with consumers. Coping with a very high volume of enquiries requires some kind of structuring of the process of communicating with customers. This is often achieved by using a carefully designed enquiry process (sometimes known as a 'script').

Critical commentary

Although the idea of process types is useful insomuch as it reinforces the, sometimes important, distinctions between different types of process, it is in many ways simplistic. In reality there is no clear boundary between process types. For example, a specialist camera retailer would normally be categorized as a service shop, yet it also will give, sometimes very specialized, technical advice to customers. It is not a professional service like a consultancy of course, but it does have elements of a professional service process within its design. This is why the volume and variety characteristics of a process are sometimes seen as being a more realistic way of describing processes. The product–process matrix described next adopts this approach.

The product–process matrix

Product–process matrix

Making comparisons between different processes along a spectrum which goes, for example, from shipbuilding at one extreme to electricity generation at the other has limited value. No one grumbles that yachts are so much more expensive than electricity. The real point is that because the different process types overlap, organizations often have a choice of what type of process to employ. This choice will have consequences to the operation, especially in terms of its cost and flexibility. The classic representation of how cost and flexibility vary with process choice is the **product–process matrix** that comes from Professors Hayes and Wheelwright of Harvard University.[3] They represent process choices on a matrix with the volume–variety as one dimension, and process types as the other (our matrix has been updated to incorporate both product and service operations). Figure 5.3 shows their matrix adapted to fit with the terminology used here. Most operations stick to **the 'natural' diagonal** of the matrix, and few, if any, are found in the extreme corners of the matrix. However, because there is some overlap between the various process types, operations might be positioned slightly off the diagonal.

The 'natural' diagonal

The diagonal of the matrix shown in Figure 5.3 represents a 'natural' lowest cost position for an operation. Operations which are on the right of the 'natural' diagonal have processes which would normally be associated with lower volumes and higher variety. This means that their processes are likely to be more flexible than seems to be warranted by their actual volume–variety position. Put another way, they are not taking advantage of their ability to standardize their processes. Therefore, their costs are likely to be higher than they would be with a process that was closer to the diagonal. Conversely, operations that are on the left of the diagonal have adopted processes which would normally be used in a higher-volume and lower-variety situation. Their processes will therefore be 'over-standardized' and probably too inflexible for their volume–variety position. This lack of flexibility can also lead to high costs because the process will not be able to change from one activity to another as efficiently as a more flexible process.

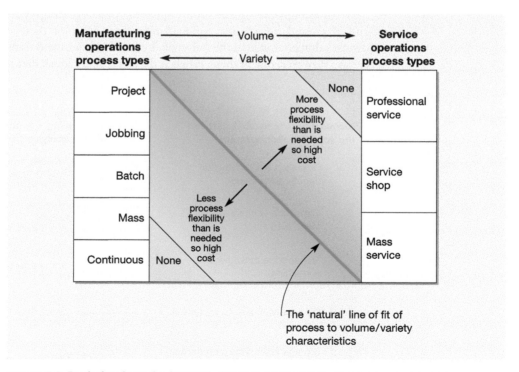

Figure 5.3 Deviating from the 'natural' diagonal on the product–process matrix has consequences for cost and flexibility

Source: Based on Hayes and Wheelwright[4]

Detailed process design

After the overall design of a process has been determined, its individual activities must be configured. At its simplest this detailed design of a process involves identifying all the individual activities that are needed to fulfil the objectives of the process and deciding on the sequence in which these activities are to be performed and who is going to do them. There will, of course, be some constraints on this. Some activities must be carried out before others and some activities can only be done by certain people or machines. Nevertheless, for a process of any reasonable size, the number of alternative process designs is usually large. This means that process design is often done using some simple visual approach such as **process mapping**.

Process mapping

Process mapping

Process mapping simply involves describing processes in terms of how the activities within the process relate to each other. There are many techniques which can be used for *process mapping* (or **process blueprinting**, or **process analysis**, as it is sometimes called). However, all the techniques identify the different *types of* activity that take place during the process and show the flow of materials or people or information through the process.

Process blueprinting
Process analysis

Process mapping symbols

Process mapping symbols

Process mapping symbols are used to classify different types of activity. And although there is no universal set of symbols used all over the world for any type of process, there are some that are commonly used. Most of these derive either from the early days of 'scientific' management around a century ago or, more recently, from information system flowcharting. Figure 5.4 shows the symbols we shall use here.

These symbols can be arranged in order, and in series or in parallel, to describe any process. For example, the retail catering operation of a large campus university has a number of outlets around the campus selling sandwiches. Most of these outlets sell 'standard' sandwiches that are made in the university's central kitchens and transported to each outlet every day. However, one of these outlets is different; it is a kiosk that makes more expensive

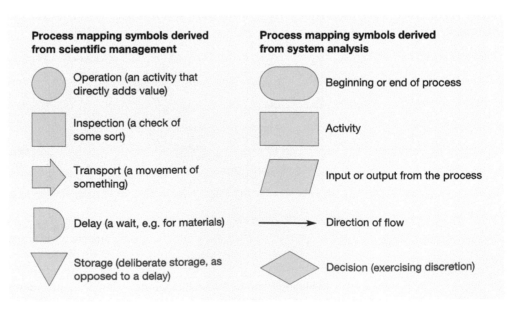

Figure 5.4 Some common process mapping symbols

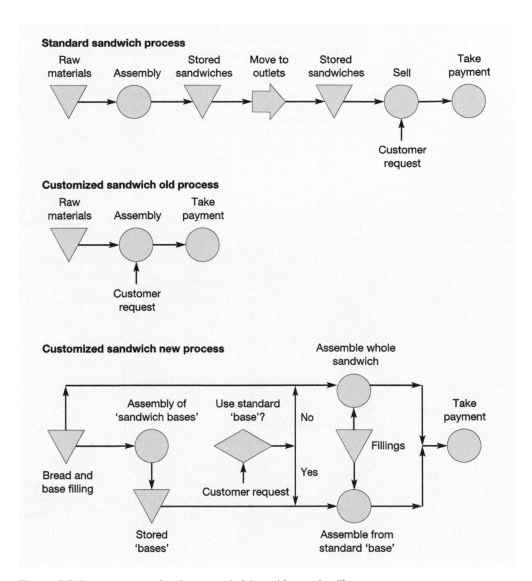

Figure 5.5 Process maps for three sandwich making and selling processes

'customized' sandwiches to order. Customers can specify the type of bread they want and choose from a very wide combination of different fillings. As queues for this customized service are becoming excessive, the catering manager is considering redesigning the process to speed it up. This new process design is based on the findings from a recent student study of the current process which proved that 95 per cent of all customers ordered only two types of bread (soft roll and Italian bread) and three types of protein filling (cheese, ham and chicken). Therefore the six 'sandwich bases' (2 types of bread × 3 protein fillings) could be prepared in advance and customized with salad, mayonnaise, etc. as customers ordered them. The process maps for making and selling the standard sandwiches, the current customized sandwiches and the new customized process are shown in Figure 5.5.

Note how the introduction of some degree of discretion in the new process makes it more complex to map at this detailed level. This is one reason why processes are often mapped at a more aggregated level, called **high-level process mapping**, before more detailed maps are drawn. Figure 5.6 illustrates this for the new customized sandwich operation. At the highest level the process can be drawn simply as an input–transformation–output process with sandwich materials and customers as its input resources and satisfied

High-level process
mapping

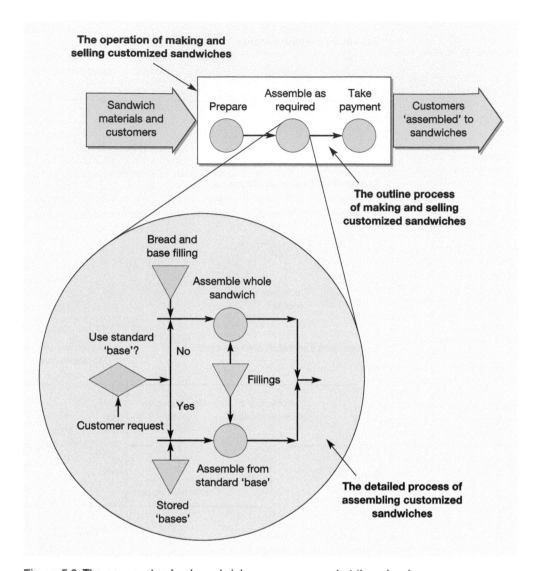

Figure 5.6 The new customized sandwich process mapped at three levels

customers with 'assembled' sandwiches as outputs. No details of how inputs are transformed into outputs are included. At a slightly lower, or more detailed level, what is sometimes called an **outline process map** (or chart) identifies the sequence of activities but only in a general way. So the activity of finding out what type of sandwich a customer wants, deciding if it can be assembled from a sandwich 'base' and then assembling it to meet the customer's request, is all contained in the general activity 'assemble as required'. At the more detailed level, all the activities are shown (we have shown the activities within 'assemble as required').

Using process maps to improve processes

One significant advantage of mapping processes is that each activity can be systematically challenged in an attempt to improve the process. For example, Figure 5.7 shows the flow process chart which Intel Corporation, the computer chip company, drew to describe its method of processing expense reports (claims forms). It also shows the process chart for the same process after critically examining and improving the process. The new process cut the number

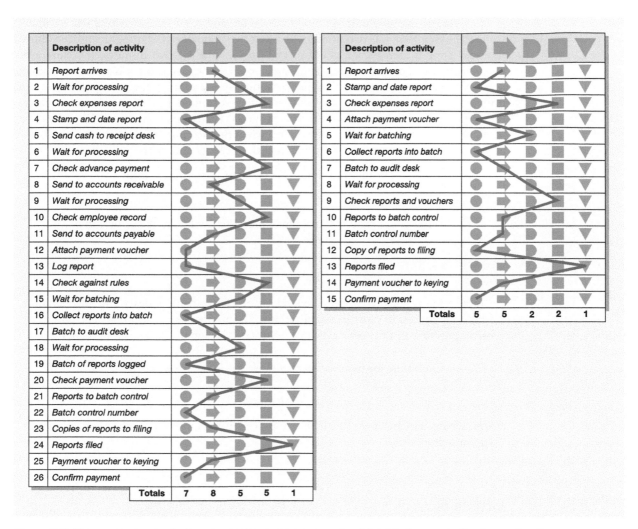

	Description of activity	●	➡	D	■	▼
1	Report arrives	●	➡	D	■	▼
2	Wait for processing	●	➡	D	■	▼
3	Check expenses report	●	➡	D	■	▼
4	Stamp and date report	●	➡	D	■	▼
5	Send cash to receipt desk	●	➡	D	■	▼
6	Wait for processing	●	➡	D	■	▼
7	Check advance payment	●	➡	D	■	▼
8	Send to accounts receivable	●	➡	D	■	▼
9	Wait for processing	●	➡	D	■	▼
10	Check employee record	●	➡	D	■	▼
11	Send to accounts payable	●	➡	D	■	▼
12	Attach payment voucher	●	➡	D	■	▼
13	Log report	●	➡	D	■	▼
14	Check against rules	●	➡	D	■	▼
15	Wait for batching	●	➡	D	■	▼
16	Collect reports into batch	●	➡	D	■	▼
17	Batch to audit desk	●	➡	D	■	▼
18	Wait for processing	●	➡	D	■	▼
19	Batch of reports logged	●	➡	D	■	▼
20	Check payment voucher	●	➡	D	■	▼
21	Reports to batch control	●	➡	D	■	▼
22	Batch control number	●	➡	D	■	▼
23	Copies of reports to filing	●	➡	D	■	▼
24	Reports filed	●	➡	D	■	▼
25	Payment voucher to keying	●	➡	D	■	▼
26	Confirm payment	●	➡	D	■	▼
	Totals	**7**	**8**	**5**	**5**	**1**

	Description of activity	●	➡	D	■	▼
1	Report arrives	●	➡	D	■	▼
2	Stamp and date report	●	➡	D	■	▼
3	Check expenses report	●	➡	D	■	▼
4	Attach payment voucher	●	➡	D	■	▼
5	Wait for batching	●	➡	D	■	▼
6	Collect reports into batch	●	➡	D	■	▼
7	Batch to audit desk	●	➡	D	■	▼
8	Wait for processing	●	➡	D	■	▼
9	Check reports and vouchers	●	➡	D	■	▼
10	Reports to batch control	●	➡	D	■	▼
11	Batch control number	●	➡	D	■	▼
12	Copy of reports to filing	●	➡	D	■	▼
13	Reports filed	●	➡	D	■	▼
14	Payment voucher to keying	●	➡	D	■	▼
15	Confirm payment	●	➡	D	■	▼
	Totals	**5**	**5**	**2**	**2**	**1**

Figure 5.7 Flow process charts for processing expense reports at Intel before and after improving the process

of activities from 26 down to 15. The accounts payable's activities were combined with the cash-receipt's activities of checking employees' past expense accounts (activities 8, 10 and 11) which also eliminated activities 5 and 7. After consideration, it was decided to eliminate the activity of checking items against company rules, because it seemed '*more trouble than it was worth*'. Also, logging the batches was deemed unnecessary. All this combination and elimination of activities had the effect of removing several 'delays' from the process. The end-result was a much-simplified process which reduced the staff time needed to do the job by 28 per cent and considerably speeded up the whole process.

Throughput, cycle time and work-in-process

The new customized sandwich process has one indisputable advantage over the old process: it is faster in the sense that customers spend less time in the process. The additional benefit this brings is a reduction in cost per customer served (because more customers can be served without increasing resources). Note, however, that the total amount of work needed to make and sell a sandwich has not reduced. All the new process has done is to move some of the work to a less busy time. So the **work content** (the total amount of work required to produce a unit of output) has not changed but customer **throughput time** (the time for a unit to move through the process) has improved.

Work content

Throughput time

For example, suppose that the time to assemble and sell a sandwich (the work content) using the old process was two minutes and that two people were staffing the process during the busy period. Each person could serve a customer every two minutes, therefore every two minutes two customers were being served, so on average a customer is emerging from the process every minute. This is called the **cycle time** of the process, the average time between units of output emerging from the process. When customers join the queue in the process they become **work-in-process** (or work-in-progress) sometimes written as WIP. If the queue is ten people long (including that customer) when the customer joins it, he or she will have to wait ten minutes to emerge from the process. Put more succinctly:

Cycle time

Work-in-process

$$\text{Throughput time} = \text{Work-in-process} \times \text{Cycle time}$$

In this case,

$$10 \text{ minutes wait} = 10 \text{ people in the system} \times 1 \text{ minute per person}$$

Worked example

Suppose the regional back-office operation of a large bank is designing an operation which will process its mortgage applications. The number of applications to be processed is 160 per week and the time available to process the applications is 40 hours per week.

$$\text{Cycle time for the process} = \frac{\text{time available}}{\text{number to be processed}} = \frac{40}{160} = \frac{1}{4} \text{ hour}$$

$$= 15 \text{ minutes}$$

So the bank's layout must be capable of processing a completed application once every 15 minutes.

Little's law

Little's law

This mathematical relationship (throughput time = work-in-process × cycle time) is called **Little's law**. It is simple but very useful, and it works for any stable process. For example, suppose it is decided that, when the new process is introduced, the average number of customers in the process should be limited to around ten and the maximum time a customer is in the process should be on average four minutes. If the time to assemble and sell a sandwich (from customer request to the customer leaving the process) in the new process has reduced to 1.2 minutes, how many staff should be serving?

Putting this into Little's law:

$$\text{Throughput time} = 4 \text{ minutes}$$

and

$$\text{Work-in-progress, WIP} = 10$$

So, since

$$\text{Throughput time} = \text{WIP} \times \text{Cycle time}$$

$$\text{Cycle time} = \frac{\text{Throughput time}}{\text{WIP}}$$

$$\text{Cycle time for the process} = \frac{4}{10} = 0.4 \text{ minute}$$

That is, a customer should emerge from the process every 0.4 minute, on average.

Given that an individual can be served in 1.2 minutes,

$$\text{Number of servers required} = \frac{1.2}{0.4} = 3$$

In other words, three servers would serve three customers in 1.2 minutes. Or one customer in 0.4 minute.

Worked example

Mike was totally confident in his judgement, *'You'll never get them back in time'*, he said. *'They aren't just wasting time, the process won't allow them to all have their coffee and get back for 11 o'clock.'* Looking outside the lecture theatre, Mike and his colleague Silvia were watching the 20 business people who were attending the seminar queuing to be served coffee and biscuits. The time was 10.45 and Silvia knew that unless they were all back in the lecture theatre at 11 o'clock there was no hope of finishing his presentation before lunch. *'I'm not sure why you're so pessimistic'*, said Silvia. *'They seem to be interested in what I have to say and I think they will want to get back to hear how operations management will change their lives.'* Mike shook his head. *'I'm not questioning their motivation'*, he said, *'I'm questioning the ability of the process out there to get through them all in time. I have been timing how long it takes to serve the coffee and biscuits. Each coffee is being made fresh and the time between the server asking each customer what they want and them walking away with their coffee and biscuits is taking 48 seconds. Remember that, according to Little's law, throughput equals work-in-process multiplied by cycle time. If the work-in-process is the 20 managers in the queue and cycle time is 48 seconds, the total throughput time is going to be 20 multiplied by 0.8 minute which equals 16 minutes. Add to that sufficient time for the last person to drink their coffee and you must expect a total throughput time of a bit over 20 minutes. You just haven't allowed long enough for the process.'* Silvia was impressed. *'Err . . . what did you say that law was called again?'* *'Little's law'*, said Mike.

Worked example

Every year it was the same. All the workstations in the building had to be renovated (tested, new software installed, etc.) and there was only one week in which to do it. The one week fell in the middle of the August vacation period when the renovation process would cause minimum disruption to normal working. Last year the company's 500 workstations had all been renovated within one working week (40 hours). Each renovation last year took on average 2 hours and 25 technicians had completed the process within the week. This year there would be 530 workstations to renovate but the company's IT support unit had devised a faster testing and renovation routine that would only take on average $1^{1}/_{2}$ hours instead of 2 hours. How many technicians will be needed this year to complete the renovation processes within the week?

Last year:

$$\text{Work-in-progress (WIP)} = 500 \text{ workstations}$$
$$\text{Time available } (T_{t}) = 40 \text{ hours}$$
$$\text{Average time to renovate} = 2 \text{ hours}$$
$$\text{Therefore throughput rate } (T_{r}) = {}^{1}/_{2} \text{ hour per technician}$$
$$= 0.5N$$

where $N = \text{Number of technicians}$

Little's law:

$$\text{WIP} = T_t \times T_r$$

$$500 = 40 \times 0.5N$$

$$N = \frac{500}{40 \times 0.5}$$

$$= 25 \text{ technicians}$$

This year:

$$\text{Work-in-progress (WIP)} = 530 \text{ workstations}$$

$$\text{Time available} = 40 \text{ hours}$$

$$\text{Average time to renovate} = 1.5 \text{ hours}$$

$$\text{Throughput rate } (T_r) = 1/1.5 \text{ per technician}$$

$$= 0.67N$$

where

$$N = \text{Number of technicians}$$

Little's law:

$$\text{WIP} = T_t \times T_r$$

$$530 = 40 \times 0.67N$$

$$N = \frac{530}{40 \times 0.67}$$

$$= 19.88 \text{ technicians}$$

$$\approx 20 \text{ technicians}$$

Balancing and bottlenecks

Balancing

One of the most important design decisions in layout is that of **balancing**. Perfect balancing would mean that work content is allocated equally to each stage in the process. This is nearly always impossible to achieve in practice and some imbalance in the work allocation results. Inevitably this will increase the effective cycle time of the process. If it becomes greater than the required cycle time, it may be necessary to devote extra resources, in the shape of a further stage, to compensate for the imbalance. The effectiveness of the balancing activity is measured by **balancing loss**. This is the time wasted through the unequal allocation of work as a percentage of the total time invested in processing the product or service. The longest stage in the process is called a '**bottleneck**'. It will govern the flow of items through the whole process.

Balancing loss

Bottleneck

Worked example

In Figure 5.8 the work allocations in a four-stage process are illustrated. The total amount of time invested in creating each service or product is four times the cycle time because, for every unit produced, all four stages have been working for the cycle time. When the work is equally allocated between the stages, the total time invested in each service or product is $4 \times 2.5 = 10$ minutes. However, when work is unequally allocated, as illustrated, the time invested is $3.0 \times 4 = 12$ minutes, i.e. 2.0 minutes of time, 16.67 per cent of the total, is wasted.

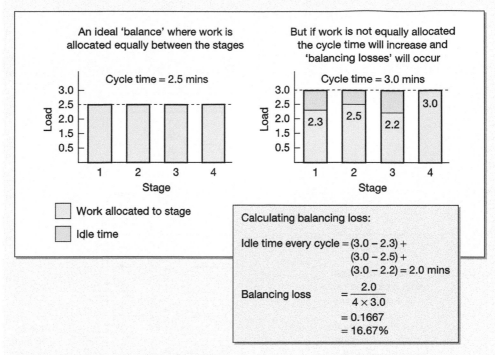

Figure 5.8 Balancing loss is that proportion of the time invested in processing the product or service which is not used productively

'Long thin' on 'short fat' processes

Return to the mortgage-processing process in the earlier worked example. It requires four stages working on the task to maintain a cycle time of one processed application every 15 minutes. The conventional arrangement of the four stages would be to lay them out in one line, each stage having 15 minutes' worth of work. However, nominally, the same output rate could also be achieved by arranging the four stages as two shorter lines, each of two stages with 30 minutes' worth of work each. Alternatively, following this logic to its ultimate conclusion, the stages could be arranged as four parallel stages, each responsible for the whole work content. Figure 5.9 shows these options.

This may be a simplified example, but it represents a genuine issue. Should the process be arranged as a single **long thin** line, as several **short fat** parallel lines, or somewhere in between? (Note that 'long' refers to the number of stages and 'fat' to the amount of work allocated to each stage.) In any particular situation there are usually technical constraints which limit either how 'long and thin' or how 'short and fat' the process can be, but there is usually a range of possible options within which a choice needs to be made.

The advantages of long thin processes include:

- *Controlled flow of materials or customers* – which is easy to manage.
- *Simple materials handling* – especially if a product being manufactured is heavy, large or difficult to move.
- *Lower capital requirements*. If a specialist piece of equipment is needed for one element in the job, only one piece of equipment would need to be purchased; on short fat arrangements every stage would need one.
- *More efficient operation*. If each stage is only performing a small part of the total job, the person at the stage will have a higher proportion of direct productive work as opposed to the non-productive parts of the job, such as picking up tools and materials.

Long thin
Short fat

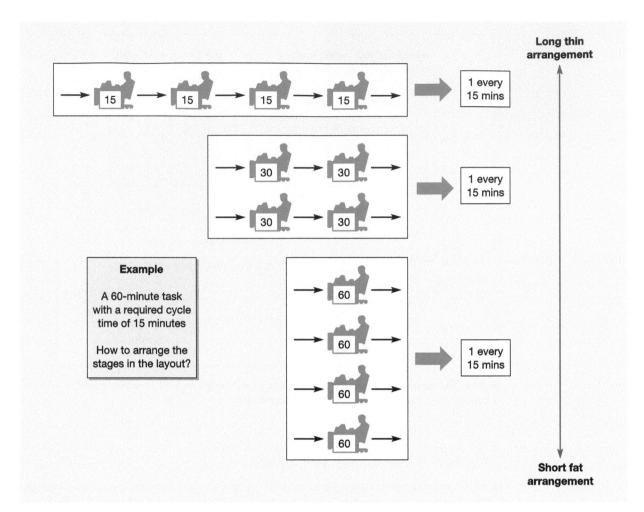

Figure 5.9 The arrangement of stages in product layout can be described on a spectrum from 'long thin' to 'short fat'

The advantages of the short fat processes include:

- *Higher mix flexibility*. If the layout needs to process several types of product or service, each stage or line could specialize in different types.
- *Higher volume flexibility*. As volume varies, stages can simply be closed down or started up as required; long thin processes would need rebalancing each time the cycle time changed.
- *Higher robustness*. If one stage breaks down or ceases operation in some way, the other parallel stages are unaffected; a long thin process would cease operating completely.
- *Less monotonous work*. In the mortgage example, the staff in the short fat arrangement are repeating their tasks only every hour; in the long thin arrangement it is every 15 minutes.

Throughput efficiency

This idea that the throughput time of a process is different from the work content of whatever it is processing has important implications. What it means is that for significant amounts of time no useful work is being done to the materials, information or customers that are progressing through the process. In the case of the simple example of the sandwich process described earlier, customer throughput time is restricted to 4 minutes, but the work content of the task (serving the customer) is only 1.2 minutes. So, the item being processed (the customer) is only being 'worked on' for 1.2/4 = 30 per cent of its time. This is called the **throughput efficiency** of the process.

Throughput efficiency

$$\text{Percentage throughput efficiency} = \frac{\text{Work content}}{\text{Throughput time}} \times 100$$

In this case the throughput efficiency is very high, relative to most processes, perhaps because the 'items' being processed are customers who react badly to waiting. In most material and information transforming processes, throughput efficiency is far lower, usually in single percentage figures.

Worked example

A vehicle licensing centre receives application documents, keys in details, checks the information provided on the application, classifies the application according to the type of licence required, confirms payment and then issues and mails the licence. It is currently processing an average of 5,000 licences every 8-hour day. A recent spot check found 15,000 applications that were 'in progress' or waiting to be processed. The sum of all activities that are required to process an application is 25 minutes. What is the throughput efficiency of the process?

$$\text{Work-in-progress} = 15,000 \text{ applications}$$

$$\text{Cycle time} =$$

$$\frac{\text{Time producing}}{\text{Number produced}} = \frac{8 \text{ hours}}{5,000} = \frac{480 \text{ minutes}}{5,000} = 0.096 \text{ minute}$$

From Little's law,

$$\text{Throughput time} = \text{WIP} \times \text{Cycle time}$$

$$\text{Throughput time} = 15,000 \times 0.096$$

$$= 1,440 \text{ minutes}$$

$$\text{Throughput efficiency} = \frac{\text{Work content}}{\text{Throughput time}} = \frac{25}{1,440} = 1.74 \text{ per cent}$$

Although the process is achieving a throughput time of 24 hours (which seems reasonable for this kind of process) the applications are only being worked on for 1.74 per cent of the time they are in the process.

Value-added throughput efficiency

The approach to calculating throughput efficiency that is described above assumes that all the 'work content' is actually needed. Yet we have already seen from the Intel expense report example that changing a process can significantly reduce the time that is needed to complete the task. Therefore, work content is actually dependent upon the methods and technology used to perform the task. It may be also that individual elements of a task may not be considered 'value-added'. In the Intel expense report example the new method eliminated some steps because they were 'not worth it', that is, they were not seen as adding value. So, **value-added throughput efficiency** restricts the concept of work content to only those tasks that are actually adding value to whatever is being processed. This often eliminates activities such as movement, delays and some inspections.

For example, if in the licensing worked example, of the 25 minutes of work content only 20 minutes were actually adding value, then

Value-added throughput efficiency

$$\text{Value-added throughput efficiency} = \frac{20}{1,440} = 1.39 \text{ per cent}$$

Workflow[5]

When the transformed resource in a process is information (or documents containing information), and when information technology is used to move, store and manage the information, process design is sometimes called 'workflow' or 'workflow management'. It is defined as 'the automation of procedures where documents, information or tasks are passed between participants according to a defined set of rules to achieve, or contribute to, an overall business goal'. Although workflow may be managed manually, it is almost always managed using an IT system. More specifically, workflow is concerned with the following:

- analysis, modelling, definition and subsequent operational implementation of business processes;
- the technology that supports the processes;
- the procedural (decision) rules that move information or documents through processes;
- defining the process in terms of the sequence of work activities, the human skills needed to perform each activity and the appropriate IT resources.

The effects of process variability

So far in our treatment of process design we have assumed that there is no significant variability either in the demand to which the process is expected to respond or in the time taken for the process to perform its various activities. Clearly, this is not the case in reality. So, it is important to take account of variability in process design.

Process variability

There are many reasons why **variability** occurs in processes. These can include: the late or early arrival of material, information or customers, a temporary malfunction or breakdown of process technology within a stage of the process, the recycling of 'mis-processed' materials, information or customers to an earlier stage in the process, and variation in the requirements of items being processed. All these sources of variation interact with each other, but result in two fundamental types of variability.

- Variability in the demand for processing at an individual stage within the process, usually expressed in terms of variation in the inter-arrival times of units to be processed.
- Variation in the time taken to perform the activities (i.e. process a unit) at each stage.

To understand the effect of arrival variability on process performance, it is first useful to examine what happens to process performance in a very simple process as arrival time changes under conditions of no variability. For example, the simple process shown in Figure 5.10 is composed of one stage that performs exactly 10 minutes of work. Units arrive at the process at a constant and predictable rate. If the arrival rate is one unit every 30 minutes, then the process will be utilized for only 33.33% of the time, and the units will never have to wait to be processed. This is shown as point A on Figure 5.10. If the arrival rate increases to one arrival every 20 minutes, the utilization increases to 50%, and again the units will not have to wait to be processed. This is point B on Figure 5.10. If the arrival rate increases to one arrival every 10 minutes, the process is now fully utilized, but, because a unit arrives just as the previous one has finished being processed, no unit has to wait. This is point C on Figure 5.10. However, if the arrival rate ever exceeded one unit every 10 minutes, the waiting line in front of the process activity would build up indefinitely, as is shown as point D in Figure 5.10. So, in a perfectly constant and predictable world, the relationship between process waiting time and utilization is a rectangular function as shown by the red dotted line in Figure 5.10.

However, when arrival and process times are variable, then sometimes the process will have units waiting to be processed, while at other times the process will be idle, waiting for units to arrive. Therefore the process will have both a 'non-zero' average queue and be under-utilized in the same period. So, a more realistic point is that shown as point X in Figure 5.10. If the average arrival time were to be changed with the same variability, the blue line in Figure 5.10 would show **the relationship between average waiting time and process utilization**. As the process moves closer to 100% utilization the higher the average waiting time will become. To put it another way, the only way to guarantee very low waiting times for the units is to suffer low process utilization.

The relationship between average waiting time and process utilization is a particularly important one

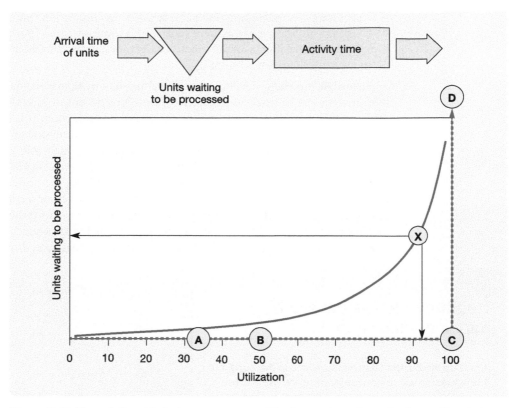

Figure 5.10 The relationship between process utilization and number of units waiting to be processed for constant, and variable, arrival and process times

The greater the variability in the process, the more the waiting time utilization deviates from the simple rectangular function of the 'no variability' conditions that was shown in Figure 5.10. A set of curves for a typical process is shown in Figure 5.11(a). This phenomenon has important implications for the design of processes. In effect it presents three options to process designers wishing to improve the waiting time or utilization performance of their processes, as shown in Figure 5.11(b):

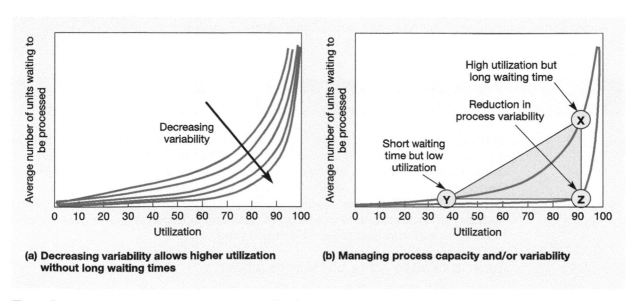

Figure 5.11 The relationship between process utilization and number of units waiting to be processed for variable arrival and activity times

- accept long average waiting times and achieve high utilization (point X);
- accept low utilization and achieve short average waiting times (point Y); or
- reduce the variability in arrival times, activity times, or both, and achieve higher utilization and short waiting times (point Z).

To analyse processes with both inter-arrival and activity time variability, queuing or 'waiting line' analysis can be used (see Chapter 8). However, do not dismiss the relationship shown in Figures 5.10 and 5.11 as some minor technical phenomenon. It is far more than this. It identifies an important choice in process design that could have strategic implications. Which is more important to a business, fast throughput time or high utilization of its resources? The only way to have both of these simultaneously is to reduce variability in its processes, which may itself require strategic decisions such as limiting the degree of customization of products or services, or imposing stricter limits on how products or services can be delivered to customers, and so on. It also demonstrates an important point concerned with the day-to-day management of processes – the only way to absolutely guarantee a hundred per cent utilization of resources is to accept an infinite amount of work-in-progress and/or waiting time.

Short case
Heathrow delays caused by capacity utilization[6]

Source: Alamy Images

It may be the busiest international airport in the world, but it is unlikely to win any prizes for being the most loved. Long delays, overcrowding and a shortage of capacity has meant that Heathrow is often a cause of frustration to harassed passengers. Yet to the airlines it is an attractive hub. Its size and location give it powerful 'network effects'. This means that it can match incoming passengers with outgoing flights to hundreds of different cities. Actually it is its attractiveness to the airlines that is one of its main problems. Heathrow's runways are in such demand that they are almost always operating at, or close to, their maximum capacity. In fact, its runways operate at 99% of capacity. This compares with about 70% at most other large airports. This means that the slightest variability (bad weather or an unscheduled landing such as a plane having to turn back with engine trouble) causes delays, which in turn cause more delays. (See Figure 5.11 for the theoretical explanation of this effect.) The result is that 33% of all flights at Heathrow are delayed by at least 15 minutes. This is poor when compared with other large European airports such as Amsterdam and Frankfurt, which have 21% and 24% of flights delayed respectively.

Human implications for process design

Although we are here dealing with the human implications of process design as the last topic of this chapter, this does not mean that it should be seen as secondary, or unimportant in any way. On the contrary, it is regarded by many as by far the dominant issue of process design. However, there is a whole other field of study – organizational behaviour – that specialises in these issues. Yet, it is included in this chapter in recognition that operations managers are, in practice, the ones who have a significant influence on how people's reactions to their jobs are accommodated in the design of processes.

Task allocation – the division of labour

Division of labour

The idea of the **division of labour** – dividing the total task down into smaller parts, was first formalized as a concept by the economist Adam Smith in his *Wealth of Nations* in 1746.

Perhaps the epitome of the division of labour is the assembly line, where products move along a single path and are built up by operators continually repeating a single task. This is the predominant model of job design in most mass-produced products and in some mass-produced services (fast food, for example). There are some *real advantages* in division of labour:

- *It promotes faster learning.* It is obviously easier to learn how to do a relatively short and simple task than a long and complex one.
- *Automation becomes easier.* Dividing a total task into small parts raises the possibility of automating some of those small tasks.
- *Reduced non-productive work.* This is probably the most important benefit of division of labour. In large, complex tasks the proportion of time spent picking up tools and materials, putting them down again and generally finding, positioning and searching can be very high indeed (called non-productive elements of work). But in shorter, divided, tasks non-productive work can be considerably reduced, which would be very significant to the costs of the operation.

There are also serious drawbacks to highly divided jobs:

- *Monotony.* The shorter the task, the more often operators will need to repeat it. Repeating the same task, for example every 30 seconds, eight hours a day and five days a week, can hardly be called a fulfilling job. As well as any ethical objections, there are other, more obviously practical objections. These include the increased likelihood of absenteeism and staff turnover and the increased likelihood of error.
- *Physical injury.* The continued repetition of a very narrow range of movements can, in extreme cases, lead to physical injury. The over-use of some parts of the body (especially the arms, hands and wrists) can result in pain and a reduction in physical capability. This is sometimes called repetitive strain injury (RSI).
- *Low flexibility.* Dividing a task up into many small parts often gives the job design a rigidity which is difficult to change under changing circumstances.
- *Poor robustness.* Highly divided jobs imply customers, materials or information passing between several stages. If one of these stages is not working correctly, for example because some equipment is faulty, the whole operation is affected.

Scientific management

Scientific management

Taylorism

Related to the division of labour are the ideas of 'scientific' management. The term **scientific management** became established in 1911 with the publication of the book of the same name by Fredrick Taylor (this whole approach to job design is sometimes referred to, pejoratively, as **Taylorism**). In this work he identified what he saw as the basic tenets of scientific management:[7]

- All aspects of work should be investigated on a scientific basis to establish the laws, rules and formulae governing the best methods of working.
- Such an investigative approach to the study of work is necessary to establish what constitutes a 'fair day's work'.
- Workers should be selected, trained and developed methodically to perform their tasks.
- Managers should act as the planners of the work (analysing jobs and standardizing the best method of doing the job) while workers should be responsible for carrying out the jobs to the standards laid down.
- Cooperation should be achieved between management and workers based on the 'maximum prosperity' of both.

The important thing to remember about scientific management is that it is not 'scientific' as such, although it certainly does take an 'investigative' approach to improving operations. Perhaps a better term for it would be 'systematic management'. It gave birth to two separate, but related, fields of study, **method study**, which determines the methods and activities to be included in jobs, and **work measurement**, which is concerned with measuring the time that should be taken for performing jobs. Together, these two fields are often referred to as **work study**.

Method study
Work measurement
Work study

Critical commentary

Even in 1915, criticisms of the scientific management approach were being voiced.[8] In a submission to the United States Commission on Industrial Relations, scientific management is described as:

- being in 'spirit and essence a cunningly devised speeding up and sweating system';
- intensifying the 'modern tendency towards specialization of the work and the task';
- condemning 'the worker to a monotonous routine';
- putting 'into the hands of employers an immense mass of information and methods that may be used unscrupulously to the detriment of workers';
- tending to 'transfer to the management all the traditional knowledge, the judgement and skills of workers';
- greatly intensifying 'unnecessary managerial dictation and discipline';
- tending to 'emphasize quantity of product at the expense of quality'.

Designing the human interface – ergonomic workplace design

Ergonomics

Human factors engineering

Ergonomics is concerned primarily with the physiological aspects of job design. Physiology is about the way the body functions. It involves two aspects: firstly, how a person interfaces with his or her immediate working area; secondly, how people react to environmental conditions. Ergonomics is sometimes referred to as **human factors engineering** or just 'human factors'. Both aspects are linked by two common ideas:

- There must be a fit between people and the jobs they do. To achieve this fit there are only two alternatives. Either the job can be made to fit the people who are doing it, or, alternatively, the people can be made (or perhaps less radically, recruited) to fit the job. Ergonomics addresses the former alternative.
- It is important to take a 'scientific' approach to job design, for example collecting data to indicate how people react under different job design conditions and trying to find the best set of conditions for comfort and performance.

We will explain further some of the aspects of ergonomics in Chapter 6.

Job commitment – behavioural approaches to job design

Behavioural approach

Processes which are designed purely on division of labour, scientific management or even purely ergonomic principles can alienate the people performing them. Process design should also take into account the desire of individuals to fulfil their needs for self-esteem and personal development. This is where motivation theory and its contribution to the **behavioural approach** to process design is important. This achieves two important objectives. Firstly, it provides jobs which have an intrinsically higher quality of working life – an ethically desirable end in itself. Secondly, because of the higher levels of motivation it engenders, it is instrumental in achieving better performance for the operation, in terms of both the quality and the quantity of output.[9] This approach to job design involves two conceptual steps: firstly, exploring how the various characteristics of the job affect people's motivation; secondly, exploring how individuals' motivation towards the job affects their performance at that job.

Some of the job characteristics that are held to have a positive effect on job satisfaction are as follows.

Job rotation

Job rotation

If increasing the number of related tasks in the job is constrained in some way, for example by the technology of the process, one approach may be to encourage **job rotation**. This means moving individuals periodically between different sets of tasks to provide some variety in their activities. When successful, job rotation can increase skill flexibility and make a small contribution to reducing monotony. However, it is not viewed as universally beneficial either by management (because it can disrupt the smooth flow of work) or by the people performing the jobs (because it can interfere with their rhythm of work).

Job enlargement

Job enlargement

The most obvious method of achieving at least some of the objectives of behavioural job design is by allocating a larger number of tasks to individuals. If these extra tasks are broadly of the same type as those in the original job, the change is called **job enlargement**. This may not involve more demanding or fulfilling tasks, but it may provide a more complete and therefore slightly more meaningful job. If nothing else, people performing an enlarged job will not repeat themselves as often, which could make the job less monotonous.

Job enrichment

Job enrichment

Job enrichment, not only means increasing the number of tasks, but also allocating extra tasks which involve more decision making, greater autonomy and greater control over the job. For example, the extra tasks could include maintenance, planning and control, or monitoring quality levels. The effect is both to reduce repetition in the job and to increase autonomy and personal development. So, in the assembly-line example, each operator, as well as being allocated a job which is twice as long as that previously performed could also be allocated responsibility for carrying out routine maintenance and such tasks as record-keeping and managing the supply of materials.

Empowerment

Empowerment

Empowerment is usually taken to mean more than simple autonomy. Whereas autonomy means giving staff the *ability* to change how they do their jobs, empowerment means giving staff the *authority* to make changes to the job itself, as well as how it is performed. This can be designed into jobs to different degrees.[10] At a minimum, staff could be asked to contribute their suggestions for how the operation might be improved. Going further, staff could be empowered to redesign their jobs. Further still, staff could be included in the strategic direction and performance of the whole organization. The *benefits* of empowerment are generally seen as providing fast responses to customer needs, employees who feel better about their jobs and who will interact with customers with more enthusiasm, promoting 'word-of-mouth' advertising and customer retention. However, there are *costs* associated with empowerment, including higher selection and training costs, perceived inequity of service and the possibility of poor decisions being made by employees.

Team-working

Team-based work organization

A development in job design which is closely linked to the empowerment concept is that of **team-based work organization** (sometimes called self-managed work teams). This is where staff, often with overlapping skills, collectively perform a defined task and have a high degree of discretion over how they actually perform the task. The team would typically control such things as task allocation between members, scheduling work, quality measurement and improvement, and sometimes the hiring of staff. To some extent most work has always been a group-based activity. The concept of teamwork, however, is more prescriptive and assumes a shared set of

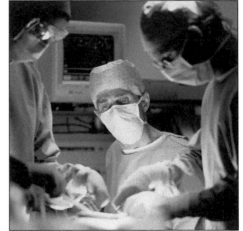

Source: Getty Images

objectives and responsibilities. Groups are described as teams when the virtues of working together are being emphasized, such as the ability to make use of the various skills within the team. Teams may also be used to compensate for other organizational changes such as the move towards flatter organizational structures. When organizations have fewer managerial levels, each manager will have a wider span of activities to control. Teams which are capable of autonomous decision-making have a clear advantage in these circumstances.

Summary answers to key questions

Check and improve your understanding of this chapter using self-assessment questions and a personalized study plan, audio and video downloads, and an eBook – all at www.myomlab.com.

➤ What is process design?

- Process design is the activity which shapes the physical form and purpose of the processes that create and deliver services and products.

- The overall purpose of process design is to meet the needs of customers through achieving appropriate levels of quality, speed, dependability, flexibility and cost.

- The design activity must also take account of environmental issues. These include examination of the source and suitability of materials, the sources and quantities of energy consumed, the amount and type of waste material, the life of the product itself, and the end-of-life state of the product.

➤ How do volume and variety affect process design?

- The overall nature of any process is strongly influenced by the volume and variety of what it has to process.

- The concept of process types summarizes how volume and variety affect overall process design.

- In manufacturing, these process types are (in order of increasing volume and decreasing variety) project, jobbing, batch, mass and continuous processes. In service operations, the terms often used (again in order of increasing volume and decreasing variety) are professional services, service shops and mass services.

➤ How are processes designed in detail?

- Processes are designed initially by breaking them down into their individual activities. Often common symbols are used to represent types of activity. The sequence of activities in a process is then indicated by the sequence of symbols representing activities. This is called 'process mapping'. Alternative process designs can be compared using process maps and improved processes considered in terms of their operations performance objectives.

- Process performance in terms of throughput time, work-in-progress, and cycle time are related by a formula known as Little's law: throughput time equals work-in-progress multiplied by cycle time.

- Variability has a significant effect on the performance of processes, particularly the relationship between waiting time and utilization.

➤ What are the human implications for process design?

- There are many ideas (and a whole field of study – organizational behaviour) that should be taken into account when designing processes. These include the division of labour, ergonomics and more behavioural approaches such as job rotation, job enlargement, job enrichment, empowerment and team-working.

Learning exercises

These problems and applications will help to improve your analysis of operations. You can find more practice problems as well as worked examples and guided solutions on MyOMLab at www.myomlab.com.

1 Read again the description of fast-food drive-through processes at the beginning of this chapter. (a) Draw a process map that reflects the types of process described. (b) What advantage do you think is given to McDonald's through its decision to establish a call centre for remote order-taking for some of its outlets?

2 A regional government office that deals with passport applications is designing a process that will check applications and issue the documents. The number of applications to be processed is 1,600 per week and the time available to process the applications is 40 hours per week. What is the required cycle time for the process?

3 For the passport office, described above, the total work content of all the activities that make up the total task of checking, processing and issuing a passport is, on average, 30 minutes. How many people will be needed to meet demand?

4 The same passport office has a 'clear desk' policy that means that all desks must be clear of work by the end of the day. How many applications should be loaded onto the process in the morning in order to ensure that every one is completed and desks are clear by the end of the day? (Assume a 7.5-hour (450-minute) working day.)

Want to know more?

Chopra, S., Anupindi, R., Deshmukh, S.D., Van Mieghem, J.A. and Zemel, E. (2006) *Managing Business Process Flows*, Prentice-Hall, Englewood Cliffs, NJ. An excellent, although mathematical, approach to process design in general.

Hammer, M. (1990) Reengineering work: don't automate, obliterate, *Harvard Business Review*, July–August. This is the paper that launched the whole idea of business processes and process management in general to a wider managerial audience. Slightly dated but worth reading.

Hopp, W.J. and Spearman, M.L. (2001) *Factory Physics*, 2nd edn, McGraw-Hill, New York. Very technical so don't bother with it if you aren't prepared to get into the maths. However, there is some fascinating analysis, especially concerning Little's law.

Smith, H. and Fingar, P. (2003) *Business Process Management: The Third Wave*, Meghan-Kiffer Press, Tampa, Fl. A popular book on process management from a business process re-engineering perspective.

Useful websites

www.bpmi.org Site of the Business Process Management Initiative. Some good resources including papers and articles.

www.bptrends.com News site for trends in business process management generally. Some interesting articles.

www.bls.gov/oes/ US Department of Labor employment statistics.

www.fedee.com Federation of European Employers guide to employment and job trends in Europe.

www.iienet.org The Global Association of Productivity and Efficiency Professionals site. This is an important professional body for process design and related topics.

www.opsman.org Lots of useful stuff.

www.waria.com A Workflow and Reengineering Association web site. Some useful topics.

Now that you have finished reading this chapter, why not visit MyOMLab at www.myomlab.com where you'll find more learning resources to help you make the most of your studies and get a better grade.

Chapter 6

Location, layout and flow

Key questions

➤ Where should operations be located?

➤ What is 'layout' and what are the types used in operations?

➤ What type of layout should an operation choose?

➤ How should items be positioned in a workplace?

Introduction

This chapter is about where you put things or, more formally, how operations resources are positioned relative to each other. We shall examine this positioning at three levels from macro to micro. Firstly, we look at how operations locate their sites geographically. Secondly (and this constitutes the majority of the chapter), we look at the layout of resources within operations and processes. Finally, we briefly examine how equipment is positioned within individuals' work areas. This positioning decision is important because it determines the way transformed resources flow through supply networks, operations and processes. Relatively small changes in the position of products in a supermarket, or changing rooms in a sports centre, or the position of a machine in a factory, can affect the flow through the operation which, in turn, affects the costs and general effectiveness of the operation. Figure 6.1 shows where this chapter fits into the overall operations model.

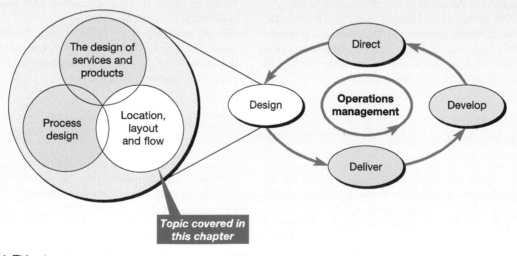

Figure 6.1 This chapter examines location, layout and flow

Check and improve your understanding of this chapter using self-assessment questions and a personalized study plan, audio and video downloads, and an eBook – all at www.myomlab.com.

Operations in practice Tesco's store flow processes[1]

Finding, purchasing and developing the sites for its retail stores is a major (and controversial) part of Tesco's activities. In its UK market, the main issue is obtaining permission from local government authorities. The UK's planning regime, once relatively relaxed to encourage retail development and stimulate economic growth, is now far stricter, more complicated and takes longer. Frequently there are local objections to supermarket development. Some are from smaller retailers who fear loss of business, some are from residents wary of traffic congestion, and some from people who dislike the dominance of firms like Tesco. To go through all this effort, Tesco must be convinced that any potential location represents a sound business investment. Location (or, more accurately, layout) within their stores is equally important.

Successful supermarkets like Tesco also know that the design of their stores has a huge impact on profitability. They must maximize their revenue per square metre and minimize the costs of operating the store, while keeping customers happy. At a basic level, supermarkets have to get the amount of space allocated to the different areas right. Tesco's 'One in front' campaign, for example, tries to avoid long waiting times by opening additional tills if more than one customer is waiting at a checkout. Tesco also uses technology to understand exactly how customers flow through their stores. The 'Smartlane' system from Irisys, a specialist in intelligent infrared technologies, counts the number and type of customers entering the store (in family or other groups known as 'shopping units'), tracks their movement using infrared sensors, and predicts the likely demand at the checkouts up to an hour in advance. The circulation of customers through the store must be right and the right layout can make customers buy more. Some supermarkets put their entrance on the left-hand side of a building with a layout designed to take customers in a clockwise direction around the store. Aisles are made wide to ensure a relatively slow flow of trolleys so that customers pay more attention to the products on display (and buy more). However, wide aisles can come at the expense of reduced shelf space that would allow a wider range of products to be stocked.

The actual location of all the products is a critical decision, directly affecting the convenience to customers, their level of spontaneous purchase and the cost of filling the shelves. Although the majority of supermarket sales are packaged, tinned or frozen goods, the displays of fruit and vegetables are usually located adjacent to the main entrance, as a signal of freshness and wholesomeness, providing an attractive and welcoming point of entry. Basic products that figure on most people's shopping lists, such as flour, sugar and bread, may be located at the back of the store and apart from each other so that customers have to pass higher-margin items as they search. High-margin items are usually put at eye level on shelves (where they are more likely to be seen) and low-margin products lower down or higher up. Some customers also go a few paces up an aisle before they start looking for what they need. Some supermarkets call the shelves occupying the first metre of an aisle 'dead space' – not a place to put impulse-bought goods. The prime site in a supermarket is the 'gondola-end', the shelves at the end of the aisle. Moving products to this location can increase sales 200 or 300 per cent. It's not surprising that suppliers are willing to pay for their products to be located here. The supermarkets themselves are keen to point out that, although they obviously lay out their stores with customers' buying behaviour in mind, it is counterproductive to be too manipulative. Some commonly held beliefs about supermarket layout are not always true. They deny that they periodically change the location of foodstuffs in order to jolt customers out of their habitual shopping patterns so that they are more attentive to other products and end up buying more. Occasionally layouts are changed, they say mainly to accommodate changing tastes and new ranges. At a more micro-level, Tesco will be concerned to make its checkout areas safe and convenient for its staff and customers. Similarly the design of self checkout equipment must be conveniently designed. So positioning, whether it is location, store layout, or workstation design, will have an impact on Tesco's performance.

The location of operations

It was reputedly Lord Sieff, one-time boss of Marks and Spencer, the UK-based retail organization, who said, '*There are three important things in retailing – location, location and location*', and any retailing operation knows exactly what he meant. Get the location wrong and it can have a significant impact on profits. For example, mislocating a fire service station can slow down the average journey time of the fire crews in getting to the fires; locating a factory where there is difficulty attracting labour with appropriate skills will affect the effectiveness of the factory's operations. Location decisions will usually have an effect on an operation's costs as well as its ability to serve its customers (and therefore its revenues). Also, location decisions, once taken, are difficult to undo. The costs of moving an operation can be hugely expensive and the risks of inconveniencing customers very high. No operation wants to move very often.

Reasons for location decisions

Whilst the location of some operations is largely historical, they are implicitly making a decision not to move. Presumably their assumption is that the cost and disruption involved in changing location would outweigh any potential benefits of a new location. Two stimuli often cause organizations to change locations: changes in demand for their services and products, and changes in supply of their inputs.

Changes in demand. A change in location may be prompted by customer demand shifting. For example, as garment manufacturers moved from Europe to Asia, suppliers of zips, threads, etc. started to follow them. Changes in the volume of demand can also prompt relocation. To meet higher demand, an operation could expand its existing site, choose a larger site in another location, or keep its existing location and find a second location for an additional operation; the last two options will involve a location decision. High-visibility operations may not have the choice of expanding on the same site to meet rising demand. A dry cleaning service may attract only marginally more business by expanding an existing site because it offers a local, and therefore convenient, service. Finding a new location for an additional operation is probably its only option for expansion.

Changes in supply. The other stimulus for relocation is changes in the cost or availability of supply of inputs to the operation. For example, a mining or oil company will need to relocate as the minerals it is extracting become depleted. A manufacturing company might choose to relocate its operations to a part of the world where labour costs are low, because the equivalent resources (people) in its original location have become relatively expensive. Sometimes a business might choose to relocate to release funds if the value of the land it occupies is worth more than an alternative, equally good, location.

The objectives of the location decision

The aim of the location decision is to achieve an appropriate balance between three related objectives:

Spatially variable costs
- the **spatially variable costs** of the operation (spatially variable means that something changes with geographical location);
- the service the operation is able to provide to its customers;
- the revenue potential of the operation.

In for-profit organizations the last two objectives are related. The assumption is that the better the service the operation can provide to its customers, the better will be its potential to attract custom and therefore generate revenue. In not-for-profit organizations, revenue

Short case
The Tata Nano finds a new home[2]

Finding a suitable site for any operation can be a political as well as an economic problem. It certainly was when Tata, the Indian company, unveiled its plans for the Nano in 2007. Named the '1 lakh car' (in India one lakh means 100,000), it would be the cheapest car in the world, with the basic model priced at 100,000 rupees, or $2,500, excluding taxes. The price was about half of existing low-cost cars. The site chosen by Tata was equally bold. It was to be made at Singur, in the Indian state of West Bengal, a populous state with Calcutta (now called Kolkata) as its capital. Although the Communist Party had ruled the state for four decades, the West Bengal government was keen to encourage the Nano plant. It would bring much-needed jobs and send a message that the state welcomed inward investment. In fact, it had won the plant against stiff competition from rival states.

Controversially, the state government had expropriated land for the factory using an old law dating from 1894, which requires private owners to sell land for a 'public purpose'. The government justified this action by pointing out that over 13,000 people had some kind of claim to parts of the land required for the new plant. Tata could not be expected to negotiate, one by one, with all of them. Also financial compensation was offered at

significantly above market rates. Unfortunately about 2,250 people refused to accept the offered compensation. The political opposition organized mass protests in support of the farmers who did not want to move. They blocked roads, threatened staff and even assaulted an employee of a Tata supplier. In response, Ratan Tata, chairman of the Tata group, threatened to move the Nano plant from the state if the company really was not wanted, even though the company had already invested 15 billion rupees in the project. Eventually, exasperated with being caught in the 'political crossfire', Tata said it would abandon its factory in the state. Instead, the company selected a location in Gujarat, one of India's most industrialized states, which quickly approved even more land than the West Bengal site.

potential might not be a relevant objective and so cost and customer service are often taken as the twin objectives of location. In making decisions about where to locate an operation, operations managers are concerned with minimizing spatially variable costs and maximizing revenue and customer service. Location affects both of these but not equally for all types of operation. For example, with most products, customers may not care very much where they were made. Location is unlikely to affect the operation's revenues significantly. However, the costs of the operation will probably be very greatly affected by location. Services, on the other hand, often have both costs and revenues affected by location. The location decision for any operation is determined by the relative strength of supply-side and demand-side factors (see Figure 6.2).

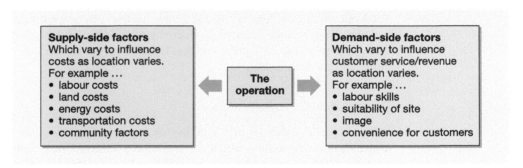

Figure 6.2 Supply-side and demand-side factors in location decisions

Supply-side influences

Labour costs. The costs of employing people with particular skills can vary between different areas in any country, but are likely to be more significant when international comparisons are made. Labour costs can be expressed in two ways. The 'hourly cost' is what firms have to pay workers on average per hour. However, the 'unit cost' is an indication of the labour cost per unit of production. This includes the effects both of productivity differences between countries and of differing currency exchange rates. Exchange rate variation can cause unit costs to change dramatically over time. Yet, labour costs exert a major influence on the location decision, especially in some industries such as clothing, where labour costs as a proportion of total costs are relatively high.

Land costs. The cost of acquiring the site itself is sometimes a relevant factor in choosing a location. Land and rental costs vary between countries and cities. At a more local level, land costs are also important. A retail operation, when choosing 'high-street' sites, will pay a particular level of rent only if it believes it can generate a certain level of revenue from the site.

Energy costs. Operations which use large amounts of energy, such as aluminium smelters, can be influenced in their location decisions by the availability of relatively inexpensive energy. This may be direct, as in the availability of hydroelectric generation in an area, or indirect, such as low-cost coal which can be used to generate inexpensive electricity.

Transportation costs. Transportation costs include both the cost of transporting inputs from their source to the site of the operation, and the cost of transporting goods from the site to customers. Whereas almost all operations are concerned to some extent with the former, not all operations transport goods to customers; rather, customers come to them (for example, hotels). Even for operations that do transport their goods to customers (most manufacturers, for example), we consider transportation as a supply-side factor because as location changes, transportation costs also change. Proximity to sources of *supply* dominates the location decision where the cost of transporting input materials is high or difficult. Food processing and other agriculture-based activities, for example, are often carried out close to growing areas. Conversely, transportation to *customers* dominates location decisions where this is expensive or difficult. Civil engineering projects, for example, are constructed mainly where they will be needed.

Community factors. Community factors are those influences on an operation's costs which derive from the social, political and economic environment of its site. These include:

- local tax rates
- government financial and planning assistance
- political stability, and local attitudes to 'inward investment'
- language
- availability of support services
- history of labour relations and behaviour
- environmental restrictions and waste disposal.

A major influence in where businesses locate is the cost of operating at different locations. Total operating cost depends on more than wage costs, or even total labour costs (which includes allowances for different productivity rates). Figure 6.3 illustrates what makes up the cost of shirts sold in different countries. Remember, the retailer will often sell the item for more than double the cost.[3]

Demand-side influences

Labour skills. The abilities of a local labour force can have an effect on customer reaction to the services or products which the operation produces. For example, 'science parks' are usually located close to universities because they hope to attract companies that are interested in using the skills available at the university.

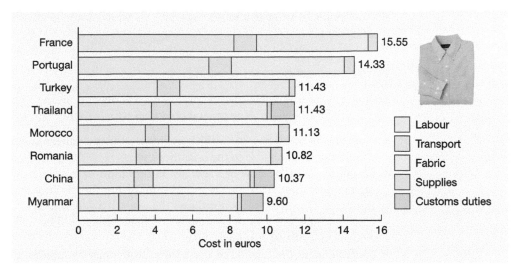

Figure 6.3 The cost of a shirt

The suitability of the site itself. Different sites are likely to have different intrinsic characteristics which can affect an operation's ability to serve customers and generate revenue. For example, the location of a luxury resort hotel which offers up-market holiday accommodation is very largely dependent on the intrinsic characteristics of the site. Located next to the beach, surrounded by waving palm trees and overlooking a picturesque bay, the hotel is very attractive to its customers. Move it a few kilometres away into the centre of an industrial estate and it rapidly loses its attraction.

Image of the location. Some locations are firmly associated in customers' minds with a particular image. Suits from Savile Row (the centre of the up-market bespoke tailoring district in London) may be no better than high-quality suits made elsewhere but, by locating its operation there, a tailor has probably enhanced its reputation and therefore its revenue. The product and fashion design houses of Milan and the financial services in the City of London also enjoy a reputation shaped partly by that of their location.

Convenience for customers. Of all the demand-side factors, this is, for many operations, the most important. Locating a general hospital, for instance, in the middle of the countryside may have many advantages for its staff, and even perhaps for its costs, but it clearly would be very inconvenient to its customers. Those visiting the hospital would need to travel long distances. This means that general hospitals are located close to centres of demand. Similarly with other public services and restaurants, stores, banks, petrol filling stations etc., location determines the effort to which customers have to go in order to use the operation.

What is layout and what are the types used in operations?

The 'layout' of an operation or process means how its transformed resources are positioned relative to each other and how its various tasks are allocated to these transforming resources. Together these two decisions will dictate the pattern of flow for transformed resources as they progress through the operation or process. It is an important decision because, if the layout proves wrong, it can lead to over-long or confused flow patterns, customer queues, long process times, inflexible operations, unpredictable flow and high cost. Also, re-laying out an existing operation can cause disruption, leading to customer dissatisfaction or lost operating time. So, because the **layout decision** can be difficult and expensive, operations managers are reluctant to do it too often. Therefore layout must start with a full appreciation of the objectives that the layout should be trying to achieve. However, this is only the

The layout decision is relatively infrequent but important

starting point of what is a multi-stage process which leads to the final physical layout of the operation.

What makes a good layout?

To a large extent the objectives of any layout will depend on the strategic objectives of the operation, but there are some general objectives which are relevant to all operations:

- *Inherent safety.* All processes which might constitute a danger to either staff or customers should not be accessible to the unauthorized.
- *Length of flow.* The flow of materials, information or customers should be appropriate for the operation. This usually means minimizing the distance travelled by transformed resources. However, this is not always the case (in a supermarket, for example).
- *Clarity of flow.* All flow of customers and materials should be well signposted, clear and evident to staff and customers alike.
- *Staff conditions.* Staff should be located away from noisy or unpleasant parts of the operation.
- *Management coordination.* Supervision and communication should be assisted by the location of staff and communication devices.
- *Accessibility.* All machines and facilities should be accessible for proper cleaning and maintenance.
- *Use of space.* All layouts should use space appropriately. This usually means minimizing the space used, but sometimes can mean achieving an impression of spacious luxury, as in the entrance lobby of a high-class hotel.
- *Long-term flexibility.* Layouts need to be changed periodically. A good layout will have been devised with the possible future needs of the operation in mind.

The basic layout types

Most practical layouts are derived from only four **basic layout types**. These are:

Basic layout type

Fixed-position layout
Functional layout
Cell layout
Line layout

- **fixed-position layout**
- **functional layout**
- **cell layout**
- **line layout** (also called **product layout**)

Which type of layout is used will (partly) depend on which type of process is being used. Process 'types' (described in Chapter 5) represent the broad approaches to the organization of processes and activities. Layout is a narrower, but related concept. It is the physical mani-

Layout is influenced by process types

festation of a process type, but there is often some overlap between **process types** and the layouts that they could use. As Table 6.1 indicates, a process type does not necessarily imply only one particular basic layout.

Fixed-position layout

Fixed-position layout is in some ways a contradiction in terms, since the transformed resources do not move between the transforming resources. Instead of materials, information or customers flowing through an operation, the recipient of the processing is stationary and the equipment, machinery, plant and people who do the processing move as necessary. This could be because the product or the recipient of the service is too large to be moved conveniently, or it might be too delicate to move, or perhaps it could object to being moved; for example:

- *Motorway construction* – the product is too large to move.
- *Open-heart surgery* – patients are too delicate to move.
- *High-class service restaurant* – customers would object to being moved to where food is prepared.

Table 6.1 The relationship between process types and basic layout types

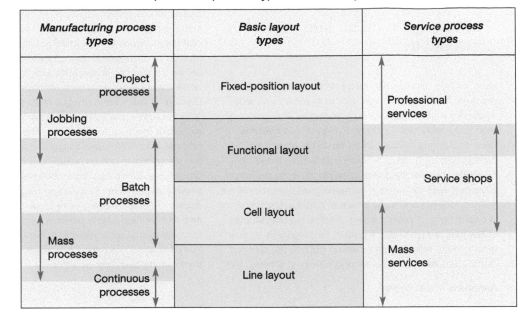

- *Mainframe computer maintenance* – the product is too big and probably also too delicate to move, and the customer might object to bringing it in for repair.

A construction site is typical of a fixed-position layout in that there is a limited amount of space which must be allocated to the various transforming resources. The main problem in designing this layout will be to allocate areas of the site to the various contractors so that they have adequate space, they can receive and store their deliveries of materials, they can have access to their parts of the project without interfering with each other's movements, they minimize movement, and so on.

Functional layout

Functional layout is so called because it conforms to the needs and convenience of the functions performed by the transforming resources within the processes. (Confusingly, functional layout is also referred to as 'process layout' but this term is being superseded.) In functional layout, similar resources or processes are located together. This may be because it is convenient to group them together, or that the utilization of transforming resources is improved. It means that when materials, information or customers flow through the operation, their route is determined according to their needs. Different customers or products will have different needs and therefore take different routes. Usually this makes the flow pattern in the operation very complex. Examples of functional layouts include:

- *Hospital* – some processes (e.g. X-ray machines and laboratories) are required by several types of patient; some processes (e.g. general wards) can achieve high staff- and bed-utilization.
- *Machining the parts which go into aircraft engines* – some processes (e.g. heat treatment) need specialist support (heat and fume extraction); some processes (e.g. machining centres) require the same technical support from specialist setter–operators; some processes (e.g. grinding machines) get high machine utilization as all parts which need grinding pass through a single grinding section.
- *Supermarket* – some products, such as tinned goods, are convenient to restock if grouped together. Some areas, such as those holding frozen vegetables, need the common technology of freezer cabinets. Others, such as the areas holding fresh vegetables, might be together because that way they can be made to look attractive to customers (see the opening short case).

Short case
'Factory flow' helps surgery productivity[4]

Even surgery can be seen as a process, and like any process, it can be improved. Normally patients remain stationary with surgeons and other theatre staff performing their tasks around the patient. However, this idea has been challenged by John Petri, an Italian consultant orthopaedic surgeon at a hospital in Norfolk in the UK. Frustrated by spending time drinking tea while patients were prepared for surgery, he redesigned the process so now he moves continually between two theatres. While he is operating on a patient in one theatre, his anaesthetist colleagues are preparing a patient for surgery in another theatre. After finishing with the first patient, the surgeon 'scrubs up', moves to the second operating theatre, and

begins the surgery on the second patient. While he is doing this the first patient is moved out of the first operating theatre and the third patient is prepared. This method of overlapping operations in different theatres allows the surgeon to work for five hours at a time rather than the previous standard three-and-a-half-hour session. *'If you were running a factory'*, says the surgeon, *'you wouldn't allow your most important and most expensive machine to stand idle. The same is true in a hospital.'* Currently used on hip and knee replacements, this layout would not be suitable for all surgical procedures. Since its introduction the surgeon's waiting list has fallen to zero and his productivity has doubled. *'For a small increase in running costs we are able to treat many more patients'*, said a spokesperson for the hospital management. *'What is important is that clinicians . . . produce innovative ideas and we demonstrate that they are effective.'*

Assembly line surgery

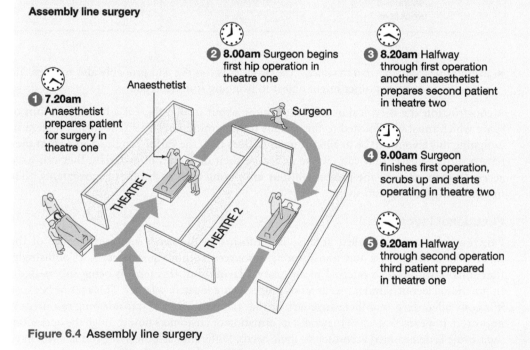

❶ **7.20am** Anaesthetist prepares patient for surgery in theatre one

Anaesthetist

Surgeon

❷ **8.00am** Surgeon begins first hip operation in theatre one

❸ **8.20am** Halfway through first operation another anaesthetist prepares second patient in theatre two

❹ **9.00am** Surgeon finishes first operation, scrubs up and starts operating in theatre two

❺ **9.20am** Halfway through second operation third patient prepared in theatre one

THEATRE 1

THEATRE 2

Figure 6.4 Assembly line surgery

Figure 6.5 shows a functional layout in a university library. The various areas – reference books, enquiry desk, journals, and so on – are located in different parts of the operation. The customer is free to move between the areas depending on his or her requirements. The figure also shows the route taken by one customer on one visit to the library. If the routes for the customers were superimposed on the plan, the pattern of the traffic between the various parts of the operation would be revealed. The density of this traffic flow is an important piece of information in the detailed design of this type of layout. Changing the location of the various areas in the library will change the pattern of flow for the library as a whole.

The detailed design of functional layouts is complex, as is flow in this type of layout. Chief among the factors which lead to this complexity is the very large number of different options. For example, in the very simplest case of just two work centres, there are only two ways of arranging these *relative to each other*. But there are six ways of arranging three centres and 120 ways of arranging five centres. This relationship is a factorial one. For N centres there are factorial N (N!) different ways of arranging the centres, where:

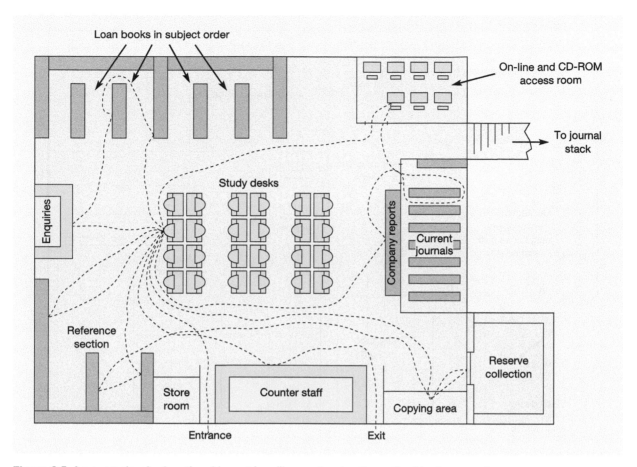

Figure 6.5 An example of a functional layout in a library showing the path of just one customer

$$N! = N \times (N-1) \times (N-2) \times \ldots \times (1)$$

So for a relatively simple functional layout with, say, 20 work centres, there are $20! = 2.433 \times 10^{18}$

Combinatorial complexity ways of arranging the operation. This **combinatorial complexity** of functional layouts makes optimal solutions difficult to achieve in practice. Most functional layouts are designed by a combination of intuition, common sense and systematic trial and error.

Cell layout

A cell layout is one where the transformed resources entering the operation are pre-selected (or pre-select themselves) to move to one part of the operation (or cell) in which all the transforming resources, to meet their immediate processing needs, are located. After being processed in the cell, the transformed resources may go on to another cell. In effect, cell layout is an attempt to bring some order to the complexity of flow which characterizes functional layout. Examples of cell layouts include:

- *Maternity unit in a hospital* – customers needing maternity attention are a well-defined group who can be treated together and who are unlikely to need the other facilities of the hospital at the same time that they need the maternity unit.
- *Some laptop assembly* – within a contract manufacturer's factory, the assembly of different laptop brands may be done in a special area dedicated to that one brand that has special requirements such as particularly high quality levels.
- *'Lunch' products area in a supermarket* – some customers use the supermarket just to purchase sandwiches, savoury snacks, etc. for their lunch. These products may be located together so that these customers do not have to search around the store.

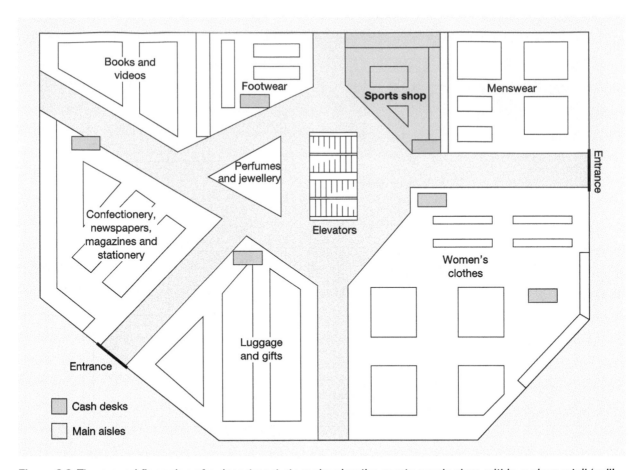

Figure 6.6 The ground floor plan of a department store showing the sports goods shop-within-a-shop retail 'cell'

Shop-within-a-shop

In Figure 6.6 the ground floor of a department store is shown, comprising displays of various types of goods in different parts of the store. In this sense the predominant layout of the store is a functional layout. However, some 'themed' products may be put together, such as in the sports shop. This area is a **shop-within-a-shop** which will stock sports clothes, sports shoes, sports bags, sports books and DVDs, sports equipment and energy drinks, which are also located elsewhere in the store. They have been located in the 'cell' not because they are similar goods (shoes, books and drinks would not usually be located together) but because they are needed to satisfy the needs of a particular type of customer. Enough customers come to the store to buy 'sports goods' in particular to devote an area specifically for them. Also, customers intending to buy sports shoes might also be persuaded to buy other sports goods if they are placed in the same area.

Line layout

Line layout

Line layout (also called product layout) involves locating the transforming resources entirely for the convenience of the transformed resources. Customers, products or pieces of information follow a prearranged route in which the sequence of activities that are required matches the sequence in which the processes have been located. The transformed resources 'flow' as in a 'line' through the process. Flow is predictable and therefore relatively easy to control. Examples of line layout include:

- *Loan application processing* – all applications require the same sequence of clerical and decision-making activities.
- *Self-service cafeteria* – generally the sequence of customer requirements (starter, main course, dessert, drink) is common to all customers, but layout also helps control customer flow.

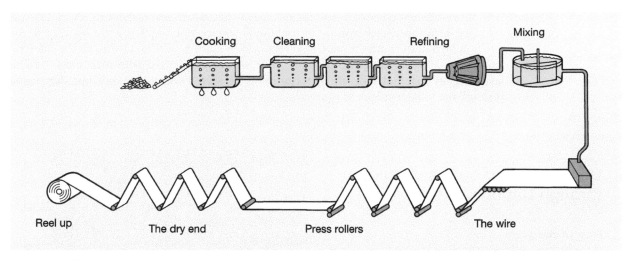

Figure 6.7 The sequence of processes in paper-making; each process will be laid out in the same sequence

- *Automobile assembly* – almost all variants of the same model require the same sequence of processes.

Figure 6.7 shows the sequence of processes in a paper-making operation. Such an operation would use product layout. Gone are the complexities of flow which characterized functional layouts, and to a lesser extent cell layouts, and although different types of paper are produced in this operation, all types have the same processing requirements.

Mixed layouts

Many operations either design themselves hybrid layouts which combine elements of some or all of the basic layout types, or use the 'pure' basic layout types in different parts of the operation. For example, a hospital would normally be arranged on functional-layout principles, each department representing a particular type of process (the X-ray department, the surgical theatres, the blood-processing laboratory, and so on). Yet within each department, quite different layouts are used. The X-ray department is probably arranged in a functional layout, the surgical theatres in a fixed-position layout, and the blood-processing laboratory in a line layout. Another example is shown in Figure 6.8. Here a restaurant complex is shown

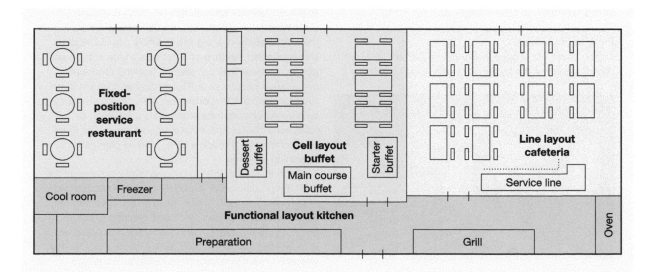

Figure 6.8 A restaurant complex with all four basic layout types

with three different types of restaurant and the kitchen which serves them all. The kitchen is arranged in a functional layout, the traditional service restaurant is arranged in a fixed-position layout, the buffet restaurant is arranged in a cell-type layout, while in the cafeteria restaurant, all customers take the same route when being served with their meal – a line layout. They may not take the opportunity to be served with every dish but they move through the same sequence of processes.

Short case
Chocolate and customers flow through Cadbury's[5]

Customers being processed

Flow of chocolate

In the famous Cadbury's chocolate factory at Bourneville, on the outskirts of Birmingham, UK, chocolate products are manufactured to a high degree of consistency and efficiency. Production processes are based on a *product layout*. This has allowed Cadbury's engineers to develop and procure machinery to meet the technical and capacity requirements of each stage of the process. Consider, for example, the production of Cadbury's Dairy Milk bars. First, the standard liquid chocolate is prepared from cocoa beans, fresh milk and sugar using specialized equipment, connected together with pipes and conveyors. These processes operate continuously, day and night, to ensure consistency of both the chocolate itself and the rate of output. Next, the liquid is pumped through heated pipework to the moulding department, where it is automatically dispensed into a moving line of precision-made plastic moulds which form the chocolate bars and vibrate them to remove any trapped air bubbles. The moulds are continuously conveyed into a large refrigerator, allowing sufficient time for the chocolate to harden. The next stage inverts the moulds and shakes out the moulded bars. These then pass directly to a set of highly automated wrapping and packing machines, from where they go to the warehouse.

Flow of customers

Cadbury also has a large visitor centre called 'Cadbury World' alongside the factory (linked to a viewing area

Chocolate being processed

which looks onto the packaging area described above). Cadbury World is a permanent exhibition devoted entirely to chocolate and the part Cadbury has played in its fascinating history. As most of the attractions are indoors, with limited circulation space, the main exhibition and demonstration areas are designed to allow a smooth flow of customers, where possible avoiding bottlenecks and delays. The design is also a line layout with a single route for all customers. Entry to the Exhibition Area is by timed ticket, to ensure a constant flow of input customers, who are free to walk around at their preferred speed, but are constrained to keep to the single track through the sequence of displays. On leaving this section, they are directed upstairs to the Chocolate Packaging Plant, where a guide escorts standard-sized batches of customers to the appropriate positions where they can see the packing processes and a video presentation. The groups are then led down to and around the Demonstration Area, where skilled employees demonstrate small-scale production of handmade chocolates. Finally, visitors are free to roam unaccompanied through a long, winding path of the remaining exhibits.

Cadbury has chosen to use the line layout design for both the production of chocolates and the processing of its visitors. In both cases, volumes are large and the variety offered is limited. Sufficient demand exists for each standard 'product', and the operations objective is to achieve consistent high quality at low cost. Neither operation has much volume flexibility, and both are expensive to change.

What is layout and what are the types used in operations?

The volume and variety characteristics of an operation will influence its layout

The importance of flow to an operation will depend on its **volume and variety characteristics**. When volume is very low and variety is relatively high, 'flow' is not a major issue. For example, in telecommunications satellite manufacture, a fixed-position layout is likely to be appropriate because each product is different and because products 'flow' through the operation very infrequently, so it is just not worth arranging facilities to minimize the flow of parts through the operation. With higher volume and lower variety, flow becomes an issue. If the variety is still high, however, an entirely flow-dominated arrangement is difficult because there will be different flow patterns. For example, the library in Figure 6.5 will arrange its different categories of books and its other services partly to minimize the average distance its customers have to 'flow' through the operation. But, because its customers' needs vary, it will arrange its layout to satisfy the majority of its customers (but perhaps inconvenience a minority). When the variety of products or services reduces to the point where a distinct 'category' with similar requirements becomes evident but variety is still not small, cell layout could become appropriate, as in the sports goods cell in Figure 6.6. When variety is relatively small and volume is high, flow can become regularized and a line layout is likely to be appropriate (see Figure 6.7).

Selecting a layout type

The volume–variety characteristics of the operation will, to a large extent, narrow the choice down to one or two layout options. The decision as to which layout type to adopt will be influenced by an understanding of their relative advantages and disadvantages. Table 6.2 shows some of the more significant advantages and disadvantages associated with each layout

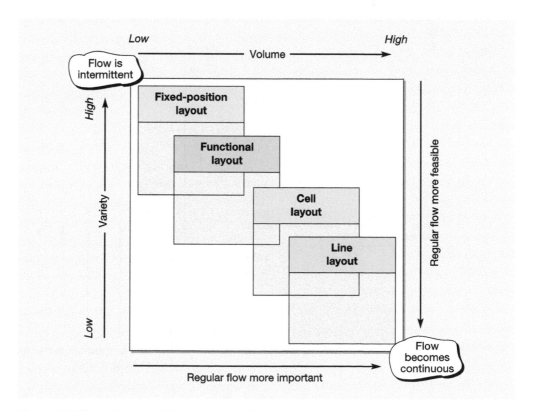

Figure 6.9 The volume–variety process position of an operation influences its layout and, in turn, the flow of transformed resources

Table 6.2 The advantages and disadvantages of the basic layout types

	Advantages	*Disadvantages*
Fixed-position	Very high mix and product flexibility Product or customer not moved or disturbed High variety of tasks for staff	Very high unit costs Scheduling of space and activities can be difficult Can mean much movement of plant and staff
Functional	High mix and product flexibility Relatively robust in the case of disruptions Relatively easy supervision of equipment or plant	Low facilities utilization Can have very high work-in-progress or customer queuing Complex flow can be difficult to control
Cell	Can give a good compromise between cost and flexibility for relatively high-variety operations Fast throughput Group work can result in good motivation	Can be costly to rearrange existing layout Can need more plant and equipment Can give lower plant utilization
Line	Low unit costs for high volume Gives opportunities for specialization of equipment Materials or customer movement is convenient	Can have low mix flexibility Not very robust if there is disruption Work can be very repetitive

type. It should be stressed, however, that the type of operation will influence their relative importance. For example, a high-volume television manufacturer may find the low-cost characteristics of a line layout attractive, but an amusement theme park may adopt the same layout type primarily because of the way it 'controls' customer flow.

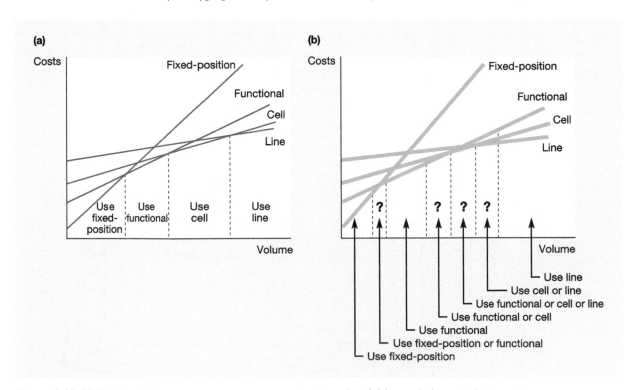

Figure 6.10 (a) The basic layout types have different fixed- and variable-cost characteristics which seem to determine which one to use. (b) In practice the uncertainty about the exact fixed and variable costs of each layout means the decision can rarely be made on cost alone

Of all the characteristics of the various layout types, perhaps the most generally significant are the unit cost implications of layout choice. This is best understood by distinguishing between the fixed- and variable-cost elements of adopting each layout type. For any particular product or service, the fixed costs of physically constructing a fixed-position layout are relatively small compared with any other way of producing the same product or service. However, the variable costs of producing each individual product or service are relatively high compared to the alternative layout types. Fixed costs then tend to increase as one moves from fixed-position, through functional and cell, to line layout. Variable costs per product or service tend to decrease, however. The total costs for each layout type will depend on the volume of products or services produced and are shown in Figure 6.10(a). This seems to show that for any volume there is a lowest-cost basic layout. However, in practice, the cost analysis of layout selection is rarely as clear as this. The exact cost of operating the layout is difficult to forecast and will probably depend on many often-difficult-to-predict factors. Rather than use lines to represent the cost of layout as volume increases, broad bands, within which the real cost is likely to lie, are probably more appropriate (see Figure 6.10(b)). The discrimination between the different layout types is now far less clear. There are ranges of volume for which any of two or three layout types might provide the lowest operating cost. The less certainty there is over the costs, the broader the cost 'bands' will be, and the less clear the choice will be. The probable costs of adopting a particular layout need to be set in the broader context of advantages and disadvantages in Table 6.2.

Workplace layout

At a micro and detailed level, the 'positioning' of equipment has the same purpose as the positioning of operations geographically or the positioning of resources within the operation; this is to minimize cost and maximize some combination of safety, quality, speed, dependability and flexibility. In the workplace, this usually translates to mean minimizing human effort, promoting good-quality work and preventing injury. This may mean positioning equipment so that it does not place undue physical demands on staff, providing mechanical assistance where required and ensuring that items are placed clearly and conveniently. The subject of ergonomics that we mentioned in the process design chapter can help in achieving these aims.

Anthropometric aspects

Anthropometric data

Many ergonomic improvements are primarily concerned with what are called the anthropometric aspects of jobs – that is, the aspects related to people's size, shape and other physical abilities. The design of an assembly task, for example, should be governed partly by the size and strength of the operators who do the job. The data which ergonomists use when doing this is called **anthropometric data**. Because we all vary in our size and capabilities, ergonomists are particularly interested in our range of capabilities, which is why anthropometric data is usually expressed in percentile terms. Figure 6.11 illustrates this idea. This shows the idea of size (in this case height) variation. Only 5 per cent of the population are smaller than the person on the extreme left (5th percentile), whereas 95 per cent of the population are smaller than the person on the extreme right (95th percentile). When this principle is applied to other dimensions of the body, for example arm length, it can be used to design work areas. Figure 6.11 also shows the normal and maximum work areas derived from anthropometric data. It would be inadvisable, for example, to place frequently used components or tools outside the maximum work area derived from the 5th percentile dimensions of human reach.

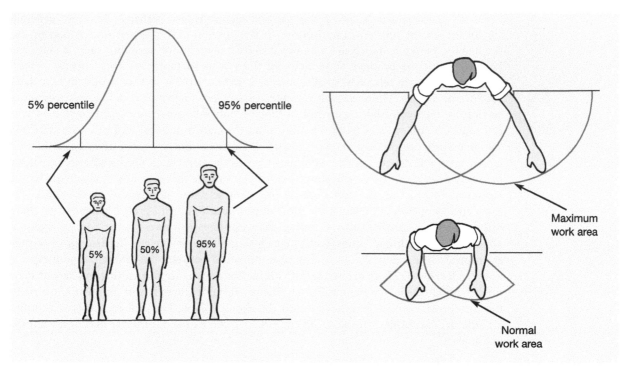

Figure 6.11 The use of anthropometric data in job design

Summary answers to key questions

Check and improve your understanding of this chapter using self-assessment questions and a personalized study plan, audio and video downloads, and an eBook – all at www.myomlab.com.

➤ Where should operations be located?

■ The stimuli which act on an organization during the location decision can be divided into supply-side and demand-side influences. Supply-side influences are the factors such as labour, land and utility costs which change as location changes. Demand-side influences include such things as the image of the location, its convenience for customers and the suitability of the site itself.

➤ What is layout and what are the types used in operations?

■ The 'layout' of an operation or process means how its transformed resources are positioned relative to each other and how its various tasks are allocated to these transforming resources.

■ There are four basic layout types. They are fixed-position layout, functional layout, cell layout and line layout.

➤ What type of layout should an operation choose?

■ Partly this is influenced by the nature of the process type, which in turn depends on the volume–variety characteristics of the operation. Partly also the decision will depend on the objectives of the operation. Cost and flexibility are particularly affected by the layout decision.

- The fixed and variable costs implied by each layout differ such that, in theory, one particular layout will have the minimum costs for a particular volume level. However, in practice, uncertainty over the real costs involved in layout makes it difficult to be precise on which is the minimum-cost layout.

> ➤ **How should items be positioned in a workplace?**

- Usually workplace design involves positioning equipment to minimize effort, minimize the risk of injury, and maximize quality of work.

Learning exercises

These problems and applications will help to improve your analysis of operations. You can find more practice problems as well as worked examples and guided solutions on MyOMLab at www.myomlab.com.

1 Sketch the layout of your local shop, coffee bar or sports hall reception area. Observe the area and draw onto your sketch the movements of people through the area over a sufficient period of time to get over 20 observations. Assess the flow in terms of volume, variety and type of layout.

2 Revisit the opening short case in this chapter that examines some of the principles behind supermarket layout. Then visit a supermarket and observe people's behaviour. You may wish to try and observe which areas they move slowly past and which areas they seem to move past without paying attention to the products. (You may have to exercise some discretion when doing this; people generally don't like to be stalked round the supermarket too obviously.) Try and verify, as far as you can, some of the principles that were outlined in the opening short case. If you were to redesign the supermarket what would you recommend?

3 Draw a rough plan of your (or someone else's) kitchen. Note (or observe) movements around the kitchen during food preparation and cleaning. How could its layout be improved?

Want to know more?

This is a relatively technical chapter and, as you would expect, most books on the subject are technical. Here are a few of the more accessible.

Karlsson, C. (1996) Radically new production systems, *International Journal of Operations and Production Management*, vol. 16, no. 11. An interesting paper because it traces the development of Volvo's factory layouts over the years.

Meyers, F.E. and Stephens, M.P. (2000) *Manufacturing Facilities Design and Material Handling*, Prentice-Hall, Upper Saddle River, NJ. Exactly what it says, thorough.

Meller, R.D. and Kai-Yin Gau (1996) The facility layout problem: recent and emerging trends and perspectives, *Journal of Manufacturing Systems*, vol. 15, issue 5, 351–66. A review of the literature in the area.

Useful websites

www.bpmi.org Site of the Business Process Management Initiative. Some good resources including papers and articles.

www.bptrends.com News site for trends in business process management generally. Some interesting articles.

www.iienet.org The Global Association of Productivity and Efficiency Professionals site. They are an important professional body for process design and related topics.

www.waria.com A Workflow and Reengineering Association website. Some useful topics.

www.opsman.org Lots of useful stuff.

Now that you have finished reading this chapter, why not visit MyOMLab at www.myomlab.com where you'll find more learning resources to help you make the most of your studies and get a better grade.

Chapter 7

Supply network management

Key questions

➤ Why should an organization take a supply network perspective?

➤ What is involved in managing supply networks?

➤ What is involved in designing a supply network?

➤ What are the types of relationships between operations in supply networks?

➤ What is the 'natural' dynamic of a supply network?

➤ How can supply networks be improved?

Introduction

No operation exists in isolation. Every operation is part of a larger and interconnected *supply network.* These networks not only include suppliers and customers, but also suppliers' suppliers and customers' customers, and so on. As operations outsource many of their activities, the way they manage the supply of services and products is hugely important. At a strategic level, operations managers are involved in 'designing' the shape of their network and determining what to do and what to buy. At a more operational level, operations managers must consider the type of relationships they wish to develop with suppliers, understand the dynamics of their network, and improve their supply networks in order to ultimately satisfy end customers. Figure 7.1 shows where this chapter fits into the overall operations model.

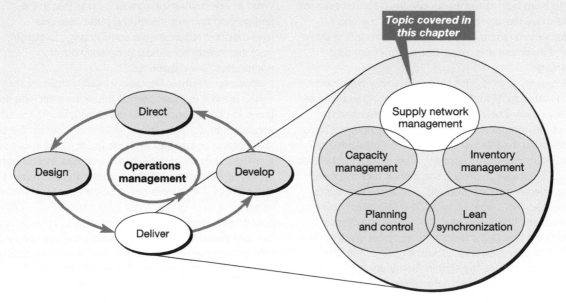

Figure 7.1 This chapter examines supply network management

Operations in practice Dell: no operating model lasts forever[1]

When he was a student at the University of Texas at Austin, Michael Dell's sideline of buying unused stock of PCs from local dealers, adding components, and re-selling the now higher-specification machines to local businesses was so successful that he quit university and founded a computer company which was to revolutionize the industry's supply network management. His fledgling company was just too small to make its own components. Better, he figured to learn how to manage a network of committed specialist component manufacturers and take the best of what was available in the market. Dell says that his commitment to outsourcing was always done for the most positive of reasons. '*We focus on how we can coordinate our activities to create the most value for customers*'. Yet Dell still faced a cost disadvantage against its far bigger competitors, so they decided to sell its computers direct to its customers, bypassing retailers. This allowed the company to cut out the retailer's (often considerable) margin, which in turn allowed Dell to offer lower prices. Dell also realized that cutting out the link in the supply network between them and the customer also provided them with significant learning opportunities to get to know their customers' needs far more intimately. Most importantly it allowed Dell to learn how to run its supply chain so that products could move through the supply chain to the end-customer in a fast and efficient manner, reducing Dell's level of inventory and giving Dell a significant cost advantage.

However, what is right at one time may become a liability later on. Two decades later Dell's growth started to slow down. The irony of this is that, what had been one of the company's main advantages, its direct sales model using the Internet and its market power to squeeze price reductions from suppliers, were starting to be seen as disadvantages. Although the market had changed, Dell's operating model had not. Some commentators questioned Dell's size. How could a $56 billion company remain lean, sharp, and alert? Other commentators pointed out that Dell's rivals had also now learnt to run efficient supply networks. However, one of the main factors was seen as the shift in the nature of the market itself. Sales of PCs to business users had become largely a commodity business with wafer-thin margins, and this part of the market was growing slowly

Source: Corbis/Gianni Giansanti/Sygma

compared to the sale of computers to individuals. Selling computers to individuals provided slightly better margins than the corporate market, but they increasingly wanted up-to-date computers with a high design value, and most significantly, they wanted to see, touch and feel the products before buying them. This was clearly a problem for a company like Dell which had spent 20 years investing in its telephone- and later, internet-based sales channels. What all commentators agreed on was that in the fast-moving and cut-throat computer business, where market requirements could change overnight, operations resources must constantly develop appropriate new capabilities.

However, Michael Dell said it could regain its spot as the world's number one PC maker by switching its focus to consumers and the developing world. He also conceded that the company had missed out on the boom in supplying computers to home users – who make up just 15% of its revenues – because it was focused on supplying businesses. '*Let's say you wanted to buy a Dell computer in a store nine months ago – you'd have searched a long time and not found one. Now we have over 10,000 stores that sell our products.*' He rejected the idea that design was not important to his company, though he accepted that it had not been a top priority when all the focus was on business customers. '*As we've gone to the consumer we've been paying quite a bit more attention to design, fashion, colors, textures and materials.*'

The supply network perspective

A **supply network** perspective means setting an operation in the context of all the customers and suppliers that interact with it. Materials, parts, information, ideas and people may all flow through the supply network. On its **supply side**, an operation has its suppliers of materials, information or services. These are often called **first-tier suppliers**. These suppliers themselves have their own **second-tier suppliers** who in turn could also have suppliers, and so on. On the **demand side** the operation has customers. These customers might not be the final consumers of the operation's services or products; they might have their own set of customers. 'First-tier' customers are the main customer group for the operation, who in turn supply 'second-tier' customers.

Figure 7.2 illustrates the simplified supply network for two operations. First is a plastic homeware (kitchen bowls, food containers, etc.) manufacturer. Note that on the demand side the homeware manufacturer supplies some of its basic products to wholesalers which supply retail outlets. However, it also supplies some retailers directly with 'made-to-order' products. The second example, an enclosed shopping mall, also has suppliers and customers that themselves have their own suppliers and customers. Along with the flow of services and products in the network, each link in the network will feed back orders and information to its suppliers. It is a two-way process with goods flowing one way and information flowing the other.

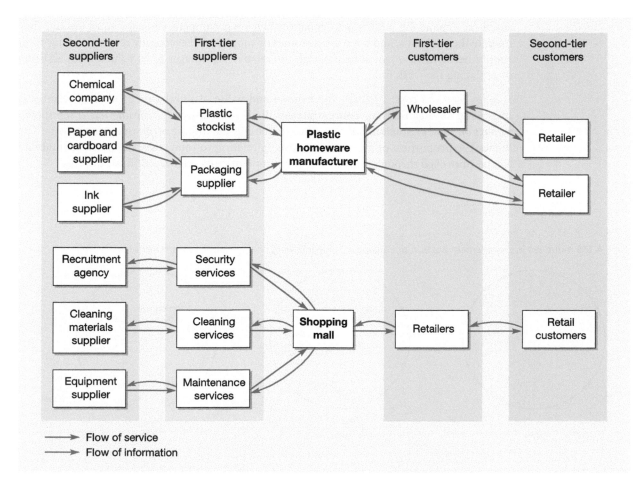

Figure 7.2 Operations network for a plastic homeware company and a shopping mall

Why consider the whole supply network?

There are a number of important reasons for taking a supply network perspective:

It helps an understanding of competitiveness. Immediate customers and immediate suppliers, quite understandably, are the main concern to competitively minded companies. Yet sometimes they need to look beyond these immediate contacts to understand why customers and suppliers act as they do. If it wants to understand its ultimate customers' needs at the end of the network, an operation can and should rely on the intermediate links in the network between itself and its end customers.

Downstream

Upstream

It helps identify significant links in the network. The key to understanding supply networks lies in identifying the parts of the network which contribute to those performance objectives valued by end-customers. Any analysis of networks must start, therefore, by understanding the **downstream** end of the network. After this, the **upstream** parts of the network which contribute most to end-customer service will need to be identified. For example, the important end-customers for domestic plumbing appliances are the installers and service companies that deal directly with domestic consumers. They are supplied by 'stock holders' which must have all parts in stock and deliver them fast. Suppliers of parts to the stock holders can best contribute to their end-customers' competitiveness partly by offering a short delivery lead time but mainly through dependable delivery. The key players in this example are the stock holders. The best way of winning end-customer business in this case is to give the stock holder prompt delivery which helps keep costs down while providing high availability of parts.

It helps focus on long-term issues. There are times when circumstances render parts of a supply network weaker than its adjacent links. A major machine breakdown, for example, or a labour dispute might disrupt a whole network. Should its immediate customers and suppliers exploit the weakness to enhance their own competitive position, or should they tolerate the problems, and hope the customer or supplier will eventually recover? A long-term supply-network view would be to weigh the relative advantages to be gained from assisting or replacing the weak link.

It helps focus on cost. Typically the volume and value of purchased goods and services is increasing as organizations concentrate on their 'core tasks'. ***Purchasing has a significant impact on total organizational costs***, thus increasing the impact on an operation's costs. The higher the proportion of procurement costs in relation to total costs, the more profitability can be improved through reduction in procurement costs. Figure 7.3 illustrates this.

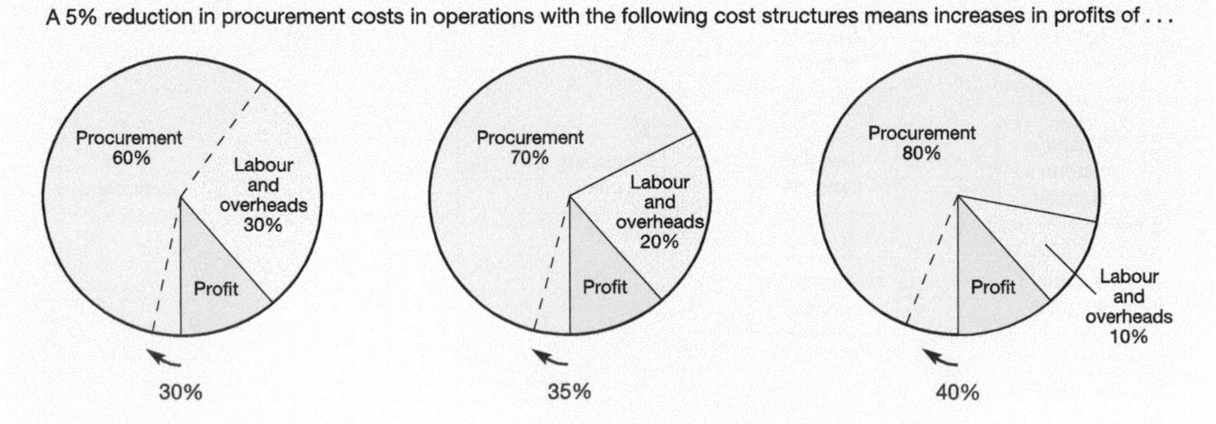

Figure 7.3 Impact of reduced procurement costs on total costs and profit

Designing and managing supply networks

A supply network is all the operations linked together to provide services and products through to the end-customers

A supply chain is a strand of linked operations

Designing and managing **supply networks** is a holistic approach to managing the interconnection of organizations that combine to produce value to the ultimate consumer in the form of services and products. Within supply networks, there can be many hundreds of strands of linked operations, commonly referred to as **supply chains**. An analogy often used to describe supply chains is that of the 'pipeline'. Just as liquids flow through a pipeline, so services and products flow down a supply chain. Long pipelines will, of course, contain more liquid than short ones, so the time taken for liquid to flow all the way through a long pipeline will be longer.

Some of the terms used in supply network management are not universally applied. Furthermore, some of the concepts behind the terminology overlap in the sense that they refer to common parts of the total supply network (Figure 7.4). *Supply network management* (also called supply chain management) coordinates all the operations on the supply side and the demand side. *Purchasing and supply management* deals with the operation's interface with its supply markets. *Physical distribution management* may mean supplying immediate customers, while *logistics* is an extension that often refers to materials and information flow down through a distribution channel, to the retail store or consumers (increasingly common because of the growth of internet-based retailing). The term *third-party logistics* (TPL) indicates outsourcing to a specialist logistics company. *Materials management* is a more limited term and refers to the flow of materials and information only through the immediate supply network.

Performance objectives of supply networks

The key objective in managing supply networks is the satisfaction of the end-customer. All parts of the network must consider the final customer, no matter how far an individual operation is from them. When customers decide to make a purchase, they trigger action across the whole network. All the businesses in the supply network pass on portions of

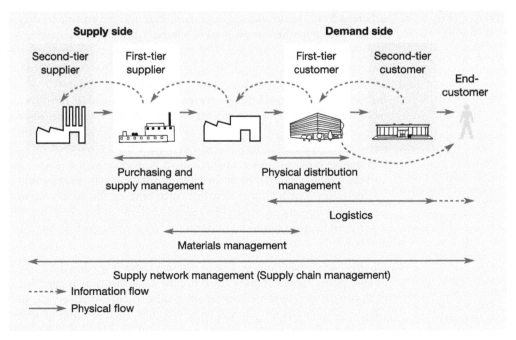

Figure 7.4 Some of the terms used to describe the management of different parts of the supply network

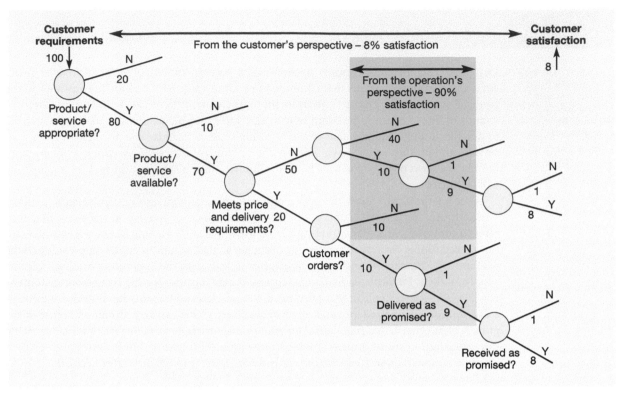

Figure 7.5 Taking a customer perspective of supply network performance can lead to very different conclusions

that end-customer's money to each other, each retaining a margin for the value it has added. Each operation in the network should be satisfying its own customer, but also making sure that eventually the end-customer is satisfied.

For a demonstration of how end-customer perceptions of supply satisfaction can be very different from that of a single operation, examine the customer 'decision tree' in Figure 7.5. It charts the hypothetical progress of a hundred customers requiring service from a business. Supply performance, as seen by the core operation, is represented by the shaded part of the diagram. It has received 20 orders, 18 of which were delivered as promised (on time, and in full). However, of the original customers who requested the service, 20 found it was inappropriate, 10 could not be served due to unavailability, 50 were not satisfied with the price and/or delivery requirements (though 10 did still place an order). So what seems a 90 per cent supply performance is in fact an 8 per cent performance from the customer's perspective. Note that this is just one operation from the operation's perspective. Include the cumulative effect of similar reductions in performance for all the operations in a network, and the probability that the end-customer is adequately served could become remote.

The point here is that the performance both of the supply network as a whole, and its constituent operations, should be judged in terms of how end-customer needs are satisfied, in terms of the five operations performance objectives: quality, speed, dependability, flexibility and cost.

Quality – the quality of a service or product when it reaches the customer is a function of the quality performance of every operation in the network that supplied it. Errors in each stage of the chain can multiply in their effect on end-customer service, so if each of 7 stages in a supply network has a 1 per cent error rate, only 93.2 per cent of services or products will be of good quality on reaching the end-customer. This is why, only by every stage taking some responsibility for its own *and its suppliers'* performance, can a supply network achieve high end-customer quality.

Speed has two meanings in a supply network context. The first is how fast customers can be served. However, fast customer response can be achieved simply by over-resourcing or over-stocking within the network. For example, an accounting firm may be able to respond quickly to customer demand by having a large number of accountants on standby waiting for demand that may (or may not) occur. An alternative perspective on speed is the time taken for services and products to move through the network. So, for example, products that move quickly across a supply network will spend little time as inventory, which in turn reduces inventory-related costs in the network.

Dependability – like speed, one can almost guarantee 'on-time' delivery by keeping excessive resources, such as inventory, within the network. However, dependability of throughput time is a much more desirable aim because it reduces uncertainty. If individual operations do not deliver as promised, there will be a tendency for customers to over-order, or order early, in order to provide some kind of insurance against late delivery. This is why delivery dependability is often measured as 'on time, in full' in supply networks.

Flexibility – in a supply network context, flexibility is usually taken to mean the ability to cope with changes and disturbances. Very often this is referred to as agility. The concept of agility includes previously discussed issues such as focusing on the end-customer and ensuring fast throughput and responsiveness to customer needs. But, in addition, agile supply networks are sufficiently flexible to cope with changes, either in the nature of customer demand or in the supply capabilities of operations within the network.

Cost – in addition to the costs incurred within each operation, the supply network as a whole incurs additional costs that derive from operations doing business with each other. These may include such things as the costs of finding appropriate suppliers, setting up contractual agreements, monitoring supply performance, transporting products between operations, holding inventories, and so on. Many developments in supply network management, such as partnership agreements or reducing the number of suppliers, are attempts to minimize transaction costs.

Short case
Ford Motors' team value management[2]

Purchasing managers are a vital link between an operation and its suppliers. They work best when teamed up with mainstream operations managers who know what the operation really needs, especially if, between them, they take a role that challenges previous assumptions. That is the basis behind Ford Motor Company's 'team value management' (TVM) approach. Reputedly, it all started when Ford's Head of Global Purchasing, David Thursfield, discovered that a roof rack designed for one of Ford's smaller cars was made of plastic-coated aluminium and capable of bearing a 100 kg load. This prompted the questions, *'Why is this rack covered in plastic? Why would anyone want to put 100 kg on the roof of a car that small?'* He found that no one had ever questioned the original specification. When Ford switched to using steel roof racks capable of bearing a smaller weight, they halved the cost. *'It is important'*, he says, *'to check whether the company is getting the best price for parts and raw material that provide the appropriate level of performance without being too expensive.'* The savings in a large company

Source: Getty Images/Getty Images News

such as Ford can be huge. Often in multinationals, each part of the business makes sourcing and design decisions independently and does not exploit opportunities for cross-usage of components. The TVM approach is designed to bring together engineering and purchasing staff and identify where cost can be taken out of purchased parts and where there is opportunity for parts commonality (see Chapter 4) between different models. When a company's global purchasing budget is $75bn like Ford's, the potential for cost savings is significant.

Supply network design

Taking a supply network perspective is useful because it prompts a number of important design decisions. These combine to determine how a supply network can operate and its ability to deliver value to customers. These decisions include:

1 Who should do what in the network? How many steps should there be in the network? What is the role of customers, suppliers, complementors and competitors? This is called the network shape decision.
2 How much of the network should the operation own? This is called the do-or-buy, outsourcing or vertical integration decision.
3 How should supply networks be configured when operations compete in different ways in different markets? This is called the supply network matching decision.

The network shape decision

Supply base reduction

Reconfiguring a supply network sometimes involves parts of the operation being merged – not necessarily in the sense of a change of ownership of any parts of an operation, but rather in the way responsibility is allocated for carrying out activities. The most common example of network reconfiguration has come through the many companies that have recently reduced the number of direct suppliers. The complexity of dealing with many thousands of suppliers may both be expensive for an operation and (sometimes more important) prevent the operation from developing a close relationship with a supplier. It is not easy to be close to so many different suppliers.

Disintermediation

Disintermediation

Another trend in some supply networks is that of companies within a network bypassing customers or suppliers to make contact directly with customers' customers or suppliers' suppliers. 'Cutting out the middlemen' in this way is called **disintermediation**. An obvious example of this is the way the Internet has allowed some suppliers to 'disintermediate' traditional retailers in supplying services and products to consumers. So, for example, many services in the travel industry that used to be sold through retail outlets (travel agents) are now also available direct from the suppliers. The option of purchasing the individual components of a vacation through the websites of the airline, hotel, car hire company, etc., is now easier for consumers. Of course, they may still wish to purchase an 'assembled' product from retail travel agents which can have the advantage of convenience.

Co-opetition

One approach to thinking about supply networks sees any business as being surrounded by four types of players: suppliers, customers, competitors and complementors. Complementors enable one's services or products to be valued more by customers because they can also have the complementor's products or services, as opposed to when they have yours alone. Competitors are the opposite: they make customers value your service or product less when they can have their product or service, rather than yours alone. Competitors can also be complementors and vice versa. For example, adjacent restaurants may see themselves as competitors for customers' business. A customer standing outside and wanting a meal will choose between the two of them. Yet, in another way they are complementors. Would that customer have come to this part of town unless there was more than one restaurant to choose from? Restaurants, theatres, art galleries and tourist attractions generally, all cluster together in a form of cooperation to increase the total size of their joint market. It is important to distinguish between the way companies cooperate in increasing the total size of a market and the way in which they then compete for a share of that market. In the long term it creates value for the total network to find ways of increasing value for suppliers and well as customers. All the players in the supply network, whether they are customers, suppliers, competitors or complementors, can be both friends and enemies at different times. The term used to capture this idea is '**co-opetition**'.[3]

Co-opetition

The do-or-buy decision

No single business does everything that is required to deliver its services and products. Bakers do not grow wheat or even mill it into flour. Banks do not usually do their own credit checking: they retain the services of specialist agencies that have the information systems and expertise to do it better. Although most companies have always outsourced some of their activities, a larger proportion of direct activities are now being bought from suppliers. In addition, many indirect processes are also being outsourced, often referred to as '**business process outsourcing**' (BPO). Financial service companies in particular are starting to outsource some of their more routine back-office processes. In a similar way many processes within the human resource function, from payroll services through to more complex training and development processes, are being outsourced to specialist companies. The processes may still be physically located where they were before, but the staff and technology are managed by the outsourcing service provider. The reason for doing this is often primarily to reduce cost. However, there can also be significant gains in the quality and flexibility of service offered. Deciding what to do itself in-house and what to outsource is often called the 'do or buy' decision, when individual components or activities are being considered, or the 'vertical integration decision' when it is the ownership of whole operations that is being decided. Vertical integration can be defined in terms of three factors.[4]

Business process
outsourcing (BPO)

1 *The direction of vertical integration.* Should an operation expand by buying one of its suppliers or by buying one of its customers? The strategy of expanding on the supply side of the network is sometimes called 'backward' or 'upstream' vertical integration, and expanding on the demand side is sometimes called 'forward' or 'downstream' vertical integration.
2 *The extent of vertical integration.* How far should an operation take the extent of its vertical integration? Some organizations deliberately choose not to integrate far, if at all, from their original part of the network. Alternatively, some organizations choose to become very vertically integrated.
3 *The balance among stages.* How exclusive should the relationship be between operations? A totally balanced network relationship is one where an operation produces only for the next stage in the network and totally satisfies its requirements. Less than full balance allows each operation to sell its output to other companies or to buy in some of its supplies from other companies.

Making the do-or-buy decision

Whether it is referred to as the do-or-buy, vertical integration or the outsourcing decision, the choice facing operations is rarely simple. Organizations in different circumstances with different objectives are likely to take different decisions. Yet the question itself is relatively simple, even if the decision itself is not: 'Does in-house or outsourced supply in a particular set of circumstances give the appropriate performance objectives that it requires to compete more effectively in its markets?' For example, if the main performance objectives for an operation are dependable delivery and meeting short-term changes in customers' delivery requirements, the key question should be: 'How does in-house or outsourcing give better dependability and delivery flexibility performance?' Table 7.1 summarizes some arguments for in-house supply and outsourcing in terms of each performance objective.

Although the effect of outsourcing on the operation's performance objective is important, there are other factors that companies take into account when deciding if outsourcing an activity is a sensible option. If an activity has long-term **strategic importance** to a company,

Outsourcing is a
strategic decision

Table 7.1 How in-house and outsourced supply may affect an operation's performance objectives

Performance objective	'Do it yourself' in-house supply	'Buy it in' outsourced supply
Quality	The origins of any quality problems are usually easier to trace in-house and improvement can be more immediate but there can be some risk of complacency.	Supplier may have specialized knowledge and more experience, also may be motivated through market pressures, but communication more difficult.
Speed	Can mean synchronized schedules which speeds throughput of materials and information, but if the operation has external customers, internal customers may be low-priority.	Speed of response can be built into the supply contract where commercial pressures will encourage good performance, but there may be significant transport/delivery delays.
Dependability	Easier communications can help dependability, but, if the operation also has external customers, internal customers may be low priority.	Late-delivery penalties in the supply contract can encourage good delivery performance, but organizational barriers may inhibit in communication.
Flexibility	Closeness to real business needs can alert the in-house operation to required changes, but the ability to respond may be limited by the scale and scope of internal operations.	Outsourced suppliers may be larger with wider capabilities and have more ability to respond to changes, but may have to balance conflicting needs of different customers.
Cost	In-house operations do not have to make the margin required by outside suppliers so the business can capture the profits which would otherwise be given to the supplier, but relatively low volumes may mean that it is difficult to gain economies of scale or the benefits of process innovation.	Probably the main reason why outsourcing is so popular. Outsourced companies can achieve economies of scale and they are motivated to reduce their own costs because it directly impacts on their profits, but costs of communication and coordination with supplier need to be taken into account.

it is unlikely to outsource it. For example, a retailer might choose to keep the design and development of its website in-house even though specialists could perform the activity at less cost because it plans to move into web-based retailing at some point in the future. Nor would a company usually outsource an activity where it had specialized skills or knowledge. For example, a company making laser printers may have built up specialized knowledge in the production of sophisticated laser drives. This capability may allow it to introduce product or process innovations in the future. It would be foolish to 'give away' such capability. After these two more strategic factors have been considered, the company's operations performance can be taken into account. Obviously if its operations performance is already superior to any potential supplier, it would be unlikely to outsource the activity. Even if its performance was currently below that of potential suppliers, it may not outsource the activity if it feels that it could significantly improve its performance. Figure 7.6 illustrates this decision logic.

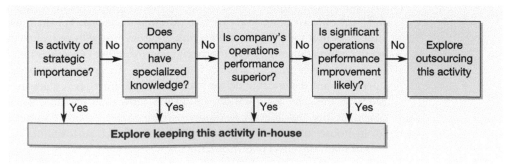

Figure 7.6 The decision logic of outsourcing

Short case
Behind the brand names[5]

The market for notebook computers is a fast-evolving and competitive one. Yet few who buy these products know that the majority of the world's notebooks are made by a small number of Taiwanese and Korean manufacturers. Taiwanese firms alone make around 60 per cent of all notebooks in the world, including most of Dell, Compaq and Apple machines. In a market with unremitting technological innovation and fierce price competition, it makes sense to outsource production to companies that can achieve the economies that come with high-volume manufacture as well as develop the expertise which enables new designs to be put into production without the usual cost overruns and delays. However, the big brand names are keen to defend their products' performance. Dell, for example, admits that a major driver of its outsourcing policy is the requirement to keep costs at a competitive level, but says that it can ensure product quality and performance through

Source: Rex Features

its relationship with its suppliers. *'The production lines are set up by Dell and managed by Dell'*, says Tony Bonadero, Director of Product Marketing for Dell's laptop range. Dell also imposes strict quality control and manages the overall design of the product.

Supply network alignment

An important question for supply managers to consider is 'How should supply networks be configured when operations compete in different ways in different markets?' One answer, proposed by Professor Marshall Fisher of Wharton Business School, is to organize the supply network serving those individual markets in different ways.[6] He points out that many companies have seemingly similar products which, in fact, compete in different ways. Shoe manufacturers may produce classics which change little over the years, as well as fashions which last only one or two seasons. Chocolate manufacturers have stable lines which have been sold for 50 years, but also create 'specials' associated with an event or film release, maybe selling only for a few months. Demand for the former products will be relatively stable and predictable, but demand for the latter will be far more uncertain. Also, the profit margin commanded by the innovative product will probably be higher than that of the more functional product. However, the price (and therefore the margin) of the innovative product may drop rapidly once it has become unfashionable in the market.

Efficient supply networks
Responsive supply networks

The supply network policies which are seen to be appropriate for functional services and products and innovative services and products are termed by Fisher **efficient supply network** policies and **responsive supply network** policies, respectively. Efficient supply network policies include keeping inventories low, especially in the downstream parts of the network, so as to maintain fast throughput and reduce the amount of working capital tied up in the inventory. What inventory there is in the network is concentrated mainly in the manufacturing operation, where it can keep utilization high and therefore manufacturing costs low. Information must flow quickly up and down the chain from retail outlets back up to the manufacturer so that schedules can be given the maximum amount of time to adjust efficiently. The network is then managed to make sure that products flow as quickly as possible down the chain to replenish what few stocks are kept in the network. By contrast, responsive supply policies stress high service levels and responsive supply to the end-customer. The inventory in the network will be deployed as closely as possible to the customer. In this way, the network can still supply even when dramatic changes occur in customer demand. Fast throughput from the upstream parts of the network will still be needed to replenish downstream stocks. But

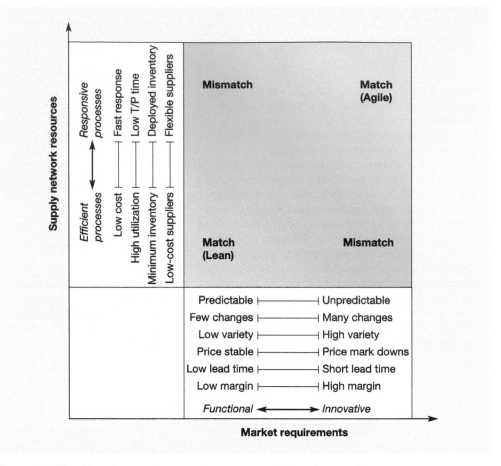

Figure 7.7 Matching the supply network resources with market requirements

Source: Adapted from Fisher, M.C. (1997) What is the right supply chain for your product? *Harvard Business Review*, March–April, 105–16.

those downstream stocks are needed to ensure high levels of availability to end-customers. Figure 7.7 illustrates how the different supply network policies match the different market requirements implied by functional and innovative products.

Types of relationships in supply networks

One of the key issues within a supply network is how relationships with suppliers and customers should be managed. The behaviour of the supply network as a whole is, after all, made up of the relationships which are formed between individual pairs of operations. It is important, therefore, to have some framework which helps us to understand the different ways in which supply relationships can be developed.

Business or consumer relationships?

We can distinguish between relationships that are the final link in the supply network, involving the ultimate consumer, and those involving two commercial businesses (Figure 7.8). So, **business-to-business** (B2B) relationships are by far the most common in a supply network context. **Business-to-consumer** (B2C) relationships include both 'bricks and mortar' retailers

Business to business

Business to consumer

	Relationship – to . . .	
	Business	Consumer (Peer)
Business	**B2B** *Relationship* • Most common, all but the last link in the supply network *E-commerce examples* • Electronic marketplaces • e.g. b2b Index	**B2C** *Relationship* • Retail operations • Comparison web sites *E-commerce examples* • Online retailers • e.g. Amazon.com
Consumer (Peer)	**C2B** *Relationship* • Consumers offer, business responds *E-commerce examples* • Usually focused on specialist area • e.g. Google Adsense	**C2C (P2P)** *Relationship* • Originally one of the driving forces behind the modern Internet (ARPANET) *E-commerce examples* • File sharing networks (legal and illegal) • e.g. Napster, Gnutella

(Left axis label: Relationship – from . . .)

Figure 7.8 The business–consumer relationship matrix

Consumer to business

Customer to customer

and online retailers. **Consumer-to-business** (C2B) relationships involve consumers posting their needs on the web (sometimes stating the price they are willing to pay), and companies then deciding whether to offer. **Customer-to-customer** (C2C) or peer-to-peer (P2P) relationships include the online exchange and auction services and file-sharing services. In this chapter we deal almost exclusively with B2B relationships.

Types of business-to-business relationship

A convenient way of categorizing supply relationships is to examine the extent and nature of what a company chooses to buy in from suppliers. Two dimensions are particularly important – *what* the company chooses to outsource, and *who* it chooses to supply it. In terms of what is outsourced, a key question is, 'how many activities are outsourced?' from doing everything in-house at one extreme, to outsourcing everything at the other extreme. In terms of who is chosen to supply products and services, two questions are important, 'how many suppliers will be used by the operation?' and 'how close are the relationships?' Figure 7.9 illustrates this way of characterizing relationships. It also identifies some of the more common types of relationship and shows some of the trends in how supply relationships have moved.

Traditional market supply relationships

Short-term transactional relationships

The very opposite of performing an operation in-house is to purchase services and products from outside in a 'pure' market fashion, often seeking the 'best' supplier every time it is necessary to purchase. Each transaction effectively becomes a separate decision. The **relationship** between buyer and seller, therefore, can be very short-term. Once the services or products are delivered and payment is made, there may be no further trading between the parties. Short-term relationships may be used on a trial basis when new companies are being considered as more regular suppliers. Also, many purchases which are made by operations are

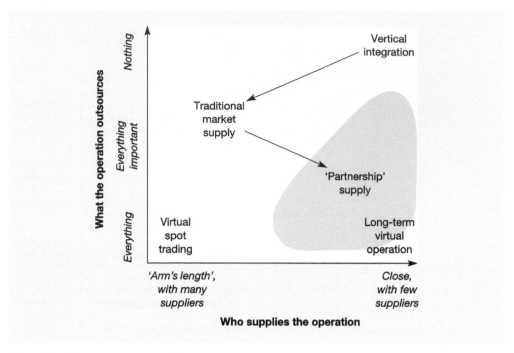

Figure 7.9 Types of supply chain relationship

one-off or very irregular. The advantages of traditional market supplier relationships are usually seen as follows:

- They maintain competition between alternative suppliers. This promotes a constant drive between suppliers to provide best value.
- A supplier specializing in a small number of services or products, but supplying them to many customers, can gain natural economies of scale. This enables the supplier to offer the products and services at a lower price than would be obtained if customers performed the activities themselves.
- There is inherent flexibility in outsourced supplies. If demand changes, customers can simply change the number and type of suppliers. This is a far faster and simpler alternative to having to redirect internal activities.
- Innovations can be exploited no matter where they originate. Specialist suppliers are more likely to come up with innovative products and services which can be bought in faster and cheaper than would be the case if the company were itself trying to innovate.
- They help operations to concentrate on their core activities. One business cannot be good at everything. It is sensible therefore to concentrate on the important activities and outsource the rest.

There are, however, disadvantages in buying in a totally 'free market' manner:

- There may be supply uncertainties. Once an order has been placed, it is difficult to maintain control over how that order is fulfilled. This is a particular problem if the buyer is small relative to the supplier, so lacks power to influence their behaviour.
- Choosing who to buy from takes time and effort. Gathering sufficient information and making decisions continually are, in themselves, activities which need to be resourced.
- There are strategic risks in subcontracting activities to other businesses. An over-reliance on outsourcing can 'hollow out' the company, leaving it with few internal capabilities to exploit in its markets.
- Short-term, price-oriented types of relationship can have a downside in terms of ongoing support and reliability. This may mean that a short-term 'least-cost' purchase decision will lead to long-term high cost.

Short case
Northern Foods wins a slice of the in-flight meals business[7]

The companies that provide airline catering services are in a tough business. Meals must be of a quality that is appropriate for the class and type of flight, yet the airlines that are their customers are always looking to keep costs as low as possible, menus must change frequently and the airlines must respond promptly to customer feedback. If this were not enough, forecasting passenger numbers is difficult. Catering suppliers are advised of the likely numbers of passengers for each flight several days in advance, but the actual minimum number of passengers for each class is only fixed six hours before take-off. Also, flight arrivals are sometimes delayed, putting pressure on everyone to reduce the turnaround time, and upsetting work schedules. Even when a flight lands on time no more than 40 minutes are allowed before the flight is ready for take-off again, so complete preparation and a well-ordered sequence of working is essential. It is a specialized business, and in order to maintain a fast, responsive and agile service, airline caterers have traditionally produced food on, or near, airport sites using their own chefs and staff to cook and tray-set meals. The catering companies' suppliers are also usually airline specialists who themselves are located near the caterers so that they can offer very short response times.

The companies that provide catering services may also provide related services. For example, LSG Sky Chefs (a subsidiary of Deutsche Lufthansa AG) is a provider of tailor-made in-flight services for all types of airlines around the world. Their main areas of service are Airline Catering, In-flight Equipment and Logistics and In-flight Management. They are also large, employing 30,000 people at 200 customer service centres in 49 countries. In 2007 they produced 418 million meals for more than 300 airlines, representing more than 30 per cent of the global airline catering market.

The airline sector has over recent years suffered a series of shocks including 9/11, oil price volatility, financial

Source: Virgin Atlantic

Specialized companies have developed that prepare food in specialized factories, often for several airlines.

crises and world recession. This has meant that airlines are reviewing their catering supply solutions. In December 2008 Gate Gourmet, the world's largest independent provider of airline catering lost the contract to supply British Airways' short-haul flights out of Heathrow to new entrants into the airline catering market, a consortium of Northern Foods, a leading food producer, whose normal business is supplying retailers with own-label and branded food, and DHL, a subsidiary of Deutsche Post and the market-leading international express and logistics company. DHL is already a large supplier to 'airside' caterers at Heathrow and already has its own premises at the airport. Northern Foods will make the food at its existing factories and deliver it to DHL, which will assemble onto airline catering trays and transfer them onto aircraft. The new contract is the first time that Northern Foods, whose biggest customer is Marks and Spencer, the UK retail chain, has developed new business outside its normal supermarket customer base.

'Partnership' supply relationships

Partnership relationships   **Partnership relationships** in supply networks are sometimes seen as a compromise between vertical integration on the one hand (owning the resources which supply you) and pure market relationships on the other (having only a transactional relationship with those who supply you). Although to some extent this is true, partnership relationships are not only a simple mixture of vertical integration and market trading, although they do attempt to achieve some of the closeness and coordination efficiencies of vertical integration, but at the same time attempt to achieve a relationship that has a constant incentive to improve. Partnership relationships are defined as: *'relatively enduring inter-firm cooperative agreements, involving flows and linkages that use resources and/or governance structures from autonomous organizations, for the joint accomplishment of individual goals linked to the corporate mission of each* *sponsoring firm'.*[8] What this means is that suppliers and customers are expected to cooperate, even to the extent of sharing skills and resources, to achieve joint benefits beyond those they could have achieved by acting alone. At the heart of the concept of partnership lies the issue of the *closeness* of the relationship. Partnerships are close relationships, the degree of which is influenced by a number of factors:

- *Sharing success.* An attitude of shared success means that both partners work together in order to increase the total amount of joint benefit they receive, rather than manoeuvring to maximize their own individual contribution.
- *Long-term expectations.* Partnership relationships imply relatively long-term commitments, but not necessarily permanent ones.
- *Multiple points of contact.* Communication between partners is not only through formal channels, but may take place between many individuals in both organizations.
- *Joint learning.* Partners in a relationship are committed to learn from each other's experience and perceptions of the other operations in the chain.
- *Few relationships.* Although partnership relationships do not necessarily imply single sourcing by customers, they do imply a commitment on the part of both parties to limit the number of customers or suppliers with whom they do business. It is difficult to maintain close relationships with many different trading partners.
- *Joint coordination of activities.* As there are fewer relationships, it becomes possible jointly to coordinate activities such as the flow of materials or service, payment, and so on.
- *Information transparency.* An open and efficient information exchange is seen as a key element in partnerships because it helps to build confidence between the partners.
- *Joint problem-solving.* Although partnerships do not always run smoothly, jointly approaching problems can increase closeness over time.
- *Trust.* This is probably the key element in partnership relationships. In this context, trust means the willingness of one party to relate to the other on the understanding that the relationship will be beneficial to both, even though that cannot be guaranteed. Trust is widely held to be both the key issue in successful partnerships, but also, by far, the most difficult element to develop and maintain.

Virtual operations

Virtual operation

An extreme form of outsourcing operational activities is that of the **virtual operation**. Virtual operations do relatively little themselves, but rely on a network of suppliers that can provide services and products on demand. A network may be formed for only one project and then disbanded once that project ends. For example, some software and Internet companies are virtual in the sense that they buy in all the services needed for a particular development. This may include not only the specific software development skills but also such things as project management, testing, applications prototyping, marketing, physical production, and so on. Much of the Hollywood film industry also operates in this way. A production company may buy and develop an idea for a movie, but it is created, edited and distributed by a loose network of agents, actors, technicians, studios and distribution companies. The advantage of virtual operations is their flexibility and the fact that the risks of investing in production facilities are far lower than in a conventional operation. However, without any solid base of resources, a company may find it difficult to hold onto and develop a unique core of technical expertise. The resources used by virtual companies will almost certainly be available to competitors. In effect, the core competence of a virtual operation lies in the way it is able to manage its supply network.

Selecting suppliers

Choosing appropriate suppliers should involve trading off alternative attributes. Rarely are potential suppliers so clearly superior to their competitors that the decision is self-evident.

Table 7.2 Factors for rating alternative suppliers

Short-term ability to supply	Longer-term ability to supply
Range of services or products provided	Potential for innovation
Quality of services or products	Ease of doing business
Responsiveness	Willingness to share risk
Dependability of supply	Long-term commitment to supply
Delivery and volume flexibility	Ability to transfer knowledge as well as products and services
Total cost of being supplied	Technical capability
Ability to supply in the required quantity	Operations capability
	Financial capability
	Managerial capability

Most businesses find it best to adopt some kind of supplier 'scoring' or assessment procedure. This should be capable of rating alternative suppliers in terms of factors such as those in Table 7.2.

Supplier selection

Selecting suppliers should involve evaluating the relative importance of all these factors. So, for example, a business might choose a supplier that, although more expensive than alternative suppliers, has an excellent reputation for on-time delivery, or because the high level of supply dependability allows the business to hold lower stock levels. Other trade-offs may be more difficult to calculate. For example, a potential supplier may have high levels of technical capability, but may be financially weak, with a small but finite risk of going out of business. Other suppliers may have little track record of supplying the products or services required, but show the managerial talent and energy for potential customers to view developing a supply relationship as an investment in future capability.

Worked example

A hotel chain has decided to change its supplier of cleaning supplies because its current supplier has become unreliable in its delivery performance. The two alternative suppliers that it is considering have been evaluated, on a 1–10 scale, against the criteria shown in Table 7.3. That also shows the relative importance of each criterion, also on a 1–10 scale. Based on this evaluation, Supplier B has the superior overall score.

Table 7.3 Weighted supplier selection criteria for the hotel chain

Factor	Weight	Supplier A score	Supplier B score
Cost performance	10	8 (8 × 10 = 80)	5 (5 × 10 = 50)
Quality record	10	7 (7 × 10 = 70)	9 (9 × 10 = 90)
Delivery speed promised	7	5 (5 × 7 = 35)	5 (5 × 7 = 35)
Delivery speed achieved	7	4 (4 × 7 = 28)	8 (8 × 7 = 56)
Dependability record	8	6 (6 × 8 = 48)	8 (8 × 8 = 64)
Range provided	5	8 (8 × 5 = 40)	5 (5 × 5 = 25)
Innovation capability	4	6 (6 × 4 = 24)	9 (9 × 4 = 36)
Total weighted score		325	356

An important decision facing most purchasing managers is whether to source each individual product or service from one or more than one supplier, known, respectively, as **single-sourcing** and **multi-sourcing**. Some of the advantages and disadvantages of single- and multi-sourcing are shown in Table 7.4.

Single-sourcing
Multi-sourcing

Table 7.4 Advantages and disadvantages of single- and multi-sourcing

	Single-sourcing	Multi-sourcing
Advantages	• Potentially better quality because more supplier quality assurance possibilities • Strong relationships which are more durable • Greater dependency encourages more commitment and effort • Better communication • Easier to cooperate on new innovation • More scale economies • Higher confidentiality	• Purchaser can drive price down by competitive tendering • Reduces dependency on individual suppliers • Can switch sources in case of supply failure • Wide sources of knowledge and expertise to tap
Disadvantages	• More vulnerable to disruption if a failure to supply occurs • Individual supplier more affected by volume fluctuations • Supplier might exert upward pressure on prices if no alternative supplier is available	• Difficult to encourage commitment by supplier • Less easy to develop effective SQA • More effort needed to communicate • Suppliers less likely to invest in new processes • More difficult to obtain scale economies

It may seem as though companies that multi-source do so exclusively for their own short-term benefit. However, this is not always the case: multi-sourcing can bring benefits to both supplier and purchaser in the long term. For example, Robert Bosch GmbH, the German automotive components business, required that subcontractors do no more than 20 per cent of their total business with them. This was to prevent suppliers becoming too dependent and allow volumes to be fluctuated without pushing the supplier into bankruptcy. However, there has been a trend for purchasing functions to reduce the number of companies supplying any one part or service.

Dual sourcing

Parallel sourcing

Dual sourcing or **parallel sourcing** is often seen as a way to balance the relative merits of single and multi-sourcing. This involves using two suppliers for similar goods or services. Whilst dual suppliers are usually required to cooperate, an element of competition may also be encouraged by adjusting the percentage of the contract awarded to each supplier based on previous performance.

Global sourcing

Global sourcing

One of the major developments of recent years has been the expansion in the proportion of services and products which businesses source from outside their home country; this is called **global sourcing**. Traditionally, even companies that exported their goods and services all over the world (that is, they were international on their demand side) still sourced the majority of their supplies locally. There are a number of factors promoting global sourcing:

● The formation of trading blocs in different parts of the world has lowered tariff barriers, at least within those blocs. For example, the single market developments within the European Union (EU), the North American Free Trade Agreement (NAFTA) and the South American Trade Group (MERCOSUR) have all made it easier to trade internationally within the regions.

● Transportation infrastructures are considerably more sophisticated and cheaper than they once were. Super-efficient port operations in Rotterdam and Singapore, for example, integrated road–rail systems, jointly developed autoroute systems, and cheaper air freight have all reduced some of the cost barriers to international trade.

● Perhaps most significantly, far tougher world competition has forced companies to look to reducing their total costs. Given that in many industries bought-in items are the largest single part of operations costs, an obvious strategy is to source from wherever is cheapest.

There are, of course, challenges to global sourcing. Suppliers that are further away need to transport their products across long distances. The risks of delays and hold-ups can be far greater than when sourcing locally. Also, negotiating with suppliers whose native language is different from one's own makes communication more difficult and can lead to misunderstandings over contract terms. Therefore global sourcing decisions require businesses to balance cost, performance, service and risk factors, not all of which are obvious. These factors are important in global sourcing because of non-price or 'hidden' cost factors such as cross-border freight and handling fees, complex inventory stocking and handling requirements, more complex administrative, documentation and regulatory requirements, and increased operational risk caused by geopolitical factors.

Supply network dynamics

The bullwhip effect

The 'bullwhip effect' is used to describe how a small disturbance at the downstream end of a supply network causes increasingly large disturbances, errors, inaccuracies and volatility as it works its way upstream. Its main cause is an understandable desire by the different links in the supply network to manage their production rates and inventory levels sensibly. To demonstrate this, examine the production rate and stock levels for the supply network shown in Table 7.5. This is a four-stage supply network where the focal operation is served by three tiers of suppliers. The demand from the market has been running at a rate of 100 items per period, but in period 2 demand reduces to 95 items. All stages in the supply chain work on the principle that they will keep in stock one period's demand (a simplification but not a gross one). The 'stock' column shows the starting stock at the beginning, and the finish stock at the end, of the period. At the beginning of period 2, the focal operation has

Table 7.5 Fluctuations of production levels along supply chain in response to small change in end-customer demand

Period	Third-tier supplier		Second-tier supplier		First-tier supplier		Focal operation		Demand
	Prodn.	Stock	Prodn.	Stock	Prodn.	Stock	Prodn.	Stock	
1	100	100	100	100	100	100	100	100	100
		100		100		100		100	
2	20	100	60	100	80	100	90	100	95
		60		80		90		95	
3	180	60	120	80	100	90	95	95	95
		120		100		95		95	
4	60	120	90	100	95	95	95	95	95
		90		95		95		95	
5	100	90	95	95	95	95	95	95	95
		95		95		95		95	
6	95	95	95	95	95	95	95	95	95
		95		95		95		95	

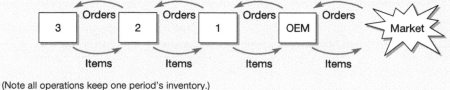

(Note all operations keep one period's inventory.)

100 units in stock. Demand in period 2 is 95 and the operation must produce enough to finish up at the end of the period with 95 in stock (this being the new demand rate). To do this, it need only manufacture 90 items; these, together with 5 items taken out of the starting stock, will supply demand and leave a finished stock of 95 items. Note, however, that a change in demand of only 5 items has produced a fluctuation of 10 items in the operation's production rate.

Now carry this same logic through to the first-tier supplier. At the beginning of period 2, the second-tier supplier has 100 items in stock. The demand which it has to supply in period 2 is derived from the production rate of the focal operation. This has dropped down to 90 in period 2. The first-tier supplier therefore has to produce enough to supply the demand of 90 and leave one month's demand (now 90 items) as its finished stock. A production rate of 80 items per month will achieve this. It will therefore start period 3 with an opening stock of 90 items, but the demand from its customers has now risen to 95 items. It therefore has to produce sufficient to fulfil this demand of 95 items and leave 95 items in stock. To do this, it must produce 100 items in period 3. This logic can be extended right back to the third-tier supplier. The further back up the supply chain an operation is placed, the more drastic are the fluctuations caused by the relatively small change in demand from the final customer. The decision of how much to produce each month is governed by the following relationship:

Total available for sale in any period = Total required in the same period
Starting stock + Production rate = Demand + Closing stock
Starting stock + Production rate = 2 × Demand (because closing stock must be equal to demand)
Production rate = 2 × Demand − Starting stock

Causes of the bullwhip effect

Whenever two operations in a supply network arrange for one to provide services or products to the other, there is the potential for misunderstanding and miscommunication. This may be caused simply by not being sufficiently clear about what a customer expects or what a supplier is capable of delivering. Other causes of the bullwhip effect include errors in forecasting, long or variable lead times, order batching, volatility in demand caused by price fluctuations or promotions, panic ordering (shortage gaming), and the perceived risk of other's bounded rationality within a supply network. Figure 7.10 shows the bullwhip effect in a typical supply network, with relatively small fluctuations in the market causing increasing volatility further back in the network.

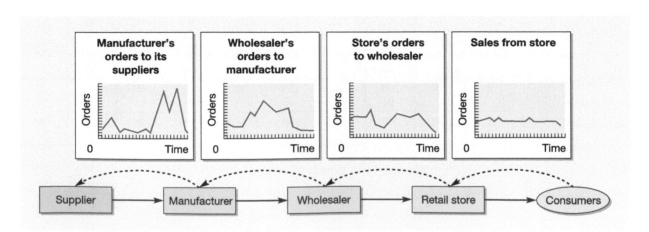

Figure 7.10 Typical supply chain dynamics

Improving supply networks

Increasingly important for operations managers are attempts to improve performance of supply networks. These are usually attempts to either coordinate activities throughout the network or to better understand the complexity of supply processes.

Operational efficiency

Operational efficiency helps improve supply network performance

'Operational efficiency' means the efforts that each operation in the network can make to reduce its own complexity, reduce the cost of doing business with other operations and increase throughput time. The cumulative effect of these individual activities is to simplify the whole **network**. For example, imagine a network of operations whose performance level is relatively poor: quality defects are frequent, the lead time to order products and services is long, and delivery is unreliable and so on. The behaviour of the network would be a continual sequence of errors and effort wasted in replanning to compensate for the errors. Poor quality would mean extra and unplanned orders being placed, and unreliable delivery and slow delivery lead times would mean high safety stocks. Just as important, most operations managers' time would be spent coping with the inefficiency. By contrast, a network whose operations had high levels of operations performance would be more predictable and have faster throughput, both of which would help to minimize supply chain fluctuations.

Supply network time compression

One of the most important approaches to improving the operational efficiency of supply networks is known as **time compression**. This means speeding up the flow of materials and information through the network. The bullwhip effect we observed in Table 7.5 and Figure 7.10 was due partly to the slowness of information moving back up the chain. Figure 7.11 illustrates the advantages of time compression in terms of its overall impact on profitability.[9]

The use of e-business to improve supply networks

New information technology applications combined with internet-based e-business have transformed supply networks. Without appropriate information, supply managers cannot make the decisions that coordinate activities and flows through the network. To some extent, they are 'driving blind' and have to rely on the most obvious of mismatches between the activities of different stages in the network (such as excess inventory) to inform their decisions. Conversely, with accurate and 'near real-time' information, integration is possible and can benefit the network and, eventually, the end-customer. Just as importantly, the collection, analysis and distribution of information using e-business technologies is far less expensive to arrange than previous, less automated methods. Table 7.6 summarizes some of the effects of

Table 7.6 Some effects of e-business on supply chain management practice

	Market/sales information flow	Product/service flow	Cash flow
Supply-chain-related activities	Understanding customers' needs Designing appropriate services/products Demand forecasting	Purchasing Inventory management Throughput / waiting times Distribution	Supplier payments Customer invoicing Customer receipts
Beneficial effects of e-business practices	Better customer relationship management Monitoring real-time demand On-line customization Ability to coordinate output with demand	Lower purchasing administration costs Better purchasing deals Reduced bullwhip effect Reduced inventory More efficient distribution	Faster movement of cash Automated cash movement Integration of financial information with sales and operations activities

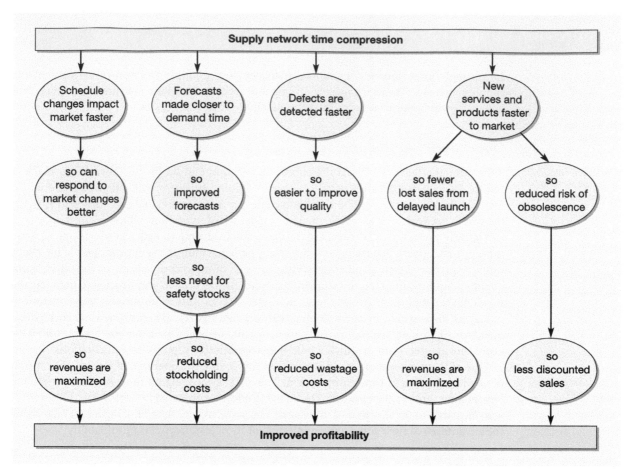

Figure 7.11 Supply network time compression can both reduce costs and increase revenues
Source: Based on Towill

e-business on three important aspects of supply network management – business and market information flow, product and service flow, and the cash flow.

E-procurement

E-procurement

E-procurement is the generic term used to describe the use of electronic methods in every stage of the purchasing process from identification of requirement through to payment, and potentially to contract management.[10] For some years, electronic means have been used by businesses to confirm purchased orders and ensure payment to suppliers. The rapid development of the Internet, however, opened up the potential for far more fundamental changes in purchasing behaviour. Partly this was as the result of supplier information made available through the Internet. By making it easier to search for alternative suppliers, the Internet has changed the economies of the search process and offers the potential for wider searches. It also changed the economies of scale in purchasing. For example, purchasers requiring relatively low volumes find it easier to group together in order to create orders of sufficient size to warrant lower prices. However, whilst the cost savings from purchased goods and services may be the most visible advantage of e-procurement, some managers say that it is just the tip of the iceberg. It can also be far more efficient because purchasing staff are no longer chasing purchase orders and performing routine administrative tasks. Much of the advantage and time savings comes from the decreased need to re-enter information, from streamlining the interaction with suppliers and from having a central repository for data with everything contained in one system. Purchasing staff can negotiate with vendors faster and more effectively. Online auctions can compress negotiations from months to one or two hours, or even minutes.

E-procurement has grown largely because of the development over the last ten years of electronic marketplaces (also sometimes called infomediaries or cybermediaries). These intermediaries allow buyers and sellers in a B2B context to exchange information about prices and offerings. They can be categorized as consortium, private or third party.

- A private e-marketplace is where buyers or sellers conduct business in the market only with their partners and suppliers by previous arrangement.
- The consortium e-marketplace is where several large businesses combine to create an e-marketplace controlled by the consortium.
- A third-party e-marketplace is where an independent party creates an unbiased, market-driven e-marketplace for buyers and sellers in an industry.

The Internet is an important source of purchasing information, even if the purchase itself is made using more traditional methods. Also, even though many businesses have gained advantages by using e-procurement, it does not mean that everything should be bought electronically. When businesses purchase very large amounts of strategically important products or services, they will negotiate multimillion-euro deals, which involve months of discussion, arranging for deliveries up to a year ahead. In such environments, e-procurement may add little value.

Logistics and the Internet

In supply networks dealing with physical assets, transportation is required. Internet communications in this area of supply management have had two major effects. The first is to make information more readily available along the **distribution chain**. This means that the transport companies, warehouses, suppliers and customers that make up the network can share knowledge of where things are at any given time. This allows the operations within the network to coordinate their activities more readily, with potentially significant cost savings. For example, an important issue for transportation companies is **back-loading**. When the company is contracted to transport goods from A to B, its vehicles may have to return from B to A empty. Back-loading means finding a potential customer that wants their goods transported from B to A in the right time frame. Companies which can fill their vehicles on both the outward and return journeys will have significantly lower costs per distance travelled than those whose vehicles are empty for half the total journey.

The second impact of the Internet on logistics has been in the 'business to consumer' part of the supply network. While the last few years have seen an increase in the number of goods bought by consumers online, most goods still have to be physically transported to the customer. Often early e-retailers ran into major problems in the **order fulfilment** task of actually supplying their customers. Partly this was because many traditional warehouse and distribution operations were not designed for e-commerce fulfilment. Supplying a conventional retail operation requires relatively large vehicles to move relatively large quantities of goods from warehouses to shops. Distributing to individual customers requires a large number of smaller deliveries.

Information-sharing

One of the reasons for the fluctuations in output described in the bullwhip example earlier was that each operation in the network reacted to the orders placed by its immediate customer. None of the operations had an overview of what was happening throughout the chain. If information had been available and **shared throughout the chain**, it is unlikely that such wild fluctuations would have occurred. It is sensible therefore to try to transmit information throughout the chain so that all the operations can monitor true demand, free of these distortions. An obvious improvement is to make information on end-customer demand

Distribution chain

Back-loading

Order fulfilment

Information sharing helps improve supply chain performance

Short case
TDG serving the whole supply chain[11]

Source: TDG Logistics

TDG are specialists in providing *third-party* logistics services to the growing number of manufacturers and retailers that choose not to do their own distribution. Instead they outsource to companies like TDG, which have operations spread across 250 sites that cover the UK, Ireland, France, Spain, Poland and Holland, employ 8,000 people and use 1,600 vehicles.

'There are a number of different types of company providing distribution services', says David Garman, Chief Executive Officer of TDG, 'each with different propositions for the market. At the simplest level, there are the "haulage" and "storage" businesses. These companies either move goods around or they store them in warehouses. Clients plan what has to be done and it is done to order. One level up from the haulage or storage operations are the physical distribution companies, who bring haulage and storage together. These companies collect clients' products, put them into storage facilities and deliver them to the end-customer as and when required. After that there are the companies who offer contract logistics. As a contract logistics service provider, you are likely to be dealing with the more sophisticated clients who are looking for better quality facilities and management and the capability to deal with more complex operations. One level further up is the market for supply chain management services. To do this you have to be able to manage supply chains from end to end, or at least some significant part of the whole chain. Doing this requires a much greater degree of

analytical and modelling capability, business process reengineering and consultancy skills.'

TDG, along with other prominent logistics companies, describes itself as a 'lead logistics provider'. This means that they can provide the consultancy-led, analytical and strategic services integrated with a sound base of practical experience in running successful 'on-the-road' operations. 'In 1999 TDG was a UK distribution company', says David Garman, 'now we are a European contract logistics provider with a vision to becoming a full supply chain management company. Providing such services requires sophisticated operations capability, especially in terms of information technology and management dynamism. Because our sites are physically dispersed with our vehicles at any time spread around the motorways of Europe, IT is fundamental to this industry. It gives you visibility of your operation. We need the best operations managers, supported by the best IT.'

available to upstream operations. Electronic point-of-sale (EPOS) systems used by many retailers attempt to do this. Sales data from checkouts or cash registers are consolidated and transmitted to the warehouses, transportation companies and supplier manufacturing operations that form their supply network. Similarly, electronic data interchange (EDI) helps to share information (see the short case on Seven-Eleven Japan). EDI can also affect the economic order quantities shipped between operations in the supply chain.

Channel alignment

Channel alignment focuses on harmonizing the network

Channel alignment means the adjustment of scheduling, material movements, stock levels, pricing and other sales strategies so as to bring all the operations in the network into line with each other. This goes beyond the provision of information. It means that the systems and methods of planning and control decision-making are harmonized through the network. For example, even when using the same information, differences in forecasing methods or purchasing practices can lead to fluctuations in orders between operations in the chain. One way of avoiding this is to allow an upstream supplier to manage the inventories of its downstream customer. This is known as **vendor-managed inventory** (VMI). So, for example, a packaging supplier could take responsibility for the stocks of packaging materials held by a food manufacturing customer. In turn, the food manufacturer takes responsibility for the stocks of its products which are held in its customer's, the supermarket's warehouses.

Vendor-managed inventory

Seven-Eleven Japan's agile supply chain[12]

Seven-Eleven Japan (SEJ) is Japan's largest and most successful retailer. The average amount of stock in an SEJ store is between 7 and 8.4 days of demand, a remarkably fast stock turnover for any retailer. Industry analysts see SEJ's agile supply management as being the driving force behind its success. It is an agility that is supported by a fully integrated information system that provides visibility of the whole supply network and ensures fast replenishment of goods in its stores customized exactly to the needs of individual stores. As a customer comes to the checkout counter the assistant first keys in the customer's gender and approximate age and then scans the bar codes of the purchased goods. This sales data is transmitted to the Seven-Eleven headquarters through its own high-speed lines. Simultaneously, the store's own computer system records and analyzes the information so that store managers and headquarters have immediate point-of-sale information. This allows both store managers and headquarters to, hour by hour, analyze sales trends, any stock-outs, types of customer buying certain products, and so on. The headquarter's computer aggregates all this data by region, product and time so that all parts of the supply network, from suppliers through to the stores, have the information by the next morning. Every Monday, the company chairman and top executives review all performance information for the previous week and develop plans for the up-coming week. These plans are presented on Tuesday morning to SEJ's 'operations field counsellors' each of which is responsible for facilitating performance improvement in around eight stores. On Tuesday afternoon the field counsellors for each region meet to decide how they will implement the overall plans

for their region. On Tuesday night the counsellors fly back to their regions and by next morning are visiting their stores to deliver the messages developed at headquarters which will help the stores implement their plans. SEJ's physical distribution is also organized on an agile basis. The distribution company maintains radio communications with all drivers and SEJ's headquarters keeps track of all delivery activities. Delivery times and routes are planned in great detail and published in the form of a delivery time-table. On average each delivery takes only one and a half minutes at each store, and drivers are expected to make their deliveries within ten minutes of scheduled time. If a delivery is late by more than thirty minutes the distribution company has to pay the store a fine equivalent to the gross profit on the goods being delivered. The agility of the whole supply system also allows SEJ headquarters and the distribution company to respond to disruptions. For example, on the day of the Kobe earthquake, SEJ used 7 helicopters and 125 motor cycles to rush through a delivery of 64,000 rice balls to earthquake victims.

The SCOR model

The Supply Chain Operations Reference model (SCOR) is a broad, but highly structured and systematic, framework for improving supply networks. The framework uses a methodology, diagnostic and benchmarking tools that are increasingly widely accepted for evaluating and comparing supply activities and their performance. Just as important, the SCOR model allows its users to improve, and communicate management practices within and between all interested parties in their supply network by using a standard language and a set of structured definitions. Companies that have used the model include BP, AstraZeneca, Shell, SAP AG, Siemens AG and Bayer. Claimed benefits from using the SCOR model include improved process understanding and performance, improved supply network performance, increased customer satisfaction and retention, a decrease in required capital, better profitability and return on investment, and increased productivity. The model uses three individual techniques turned into an integrated approach. These are:

- Business process modelling.
- Benchmarking performance.
- Best practice analysis.

Business process modelling

SCOR does not represent organizations or functions, but rather processes. Each basic 'link' in the supply network is made up of five types of process, each process being a 'supplier–customer' relationship, see Figure 7.12.

- 'Source' is the procurement, delivery, receipt and transfer of raw material items, sub-assemblies, and/or services.
- 'Make' is the transformation process of adding value to products and services through mixing operations processes.
- 'Deliver' processes perform all customer-facing order management and fulfilment activities including outbound logistics.
- 'Plan' processes manage each of these customer–supplier links and balance the activity of the supply network. They are the supply and demand reconciliation process, which includes prioritization when needed.
- 'Return' processes look after the reverse logistics flow of moving material back from end-customers upstream in the supply chain because of product defects, post-delivery customer support, or recycling (end-of-life reverse supply).

All these processes are modelled at increasingly detailed levels from level 1 through to level 3.

Benchmarking performance

Performance metrics in the SCOR model are also structured by level. Level 1 metrics are the yardsticks by which an organization can measure how successful it is in achieving its desired positioning within the competitive environment, as measured by the performance of a particular supply chain. These level 1 metrics are the key performance indicators (KPIs) of the chain and are created from lower-level diagnostic metrics (called level 2 and level 3 metrics) which are calculated on the performance of lower-level processes.

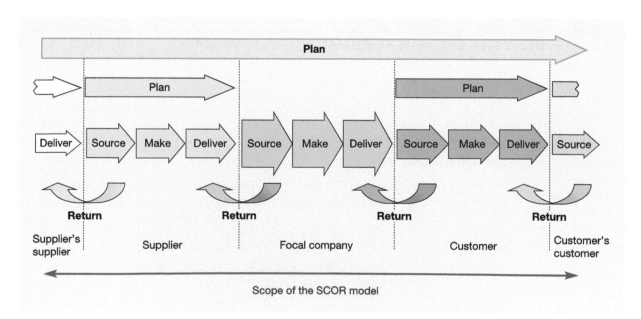

Figure 7.12 Matching the operations resources in the supply network with market requirements

Best practice analysis

Best practice analysis follows the benchmarking activity that should have measured the performance of the supply network processes and identified the main performance gaps. Best practice analysis identifies the activities that need to be performed to close the gaps. The definition of a 'best practice' in the SCOR model is one that:

- Is current – neither untested (emerging) nor outdated.
- Is structured – it has clearly defined goals, scope and processes.
- Is proven – there has been some clearly demonstrated success.
- Is repeatable – it has been demonstrated to be effective in various contexts.
- Has an unambiguous method – the practice can be connected to business processes, operations strategy, technology, supply relationships, and information or knowledge management systems.
- Has a positive impact on results – operations improvement can be linked to KPIs.

The SCOR roadmap

The SCOR model can be implemented by using a five-phase project 'roadmap'. Within this roadmap lies a collection of tools and techniques that both help to implement and support the SCOR framework. In fact many of these tools are commonly used management decision tools such as Pareto charts, cause–effect diagrams, maps of material flow and brainstorming.

Phase 1: Discover – Involves supply-network definition and prioritization where a 'Project Charter' sets the scope for the project. This identifies logic groupings of supply network within the scope of the project. The priorities, based on a weighted rating method, determine which supply network should be dealt with first. This phase also identifies the resources that are required, identified and secured through business process owners or actors.

Phase 2: Analyse – Using data from benchmarking and competitive analysis, the appropriate level of performance metrics are identified; that will define the strategic requirements of each supply network.

Phase 3: Material flow design – In this phase the project teams have their first go at creating a common understanding of how processes can be developed. The current state of processes is identified and an initial analysis attempts to see where there are opportunities for improvement.

Phase 4: Work and information flow design – The project teams collect and analyse the work involved in all relevant processes (plan, source, make, deliver and return) and map the productivity and yield of all transactions.

Phase 5: Implementation planning – This is the final and preparation phase for communicating the findings of the project. Its purpose is to transfer the knowledge of the SCOR team(s) to individual implementation or deployment teams.

Summary answers to key questions

Check and improve your understanding of this chapter using self-assessment questions and a personalized study plan, audio and video downloads, and an eBook – all at www.myomlab.com.

➤ Why should an organization take a supply network perspective?

■ The main advantage is that it helps any operation to understand how it can compete effectively within the network. This is because a supply network approach requires operations managers to think about their suppliers and their customers *as operations*. It can also help to identify particularly significant links within the network and hence identify long-term strategic changes which will affect the operation.

➤ What is involved in managing supply networks?

■ Managing supply networks involves understanding and influencing the various linkages between upstream and downstream operations with the objective of delivering better performance to the end-customer.

■ Key activities include designing the supply network, determining the type of supply relationships, understanding supply dynamics and improving supply networks.

➤ What is involved in designing a supply network?

■ Deciding the 'shape' of the supply network: This may involve reducing the number of suppliers to the operation so as to develop closer relationships, bypassing or disintermediating operations in the network, and co-opetition.

■ Deciding what to do and what to buy: This concerns the nature of the ownership of the operations within a supply network. The direction of vertical integration refers to whether an organization wants to own operations on its supply side or demand side (backwards or forwards integration). The extent of vertical integration relates to whether an organization wants to own a wide span of the supply network. The balance of integration refers to whether operations can trade with only their vertically integrated partners or with organizations as well.

■ Deciding how to align supply and demand in the network: Marshall Fisher distinguishes between functional markets and innovative markets. He argues that functional markets, which are relatively predictable, require efficient supply networks, whereas innovative markets, which are less predictable, require responsive supply networks.

➤ What are the types of relationship between operations in supply networks?

■ Supply networks are made up of individual pairs of buyer–supplier relationships. Business-to-business (B2B) relationships are of the most interest to operations managers. They can be characterized on two dimensions – what is outsourced to a supplier, and the number and closeness of the relationships.

■ Traditional market supplier relationships are where a purchaser chooses suppliers on an individual periodic basis. No long-term relationship is usually implied by such 'transactional' relationships, but it makes it difficult to build internal capabilities.

■ Partnership supplier relationships involve customers forming long-term relationships with suppliers. In return for the stability of demand, suppliers are expected to commit to high levels of service. True partnerships are difficult to sustain and rely heavily on the degree of trust which is allowed to build up between partners.

- Virtual operations are an extreme form of outsourcing where an operation does relatively little itself and subcontracts almost all its activities.

- Selecting suppliers involves deciding whether to source from one (single), two (dual or parallel) or many (multi) suppliers. One must then consider the relative merits of alternative suppliers.

> ➤ What is the 'natural' dynamic of a supply network?

- Supply networks exhibit a dynamic behaviour known as the 'bullwhip' effect. This shows how small changes at the demand end of a supply chain are progressively amplified for operations further back in the network.

- Common causes of the bullwhip effect include errors in forecasting, long and variable lead-times, order batching, demand volatility, panic ordering, and bounded rationality.

> ➤ How can supply networks be improved?

- To reduce the 'bullwhip' effect, operations can adopt some mixture of coordination strategies:
  - operational efficiency: this means eliminating sources of inefficiency or ineffectiveness in the network; of particular importance is 'time compression', which attempts to increase the throughput speed of the operations in the network;
  - e-business: new IT applications have transformed supply networks, enabling improvements in flows of services, information, and products;
  - information-sharing: the efficient distribution of information throughout the chain can reduce demand fluctuations along the chain by linking all operations to the source of demand;
  - channel alignment: this means adopting the same or similar decision-making processes throughout the chain to coordinate how and when decisions are made.

- The Supply Chain Operations Reference model (SCOR) is a highly structured framework for supply network improvement using business process modelling, benchmarking and best practice analysis in an integrated approach.

Learning exercises

These problems and applications will help to improve your analysis of operations. You can find more practice problems as well as worked examples and guided solutions on MyOMLab at **www.myomlab.com.**

1 Visit sites on the Internet that offer (legal) downloadable music using MP3 or other compression formats. Consider the music business supply network, **(a)** for the recordings of a well-known popular music artist, and **(b)** for a less well-known (or even largely unknown) artist struggling to gain recognition. How might the transmission of music over the Internet affect each of these artists' sales? What implications does electronic music transmission have for record shops?

2 'Look, why should we waste our time dealing with suppliers who can merely deliver good product, on time, and in full? There are any number of suppliers who can do that. What we are interested in is developing a set of suppliers who will be able to supply us with suitable components for the generation of products that comes after the next products we launch. It's the underlying capability of suppliers that we are really interested in.'

(a) Devise a set of criteria that this manager could use to evaluate alternative suppliers.
(b) Suggest ways in which she could determine how to weight each criterion.

3 The example of the bullwhip effect shown in Table 7.5 shows how a simple 5 per cent reduction in demand at the end of the supply network causes fluctuations that increase in severity the further back an operation is placed in the chain.

(a) Using the same logic and the same rules (i.e. all operations keep one period's inventory), what would the effect on the chain be if demand fluctuated period by period between 100 and 95? That is, period 1 has a demand of 100, period 2 has a demand of 95, period 3 a demand of 100, period 4 a demand of 95, and so on?

(b) What happens if all operations in the supply network decided to keep only half of the period's demand as inventory?

4 Visit a C2C auction site (for example eBay) and analyse the function of the site in terms of the way it facilitates transactions. What does such a site have to get right to be successful?

Want to know more?

Carmel, E. and Tjia, P. (2005) *Offshoring Information Technology: Sourcing and Outsourcing to a Global Workforce*, Cambridge University Press, Cambridge. An academic book on outsourcing.

Chopra, S. and Meindl, P. (2001) *Supply Chain Management: Strategy, Planning and Operations*, Prentice Hall, Upper Saddle River, NJ. A good textbook that covers both strategic and operations issues.

Fisher, M.L. (1997) What is the right supply chain for your product?, *Harvard Business Review*, vol. 75, no. 2.

A particularly influential article that explores the issue of how supply networks are not all the same.

Harrison, A. and van Hoek, R. (2002) *Logistics Management and Strategy*, Financial Times Prentice Hall, Harlow. A short but readable book that explains many of the modern ideas in supply network management including lean supply networks and agile supply networks.

Vashistha, A. and Vashistha, A. (2006) *The Offshore Nation: Strategies for Success in Global Outsourcing and Offshoring*, McGraw-Hill Higher Education. A topical book on outsourcing.

Useful websites

www.cio.com/topic/3207/supply_chain_management Site of CIO's Supply Chain Management Research Center. Topics include procurement and fulfilment, with case studies.

www.gsb.stanford.edu/scforum/ Stanford University's supply chain forum. Interesting debate.

www.rfidc.com/ Site of the RFID Centre that contains RFID demonstrations and articles to download.

www.spychips.com/ Vehemently anti-RFID site. If you want to understand the nature of some activists' concern over RFID, this site provides the arguments.

www.cips.org/ The Chartered Institute of Purchasing and Supply (CIPS) is an international organization, serving the purchasing and supply profession and dedicated to promoting best practice. Some good links.

www.opsman.org Lots of useful stuff.

 PEARSON

Now that you have finished reading this chapter, why not visit MyOMLab at www.myomlab.com where you'll find more learning resources to help you make the most of your studies and get a better grade.

Chapter 10

Planning and control

Key questions

➤ What is planning and control?

➤ How do supply and demand affect planning and control?

➤ What are the activities of planning and control?

➤ How can enterprise resource planning (ERP) help planning and control?

Introduction

Within the constraints imposed by its design, an operation has to be run on an ongoing basis. 'Planning and control' is concerned with managing the ongoing activities of the operation so as to satisfy customer demand. All operations require plans and require controlling, although the degree of formality and detail may vary. This chapter introduces and provides an overview of some of the principles and methods of planning and control. We also examine information technology (IT), in the form of ERP (enterprise resources planning) systems. The different aspects of planning and control can be viewed as representing the reconciliation of supply with demand. Figure 10.1 shows where this chapter fits into the overall operations model.

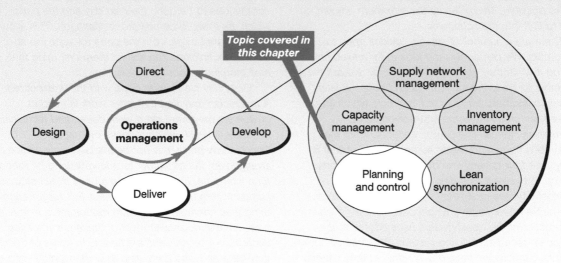

Figure 10.1 This chapter examines planning and control

Operations in practice Joanne manages the schedule[1]

Joanne Cheung is the Senior Service Adviser at a premier BMW dealership. She and her team act as the interface between customers who want their cars serviced and repaired; and the 16 technicians who carry out the work in their state-of-the-art workshop. *'There are three types of work that we have to organize'*, says Joanne. *'The first is performing repairs on customers' vehicles. They usually want this doing as soon as possible. The second type of job is routine servicing. It is usually not urgent so customers are generally willing to negotiate a time for this. The remainder of our work involves working on the pre-owned cars which our buyer has bought-in to sell on to customers. Before any of these cars can be sold they have to undergo extensive checks. To some extent we treat these categories of work slightly differently. We have to give good service to our internal car buyers, but there is some flexibility in planning these jobs. At the other extreme, emergency repair work for customers has to be fitted into our schedule as quickly as possible. If someone is desperate to have their car repaired at very short notice, we sometimes ask them to drop their car in as early as they can and pick it up as late as possible. This gives us the maximum amount of time to fit it into the schedule.*

'There are a number of service options open to customers. We can book short jobs in for a fixed time and do it while they wait. Most commonly, we ask the customer to leave the car with us and collect it later. To help customers we have ten loan cars which are booked out on a first-come first-served basis. Alternatively, the vehicle can be collected from the customer's home and delivered back there when it is ready. Our four drivers who do this are able to cope with up to twelve jobs a day.

'Most days we deal with fifty to eighty jobs, taking from half-an-hour up to a whole day. To enter a job into our process all Service Advisers have access to the computer-based scheduling system. On-screen it shows the total capacity we have day-by-day, all the jobs that are booked in, the amount of free capacity still available, the number of loan cars available, and so on. We use this to see when we have the capacity to book a customer in, and then enter all the customer's details. BMW have

Source: © BMW Group

Joanne has to balance the needs of customers and the constraints of the workshop

issued *"standard times"* for all the major jobs. However, you have to modify these standard times a bit to take account of circumstances. That is where the Service Adviser's experience comes in.

'We keep all the most commonly used parts in stock, but if a repair needs a part which is not in stock, we can usually get it from the BMW parts distributors within a day. Every evening our planning system prints out the jobs to be done the next day and the parts which are likely to be needed for each job. This allows the parts staff to pick out the parts for each job so that the technicians can collect them first thing the next morning without any delay.

'Every day we have to cope with the unexpected. A technician may find that extra work is needed, customers may want extra work doing, and technicians are sometimes ill, which reduces our capacity. Occasionally parts may not be available so we have to arrange with the customer for the vehicle to be rebooked for a later time. Every day up to four or five customers just don't turn up. Usually they have just forgotten to bring their car in so we have to rebook them in at a later time. We can cope with most of these uncertainties because our technicians are flexible in terms of the skills they have and also are willing to work overtime when needed. Also, it is important to manage customers' expectations. If there is a chance that the vehicle may not be ready for them, it shouldn't come as a surprise when they try and collect it.'

What is planning and control?

Planning and control is concerned with the reconciliation between what the market requires and what the operation's resources can deliver. **Planning and control** activities provide the systems, procedures and decisions which bring different aspects of supply and demand together. The purpose is always the same – to make a connection between supply and demand that will ensure that the operation's processes run effectively and efficiently and produce products and services as required by customers. Consider, for example, the way in which routine surgery is organized in a hospital. When a patient arrives and is admitted to the hospital, much of the planning for the surgery will already have happened. The operating theatre will have been reserved, and the doctors and nurses who staff the operating theatre will have been provided with all the information regarding the patient's condition. Appropriate preoperative and postoperative care will have been organized. All this will involve staff and facilities in different parts of the hospital. All must be given the same information and their activities coordinated. Soon after the patient arrives, he or she will be checked to make sure that their condition is as expected. Blood, if required, will be cross-matched and reserved, and any medication will be made ready. Any last-minute changes may require some degree of replanning. For example, if the patient shows unexpected symptoms, observation may be necessary before the surgery can take place. Not only will this affect the patient's own treatment, but other patients' treatment may also have to be rescheduled. All these activities of scheduling, coordination and organization are concerned with the planning and control of the hospital.

The difference between planning and control

We have chosen to treat planning and control together. This is because the division between planning and control is not always clear. However, there are some general features that help to distinguish between the two. **Planning** is a formalization of what is intended to happen at some time in the future. But a plan does not guarantee that an event will actually happen. Customers change their minds about what they want and when they want it. Suppliers may not always deliver on time, machines may fail, or staff may be absent through illness. **Control** is the process of coping with changes. It may mean that plans need to be redrawn. It may also mean that an 'intervention' will need to be made in the operation to bring it back 'on track' – for example, finding a new supplier that can deliver quickly, repairing the machine which failed, or moving staff from another part of the operation to cover for the absentees. Control makes the adjustments which allow the operation to achieve the objectives that the plan has set, even when the assumptions on which the plan was based do not hold true.

Long-, medium- and short-term planning and control

The nature of planning and control activities changes over time. In the very long term, operations managers make plans concerning what they intend to do, what resources they need, and what objectives they hope to achieve. The emphasis is on planning rather than control, because there is little to control as such. They will use forecasts of likely demand which are described in aggregated terms. For example, a hospital will make plans for '2,000 patients' without necessarily going into the details of the individual needs of those patients. Similarly, the hospital might plan to have 100 nurses and 20 doctors but again without deciding on the specific attributes of the staff. Operations managers will be concerned mainly to achieve financial targets. Budgets will be put in place which identify its costs and revenue targets.

Medium-term planning and control is more detailed. It looks ahead to assess the overall demand which the operation must meet in a partially disaggregated manner. By this time, for example, the hospital must distinguish between different types of demand. The number of patients coming as accident and emergency cases will need to be distinguished from those requiring routine operations. Similarly, different categories of staff will have been identified

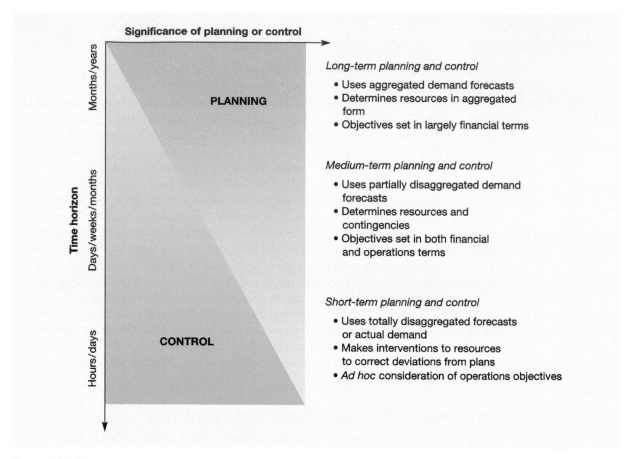

Figure 10.2 The balance between planning and control activities changes in the long, medium and short term

and broad staffing levels in each category set. Just as important, contingencies will have been put in place which allow for slight deviations from the plans.

In short-term planning and control, many of the resources will have been set and it will be difficult to make large changes. However, short-term interventions are possible if things are not going to plan. By this time, demand will be assessed on a totally disaggregated basis, with all types of surgical procedures treated as individual activities. More importantly, individual patients will have been identified by name, and specific time slots booked for their treatment. In making short-term interventions and changes to the plan, operations managers will be attempting to balance the quality, speed, dependability, flexibility and costs of their operation on an *ad hoc* basis. It is unlikely that they will have the time to carry out detailed calculations of the effects of their short-term planning and control decisions on all these objectives, but a general understanding of priorities will form the background to their decision making. Figure 10.2 shows how the control aspects of planning and control increase in significance closer to the date of the event.

Supply and demand effects on planning and control

If planning and control is the process of reconciling demand with supply, then the nature of the decisions taken to plan and control an operation will depend on both the nature of demand and the nature of supply in that operation. In this section, we examine some differences in

Short case
Operations control at Air France[2]

'In many ways a major airline can be viewed as one large planning problem which is usually approached as many independent, smaller (but still difficult) planning problems. The list of things which need planning seems endless: crews, reservation agents, luggage, flights, through trips, maintenance, gates, inventory, equipment purchases. Each planning problem has its own considerations, its own complexities, its own set of time horizons, its own objectives, but all are interrelated.'

Air France has eighty flight planners working 24-hour shifts in their flight planning office at Roissy, Charles de Gaulle. Their job is to establish the optimum flight routes, anticipate any problems such as weather changes, and minimize fuel consumption. Overall the goals of the flight planning activity are first, and most important, safety followed by economy and passenger comfort. Increasingly powerful computer programs process the mountain of data necessary to plan the flights, but in the end many decisions still rely on human judgement. Even the most sophisticated expert systems only serve as support for the flight planners. Planning Air France's schedule is a massive job. Just some of the considerations which need to be taken into account include the following.

- *Frequency* – for each airport how many separate services should the airline provide?
- *Fleet assignment* – which type of plane should be used on each leg of a flight?
- *Banks* – at any airline hub where passengers arrive and may transfer to other flights to continue their journey, airlines like to organize flights into 'banks' of several planes which arrive close together, pause to let passengers change planes, and all depart close together. So, how many banks should there be and when should they occur?

- *Block times* – a block time is the elapsed time between a plane leaving the departure gate at an airport and arriving at its gate in the arrival airport. The longer the allowed block time the more likely a plane will be to keep to schedule even if it suffers minor delays. However, longer block times also mean fewer flights can be scheduled.
- *Planned maintenance* – any schedule must allow time for planes to have time at a maintenance base.
- *Crew planning* – pilot and cabin crew must be scheduled to allocate pilots to fly planes on which they are licensed and to keep within maximum 'on duty' times for all staff.
- *Gate plotting* – if many planes are on the ground at the same time there may be problems in loading and unloading them simultaneously.
- *Recovery* – many things can cause deviations from any plan in the airline industry. Allowances must be built in to allow for recovery.

For flights within and between Air France's 12 geographic zones, the planners construct a flight plan that will form the basis of the actual flight only a few hours later. All planning documents need to be ready for the flight crew who arrive two hours before the scheduled departure time. Being responsible for passenger safety and comfort, the captain always has the final say and, when satisfied, co-signs the flight plan together with the planning officer.

demand and supply which can affect the way in which operations managers plan and control their activities.

Uncertainty in supply and demand

Uncertainty makes both planning and control more difficult. Local village carnivals, for example, rarely work to plan. Events take longer than expected, some of the acts scheduled in the programme may be delayed *en route*, and some traders may not arrive. The event requires a good compère to keep it moving, keep the crowd amused, and in effect control the event. Demand may also be unpredictable. A fast-food outlet inside a shopping centre does not know how many people will arrive, when they will arrive and what they will order. It may be possible to predict certain patterns, such as an increase in demand over the lunch and tea-time periods, but a sudden rainstorm that drives shoppers indoors into the centre could significantly increase demand. Conversely, other operations are reasonably predictable, and the need for control is minimal. For example, cable TV services provide programmes to a schedule into subscribers' homes. It is rare to change the programme plan. Demand may also be predictable. In a school, for example, once classes are fixed and the term or semester has started, a teacher knows how many pupils are in the class. A combination of uncertainty in the operation's ability to supply, and in the demand for its products and services, is particularly difficult to plan and control.

Dependent and independent demand

Some operations can predict demand with more certainty than others. For example, consider an operation providing professional decorating and refurbishment services which has as its customers a number of large hotel chains. Most of these customers plan the refurbishment and decoration of their hotels months or even years in advance. Because of this, the decoration company can itself plan its activities in advance. Its own demand is dependent upon the relatively predictable activities of its customers. By contrast, a small painter and decorator serves the domestic and small business market. Some business also comes from house construction companies, but only when their own painters and decorators are fully occupied. In this case, demand on the painting and decorating company is relatively unpredictable. To some extent, there is a random element in demand which is virtually independent of any factors obvious to the company.

Dependent demand | **Dependent demand**, then, is demand which is relatively predictable because it is dependent upon some factor which is known. For example, the manager who is in charge of ensuring that there are sufficient tyres in an automobile factory will not treat the demand for tyres as a totally random variable. He or she will not be totally surprised by the exact quantity of tyres which are required by the plant every day. The process of demand forecasting is relatively straightforward. It will consist of examining the manufacturing schedules in the car plant and deriving the demand for tyres from these. If 200 cars are to be manufactured on a particular day, then it is simple to calculate that 1,000 tyres will be demanded by the car plant (each car has five tyres) – demand is dependent on a known factor, the number of cars to be manufactured. Because of this, the tyres can be ordered from the tyre manufacturer to a delivery schedule which is closely in line with the demand for tyres from the plant (as in Figure 10.3). In fact, the demand for every part of the car plant will be derived from the assembly schedule for the finished cars. Manufacturing instructions and purchasing requests will all be dependent upon this figure.

Independent demand | Some operations are subject to **independent demand**. They will supply demand without having any firm forward visibility of customer orders. For example, customers do not have to inform a supermarket when they are arriving and what they will buy. The supermarket takes its planning and control decisions based on its experience and understanding of the market, independent of what may actually happen. They run the risk of being out of stock of items when demand does not match their expectations. For example, the Ace Tyre Company, which operates a drive-in tyre replacement service, will need to manage a stock of tyres. In that sense it is exactly the same task that faced the manager of tyre stocks in the car plant. However, demand is very different for Ace Tyre. It cannot predict either the volume or the specific needs of customers. It must make decisions on how many and what type of tyres to stock, based on demand forecasts and in the light of the risks it is prepared to run of being out of stock. This is the nature of *independent demand planning and control*. It makes 'best guesses' concerning future demand, attempts to put the resources in place which can satisfy this demand, and attempts to respond quickly if actual demand does not match the forecast.

Responding to demand

In conditions of dependent demand, an operation will only start the process of producing goods or services when it needs to. Each order triggers the planning and control activities to

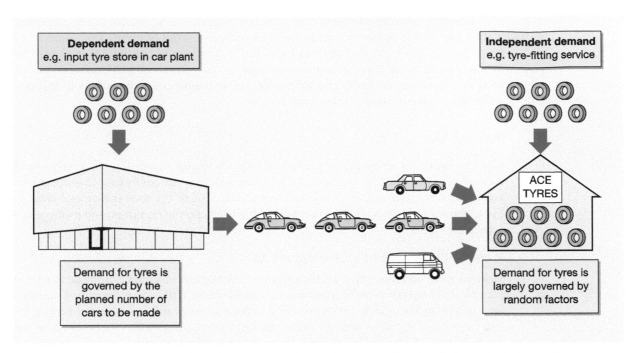

Figure 10.3 Dependent demand is derived from the demand for something else; independent demand is more random

organize their production. For example, a specialist housebuilder might only start the process of planning and controlling the construction of a house when requested to do so by the customer. The builder might not even have the resources to start building before the order is received. The material that will be necessary to build the house will be purchased only when the timing and nature of the house are certain. The staff and the construction equipment might also be 'purchased' only when the nature of demand is clear. In a similar way, a specialist conference organizer will start planning for an event only when specifically requested to do so by the clients. A venue will be booked, speakers organized, meals arranged and the delegates contacted only when the nature of the service is clear. The planning and control necessary for this kind of operation can be called **resource-to-order** planning and control.

Resource-to-order

Other operations might be sufficiently confident of the nature of demand, if not its volume and timing, to keep 'in stock' most of the resources it requires to satisfy its customers. Certainly it will keep its transforming resources, if not its transformed resources. However, it would still make the actual product or service only to a firm customer order. For example, a house builder who has standard designs might choose to build each house only when a customer places a firm order. Because the design of the house is relatively standard, suppliers of materials will have been identified, even if the building operation does not keep the items in stock itself. The equivalent in the conference business would be a conference centre which has its own 'stored' permanent resources (the building, staff, etc.) but only starts planning a conference when it has a firm booking. In both cases, the operations would need **create-to-order or make-to-order** planning and control.

Create-to-order and make-to-order

Some operations produce services or products ahead of any firm orders 'to stock'. For example, some builders will construct pre-designed standard houses or apartments ahead of any firm demand for them. This will be done either because it is less expensive to do so or because it is difficult to create the goods or services on a one-off basis (it is difficult to make each apartment only when a customer chooses to buy one). If demand is high, customers may place requests for houses before they are started or during their construction. In this case, the customer will form a backlog of demand and must wait. The builder is also taking the risk, however, of holding a stock of unsold houses if buyers do not come along before they are finished. In fact, it is difficult for small builders to operate in this way, but less so for (say) a bottled cola manufacturer or other mass producer. The equivalent in the conference market would be a conference centre which schedules a series of events and conferences, programmed in advance and open to individual customers to book into or even turn up on the day. Cinemas and theatres usually work in this manner. Their performances are produced and supplied irrespective of the level of actual demand. Operations of this type will require **make-to-stock** planning and control.

Make-to-stock

P:D ratios[3]

P:D ratio

Another way of characterizing the graduation between resource-to-order and make-to-stock is by using a **P:D ratio**. This contrasts the total length of time customers have to wait between asking for the service and receiving it, demand time, D, and the total throughput time, P. Throughput time is how long the operation takes to obtain the resources, and produce and deliver the service.

P and D times depend on the operation

Make-to-stock operations produce their services and products in advance of any demand. For example, in an operation making consumer durables, demand time, D, is the sum of the times for transmitting the order to the company's warehouse or stock point, picking and packing the order and physically transporting it to the customer. Behind this visible order cycle, however, lie other cycles. Reduction in the finished goods stock will eventually trigger the decision to manufacture a replenishment batch. This 'produce' cycle involves scheduling work in the manufacturing process. Behind the 'produce' cycle lies the 'obtain resources' cycle – the time for obtaining the input stocks. So, for this type of operation, the 'demand' time which the customer sees is very short compared with the total 'throughput' cycle. Contrast this with a resource-to-order operation. Here, D is the same as P. Both include the 'obtain resources', 'produce' and 'delivery' cycles. The produce-to-order operation lies in between these two (see Figure 10.4).

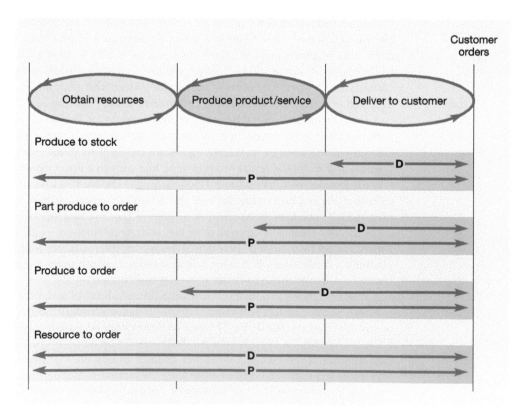

Figure 10.4 *P* and *D* for the different types of planning and control

P:D **ratios indicate the degree of speculation**

Reducing total throughput time *P* will have varying effects on the time the customer has to wait for demand to be filled. In resource-to-order operations, *P* and *D* are the same. Speeding up any part of *P* will reduce customer's waiting time, *D*. On the other hand, in 'produce-to-stock' operations, customers would only see reduced *D* time if the 'deliver' part of *P* were reduced. Also, in Figure 10.4, *D* is always shown as being smaller than *P*, which is the case for most companies. How much smaller *D* is than *P* is important because it indicates the proportion of the operation's activities which are speculative, that is, carried out on the expectation of eventually receiving a firm order for its efforts. The larger *P* is compared with *D*, the higher the proportion of speculative activity in the operation and the greater the risk the operation carries. The speculative element in the operation is there because demand cannot be forecast perfectly. With exact or close to exact forecasts, risk would be non-existent or very low, no matter how much bigger *P* was than *D*. Expressed another way: when *P* and *D* are equal, no matter how inaccurate the forecasts are, speculation is eliminated because everything is resourced and made to a firm order (although bad forecasting will lead to other problems). Reducing the *P:D* ratio becomes, in effect, a way of taking some of the risk out of operations planning and control.

Planning and control activities

There are four overlapping activities: loading, sequencing, scheduling, and monitoring and control that together form the planning and control task (see Figure 10.5). Some caution is needed when using these terms. Different organizations may use them in different ways, and even textbooks in the area adopt different definitions. For example, some authorities describe what we have called 'planning and control' as 'operations scheduling'. However, the terminology of planning and control is less important than understanding the basic ideas.

Loading

Loading

Loading is the amount of work that is allocated to a part of an operation. For example, a machine on the shop floor of a manufacturing business is available, in theory, 168 hours

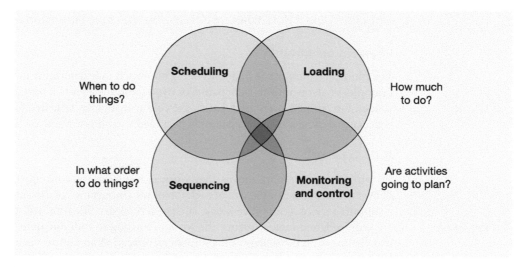

Figure 10.5 Planning and control activities

a week. However, this does not necessarily mean that 168 hours of work can be loaded onto that machine. For some periods the machine cannot be worked; for example, it may not be available on statutory holidays and weekends. Therefore, the load put onto the machine must take this into account. Of the time that the machine is available for work, other losses further reduce the available time. For example, time may be lost while changing over from making one component to another. If the machine breaks down, it will not be available. If there is machine reliability data available, this must also be taken into account. Sometimes the machine may be waiting for parts to arrive or be 'idling' for some other reason. Other losses could include an allowance for the machine being run below its optimum speed (for example, because it has not been maintained properly) and an allowance for the 'quality losses' or defects which the machine may produce. Likewise, in a service-dominant operation it may not be appropriate to schedule workers for 8 hours per day. Loading will need to take into account rest breaks, idle time, changing from one task to another, and boredom reducing actual time available, for example. Of course, many of these losses should be small or non-existent in a well-managed operation. However, the **valuable operating time** available for productive working, even in the best operations, can be significantly below the maximum time available.

Valuable operating time

Sequencing

Sequencing

When work arrives at any part of an operation decisions must be taken on the order in which the work will be tackled. This activity is termed **sequencing**. The priorities given to work in an operation are often determined by some predefined set of rules, some of which are summarized below.

Customer priority

Customer priority sequencing

Operations will sometimes use **customer priority sequencing**, which allows an important or aggrieved customer (or item) to be 'processed' prior to others, irrespective of the order of arrival. This approach is typically used by operations whose customer base is skewed, containing a mass of small customers and a few large, very important customers. Some banks, for example, give priority to important customers. The emergency services often have to use their judgement in prioritizing the urgency of requests for service. For example, in the priority system used by police forces the operators receiving emergency and other calls are trained to grade the calls into priority categories. The response by the police is then organized to match the level of priority. The triage system in hospitals operates in a similar way (see short case). However, customer priority sequencing, although giving a high level of service to some customers, may erode the service given to many others. This may lower the overall performance of the operation if work flows are disrupted to accommodate important customers.

Physical constraints

The physical nature of the materials being processed may determine the priority of work. For example, in an operation using paints or dyes, lighter shades will be sequenced before darker shades. On completion of each batch, the colour is slightly darkened for the next batch. This is because darkness of colour can only be added to and not removed from the colour mix.

Due date (DD)

Due date sequencing

Prioritizing by due date means that work is sequenced according to when it is 'due' for delivery, irrespective of the size of each job or the importance of each customer. For example, a support service in an office block, such as a reprographic unit, will often ask when copies are required, and then sequence the work according to that due date. **Due date sequencing** usually improves the delivery reliability of an operation and improves average delivery speed. However, it may not provide optimal productivity, as a more efficient sequencing of work may reduce total costs.

Short case
The hospital triage system[4]

One of the hospital environments that is most difficult to sequence is the Accident and Emergency department, where patients arrive at random, without any prior warning, throughout the day. It is up to the hospital's reception and the medical staff to devise very rapidly a schedule which meets most of the necessary criteria. In particular, patients who arrive having had very serious accidents, or presenting symptoms of a serious illness, need to be attended to urgently. Therefore, the hospital will sequence these cases first. Less urgent cases – perhaps patients who are in some discomfort, but whose injuries or illnesses are not life-threatening – will have to wait until the urgent cases are treated. Routine non-urgent cases will have the lowest priority of all. In many circumstances, these patients will have to wait for the longest time, which may be many hours, especially if the hospital is busy. Sometimes these non-urgent cases may even be turned away if the hospital is too busy with more important cases. In situations where hospitals expect sudden influxes of patients, they have developed what is known as a triage system, whereby

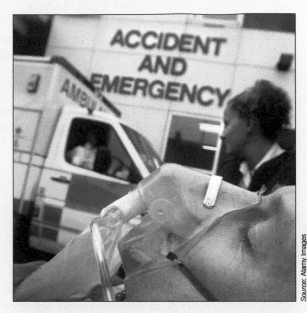

Source: Alamy Images

medical staff hurriedly sort through the patients who have arrived to determine which category of urgency each patient fits into. In this way a suitable schedule for the various treatments can be devised in a short period of time.

Last-in first-out (LIFO)

Last-in first-out
sequencing

Last-in first-out (LIFO) is a method of sequencing usually selected for practical reasons. For example, unloading an elevator is more convenient on a LIFO basis, as there is only one entrance and exit. However, it is not an equitable approach. Patients at hospital clinics may be infuriated if they see newly arrived patients examined first.

First-in first-out (FIFO)

First-in first-out
sequencing

Some operations serve customers in exactly the sequence they arrive in. This is called **first-in first-out sequencing** (FIFO), or sometimes 'first come, first served' (FCFS). For example, passport offices receive mail, and sort it according to the day when it arrived. They work through the mail, opening it in sequence, and process the passport applications in order of arrival.

Longest operation time (LOT)

Longest operation time
sequencing

Operations may feel obliged to sequence their longest jobs first in the system called **longest operation time sequencing**. This has the advantage of occupying work centres for long periods. By contrast, relatively small jobs progressing through an operation will take up time at each work centre because of the need to change over from one job to the next. However, although longest operation time sequencing keeps utilization high, this rule does not take into account delivery speed, reliability or flexibility.

Shortest operation time first (SOT)

Shortest operation time
sequencing

Most operations at some stage become cash-constrained. Larger jobs that take more time will not enable the business to invoice as quickly. In these situations, the sequencing rules may be adjusted to tackle short jobs first in the system, called **shortest operation time sequencing**. These jobs can then be invoiced and payment received to ease cash-flow problems. This has an effect of improving delivery performance, if the unit of measurement is delivery of jobs. However, it may adversely affect total productivity and can damage service to larger customers.

Judging sequencing rules

All five performance objectives, or some variant of them, could be used to judge the effectiveness of sequencing rules. However, the objectives of dependability, speed and cost are particularly important. So, for example, the following performance objectives are often used:

- Meeting 'due date' promised to customer (dependability);
- Minimizing the time the job spends in the process, also known as 'flow time' (speed);
- Minimizing work-in-progress inventory (an element of cost);
- Minimizing idle time of work centres (another element of cost).

Scheduling

Having determined the sequence that work is to be tackled in, some operations require a detailed timetable showing at what time or date jobs should start and when they should end – this is **scheduling**. Schedules are familiar statements of volume and timing in many consumer environments. For example, a bus schedule shows that more buses are put on routes at more frequent intervals during rush-hour periods. The bus schedule shows the time each bus is due to arrive at each stage of the route. Schedules of work are used in operations where some planning is required to ensure that customer demand is met. Other operations, such as rapid-response service operations where customers arrive in an unplanned way, cannot schedule the operation in a short-term sense. They can only respond at the time demand is placed upon them.

The complexity of scheduling[5]

The scheduling activity is one of the most complex tasks in operations management. Firstly, schedulers must deal with several different types of resource simultaneously. Machines will have different capabilities and capacities; staff will have different skills. More importantly, the number of possible schedules increases rapidly as the number of activities and processes increases. For example, suppose one machine has five different jobs to process. Any of the five jobs could be processed first and, following that, any one of the remaining four jobs, and so on. This means that there are:

$$5 \times 4 \times 3 \times 2 = 120 \text{ different schedules possible}$$

More generally, for n jobs there are $n!$ (factorial n) different ways of scheduling the jobs through a single process. We can now consider what impact there would be if, in the same situation, there was more than one type of machine. If we were trying to minimize the number of set-ups on two machines, there is no reason why the sequence on machine 1 would be the same as the sequence on machine 2. If we consider the two sequencing tasks to be independent of each other, for two machines there would be:

$$120 \times 120 = 14,400 \text{ possible schedules of the two machines and five jobs.}$$

A general formula can be devised to calculate the number of possible schedules in any given situation, as follows:

$$\text{Number of possible schedules} = (n!)m$$

where n is the number of jobs and m is the number of machines. In practical terms, this means that there are often many millions of feasible schedules, even for relatively small operations. This is why scheduling rarely attempts to provide an 'optimal' solution but rather satisfies itself with an 'acceptable' feasible one.

Forward and backward scheduling

Forward scheduling involves starting work as soon as it arrives. **Backward scheduling** involves starting jobs at the last possible moment to prevent them from being late. For example, assume that it takes six hours for a contract laundry to wash, dry and press a batch of overalls. If

(margin notes: Scheduling; Forward scheduling; Backward scheduling)

the work is collected at 8.00 am and is due to be picked up at 4.00 pm, there are more than six hours available to do it. Table 10.1 shows the different start times of each job, depending on whether they are forward- or backward-scheduled.

Table 10.1 The effects of forward and backward scheduling

Task	Duration	Start time (backwards)	Start time (forwards)
Press	1 hour	3.00 pm	1.00 pm
Dry	2 hours	1.00 pm	11.00 am
Wash	3 hours	10.00 am	8.00 am

The choice of backward or forward scheduling depends largely upon the circumstances. Table 10.2 lists some advantages and disadvantages of the two approaches.

Table 10.2 Advantages of forward and backward scheduling

Advantages of forward scheduling	Advantages of backward scheduling
High labour utilization – workers always start work to keep busy	Lower material costs – materials are not used until they have to be, therefore delaying added value until the last moment
Flexible – the time slack in the system allows unexpected work to be loaded	Less exposed to risk in case of schedule change by the customer Tends to focus the operation on customer due dates

Gantt charts

Gantt chart

The most common method of scheduling is by use of the **Gantt chart**. This is a simple device which represents time as a bar, or channel, on a chart. The start and finish times for activities can be indicated on the chart and sometimes the actual progress of the job is also indicated. The advantages of Gantt charts are that they provide a simple visual representation both of what should be happening and of what actually is happening in the operation. Furthermore, they can be used to 'test out' alternative schedules. It is a relatively simple task to represent alternative schedules (even if it is a far from simple task to find a schedule which fits all the resources satisfactorily). Figure 10.6 illustrates a Gantt chart for a specialist software developer. It indicates the progress of several jobs as they are expected to progress through five stages of the process. Gantt charts are not an optimizing tool, they merely facilitate the development of alternative schedules by communicating them effectively.

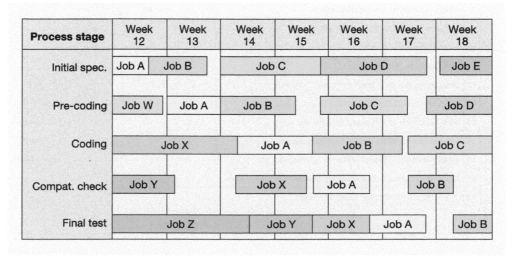

Figure 10.6 Gantt chart showing the schedule for jobs at each process stage

The life and times of a chicken salad sandwich[6]

Pre-packed sandwiches are a growth product around the world as consumers put convenience and speed above relaxation and cost. But if you have recently consumed a pre-packed sandwich, think about the schedule of events which has gone into its making. For example, take a chicken salad sandwich. Less than 5 days ago, the chicken was on the farm unaware that it would never see another weekend. The Gantt chart schedule shown in Figure 10.7 tells the story of the sandwich, and (posthumously), of the chicken.

From the forecast, orders for non-perishable items are placed for goods to arrive up to a week in advance of their use. Orders for perishable items will be placed daily, a day or two before the items are required. Tomatoes, cucumbers and lettuces have a three-day shelf life so may be received up to three days before production. Stock is held on a strict first-in-first-out (FIFO) basis. If today is Wednesday, vegetables are processed that have been received during the last three days. This morning the bread arrived from a local bakery and the chicken arrived fresh,

cooked and in strips ready to be placed directly in the sandwich during assembly. Yesterday (Tuesday) it had been killed, cooked, prepared and sent on its journey to the factory. By midday orders for tonight's production will have been received on the Internet. From 2.00 pm until 10.00 pm the production lines are closed down for maintenance and a very thorough cleaning. During this time the production planning team is busy planning the night's production run. Production for delivery to customers furthest away from the factory will have to be scheduled first. By 10 pm production is ready to start. Sandwiches are made on production lines. The bread is loaded onto a conveyor belt by hand and butter is spread automatically by a machine. Next the various fillings are applied at each stage according to the specified sandwich 'design', see Figure 10.8. After the filling has been assembled the top slice of bread is placed on the sandwich and machine-chopped into two triangles, packed and sealed by machine. It is now early Thursday morning and by 2.00 am the first refrigerated lorries are already departing on their journeys to various customers. Production continues through until 2.00 pm on the Thursday, after which once again the maintenance and cleaning teams move in. The last sandwiches are dispatched by 4.00 pm on the Thursday. There is no finished goods stock.

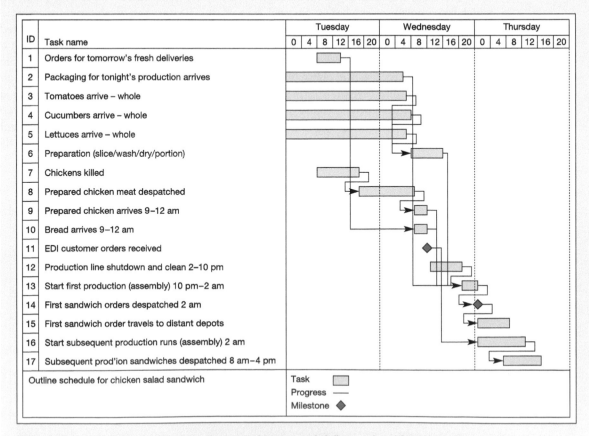

Figure 10.7 Simplified schedule for the manufacture and delivery of a chicken salad sandwich

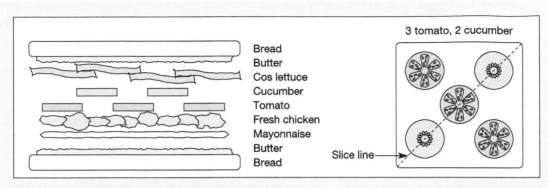

Figure 10.8 Design for a chicken salad sandwich

Scheduling work patterns

Where the dominant resource in an operation is its staff, then the schedule of work times effectively determines the capacity of the operation itself. The main task of scheduling, therefore, is to make sure that sufficient numbers of people are working at any point in time to provide a capacity appropriate for the level of demand at that point in time. This is often called **staff rostering**. Operations such as call centres, postal delivery, policing, holiday couriers, retail shops and hospitals will all need to schedule the working hours of their staff with demand in mind. This is a direct consequence of these operations having relatively high 'visibility'. Such operations cannot store their outputs in inventories and so must respond directly to customer demand. For example, Figure 10.9 shows the scheduling of shifts for a small technical 'hot line' support service for a small software company. It gives advice to customers on their technical problems. Its service times are 04.00 hrs to 20.00 hrs on Monday, 04.00 hrs to 22.00 hrs Tuesday to Friday, 06.00 hrs to 22.00 hrs on Saturday, and 10.00 hrs to 20.00 hrs on Sunday. Demand is heaviest Tuesday to Thursday, starts to decrease on Friday, is low over the weekend and starts to increase again on Monday.

The scheduling task for this kind of problem can be considered over different timescales, two of which are shown in Figure 10.9. During the day, working hours need to be agreed with individual staff members. During the week, days off need to be agreed. During the year, vacations, training periods and other blocks of time where staff are unavailable need to be agreed. All this has to be scheduled such that:

● capacity matches demand;
● the length of each shift is neither excessively long nor too short to be attractive to staff;

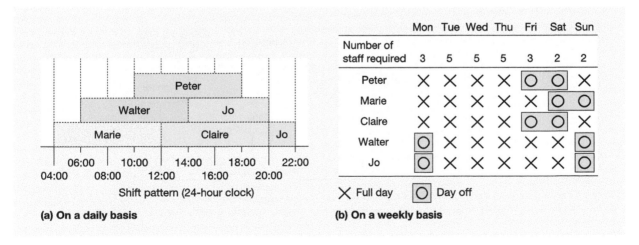

Figure 10.9 Shift scheduling in a home-banking enquiry service

- working at unsocial hours is minimized;
- days off match agreed staff conditions (for example) in this example – staff prefer two consecutive days off every week;
- vacation and other 'time-off' blocks are accommodated;
- sufficient flexibility is built into the schedule to cover for unexpected changes in supply (staff illness) and demand (surge in customer calls).

Scheduling staff times is one of the most complex of scheduling problems. In the relatively simple example shown in Figure 10.9 we have assumed that all staff have the same level and type of skill. In very large operations with many types of skill to schedule and uncertain demand (for example a large hospital) the scheduling problem becomes extremely complex. Some mathematical techniques are available but most scheduling of this type is, in practice, solved using heuristics (rules of thumb), some of which are incorporated into commercially available software packages.

Monitoring and controlling the operation

Having created a plan for the operation through loading, sequencing and scheduling, each part of the operation has to be monitored to ensure that planned activities are indeed happening. Any deviation from the plans can then be rectified through some kind of intervention in the operation, which itself will probably involve some replanning. Figure 10.10 illustrates a simple view of control. The output from a work centre is monitored and compared with the plan which indicates what the work centre is supposed to be doing. Deviations from this plan are taken into account through a replanning activity and the necessary interventions made to the work centre which will ensure that the new plan is carried out. Eventually, some further deviation from planned activity will be detected and the cycle is repeated.

Push and pull control

One element of control is periodic intervention into the activities of the operation. An important decision is how this intervention takes place. The key distinction is between intervention signals which **push** work through the processes within the operation and those which **pull** work only when it is required. In a push system of control, activities are scheduled by means of a central system and completed in line with central instructions, such as an ERP system (see later). Each work centre pushes out work without considering whether the succeeding work centre can make use of it. Work centres are coordinated by means of the

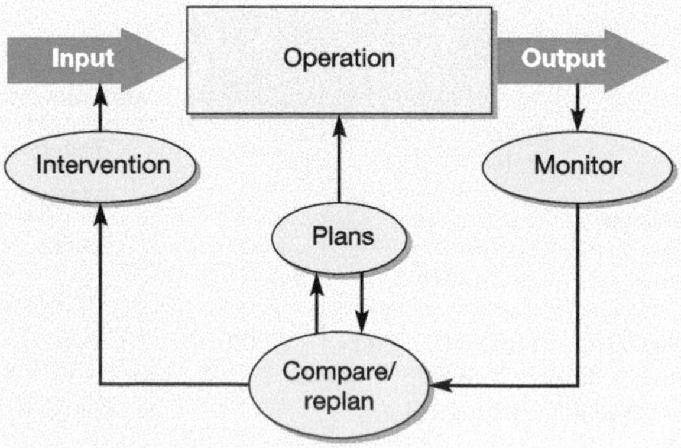

Push control
Pull control

Figure 10.10 A simple model of control

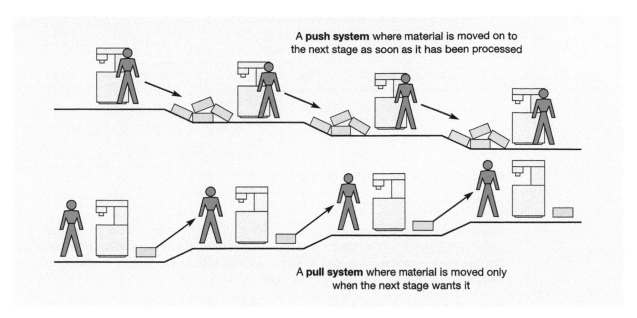

Figure 10.11 Push versus pull: the gravity analogy

central operations planning and control system. In practice, however, there are many reasons why actual conditions differ from those planned. As a consequence, idle time, queues and inventory often characterize push systems. By contrast, in a pull system of control, the pace and specification of what is done are set by the 'customer' workstation, which 'pulls' work from the preceding (supplier) workstation. The customer acts as the only 'trigger' for movement. If a request is not passed back from the customer to the supplier, the supplier cannot do anything. A request from a customer not only triggers activity at the supplying stage, but also prompts the supplying stage to request a further delivery from its own suppliers. In this way, demand is transmitted back through the stages from the original point of demand by the original customer.

Understanding the differing principles of push and pull is important because they have different effects in terms of their propensities to accumulate inventory in the operation. Pull systems are far less likely to result in inventory build-up and are therefore favoured by lean operations (see Chapter 11).

Drum, buffer, rope

Drum, buffer, rope
Theory of constraints

The **drum, buffer, rope** concept comes from the **theory of constraints** (TOC) originally described by Eli Goldratt in his novel *The Goal*.[7] It is an idea that helps to decide exactly *where* in a process control should occur. Most operations do not have the same amount of work loaded onto each separate work centre (that is, they are not perfectly balanced). This means there is likely to be a part of the process which is acting as a bottleneck on the work flowing through the process. Goldratt argued that the bottleneck in the process should be the control point of the whole process. It is called the *drum* because it sets the 'beat' for the rest of the process to follow. Because it does not have sufficient capacity, a bottleneck is (or should be) working all the time. Therefore, it is sensible to keep a *buffer* of inventory in front of it to make sure that it always has something to work on. Because it constrains the output of the whole process, any time lost at the bottleneck will affect the output from the whole process. Therefore, it is not worthwhile for the parts of the process before the bottleneck to work to their full capacity. All they would do is produce work which

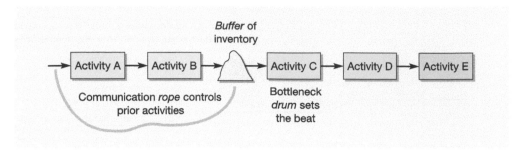

Figure 10.12 The drum, buffer, rope concept

would accumulate further along in the process up to the point where the bottleneck is constraining the flow. Therefore, some form of communication between the bottleneck and the input to the process is needed to make sure that activities before the bottleneck do not overproduce. This is called the *rope* (see Figure 10.12).

Critical commentary

Most of the perspectives on control taken in this chapter are simplifications of a far more messy reality. They are based on models used to understand mechanical systems such as car engines. But anyone who has worked in real organizations knows that organizations are not machines. They are social systems, full of complex and ambiguous interactions. Simple models such as these assume that operations objectives are always clear and agreed, yet organizations are political entities where different and often conflicting objectives compete. Local government operations, for example, are overtly political. Furthermore, the outputs from operations are not always easily measured. A university may be able to measure the number and qualifications of its students, for example, but it cannot measure the full impact of its education on their future happiness. Also, even if it is possible to work out an appropriate intervention to bring an operation back into 'control', most operations cannot perfectly predict what effect the intervention will have. Even the largest burger bar chain does not know *exactly* how a new shift allocation system will affect performance. Also, some operations never do the same thing more than once anyway. Most of the work done by construction operations is one-offs. If every output is different, how can 'controllers' ever know what is supposed to happen? Their plans themselves are mere speculation.

Enterprise resource planning (ERP)

One of the most important issues in planning and controlling operations is managing the sometimes vast amounts of information generated by the activity. It is not just the operations function that is the author and recipient of this information – almost every other function of a business will be involved. So, it is important that all relevant information that is spread throughout the organization is brought together. Then it can inform planning and control decisions such as when activities should take place, where they should happen, who should be doing them, how much capacity will be needed, and so on. This is what enterprise resource planning (ERP) does.

What is ERP?

Enterprise resource
planning

An easy way of thinking about **enterprise resource planning** (ERP) is to imagine that you have decided to hold a party in two weeks' time and expect about 40 people to attend. As well as drinks, you decide to provide sandwiches and snacks. You will probably do some simple calculations, estimating guests' preferences and how much people are likely to drink and eat. You may already have some food and drink in the house which you will use, so you will take that into account when making your shopping list. If any of the food is to be cooked from a recipe, you may have to multiply up the ingredients to cater for 40 people. Also, you may also wish to take into account the fact that you will prepare some of the food the week before and freeze it, while you will leave the rest to either the day before or the day of the party. So, you will need to decide when each item is required so that you can shop in time. In fact, planning a party requires a series of interrelated decisions about the volume (quantity) and timing of the *materials* needed. This is the basis of the foundation concept for ERP called

Materials requirement
planning

materials requirement planning (MRP). It is a process that helps companies make volume and timing calculations (similar to those in the party, but on a much larger scale, and with a greater degree of complexity). But your planning may extend beyond 'materials'. You may want to hire in a sound system from a local supplier – you will have to plan for this. The party also has financial implications. You may have to agree a temporary increase to your credit card limit. Again, this requires some forward planning and calculations of how much it is going to cost, and how much extra credit you require. Both the equipment and financial implications may vary if you increase the number of guests. But, if you postpone the party for a month, these arrangements will change. Also, there are also other implications of organizing the party. You will need to give friends, who are helping with the organization, an idea of when they should come and for how long. This will depend on the timing of the various tasks to be done (making sandwiches etc.).

So, even for this relatively simple activity, the key to successful planning is how we generate, integrate and organize all the information on which planning and control depends. Of course, in business operations it is more complex than this. Companies usually sell many different services and products to many hundreds of customers with constantly changing demands. This is a bit like organizing 200 parties one week, 250 the next and 225 the following week, all for different groups of guests with different requirements who keep changing their minds about what they want to eat and drink. This is what ERP does, it helps companies 'forward-plan' these types of decisions and understand all the implications of any changes to the plan.

How did ERP develop?

Enterprise resource planning is the latest, and the most significant, development of the original materials requirements planning (MRP) philosophy. The large companies which have grown almost exclusively on the basis of providing ERP systems include SAP and Oracle. Yet to understand ERP, it is important to understand the various stages in its development, summarized in Figure 10.13. The original MRP became popular during the 1970s, although the planning and control logic that underlies it had, by then, been known for some time. What popularized MRP was the availability of computer power to drive the basic planning and control mathematics.

Manufacturing Resource
Planning

Manufacturing Resource Planning (MRP II) expanded out of MRP during the 1980s. Again, it was a technology innovation that allowed the development. Local-area networks (LANs), together with increasingly powerful desktop computers, allowed a much higher degree of processing power and communication between different parts of a business. Also MRP II's extra sophistication allowed the forward modelling of 'what-if' scenarios. The strength of MRP and MRP II lay always in the fact that it could explore the *consequences* of any changes to what an operation was required to do. So, if demand changed, the MRP system would calculate all the 'knock-on' effects and issue instructions accordingly. This

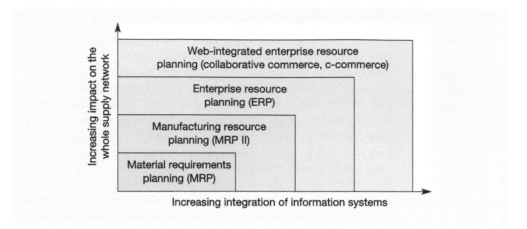

Figure 10.13 The development of ERP

Enterprise resource
planning same principle also applies to ERP, but on a much wider basis. **Enterprise resource planning (ERP)** has been defined as,

> '*a complete enterprise wide business solution. The ERP system consists of software support modules such as: marketing and sales, field service, product design and development, production and inventory control, procurement, distribution, industrial facilities management, process design and development, manufacturing, quality, human resources, finance and accounting, and information services. Integration between the modules is stressed without the duplication of information.*'[8]

So, ERP systems allow decisions and databases from all parts of the organization to be integrated so that the consequences of decisions in one part of the organization are reflected in the planning and control systems of the rest of the organization (see Figure 10.14). ERP is the equivalent of the organization's central nervous system, sensing information about the condition of different parts of the business and relaying the information to other parts of

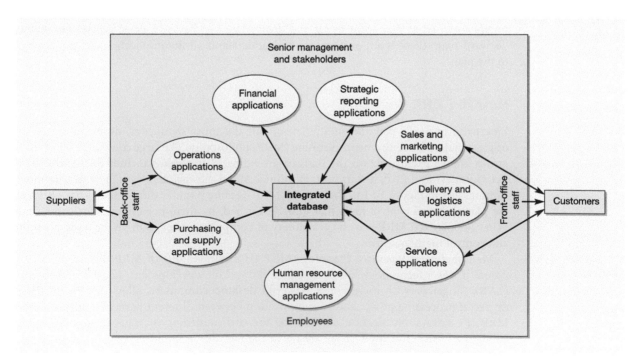

Figure 10.14 ERP integrates information from all parts of the organization

the business that need it. The information is updated in real time by those who use it and yet is always available to everyone connected to the ERP system.

Also, the potential of web-based communication has provided a further boost to ERP development. Many companies have suppliers, customers and other businesses with whom they collaborate who themselves have ERP-type systems. An obvious development is to allow these systems to communicate across supply networks. However, the technical, as well as organizational and strategic consequences of this can be formidable. Nevertheless, many authorities believe that the true value of ERP systems is only fully exploited when such **web-integrated ERP** (known by some people as 'collaborative commerce', or c-commerce) becomes widely implemented.

Web-integrated ERP

Summary answers to key questions

Check and improve your understanding of this chapter using self-assessment questions and a personalized study plan, audio and video downloads, and an eBook – all at www.myomlab.com.

➤ What is planning and control?

■ Planning and control is the reconciliation of the potential of the operation to supply services and products, with the demands of its customers on the operation. It is the set of day-to-day activities that run the operation.

■ A plan is a formalization of what is intended to happen at some time in the future. Control is the process of coping with changes to the plan and the operation to which it relates. Although planning and control are theoretically separable, they are usually treated together.

■ The balance between planning and control changes over time. Planning dominates in the long term and is usually done on an aggregated basis. At the other extreme, in the short term, control usually operates within the resource constraints of the operation but makes interventions into the operation in order to cope with short-term changes in circumstances.

➤ How do supply and demand affect planning and control?

■ The degree of uncertainty in demand affects the balance between planning and control. The greater the uncertainty, the more difficult it is to plan, and greater emphasis must be placed on control.

■ This idea of uncertainty is linked with the concepts of dependent and independent demand. Dependent demand is relatively predictable because it is dependent on some known factor. Independent demand is less predictable because it depends on the chances of the market or customer behaviour.

■ The different ways of responding to demand can be characterized by differences in the $P:D$ ratio of the operation. The $P:D$ ratio is the ratio of total throughput time of goods or services to demand time.

➤ What are the activities of planning and control?

■ In planning and controlling the volume and timing of activity in operations, four distinct activities are necessary:
  – loading, which dictates the amount of work that is allocated to each part of the operation;
  – sequencing, which decides the order in which work is tackled within the operation;

– scheduling, which determines the detailed timetable of activities and when activities are started and finished;

– monitoring and control, which involve detecting what is happening in the operation, replanning if necessary, and intervening in order to impose new plans. Two important types are 'pull' and 'push' control. Pull control is a system whereby demand is triggered by requests from a work centre's (internal) customer. Push control is a centralized system whereby decisions are issued to work centres which are then required to perform the task and supply the next workstation.

➤ How can enterprise resource planning (ERP) help planning and control?

- ERP is an enterprise-wide information system that integrates all the information from many functions, that is needed for planning and controlling operations activities. This integration around a common database allows for transparency.

- ERP can be seen as the latest development from the original planning and control approach known as materials requirements planning (MRP).

- Although ERP is becoming increasingly competent at the integration of internal systems and databases, there is the even more significant potential of integration with other organizations' ERP (and equivalent) systems.

Learning exercises

These problems and applications will help to improve your analysis of operations. You can find more practice problems as well as worked examples and guided solutions on MyOMLab at www.myomlab.com.

1 Re-read the 'operations management in practice' at the beginning of the chapter, 'Joanne manages the schedule', and also the short case on Air France. What are the differences and what are the similarities between the planning and control tasks in these two operations?

2 A specialist sandwich retailer must order sandwiches at least 8 hours before they are delivered. When they arrive in the shop, they are immediately displayed in a temperature-controlled cabinet. The average time that the sandwiches spend in the cabinet is 6 hours. What is the *P:D* ratio for this retail operation?

3 *Step 1* – Make a list of all the jobs you have to do in the next week. Include in this list jobs relating to your work and/or study, jobs relating to your domestic life, in fact all the things you have to do.

Step 2 – Prioritize all these jobs on a 'most important' to 'least important' basis.

Step 3 – Draw up an outline schedule of exactly when you will do each of these jobs.

Step 4 – At the end of the week compare what your schedule said you *would* do with what you actually *have* done. If there is a discrepancy, why did it occur?

Step 5 – Draw up your own list of planning and control rules from your experience in this exercise in personal planning and control.

4 From your own experience of making appointments at your general practitioner's surgery, or by visiting whoever provides you with primary medical care, reflect on how patients are scheduled to see a doctor or nurse.

(a) What do you think planning and control objectives are for a general practitioner's surgery?
(b) How could your own medical practice be improved?

Want to know more?

Goldratt, E.Y. and Cox, J. (1984) *The Goal*, North River Press, Great Barrington, MA. Don't read this if you like good novels but do read it if you want an enjoyable way of understanding some of the complexities of scheduling. It particularly applies to the drum, buffer, rope concept described in this chapter.

Kehoe, D.F. and Boughton, N.J. (2001) New paradigms in planning and control across manufacturing supply chains – the utilization of Internet technologies, *International Journal of Operations and Production Management*, vol. 21, issue 5/6, 582–93.

Vollmann, T., Berry, W., Whybark, D.C. and Jacobs, F.R. (2004) *Manufacturing Planning and Control Systems for Supply Chain Management: The Definitive Guide for Professionals*, McGraw-Hill Higher Education, New York. The latest version of the 'bible' of planning and control.

Useful websites

www.bpic.co.uk/ Some useful information on general planning and control topics.

www.apics.org The American professional and education body that has its roots in planning and control activities.

www.opsman.org Lots of useful stuff.

Now that you have finished reading this chapter, why not visit MyOMLab at www.myomlab.com where you'll find more learning resources to help you make the most of your studies and get a better grade.

Chapter 12

Quality management

Key questions

➤ What is quality and why is it so important?

➤ How can quality problems be diagnosed?

➤ What steps lead towards conformance to specification?

➤ What is total quality management (TQM)?

Introduction

Quality is the only one of the five operations performance criteria to have its own dedicated chapter in this book. There are two reasons for this. Firstly, in some organizations a separate function is devoted exclusively to the management of quality. Secondly, quality is a key concern of almost all organizations. High-quality offerings can give an organization a considerable competitive edge. Good quality reduces the costs of rework, waste, complaints and returns and, most importantly, generates satisfied customers. Some operations managers believe that, in the long run, quality is the most important single factor affecting an organization's performance relative to its competitors. Figure 12.1 shows where this chapter fits into the overall operations model.

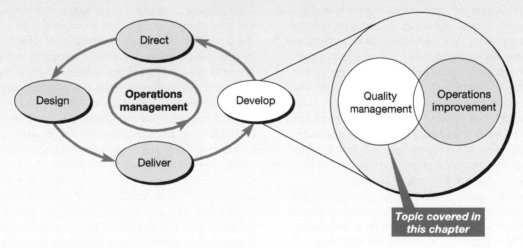

Figure 12.1 This chapter examines quality management

*Check and improve your understanding of this chapter using self-assessment questions and a personalized study plan, audio and video downloads, and an eBook – all at **www.myomlab.com**.*

Operations in practice Quality at the Four Seasons Canary Wharf[1]

The first Four Seasons Hotel opened over 45 years ago. Since then the company has grown to 81 properties in 34 countries. Famed for its quality of service, the hotel group has won countless awards including the prestigious Zagat survey and numerous AAA Five Diamond Awards, and it is also one of only 14 organizations that have been on the *Fortune* magazine's list of '100 Best Companies to Work For' every year since it launched in 1998, thus ranking as 'top hotel chain' internationally. From its inception the group has had the same guiding principle, 'to make the quality of our service our competitive advantage'. The company has what it calls its Golden Rule: 'Do to others (guests and staff) as you would wish others to do to you.' It is a simple rule, but it guides the whole organization's approach to quality.

Source: Four Seasons Hotels, Photographer Robert Miller

'*Quality service is our distinguishing edge and the company continues to evolve in that direction. We are always looking for better, more creative and innovative ways of serving our guests*', says Michael Purtill, the General Manager of the Four Seasons Hotel Canary Wharf in London. '*We have recently refined all of our operating standards across the company, enabling us to further enhance the personalized, intuitive service that all our guests receive. All employees are empowered to use their creativity and judgement in delivering exceptional service and making their own decisions to enhance our guests' stay. For example, one morning an employee noticed that a guest had a flat tyre on their car and decided of his own accord to change it for them, which was very much appreciated by the guest.*

'*The golden rule means that we treat our employees with dignity, respect and appreciation. This approach encourages them to be equally sensitive to our guests' needs and offer sincere and genuine service that exceeds expectations. Just recently one of our employees accompanied a guest to the hospital and stayed there with him for the entire afternoon. He wanted to ensure that the guest wasn't alone and was given the medical attention he needed. The following day that same employee took the initiative to return to the hospital (even though it was his day off) to visit and made sure that the guest's family in America was kept informed about his progress. We ensure that we have an ongoing focus on recognizing these successes and publicly praise and celebrate all individuals who deliver these warm, spontaneous, thoughtful touches.*

'*At Four Seasons we believe that our greatest asset and strength is our people. We pay a great deal of attention to selecting the right people with an attitude that takes great pride in delivering exceptional service. We know that motivated and happy employees are essential to our service culture and are committed to developing our employees to*

their highest potential. Our extensive training programmes and career development plans are designed with care and attention to support the individual needs of our employees as well as operational and business demands. In conjunction with traditional classroom-based learning, we offer tailor-made internet-based learning featuring exceptional quality courses for all levels of employee. Such importance is given to learning and development that the hotel has created two specialized rooms, designated for learning and development. One is intended for group learning and the other is equipped with private computer stations for internet-based individual learning. There is also a library equipped with a broad variety of hospitality-related books, CDs and DVDs that can be taken home at any time. This encourages our employees to learn and develop at an individual pace. This is very motivating for our employees and in the same instance their development is invaluable to the growth of our company. Career-wise, the sky is the limit and our goal is to build lifelong, international careers with Four Seasons.

'*Our objective is to exceed guest expectations and feedback from our guests and our employees is an invaluable barometer of our performance. We have created an in-house database that is used to record all guest feedback (whether positive or negative). We also use an online guest survey and guest comment cards which are all personally responded to and analysed to identify any potential service gaps. We continue to focus on delivering individual personalized experiences and our Guest History database remains vital in helping us to achieve this. All preferences and specific comments about service experience are logged on the database. Every comment and every preference is discussed and planned for, for every guest, for every visit. It is our culture that sets Four Seasons apart: the drive to deliver the best service in the industry that keeps our guests returning again and again.*'

What is quality and why is it so important?

It is worth revisiting some of the arguments which were presented in Chapter 3 regarding the benefits of high quality. This will explain why quality is seen as being so important by most operations. There are ways in which quality improvements can affect other aspects of operations performance. Revenues can be increased by better sales and enhanced prices in the market. At the same time, costs can be brought down by improved efficiencies, productivity and the use of capital. So, a key task of the operations function must be to ensure that it provides quality services and goods, to both its internal and external customers.

The operation's view of quality

There are many definitions of quality

There are many definitions of **quality**; here we define it as *'consistent conformance to customers' expectations'*. The use of the word 'conformance' implies that there is a need to meet a clear specification. Ensuring a service or product conforms to specification is a key operations task. 'Consistent' implies that conformance to specification is not an *ad hoc* event but that the service or product meets the specification because quality requirements are used to design and run the processes that create services and products. The use of 'customers' expectations' recognizes that the service or product must take the views of customers into account, which may be influenced by price. Also note the use of the word 'expectations' in this definition, rather than 'needs' or 'wants'.

Customers' view of quality

Past experiences, individual knowledge and history will all shape customers' expectations. Furthermore, customers may each *perceive* a service or product in different ways. One person may perceive a long-haul flight as an exciting part of a holiday; the person on the next seat may see it as a necessary chore to get to a business meeting. So quality needs to be understood from a customer's point of view because, to the customer, the quality of a particular offering is whatever he or she perceives it to be. If the passengers on a skiing charter flight perceive it to be of good quality, despite long queues at check-in or cramped seating and poor meals, then the flight really is of good perceived quality.[2] Also customers may be unable to judge the 'technical' specification of the service or product and so use surrogate measures as a basis for their perception of quality.[3] For example, a customer may find it difficult to judge the technical quality of dental treatment, except insofar as it does not give any more trouble. The customer may therefore perceive quality in terms of the attire and demeanour of the dentist and technician, décor of the surgery, and how they were treated.

Reconciling the operation's and the customer's views of quality

Customer expectations

Customer perception

A customer's view of quality is shaped by the gap between perception and expectation

The operation's view of quality is concerned with trying to meet **customer expectations**. The customer's view of quality is what he or she *perceives* the service or product to be. To create a unified view, quality can be defined as the degree of fit between customers' expectations and **customer perception** of the service or product.[4] Using this idea allows us to see the customers' view of quality of the service or product as the result of the customers comparing their expectations of performance with their perception of performance. If the service or product experience was better than expected then the customer is satisfied and quality is perceived to be high. If the service or product was less than his or her expectations then quality is low and the customer may be dissatisfied. If the service or product matches expectations then the perceived quality of the product or service is seen to be **acceptable**. These relationships are summarized in Figure 12.2.

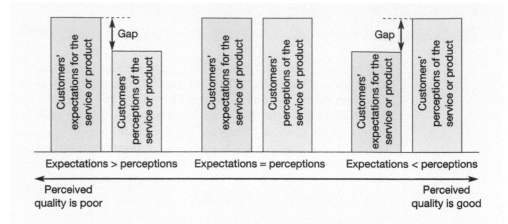

Figure 12.2 Perceived quality is governed by the magnitude and direction of the gap between customers' expectations and their perceptions of the service or product

Short case
Tea and Sympathy[5]

Defining quality in terms of perception and expectation can sometimes reveal some surprising results. For example, Tea and Sympathy is a British restaurant and café in the heart of New York's West Village. Over the last ten years it has become a fashionable landmark in a city with one of the broadest range of restaurants in the world. Yet it is tiny, around a dozen tables packed into an area little bigger than the average British sitting room. Not only expatriate Brits but also native New Yorkers and celebrities queue to get in. As the only British restaurant in New York, it has a novelty factor, but also it has become famous for the unusual nature of its service. *'Everyone is treated in the same way',* says Nicky Perry, one of the two ex-Londoners who run it, *'We have a firm policy that we don't take any shit.'* This robust attitude to the treatment of customers is reinforced by 'Nicky's Rules' which are printed on the menu.

1 Be pleasant to the waitresses – remember Tea and Sympathy girls are always right.
2 You will have to wait outside the restaurant until your entire party is present – no exceptions.
3 Occasionally, you may be asked to change tables so that we can accommodate all of you.
4 If we don't need the table you may stay all day, but if people are waiting it's time to naff off.

5 These rules are strictly enforced. Any argument will incur Nicky's wrath. You have been warned.

Most of the waitresses are also British and enforce Nicky's Rules strictly. If customers object they are thrown out. Nicky says that she has had to train 'her girls' to toughen up. *'I've taught them that when people cross the line they can tear their throats out as far as I'm concerned. What we've discovered over the years is that if you are really sweet, people see it as a weakness. People get thrown out of the restaurant about twice a week and yet customers still queue for the genuine shepherd's pie, a real cup of tea, and of course the service.'*

Both customers' expectations and perceptions are influenced by a number of factors, some of which cannot be controlled by the operation and some of which, to a certain extent, can be managed. Figure 12.3 shows some of the factors that will influence the gap between expectations and perceptions. This model of customer-perceived quality can help us understand how operations can manage quality and identifies some of the problems in so doing. The bottom part of the diagram represents the operation's 'domain' of quality and the top part the customer's 'domain'. These two domains meet in the actual service or product, which is provided by the

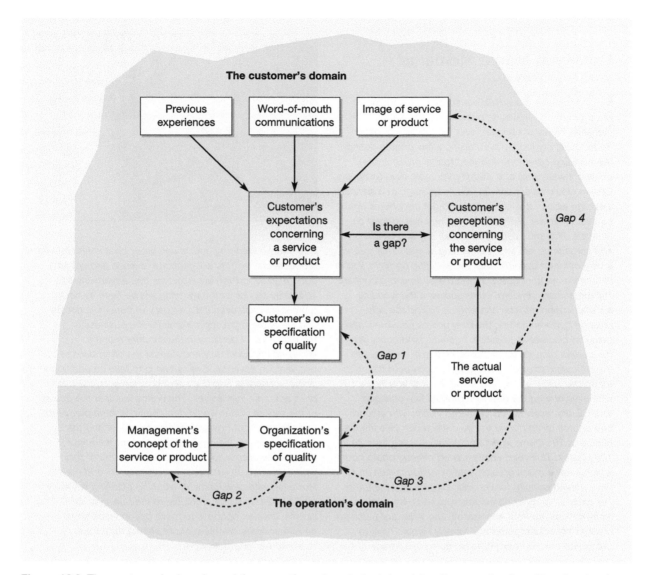

Figure 12.3 The customer's domain and the operations domain in determining the perceived quality, showing how the gap between customers' expectations and their perception of a service or product could be explained by one or more gaps elsewhere in the model

Source: Adapted from Parasuraman, A. *et al.* (1985) A conceptual model of service quality and implications for future research, *Journal of Marketing*, vol. 49, Fall, pp. 41–50. Reproduced with permission from the American Marketing Association.

organization and experienced by the customer. Within the operation's domain, management is responsible for designing the service or product and providing a specification of the quality to which the service or product has to be created. Within the customer's domain, his or her expectations are shaped by such factors as previous experiences with the particular service or product, the marketing image provided by the organization and word-of-mouth information from other users. These expectations are internalized as a set of quality characteristics.

Diagnosing quality problems[6]

Figure 12.3 shows how quality problems can be diagnosed. If the perceived quality gap is such that customers' perceptions of the offering fail to match their expectations of it, then the reason (or reasons) must lie in other gaps elsewhere in the model as follows.

Short case
Quality at Magic Moments

Source: Alamy Images

Magic Moments is a small, but successful wedding photography business. Its owner, Richard Webber, has seen plenty of changes over the last twenty years. *'In the past, my job involved taking a few photos during the wedding ceremony and then formal group shots outside. I was rarely at a wedding for more than two hours. Clients would select around 30 photos to go in a standard wedding album. It was important to get the photos right, because that was really the only thing I was judged on. Now it's different. I usually spend all day at a wedding, and sometimes late into the evening as well. This creates a very different dynamic with the wedding party, as you're almost like another guest. Whilst the bride and groom are still my primary concern, other guests at the wedding are also important. The challenge is to find the right balance between getting the best photos possible whilst being as discreet as possible. I could spend hours getting the perfect picture, but annoy everyone in the process. It's difficult, because clients judge you on both the technical quality of your work and the way you interact with everyone on the day. The product has changed too. Clients receive a CD or memory stick with around 500 photos taken during the day. Also I can give them a choice of 10 albums in different sizes, ranging from 30 to 100 photos. This year, I have started offering photo books which allow a much greater level of customization and have proved popular for younger couples. For the future, I'm considering offering albums with wedding items such as invitations, confetti and menus, and individual paintings created from photographs. Obviously I would have to outsource the paintings. I'm also going to upgrade our* web site, so wedding guests can order photos and related products online. This will generate revenue and act as a good marketing tool. My anxiety is that advertising this additional service at the wedding will be seen as being too commercial, even if it's actually of benefit to guests.

One of the biggest problems for the business is the high level of demand in the summer months. Weekends in June, July and August are often booked up two years in advance. One option is to take on additional photographers during busy periods. However, the best ones are busy themselves. The concern is that the quality of the service I offer would deteriorate. A large part of the business is about how one relates to clients and that's hard to replicate. Having been to so many weddings, I often offer clients advice on various aspects of their wedding, such as locations, bands, caterers and florists. However, with development, wedding planning is clearly an area that could be profitable to the business. Of course, another option is to move beyond weddings into other areas, such as school photos, birthdays, celebrations, or studio work.'

Gap 1: The customer's specification–operation's specification gap. Perceived quality could be poor because there may be a mismatch between the organization's own internal quality specification and the specification which is expected by the customer. For example, a car may be designed to need servicing every 10,000 kilometres but the customer may expect 15,000-kilometre service intervals.

Gap 2: The concept–specification gap. Perceived quality could be poor because there is a mismatch between the concept (see Chapter 4) and the way the organization has specified quality internally. For example, the concept of a car might have been for an inexpensive, energy-efficient means of transportation, but the inclusion of a climate control system may have both added to its cost and made it less energy-efficient.

Gap 3: The quality-specification–actual-quality gap. Perceived quality could be poor because there is a mismatch between actual quality and the internal quality specification (often called 'conformance to specification'). For example, the internal quality specification for a car may be that the gap between its doors and body, when closed, must not exceed 7 mm. However, because of inadequate equipment, the gap in reality is 9 mm.

Gap 4: The actual-quality–communicated-image gap. Perceived quality could be poor because there is a gap between the organization's external communications or market image and the actual quality delivered to the customer. This may be because the marketing function has set unachievable expectations or operations is not capable of the level of quality expected by the customer. For example, an advertising campaign for an airline might show a cabin attendant offering to replace a customer's shirt on which food or drink has been spilt, whereas such a service may not in fact be available should this happen.

Conformance to specification

Conformance to specification means producing a product or providing a service to its design specification. It is usually seen as the most important contribution that operations management can make to the customer's perception of quality. Achieving conformance can be summarized in six sequential steps.

Step 1   Define the quality characteristics of the service or product.
Step 2   Decide how to measure each quality characteristic.
Step 3   Set quality standards for each quality characteristic.
Step 4   Control quality against those standards.
Step 5   Find and correct causes of poor quality.
Step 6   Continue to make improvements.

Step 1 – Define the quality characteristics

Much of the 'quality' of an offering will have been specified in its design. But not all the design details are useful in controlling quality. For example, the design of a television may specify that its outer cabinet is made with a particular veneer. Each television is not checked, however, to make sure that the cabinet is indeed made from that particular veneer. Rather it is the *consequences* of the design specification which are examined – the appearance of the cabinet, for example. These consequences for quality planning and control of the design

Quality characteristics

are called the **quality characteristics** of the offering. Table 12.1, overleaf, shows a list of the quality characteristics which are generally useful.

Step 2 – Decide how to measure each characteristic

These characteristics must be defined in such a way as to enable them to be measured and then controlled. This involves taking a very general quality characteristic such as 'appearance' and breaking it down, as far as one can, into its constituent elements. 'Appearance' is difficult to measure as such, but 'colour match', 'surface finish' and 'number of visible scratches' are all capable of being described in a more objective manner. They may even be quantifiable. Other quality characteristics pose more difficulty. The 'courtesy' of airline staff, for example, has no objective quantified measure. Yet operations with high customer contact, such as airlines, place a great deal of importance on the need to ensure courtesy in their staff. In cases like this, the operation will have to attempt to measure customer *perceptions* of courtesy.

Variables and attributes

Variables
Attributes

The measures used by operations to describe quality characteristics are of two types: **variables** and **attributes**. Variable measures are those that can be measured on a continuously variable scale (for example, length, diameter, weight or time). Attributes are those which are assessed by judgement and are dichotomous, i.e. have two states (for example, right or wrong, works or does not work, looks OK or not OK). Table 12.2 categorizes some of the measures which might be used for the quality characteristics of the car and the airline journey.

Table 12.1 Quality characteristics for a car, a bank loan and an air journey

Quality characteristic	Car (material transformation process)	Bank loan (information transformation process)	Air journey (customer transformation process)
Functionality – how well the product or service does its job	Speed, acceleration, fuel consumption, ride quality, road-holding, etc.	Interest rate, terms and conditions	Safety and duration of journey, onboard meals and drinks, car and hotel booking services
Appearance – the sensory characteristics of the product or service: its aesthetic appeal, look, feel, etc.	Aesthetics, shape, finish, door gaps, etc.	Aesthetics of information, web site, etc.	Décor and cleanliness of aircraft, lounges and crew
Reliability – the consistency of the product's or service's performance over time	Mean time to failure	Keeping promises (implicit and explicit)	Keeping to the published flight times
Durability – the total useful life of the product or service	Useful life (with repair)	Stability of terms and conditions	Keeping up with trends in the industry
Recovery – the ease with which problems with the product or service can be resolved	Ease of repair	Resolution of service failures	Resolution of service failures
Contact – the nature of the person-to-person contact which might take place	Knowledge and courtesy of sales staff	Knowledge and courtesy of branch and call centre staff	Knowledge, courtesy and sensitivity of airline staff

Table 12.2 Variable and attribute measures for quality characteristics

Quality characteristic	Car		Airline journey	
	Variable	Attribute	Variable	Attribute
Functionality	Acceleration and braking characteristics from test bed	Is the ride quality satisfactory?	Number of journeys which actually arrived at the destination (i.e. didn't crash!)	Was the food acceptable?
Appearance	Number of blemishes visible on car	Is the colour to specification?	Number of seats not cleaned satisfactorily	Is the crew dressed smartly?
Reliability	Average time between faults	Is the reliability satisfactory?	Proportion of journeys which arrived on time	Were there any complaints?
Durability	Life of the car	Is the useful life as predicted?	Number of times service innovations lagged competitors	Generally, is the airline updating its services in a satisfactory manner?
Recovery	Time from fault discovered to fault repaired	Is the serviceability of the car acceptable?	Proportion of service failures resolved satisfactorily	Do customers feel that staff deal satisfactorily with complaints?
Contact	Level of help provided by sales staff (1 to 5 scale)	Did customers feel well served (yes or no)?	The extent to which customers feel well treated by staff (1 to 5 scale)	Did customers feel that the staff were helpful (yes or no)?

Step 3 – Set quality standards

When operations managers have identified how any quality characteristic can be measured, they need a quality standard against which it can be checked; otherwise they will not know whether it indicates good or bad performance. The quality standard is that level of quality which defines the boundary between acceptable and unacceptable. Such standards may well be constrained by operational factors such as the state of technology in the factory, and the cost limits of making the product. At the same time, however, they need to be appropriate to the expectations of customers. But quality judgements can be difficult. If one airline passenger out of every 10,000 complains about the food, is that good because 9,999 passengers out of 10,000 are satisfied? Or is it bad because, if one passenger complains, there must be others who, although dissatisfied, did not bother to complain? And if that level of complaint is similar for other airlines, should it regard its quality as satisfactory?

Step 4 – Control quality against those standards

After setting up appropriate standards, the operation will then need to check that the services or products conform to those standards: doing things right, first time, every time. This involves three decisions:

1 Where in the operation should they check that it is conforming to standards?
2 Should they check everything or take a sample?
3 How should the checks be performed?

Where should the checks take place?

At the start of the process incoming resources may be inspected to make sure that they are to the correct specification. For example, a university will screen applicants to try to ensure that they have a high chance of getting through the programme. A car manufacturer will check that components are of the right specification. During the process, checks may take place before a particularly costly process, prior to 'difficult to check', immediately after a process with a high defective rate, before potential damage or distress might be caused, and so on. Checks may also take place after the process itself to ensure that customers do not experience non-conformance.

Check everything or take a sample?

Quality sampling

While it might seem ideal to check every single service or product, a **sample** may be more practical for a number of reasons.

- It might be dangerous to inspect everything. A doctor, for example, checks just a small sample of blood rather than taking all of a patient's blood! The characteristics of this sample are taken to represent those of the rest of the patient's blood.
- Checking everything might destroy the product or interfere with the service. Not every light bulb is checked for how long it lasts – it would destroy every bulb. Waiters do not check that customers are enjoying the meal every 30 seconds.
- Checking everything can be time-consuming and costly. It may not be feasible to check the feelings of every bus commuter every day or to check all output from a high-volume machine.

Also 100 per cent checking may not guarantee that all defects will be identified. Sometimesit is intrinsically difficult. For example, although a physician may undertake the correct testing procedure, he or she may not necessarily diagnose a disease. Nor is it easy to notice everything. For example, try counting the number of 'e's on this page. Count them again and see if you get the same score!

Type I and type II errors

Although it reduces checking time, using a sample to make a decision about quality does have its own inherent problems. Like any decision activity, we may get the decision wrong. Take the example of a pedestrian waiting to cross a street. He or she has two main decisions: whether to continue waiting or to cross. If there is a satisfactory break in the traffic and the pedestrian crosses then a correct decision has been made. Similarly, if that person continues to wait because the traffic is too dense then he or she has again made a correct decision. There are two types of incorrect decisions or errors, however. One incorrect decision would be if he or she decides to cross when there is not an adequate break in the traffic, resulting in an accident – this is referred to as a type I error. Another incorrect decision would occur if he or she decides not to cross even though there was an adequate gap in the traffic – this is called a type II error. In crossing the road, therefore, there are four outcomes, which are summarized in Table 12.3.

Table 12.3 Type I and type II errors for a pedestrian crossing the road

	Road conditions	
Decision	Unsafe	Safe
Cross	Type I error	Correct decision
Wait	Correct decision	Type II error

Type I errors are those which occur when a decision was made to do something and the situation did not warrant it. Type II errors are those which occur when nothing was done, yet a decision to do something should have been taken as the situation did indeed warrant it. For example, if a school's inspector checks the work of a sample of 20 out of 1,000 pupils and all 20 of the pupils in the sample have failed, the inspector might draw the conclusion that all the pupils have failed. In fact, the sample just happened to contain 20 out of the 50 students who had failed the course. The inspector, by assuming a high fail rate would be making a type I error. Alternatively, if the inspector checked 20 pieces of work all of which were of a high standard, he or she might conclude that all the pupils' work was good despite having been given, or having chosen, the only pieces of good work in the whole school. This would be a type II error. Although these situations are not likely, they are possible. Therefore any sampling procedure has to be aware of these risks (see the short case on 'Surgical statistics').

Short case
Surgical statistics[7]

Understanding the nature of type I and type II errors is an essential part of any surgeon's quality planning. Take the well-known appendectomy operation, for example. This is the removal of the appendix when it becomes infected or inflamed. Removal is necessary because of the risk of the appendix bursting and causing peritonitis, a potentially fatal poisoning of the blood. The surgical procedure itself is a relatively simple operation with expected good results but there is always a small risk associated with any invasive surgery needing a general anaesthetic. In addition, like any surgical procedure, it is expensive. The cost of the USA's approximately quarter-of-a-million appendectomies averages out to around $4,500 per operation. Unfortunately, appendicitis is difficult to diagnose accurately. Using standard X-ray procedures a definite diagnosis can only be obtained about 10 per cent of the time. But now a new technique, developed in the Massachusetts General Hospital in Boston, claims to be able to identify 100 per cent of true appendicitis cases before surgery is carried out.

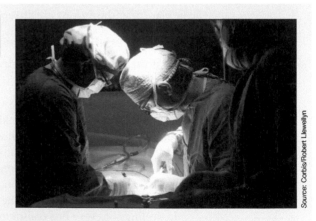

Source: Corbis/Robert Llewellyn

The new technique (Focused Appendix Computed Tomography) uses spiral X-ray images together with a special dye. It scans only the relevant part of the body, so exposure to radiation is not as major an issue as with conventional X-ray techniques. The technique can also help in providing an alternative diagnosis when an appendectomy is not needed. Most significantly, the potential cost savings are very great. The test itself costs less than $250, which means that one single avoided surgery pays for around 20 tests.

How should the checks be performed?

Statistical process
control

In practice most operations will use some form of sampling to check the quality of their services or products. The decision then is what kind of sample procedure to adopt. By far the best known method of doing this is the procedure called **statistical process control** (SPC). SPC is concerned with sampling the process during the production of the goods or the delivery of service. Based on this sample, decisions are made as to whether the process is 'in control', that is, operating as it should be. The value of SPC is not just to make checks of a single sample but to monitor the quality over a period of time. It does this by using **control charts** to see if the process seems to be performing as it should, or alternatively if it is 'out of control'. If the process does seem to be going out of control, then steps can be taken *before* there is a problem. Actually, most operations chart their quality performance in some way. Figure 12.4, or something like it, could be found in almost any operation. The chart could, for example, represent the percentage of customers in a sample of 1,000 who, each month, were dissatisfied with the restaurant's cleanliness. While the amount of dissatisfaction may be acceptably small, management should be concerned that it has been steadily increasing over time and may wish to investigate why this is so. In this case, the control chart is plotting an attribute measure of quality (satisfied or not). Looking for trends is an important use of control charts. If the trend suggests the process is getting steadily worse, then it will be worth investigating the process. If the trend is steadily improving, it may still be worthy of investigation to try to identify what is happening that is making the process better.

Control charts

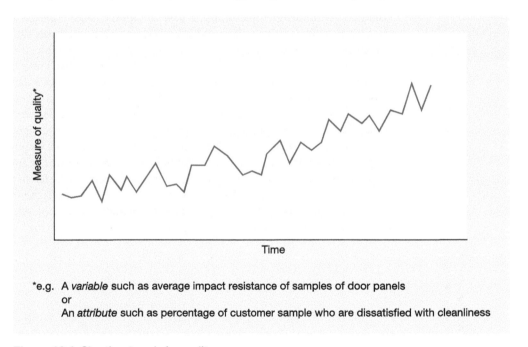

*e.g. A *variable* such as average impact resistance of samples of door panels
or
An *attribute* such as percentage of customer sample who are dissatisfied with cleanliness

Figure 12.4 Charting trends in quality measures

Common causes of variability

Common causes

The processes charted in Figure 12.4 showed an upwards trend. But the trend was neither steady nor smooth: it varied, sometimes up, sometimes down. All processes vary to some extent. People perform tasks slightly differently each time. No machine will give precisely the same result each time it is used. Given this, it is not surprising that the measure of quality will also vary. Variations which derive from these *common causes* can never be entirely eliminated (although they can be reduced). For example, if a machine is filling boxes with rice, it will not place *exactly* the same weight of rice in every box it fills. Usually this type of variation can be described by a normal distribution with 99.7 per cent of the variation lying within ±3 standard deviations. The obvious question for any operations manager would be:

'Is this variation in the process performance acceptable?' The answer will depend on the acceptable range of weights which can be tolerated by the operation. This range is called the **specification range**. If the weight of rice in the box is too small then the organization might infringe labelling regulations; if it is too large, the organization is 'giving away' too much of its product for free.

Specification range

Assignable causes of variation

Not all variation in processes is the result of common causes. There may be something wrong with the process which is assignable to a particular and preventable cause. An untrained person may not be following prescribed procedures. Machinery may have worn or been set up badly. The causes of such variation are called *assignable causes*. The question is whether the results from any particular sample, when plotted on the control chart, simply represent the variation due to common causes or due to some specific and correctable *assignable* cause. Figure 12.5, for example, shows the control chart for the average impact resistance of samples of door panels taken over time. Like any process the results vary, but the last three points seem to be lower than usual. So, is this natural (common cause) variation, or the symptom of some more serious (assignable) cause?

Assignable causes

To help make this decision, **control limits** can be added to the control chart (the red dashed lines) which indicates the expected extent of 'common-cause' variation. If any points lie outside these control limits (the shaded zone) then the process can be deemed out of control in the sense that variation is likely to be due to assignable causes. These control limits could be set intuitively by examining past variation during a period when the process was thought to be free of any variation which could be due to assignable causes. But control limits can also be set in a more statistically revealing manner. For example, if the process which tests door panels had been measured to determine the normal distribution which represents its common-cause variation, then control limits can be based on this distribution. Figure 12.5 also shows how control limits can be added; here they are put at ±3 standard deviations (of the population of sample means) away from the mean of sample averages. It shows that the probability of the final point on the chart being influenced by an assignable cause is very high indeed. When the process is exhibiting behaviour which is outside its normal 'common-cause' range, it is said to be 'out of control'. Yet there is a small but finite chance that the (seemingly out of limits) point is just one of the rare but natural results at the tail of the distribution which describes perfectly normal behaviour. Stopping the process under these circumstances would represent a type I error because the process is actually in control. Alternatively, ignoring a result which in reality is due to an assignable cause is a type II error.

Control limits

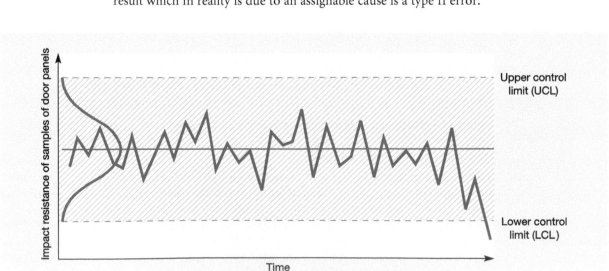

Figure 12.5 Control chart for the impact resistance of door panels, together with control limits

Why variability is a bad thing

Assignable variation is a signal that something has changed in the process which therefore must be investigated. But normal variation is itself a problem because it masks any changes in process behaviour. Figure 12.6 shows the performance of two processes both of which are subjected to a change in their process behaviour at the same time. The process on the left has such a wide natural variation that it is not immediately apparent that any change has taken place. Eventually it will become apparent because the likelihood of process performance violating the lower (in this case) control limit has increased, but this may take some time. By contrast, the process on the right has a far narrower band of natural variation. Because of this, the same change in average performance is more easily noticed (both visually and statistically). So, the narrower the natural variation of a process, the more obvious are changes in the behaviour of that process. And the more obvious are process changes, the easier it is to understand how and why the process is behaving in a particular way. Accepting any variation in any process is, to some degree, admitting to ignorance of how that process works.

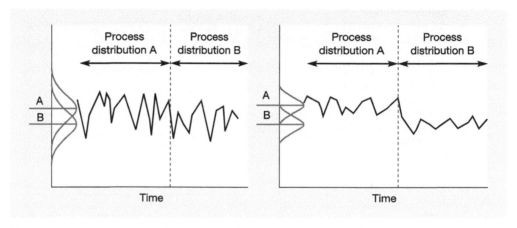

Figure 12.6 Low process variation allows changes in process performance to be readily detected

Steps 5 and 6 – Find and correct causes of poor quality and continue to make improvements

The final two steps in our list of quality management activities are, in some ways, the most important yet also the most difficult. They also blend into the general area of operations improvement covered in the next chapter. Nevertheless, there is an aspect of quality management that has been particularly important in shaping how quality is improved and the improvement activity made self-sustaining. This is total quality management (TQM).

Total quality management (TQM)

Total quality management

Total quality management (TQM) was one of the earliest of the current wave of management 'fashions'. Its peak of popularity was in the late 1980s and early 1990s. As such it has suffered from something of a backlash in recent years and there is little doubt that many companies adopted TQM in the simplistic belief that it would transform their operations performance overnight. Yet the general precepts and principles that constitute TQM are still the dominant mode of organizing operations improvement. The approach we take here is to stress the importance of the 'total' in total quality management and how it can guide the agenda for improvement.

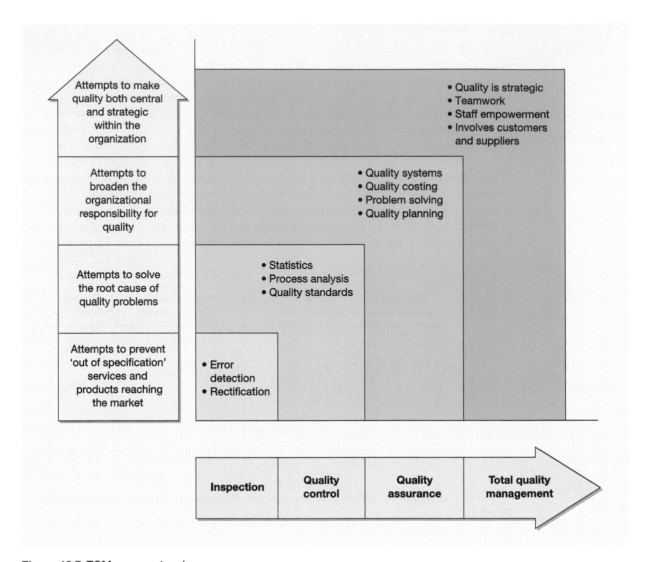

Figure 12.7 TQM as an extension

TQM as an extension of previous practice

Inspection

Quality control

Quality assurance

TQM can be viewed as a logical extension of the way in which quality-related practice has progressed (see Figure 12.7). Originally quality was achieved by **inspection** – screening out defects before they were noticed by customers. The **quality control** (QC) concept developed a more systematic approach to not only detecting, but also treating quality problems. **Quality assurance** (QA) widened the responsibility for quality to include functions other than direct operations. It also made increasing use of more sophisticated statistical quality techniques. TQM included much of what went before but developed its own distinctive themes. We will use some of these themes to describe how TQM represents a clear shift from traditional approaches to quality.

What is TQM?

TQM is a philosophy of how to approach the organization of quality improvement

TQM is 'an effective system for integrating the quality development, quality maintenance and quality improvement efforts of the various groups in an organization so as to enable production and service at the most economical levels which allow for full customer satisfaction'.[8] However, it was the Japanese who first made the concept work on a wide scale and subsequently popularized the approach and the term 'TQM'. It was then developed further by several, so-called, 'quality gurus'. Each 'guru' stressed a different set of issues, from which emerged the TQM approach. It is best thought of as a philosophy of how to approach quality improvement. This philosophy, above everything, stresses the 'total' of TQM. It is an approach that puts quality at the heart of everything that is done by an operation and includes all activities within an operation. This totality can be summarized by the way TQM lays particular stress on the following:

- meeting the needs and expectations of customers;
- covering all parts of the organization;
- including every person in the organization;
- examining all costs which are related to quality, especially failure costs and getting things 'right first time';
- developing the systems and procedures which support quality and improvement;
- developing a continuous process of improvement (this will be treated in the broader context of improvement, in Chapter 13).

TQM means meeting the needs and expectations of customers

Customer-centricity
Voice of the customer

Earlier in this chapter we defined quality as 'consistent conformance to customers' expectations'. Therefore any approach to quality management must necessarily include the customer perspective. In TQM this customer perspective is particularly important. It may be referred to as '**customer-centricity**' or the '**voice of the customer**'. However, the term TQM stresses the importance of starting with an insight into customer needs, wants, perceptions and preferences. This can then be translated into quality objectives and used to drive quality improvement.

TQM means covering all parts of the organization

Internal customer or
supplier

For an organization to be truly effective, every single part of it, each department, each activity, and each person must work properly together, because of the affect they have on one another. One of the most powerful concepts that has emerged from various improvement approaches is the concept of the **internal customer or supplier**. This is recognition that everyone is a customer within the organization and consumes services or products provided by other internal suppliers, and everyone is also an internal supplier for other internal customers. The implication of this is that errors in the service provided within an organization will eventually affect the service or product which reaches the external customer.

Service-level agreements

Service-level agreements

Some organizations bring a degree of formality to the internal customer concept by encouraging different parts of the operation to agree **service-level agreements** (SLAs) with each other. SLAs are formal definitions of the dimensions of service and the relationship between two parts of an organization. The type of issues which would be covered by such an agreement could include response times, the range of services, dependability of service supply, and so on. Boundaries of responsibility and appropriate performance measures could also be agreed. For example, an SLA between an information systems support unit and a research unit in the laboratories of a large company could define such performance measures as:

- the types of information network services which may be provided as 'standard';
- the range of special information services which may be available at different periods of the day;
- the minimum 'up-time', i.e. the proportion of time the system will be available at different periods of the day;

- the maximum response time and average response time to get the system fully operational should it fail;
- the maximum response time to provide 'special' services, and so on.

TQM means including every person in the organization

Every person in the organization has the potential to contribute to quality. Although it may be necessary to develop some specialists to assist with maintaining quality levels, TQM was amongst the first approaches to stress the centrality of harnessing everyone's impact on quality and therefore their potential contribution to quality. There is scope for creativity and innovation even in relatively routine activities, claim TQM proponents. The shift in attitude which is needed to view employees as the most valuable intellectual and creative resource which the organization possesses can still prove difficult for some organizations. When TQM practices first began to migrate from Japan in the late 1970s, the ideas seemed even more radical. Some Japanese industrialists even thought (mistakenly) that companies in Western economies would never manage to change.

TQM means all costs of quality are considered

The costs of controlling quality may not be small, whether the responsibility lies with each individual or a dedicated quality control department. It is therefore necessary to examine all the costs and benefits associated with quality (in fact 'cost of quality' is usually taken to refer to both costs and benefits of quality). These costs of quality are usually categorized as *prevention costs, appraisal costs, internal failure costs* and *external failure costs*.

Prevention costs

Prevention costs are those costs incurred in trying to prevent problems, failures and errors from occurring in the first place. They include such things as:

- identifying potential problems and putting the process right before poor quality occurs;
- designing and improving the design of services, products and processes to reduce quality problems;
- training and development of personnel in the best way to perform their jobs;
- process control through SPC.

Appraisal costs

Appraisal costs are those costs associated with controlling quality to check to see if problems or errors have occurred during and after the creation of the product or service. They might include such things as:

- the setting up of statistical acceptance sampling plans;
- the time and effort required to inspect inputs, processes and outputs;
- obtaining processing inspection and test data;
- investigating quality problems and providing quality reports;
- conducting customer surveys and quality audits.

Internal failure costs

Internal failure costs are failure costs associated with errors which are dealt with inside the operation. These costs might include such things as:

- the cost of scrapped parts and material;
- reworked parts and materials;
- the lost production time as a result of coping with errors;
- lack of concentration due to time spent troubleshooting rather than improvement.

External failure costs

External failure costs are those which are associated with an error going out of the operation to a customer. These costs include such things as:

- loss of customer goodwill affecting future business;
- aggrieved customers who may take up time;

- litigation (or payments to avoid litigation);
- guarantee and warranty costs;
- the cost to the company of providing excessive capability (too much coffee in the pack or too much information to a client).

The relationship between quality costs

In traditional quality management it was assumed that failure costs reduce as the money spent on appraisal and prevention increases. Furthermore, it was assumed that there is an *optimum* amount of quality effort to be applied in any situation, which minimizes the total costs of quality. The argument is that there must be a point beyond which diminishing returns set in – that is, the cost of improving quality gets larger than the benefits which it brings. Figure 12.8(a) sums up this idea. As quality effort is increased, the costs of providing the effort – through extra quality controllers, inspection procedures, and so on – increases proportionally. At the same time, however, the cost of errors, faulty products, and so on, decreases because there are fewer of them. However, TQM proponents believe that this logic is flawed. Firstly, it implies that failure and poor quality are acceptable. Why, TQM proponents argue, should any operation accept the *inevitability* of errors? Some occupations seem to be able to accept a zero-defect standard. No one accepts that pilots are allowed to crash a certain proportion of their aircraft, or that nurses will drop a certain proportion of the babies they deliver. Secondly, it assumes that costs are known and measurable. In fact putting realistic figures to the cost of quality is not a straightforward matter. Thirdly, it is argued that failure costs in the traditional model are greatly underestimated. In particular, all the management time wasted by failures and the loss of concentration it causes are rarely accounted for. Fourthly, it implies that prevention costs are inevitably high because it involves expensive inspection. But why shouldn't quality be an integral part of everyone's work rather than employing extra people to inspect. Finally, the 'optimum-quality level' approach, by accepting compromise, does little to challenge operations managers and staff to find ways of improving quality. Put these corrections into the optimum-quality effort calculation and the picture looks very different (see Figure 12.8b). If there is an 'optimum', it is a lot further to the right, in the direction of putting more effort (but not necessarily cost) into quality.

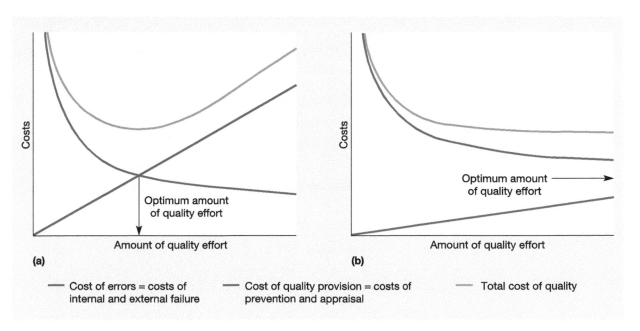

Figure 12.8 (a) The traditional cost of quality model, and (b) the traditional cost of quality model with adjustments to reflect TQM criticisms

A story which illustrates the difference in attitude between a TQM and a non-TQM company has become almost a legend among TQM proponents. It concerns a plant in Ontario, Canada, of IBM, the computer company. It ordered a batch of components from a Japanese manufacturer and specified that the batch should have an acceptable quality level (AQL) of three defective parts per thousand. When the parts arrived in Ontario they were accompanied by a letter which expressed the supplier's bewilderment at being asked to supply defective parts as well as good ones. The letter also explained that they had found it difficult to make parts which were defective, but had indeed managed it. These three defective parts per thousand had been included and were wrapped separately for the convenience of the customer!

The TQM quality cost model

TQM rejects the optimum-quality level concept and strives to reduce all known and unknown failure costs by preventing errors and failure taking place. Rather than looking for 'optimum' levels of quality effort, TQM stresses the relative balance between different types of quality cost. Of the four cost categories, two (costs of prevention and costs of appraisal) are open to managerial influence, while the other two (internal costs of failure and external costs of failure) show the consequences of a lack of prevention and appraisal. So, rather than placing most emphasis on appraisal (so that 'bad products and service don't get through to the customer') TQM emphasizes prevention (to stop errors happening in the first place). That is because the more effort that is put into error prevention, the more internal and external failure costs are reduced. Then, once confidence has been firmly established, appraisal costs can be reduced. Eventually even prevention costs can be stepped down in absolute terms, though prevention remains a significant cost in relative terms. Figure 12.9 illustrates this idea. Initially total quality costs may rise as investment in some aspects of prevention – mainly training – is increased. However, a reduction in total costs can quickly follow.

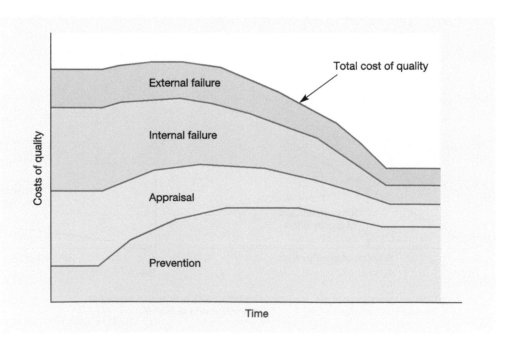

Figure 12.9 Increasing the effort spent on preventing errors occurring in the first place brings a more than equivalent reduction in other cost categories

Getting things 'right first time'

Accepting the relationships between categories of quality cost as illustrated in Figure 12.9 has a particularly important implication for how quality is managed. It shifts the emphasis from *reactive* (waiting for something to happen) to *proactive* (doing something before anything happens). This change in the view of quality costs has come about with a movement from an inspect-in (appraisal-driven) approach to a design-in (**getting it right first time**) approach.

Getting it right first time

Developing the systems and procedures which support quality and improvement

The emphasis on highly formalized systems and procedures to support TQM has declined in recent years, yet one aspect is still active for many companies. This is the adoption of the ISO 9000 standard. And although ISO 9000 can be regarded as a stand-alone issue, it is very closely associated with TQM.

ISO 9000

The **ISO 9000** series is a set of worldwide standards that establishes requirements for companies' quality management systems. ISO 9000 is being used worldwide to provide a framework for quality assurance. Registration requires a third-party assessment of a company's quality standards and procedures and regular audits are made to ensure that the systems do not deteriorate. Rather than using different standards for different functions within a business it takes a 'process' approach that focuses on outputs from any operation's process rather than detailed procedures. This process orientation requires operations to define and record core processes and sub-processes (in a manner very similar to the 'hierarchy of processes' principle that was outlined in Chapter 1). In addition, processes are documented using the process mapping approach that was described in Chapter 5.

ISO 9000 is seen as providing benefits both to the organizations adopting it (because it gives them detailed guidance on how to design their control procedures) and especially to customers (who have the assurance of knowing that the services and products they purchase are produced by an operation working to a defined standard). It may also provide a useful discipline to stick to 'sensible' process-oriented procedures which lead to error reduction, reduced customer complaints and reduced costs of quality, and may even identify existing procedures which can be eliminated. Moreover, gaining the certificate demonstrates that the company takes quality seriously; it therefore has a marketing benefit.

Critical commentary

Notwithstanding its widespread adoption (and its revision to take into account some of its perceived failings), ISO 9000 is not seen as beneficial by all authorities, and is still subject to some specific criticisms. These include the following:

- The use of standards and procedures encourages 'management by manual' and over-systematized decision-making.
- The whole process of documenting processes, writing procedures, training staff and conducting internal audits is expensive and time-consuming.
- Similarly, the time and cost of achieving and maintaining ISO 9000 registration are excessive.
- It is too formulaic. It encourages operations to substitute a 'recipe' for a more customized and creative approach to managing operations improvement.

Summary answers to key questions

 *Check and improve your understanding of this chapter using self-assessment questions and a personalized study plan, audio and video downloads, and an eBook – all at* **www.myomlab.com.**

➤ What is quality and why is it so important?

- The definition of quality used in this book defines quality as 'consistent conformance to customers' expectations'.

- High quality offerings are a key driver of competitive advantage for organizations.

➤ How can quality problems be diagnosed?

- At a broad level, quality is best modelled as the gap between customers' expectations concerning the service or product and their perceptions concerning the service or product.

- Modelling quality this way will allow the development of a diagnostic tool which is based around the perception–expectation gap. Such a gap may be explained by four other gaps:
  - the gap between a customer's specification and the operation's specification;
  - the gap between the concept and the way the organization has specified it;
  - the gap between the way quality has been specified and the actual delivered quality;
  - the gap between the actual delivered quality and the way the offering has been described to the customer.

➤ What steps lead towards conformance to specification?

- There are six steps:
  - define quality characteristics;
  - decide how to measure each of the quality characteristics;
  - set quality standards for each characteristic;
  - control quality against these standards;
  - find and correct the causes of poor quality;
  - continue to make improvements.

- Most quality planning and control involves sampling the operations performance in some way. Sampling can give rise to erroneous judgements which are classed as either type I or type II errors. Type I errors involve making corrections where none are needed. Type II errors involve not making corrections where they are in fact needed.

- Statistical process control (SPC) involves using control charts to track the performance of one or more quality characteristics in the operation. The power of control charting lies in its ability to set control limits derived from the statistics of the natural variation of processes. These control limits are often set at ± 3 standard deviations of the natural variation of the process samples.

➤ What is total quality management (TQM)?

- TQM is 'an effective system for integrating the quality development, quality maintenance and quality improvement efforts of the various groups in an organization so as to enable production and service at the most economical levels which allow for full customer satisfaction'.

- It is best thought of as a philosophy that stresses the 'total' of TQM and puts quality at the heart of everything that is done by an operation.
- 'Total' in TQM means the following:
  - meeting the needs and expectations of customers;
  - covering all parts of the organization;
  - including every person in the organization;
  - examining all costs which are related to quality, and getting things 'right first time';
  - developing the systems and procedures which support quality and improvement;
  - developing a continuous process of improvement.

Learning exercises

These problems and applications will help to improve your analysis of operations. You can find more practice problems as well as worked examples and guided solutions on MyOMLab at www.myomlab.com.

1 Find two products, one a manufactured food item (for example, a pack of breakfast cereals, packet of biscuits, etc.) and the other a domestic electrical item (for example, electric toaster, coffee maker, etc.).

(a) Identify the important quality characteristics for these two products.
(b) How could each of these quality characteristics be specified?
(c) How could each of these quality characteristics be measured?

2 Many organizations check up on their own level of quality by using 'mystery shoppers'. This involves an employee of the company acting the role of a customer and recording how they are treated by the operation. Choose two or three high-visibility operations (for example, a cinema, a department store, the branch of a retail bank, etc.) and discuss how you would put together a mystery shopper approach to testing their quality. This may involve you determining the types of characteristics you would wish to observe, the way in which you would measure these characteristics, an appropriate sampling rate, and so on. Try out your mystery shopper plan by visiting these operations.

3 Re-read the short case 'Quality at Magic Moments'. What does 'quality' mean for Richard Webber's service? How might his customers' expectations and perceptions influence perceived quality?

4 Find any website selling clothes. How would you judge the quality of its services?

Want to know more?

Dale, B.G. (ed.) (2003) *Managing Quality*, Blackwell, Oxford. This latest version of a long-established, comprehensive and authoritative text.

Garvin, D.A. (1988) *Managing Quality*, The Free Press, New York. Somewhat dated now but relates to our discussion at the beginning of this chapter.

George, M.L., Rowlands, D. and Kastle, B. (2003) *What Is Lean Six Sigma?* McGraw-Hill, New York. Very much a quick introduction on what Lean Six Sigma is and how to use it.

Pande, P.S., Neuman, R.P. and Kavanagh, R.R. (2000) *The Six Sigma Way*, McGraw-Hill, New York. There are many books written by consultants for practising managers on the now fashionable Six Sigma Approach. This is as readable as any.

Useful websites

www.bqf.org.uk/ The British Quality Foundation is a not-for-profit organization promoting business excellence.

www.juran.com The Juran Institute's mission statement is to provide clients with the concepts, methods and guidance for attaining leadership in quality.

www.asq.org/ The American Society for Quality site. Good professional insights.

www.opsman.org Lots of useful stuff.

www.nist.gov/baldrige American Quality Assurance Institute. Well-established institution for all types of business quality assurance.

www.gslis.utexas.edu/~rpollock/tqm.html Non-commercial site on total quality management with some good links.

www.iso.org/iso/home.htm Site of the International Standards Organization that runs the ISO 9000 and ISO 14000 families of standards. ISO 9000 has become an international reference for quality management requirements.

Now that you have finished reading this chapter, why not visit MyOMLab at www.myomlab.com where you'll find more learning resources to help you make the most of your studies and get a better grade.

Accounting and Finance for Non-Specialists

Peter Atrill
Eddie McLaney

Chapter 1

Introduction to accounting and finance

Introduction

Welcome to the world of accounting and finance! In this opening chapter we provide a broad outline of these subjects. We begin by considering the roles of accounting and finance and then go on to identify the main users of financial information. We shall see how both accounting and finance can be valuable tools in helping these users improve the quality of their decisions. In subsequent chapters, we develop this decision-making theme by examining in some detail the kinds of financial reports and methods used to aid decision making.

For many of you, accounting and finance are not the main focus of your studies and you may well be asking 'Why do I need to study these subjects?' So, after we have considered the key features of accounting and finance, we shall go on to discuss why some understanding of them is likely to be relevant to you.

Learning outcomes

When you have completed this chapter, you should be able to:

■ explain the nature and roles of accounting and finance;
■ identify the main users of financial information and discuss their needs;
■ distinguish between financial accounting and management accounting;
■ explain why an understanding of accounting and finance is likely to be relevant to your needs.

What are accounting and finance?

 Let us start our study of accounting and finance by trying to understand the purpose of each. Accounting is concerned with collecting, analysing and communicating financial information. The ultimate aim is to help those using this information to make more informed decisions. If the financial information that is communicated is not capable of improving the quality of decisions made, there would be no point in producing it.

Accounting information should be useful to anyone wishing to make decisions and plans about businesses, including those who control and manage them. Thus, the managers of businesses may need accounting information to decide whether to:

- develop new products or services (as with a computer manufacturer developing a new range of computers);
- increase or decrease the price or quantity of existing products or services (as with a telecommunications business changing its mobile phone call and text charges);
- borrow money to help finance the business (as with a supermarket wishing to increase the number of stores it owns);
- increase or decrease the operating capacity of the business (as with a beef farming business reviewing the size of its herd); and
- change the methods of purchasing, production or distribution (as with a clothes retailer switching from UK to overseas suppliers).

The information provided should help in identifying and assessing the financial consequences of these sorts of decisions.

Though managers are likely to be important users of accounting information relating to their particular business, they are by no means the only users. There are others outside the business who may also need accounting information. These users will be considered in some detail a little later but examples include those deciding whether to:

- invest or disinvest in the ownership of the business (for example, investors who buy or sell shares);
- lend money to the business (for example, a bank providing a loan);
- offer credit facilities (for example, a supplier of goods or services offering delayed payment).

Sometimes the impression is given that the purpose of accounting is simply to prepare financial reports on a regular basis. While it is true that accountants undertake this kind of work, it does not represent an end in itself. As already mentioned, the ultimate aim of the accountant's work is to give people better financial information on which to base their decisions. This decision-making perspective of accounting fits in with the theme of this book and shapes the way in which we deal with each topic.

 Finance (or financial management), like accounting, exists to help decision makers. It is concerned with the ways in which funds for a business are raised and invested. This lies at the very heart of what a business is about. In essence, a business exists to raise funds from investors (owners and lenders) and then to use those funds to make investments (in equipment, premises, inventories and so on) in an attempt to make the business, and its owners, wealthier. It is important that funds are raised in a way that is appropriate to the particular needs of the business. An understanding of finance should help in identifying:

- the main forms of finance available;
- the costs and benefits of each form of finance;
- the risks associated with each form of finance; and
- the role of financial markets in supplying finance.

Once the funds are raised, they must be invested in a way that will provide the business with a worthwhile return. An understanding of finance should help in evaluating

- the returns from that investment; and
- the risks associated with that investment.

Businesses tend to raise and invest funds in large amounts for long periods of time. The quality of the investment decisions made can, therefore, have a profound impact on the fortunes of the business.

There is little point in trying to make a sharp distinction between accounting and finance. We have already seen that both are concerned with the financial aspects of decision making. There is considerable overlap between the two subjects: for example, accounting reports are a major source of information for financing and investment decision making. In this book, we shall not emphasise the distinctions between accounting and finance.

Who are the users of accounting information?

For accounting information to be useful, the accountant must be clear *for whom* the information is being prepared and *for what purpose* the information will be used. There are likely to be various groups of people (known as 'user groups') with an interest in a particular organisation, in the sense of needing to make decisions about it. For the typical private sector business, the more important of these groups are shown in Figure 1.1. Take a look at this figure and then try Activity 1.1.

Activity 1.1

Ptarmigan Insurance plc (PI) is a large motor insurance business. Taking the user groups identified in Figure 1.1, suggest, for each group, the sorts of decisions likely to be made about PI and the factors to be taken into account when making these decisions.

Your answer may be along the following lines:

User group	Decision
Customers	Whether to take further motor policies with PI. This might involve an assessment of PI's ability to continue in business and to meet their needs, particularly in respect of any insurance claims made.

User group	Decision
Competitors	How best to compete against PI or, perhaps, whether to leave the market on the grounds that it is not possible to compete profitably with PI. This might involve competitors using PI's performance in various respects as a 'benchmark' when evaluating their own performance. They might also try to assess PI's financial strength and to identify significant changes that may signal PI's future actions (for example, raising funds as a prelude to market expansion).
Employees	Whether to continue working for PI and, if so, whether to demand higher rewards for doing so. The future plans, profits and financial strength of the business are likely to be of particular interest when making these decisions.
Government	Whether PI should pay tax and, if so, how much, whether it complies with agreed pricing policies, whether financial support is needed and so on. In making these decisions an assessment of PI's profits, sales revenues and financial strength would be made.
Community representatives	Whether to allow PI to expand its premises and/or whether to provide economic support for the business. When making such decisions, PI's ability to continue to provide employment for the community and its willingness to use community resources and to fund environmental improvements are likely to be important considerations.
Investment analysts	Whether to advise clients to invest in PI. This would involve an assessment of the likely risks and future returns associated with PI.
Suppliers	Whether to continue to supply PI and, if so, whether to supply on credit. This would involve an assessment of PI's ability to pay for any goods and services supplied.
Lenders	Whether to lend money to PI and/or whether to require repayment of any existing loans. PI's ability to pay the interest and to repay the principal sum would be important factors in such decisions.
Managers	Whether the performance of the business needs to be improved. Performance to date would be compared with earlier plans or some other 'benchmark' to decide whether action needs to be taken. Managers may also wish to decide whether there should be a change in PI's future direction. This would involve looking at PI's ability to perform and at the opportunities available to it.
Owners	Whether to invest more in PI or to sell all, or part, of the investment currently held. This would involve an assessment of the likely risks and returns associated with PI. Owners may also be involved with decisions on rewarding senior managers. The financial performance of the business would normally be considered when making such a decision.

Although this answer covers many of the key points, you may have identified other decisions and/or other factors to be taken into account by each group.

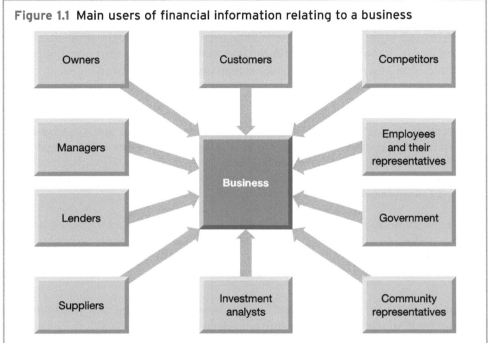

Figure 1.1 Main users of financial information relating to a business

Owners

Customers

Competitors

Managers

Business

Employees and their representatives

Lenders

Government

Suppliers

Investment analysts

Community representatives

Several user groups have an interest in accounting information relating to a business. The majority of these are outside the business but, nevertheless, have a stake in it. This is not meant to be an exhaustive list of potential users; however, the groups identified are normally the most important.

Providing a service

One way of viewing accounting is as a form of service. Accountants provide economic information to their 'clients', who are the various users identified in Figure 1.1. The quality of the service provided is determined by the extent to which the needs of the various user groups have been met. To meet these users' needs, it can be argued that accounting information should possess certain key qualities, or characteristics: relevance, reliability, comparability and understandability.

■ Relevance. It must be possible for accounting information to influence decisions. Unless this characteristic is present, there is really no point in producing the information. The information may be relevant to the prediction of future events (for example, in predicting how much profit is likely to be earned next year) or relevant in helping to confirm past events (for example, in establishing how much profit was earned last year). The role of accounting in confirming past events is important because users often wish to check the accuracy of earlier predictions that they have made. The accuracy of earlier predictions may help users to judge the accuracy of current predictions. To influence a decision, the information must, of course, be available when the decision is being made. Thus, relevant information must be timely.

→ ■ Reliability. Accounting should be free from significant error or bias. It should be capable of being relied upon by managers to represent what it is supposed to represent. Though both relevance and reliability are very important, the problem that we often face in accounting is that information that is highly relevant may not be very reliable. Similarly, that which is reliable may not be very relevant.

Activity 1.2

To illustrate this last point, let us assume that a manager has to sell a custom-built machine owned by the business and has recently received a bid for it. This machine is very unusual and there is no ready market for it.

What information would be relevant to the manager when deciding whether to accept the bid? How reliable would that information be?

The manager would probably like to know the current market value of the machine before deciding whether or not to accept the bid. The current market value would be highly relevant to the final decision, but it might not be very reliable because the machine is unique and there is likely to be little information concerning market values.

When seeking to strike the right balance between relevance and reliability, the needs of users should be the overriding consideration.

→ ■ Comparability. This quality will enable users to identify changes in the business over time (for example, the trend in sales revenue over the past five years). It will also help them to evaluate the performance of the business in relation to similar businesses. Comparability is achieved by treating items that are basically the same in the same manner for accounting purposes. Comparability may also be enhanced by making clear the policies adopted in measuring and presenting the information.

→ ■ Understandability. Accounting reports should be expressed as clearly as possible and should be understood by those at whom the information is aimed.

Activity 1.3

Do you think that accounting reports should be understandable to those who have not studied accounting?

It would be very useful if accounting reports could be understood by everyone. This, however, is unrealistic, as complex financial events and transactions cannot normally be expressed in simple terms. It is probably best that we regard accounting reports in the same way that we regard a report written in a foreign language. To understand either of these, we need to have had some preparation. Generally speaking, accounting reports assume that the user not only has a reasonable knowledge of business and accounting but is also prepared to invest some time in studying the reports.

Despite the answer to Activity 1.3, the onus is clearly on accountants to provide information in a way that makes it as understandable as possible to non-accountants.

But . . . is it material?

The qualities, or characteristics, that have just been described will help us to decide whether accounting information is potentially useful. If a particular piece of information has these qualities then it may be useful. However, this does not automatically mean that it should be reported to users. We also have to consider whether the information is material, or significant. This means that we should ask whether its omission or misrepresentation in the accounting reports would really alter the decisions that users make. Thus, in addition to possessing the characteristics mentioned above, accounting information must also cross the threshold of materiality. If the information is not regarded as material, it should not be included within the reports as it will merely clutter them up and, perhaps, interfere with the users' ability to interpret the financial results. The type of information and amounts involved will normally determine whether it is material.

Weighing up the costs and benefits

Having read the previous sections you may feel that, when considering a piece of accounting information, provided the four main qualities identified are present and it is material it should be gathered and made available to users. Unfortunately, there is one more hurdle to jump. Something may still exclude a piece of accounting information from the reports even when it is considered to be useful. Consider Activity 1.4.

Activity 1.4

Suppose an item of information is capable of being provided. It is relevant to a particular decision, it is also reliable, comparable, can be understood by the decision maker concerned and is material.

Can you think of the reason why, in practice, you might choose not to produce, or discover, the information?

The reason is that you judge the cost of doing so to be greater than the potential benefit of having the information. This cost–benefit issue will limit the amount of accounting information provided.

In theory, a particular item of accounting information should only be produced if the costs of providing it are less than the benefits, or value, to be derived from its use. In practice, however, these costs and benefits are often difficult to assess.

To illustrate the practical problems of establishing the value of information, let us assume that someone has collided with our car in a car park and dented one of the doors and scraped the paintwork. We want to have the dent taken out and the door resprayed at a local garage. We know that the nearest garage would charge £250 but we believe that other local garages may offer to do the job for a lower price. The only way of finding out the prices at other garages is to visit them, so that they can see the extent of the damage. Visiting the garages will involve using some petrol and will take up some of our time. Is it worth the cost of finding out the price for the job at the various local garages? The answer, as we have seen, is that if the cost of discovering the price is less than the potential benefit, it is worth having that information.

To identify the various prices for the job, there are several points to be considered, including:

■ How many garages shall we visit?
■ What is the cost of petrol to visit each garage?
■ How long will it take to make all the garage visits?
■ At what price do we value our time?

The economic benefit of having the information on the price of the job is probably even harder to assess. The following points need to be considered:

■ What is the cheapest price that we might be quoted for the job?
■ How likely is it that we shall be quoted a price cheaper than £250?

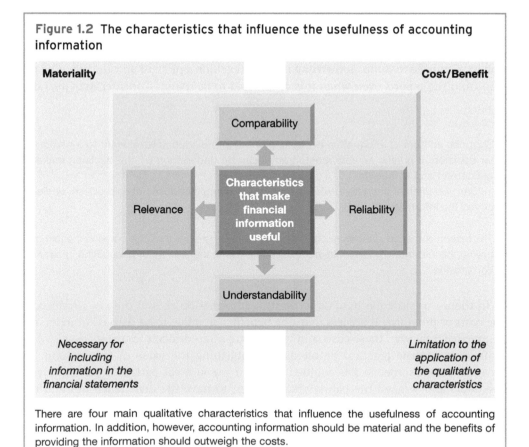

Figure 1.2 The characteristics that influence the usefulness of accounting information

There are four main qualitative characteristics that influence the usefulness of accounting information. In addition, however, accounting information should be material and the benefits of providing the information should outweigh the costs.

As we can imagine, the answers to these questions may be far from clear – remember that we have only contacted the local garage so far. When assessing the value of accounting information we are confronted with similar problems.

Producing accounting information can be very costly; however, the costs are often difficult to quantify. The direct, out-of-pocket costs, such as salaries of accounting staff, are not really a problem to identify, but these are only part of the total costs involved. There are also less direct costs such as the cost of the user's time spent on analysing and interpreting the information contained in reports.

The economic benefit of having accounting information is even harder to assess. It is possible to apply some 'science' to the problem of weighing the costs and benefits, but a lot of subjective judgement is likely to be involved. No one would seriously advocate that the typical business should produce no accounting information. At the same time, no one would advocate that every item of information that could be seen as possessing one or more of the key characteristics should be produced, irrespective of the cost of producing it.

The characteristics that influence the usefulness of accounting information, and which have been discussed in this section, and the preceding section are set out in Figure 1.2.

Accounting as an information system

We have already seen that accounting can be seen as the provision of a service to 'clients'. Another way of viewing accounting is as a part of the business's total information system. Users, both inside and outside the business, have to make decisions concerning the allocation of scarce economic resources. To ensure that these resources are efficiently allocated, users need economic information on which to base decisions. It is the role of the accounting system to provide this information.

The accounting information system should have certain features that are common to all valid information systems within a business. These are:

- identifying and capturing relevant information (in this case financial information);
- recording, in a systematic way, the information collected;
- analysing and interpreting the information collected; and
- reporting the information in a manner that suits the needs of users.

The relationship between these features is set out in Figure 1.3.

Figure 1.3 The accounting information system

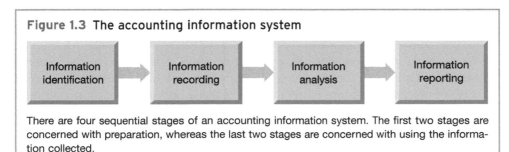

There are four sequential stages of an accounting information system. The first two stages are concerned with preparation, whereas the last two stages are concerned with using the information collected.

Given the decision-making emphasis of this book, we shall be concerned primarily with the final two elements of the process: the analysis and reporting of accounting information. We shall consider the way in which information is used by, and is useful to, users rather than the way in which it is identified and recorded.

Efficient accounting systems are an essential ingredient of an efficient business. When the accounting systems fail, the results can be disastrous. Real World 1.1 provides an example of one such failure and its impact on the business.

Real World 1.1

System failure

Cohort, the defence services group, will shift its focus towards internal restructuring and away from the external expansion strategy it has followed in recent years in the wake of serious accounting problems, according to Andy Thomis, chief executive.

'[Acquisitions and international expansion] will follow in due course . . . at the moment we've got to sort the problems out and restore shareholder value,' Mr Thomis said.

Last week Cohort surprised the market with a profits warning and said it would miss full year results expectations. An IT changeover and accounting errors caused it to significantly overstate income on certain contracts at its SCS unit.

Since then the shares have slumped more than 40 per cent to around 95p.

Mr Thomis said he had suspended the financial controller of SCS, which provides consultancy services to the Ministry of Defence, pending the results of an ongoing investigation, and would take further steps to cut costs.

The comments came as Cohort reported its results for the six months to the end of October. Over the period, pre-tax profits fell by more than half to £1.2 million.

Source: 'Cohort to restructure', The Financial Times, 09/12/2009 (Lemer, J.), copyright © The Financial Times Ltd.

Management accounting and financial accounting

Accounting is usually seen as having two distinct strands. These are:

■ management accounting, which seeks to meet the accounting needs of managers; and
■ financial accounting, which seeks to meet those of all of the other users identified earlier in the chapter (see Figure 1.1).

The difference in their targeted user groups has led to each strand of accounting developing along different lines. The main areas of difference are as follows.

■ *Nature of the reports produced.* Financial accounting reports tend to be general-purpose, that is, they contain financial information that will be useful for a broad range of users and decisions rather than being specifically designed for the needs of a particular group or set of decisions. Management accounting reports, on the other hand, are often specific-purpose reports. They are designed with a particular decision in mind and/or for a particular manager.

- *Level of detail.* Financial accounting reports provide users with a broad overview of the performance and position of the business for a period. As a result, information is aggregated and detail is often lost. Management accounting reports, however, often provide managers with considerable detail to help them with a particular operational decision.
- *Regulations.* Financial accounting reports, for many businesses, are subject to accounting regulations that try to ensure that they are produced with standard content and in a standard format. The law and accounting rule makers impose these regulations. As management accounting reports are for internal use only, there are no regulations from external sources concerning the form and content of the reports. They can be designed to meet the needs of particular managers.
- *Reporting interval.* For most businesses, financial accounting reports are produced on an annual basis, though some large businesses produce half-yearly reports and a few produce quarterly ones. Management accounting reports may be produced as frequently as required by managers. In many businesses, managers are provided with certain reports on a daily, weekly or monthly basis, which allows them to check progress frequently. In addition, special-purpose reports will be prepared when required (for example, to evaluate a proposal to purchase a piece of equipment).
- *Time orientation.* Financial accounting reports reflect the performance and position of the business for the past period. In essence, they are backward-looking. Management accounting reports, on the other hand, often provide information concerning future performance as well as past performance. It is an oversimplification, however, to suggest that financial accounting reports never incorporate expectations concerning the future. Occasionally, businesses will release projected information to other users in an attempt to raise capital or to fight off unwanted takeover bids. Even preparation of the routine financial accounting reports typically requires making some judgements about the future, as we shall see in Chapter 3.
- *Range and quality of information.* Financial accounting reports concentrate on information that can be quantified in monetary terms. Management accounting also produces such reports, but is also more likely to produce reports that contain information of a non-financial nature, such as physical volume of inventories, number of sales orders received, number of new products launched, physical output per employee and so on. Financial accounting places greater emphasis on the use of objective, verifiable evidence when preparing reports. Management accounting reports may use information that is less objective and verifiable, but nevertheless provide managers with the information they need.

We can see from this that management accounting is less constrained than financial accounting. It may draw from a variety of sources and use information that has varying degrees of reliability. The only real test to be applied when assessing the value of the information produced for managers is whether or not it improves the quality of the decisions made.

The distinctions between management accounting and financial accounting suggest that there are differences between the information needs of managers and those of other users. While differences undoubtedly exist, there is also a good deal of overlap between these needs.

Activity 1.5

Can you think of any areas of overlap between the information needs of managers and those of other users?

We thought of two points:

■ Managers will, at times, be interested in receiving a historical overview of business operations of the sort provided to other users.

■ Other users would be interested in receiving information relating to the future, such as the planned level of profits, and non-financial information, such as the state of the sales order book and the extent of product innovations.

The distinction between the two areas of accounting reflects, to some extent, the differences in access to financial information. Managers have much more control over the form and content of information they receive. Other users have to rely on what managers are prepared to provide or what must be provided to satisfy the financial reporting regulations. Though the scope of financial accounting reports has increased over time, fears concerning loss of competitive advantage and user ignorance concerning the reliability of forecast data have led businesses to resist providing other users with the same detailed and wide-ranging information as is available to managers.

Scope of this book

This book covers both financial accounting and management accounting topics. Broadly speaking, the next five chapters (Part 1, Chapters 2 to 6) are concerned with financial accounting topics and the following three (Part 2, Chapters 7 to 9) with management accounting topics. The final part of the book (Part 3, Chapters 10 to 12) is concerned with the financial management of the business, that is, the chapters examine issues relating to the financing and investing activities of the business. As we have seen, accounting information is usually vitally important for these kinds of decisions.

Has accounting become too interesting?

In recent years, accounting has become front-page news and has been a major talking point among those connected with the world of business. Unfortunately, the attention that accounting has attracted has been for all the wrong reasons. We have seen that investors rely on financial reports to help to keep an eye both on their investment and on the performance of the managers. What, though, if the managers provide misleading financial reports to investors? Recent revelations suggest that the managers of some large businesses have been doing just this.

Two of the most notorious cases have been those of:

- Enron, an energy-trading business based in Texas, which was accused of entering into complicated financial arrangements in an attempt to obscure losses and to inflate profits; and
- WorldCom, a major long-distance telephone operator in the US, which was accused of reclassifying $3.9 billion of expenses so as to falsely inflate the profit figures that the business reported to its owners (shareholders) and to others.

In the wake of these scandals, there was much closer scrutiny by investment analysts and investors of the financial reports that businesses produce. This led to further businesses, in both the US and Europe, being accused of using dubious accounting practices to bolster reported profits.

Accounting scandals can have a profound effect on all those connected with the business. The Enron scandal, for example, ultimately led to the collapse of the company, which, in turn, resulted in lost jobs and large financial losses for lenders, suppliers and investors. Confidence in the world of business can be badly shaken by such events and this can pose problems for society as a whole. Not surprisingly, therefore, the relevant authorities tend to deal severely with those who perpetrate such scandals. For example, in the US, Bernie Ebbers, the former chief executive of WorldCom, received twenty-five years in prison for his part in the fraud.

Various reasons have been put forward to explain this spate of scandals. Some scandals may have been caused by the pressures on managers to meet unrealistic expectations of investors for continually rising profits, others by the greed of unscrupulous executives whose pay is linked to financial performance. However, they may all reflect a particular economic environment.

Real World 1.2 offers the view that, when all appears to be going well with a business, people can be quite gullible and over-trusting.

Real World 1.2

The thoughts of Warren Buffett

Warren Buffett is one of the world's shrewdest and most successful investors. He believes that the accounting scandals mentioned above were perpetrated during the 'new economy boom' of the late 1990s when confidence was high and exaggerated predictions were being made concerning the future. He states that during that period

> You had an erosion of accounting standards. You had an erosion, to some extent, of executive behaviour. But during a period when everybody 'believes', people who are inclined to take advantage of other people can get away with a lot.

He believes that the worst is now over and that the 'dirty laundry' created during this heady period was later washed away when the washing machine entered the 'rinse cycle'.

Source: 'Buffett expects markets to get worse', The Times, 26 September 2002, p. 25, John Ashworth.

Whatever the causes, the result of these accounting scandals has been to undermine the credibility of financial statements and to introduce much stricter regulations concerning the quality of financial information. We shall return to this issue in later chapters when we consider the financial statements.

The changing face of accounting

Over the past three decades, the environment within which businesses operate has become increasingly turbulent and competitive. Various reasons have been identified to explain these changes, including:

- the increasing sophistication of customers;
- the development of a global economy where national frontiers become less important;
- rapid changes in technology;
- the deregulation of domestic markets (for example, electricity, water and gas);
- increasing pressure from owners (shareholders) for competitive economic returns; and
- the increasing volatility of financial markets.

This new, more complex, environment has brought new challenges for managers and other users of accounting information. Their needs have changed and both financial accounting and management accounting have had to respond. To meet the changing needs of users there has been a radical review of the kind of information to be reported.

The changing business environment has given added impetus to the search for a clear framework and principles upon which to base financial accounting reports. Various attempts have been made to clarify the purpose of financial accounting reports and to provide a more solid foundation for the development of accounting rules. The frameworks and principles that have been developed try to address fundamental questions such as:

- Who are the users of financial accounting information?
- What kinds of financial accounting reports should be prepared and what should they contain?
- How should items such as profit and asset values be measured?

In response to criticisms that the financial reports of some businesses are not clear enough to users, accounting rule makers have tried to improve reporting rules to ensure that the accounting policies of businesses are more comparable and more transparent and that they portray economic reality more faithfully. While this has had a generally beneficial effect, the recent accounting scandals have highlighted the limitations of accounting rules in protecting investors and others.

The internationalisation of businesses has created a need for accounting rules to have an international reach. It can no longer be assumed that users of accounting information relating to a particular business are based in the country in which the business operates or are familiar with the accounting rules of that country. Thus, there has been increasing harmonisation of accounting rules across national frontiers.

Management accounting has also changed by becoming more outward-looking in its focus. In the past, information provided to managers has been largely restricted to that collected within the business. However, the attitude and behaviour of customers and rival businesses have now become the object of much information-gathering. Increasingly, successful businesses are those that are able to secure and maintain competitive advantage over their rivals.

To obtain this advantage, businesses have become more 'customer driven' (that is, concerned with satisfying customer needs). This has led to the production of management accounting information that provides details of customers and the market, such as customer evaluation of services provided and market share. In addition, information about the costs and profits of rival businesses, which can be used as 'benchmarks' by which to gauge competitiveness, is gathered and reported.

To compete successfully, businesses must also find ways of managing costs. The cost base of modern businesses is under continual review and this, in turn, has led to the development of more sophisticated methods of measuring and controlling costs.

How are businesses managed?

We have already seen that the environment in which businesses operate has become increasingly turbulent and competitive. The effect of these environmental changes has been to make the role of managers more complex and demanding. It has meant that managers have had to find new ways to manage their business. This has increasingly led to the introduction of strategic management.

Strategic management is designed to provide a business with a clear sense of purpose and to ensure that appropriate action is taken to achieve that purpose. The action taken should link the internal resources of the business to the external environment of competitors, suppliers, customers and so on. This should be done in such a way that any business strengths, such as having a skilled workforce, are exploited and any weaknesses, such as being short of investment finance, are not exposed. To achieve this requires the development of strategies and plans that take account of the business's strengths and weaknesses, as well as the opportunities offered and threats posed by the external environment. Access to a new, expanding market is an example of an opportunity; the decision of a major competitor to reduce prices is an example of a threat. This topic will be considered in more depth in Chapter 9 when we consider business planning and budgeting.

What is the financial objective of a business?

A business is normally created to enhance the wealth of its owners. Throughout this book we shall assume that this is its main objective. This may come as a surprise, as there are other objectives that a business may pursue that are related to the needs of others associated with the business. For example, a business may seek to provide good working conditions for its employees, or it may seek to conserve the environment for the local community. While a business may pursue these objectives, it is normally set up with a view to increasing the wealth of its owners. In practice, the behaviour of businesses over time appears to be consistent with this objective.

Real World 1.3 explains how one well-known business has changed its focus in order to improve profits for its owners.

Real World 1.3

Profiting from change

It speaks volumes for the work done by Kate Swann in turning around W H Smith that when she became chief executive five years ago, the company was being spoken of in similar terms to Woolworths. Comments such as 'You wouldn't invent it if you were starting out today' and 'What is it actually for these days?' were typical among analysts, as they were with Woolies. Indeed, many thought that W H Smith was beyond help and argued that the supermarkets were eating away at sales.

Ms Swann has defied the sceptics, achieving an impressive turnaround. The company's magazine and newspaper distribution division was hived off as a separate entity and new outlets were opened at airports and railway stations – so much so that sales by W H Smith's travel unit now threaten to overtake those of its traditional high street stores. Lines with lower profit margins, such as CDs and DVDs, have been cleared from the shelves to make way for items with higher profit margins, such as stationery.

The last plank of the strategy was in evidence again in yesterday's update, in which Ms Swann reported that sales in the nine weeks to 17 January were down by 7 per cent in the high street stores and by 2 per cent in the travel stores, partly because W H Smith is continuing to reduce its exposure to the entertainment category.

That was the bad news. The good news was that, although sales overall were down, the reduced focus on entertainment was good for profits. W H Smith made an extra 2p of profit in every £1 of sales, compared with the same period a year earlier, a stunning achievement given the deflation hitting the high street.

Source: 'Business big shot: Kate Swann of WH Smith', *The Times*, 27 January 2009, p. 39 (Ian King), http://business.timesonline.co.uk/tol/business/movers_and_shakers/article5594430.ece.

Within a market economy there are strong competitive forces at work that ensure that failure to enhance owners' wealth will not be tolerated for long. Competition for the funds provided by the owners and competition for managers' jobs will normally mean that the owners' interests will prevail. If the managers do not provide the expected increase in ownership wealth, the owners have the power to replace the existing management team with a new team that is more responsive to owners' needs.

Does this mean that the needs of other groups associated with the business (employees, customers, suppliers, the community and so on) are not really important? The answer to this question is certainly no, if the business wishes to survive and prosper over the longer term. Satisfying the needs of other groups will normally be consistent with increasing the wealth of the owners over the longer term.

The importance of customers to a business cannot be overstated. Dissatisfied customers will take their business to another supplier and this will, in turn, lead to a loss of wealth for the owners of the business losing the customers. Real World 1.4 provides an illustration of the way in which one business acknowledges the link between customer satisfaction and creating wealth for its owners.

Real World 1.4

Checking out Sainsbury's objectives

J. Sainsbury plc is a leading food retailer that recognises the importance of customers to increasing the wealth of the owners (shareholders) as follows:

Our objective is to serve customers well and thereby provide shareholders with good, sustainable financial returns.

Source: Investor FAQs, www.j-sainsbury.co.uk, November 2009, p. 2.

A dissatisfied workforce may result in low productivity, strikes and so forth, which will in turn have an adverse effect on owners' wealth. Similarly, a business that upsets the local community by unacceptable behaviour, such as polluting the environment, may attract bad publicity, resulting in a loss of customers. It may also attract heavy fines.

Real World 1.5 provides an example of how two businesses responded to potentially damaging allegations.

Real World 1.5

The price of clothes

US clothing and sportswear manufacturers Gap and Nike have many of their clothes produced in Asia where labour tends to be cheap. However, some of the contractors that produce clothes on behalf of the two companies have been accused of unacceptable practices.

Campaigners visited the factories and came up with damaging allegations. The factories were employing minors, they said, and managers were harassing female employees.

Nike and Gap reacted by allowing independent inspectors into the factories. They promised to ensure their contractors obeyed minimum standards of employment. Earlier this year, Nike took the extraordinary step of publishing the names and addresses of all its contractors' factories on the internet. The company said it could not be sure all the abuse had stopped. It said that if campaigners visited its contractors' factories and found examples of continued malpractice, it would take action.

Nike and Gap said the approach made business sense. They needed society's approval if they were to prosper. Nike said it was concerned about the reaction of potential US recruits to the campaigners' allegations. They would not want to work for a company that was constantly in the news because of the allegedly cruel treatment of those who made its products.

Source: 'Fair shares?', *The Financial Times*, 11/06/2005 (Skapinker, M.), copyright © The Financial Times Ltd.

It is important to recognise that generating wealth for the owners is not the same as seeking to maximise the current year's profit. Wealth creation is a longer-term concept, which relates not only to this year's profit but to that of future years as well. In the short term, corners can be cut and risks taken that improve current profit at the expense of future profit. Real World 1.6 provides some examples of how emphasis on short-term profit can be damaging.

Real World 1.6

Short-term gains, long-term problems

For many years, under the guise of defending capitalism, we have been allowing ourselves to degrade it. We have been poisoning the well from which we have drawn wealth.

We have misunderstood the importance of values to capitalism. We have surrendered to the idea that success is pursued by making as much money as the law allowed without regard to how it was made.

Thirty years ago, retailers would be quite content to source the shoes they wanted to sell as cheaply as possible. The working conditions of those who produced them was not their concern.

Then headlines and protests developed. Society started to hold them responsible for previously invisible working conditions.

Companies like Nike went through a transformation. They realised they were polluting their brand. Global sourcing became visible. It was no longer viable to define success simply in terms of buying at the lowest price and selling at the highest.

Financial services and investment are today where footwear was thirty years ago. Public anger at the crisis will make visible what was previously hidden.

Take the building up of huge portfolios of loans to poor people on US trailer parks. These loans were authorised without proper scrutiny of the circumstances of the borrowers. Somebody else then deemed them fit to be securitised and so on through credit default swaps and the rest without anyone seeing the transaction in terms of its ultimate human origin.

Each of the decision makers thought it okay to act like the thoughtless footwear buyer of the 1970s. The price was attractive. There was money to make on the deal. Was it responsible? Irrelevant. It was legal, and others were making money that way.

And the consequences for the banking system if everybody did it? Not our problem.

Now we are paying the price in trillions of dollars for that imprudent attitude.

One senior investment banker whose business has survived the crisis in good shape recently confirmed this analysis to me. Again and again new product ideas had been put in front of him, without any prior thought about their ethical content.

The consumer has had a profound shock. Surely we could have expected the clever and wise people who invested our money to be better at risk management than they have shown themselves to be in the present crisis?

How could they have been so gullible in not challenging the bankers whose lending proved so flaky? How could they have believed that the levels of bonuses that were, at least in part, coming out of their savings could have been justified in 'incentivising' a better performance? How could they have believed that a 'better' performance would be one that is achieved for one bank without regard to its effect on the whole banking system? Where was the stewardship from those exercising investment on their behalf?

The answer has been that very few of them do exercise that stewardship. Most have stood back and said it doesn't really pay them to do so.

The failure of stewardship comes from the same mindset that created the irresponsible lending in the first place. We are back to the mindset that has allowed us to poison the well: never mind the health of the system as a whole, I'm making money out of it at the moment.

Responsibility means awareness for the system consequences of our actions. It is not a luxury. It is the cornerstone of prudence.

Source: Goyder, M., 'How we've poisoned the well of wealth', *The Financial Times*, 15 February 2009.

Balancing risk and return

All decision making involves the future, and business decision making is no exception. The only thing certain about the future, however, is that we cannot be sure what will happen. Things may not turn out as planned and this risk should be carefully considered when making financial decisions.

As in other aspects of life, risk and return tend to be related. Evidence shows that returns relate to risk in something like the way shown in Figure 1.4.

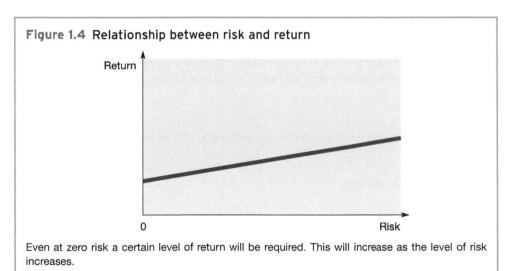

Figure 1.4 Relationship between risk and return

Even at zero risk a certain level of return will be required. This will increase as the level of risk increases.

This relationship between risk and return has important implications for setting financial objectives for a business. The owners will require a minimum return to induce them to invest at all, but will require an additional return to compensate for taking risks; the higher the risk, the higher the required return. Managers must be aware of this and must strike the appropriate balance between risk and return when setting objectives and pursuing particular courses of action.

Real World 1.7 describes how some businesses have been making higher-risk investments in pursuit of higher returns.

Appetite for risk drives businesses

Over the last few years, companies from the US and western Europe, joined increasingly by competitors from China and India, have looked to new markets abroad both to source and sell their products.

Driven by intensifying competition at home, companies have been drawn into direct investment in markets that not long ago were considered beyond the pale. But in the drive to increase returns, they have also been forced to accept higher risks.

Over time, the balance between risk and reward changes. For example, companies flooded into Russia early in the decade. But recently returns have fallen, largely due to booming raw materials prices. Meanwhile the apparent risk of investing in Russia has grown significantly.

As the risk/reward calculation has changed in Russia, companies have looked to other countries such as Libya and Vietnam where the rewards may be substantial, and the threats, though high, may be more manageable.

Source: adapted from 'Appetite for risk drives industry', *The Financial Times*, 27/06/2007 (Fidler, S.), copyright © The Financial Times Ltd.

Not-for-profit organisations

Though the focus of this book is accounting as it relates to private sector businesses, there are many organisations that do not exist mainly for the pursuit of profit.

Activity 1.6

Can you think of at least four types of organisation that are not primarily concerned with making profits?

We thought of the following:

- charities
- clubs and associations
- universities
- local government authorities
- national government departments
- churches
- trade unions.

All of these organisations need to produce accounting information for decision-making purposes. Once again, various user groups need this information to help them to make decisions. These user groups are often the same as, or similar to, those identified for private sector businesses. They may have a stake in the future viability of the organisation and may use accounting information to check that the wealth of the organisation is being properly controlled and used in a way that is consistent with its objectives.

Real World 1.8 provides an example of the importance of accounting to relief agencies.

Real World 1.8

Accounting for disasters

In the aftermath of the Asian tsunami more than £400 million was raised from charitable donations. It was important that his huge amount of money for aid and reconstruction was used as efficiently and effectively as possible. That did not just mean medical staff and engineers. It also meant accountants.

The charity that exerts financial control over aid donations is Mango: Management Accounting for Non-Governmental Organisations (NGOs). It provides accountants in the field and it provides the back-up, such as financial training and all the other services that should result in really robust financial management in a disaster area.

The world of aid has changed completely as a result of the tsunami. According to Mango's director, Alex Jacobs, 'Accounting is just as important as blankets. Agencies have been aware of this for years. But when you move on to a bigger scale there is more pressure to show the donations are being used appropriately.'

More recently, the earthquake in Haiti led to a call from Mango for French-speaking accountants to help support the relief programme and to help in the longer-term rebuilding of Haiti.

Sources: adapted from Bruce, R., 'Tsunami: finding the right figures for disaster relief', FT.com, 7 March 2005; Bruce, R., 'The work of Mango: coping with generous donations', FT.com, 27 February 2006; and Grant, P., 'Accountants needed in Haiti', *Accountancy Age,* 5 February 2010.

Why do I need to know anything about accounting and finance?

If you are planning a career in accounting or finance, you will be clear as to why you are now studying these subjects.

If your career plans do not lie in that direction, you may be asking yourself at this point 'Why do I need to study accounting and finance? I don't intend to become an accountant!' Well, from the explanation of what accounting and finance is about, which has broadly been the subject of this chapter, it should be clear that the accounting/finance function within a business is a central part of its management information system. On the basis of information provided by the system, managers make decisions concerning the allocation of resources. These decisions may concern whether to:

- continue with certain business operations;
- invest in particular projects; or
- sell particular products.

Such decisions can have a profound effect on all those connected with the business. It is important, therefore, that *all* those who intend to work in a business should have a fairly clear idea of certain important aspects of accounting and finance. These aspects include

■ how accounting reports should be read and interpreted;
■ how financial plans are made;
■ how investment decisions are made; and
■ how businesses are financed.

Many, perhaps most, students have a career goal of being a manager within a business – perhaps a personnel manager, production manager, marketing manager or IT manager. If you are one of these students, an understanding of accounting and finance is very important. When you become a manager, even a junior one, it is almost certain that you will have to use financial reports to help you to carry out your management tasks. It is equally certain that it is largely on the basis of financial information and reports that your performance as a manager will be judged.

As a manager, it is likely that you will be expected to help in forward planning for the business. This will often involve the preparation of projected financial statements and setting of financial targets. If you do not understand what the financial statements really mean and the extent to which the financial information is reliable, you will find yourself at a distinct disadvantage to others who know their way round the system. As a manager, you will also be expected to help decide how the limited resources available to the business should be allocated between competing options. This will require an ability to evaluate the costs and benefits of the different options available. Once again, an understanding of accounting and finance is important to carrying out this management task.

This is not to say that you cannot be an effective and successful personnel, production, marketing or IT manager unless you are also a qualified accountant. It does mean, however, that you need to become a bit 'streetwise' in accounting and finance in order to succeed. This book should give you that street wisdom.

Summary

The main points of this chapter may be summarised as follows.

What are accounting and finance?
■ Accounting provides financial information to help various user groups make better judgements and decisions.
■ Finance is concerned with the financing and investing activities of the business and is also concerned with improving the quality of user decisions.

Accounting and user needs
■ For accounting to be useful, there must be a clear understanding of *for whom* and *for what purpose* the information will be used.
■ Owners, managers and lenders are important user groups, but there are several others.

Providing a service

- Accounting can be viewed as a form of service as it involves providing financial information required by the various users.

- To provide a useful service, accounting must possess certain qualities, or characteristics. These are relevance, reliability, comparability and understandability. In addition, accounting information must be material.

- Providing a service to users can be costly and financial information should be produced only if the cost of providing the information is less than the benefits gained.

Accounting information

- Accounting is part of the total information system within a business. It shares the features that are common to all information systems within a business, which are the identification, recording, analysis and reporting of information.

Management accounting and financial accounting

- Accounting has two main strands – management accounting and financial accounting.

- Management accounting seeks to meet the needs of the business's managers, and financial accounting seeks to meet the needs of the other user groups.

- These two strands differ in terms of the types of reports produced, the level of reporting detail, the time horizon, the degree of regulation and the range and quality of information provided.

Is accounting too interesting?

- In recent years, there has been a wave of accounting scandals in the US and Europe.

- This appears to reflect a particular economic environment, although other factors may also play a part.

The changing face of accounting

- Changes in the economic environment have led to changes in the nature and scope of accounting.

- Financial accounting has improved its framework of rules and there has been greater international harmonisation of accounting rules.

- Management accounting has become more outward-looking, and new methods for managing costs have emerged.

How are businesses managed?

- Strategic management has been increasingly adopted to cope with the more complex and more competitive business environment.

- It is designed to provide a clear sense of purpose and to ensure that any action taken is consistent with this purpose.

What is the financial objective of a business?

- The key financial objective is to enhance the wealth of the owners. To achieve this objective, the needs of other groups connected with the business, such as employees, cannot be ignored.

- When setting financial objectives, the right balance must be struck between risk and return.

Why study accounting?

- Everyone connected with business should be a little 'streetwise' about accounting and finance because they exert such an enormous influence over business operations.

→ **Key terms**

accounting	materiality
finance	accounting information system
relevance	management accounting
reliability	financial accounting
comparability	strategic management
understandability	

Further reading

If you would like to explore the topics covered in this chapter in more depth, we recommend the following books:

Atrill, P. and McLaney, E., *Management Accounting for Decision Makers* (6th edn), Financial Times Prentice Hall, 2009, chapter 1.

Elliot, B. and Elliot, J., *Financial Accounting and Reporting* (13th edn), Financial Times Prentice Hall, 2010, chapter 7.

Horngren, C., Bhimani, A., Datar, S. and Foster, G., *Management and Cost Accounting* (4th edn), Prentice Hall, 2007, chapter 1.

McLaney, E., *Business Finance: Theory and Practice* (9th edn), Prentice Hall, 2011, chapters 1 and 2.

? Review questions

1.1   What is the purpose of providing accounting information?

1.2   Identify the main users of accounting information for a university. For what purposes would different user groups need information? Is there a major difference in the ways in which accounting information for a university would be used compared with that of a private sector business?

1.3   Management accounting has been described as 'the eyes and ears of management'. What do you think this expression means?

1.4   Financial accounting statements tend to reflect past events. In view of this, how can they be of any assistance to a user in making a decision when decisions, by their very nature, can only be made about future actions?

Chapter 2

Measuring and reporting financial position

Introduction

We saw in Chapter 1 that accounting has two distinct strands: financial accounting and management accounting. This chapter, along with Chapters 3 to 5, examines the three major financial statements that form the core of financial accounting. We start by taking an overview of these statements to see how each contributes towards an assessment of the overall financial position and performance of a business.

Following this overview, we begin a more detailed examination by turning our attention towards one of these financial statements: the statement of financial position. We shall see how it is prepared and examine the principles underpinning it. We shall also consider its value for decision-making purposes.

Learning outcomes

When you have completed this chapter, you should be able to:

■ explain the nature and purpose of the three major financial statements;

■ prepare a simple statement of financial position and interpret the information that it contains;

■ discuss the accounting conventions underpinning the statement of financial position;

■ discuss the uses and limitations of the statement of financial position for decision-making purposes.

Making financial decisions

We have just seen that a key purpose of this chapter is to show how the statement of financial position may help users. So, let us begin by providing an example of its value for decision making. Real World 2.1 describes how the statement of financial position of a small business was used by a bank when considering whether to grant a loan.

Before we consider this financial statement in detail, however, we should first gain an overview of all three major financial accounting statements. This will help us to understand the role of each as well as their interrelationships.

The major financial statements – an overview

The major financial accounting statements aim to provide a picture of the financial position and performance of a business. To achieve this, a business's accounting system will normally produce three financial statements on a regular, recurring basis. These three statements are concerned with answering the following questions relating to a particular period:

- What cash movements took place?
- How much wealth was generated?
- What is the accumulated wealth of the business at the end of the period and what form does it take?

To address each of the above questions, there is a separate financial statement. The financial statements are:

- ■ the statement of cash flows,
- ■ the income statement (also known as the profit and loss account), and
- ■ the statement of financial position (also known as the balance sheet).

Together they provide an overall picture of the financial health of the business.

Perhaps the best way to introduce these financial statements is to look at an example of a very simple business. From this we shall be able to see the sort of information that each of the statements can usefully provide. It is, however, worth pointing out that, while a simple business is our starting point, the principles for preparing the financial statements apply equally to the largest and most complex businesses. Thus, we shall frequently encounter these principles again in later chapters.

Example 2.1

Paul was unemployed and unable to find a job. He therefore decided to embark on a business venture. With Christmas approaching, he decided to buy gift wrapping paper from a local supplier and to sell it on the corner of his local high street. He felt that the price of wrapping paper in the high street shops was too high. This provided him with a useful business opportunity.

He began the venture with £40 of his own money, in cash. On Monday, Paul's first day of trading, he bought wrapping paper for £40 and sold three-quarters of it for £45 cash.

What cash movements took place in Paul's business during Monday?

For Monday, a *statement of cash flows* showing the cash movements (that is, cash in and cash out) for the day can be prepared as follows:

Statement of cash flows for Monday

	£
Opening balance (cash introduced)	40
Cash from sales of wrapping paper	45
Cash paid to buy wrapping paper	(40)
Closing balance of cash	45

The statement shows that Paul placed £40 cash into the business. The business received £45 cash from customers, but paid £40 cash to buy the wrapping paper. This left £45 of cash by Monday evening. Note that we are taking the standard approach found in the financial statements of showing figures to be deducted (in this case the £40 paid out) in brackets. We shall take this approach consistently throughout the chapters dealing with financial statements.

How much wealth (that is, profit) was generated by the business during Monday?

An *income statement* (*profit and loss account*) can be prepared to show the wealth (profit) generated on Monday. The wealth generated arises from trading and will be the difference between the value of the sales made and the cost of the goods (that is, wrapping paper) sold.

Income statement (profit and loss account) for Monday

	£
Sales revenue	45
Cost of goods sold (¾ of £40)	(30)
Profit	15

Note that it is only the cost of the wrapping paper *sold* that is matched against (and deducted from) the sales revenue in order to find the profit, not the whole of the cost of wrapping paper acquired. Any unsold inventories (in this case ¼ of £40 = £10) will be charged against the future sales revenue that they generate.

What is the accumulated wealth on Monday evening and what form does it take?

To establish the accumulated wealth at the end of Monday's trading, we can draw up a *statement of financial position* (*balance sheet*) for Paul's business. This statement will also list the forms of wealth held at the end of that day.

**Statement of financial position (balance sheet)
as at Monday evening**

	£
Cash (closing balance)	45
Inventories of goods for resale (¼ of £40)	10
Total assets	55
Equity	55

Note the terms 'assets' and 'equity' that appear in the above statement. 'Assets' are business resources (things of value to the business) and include cash and inventories. 'Equity' is the word used in accounting to describe the investment, or stake, of the owner(s) – in this case Paul – in the business. Both of these terms will be discussed in some detail a little later in this chapter.

We can see from the financial statements in Example 2.1 that each statement provides part of a picture of the financial performance and position of the business. We begin by showing the cash movements. Cash is a vital resource that is necessary for any business to function effectively. It is required to meet debts that become due and to acquire other resources (such as inventories). Cash has been described as the 'lifeblood' of a business.

Reporting cash movements alone, however, is not enough to portray the financial health of the business. To find out how much profit was generated, we need an income statement. It is important to recognise that cash and profits rarely move in unison. During Monday, for example, the cash balance increased by £5, but the profit generated, as shown in the income statement, was £15. The cash balance did not increase in line with profit because part of the wealth generated (£10) was held in the form of inventories.

The statement of financial position that was drawn up as at the end of Monday's trading provides an insight into the total wealth of the business. This wealth can be held in various forms. For this business, wealth is held in the form of cash and inventories (also known as stock). Hence, when drawing up the statement of financial position, both forms will be listed. For a large business, many other forms of wealth may be held, such as property, equipment, motor vehicles and so on.

Let us now continue with our example.

Example 2.2

On Tuesday, Paul bought more wrapping paper for £20 cash. He managed to sell all of the new inventories and all of the earlier inventories, for a total of £48.

The statement of cash flows for Tuesday will be as follows:

Statement of cash flows for Tuesday

	£
Opening balance (from Monday evening)	45
Cash from sales of wrapping paper	48
Cash paid to buy wrapping paper	(20)
Closing balance	73

The income statement for Tuesday will be as follows:

Income statement for Tuesday

	£
Sales revenue	48
Cost of goods sold (£20 + £10)	(30)
Profit	18

The statement of financial position as at Tuesday evening will be:

Statement of financial position as at Tuesday evening

	£
Cash (closing balance)	73
Inventories	–
Total assets	73
Equity	73

We can see that the total business wealth increased to £73 by Tuesday evening. This represents an increase of £18 (that is, £73 – £55) over Monday's figure – which, of course, is the amount of profit made during Tuesday as shown on the income statement.

Activity 2.1

On Wednesday, Paul bought more wrapping paper for £46 cash. However, it was raining hard for much of the day and sales were slow. After Paul had sold half of his total inventories for £32, he decided to stop trading until Thursday morning.

Have a go at drawing up the three financial statements for Paul's business for Wednesday.

Statement of cash flows for Wednesday

	£
Opening balance (from the Tuesday evening)	73
Cash from sales of wrapping paper	32
Cash paid to buy wrapping paper	(46)
Closing balance	59

Income statement for Wednesday

	£
Sales revenue	32
Cost of goods sold (½ of £46)	(23)
Profit	9

Statement of financial position as at Wednesday evening

	£
Cash (closing balance)	59
Inventories (½ of £46)	23
Total assets	82
Equity	82

Note that the total business wealth has increased by £9 (that is, the amount of Wednesday's profit) even though the cash balance has declined. This is because the business is holding more of its wealth in the form of inventories rather than cash, compared with the position on Tuesday evening.

By Wednesday evening, the equity stood at £82. This arose from Paul's initial investment of £40, plus his profits for Monday (£15), Tuesday (£18) and Wednesday (£9). This represents Paul's total investment in his business at that time. The equity of most businesses will similarly be made up of injections of funds by the owner plus any accumulated profits.

We can see that the income statement and statement of cash flows are both concerned with measuring flows (of wealth and cash respectively) during a particular period. The statement of financial position, however, is concerned with the financial position at a particular moment in time. Figure 2.1 illustrates this point.

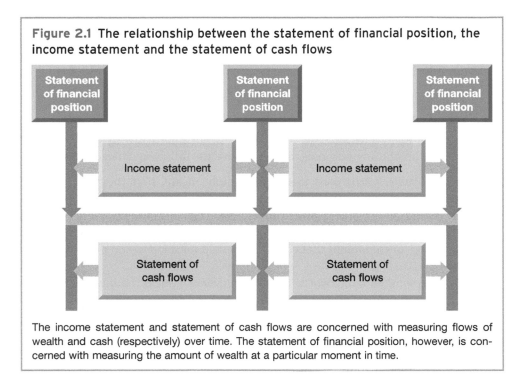

Figure 2.1 The relationship between the statement of financial position, the income statement and the statement of cash flows

The income statement and statement of cash flows are concerned with measuring flows of wealth and cash (respectively) over time. The statement of financial position, however, is concerned with measuring the amount of wealth at a particular moment in time.

The three financial statements discussed are often referred to as the final accounts of the business.

For external users (that is, virtually all users except the managers of the business concerned), these statements are normally backward-looking because they are based on information concerning past events and transactions. This can be useful in providing feedback on past performance and in identifying trends that provide clues to future performance. However, the statements can also be prepared using projected data to help assess likely future profits, cash flows and so on. The financial statements are normally prepared on a projected basis for internal decision-making purposes only. Managers are usually reluctant to publish these projected statements for external users, as they may reveal valuable information to competitors.

Now that we have an overview of the financial statements, we shall consider each one in detail. The remainder of this chapter is devoted to the statement of financial position. Chapter 3 looks at the income statement and Chapter 5 looks at the statement of cash flows. (Chapter 4 looks at the statements of financial position and income statements of limited companies.)

The statement of financial position

We saw a little earlier that this statement shows the forms in which the wealth of a business is held and how much wealth is held in each form. We can, however, be more

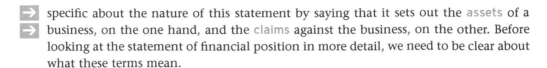 specific about the nature of this statement by saying that it sets out the assets of a business, on the one hand, and the claims against the business, on the other. Before looking at the statement of financial position in more detail, we need to be clear about what these terms mean.

Assets

An asset is essentially a resource held by a business. For a particular item to be treated as an asset for accounting purposes, it should have the following characteristics:

- *A probable future benefit must exist.* This simply means that the item must be expected to have some future monetary value. This value can arise through its use within the business or through its hire or sale. Thus, an obsolete piece of equipment that could be sold for scrap would still be considered an asset, whereas an obsolete piece of equipment that could not be sold for scrap would not be regarded as one.
- *The business must have the right to control the resource.* Unless the business controls the resource, it cannot be regarded as an asset for accounting purposes. Thus, for a business offering holidays on barges, the canal system may be a very valuable resource, but as the business will not be able to control the access of others to the canal system, it cannot be regarded as an asset of the business. (However, the barges owned by the business would be regarded as assets.)
- *The benefit must arise from some past transaction or event.* This means that the transaction (or other event) giving rise to a business's right to the benefit must have already occurred and will not arise at some future date. Thus an agreement by a business to buy a piece of equipment at some future date would not mean the item is currently an asset of the business.
- *The asset must be capable of measurement in monetary terms.* Unless the item can be measured in monetary terms, with a reasonable degree of reliability, it will not be regarded as an asset for inclusion on the statement of financial position. Thus, the title of a magazine (for example *Hello!* or *Vogue*) that was created by its publisher may be extremely valuable to that publishing business, but this value is usually difficult to quantify. It will not, therefore, be treated as an asset.

Note that all four of these conditions must apply. If one of them is missing, the item will not be treated as an asset for accounting purposes and will not, therefore, appear on the statement of financial position.

We can see that these conditions will strictly limit the kind of items that may be referred to as 'assets' in the statement of financial position. Certainly not all resources exploited by a business will be assets of the business for accounting purposes. Some, like the canal system or the magazine title *Hello!*, may well be assets in a broader sense, but not for accounting purposes. Once an asset has been acquired by a business, it will continue to be considered an asset until the benefits are exhausted or the business disposes of it in some way.

Indicate which of the following items could appear as an asset on the statement of financial position of a business. Explain your reasoning in each case.

1 £1,000 owed to the business by a customer who is unable to pay.
2 A patent, bought from an inventor, that gives the business the right to produce a new product. Production of the new product is expected to increase profits over the period during which the patent is held.
3 A new marketing director, whom the business had recently hired, who is confidently expected to increase profits by over 30 per cent during the next three years.
4 A recently purchased machine that will save the business £10,000 each year. It is already being used by the business but it has been acquired on credit and is not yet paid for.

Your answer should be along the following lines.

1 Under normal circumstances, a business would expect a customer to pay the amount owed. Such an amount is therefore typically shown as an asset under the heading 'trade receivables' (or 'debtors'). However, in this particular case the customer is unable to pay. As a result, the item is incapable of providing future benefits and the £1,000 owing would not be regarded as an asset. Debts that are not paid are referred to as 'bad debts'.
2 The patent would meet all of the conditions set out above and would therefore be regarded as an asset.
3 The new marketing director would not be considered as an asset. One argument for this is that the business does not have exclusive rights of control over the director. (Nevertheless, it may have an exclusive right to the services that the director provides.) Perhaps a stronger argument is that the value of the director cannot be measured in monetary terms with any degree of reliability.
4 The machine would be considered an asset even though it is not yet paid for. Once the business has agreed to buy the machine and has accepted it, the machine represents an asset even though payment is still outstanding. (The amount outstanding would be shown as a claim, as we shall see below.)

The sorts of items that often appear as assets in the statement of financial position of a business include:

- property
- plant and equipment
- fixtures and fittings
- patents and trademarks
- trade receivables (debtors)
- investments outside the business.

Activity 2.3

Can you think of two additional items that might appear as assets in the statement of financial position of a typical business?

You may be able to think of a number of other items. Two that we have met so far, because they were held by Paul's wrapping-paper business (in Example 2.1), are inventories and cash.

Note that an asset does not have to be a physical item – it may be a non-physical item that gives a right to certain benefits. Assets that have a physical substance and can be touched (such as inventories) are referred to as tangible assets. Assets that have no physical substance but which, nevertheless, provide expected future benefits (such as patents) are referred to as intangible assets.

Claims

A claim is an obligation of the business to provide cash, or some other form of benefit, to an outside party. It will normally arise as a result of the outside party providing assets for use by the business. There are essentially two types of claim against a business:

- Equity. This represents the claim of the owner(s) against the business. This claim is sometimes referred to as the *owner's capital*. Some find it hard to understand how the owner can have a claim against the business, particularly when we consider the example of a sole-proprietor-type business where the owner *is*, in effect, the business. For accounting purposes, however, a clear distinction is made between the business and the owner(s). The business is viewed as being quite separate from the owner. It is seen as a separate entity with its own separate existence and when financial statements are prepared, they relate to the business rather than to the owner(s). Viewed from this perspective, any funds contributed by the owner will be seen as coming from outside the business and will appear as a claim against the business in its statement of financial position.

  The equity section of the statement of financial position is broadly the same irrespective of the type of business concerned. We shall see in Chapter 4 that, with limited companies, the total equity figure must be analysed according to how each part of it first arose. For example, companies must make a distinction between that part of it that arose from retained earnings (or profits) and that part that arose from the owners putting in cash to start up the business, usually by buying shares in the company.

- Liabilities. Liabilities represent the claims of all individuals and organisations other than the owner(s). They arise from past transactions or events such as supplying goods or lending money to the business. A liability will be settled through an outflow of assets (usually cash).

Once a claim from the owners or outsiders has been incurred by a business, it will remain as an obligation until it is settled.

Now that the meanings of the terms *assets*, *equity* and *liabilities* have been established, we can consider the relationship between them. This relationship is quite straightforward. If a business wishes to acquire assets, it must raise the necessary funds from somewhere. It may raise these funds from the owner(s), or from other outside parties, or from both. Example 2.3 illustrates this relationship.

Example 2.3

Jerry and Company is a new business that was created by depositing £20,000 in a bank account on 1 March. This amount was raised partly from the owner (£6,000) and partly from borrowing (£14,000). Raising funds in this way will give rise to a claim on the business by both the owner (equity) and the lender (liability). If a statement of financial position of Jerry and Company is prepared following the above transactions, it will appear as follows:

Jerry and Company
Statement of financial position as at 1 March

	£
ASSETS	
Cash at bank	20,000
Total assets	20,000
EQUITY AND LIABILITIES	
Equity	6,000
Liabilities – borrowing	14,000
Total equity and liabilities	20,000

We can see from the statement of financial position that the total claims (equity and liabilities) are the same as the total assets. Thus:

$$\text{Assets} = \text{Equity} + \text{Liabilities}$$

This equation – which we shall refer to as the *accounting equation* – will always hold true. Whatever changes may occur to the assets of the business or the claims against it, there will be compensating changes elsewhere that will ensure that the statement of financial position always 'balances'. By way of illustration, consider the following transactions for Jerry and Company:

2 March	Bought a motor van for £5,000, paying by cheque.
3 March	Bought inventories (that is, goods to be sold) on one month's credit for £3,000. (This means that the inventories were bought on 3 March, but payment will not be made to the supplier until 3 April.)
4 March	Repaid £2,000 of the amount borrowed to the lender, by cheque.
6 March	Owner introduced another £4,000 into the business bank account.

A statement of financial position may be drawn up after each day in which transactions have taken place. In this way, we can see the effect of each transaction on the assets and claims of the business. The statement of financial position as at 2 March will be:

Jerry and Company
Statement of financial position as at 2 March

	£
ASSETS	
Cash at bank (20,000 – 5,000)	15,000
Motor van	5,000
Total assets	20,000
EQUITY AND LIABILITIES	
Equity	6,000
Liabilities – borrowing	14,000
Total equity and liabilities	20,000

As we can see, the effect of buying the motor van is to decrease the balance at the bank by £5,000 and to introduce a new asset – a motor van – to the statement of financial position. The total assets remain unchanged. It is only the 'mix' of assets that has changed. The claims against the business remain the same because there has been no change in the way in which the business has been funded.

The statement of financial position as at 3 March, following the purchase of inventories, will be:

Jerry and Company
Statement of financial position as at 3 March

	£
ASSETS	
Cash at bank	15,000
Motor van	5,000
Inventories	3,000
Total assets	23,000
EQUITY AND LIABILITIES	
Equity	6,000
Liabilities – borrowing	14,000
Liabilities – trade payable	3,000
Total equity and liabilities	23,000

The effect of buying inventories has been to introduce another new asset (inventories) to the statement of financial position. Furthermore, the fact that the goods have not yet been paid for means that the claims against the business will be increased by the £3,000 owed to the supplier, who is referred to as a trade payable (or trade creditor) on the statement of financial position.

Activity 2.4

Try drawing up a statement of financial position for Jerry and Company as at 4 March.

The statement of financial postion as at 4 March, following the repayment of part of the borrowing, will be:

Jerry and Company
Statement of financial position as at 4 March

	£
ASSETS	
Cash at bank (15,000 – 2,000)	13,000
Motor van	5,000
Inventories	3,000
Total assets	21,000
EQUITY AND LIABILITIES	
Equity	6,000
Liabilities – borrowing (14,000 – 2,000)	12,000
Liabilities – trade payable	3,000
Total equity and liabilities	21,000

The repayment of £2,000 of the borrowing will result in a decrease in the balance at the bank of £2,000 and a decrease in the lender's claim against the business by the same amount.

Activity 2.5

Try drawing up a statement of financial position as at 6 March for Jerry and Company.

The statement of financial position as at 6 March, following the introduction of more funds, will be:

Jerry and Company
Statement of financial position as at 6 March

	£
ASSETS	
Cash at bank (13,000 + 4,000)	17,000
Motor van	5,000
Inventories	3,000
Total assets	25,000
EQUITY AND LIABILITIES	
Equity (6,000 + 4,000)	10,000
Liabilities – borrowing	12,000
Liabilities – trade payable	3,000
Total equity and liabilities	25,000

The introduction of more funds by the owner will result in an increase in the equity of £4,000 and an increase in the cash at bank by the same amount.

Example 2.3 illustrates the point that the accounting equation (assets equals equity plus liabilities) will always hold true, because it reflects the fact that, if a business wishes to acquire more assets, it must raise funds equal to the cost of those assets. The funds raised must be provided by the owners (equity), or by others (liabilities) or by a combination of the two. Hence the total cost of assets acquired should always equal the total equity plus liabilities.

It is worth pointing out that businesses do not normally draw up a statement of financial position after each day, as shown in the example above. We have done this to illustrate the effect on the statement of financial position of each transaction. In practice, a statement of financial position for a business is usually prepared at the end of a defined reporting period.

Determining the length of the reporting period will involve weighing up the costs of producing the information against the perceived benefits of the information for decision-making purposes. In practice, the reporting period will vary between businesses; it could be monthly, quarterly, half-yearly or annually. For external reporting purposes, an annual reporting period is the norm (although certain businesses, typically larger ones, report more frequently than this). However, for internal reporting purposes to managers, monthly financial statements may be prepared.

The effect of trading transactions

In Example 2.3, we dealt with the effect on the statement of financial position of a number of different types of transactions that a business might undertake. These transactions covered the purchase of assets for cash and on credit, the repayment of borrowing and the injection of equity. However, one form of transaction (trading transactions) has not yet been considered. To deal with the effect of trading transactions on the statement of financial position, let us return to Jerry and Company.

Example 2.4

The statement of financial position that we drew up for Jerry and Company as at 6 March was as follows:

Jerry and Company
Statement of financial position as at 6 March

	£
ASSETS	
Cash at bank	17,000
Motor van	5,000
Inventories	3,000
Total assets	25,000
EQUITY AND LIABILITIES	
Equity	10,000
Liabilities – borrowing	12,000
Liabilities – trade payable	3,000
Total equity and liabilities	25,000

On 7 March, the business managed to sell all of the inventories for £5,000 and received a cheque immediately from the customer for this amount. The statement of financial position on 7 March, after this transaction has taken place, will be:

Jerry and Company
Statement of financial position as at 7 March

	£
ASSETS	
Cash at bank (17,000 + 5,000)	22,000
Motor van	5,000
Inventories (3,000 – 3,000)	–
Total assets	27,000
EQUITY AND LIABILITIES	
Equity (10,000 + (5,000 – 3,000))	12,000
Liabilities – borrowing	12,000
Liabilities – trade payable	3,000
Total equity and liabilities	27,000

We can see that the inventories (£3,000) have now disappeared from the statement of financial position, but the cash at bank has increased by the selling price of the inventories (£5,000). The net effect has therefore been to increase assets by £2,000 (that is, £5,000 less £3,000). This increase represents the net increase in wealth (the profit) that has arisen from trading. Also note that the equity of the business has increased by £2,000, in line with the increase in assets. This increase in equity reflects the fact that increases in wealth, as a result of trading or other operations, will be to the benefit of the owners and will increase their stake in the business.

Activity 2.6

What would have been the effect on the statement of financial position if the inventories had been sold on 7 March for £1,000 rather than £5,000?

The statement of financial position on 7 March would then have been:

Jerry and Company
Statement of financial position as at 7 March

	£
ASSETS	
Cash at bank (17,000 + 1,000)	18,000
Motor van	5,000
Inventories (3,000 – 3,000)	–
Total assets	23,000
EQUITY AND LIABILITIES	
Equity (10,000 + (1,000 – 3,000))	8,000
Liabilities – borrowing	12,000
Liabilities – trade payable	3,000
Total equity and liabilities	23,000

As we can see, the inventories (£3,000) will disappear from the statement of financial position but the cash at bank will rise by only £1,000. This will mean a net reduction in assets of £2,000. This reduction represents a loss arising from trading and will be reflected in a reduction in the equity of the owners.

We can see that any decrease in wealth (that is, a loss) arising from trading or other transactions will lead to a reduction in the owner's stake in the business. If the business wished to maintain the level of assets as at 6 March, it would be necessary to obtain further funds from the owners or from borrowing, or both.

What we have just seen means that the accounting equation can be extended as follows:

Assets (at the end = Equity (amount at the start of the period
of the period)   + profit (or – loss) for the period)
**   + Liabilities (at the end of the period)**

(This is assuming that the owner makes no injections or withdrawals of equity during the period.)

Any funds introduced or withdrawn by the owner for living expenses or other reasons also affect equity. If the owners withdrew £1,500 for their own use, the equity of the owners would be reduced by £1,500. If these drawings were in cash, the balance of cash would decrease by £1,500 in the statement of financial position.

Note that, like all statement of financial position items, the amount of equity is cumulative. This means that any profit made that is not taken out as drawings by the owner(s) remains in the business. These retained (or 'ploughed-back') earnings have the effect of expanding the business.

Classifying assets

On the statement of financial position, assets and claims are usually grouped into categories. This is designed to help users, as a haphazard listing of these items could be confusing. Assets may be categorised as being either current or non-current.

Current assets

Current assets are basically assets that are held for the short term. To be more precise, they are assets that meet any of the following conditions:

- they are held for sale or consumption during the business's normal operating cycle;
- they are expected to be sold within the next year;
- they are held principally for trading;
- they are cash, or near equivalents to cash such as easily marketable, short-term investments.

The operating cycle of a business is the time between buying and/or creating a product or service and receiving the cash on its sale. For most businesses, this will be less than a year.

The most common current assets are inventories (stock), trade receivables (customers who owe amounts for goods or services supplied on credit) and cash.

It is worth making the point here that most sales made by most businesses are made on credit. This is to say that the goods pass to, or the service is rendered to, the customer at one point but the customer pays later. Retail sales are the only significant exception to this general point.

For businesses that sell goods, rather than render a service, the current assets of inventories, trade receivables and cash are interrelated. They circulate within a business as shown in Figure 2.2. We can see that cash can be used to buy inventories, which are then sold on credit. When the credit customers (trade receivables) pay, the business receives an injection of cash and so on.

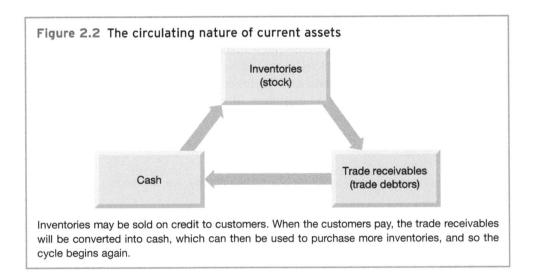

Figure 2.2 The circulating nature of current assets

Inventories may be sold on credit to customers. When the customers pay, the trade receivables will be converted into cash, which can then be used to purchase more inventories, and so the cycle begins again.

For purely service businesses, the situation is similar, except that inventories are not involved.

Non-current assets

Non-current assets (also called fixed assets) are simply assets that do not meet the definition of current assets. They tend to be held for long-term operations.

This distinction between assets that are continuously circulating within the business (current) and assets used for long-term operations (non-current) may be helpful when trying to assess the appropriateness of the mix of assets held. Most businesses will need a certain amount of both types of asset to operate effectively.

Activity 2.7

Can you think of two examples of assets that may be classified as non-current assets for an insurance business?

Examples of assets that may be defined as being non-current are:

- property
- furniture
- motor vehicles
- computers
- computer software
- reference books.

This is not an exhaustive list. You may have thought of others.

It is important to appreciate that how a particular asset is classified (that is, between current and non-current) may vary according to the nature of the business. This is because the *purpose* for which a particular type of asset is held may differ from business to business. For example, a motor vehicle manufacturer will normally hold inventories of the finished motor vehicles produced for resale; it would, therefore, classify them as part of the current assets. On the other hand, a business that uses motor vehicles for delivering its goods to customers (that is, as part of its long-term operations) would classify them as non-current assets.

Activity 2.8

The assets of Kunalun and Co., a large advertising agency, are as follows:

- cash at bank
- fixtures and fittings
- office equipment
- motor vehicles
- property
- computer equipment
- work in progress (that is, partly completed work for clients).

Which of these do you think should be defined as non-current assets and which should be defined as current assets?

Your answer should be as follows:

Non-current assets	*Current assets*
Fixtures and fittings	Cash at bank
Office equipment	Work in progress
Motor vehicles	
Property	
Computer equipment	

Classifying claims

As we have already seen, claims are normally classified into equity (owner's claim) and liabilities (claims of outsiders). Liabilities are further classified as either current or non-current.

Current liabilities

Current liabilities are basically amounts due for settlement in the short term. To be more precise, they are liabilities that meet any of the following conditions:

- they are expected to be settled within the business's normal operating cycle;
- they are held principally for trading purposes;
- they are due to be settled within a year after the date of the relevant statement of financial position;
- there is no right to defer settlement beyond a year after the date of the relevant statement of financial position.

Non-current liabilities

Non-current liabilities represent amounts due that do not meet the definition of current liabilities and so represent longer-term liabilities.

It is quite common for non-current liabilities to become current liabilities. For example, borrowings to be repaid eighteen months after the date of a particular statement of financial position will appear as a non-current liability, but will appear as a current liability in the statement of financial position in the following year.

This classification of liabilities between current and non-current helps to highlight those financial obligations that must shortly be met. Users can compare the amount of current liabilities with the amount of current assets (that is, the assets that either are cash or will turn into cash within the normal operating cycle) to see whether a business can cover its maturing obligations.

The classification of liabilities between current and non-current should also help to indicate how long-term finance is raised. If a business relies on long-term borrowings to finance the business, the financial risks associated with the business will increase. This is because these borrowings will bring a commitment to make periodic interest payments and capital repayments. The business may be forced to stop trading if this commitment is not fulfilled. Thus, when raising long-term finance, a business must try to strike the right balance between non-current liabilities and owner's equity. We shall consider this issue in more detail in Chapter 6.

Activity 2.9

Can you think of one example of a current liability and one of a non-current liability?

An example of a current liability would be amounts owing to suppliers for goods supplied on credit (trade payables) or a bank overdraft (a form of short-term bank borrowing that is repayable on demand). An example of a non-current liability would be long-term borrowings.

Statement layouts

Now that we have looked at the classification of assets and liabilities, we shall consider the layout of the statement of financial position. Although there is an almost infinite number of ways in which the same information on assets and claims could be presented, we shall consider two basic layouts. The first of these follows the style that we adopted with Jerry and Company earlier (see pages 39 to 43). A more comprehensive example of this style is shown in Example 2.5.

Example 2.5

Brie Manufacturing
Statement of financial position as at 31 December 2009

	£000
ASSETS	
Non-current assets	
Property	45
Plant and equipment	30
Motor vans	19
	94
Current assets	
Inventories	23
Trade receivables	18
Cash at bank	12
	53
Total assets	147
EQUITY AND LIABILITIES	
Equity	60
Non-current liabilities	
Long-term borrowings	50
Current liabilities	
Trade payables	37
Total equity and liabilities	147

The non-current assets have a total of £94,000, which together with the current assets total of £53,000 gives a total of £147,000 for assets. Similarly, the equity totals £60,000, which together with the £50,000 for non-current liabilities and £37,000 for current liabilities gives a total for equity and liabilities of £147,000.

Within each category of asset (non-current and current) shown in Example 2.5, the items are listed in reverse order of liquidity (nearness to cash). Thus, the assets that are furthest from cash come first and the assets that are closest to cash come last. In the case of non-current assets, property is listed first as this asset is usually the most difficult to turn into cash, and motor vans are listed last as there is usually a ready market for them. In the case of current assets, we have already seen that inventories are converted to trade receivables and then trade receivables are converted to cash. Hence, under the heading of current assets, inventories are listed first, followed by trade receivables and finally cash itself. This ordering of assets is a normal practice, which is followed irrespective of the layout used.

Note that, in addition to a grand total for assets held, subtotals for non-current assets and current assets are shown. Subtotals are also used for non-current liabilities and current liabilities when more than one item appears within these categories.

This layout is the most popular in practice in the UK.

A slight variation from the standard layout illustrated in Example 2.5 is as shown in Example 2.6.

Example 2.6

Brie Manufacturing
Statement of financial position as at 31 December 2009

	£000
ASSETS	
Non-current assets	
Property	45
Plant and equipment	30
Motor vans	19
	94
Current assets	
Inventories	23
Trade receivables	18
Cash at bank	12
	53
Total assets	147
LIABILITIES	
Non-current liabilities	
Long-term borrowings	(50)
Current liabilities	
Trade payables	(37)
Total liabilities	(87)
Net assets	60
EQUITY	60

We can see that the total liabilities are deducted from the total assets. This derives a figure for net assets – which is equal to equity. Using this format, the basic accounting equation is rearranged so that

$$\text{Assets} - \text{Liabilities} = \text{Equity}$$

This rearranged equation highlights the fact that equity represents the residual interest of the owner(s) after deducting all liabilities of the business.

? Self-assessment question 2.1

The following information relates to Simonson Engineering as at 30 September 2010:

	£
Plant and machinery	25,000
Trade payables	18,000
Short-term borrowings	26,000
Inventories	45,000
Property	72,000
Long-term borrowings	51,000
Trade receivables	48,000
Equity at 1 October 2009	117,500
Cash in hand	1,500
Motor vehicles	15,000
Fixtures and fittings	9,000
Profit for the year to 30 September 2010	18,000
Drawings for the year to 30 September 2010	15,000

Required:
Prepare a statement of financial position for the business using the standard layout illustrated in Example 2.5.

Capturing a moment in time

As we have already seen, the statement of financial position reflects the assets, equity and liabilities of a business at *a specified point in time*. It has been compared to a photograph. A photograph 'freezes' a particular moment in time and will represent the situation only at that moment. Hence, events may be quite different immediately before and immediately after the photograph was taken. When examining a statement of financial position, therefore, it is important to establish the date for which it has been drawn up. This information should be prominently displayed in the heading to the statement, as shown above in Examples 2.5 and 2.6. When we are trying to assess current financial position, the more recent the statement of financial position date, the better.

A business will normally prepare a statement of financial position as at the close of business on the last day of its annual reporting period. In the UK, businesses are free to choose their accounting year. When making a decision on which year-end date to choose, commercial convenience can often be a deciding factor. For example, a business operating in the retail trade may choose to have a year-end date early in the calendar year (for example, 31 January) because trade tends to be slack during that period and more staff time is available to help with the tasks involved in the preparation of the annual financial statements (such as checking the amount of inventories held). Since trade is slack, it is also a time when the amount of inventories held by the retail business is likely to be unusually low as compared with other times of the year. Thus the statement of financial position, though showing a fair view of what it purports to show, may not show a picture of what is more typically the position of the business over the rest of the year.

The role of accounting conventions

As we saw in Chapter 1, accounting has a number of rules or conventions that have evolved over time. They have evolved as attempts to deal with practical problems experienced by preparers and users of financial statements, rather than to reflect some theoretical ideal. In preparing the statements of financial position earlier, we have followed various accounting conventions, though they have not been explicitly mentioned. We shall now identify and discuss the major conventions that we have applied.

Business entity convention

For accounting purposes, the business and its owner(s) are treated as being quite separate and distinct. This is why owners are treated as being claimants against their own business in respect of their investment. The business entity convention must be distinguished from the legal position that may exist between businesses and their owners. For sole proprietorships and partnerships, the law does not make any distinction between the business and its owner(s). For limited companies, on the other hand, there is a clear legal distinction between the business and its owners. (As we shall see in Chapter 4, the limited company is regarded as having a separate legal existence.) For accounting purposes, these legal distinctions are irrelevant and the business entity convention applies to all businesses.

Historic cost convention

The historic cost convention holds that the value of assets shown on the statement of financial position should be based on their acquisition cost (that is, historic cost). This method of measuring asset value takes preference over other methods based on some form of current value. Many people, however, find the historic cost convention difficult to support, as outdated historic costs are unlikely to help in the assessment of the current financial position. It is often argued that recording assets at their current value would provide a more realistic view of financial position and would be relevant for a wide range of decisions. However, a system of measurement based on current values can present a number of problems.

The term 'current value' can be defined in different ways. It can be defined broadly as either the current replacement cost or the current realisable value (selling price) of an asset. These two types of valuation may result in quite different figures being produced to represent the current value of an item. Furthermore, the broad terms 'replacement cost' and 'realisable value' can be defined in different ways. We must therefore be clear about what kind of current value accounting we wish to use.

Current values, however defined, are often difficult to establish with any real degree of objectivity. Activity 2.10 illustrates the practical problems associated with current value accounting.

Activity 2.10

Plumber and Company has some motor vans that are used by staff when visiting customers' premises to carry out work. It is now the last day of the business's reporting period. If it were decided to show the vans on the statement of financial position at a current value (rather than a value based on their historic cost), how might the business arrive at a suitable value and how reliable would this figure be?

Two ways of deriving a current value are to find out:

– how much would have to be paid to buy vans of a similar type and condition (current replacement cost);
– how much a motor van dealer would pay for the vans, were the business to sell them (current realisable value).

Both options will normally rely on opinion and so a range of possible values could be produced for each. For example, both the cost to replace the vans and the proceeds of selling them is likely to vary from one dealer to another. Moreover, the range of values for each option could be significantly different from one option to the other. (The selling prices of the vans are likely to be lower than the amount required to replace them.) Thus, any value finally decided upon could arouse some debate.

The figures produced under a system of current value accounting may be heavily dependent on the opinion of managers. Unless these figures are capable of some form of independent verification, there is a danger that the financial statements will lose their credibility among users. The motor vans discussed in Activity 2.10 are less of a problem than many types of asset. There is a ready market for motor vans, which means that a value can be obtained by contacting a dealer. For a custom-built piece of equipment, however, identifying a replacement cost, or worse still a selling price, could be very difficult.

By reporting assets at their historic cost, it is argued that more reliable information is produced. Reporting in this way reduces the need for judgements, as the amount paid for a particular asset is usually a matter of demonstrable fact. Information based on past costs, however, may not always be relevant to the needs of users.

Later in the chapter, we shall consider the valuation of assets in the statement of financial position in more detail. We shall see that the historic cost convention is not always rigidly adhered to. Departures from this convention are becoming more frequent.

Prudence convention

→ The prudence convention holds that caution should be exercised when making accounting judgements. The application of this convention normally involves recording all losses at once and in full; this refers to both actual losses and expected losses. Profits, on the other hand, are recognised only when they actually arise. Greater emphasis is, therefore, placed on expected losses than on expected profits. To illustrate the application of this convention, let us assume that certain inventories held by a business prove unpopular with customers and so a decision is made to sell them below their original cost. The prudence convention requires that the expected loss from future sales be recognised immediately rather than when the goods are eventually sold. If, however, these inventories could have been sold above their original cost, profit would only be recognised at the time of sale.

The prudence convention evolved to counteract the excessive optimism of some managers and is designed to prevent an overstatement of financial position and performance. Applying this convention, however, requires judgement. This means that the way in which it is applied by preparers of financial statements may differ over time and between businesses. Where excessive prudence is applied, it will lead to an understatement of profits and financial position.

Activity 2.11

What might be the effect of applying excessive prudence on the quality of user decisions?

Being excessively prudent will tend to obscure the underlying financial reality and may lead to poor decisions being made. The owners, for example, may sell their stake in the business at a lower price than they would have received if a more balanced view of the financial health of the business had been presented.

In recent years, the prudence convention has weakened its grip on accounting and has become a less dominant force. Nevertheless, it remains an important convention.

Going concern convention

→ The going concern convention holds that the financial statements should be prepared on the assumption that a business will continue operations for the foreseeable future, unless there is evidence to the contrary. In other words, it is assumed that there is no intention, or need, to sell off the non-current assets of the business. Where a business is in financial difficulties, however, non-current assets may have to be sold in order to repay those who have enforceable claims against the business.

The realisable (sale) value of many non-current assets is often much lower than the values reported in the statement of financial position. Thus, if a forced sale of assets were to occur, significant losses would arise. These anticipated losses would need to be fully reported were a business's going concern status to be called into question. Where, however, there is no expectation that non-current assets need be sold, they can continue to be shown at their reported values.

Dual aspect convention

The dual aspect convention asserts that each transaction has two aspects, both of which will affect the statement of financial position. Thus, the purchase of a motor car for cash results in an increase in one asset (motor car) and a decrease in another (cash). The repayment of borrowings results in the decrease in a liability (borrowings) and the decrease in an asset (cash).

Activity 2.12

What are the two aspects of each of the following transactions?

1   Purchasing £1,000 of inventories on credit.
2   Owner withdrawing £2,000 in cash.
3   Paying a supplier for £1,000 of inventories bought on credit a few weeks earlier.

Your answer should be as follows:

1   Inventories increase by £1,000, trade payables increase by £1,000.
2   Equity reduces by £2,000, cash reduces by £2,000.
3   Trade payables reduce by £1,000, cash reduces by £1,000.

Recording the dual aspect of each transaction ensures that the statement of financial position will continue to balance.

Figure 2.3 summarises the main accounting conventions that exert an influence on the construction of the statement of financial position.

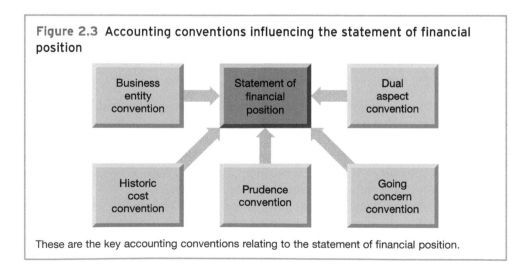

Figure 2.3 Accounting conventions influencing the statement of financial position

These are the key accounting conventions relating to the statement of financial position.

Money measurement

We saw earlier that a resource will only be regarded as an asset and included on the statement of financial position if it can be measured in monetary terms, with a reasonable degree of reliability. Some resources of a business, however, do not meet this criterion and so are excluded from the statement of financial position. As a result, the scope of the statement of financial position is limited.

Activity 2.13

Can you think of resources of a business that cannot usually be measured reliably in monetary terms?

In answering this activity you may have thought of the following:

- the quality of the human resources of the business
- the reputation of the business's products
- the location of the business
- the relationship a business enjoys with its customers.

There have been occasional attempts to measure and report resources of a business that are normally excluded from the statement of financial position so as to provide a more complete picture. These attempts, however, invariably fail the reliability test. We saw in Chapter 1 that a lack of reliability affects the quality of financial statements. Unreliable measurement can lead to inconsistency in reporting and can create uncertainty among users of the financial statements, which in turn undermines those statements' credibility.

We shall now discuss some key resources of a business that normally defy reliable measurement.

Goodwill and brands

Some intangible non-current assets are similar to tangible non-current assets: they have a clear and separate identity and the cost of acquiring the asset can be reliably measured. Examples normally include patents, trademarks, copyrights and licences. Other intangible non-current assets, however, are quite different. They lack a clear and separate identity and reflect a hotchpotch of attributes, which are part of the essence of the business. Goodwill and product brands are often examples of assets that lack a clear and separate identity.

The term 'goodwill' is often used to cover various attributes such as the quality of the products, the skill of employees and the relationship with customers. The term 'product brands' is also used to cover various attributes, such as the brand image, the quality of the product, the trademark and so on. Where goodwill and product brands have been generated internally by the business, it is often difficult to determine their cost or to measure their current market value or even to be clear that they really exist. They are, therefore, excluded from the statement of financial position.

When they are acquired through an 'arm's-length transaction', however, the problems of uncertainty about their existence and measurement are resolved. (An arm's-length transaction is one that is undertaken between two unconnected parties.) If goodwill is acquired when taking over another business, or if a business acquires a particular product brand from another business, these items will be separately identified and a price agreed for them. Under these circumstances, they can be regarded as assets (for accounting purposes) by the business that acquired them and included on the statement of financial position.

To agree a price for acquiring goodwill or product brands means that some form of valuation must take place and this raises the question as to how it is done. Usually, the valuation will be based on estimates of future earnings from holding the asset – a process that is fraught with difficulties. Nevertheless, a number of specialist businesses now exist that are prepared to take on this challenge. Real World 2.2 shows how one specialist business ranked and valued the top ten brands in the world for 2009.

Real World 2.2

Brand leaders

Millward Brown Optimor, part of WPP marketing services group, recently produced a report that ranked and valued the top ten world brands for 2009 as follows:

Ranking	Brand	Value ($m)
1	Google	100,039
2	Microsoft	76,249
3	Coca-Cola	67,625
4	IBM	66,622
5	McDonalds	66,575
6	Apple	63,113
7	China Mobile	61,283
8	GE (General Electric)	59,793
9	Vodafone	53,727
10	Marlboro	49,460

We can see that the valuations placed on the brands are quite staggering.

Source: Millward Brown Optimor, BrandZ Top 100 Most Valuable Global Brands 2009, www.millwardbrown.com.

Human resources

Attempts have been made to place a monetary measurement on the human resources of a business, but without any real success. There are, however, certain limited circumstances in which human resources are measured and reported in the statement of financial position. These circumstances normally arise with professional football clubs. While football clubs cannot own players, they can own the rights to the players' services. Where these rights are acquired by compensating other clubs for releasing the players from their contracts, an arm's-length transaction arises and the amounts paid provide a reliable basis for measurement. This means that the rights to services can be regarded as an asset of the club for accounting purposes (assuming, of course, the player will also bring benefits to the club).

Real World 2.3 describes how one leading club reports its investment in players on the statement of financial position.

Real World 2.3

Spurs players appear on the pitch and on the statement of financial position

Tottenham Hotspur Football Club (Spurs) has acquired several key players as a result of paying transfer fees to other clubs. In common with most UK football clubs, Spurs reports the cost of acquiring the rights to the players' services on its statement of financial position. The club's statement as at 30 June 2009 shows the cost of registering its squad of players at about £197 million. The club treats a proportion of each players' transfer fee as an expense each year. The exact proportion depends on the length of the particular player's contract.

The £197 million does not include 'home-grown' players such as Ledley King, because Spurs did not pay a transfer fee for them and so no clear-cut value can be placed on their services. On the surface, this is correct. However, due to capitalising cost of agents fee, a small element of Ledley King was included in the £197 million, and is allowed under FA rules. During the year to 30 June 2009, the club was very active in the transfer market and fifteen players were signed, including Jermain Defoe from Portsmouth. Defoe had previously been with Spurs and was only away at Portsmouth for 17–18 months. Fifteen players left the club (including Dimitar Berbatov to go to Manchester United), earning it transfer fees totalling £73 million.

The item of players' registrations is shown as an intangible asset in the statement of financial position as it is the rights to services, not the players, that are the assets. It is shown net of depreciation (or amortisation as it is usually termed for non-current assets). The carrying amount at 30 June 2009 was £128 million and represented 44 per cent of Spurs assets, as shown in the statement of financial position.

Source: Tottenham Hotspur plc Annual Report 2009.

Monetary stability

When using money as the unit of measurement, we normally fail to recognise the fact that it will change in value over time. In the UK and throughout much of the world, however, inflation has been a persistent problem. This has meant that the value of money has declined in relation to other assets. In past years, high rates of inflation have resulted in statements of financial position which were prepared on a historic cost basis reflecting figures for assets that were much lower than if current values were employed. Rates of inflation have been relatively low in recent years and so the disparity between historic cost values and current values has been less pronounced. Nevertheless, it can still be significant and has added fuel to the debate concerning how to measure asset values on the statement of financial position. It is to this issue that we now turn.

Valuing assets

As we saw earlier, when preparing the statement of financial position, the historic cost convention is normally applied for the reporting of assets. However, this point requires further explanation as, in practice, it is not simply a matter of recording each asset on the statement of financial position at its original cost. We shall see that things are a little more complex than this. Before discussing the valuation rules in some detail, however, we should point out that these rules are based on International Financial Reporting Standards, which are rules that are generally accepted throughout much of the world. The nature and role of financial reporting standards will be discussed in detail in Chapter 4.

Tangible non-current assets (property, plant and equipment)

Tangible non-current assets normally consist of property, plant and equipment. We shall refer to them in this way from now on. This is a rather broad term that includes items such as land and buildings, motor vehicles and fixtures and fittings. All of these items are, in essence, the 'tools' used by the business to generate wealth, that is, they are used to produce or supply goods and services or for administration purposes. They tend to be held for the longer term, which means for more than one reporting period.

Initially these items are recorded at their historic cost, which will include any amounts spent on getting them ready for use. However, they will normally be used up over time as a result of wear and tear, obsolescence and so on. The amount used up, which is referred to as *depreciation*, must be measured for each reporting period for which the assets are held. Although we shall leave a detailed examination of depreciation until Chapter 3, we need to know that when an asset has been depreciated, this must be reflected in the statement of financial position.

The total depreciation that has accumulated over the period since the asset was acquired must be deducted from its cost. This net figure (that is, the cost of the asset less the total depreciation to date) is referred to as the *carrying amount*. It is sometimes also known as *net book value* or *written-down value*. The procedure just described is not really a contravention of the historic cost convention. It is simply recognition of the fact that a proportion of the historic cost of the non-current asset has been consumed in the process of generating benefits for the business.

Although using historic cost (less any depreciation) is the standard or 'benchmark' treatment for recording these assets, an alternative is allowed. Property, plant and equipment can be recorded using fair values provided that these values can be measured reliably. The fair values, in this case, are the current market values (that is, the exchange values in an arm's-length transaction). The use of fair values, rather than depreciated cost figures, can provide users with more up-to-date information, which may well be more relevant to their needs. It may also place the business in a better light, as assets such as property (real estate) may have increased significantly in value over time. Of course, increasing the statement of financial position value of an asset does not make that asset more valuable. However, perceptions of the business may be altered by such a move.

One consequence of revaluing non-current assets is that the depreciation charge will be increased. This is because the depreciation charge is based on the increased value of the asset.

Real World 2.4 shows that one well-known business revalued its land and buildings and, by doing so, greatly improved the look of its statement of financial position.

Real World 2.4

Marks marks up land and buildings

The statement of financial position of Marks and Spencer plc, a major high street retailer, as at 28 March 2009 reveals land and buildings at a carrying amount, or net book value, of £2,458 million. These land and buildings were revalued by a firm of independent surveyors five years earlier and this has been reflected in subsequent statements of financial position. The effect of the revaluation was to give an uplift of £530.9 million against the previous carrying amount.

Source: Marks and Spencer plc Annual Report 2009, Notes to the financial statements, Note 14, www.marksandspencer.com.

Activity 2.14

Refer to the statement of financial position of Brie Manufacturing shown earlier in Example 2.5 (page 48). What would be the effect of revaluing the property to a figure of £110,000 on the statement of financial position?

The effect on the statement of financial position would be to increase the figure for the property to £110,000 and the gain on revaluation (that is, £110,000 – £45,000 = £65,000) would be added to equity, as it is the owner(s) who will benefit from the gain. The revised statement of financial position would therefore be as follows:

Brie Manufacturing
Statement of financial position as at 31 December 2009

	£000
ASSETS	
Non-current assets (property, plant and equipment)	
Property	110
Plant and equipment	30
Motor vans	19
	159
Current assets	
Inventories	23
Trade receivables	18
Cash at bank	12
	53
Total assets	212
EQUITY AND LIABILITIES	
Equity (60 + 65)	125
Non-current liabilities	
Long-term borrowings	50
Current liabilities	
Trade payables	37
Total equity and liabilities	212

Once assets are revalued, the frequency of revaluation then becomes an important issue as assets recorded at out-of-date values can mislead users. Using out-of-date revaluations on the statement of financial position is the worst of both worlds. It lacks the objectivity and verifiability of historic cost; it also lacks the realism of current values. Where fair values are used, revaluations should therefore be frequent enough to ensure that the carrying amount of the revalued asset does not differ materially from its fair value at the statement of financial position date.

When an item of property, plant or equipment is revalued on the basis of fair values, all assets within that particular group must be revalued. Thus, it is not acceptable to revalue some items of property but not others. Although this provides some degree of consistency within a particular group of assets, it does not, of course, prevent the statement of financial position from containing a mixture of valuations.

Intangible non-current assets

For these assets, the 'benchmark treatment' is, once again, that they are measured initially at historic cost. What follows, however, will depend on whether the asset has a finite or an infinite useful life. (Purchased goodwill is an example of an asset that could have an infinitely useful life, though this is not always the case.) Where the asset has a finite life, any amortisation following acquisition will be deducted from its cost.

Where, however, the asset has an infinite life, it will not be amortised. Instead, it will be tested annually to see whether there has been any fall in value. This point is discussed in more detail in the following section.

Once again, the alternative of revaluing intangible assets using fair values is available. However, this can only be used where an active market exists, which allows fair values to be properly determined. In practice, this is a rare occurrence.

The impairment of non-current assets

There is always a risk that both types of non-current asset (tangible and intangible) may suffer a significant fall in value. This may be due to factors such as changes in market conditions, technological obsolescence and so on. In some cases, this fall in value may lead to the carrying amount of the asset being higher than the amount that could be recovered from the asset through its continued use or through its sale. When this occurs, the asset value is said to be impaired and the general rule is to reduce the value on the statement of financial position to the recoverable amount. Unless this is done, the asset value will be overstated. This type of impairment in value should not be confused with routine depreciation, arising from, say, wear and tear due to normal usage.

Activity 2.15

With which one of the accounting conventions that we discussed earlier is this accounting treatment of impaired assets consistent?

The answer is the prudence convention, which states that actual or anticipated losses should be recognised in full.

In many situations, a business may use either historic cost, less any depreciation, or a value-based measure when reporting its non-current assets. However, where the value-based measure is the impaired value and is smaller than the historic-cost-based value, the business has no choice; the use of depreciated historic cost is not an option.

Real World 2.5 provides an example of where the application of the 'impairment rule', as it is called, resulted in huge write-downs (that is, reductions in the statement of financial position value of the assets) for one large business.

Real World 2.5

Painting a rosy picture

Akzo Nobel, the Dutch paints and chemicals company, on Tuesday defended its £8bn (€11.6bn) acquisition of ICI in 2007 after it took a €1.2bn (€1.5bn) impairment charge on the former UK industrial giant because of sharply lower paint sales.

The company saw the volume of paint sold fall by 10 per cent in the fourth quarter, with even steeper declines in Asia, one of the areas where ICI had been strong. This prompted the move to slash growth estimates and fair value for ICI.

'It's not a world of high growth any more, it's a world with completely different challenges,' said Hans Wijers, chief executive. 'We expect 2009 to be an uncertain year with a lot of volatility [and] with challenging volume circumstances.'

The €1.2bn impairment charge cuts into the €4.4bn of goodwill the company recorded when it acquired ICI and its Dulux brand name, but Akzo defended its previous assumptions as conservative.

'Could we have anticipated that the world economy would go down so much?' Mr Wijers said. 'I'm not sorry about [the ICI] transaction. It was the right thing to do at the right time and the company has become much stronger because of it.'

Source: adapted from 'Akzo Nobel defends ICI takeover', *The Financial Times*, 24/02/2009 (Steen, M.), copyright © The Financial Times Ltd.

We saw earlier that intangible, non-current assets with infinite lives must be tested annually to see whether there has been any impairment. Other non-current assets, however, must also be tested where events suggest that impairment has taken place.

Inventories

It is not only non-current assets that run the risk of a significant fall in value. The inventories of a business could also suffer this fate, which could be caused by factors such as reduced selling prices, obsolescence, deterioration, damage and so on. Where a fall in value means that the amount likely to be recovered from the sale of the inventories will be lower than their cost, this loss must be reflected in the statement of financial position. Thus, if the net realisable value (that is, selling price less any selling costs) falls below the historic cost of inventories held, the former should be used as the basis of valuation. This reflects, once again, the influence of the prudence convention on the statement of financial position.

Real World 2.6 reveals how one well-known business wrote down the inventories of one of its products following a sharp reduction in selling prices.

Real World 2.6

You're fired!

'You're fired!' is what some investors might like to tell Amstrad, run by Apprentice star Sir Alan Sugar. Shares in the company fell nearly 10 per cent as it revealed that sales of its much-vaunted videophone have failed to take off.

Amstrad launched the E3, a phone allowing users to hold video calls with each other, in a blaze of publicity last year. But, after cutting the price from £99 to £49, Amstrad sold just 61,000 E3s in the year to June and has taken a £5.7m stock (inventories) write-down.

Source: 'Amstrad (AMT)', *Investors Chronicle*, 7 October 2005.

The published financial statements of large businesses will normally show the basis on which inventories are valued. Real World 2.7 shows how one business reports this information.

Real World 2.7

Reporting inventories

The 2009 annual report of Ted Baker plc, a leading designer clothes brand, includes the following explanation concerning inventories:

> Inventories and work in progress are stated at the lower of cost and net realisable value. Cost includes materials, direct labour and inward transportation costs. Net realisable value is based on estimated selling price, less further costs expected to be incurred to completion and disposal. Provision is made for obsolete, slow moving or defective items where appropriate.

Source: Ted Baker plc Report and Accounts 2009, p. 44.

Meeting user needs

The statement of financial position is the oldest of the three main financial statements and many businesses prepare one on a regular basis, even where there is no regulation requiring it to be produced. This suggests that it is regarded as providing useful information. There are various ways in which the statement of financial position may help users, including the following:

- *It provides insights about how the business is financed and how its funds are deployed.* The statement of financial position shows how much finance is contributed by the owners and how much is contributed by outside lenders. It also shows the different kinds of assets acquired and how much is invested in each kind.
- *It can provide a basis for assessing the value of the business.* Since the statement of financial position lists, and places a value on, the various assets and claims, it can provide a starting point for assessing the value of the business. It is, however, severely limited in the extent to which it can do this. We have seen earlier that accounting rules may result in assets being shown at their historic cost and that the restrictive definition of assets may exclude certain business resources from the statement of financial position. Ultimately, the value of a business will be based on its ability to generate wealth in the future. Because of this, assets need to be valued on the basis of their wealth-generating potential. Also, other business resources that do not meet the restrictive definition of assets, such as brand values, need to be similarly valued and included.
- *Relationships between assets and claims can be assessed.* It can be useful to look at relationships between various statement of financial position items, for example the relationship between how much wealth is tied up in current assets and how much

is owed in the short term (current liabilities). From this relationship, we can see whether the business has sufficient short-term assets to cover its maturing obligations. We shall look at this and other relationships between statement of financial position items in some detail in Chapter 6.

■ *Performance can be assessed.* The effectiveness of a business in generating wealth can usefully be assessed against the amount of investment that was involved. Knowing the relationship between profit earned during a period and the value of the net assets invested can be helpful to many users, particularly owners and managers. This and similar relationships will also be explored in detail in Chapter 6.

Summary

The main points of this chapter may be summarised as follows.

The major financial statements

■ There are three major financial statements: the statement of cash flows, the income statement (profit and loss account) and the statement of financial position (balance sheet).

■ The statement of cash flows shows the cash movements over a particular period.

■ The income statement shows the wealth (profit) generated over a particular period.

■ The statement of financial position shows the accumulated wealth at a particular point in time.

The statement of financial position

■ This sets out the assets of the business, on the one hand, and the claims against those assets, on the other.

■ Assets are resources of the business that have certain characteristics, such as the ability to provide future benefits.

■ Claims are obligations on the part of the business to provide cash, or some other benefit, to outside parties.

■ Claims are of two types: equity and liabilities.

■ Equity represents the claim(s) of the owner(s) and liabilities represent the claims of others, apart from the owner.

■ The statement of financial position reflects the accounting equation:

$$\text{Assets} = \text{Equity} + \text{Liabilities}$$

Classification of assets and liabilities

■ Assets are normally categorised as being current or non-current.

■ Current assets are cash or near cash or are held for sale or consumption in the normal course of business, or for trading, or for the short term.

- Non-current assets are assets that are not current assets. They are normally held for the long-term operations of the business.

- Liabilities are normally categorised as being current or non-current liabilities.

- Current liabilities represent amounts due in the normal course of the business's operating cycle, or are held for trading, or are to be settled within a year of, or cannot be deferred for at least a year after, the end of the reporting period.

- Non-current liabilities represent amounts due that are not current liabilities.

Statement of financial position layouts

- The standard layout begins with assets at the top of the statement of financial position and places equity and liabilities underneath.

- A variation of the standard layout begins with the assets at the top of the statement of financial position. From the total assets figure are deducted the non-current and current liabilities to arrive at a net assets figure. Equity is placed underneath.

Accounting conventions

- Accounting conventions are the rules of accounting that have evolved to deal with practical problems experienced by those preparing financial statements.

- The main conventions relating to the statement of financial position include business entity, historic cost, prudence, going concern and dual aspect.

Money measurement

- Using money as the unit of measurement limits the scope of the statement of financial position.

- Certain resources such as goodwill, product brands and human resources are difficult to measure. An 'arm's-length transaction' is normally required before such assets can be reliably measured and reported on the statement of financial position.

- Money is not a stable unit of measurement – it changes in value over time.

Asset valuation

- The 'benchmark treatment' is to show property, plant and equipment at historic cost less any amounts written off for depreciation. However, fair values may be used rather than depreciated cost.

- The 'benchmark treatment' for intangible non-current assets is to show the items at historic cost. Only assets with a finite life will be amortised (depreciated) and fair values will rarely be used.

- Where the recoverable amount from non-current assets is below their carrying amount, this lower amount is reflected in the statement of financial position.

- Inventories are shown at the lower of cost or net realisable value.

418 Accounting and Finance for Non-Specialists

The usefulness of the statement of financial position

- It shows how finance has been raised and how it has been deployed.
- It provides a basis for valuing the business, though the conventional statement of financial position can only be a starting point.
- Relationships between various statement of financial position items can usefully be explored.
- Relationships between wealth generated and wealth invested can be helpful indicators of business effectiveness.

→ Key terms

statement of cash flows
income statement
statement of financial position
inventories
final accounts
assets
claims
tangible assets
intangible assets
equity
liabilities
trade payables
current assets

trade receivables
non-current (fixed) assets
current liabilities
non-current liabilities
accounting conventions
business entity convention
historic cost convention
prudence convention
going concern convention
dual aspect convention
property, plant and equipment
fair values

Further reading

If you would like to explore the topics covered in this chapter in more depth, we recommend the following books:

Elliott, B. and Elliott, J., *Financial Accounting and Reporting* (13th edn), Financial Times Prentice Hall, 2010, chapters 16 and 18.

IASC Foundation Education, *A Guide through IFRS 2009*, July 2009, IAS 16, IAS 36 and IAS 38.

KPMG, *Insights into IFRS* (6th edn, 2009/10), Sweet and Maxwell, 2009, sections 1.2, 3.2, 3.3, 3.8 and 3.10.

Review questions

2.1 An accountant prepared a statement of financial position for a business. In this statement, the equity of the owner was shown next to the liabilities. This confused the owner, who argued: 'My equity is my major asset and so should be shown as an asset on the statement of financial position.' How would you explain this misunderstanding to the owner?

2.2 'The statement of financial position shows how much a business is worth.' Do you agree with this statement? Explain the reasons for your response.

2.3 What is meant by the accounting equation? How does the form of this equation differ between the two statement of financial position layouts mentioned in the chapter?

2.4 In recent years there have been attempts to place a value on the 'human assets' of a business in order to derive a figure that can be included on the statement of financial position. Do you think humans should be treated as assets? Would 'human assets' meet the conventional definition of an asset for inclusion on the statement of financial position?

Exercises

Exercise 2.5 is more advanced than Exercises 2.1 to 2.4.

> If you wish to try more exercises, visit the website at www.myaccountinglab.com.

2.1 On Thursday, the fourth day of his business venture, Paul, the street trader in wrapping paper (see earlier in the chapter, pages 31–34), bought more inventories for £53 cash. During the day he sold inventories that had cost £33 for a total of £47.

Required:
Draw up the three financial statements for Paul's business venture for Thursday.

2.2 While on holiday in Bridlington, Helen had her credit cards and purse stolen from the beach while she was swimming. She was left with only £40, which she had kept in her hotel room, but she had three days of her holiday remaining. She was determined to continue her holiday and decided to make some money to enable her to do so. She decided to sell orange juice to holidaymakers using the local beach. On day 1 she bought 80 cartons of orange juice at £0.50 each for cash and sold 70 of these at £0.80 each. On the following day she bought 60 cartons at £0.50 each for cash and sold 65 at £0.80 each. On the third and final day she bought another 60 cartons at £0.50 each for cash. However, it rained and, as a result, business was poor. She managed to sell 20 at £0.80 each but sold off the rest of her inventories at £0.40 each.

Required:
Prepare an income statement and statement of cash flows for each day's trading and prepare a statement of financial position at the end of each day's trading.

2.3 On 1 March, Joe Conday started a new business. During March he carried out the following transactions:

1 March	Deposited £20,000 in a bank account.
2 March	Bought fixtures and fittings for £6,000 cash and inventories £8,000 on credit.
3 March	Borrowed £5,000 from a relative and deposited it in the bank.
4 March	Bought a motor car for £7,000 cash and withdrew £200 in cash for his own use.
5 March	A further motor car costing £9,000 was bought. The motor car bought on 4 March was given in part exchange at a value of £6,500. The balance of purchase price for the new car was paid in cash.
6 March	Conday won £2,000 in a lottery and paid the amount into the business bank account. He also repaid £1,000 of the borrowings.

Required:
Draw up a statement of financial position for the business at the end of each day.

2.4 The following is a list of the assets and claims of Crafty Engineering Ltd at 30 June last year:

	£000
Trade payables	86
Motor vehicles	38
Long-term borrowing from Industrial Finance Co.	260
Equipment and tools	207
Short-term borrowings	116
Inventories	153
Property	320
Trade receivables	185

Required:
(a) Prepare the statement of financial position of the business as at 30 June last year from the above information using the standard layout. (*Hint*: There is a missing item that needs to be deduced and inserted.)
(b) Discuss the significant features revealed by this financial statement.

2.5 The statement of financial position of a business at the start of the week is as follows:

	£
ASSETS	
Property	145,000
Furniture and fittings	63,000
Inventories	28,000
Trade receivables	33,000
Total assets	**269,000**
EQUITY AND LIABILITIES	
Equity	203,000
Short-term borrowing (bank overdraft)	43,000
Trade payables	23,000
Total equity and liabilities	**269,000**

During the week the following transactions take place:

(a) Inventories sold for £11,000 cash; these inventories had cost £8,000.
(b) Sold inventories for £23,000 on credit; these inventories had cost £17,000.
(c) Received cash from trade receivables totalling £18,000.
(d) The owners of the business introduced £100,000 of their own money, which was placed in the business bank account.
(e) The owners brought a motor van, valued at £10,000, into the business.
(f) Bought inventories on credit for £14,000.
(g) Paid trade payables £13,000.

Required:
Show the statement of financial position after all of these transactions have been reflected.

Chapter 3

Measuring and reporting financial performance

Introduction

In this chapter, we continue our examination of the major financial statements by looking at the income statement. This statement was briefly considered in Chapter 2 and we shall now look at it in some detail. We shall see how it is prepared and how it links with the statement of financial position. We shall also consider some of the key measurement problems to be faced when preparing the income statement.

Learning outcomes

When you have completed this chapter, you should be able to:

■ discuss the nature and purpose of the income statement;

■ prepare an income statement from relevant financial information and interpret the information that it contains;

■ discuss the main recognition and measurement issues that must be considered when preparing the income statement;

■ explain the main accounting conventions underpinning the income statement.

What does it mean?

Tate and Lyle plc, whose business is sweeteners, starches and sugar refining, reported sales revenue of £3,553 million and a profit of £70 million for the year ended on 31 March 2009. To understand fully the significance of these figures, we must be clear about the nature of revenue and profit. This means that we must be able to answer questions such as:

- Does the sales revenue of £3,553 million represent the cash generated from sales for the period?
- What is the relationship between the sales revenue and the profit for the period?
- Can the profit for the period of £70 million be measured with complete accuracy and certainty?
- Does the profit figure of £70 million mean that the business had £70 million more in the bank at the end of the year than it had at the beginning?
- How can the sales revenue and profit figures help in assessing performance?

The answers to these and other questions are covered in the chapter.

The income statement

In Chapter 2 we considered the statement of financial position (balance sheet). We saw that it sets out the wealth of a business, at a particular moment in time, and who contributed that wealth. However, it is not usually enough for users of financial statements to have information relating only to this aspect of financial health. Businesses exist to generate wealth, or profit, and it is the profit generated *during a period* that is the concern of many users. The main purpose of the income statement – or profit and loss account, as it is sometimes called – is to measure and report how much profit (wealth) the business has generated over a period. It also helps users to gain some impression of how that profit was made. As with the statement of financial position, which we examined in Chapter 2, the principles of preparation are the same irrespective of whether the income statement is for a sole proprietorship business or for a limited company.

The measurement of profit requires that the total revenue of the business, generated during a particular period, is identified. Revenue is simply a measure of the inflow of economic benefits arising from the ordinary activities of a business. These benefits will result in either an increase in assets (such as cash or amounts owed to the business by its customers) or a decrease in liabilities. Different forms of business enterprise will generate different forms of revenue. Some examples of the different forms that revenue can take are as follows:

- sales of goods (for example, by a manufacturer)
- fees for services (for example, of a solicitor)
- subscriptions (for example, of a club)
- interest received (for example, on an investment fund).

Real World 3.1 shows the various forms of revenue generated by a leading football club.

Real World 3.1

Gunning for revenue

Arsenal Football Club generated total revenue of £313 million for the year ended 31 May 2009. Like other leading clubs, it relies on various forms of revenue to sustain its success. Figure 3.1 shows the contribution of each form of revenue for the year. The high level of revenue from property development is unusual for a football club, even for Arsenal. It arises from the fact that the club is developing its former home Highbury Stadium for residential accommodation following its move to the Emirates Stadium.

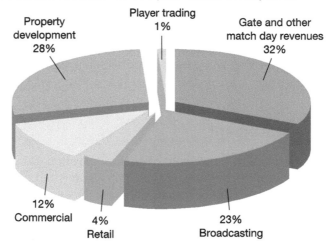

Figure 3.1 Arsenal's revenue for the year ended 31 May 2009

Player trading 1%

Property development 28%

Gate and other match day revenues 32%

12% Commercial

4% Retail

23% Broadcasting

Gate receipts and broadcasting tend to be Arsenal's main forms of revenue, although commercial activities (including sponsorship and events) are also significant. During this particular year, there was a lot of income from property development. Between them, gate receipts, broadcasting and commercial activities accounted for 93 per cent of total revenue other than property development.

Source: based on information in Arsenal Holdings plc Annual Report 2009, Note 3 to the financial statements.

The total expenses relating to each period must also be identified. Expense is really the opposite of revenue. It represents the outflow of economic benefits arising from the ordinary activities of a business. This loss of benefits will result in either a decrease in assets (such as cash) or an increase in liabilities (such as amounts owed to suppliers). Expenses are incurred in the process of generating, or attempting to generate, revenue. The nature of the business will again determine the type of expenses that will be incurred. Examples of some of the more common types of expenses are:

■ the cost of buying, or making, the goods that are sold during the period concerned – known as *cost of sales* or *cost of goods sold*
■ salaries and wages

- rent and rates
- motor vehicle running expenses
- insurance
- printing and stationery
- heat and light
- telephone and postage.

The *income statement* simply shows the total revenue generated during a particular period and deducts from this the total expenses incurred in generating that revenue. The difference between the total revenue and total expenses will represent either profit (if revenue exceeds expenses) or loss (if expenses exceed revenue). Thus, we have:

Profit (or loss) for the period = Total revenue for the period less Total expenses incurred in generating that revenue

The period over which profit or loss is normally measured is usually known as the reporting period, but is sometimes called the 'accounting period' or 'financial period'.

Different roles

The income statement and the statement of financial position should not be viewed in any way as substitutes for one another. Rather they should be seen as performing different roles. The statement of financial position, as we have seen, sets out the position at a single moment in time: it is a 'snapshot' of the make-up of the wealth held by the business. The income statement, on the other hand, is concerned with the *flow* of wealth over a period of time. The two statements are, however, closely related.

The income statement links the statements of financial position at the beginning and the end of a reporting period. Thus, at the start of a new reporting period, the statement of financial position shows the opening wealth position of the business. After an appropriate period, an income statement is prepared to show the wealth generated over that period. A statement of financial position is then also prepared to reveal the new wealth position at the end of the period. This statement of financial position will reflect the changes in wealth that have occurred since the previous statement of financial position was drawn up.

We saw in Chapter 2 (page 44) that the effect on the statement of financial position of making a profit (or loss) means that the accounting equation can be extended as follows:

Assets (at the end of the period) = Equity (amount at the start of the period + profit (or − loss) for the period) + Liabilities (at the end of the period)

(This is assuming that the owner makes no injections or withdrawals of equity during the period.)

The amount of profit or loss for the period affects the statement of financial position as an adjustment to equity.

The above equation can be extended to:

Assets (at the end of the period) = Equity (amount at the start of the period)
+ (sales revenue − expenses for the period)
+ Liabilities (at the end of the period)

In theory, it would be possible to calculate the profit (or loss) for the period by making all adjustments for revenue and expenses through the equity section of the statement of financial position. However, this would be rather cumbersome. A better solution is to have an 'appendix' to the equity section, in the form of an income statement. By deducting expenses from revenue for the period, the income statement derives the profit (or loss) by which the equity figure in the statement of financial position needs to be adjusted. This profit (or loss) figure represents the net effect of trading for the period. Through this 'appendix', users are presented with a detailed and more informative view of performance.

Income statement layout

The layout of the income statement will vary according to the type of business to which it relates. To illustrate an income statement, let us consider the case of a retail business (that is, a business that buys goods in their completed state and resells them). This type of business usually has straightforward operations and, as a result, the income statement is relatively easy to understand.

Example 3.1 sets out a typical layout for the income statement of a retail business.

Example 3.1

Better-Price Stores
Income statement for the year ended 31 October 2009

	£
Sales revenue	232,000
Cost of sales	(154,000)
Gross profit	78,000
Salaries and wages	(24,500)
Rent and rates	(14,200)
Heat and light	(7,500)
Telephone and postage	(1,200)
Insurance	(1,000)
Motor vehicle running expenses	(3,400)
Depreciation – fixtures and fittings	(1,000)
Depreciation – motor van	(600)
Operating profit	24,600
Interest received from investments	2,000
Interest on borrowings	(1,100)
Profit for the year	25,500

We saw in Chapter 2 that brackets are used to denote when an item is to be deducted. This convention is used by accountants in preference to + or − signs and will be used throughout the text.

The above income statement provides three measures of profit. Let us now consider each.

Gross profit

The first part of the income statement is concerned with calculating the gross profit for the period. We can see that revenue, which arises from selling the goods, is the first item to appear. The cost of sales (also called cost of goods sold) for the period is deducted from sales revenue. This gives the gross profit, which represents the profit from buying and selling goods, without taking into account any other revenues or expenses associated with the business.

Operating profit

Other expenses (overheads) that have been incurred in operating the business (salaries and wages, rent and rates and so on) are then deducted from the gross profit.

The resulting figure is known as the operating profit for the reporting period. This represents the wealth generated during the period from the normal activities of the business. It does not take account of any income that the business may have from activities that are not included in its normal operations. Better-Price Stores in Example 3.1 is a retailer, so the interest on some spare cash that the business has invested is not part of its operating profit. Costs of financing the business are also ignored in the calculation of the operating profit.

Profit for the year

Having established the operating profit, we add any non-operating income (such as interest receivable) and deduct any interest payable on borrowings made by the business, to arrive at the profit for the year (or net profit). This is the income that is attributable to the owner(s) of the business and which will be added to the equity figure in the statement of financial position. As can be seen, profit for the year is a residual: that is, the amount remaining after deducting all expenses incurred in generating the sales revenue for the period and taking account of non-operating income.

Further issues

Having set out the main principles involved in preparing an income statement, we need to consider some further points.

Cost of sales

The cost of sales (or cost of goods sold) figure for a period can be identified in different ways. In some businesses, the cost of sales amount for each individual sale is identified at the time of the transaction. Each item of sales revenue is closely matched with the relevant cost of that sale and so identifying the cost of sales figure for inclusion in the income statement is not a problem. Many large retailers (for example, supermarkets) have point-of-sale (checkout) devices that not only record each sale but also simultaneously pick up the cost of the goods that are the subject of the particular sale. Other businesses that sell a relatively small number of high-value items (for example, an engineering business that produces custom-made equipment) also tend to match sales revenue with the cost of the goods sold, at the time of the sale. However, some businesses (for example, small retailers) do not usually find it practical to match each sale to a particular cost of sales figure as the reporting period progresses. Instead, therefore, they identify the cost of sales figure at the end of the reporting period.

Deriving the cost of sales after the end of the reporting period

To understand how this is done, we need to remember that the cost of sales figure represents the cost of goods that were *sold* by the business during the period rather than the cost of goods that were *bought* by that business during the period. Part of the goods bought during a particular period may remain in the business, as inventories, at the reporting period end. These will normally be sold in the next period. To derive the cost of sales for a period, we need to know the amount of opening and closing inventories for the period and the cost of goods bought during the period. Example 3.2 illustrates how the cost of sales is derived.

Example 3.2

Better-Price Stores, which we considered in Example 3.1 above, began the annual reporting period with unsold inventories of £40,000 and during that year bought inventories at a cost of £189,000. At the end of the year, unsold inventories of £75,000 were still held by the business.

The opening inventories at the beginning of the year *plus* the goods bought during the year will represent the total goods available for resale. Thus:

	£
Opening inventories	40,000
Purchases (goods bought)	189,000
Goods available for resale	229,000

The closing inventories will represent that portion of the total goods available for resale that remains unsold at the end of the year. Thus, the cost of goods actually sold during the annual reporting period must be the total goods available for resale *less* the inventories remaining at the end of the year. That is:

	£
Goods available for resale	229,000
Closing inventories	(75,000)
Cost of sales (or cost of goods sold)	154,000

These calculations are sometimes shown on the face of the income statement as in Example 3.3.

Example 3.3

	£	£
Sales revenue		232,000
Cost of sales:		
Opening inventories	40,000	
Purchases (goods bought)	189,000	
Closing inventories	(75,000)	(154,000)
Gross profit		78,000

This is just an expanded version of the first section of the income statement for Better-Price Stores, as set out in Example 3.1. We have simply included the additional information concerning inventories balances and purchases for the year provided in Example 3.2.

Classifying expenses

The classifications for the revenue and expense items, as with the classifications of various assets and claims in the statement of financial position, are often a matter of judgement by those who design the accounting system. Thus, the income statement set out in Example 3.1 could have included the insurance expense with the telephone and postage expense under a single heading – say, 'general expenses'. Such decisions are normally based on how useful a particular classification will be to users. This will usually mean that expense items of material size will be shown separately. For businesses that trade as limited companies, however, there are rules that dictate the classification of various items appearing in the financial statements for external reporting purposes. These rules will be discussed in Chapter 4.

Activity 3.1

The following information relates to the activities of H & S Retailers for the year ended 30 April 2010:

	£
Motor vehicle running expenses	1,200
Closing inventories	3,000
Rent and rates payable	5,000
Motor vans – cost less depreciation	6,300
Annual depreciation – motor vans	1,500
Heat and light	900
Telephone and postage	450
Sales revenue	97,400
Goods purchased	68,350
Insurance	750
Loan interest payable	620
Balance at bank	4,780
Salaries and wages	10,400
Opening inventories	4,000

> Prepare an income statement for the year ended 30 April 2010. (*Hint*: Not all items listed should appear in the income statement.)

Your answer to this activity should be as follows:

H & S Retailers
Income statement for the year ended 30 April 2010

	£	£
Sales revenue		97,400
Cost of sales:		
Opening inventories	4,000	
Purchases	68,350	
Closing inventories	(3,000)	(69,350)
Gross profit		28,050
Salaries and wages		(10,400)
Rent and rates		(5,000)
Heat and light		(900)
Telephone and postage		(450)
Insurance		(750)
Motor vehicle running expenses		(1,200)
Depreciation – motor vans		(1,500)
Operating profit		7,850
Loan interest		(620)
Profit for the year		7,230

Note that neither the motor vans nor the bank balance are included in this statement, because they are both assets and so neither revenues nor expenses.

The reporting period

We have seen already that for reporting to those outside the business, a financial reporting cycle of one year is the norm, though some large businesses produce a half-yearly, or interim, financial statement to provide more frequent feedback on progress. For those who manage a business, however, it is probably essential to have much more frequent feedback on performance. Thus it is quite common for income statements to be prepared on a quarterly, a monthly, a weekly or even a daily basis in order to show how things are progressing.

Recognising revenue

A key issue in the measurement of profit concerns the point at which revenue is recognised. Revenue arising from the sale of goods or provision of a service could be recognised at various points. Where, for example, a motor car dealer receives an order for a new car from one of its customers, the associated revenue could be recognised by the dealer:

- at the time that the order is placed by the customer;
- at the time that the car is collected by the customer; or
- at the time that the customer pays the dealer.

These three points could well be quite far apart, particularly where the order relates to a specialist car that is sold to the customer on credit.

The point chosen is not simply a matter of academic interest: it can have a profound impact on the total revenues recognised for a particular reporting period. This, in turn, could have a profound effect on profit. If the sale transaction straddled the end of a reporting period, the choice made between the three possible times for recognising the revenue could determine whether it is included as revenue of the earlier reporting period or the later one.

When dealing with the sale of goods or the provision of services, the main criteria for recognising revenue are that:

- the amount of revenue can be measured reliably; and
- it is probable that the economic benefits will be received.

An additional criterion, however, must be applied where the revenue comes from the sale of goods, which is that:

- ownership and control of the items should pass to the buyer.

Activity 3.2 provides an opportunity to apply these criteria to a practical problem.

Activity 3.2

A manufacturing business sells goods on credit (that is, the customer pays for the goods some time after they are received). Below are four points in the production/selling cycle at which revenue might be recognised by the business:

1 when the goods are produced;
2 when an order is received from the customer;
3 when the goods are delivered to, and accepted by, the customer;
4 when the cash is received from the customer.

   A significant amount of time may elapse between these different points. At what point do you think the business should recognise revenue?

All of the three criteria mentioned above will usually be fulfilled at Point 3: when the goods are passed to, and accepted by, the customer. This is because:

- the selling price and the settlement terms will have been agreed and therefore the amount of revenue can be reliably measured;
- delivery and acceptance of the goods leads to ownership and control passing to the buyer;
- transferring ownership gives the seller legally enforceable rights that makes it probable that the buyer will pay.

We can see that the effect of applying these criteria is that a sale on credit is usually recognised *before* the cash is received. Thus, the total sales revenue figure shown in the income statement may include sales transactions for which the cash has yet to be received. The total sales revenue figure in the income statement for a period will often, therefore, be different from the total cash received from sales during that period.

For cash sales (that is sales where cash is paid at the same time as the goods are transferred), there will be no difference in timing between reporting sales revenue and the cash being received.

Real World 3.2 sets out the revenue recognition criteria for the travel business, TUI Travel plc (which owns First Choice, Thompson, Exodus and many other well-known names). We can see that, although clients may pay for flights or holidays some time before they go, any money received in advance of the departure date, or use of the service, is not treated as revenue until later.

Real World 3.2

Selling point

(i) Revenue recognition

Revenue is recognised in the income statement when the significant risks and rewards of ownership have been transferred to the buyer.

Travel agency commissions and other revenues received from the sale of third-party products are recognised when they are earned, typically on receipt of final payment. Revenue in respect of in-house product is recognised on the date of departure. Revenue from individual travel modules directly booked by the customer with airline, hotels and incoming agencies is recognised when the customer departs or uses the respective service.

No revenue is recognised if there are significant uncertainties regarding recovery of the consideration due, associated costs or possible return of goods.

(ii) Client monies received in advance (deferred income)

Client monies received at the balance sheet (statement of financial position) date relating to holidays commencing and flights departing after the year end is deferred and included within trade and other payables.

Source: TUI Travel plc Annual Report and Accounts 2009, Notes to the consolidated statements, p. 4, www.tuitravelplc.com.

Long-term contracts

Some contracts, both for goods and for services, can last for more than one reporting period. If the business providing the goods or service were to wait until the contract is completely fulfilled before recognising revenue, the income statement could give a misleading impression of the wealth generated in the various reporting periods covered by the contract. This is a particular problem for businesses that undertake major long-term contracts, where a single contract could represent a large proportion of their total activities.

Construction contracts

Construction contracts often extend over a long period of time. Suppose that a customer enters into a contract with a builder to have a new factory built that will take three years to complete. In such a situation, it is possible to recognise revenue *before* the factory is completed provided that the building work can be broken down into a number of stages and each stage can be measured reliably. Let us assume that building the factory could be broken down into the following stages:

Stage 1 – clearing and levelling the land and putting in the foundations
Stage 2 – building the walls
Stage 3 – putting on the roof
Stage 4 – putting in the windows and completing all the interior work.

Each stage can be awarded a separate price with the total for all the stages being equal to the total contract price for the factory. This means that, as each stage is completed, the builder can recognise the price for that stage as revenue and bill the customer accordingly. This is provided that the outcome of the contract as a whole can be estimated reliably.

If the builder were to wait until the factory was completed before recognising revenue, the income statement covering the final year of the contract would recognise all of the revenue on the contract, and the income statements for each preceding year would recognise no revenue. This would give a misleading impression, as it would not reflect the work done during each period.

Real World 3.3 sets out the revenue recognition criteria for one large business engaged in long-term contracts.

Real World 3.3

Contract revenue

AMEC plc is an international business offering consultancy, engineering and project management services. The point at which revenue on long-term contracts is recognised by the business is as follows:

> As soon as the outcome of a long-term contract can be estimated reliably, contract revenue and expenses are recognised in the income statement in proportion to the stage of completion of the contract. The stage of completion is assessed by reference to surveys of work performed. When the outcome of a contract cannot be estimated reliably, revenue is recognised only to the extent of contract costs incurred that it is probable will be recoverable, and contract costs are expensed as incurred. An expected loss on a contract is recognised immediately in the income statement.

Source: AMEC plc Annual Report and Accounts 2009, Notes to Consolidated Accounts, p. 68.

Services

Revenue from contracts for services may also be recognised in stages. Suppose a consultancy business has a contract to install a new computer system for the government, which will take several years to complete. Revenue can be recognised *before* the contract is completed as long as the contract can be broken down into stages and the particular stages of completion can be measured reliably. This is really the same approach as that used in the construction contract mentioned above.

Sometimes a continuous service is provided to a customer; for example, a telecommunications business may provide open access to the Internet to those who subscribe to the service. In this case, revenue is usually recognised as the service is rendered. Benefits from providing the service are usually assumed to flow evenly over time and so revenue is recognised evenly over the subscription period.

Where it is not possible to break down a service into particular stages of completion, or to assume that benefits from providing the service accrue evenly over time, revenue will not usually be recognised until the service is fully completed. A solicitor handling a house purchase for a client would normally be one such example.

Real World 3.4 provides an example of how one major business recognises revenue from providing services.

Real World 3.4

Sky-high broadcasting revenue

British Sky Broadcasting Group plc is a major satellite broadcaster that generates various forms of revenue. Here are the ways in which some of its revenues are recognised:

- Pay-per-view revenues – when the event (movie or football match) is viewed
- Subscription services, including Sky TV and Sky Broadband – as the services are provided
- Advertising revenues – when the advertising is broadcast
- Installation, hardware and service revenue – when the goods and services are delivered.

Source: based on information in British Sky Broadcasting Group plc Annual Report and Accounts 2009, p. 78.

When a service is provided, there will normally be a timing difference between the recognition of revenue and the receipt of cash. Revenue for providing services is often recognised before the cash is received, as with the sale of goods on credit. However, there are occasions when it is the other way around, usually because the service provider demands payment before rendering the service.

Activity 3.3

Can you think of any examples where cash may be demanded in advance of a service being provided? (*Hint*: Try to think of services that you may use.)

Examples of cash being received in advance of the service being provided may include:

- rent received from letting premises
- telephone line rental charges
- TV licence (BBC) or subscription (for example, Sky) fees
- subscriptions received for the use of health clubs or golf clubs.

You may have thought of others.

Recognising expenses

Having decided on the point at which revenue is recognised, we can now turn to the issue of the recognition of expenses. The matching convention of accounting is designed to provide guidance concerning the recognition of expenses. This convention states that expenses should be matched to the revenue that they helped to generate. In other words, the expenses associated with a particular item of revenue must be taken into account in the same reporting period as that in which the item of revenue is included. Applying this convention may mean that a particular expense reported in the income statement for a period may not be the same figure as the cash paid for that item during the period. The expense reported might be either more or less than the cash paid during the period. Let us consider two examples that illustrate this point.

When the expense for the period is more than the cash paid during the period

Example 3.4

Domestic Ltd sells household electrical appliances. It pays its sales staff a commission of 2 per cent of sales revenue generated. Total sales revenue for last year amounted to £300,000. This will mean that the commission to be paid in respect of the sales for the year will be £6,000. However, by the end of the year, the amount of sales commission that had actually been paid to staff was £5,000. If the business reported only the amount paid, it would mean that the income statement would not reflect the full expense for the year. This would contravene the matching convention because not all of the expenses associated with the revenue of the year would have been matched in the income statement. This will be remedied as follows:

- Sales commission expense in the income statement will include the amount paid plus the amount outstanding (that is, £6,000 = £5,000 + £1,000).
- The amount outstanding (£1,000) represents an outstanding liability at the end of the year and will be included under the heading accrued expenses, or 'accruals', in the statement of financial position. As this item will have to be paid within twelve months of the year end, it will be treated as a current liability.
- The cash will already have been reduced to reflect the commission paid (£5,000) during the period.

These points are illustrated in Figure 3.2.

In principle, all expenses should be matched to the period in which the sales revenue to which they relate is reported. However, it is sometimes difficult to match certain expenses to sales revenue in the same precise way that we have matched

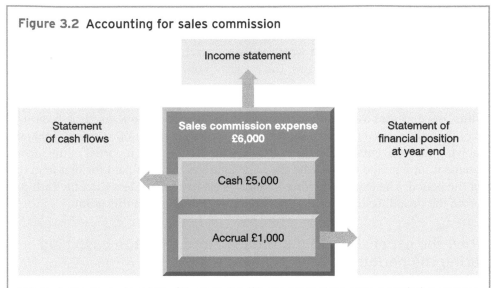

Figure 3.2 Accounting for sales commission

This illustrates the main points of Example 3.4. We can see that the sales commission expense of £6,000 (which appears in the income statement) is made up of a cash element of £5,000 and an accrued element of £1,000. The cash element appears in the statement of cash flows and the accrued element will appear as a year-end liability in the statement of financial position.

sales commission to sales revenue. It is unlikely, for example, that electricity charges incurred can be linked directly to particular sales in this way. As a result, the electricity charges incurred by, say, a retailer would be matched to the *period* to which they relate. Example 3.5 illustrates this.

Example 3.5

Domestic Ltd, a retailer, has reached the end of its annual reporting period and has only paid for electricity for the first three-quarters of the year (amounting to £1,900). This is simply because the electricity company has yet to send out bills for the quarter that ends on the same date as Domestic Ltd's year end. The amount of Domestic Ltd's bill for the last quarter is £500. In this situation, the amount of the electricity expense outstanding is dealt with as follows:

■ Electricity expense in the income statement will include the amount paid, plus the amount of the bill for the last quarter (that is, £1,900 + £500 = £2,400) in order to cover the whole year.

■ The amount of the outstanding bill (£500) represents a liability at the end of the year and will be included under the heading 'accruals' or 'accrued expenses' in the statement of financial position. This item would normally have to be paid within twelve months of the year end and will, therefore, be treated as a current liability.

- The cash will already have been reduced to reflect the electricity paid (£1,900) during the period.

This treatment will mean that the correct figure for the electricity expense for the year will be included in the income statement. It will also have the effect of showing that, at the end of the annual reporting period, Domestic Ltd owed the amount of the last quarter's electricity bill. Dealing with the outstanding amount in this way reflects the dual aspect of the item and will ensure that the accounting equation is maintained.

Domestic Ltd may wish to draw up its income statement before it is able to discover how much it owes for the last quarter's electricity. In this case it is quite normal to make a reasonable estimate of the amount of the bill and to use this estimated amount as described above.

Activity 3.4

How will the payment of the electricity bill for the last quarter be dealt with in the accounting records of Domestic Ltd?

When the electricity bill is eventually paid, it will be dealt with as follows:

- Reduce cash by the amount of the bill.
- Reduce the amount of the accrued expense as shown on the statement of financial position by the same amount.

If an estimated figure is used and there is a slight error in the estimate, a small adjustment (either negative or positive depending on the direction of the error) can be made to the following year's expense. Dealing with the estimation error in this way is not strictly correct, but the amount is likely to be insignificant.

Activity 3.5

Can you think of other expenses for a retailer, apart from electricity charges, that cannot be linked directly to sales revenue and for which matching will therefore be done on a time basis?

You may have thought of the following examples:

- rent and rates
- insurance
- interest payments
- licence fees payable
- wages and salaries (apart from any sales commission or similar payments).

This is not an exhaustive list. You may have thought of others.

When the amount paid during the period is more than the full expense for the period

It is not unusual for a business to be in a situation where it has paid more during the year than the full expense for that year. Example 3.6 illustrates how we deal with this.

Example 3.6

Images Ltd, an advertising agency, normally pays rent for its premises quarterly in advance (on 1 January, 1 April, 1 July and 1 October). On the last day of the last annual reporting period (31 December), it paid the next quarter's rent (£4,000) to the following 31 March, which was a day earlier than required. This would mean that a total of five quarters' rent was paid during the year. If Images Ltd reports all of the cash paid as an expense in the income statement, this would be more than the full expense for the year. This would contravene the matching convention because a higher figure than the expenses associated with the revenue of the year would appear in the income statement.

The problem is overcome by dealing with the rental payment as follows:

- Show the rent for four quarters as the appropriate expense in the income statement (that is, 4 × £4,000 = £16,000).
- The cash (that is, 5 × £4,000 = £20,000) would already have been paid during the year.
- Show the quarter's rent paid in advance (£4,000) as a prepaid expense under assets in the statement of financial position. (The rent paid in advance will appear as a current asset in the statement of financial position, under the heading prepaid expenses or 'prepayments'.)

In the next reporting period, this prepayment will cease to be an asset and will become an expense in the income statement of that period. This is because the rent prepaid relates to the next period and will be 'used up' during it.

These points are illustrated in Figure 3.3.

In practice, the treatment of accruals and prepayments will be subject to the materiality convention of accounting. This convention states that, where the amounts involved are immaterial, we should consider only what is reasonable. This may mean that an item will be treated as an expense in the reporting period in which it is paid, rather than being strictly matched to the revenue to which it relates. For example, a business may find that, at the end of a reporting period, a bill of £5 has been paid for stationery that has yet to be delivered. For a business of any size, the time and effort involved in recording this as a prepayment would not be justified by the little effect that this would have on the measurement of profit or financial position. The amount would, therefore, be treated as an expense when preparing the income statement for the current reporting period and ignored in the following period.

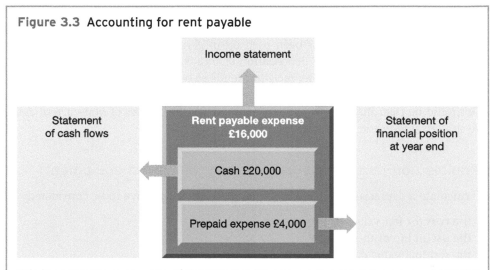

Figure 3.3 Accounting for rent payable

This illustrates the main points of Example 3.6. We can see that the rent expense of £16,000 (which appears in the income statement) is made up of four quarters' rent at £4,000 per quarter. This is the amount that relates to the period and is 'used up' during the period. The cash paid of £20,000 (which appears in the statement of cash flows) is made up of the cash paid during the period, which is five quarters at £4,000 per quarter. Finally, the prepayment of £4,000 (which appears on the statement of financial position) represents the payment made on 31 December and relates to the next annual reporting period.

Profit, cash and accruals accounting

As we have just seen, revenue does not usually represent cash received, and expenses are not the same as cash paid. As a result, the profit figure (that is, total revenue minus total expenses) will not normally represent the net cash generated during a period. It is therefore important to distinguish between profit and liquidity. Profit is a measure of achievement, or productive effort, rather than a measure of cash generated. Although making a profit will increase wealth, as we have already seen in Chapter 2, cash is only one form in which that wealth may be held.

The above points are reflected in the accruals convention of accounting, which asserts that profit is the excess of revenue over expenses for a period, not the excess of cash receipts over cash payments. Leading on from this, the approach to accounting that is based on the accruals convention is frequently referred to as accruals accounting. Thus, the statement of financial position and the income statement are both prepared on the basis of accruals accounting. The statement of cash flows, on the other hand, is not, as it simply deals with cash receipts and payments.

Depreciation

The expense of depreciation, which appeared in the income statement in Activity 3.1, requires further explanation. Most non-current assets do not have a perpetual existence.

They are eventually used up in the process of generating revenue for the business. In essence, depreciation is an attempt to measure that portion of the cost (or fair value) of a non-current asset that has been used up in generating the revenue recognised during a particular period. The depreciation charge is considered to be an expense of the period to which it relates. Depreciation tends to be relevant both to tangible non-current assets (property, plant and equipment) and to intangible non-current assets. We should be clear that the principle is the same for both types of non-current asset. We shall deal with each of the two in turn.

Tangible non-current assets (property, plant and equipment)

To calculate a depreciation charge for a period, four factors have to be considered:

- the cost (or fair value) of the asset
- the useful life of the asset
- the residual value of the asset
- the depreciation method.

The cost (or fair value) of the asset

The cost of an asset will include all costs incurred by the business to bring the asset to its required location and to make it ready for use. Thus, in addition to the costs of acquiring the asset, any delivery costs, installation costs (for example, setting up a new machine) and legal costs incurred in the transfer of legal title (for example, in purchasing property) will be included as part of the total cost of the asset. Similarly, any costs incurred in improving or altering an asset in order to make it suitable for its intended use within the business will also be included as part of the total cost.

Activity 3.6

Andrew Wu (Engineering) Ltd bought a new motor car for its marketing director. The invoice received from the motor car supplier showed the following:

	£
	£
New BMW 325i	26,350
Delivery charge	80
Alloy wheels	660
Sun roof	200
Petrol	30
Number plates	130
Road fund licence	120
	27,570
Part exchange – Reliant Robin	(1,000)
Amount outstanding	26,570

What is the total cost of the new car that will be treated as part of the business's property, plant and equipment?

The cost of the new car will be as follows:

	£
New BMW 325i	26,350
Delivery charge	80
Alloy wheels	660
Sun roof	200
Number plates	130
	27,420

This cost includes delivery charges, which are necessary to bring the asset into use. It also includes number plates, as they are a necessary and integral part of the asset. Improvements (alloy wheels and sun roof) are also regarded as part of the total cost of the motor car. The petrol and road fund licence, however, represent costs of operating the asset rather than a part of the total cost of acquiring it and making it ready for use. These amounts will, therefore, be charged as an expense in the period incurred (although part of the cost of the licence may be regarded as a prepaid expense in the period incurred).

The part-exchange figure shown is part payment of the total amount outstanding and so is not relevant to a consideration of the total cost.

The fair value of an asset was defined in Chapter 2 as the exchange value that could be obtained in an arm's-length transaction. As we saw, assets may be revalued to fair value only if this can be measured reliably. When a revaluation is carried out, all items within the same class must be revalued and revaluations must be kept up to date.

The useful life of the asset

A tangible non-current asset has both a *physical life* and an *economic life*. The physical life will be exhausted through the effects of wear and tear and/or the passage of time. It is possible, however, for the physical life to be extended considerably through careful maintenance, improvements and so on. The economic life is decided by the effects of technological progress and by changes in demand. After a while, the benefits of using the asset may be less than the costs involved. This may be because the asset is unable to compete with newer assets, or because it is no longer relevant to the needs of the business. The economic life of a non-current tangible asset may be much shorter than its physical life. For example, a computer may have a physical life of eight years, but an economic life of just three years.

It is the economic life that will determine the expected useful life for the purpose of calculating depreciation. Forecasting the economic life, however, may be extremely difficult in practice: both the rate at which technology progresses and shifts in consumer tastes can be swift and unpredictable.

Residual value (disposal value)

When a business disposes of a tangible non-current asset that may still be of value to others, some payment may be received. This payment will represent the residual value, or *disposal value*, of the asset. To calculate the total amount to be depreciated, the residual value must be deducted from the cost (or fair value) of the asset. The likely amount to be received on disposal can, once again, be difficult to predict. The best guide is often past experience of similar assets sold.

Depreciation methods

Once the amount to be depreciated (that is, the cost, or fair value, of the asset less any residual value) has been estimated, the business must select a method of allocating this depreciable amount between the annual reporting periods covering the asset's useful life. Although there are various ways in which the total depreciation may be allocated and, from this, a depreciation charge for each year derived, there are really only two methods that are commonly used in practice.

The first of these is known as the straight-line method. This method simply allocates the amount to be depreciated evenly over the useful life of the asset. In other words, an equal amount of depreciation is charged for each year that the asset is held.

Example 3.7

To illustrate this method, consider the following information:

Cost of machine	£78,124
Estimated residual value at the end of its useful life	£2,000
Estimated useful life	4 years

To calculate the depreciation charge for each year, the total amount to be depreciated must be calculated. This will be the total cost less the estimated residual value: that is, £78,124 − £2,000 = £76,124. Having done this, the annual depreciation charge can be derived by dividing the amount to be depreciated by the estimated useful life of the asset of four years. The calculation is therefore:

$$\frac{£76,124}{4} = £19,031$$

Thus, the annual depreciation charge that appears in the income statement in relation to this asset will be £19,031 for each of the four years of the asset's life.

The amount of depreciation relating to the asset will be accumulated for as long as the asset continues to be owned by the business. This accumulated depreciation figure will increase each year as a result of the annual depreciation amount charged to the income statement. This accumulated amount will be deducted from the cost of the asset on the statement of financial position. At the end of the second year, for example, the accumulated depreciation will be £19,031 × 2 = £38,062. The asset details will appear on the statement of financial position as follows:

	£
Machine at cost	78,124
Accumulated depreciation	(38,062)
	40,062

As we saw in Chapter 2, the balance of £40,062 shown above is referred to as the carrying amount (sometimes also known as the written-down value or net book value) of the asset. It represents that portion of the cost (or fair value) of the asset that has still to be charged as an expense (written off) in future years. It must be emphasised that this figure does not, except by coincidence, represent the current market value, which may be quite different. The only point at which the carrying amount is intended to equal the market value of the asset is immediately before it is to be disposed of. Thus in Example 3.7, at the end of the four-year life of the machine, the carrying amount would be £2,000 – its estimated disposal value.

The straight-line method derives its name from the fact that the carrying amount of the asset at the end of each year, when plotted against time, will result in a straight line, as shown in Figure 3.4.

Figure 3.4 Graph of carrying amount against time using the straight-line method

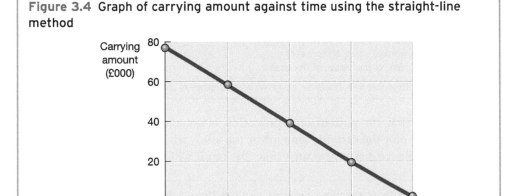

The carrying amount of the asset declines by a constant amount each year. This is because the straight-line method provides a constant depreciation charge each year. The result, when plotted on a graph, is a straight line.

The second approach to calculating annual depreciation which is found in practice is referred to as the reducing-balance method. This method applies a fixed percentage rate of depreciation to the carrying amount of the asset each year. The effect of this will be high annual depreciation charges in the early years and lower charges in the later years. To illustrate this method, let us take the same information that was used in Example 3.7. By using a fixed percentage of 60 per cent of the carrying amount to determine the annual depreciation charge, the effect will be to reduce the carrying amount to £2,000 after four years.

The calculations will be as follows:

	£
Cost of machine	78,124
Year 1 Depreciation charge (60%* of cost)	(46,874)
Carrying amount	31,250
Year 2 Depreciation charge (60% of carrying amount)	(18,750)
Carrying amount	12,500
Year 3 Depreciation charge (60% of carrying amount)	(7,500)
Carrying amount	5,000
Year 4 Depreciation charge (60% of carrying amount)	(3,000)
Residual value	2,000

* Box 3.1 explains how to derive the fixed percentage.

Box 3.1

Deriving the fixed percentage

Deriving the fixed percentage to be applied requires the use of the following formula:

$$P = (1 - \sqrt[n]{R/C}) \times 100\%$$

where: P = the depreciation percentage
  n = the useful life of the asset (in years)
  R = the residual value of the asset
  C = the cost, or fair value, of the asset.

The fixed percentage rate will, however, be given in all examples used in this text.

We can see that the pattern of depreciation is quite different between the two methods. If we plot the carrying amount of the asset, which has been derived using the reducing-balance method, against time, the result will be as shown in Figure 3.5.

Figure 3.5 Graph of carrying amount against time using the reducing-balance method

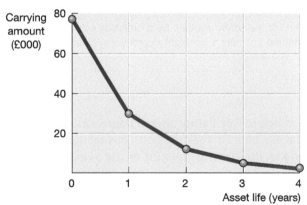

Under the reducing-balance method, the carrying amount of an asset falls by a larger amount in the earlier years than in the later years. This is because the depreciation charge is based on a fixed percentage of the carrying amount.

Activity 3.7

Assume that the machine used in the example above was owned by a business that made a profit before depreciation of £40,000 for each of the four years in which the asset was held.

Calculate the profit for the business for each year under each depreciation method, and comment on your findings.

Your answer should be as follows:

Straight-line method

	(a) Profit before depreciation £	(b) Depreciation £	(a – b) Profit £
Year 1	40,000	19,031	20,969
Year 2	40,000	19,031	20,969
Year 3	40,000	19,031	20,969
Year 4	40,000	19,031	20,969

Reducing-balance method

	(a) Profit before depreciation £	(b) Depreciation £	(a – b) Profit/(loss) £
Year 1	40,000	46,874	(6,874)
Year 2	40,000	18,750	21,250
Year 3	40,000	7,500	32,500
Year 4	40,000	3,000	37,000

The straight-line method of depreciation results in a constant profit figure over the four-year period. This is because both the profit before depreciation and the depreciation charge are constant over the period. The reducing-balance method, however, results in a changing profit figure over time, despite the fact that in this example the pre-depreciation profit is the same each year. In the first year a loss is reported and, thereafter, a rising profit.

Although the *pattern* of profit over the four-year period will be quite different, depending on the depreciation method used, the *total* profit for the period (£83,876) will remain the same. This is because both methods of depreciating will allocate the same amount of total depreciation (£76,124) over the four-year period. It is only the amount allocated *between years* that will differ.

In practice, the use of different depreciation methods may not have such a dramatic effect on profits as suggested in Activity 3.7. This is because businesses typically have more than one depreciating non-current asset. Where a business replaces some of its assets each year, the total depreciation charge calculated under the reducing-balance method will reflect a range of charges (from high through to low), as assets will be at different points in the replacement cycle. This could mean that each year's total depreciation charge may not be significantly different from the total depreciation charge that would be derived under the straight-line method.

Selecting a depreciation method

How does a business choose which depreciation method to use for a particular asset? The answer is the one that best matches the depreciation expense to the pattern of economic benefits that the asset provides. Where these benefits are provided evenly over time (buildings, for example), the straight-line method is usually appropriate. Where assets lose their efficiency (as with certain types of machinery), the benefits provided will decline over time and so the reducing-balance method may be more appropriate. Where the pattern of economic benefits provided by the asset is uncertain, the straight-line method is normally chosen.

There is an International Financial Reporting Standard (International Accounting Standard) which deals with the depreciation of property, plant and equipment. As we shall see in Chapter 4, the purpose of financial reporting standards is to narrow areas of accounting difference and to try to ensure that information provided to users is transparent and comparable. The relevant standard endorses the view that the depreciation method chosen should reflect the pattern of economic benefits provided but does not specify particular methods to be used. It states that the useful life, depreciation method and residual values of non-current assets should be reviewed at least annually and adjustments made where appropriate.

Real World 3.5 sets out the depreciation policies of Thorntons plc.

Real World 3.5

Sweet talk on depreciation policies

Thorntons plc, the manufacturer and retailer of confectionery, uses the straight-line method to depreciate all its property, plant and equipment, other than land and assets in the course of construction. The financial statements for the year ended 30 June 2009 show the period over which different classes of assets are depreciated as follows:

Long leasehold and freehold premises	50 years
Short leasehold land and buildings	Period of the lease
Other plant, vehicles and equipment	3 to 15 years
Retail fixtures and fittings	Up to 10 years

We can see that there are wide variations in the expected useful lives of the various assets held.

Source: Thorntons plc Annual Report and Accounts 2009, p. 49.

It seems that Thorntons plc is typical of UK businesses in that most use the straight-line approach. The reducing-balance method is not very much used.

The approach taken to calculating depreciation is summarised in Figure 3.6.

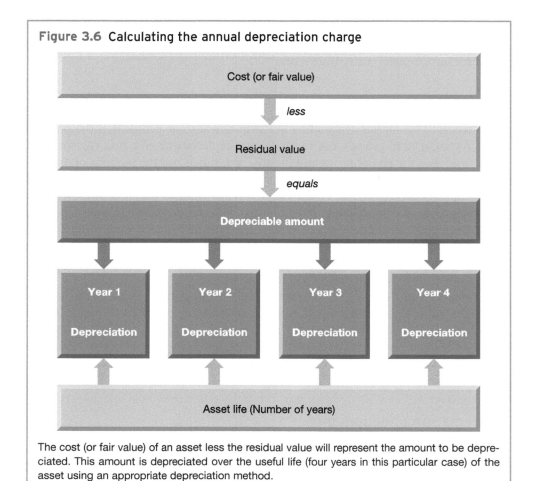

Figure 3.6 Calculating the annual depreciation charge

The cost (or fair value) of an asset less the residual value will represent the amount to be depreciated. This amount is depreciated over the useful life (four years in this particular case) of the asset using an appropriate depreciation method.

Depreciating intangible assets

Where an intangible asset has a finite life, the approach taken for the depreciation (or amortisation as it is usually called with intangibles) is broadly the same as that for property, plant and equipment (tangible non-current assets). The asset is amortised (depreciated) over its useful life and the amortisation method used should reflect the pattern of benefits provided. Some differences arise, however, because of the valuation problems surrounding these assets. Intangible assets are reported initially at cost but can, in principle, be revalued to fair value. However, this rarely occurs as there is usually no active market from which to establish fair values. For similar reasons, the residual value of an intangible asset is normally assumed to be zero.

We saw in Chapter 2 that some intangible assets, which may include acquired goodwill, have an infinite useful life. These assets are not amortised but instead are tested for impairment at least annually. While intangible assets with finite lives and property, plant and equipment are also subject to impairment testing, this will only occur when there is an indication that impairment may have taken place. They are not tested for impairment on a routine basis.

Depreciation and asset replacement

There seems to be a misunderstanding in the minds of some people that the purpose of depreciation is to provide the funds for the replacement of a non-current asset when it reaches the end of its useful life. However, this is not the purpose of depreciation as conventionally defined. It was mentioned earlier that depreciation represents an attempt to allocate the cost or fair value (less any residual value) of a non-current asset over its expected useful life. The resulting depreciation charge in each reporting period represents an expense, which is then used in the calculation of profit for the period. Calculating the depreciation charge for a period is therefore necessary for the proper measurement of financial performance. This must be done whether or not the business intends to replace the asset in the future.

If there is an intention to replace the asset, the depreciation charge in the income statement will not ensure that liquid funds are set aside by the business specifically for this purpose. Although the effect of a depreciation charge is to reduce profit and, therefore, to reduce the amount available for withdrawal by the owners, the amounts retained within the business as a result may be invested in ways that are unrelated to the replacement of the particular asset.

Depreciation and judgement

From what we have just seen about depreciation, it seems that accounting is not as precise and objective as it sometimes appears to be. There are areas where subjective judgement is required and depreciation provides a good illustration of this.

Activity 3.8

What kinds of judgements must be made to calculate a depreciation charge for a period?

You may have thought of the following:

■ the expected residual or disposal value of the asset
■ the expected useful life of the asset
■ the choice of depreciation method.

Making different judgements on these matters would result in a different pattern of depreciation charges over the life of the asset and, therefore, in a different pattern of reported profits. However, underestimations or overestimations that are made in relation to the above will be adjusted for in the final year of an asset's life. As a result, the total depreciation charge (and total profit) over the asset's life will not be affected by estimation errors.

Real World 3.6 describes the effect of extending the useful life of property, plant and equipment on the short-term profits of one large business.

Real World 3.6

Sports massage

JJB Sports plc, a leading retailer, reported interim financial results for the six months ended 30 June 2005 that caused some disquiet among investors and analysts. The business changed the estimates for the useful life of its property, plant and equipment when calculating depreciation. It explained that this was due to new requirements to adopt International Financial Reporting Standards (IFRSs) when preparing financial statements. The article below, however, suggests that not everyone believed this.

JJB massages results to boost profits

High street retailer JJB Sports massaged last week's disappointing interim results by changing its depreciation calculations, in order to boost flagging profits by £4.3 million.

Analysts admitted that they were caught on the hop, as the company reported a 35.8% drop in operating profits from £27.4 million to £17.6 million for six months ended June 2005 on revenues down 6% to £340.4 million. Operating profits would have plummeted even further to £14.3 million had the company not changed its accounting for depreciation. 'The company explained the change as coming out of its IFRS conversion review, but it was clearly there for other reasons,' said Teather & Greenwood retail analyst Sanjay Vidyarthi.

JJB said that an impairment review ahead of its IFRS transition had forced a rethink on the carrying value of property, plant and equipment.

It concluded that these items had useful economic lives that more closely matched the length of the short-term lease of the property, rather than the 10-year economic life which had formed the basis of the depreciation charge in previous reporting periods.

Richard Ratner, head of equity research at Seymour Pierce, said: 'They said the way they had depreciated assets previously was not correct but I haven't seen any other companies make this kind of change.'

JJB's share price fell from 168.2p before the results to 164.7p at the end of last week.

Source: 'JJB massages results to boost profits', *Accountancy Age*, 20 October 2005, p. 3.

Costing inventories

The way in which we measure the cost of inventories (or stock) is important because the cost of inventories sold during a reporting period will affect the calculation of profit. Furthermore, the cost of remaining inventories held at the end of the reporting period can affect the portrayal of wealth in the statement of financial position. It is tempting to think that determining the cost of inventories used or still held is pretty straightforward. However, during a period of changing prices, it can be a problem.

To determine the cost of the inventories sold and the cost of the inventories remaining at the end of the reporting period, an assumption must be made about the way in which inventories are physically handled. This assumption need not have anything to do with how the inventories are *actually* handled. It is concerned only with providing useful accounting information.

Three common assumptions used are:

- first in, first out (FIFO), in which it is assumed that the earliest acquired inventories held are the first to be used;
- last in, first out (LIFO), in which it is assumed that the latest acquired inventories held are the first to be used; and
- weighted average cost (AVCO), in which it is assumed that inventories acquired lose their separate identity and go into a 'pool'. Any issues of inventories from this pool will reflect the weighted average cost of inventories held.

Example 3.8 provides a simple illustration of the way in which each method is applied.

Example 3.8

A business commenced on 1 May to supply oil to factories. During the first month, the following transactions took place:

	Tonnes	Cost per tonne
May 2 Purchased	10,000	£10
May 10 Purchased	20,000	£13
May 18 Sold	9,000	

First in, first out (FIFO)

Using the first in, first out approach, 9,000 tonnes of the 10,000 tonnes bought on 2 May are treated as if these are the ones to be sold. The remaining inventories bought on 2 May (1,000 tonnes) and the inventories bought on 10 May (20,000 tonnes) will become the closing inventories. Thus we have:

Cost of sales	(9,000 @ £10 per tonne)	£90,000
Closing inventories		
		£
	(1,000 @ £10 per tonne)	10,000
	(20,000 @ £13 per tonne)	260,000
		270,000

Last in, first out (LIFO)

Using the last in, first out approach, 9,000 tonnes of the inventories bought on 10 May will be treated as if these are the first to be sold. The earlier inventories bought on

2 May (10,000 tonnes) and the remainder of the inventories bought on 10 May (11,000 tonnes) will become the closing inventories. Thus we have:

Cost of sales	(9,000 @ £13 per tonne)	£117,000
Closing inventories		
		£
	(11,000 @ £13 per tonne)	143,000
	(10,000 @ £10 per tonne)	100,000
		243,000

Weighted average cost (AVCO)

Since newly acquired inventories are treated, for accounting purposes, as if they lose their separate identity, any issues should reflect the weighted average cost of inventories held. Using this approach, a weighted average cost, based on the quantities of each batch purchased, is calculated. The weighted average cost is then used to derive both the cost of goods sold and the cost of remaining inventories held. This simply means that the cost of the inventories bought on 2 May and 10 May are added together and then divided by the total number of tonnes to obtain the weighted average cost per tonne. That is:

Average cost = $((10,000 \times £10) + (20,000 \times £13))/(10,000 + 20,000)$ = £12 per tonne

Both the cost of sales and the value of the closing inventories are then based on this average cost per tonne. Thus we have:

Cost of sales	(9,000 @ £12 per tonne)	£108,000
Closing inventories	(21,000 @ £12 per tonne)	£252,000

Activity 3.9

Suppose that the 9,000 tonnes of inventories in Example 3.8 were sold for £15 a tonne.

(a) Calculate the gross profit for the period under each of the three costing methods.
(b) What do you note about the different profit and closing inventories valuations when using each method, when prices are rising?

Your answer should be along the following lines:

(a) Gross profit calculation:

	FIFO £000	LIFO £000	AVCO £000
Sales revenue (9,000 @ £15)	135	135	135
Cost of sales	(90)	(117)	(108)
Gross profit	45	18	27
Closing inventories figure	270	243	252

(b) These figures show that FIFO will give the highest gross profit during a period of rising prices. This is because sales revenue is matched with the earlier (and cheaper) purchases. LIFO will give the lowest gross profit because sales revenue is matched against the more recent (and dearer) purchases. The AVCO method will normally give a figure that is between these two extremes.

The closing inventories figure in the statement of financial position will be highest with the FIFO method. This is because the cost of oil still held will be based on the more recent (and dearer) purchases. LIFO will give the lowest closing inventories figure as the oil held will be based on the earlier (and cheaper) purchases. Once again, the AVCO method will normally give a figure that is between these two extremes. During a period of falling prices, the position of FIFO and LIFO is reversed.

The different costing methods will only have an effect on the reported profit from one reporting period to the next. The figure derived for closing inventories will be carried forward and matched with sales revenue in a later period. Thus, if the cheaper purchases of inventories are matched to sales revenue in the current period, it will mean that the dearer purchases will be matched to sales revenue in a later period. Over the life of the business, therefore, the total profit will be the same either way.

Inventories – some further issues

We saw in Chapter 2 that the convention of prudence requires that inventories be valued at the lower of cost and net realisable value. (The net realisable value of inventories is the estimated selling price less any further costs necessary to complete the goods and any costs involved in selling and distributing them.) In theory, this means that the valuation method applied to inventories could switch each year, depending on which of cost and net realisable value is the lower. In practice, however, the cost of the inventories held is usually below the current net realisable value – particularly during a period of rising prices. It is, therefore, the cost figure that will normally appear in the statement of financial position.

Activity 3.10

Can you think of any circumstances where the net realisable value will be lower than the cost of inventories held, even during a period of generally rising prices?

The net realisable value may be lower where:

- goods have deteriorated or become obsolete;
- there has been a fall in the market price of the goods;
- the goods are being used as a 'loss leader';
- bad buying decisions have been made.

There is an International Financial Reporting Standard that deals with inventories. It states that, when preparing financial statements for external reporting, the cost of inventories should normally be determined using either FIFO or AVCO. The LIFO approach is not an acceptable method to use for external reporting. The standard also requires the 'lower of cost and net realisable value' rule to be used and so endorses the application of the prudence convention.

Real World 3.7 sets out the inventories costing methods of one well-known supermarket business.

Real World 3.7

Buy one, get one free

J Sainsbury plc, the supermarket chain, employs two methods of costing inventories and the particular method applied depends on where the inventories are located. The business reports:

> Inventories are valued at the lower of cost and net realisable value. Inventories at warehouses are valued on a first-in, first-out basis. Those at retail outlets are valued at calculated average cost prices.

Source: J Sainsbury plc Annual Report 2009, p. 49.

Costing inventories and depreciation provide two examples where the consistency convention must be applied. This convention holds that once a particular method of accounting is selected, it should be applied consistently over time. Thus, it would not be acceptable to switch from, say, FIFO to AVCO between periods (unless exceptional circumstances make it appropriate). The purpose of this convention is to help users make valid comparisons of performance and position from one period to the next.

Activity 3.11

Reporting inventories in the financial statements provides a further example of the need to apply subjective judgement. For the inventories of a retail business, what are the main areas where judgement is required?

The main areas are:

- the choice of cost method (FIFO, LIFO, AVCO);
- deducing the net realisable value figure for inventories held.

Trade receivables problems

We have seen that, when businesses sell goods or services on credit, revenue will usually be recognised before the customer pays the amounts owing. Recording the dual aspect of a credit sale will involve increasing sales revenue and increasing trade receivables by the amount of the revenue from the credit sale.

With this type of sale there is always the risk that the customer will not pay the amount due, however reliable they might have appeared to be at the time of the sale.

When it becomes reasonably certain that the customer will never pay, the debt owed is considered to be a **bad debt** and this must be taken into account when preparing the financial statements.

Activity 3.12

When preparing the financial statements, what would be the effect on the income statement, and on the statement of financial position, of not taking into account the fact that a debt is bad?

The effect would be to overstate the assets (trade receivables) on the statement of financial position and to overstate profit in the income statement, as the revenue which has been recognised will not result in any future benefit.

To provide a more realistic picture of financial performance and position, the bad debt must be 'written off'. This will involve reducing the trade receivables and increasing expenses (by creating an expense known as 'bad debts written off') by the amount of the bad debt.

The matching convention requires that the bad debt is written off in the same period as the sale that gave rise to the debt is recognised.

Note that, when a debt is bad, the accounting response is not simply to cancel the original sale. If this were done, the income statement would not be so informative. Reporting the bad debts as an expense can be extremely useful in assessing management performance.

Activity 3.13

The treatment of bad debts represents a further example where judgement is needed to derive an appropriate expense figure.

What will be the effect of different judgements concerning the appropriate amount of bad debts expense on the profit for a particular period and on the total profit reported over the life of the business?

Judgement is often required in deriving a figure for bad debts incurred during a period. There may be situations where views will differ concerning whether or not a debt is irrecoverable. The decision concerning whether or not to write off a bad debt will have an effect on the expenses for the period and, therefore, on the reported profit. However, over the life of the business the total reported profit would not be affected, as incorrect judgements in one period will be adjusted for in a later period.

Suppose that a debt of £100 was written off in a period and that, in a later period, the amount owing was actually received. The increase in expenses of £100 in the period in which the bad debt was written off would be compensated for by an increase in revenue of £100 when the amount outstanding was finally received (bad debt recovered). If, on the other hand, the amount owing of £100 was never written off in the first place, the profit for the two periods would not be affected by the bad debt adjustment and would, therefore, be different – but the total profit for the two periods would be the same.

Real World 3.8 describes the recent rise in bad debts among small and medium-sized businesses.

Real World 3.8

Bad debts getting worse

The average amount of bad debt being written off by small and medium-sized businesses has doubled in twelve months to £2,529, according to research by Barclays.

The bank's annual late payments survey, covering 1,000 small and medium-sized businesses, found that, on any given day, about £9 billion was owed to such companies, although this is £1 billion less than in the previous year. Although 18 per cent of those asked said that late payers were a threat to the company's survival, this was down from 32 per cent in the same survey in 2008.

One in six of the company heads interviewed said they had cancelled more debt in 2009 than in the previous twelve months.

Source: 'SMEs write off more bad debt', *The Financial Times*, 12/03/2010 (Moules, J.), copyright © The Financial Times Ltd.

Let us now try to bring together some of the points that we have raised in this chapter through a self-assessment question.

? Self-assessment question 3.1

TT and Co. is a new business that started trading on 1 January 2009. The following is a summary of transactions that occurred during the first year of trading:

1 The owners introduced £50,000 of equity, which was paid into a bank account opened in the name of the business.

2 Premises were rented from 1 January 2009 at an annual rental of £20,000. During the year, rent of £25,000 was paid to the owner of the premises.

3 Rates (a tax on business premises) were paid during the year as follows:

For the period 1 January 2009 to 31 March 2009	£500
For the period 1 April 2009 to 31 March 2010	£1,200

4 A delivery van was bought on 1 January 2009 for £12,000. This is expected to be used in the business for four years and then to be sold for £2,000.

5 Wages totalling £33,500 were paid during the year. At the end of the year, the business owed £630 of wages for the last week of the year.

6 Electricity bills for the first three quarters of the year were paid totalling £1,650. After 31 December 2009, but before the financial statements had been finalised for the year, the bill for the last quarter arrived showing a charge of £620.

7 Inventories totalling £143,000 were bought on credit.

8 Inventories totalling £12,000 were bought for cash.

9 Sales revenue on credit totalled £152,000 (cost of sales £74,000).

10 Cash sales revenue totalled £35,000 (cost of sales £16,000).
11 Receipts from trade receivables totalled £132,000.
12 Payments to trade payables totalled £121,000.
13 Van running expenses paid totalled £9,400.

At the end of the year it was clear that a credit customer (trade receivable) who owed £400 would not be able to pay any part of the debt. All of the other trade receivables were expected to settle in full.

The business uses the straight-line method for depreciating non-current assets.

Required:

Prepare an income statement for the year to 31 December 2009 and a statement of financial position as at that date.

Uses and usefulness of the income statement

The income statement, like the statement of financial position, has been around for a long time. Most large businesses prepare an income statement on a frequent basis (monthly or even more frequently). There is, however, no rule requiring this statement to be produced more frequently than once, or in some cases twice, a year. The income statement is, therefore, regarded as capable of providing useful information. In particular, this statement may help in revealing:

■ *How effective the business has been in generating wealth.* Since wealth generation is the primary reason for most businesses to exist, assessing how much wealth has been created is an important issue. Although different judgements concerning depreciation, inventories and bad debts may affect the calculation of profit for a period, this problem should not be overstated. For most businesses in most years, the effect of making different judgements would probably not significantly affect the final profit figure.

■ *How the profit was derived.* For some users, the only item of concern may be the final profit figure, or *bottom line* as it is sometimes called. While this is a primary measure of performance, and its importance is difficult to overstate, the income statement contains other information that should also be of interest. To evaluate business performance effectively, it is important to discover how the profit figure was derived. Thus the level of sales revenue, the nature and amount of expenses incurred and the profit, in relation to sales revenue, are also important to an understanding of business performance. The analysis and interpretation of financial statements are considered in detail in Chapter 6.

Summary

The main points of this chapter may be summarised as follows.

The income statement (profit and loss account)

- The income statement measures and reports how much profit (or loss) has been generated over a period.

- Profit (or loss) for the period is the difference between the total revenue and total expenses for the period.

- The income statement links the statements of financial position at the beginning and end of a reporting period.

- Normally, the income statement will first calculate gross profit and then deduct any overheads for the period. The final figure derived is the profit (or loss) for the period.

- Gross profit represents the difference between the sales revenue for the period and the cost of sales.

Expenses and revenue

- Cost of sales may be identified either by matching the cost of each sale to the particular sale or, in the case of retail and wholesaling businesses, by adjusting the goods bought during the period to take account of opening and closing inventories.

- Classifying expenses is often a matter of judgement, although there are rules for businesses that operate as limited companies.

- Revenue is recognised when the amount of revenue can be measured reliably and it is probable that the economic benefits will be received.

- Where there is a sale of goods, there is an additional criterion that ownership and control must pass to the buyer before revenue can be recognised.

- Revenue can be recognised after partial completion provided that a particular stage of completion can be measured reliably.

- The matching convention states that expenses should be matched to the revenue that they help generate.

- A particular expense reported in the income statement may not be the same as the cash paid. This will result in accruals or prepayments appearing in the statement of financial position.

- The materiality convention states that where the amounts are immaterial, we should consider only what is expedient.

- 'Accruals accounting' is preparing the income statement and statement of financial position following the accruals convention, which says that profit = revenue less expenses (not cash receipts less cash payments).

Depreciation of non-current assets

■ Depreciation requires a consideration of the cost (or fair value), useful life and residual value of an asset. It also requires a consideration of the method of depreciation.

■ The straight-line method of depreciation allocates the amount to be depreciated evenly over the useful life of the asset.

■ The reducing-balance method applies a fixed percentage rate of depreciation to the carrying amount of an asset each year.

■ The depreciation method chosen should reflect the pattern of benefits associated with the asset.

■ Depreciation is an attempt to allocate the cost (or fair value), less the residual value, of an asset over its useful life. It does not provide funds for replacement of the asset.

Costing inventories

■ The way in which we derive the cost of inventories is important in the calculation of profit and the presentation of financial position.

■ The first in, first out (FIFO) method approaches matters as if the earliest inventories held are the first to be used.

■ The last in, first out (LIFO) method approaches matters as if the latest inventories are the first to be used.

■ The weighted average cost (AVCO) method applies an average cost to all inventories used.

■ When prices are rising, FIFO gives the lowest cost of sales figure and highest closing inventories figure and LIFO gives the highest cost of sales figure and the lowest closing inventories figure. AVCO gives figures for cost of sales and closing inventories that lie between FIFO and LIFO.

■ When prices are falling, the positions of FIFO and LIFO are reversed.

■ Inventories are shown at the lower of cost and net realisable value.

■ When a particular method of accounting, such as an inventories costing method, is selected, it should be applied consistently over time.

Bad debts

■ Where it is reasonably certain that a credit customer will not pay, the debt is regarded as 'bad' and written off.

Uses of the income statement

■ It provides a profit figure.

■ It provides information on how the profit was derived.

→ **Key terms**

profit	depreciation
revenue	residual value
expense	straight-line method
reporting period	carrying amount
gross profit	written-down value
operating profit	net book value
profit for the year	reducing-balance method
cost of sales	amortisation
matching convention	first in, first out (FIFO)
accrued expenses	last in, first out (LIFO)
prepaid expenses	weighted average cost (AVCO)
materiality convention	consistency convention
accruals convention	bad debt
accruals accounting	

Further reading

If you would like to explore the topics covered in this chapter in more depth, we recommend the following books:

Elliott, B. and Elliott, J., *Financial Accounting and Reporting* (13th edn), Financial Times Prentice Hall, 2010, chapters 2, 16, 19 and 20.

IASC Foundation Education, *A Guide through IFRS 2009*, July 2009, IAS 2, IAS 16, IAS 18, IAS 36 and IAS 38.

KPMG, *Insights into IFRS* (6th edn, 2009/10), Sweet and Maxwell, 2009, sections 3.2, 3.3, 3.8, 3.10 and 4.2.

? Review questions

3.1 'Although the income statement is a record of past achievement, the calculations required for certain expenses involve estimates of the future.' What does this statement mean? Can you think of examples where estimates of the future are used?

3.2 'Depreciation is a process of allocation and not valuation.' What do you think is meant by this statement?

3.3 What is the convention of consistency? Does this convention help users in making a more valid comparison between businesses?

3.4 'An asset is similar to an expense.' Do you agree?

✳ Exercises

Exercises 3.4 and 3.5 are more advanced than Exercises 3.1 to 3.3.

If you wish to try more exercises, visit the website at www.myaccountinglab.com.

3.1 You have heard the following statements made. Comment critically on them.

(a) 'Equity only increases or decreases as a result of the owners putting more cash into the business or taking some out.'
(b) 'An accrued expense is one that relates to next year.'
(c) 'Unless we depreciate this asset we shall be unable to provide for its replacement.'
(d) 'There is no point in depreciating the factory building. It is appreciating in value each year.'

3.2 Singh Enterprises, which started business on 1 January 2007, has an annual reporting period to 31 December and uses the straight-line method of depreciation. On 1 January 2007 the business bought a machine for £10,000. The machine had an expected useful life of four years and an estimated residual value of £2,000. On 1 January 2008 the business bought another machine for £15,000. This machine had an expected useful life of five years and an estimated residual value of £2,500. On 31 December 2009 the business sold the first machine bought for £3,000.

Required:
Show the relevant income statement extract and statement of financial position extract for the years 2007, 2008 and 2009.

3.3 The owner of a business is confused and comes to you for help. The financial statements for the business, prepared by an accountant, for the last reporting period revealed a profit of £50,000. However, during the reporting period the bank balance declined by £30,000. What reasons might explain this apparent discrepancy?

3.4 The following is the statement of financial position of TT and Co. at the end of its first year of trading (from Self-assessment question 3.1):

Statement of financial position as at 31 December 2009

	£
ASSETS	
Non-current assets	
Property, plant and equipment	
Delivery van at cost	12,000
Depreciation	(2,500)
	9,500
Current assets	
Inventories	65,000
Trade receivables	19,600
Prepaid expenses*	5,300
Cash	750
	90,650
Total assets	100,150
EQUITY AND LIABILITIES	
Equity	
Original	50,000
Retained earnings	26,900
	76,900
Current liabilities	
Trade payables	22,000
Accrued expenses†	1,250
	23,250
Total equity and liabilities	100,150

* The prepaid expenses consisted of rates (£300) and rent (£5,000).

† The accrued expenses consisted of wages (£630) and electricity (£620).

During 2010, the following transactions took place:

1 The owners withdrew equity in the form of cash of £20,000.
2 Premises continued to be rented at an annual rental of £20,000. During the year, rent of £15,000 was paid to the owner of the premises.
3 Rates on the premises were paid during the year as follows: for the period 1 April 2010 to 31 March 2011 £1,300.
4 A second delivery van was bought on 1 January 2010 for £13,000. This is expected to be used in the business for four years and then to be sold for £3,000.
5 Wages totalling £36,700 were paid during the year. At the end of the year, the business owed £860 of wages for the last week of the year.
6 Electricity bills for the first three quarters of the year and £620 for the last quarter of the previous year were paid totalling £1,820. After 31 December 2010, but before the financial statements had been finalised for the year, the bill for the last quarter arrived showing a charge of £690.
7 Inventories totalling £67,000 were bought on credit.

8 Inventories totalling £8,000 were bought for cash.
9 Sales revenue on credit totalled £179,000 (cost £89,000).
10 Cash sales revenue totalled £54,000 (cost £25,000).
11 Receipts from trade receivables totalled £178,000.
12 Payments to trade payables totalled £71,000.
13 Van running expenses paid totalled £16,200.

The business uses the straight-line method for depreciating non-current assets.

Required:
Prepare an income statement for the year to 31 December 2010 and a statement of financial position as at that date.

3.5 The following is the statement of financial position of WW Associates as at 31 December 2008:

Statement of financial position as at 31 December 2008

	£
ASSETS	
Non-current assets	
Machinery	25,300
Current assets	
Inventories	12,200
Trade receivables	21,300
Prepaid expenses (rates)	400
Cash	8,300
	42,200
Total assets	67,500
EQUITY AND LIABILITIES	
Equity	
Original	25,000
Retained earnings	23,900
	48,900
Current liabilities	
Trade payables	16,900
Accrued expenses (wages)	1,700
	18,600
Total equity and liabilities	67,500

During 2009, the following transactions took place:

1 The owners withdrew equity in the form of cash of £23,000.
2 Premises were rented at an annual rental of £20,000. During the year, rent of £25,000 was paid to the owner of the premises.
3 Rates on the premises were paid during the year for the period 1 April 2009 to 31 March 2010 and amounted to £2,000.
4 Some machinery (a non-current asset), which was bought on 1 January 2008 for £13,000, has proved to be unsatisfactory. It was part-exchanged for some new machinery on 1 January 2009 and WW Associates paid a cash amount of £6,000.

The new machinery would have cost £15,000 had the business bought it without the trade-in.

5 Wages totalling £23,800 were paid during the year. At the end of the year, the business owed £860 of wages.

6 Electricity bills for the four quarters of the year were paid totalling £2,700.

7 Inventories totalling £143,000 were bought on credit.

8 Inventories totalling £12,000 were bought for cash.

9 Sales revenue on credit totalled £211,000 (cost £127,000).

10 Cash sales revenue totalled £42,000 (cost £25,000).

11 Receipts from trade receivables totalled £198,000.

12 Payments to trade payables totalled £156,000.

13 Van running expenses paid totalled £17,500.

The business uses the reducing-balance method of depreciation for non-current assets at the rate of 30 per cent each year.

Required:

Prepare an income statement for the year ended 31 December 2009 and a statement of financial position as at that date.

Chapter 4

Accounting for limited companies

Introduction

Most businesses in the UK, except the very smallest, operate in the form of limited companies. About two and a quarter million limited companies now exist and they account for the majority of UK business activity and employment. The economic significance of this type of business is not confined to the UK; it can be seen in most of the world's developed countries.

In this chapter we consider the nature of limited companies and how they differ from sole proprietorship businesses and partnerships. We examine the ways in which the owners provide finance, as well as the rules governing the way in which limited companies must account to their owners and to other interested parties. We shall also see how the financial statements, which were discussed in the previous two chapters, are prepared for this type of business.

Learning outcomes

When you have completed this chapter, you should be able to:

■ discuss the nature of the limited company;

■ describe the main features of the equity (owners' claim) in a limited company;

■ discuss the framework of rules designed to safeguard the interests of shareholders;

■ explain how the income statement and statement of financial position of a limited company differ in detail from those of sole proprietorships and partnerships.

The main features of limited companies

Legal nature

Let us begin our examination of limited companies by discussing their legal nature. A limited company has been described as an artificial person that has been created by law. This means that a company has many of the rights and obligations that 'real' people have. It can, for example, sue or be sued by others and can enter into contracts in its own name. This contrasts sharply with other types of businesses, such as sole proprietorships and partnerships (that is, unincorporated businesses), where it is the owner(s) rather than the business that must sue, enter into contracts and so on, because the business has no separate legal identity.

With the rare exceptions of those that are created by Act of Parliament or by Royal Charter, all UK companies are created (or *incorporated*) by registration. To create a company the person or persons wishing to create it (usually known as *promoters*) fill in a few simple forms and pay a modest registration fee. After having ensured that the necessary formalities have been met, the Registrar of Companies, a UK government official, enters the name of the new company on the Registry of Companies. Thus, in the UK, companies can be formed very easily and cheaply (for about £100).

A limited company may be owned by just one person, but most have more than one owner and some have many owners. The owners are usually known as *members* or *shareholders*. The ownership of a company is normally divided into a number, frequently a large number, of shares, each of equal size. Each owner, or shareholder, owns one or more shares in the company. Large companies typically have a very large number of shareholders. For example, at 31 March 2009, BT Group plc, the telecommunications business, had nearly 1.2 million different shareholders.

Since a limited company has its own legal identity, it is regarded as being quite separate from those that own and manage it. It is worth emphasising that this legal separateness of owners and the company has no connection whatsoever with the business entity convention of accounting, which we discussed in Chapter 2. This accounting convention applies equally well to all business types, including sole proprietorships and partnerships where there is certainly no legal distinction between the owner(s) and the business.

The legal separateness of the limited company and its shareholders leads to two important features of the limited company: perpetual life and limited liability. These are now explained.

Perpetual life

A company is normally granted a perpetual existence and so will continue even where an owner of some, or even all, of the shares in the company dies. The shares of the deceased person will simply pass to the beneficiary of his or her estate. The granting of perpetual existence means that the life of a company is quite separate from the lives of those individuals who own or manage it. It is not, therefore, affected by changes in ownership that arise when individuals buy and sell shares in the company.

Though a company may be granted a perpetual existence when it is first formed, it is possible for either the shareholders or the courts to bring this existence to an end. When this is done, the assets of the company are usually sold to generate cash to meet the outstanding liabilities. Any surplus arising after all liabilities have been met will then be used to pay the shareholders. Shareholders may agree to end the life of a company where it has achieved the purpose for which it was formed or where they feel that the company has no real future. The courts may bring the life of a company to an end where creditors have applied to the courts for this to be done because they have not been paid amounts owing.

Where shareholders agree to end the life of a company, it is referred to as a 'voluntary liquidation'. Real World 4.1 describes the demise of one company by this method.

Real World 4.1

Monotub Industries in a spin as founder gets Titan for £1

Monotub Industries, maker of the Titan washing machine, yesterday passed into corporate history with very little ceremony and with only a whimper of protest from minority shareholders.

At an extraordinary meeting held in a basement room of the group's West End headquarters, shareholders voted to put the company into voluntary liquidation and sell its assets and intellectual property to founder Martin Myerscough for £1. [The shares in the company were at one time worth 650p each.]

The only significant opposition came from Giuliano Gnagnatti who, along with other shareholders, has seen his investment shrink faster than a wool twin-set on a boil wash.

The not-so-proud owner of 100,000 Monotub shares, Mr Gnagnatti, the managing director of an online retailer, described the sale of Monotub as a 'free gift' to Mr Myerscough. This assessment was denied by Ian Green, the chairman of Monotub, who said the closest the beleaguered company had come to a sale was an offer for £60,000 that gave no guarantees against liabilities, which are thought to amount to £750,000.

The quiet passing of the washing machine, eventually dubbed the Titanic, was in strong contrast to its performance in many kitchens.

Originally touted as the 'great white goods hope' of the washing machine industry with its larger capacity and removable drum, the Titan ran into problems when it kept stopping during the spin cycle, causing it to emit a loud bang and leap into the air.

Summing up the demise of the Titan, Mr Green said: 'Clearly the machine had some revolutionary aspects, but you can't get away from the fact that the machine was faulty and should not have been launched with those defects.'

The usually-vocal Mr Myerscough, who has promised to pump £250,000 into the company and give Monotub shareholders £4 for every machine sold, refused to comment on his plans for the Titan or reveal who his backers were. But . . . he did say that he intended to 'take the Titan forward'.

Source: 'Monotub Industries in a spin as founder gets Titan for £1', *The Financial Times*, 23/01/2003 (Urquhart, L.), copyright © The Financial Times Ltd.

Limited liability

Since the company is a legal person in its own right, it must take responsibility for its own debts and losses. This means that, once the shareholders have paid what they have agreed to pay for the shares, their obligation to the company, and to the company's creditors, is satisfied. Thus shareholders can limit their losses to the amount that they have paid, or agreed to pay, for their shares. This is of great practical importance to potential shareholders since they know that what they can lose, as part owners of the business, is limited.

Contrast this with the position of sole proprietors or partners. They cannot 'ring-fence' assets that they do not want to put into the business. If a sole proprietorship or partnership business finds itself in a position where liabilities exceed the business assets, the law gives unsatisfied creditors the right to demand payment out of what the sole proprietor or partner may have regarded as 'non-business' assets. Thus the sole proprietor or partner could lose everything – house, car, the lot. This is because the law sees Jill, the sole proprietor, as being the same as Jill the private individual. The shareholder, by contrast, can lose only the amount committed to that company. Legally, the business operating as a limited company, in which Jack owns shares, is not the same as Jack himself. This is true even if Jack were to own all of the shares in the company.

Real World 4.2 gives an example of a well-known case where the shareholders of a particular company were able to avoid any liability to those that had lost money as a result of dealing with the company.

Real World 4.2

Carlton and Granada 1 - Nationwide Football League 0

Two television broadcasting companies, Carlton and Granada, each owned 50 per cent of a separate company, ITV Digital (formerly ON Digital). ITV Digital signed a contract to pay the Nationwide Football League (in effect the three divisions of English football below the Premiership) more than £89 million on both 1 August 2002 and 1 August 2003 for the rights to broadcast football matches over three seasons. ITV Digital was unable to sell enough subscriptions for the broadcasts and collapsed because it was unable to meet its liabilities. The Nationwide Football League tried to force Carlton and Granada (ITV Digital's only shareholders) to meet ITV Digital's contractual obligations. It was unable to do so because the shareholders could not be held legally liable for the amounts owing.

Carlton and Granada merged into one business in 2003, but at the time of ITV Digital were two independent companies.

Activity 4.1

The fact that shareholders can limit their losses to that which they have paid, or have agreed to pay, for their shares is of great practical importance to potential shareholders.

Can you think of any practical benefit to a private sector economy, in general, of this ability of shareholders to limit losses?

Business is a risky venture – in some cases very risky. People in a position to invest money will usually be happier to do so when they know the limit of their liability. If investors are given limited liability, new businesses are more likely to be formed and existing ones are likely to find it easier to raise more finance. This is good for the private sector economy and may ultimately lead to the generation of greater wealth for society as a whole.

Although limited liability has this advantage to the providers of equity finance (the shareholders), it is not necessarily to the advantage of others who have a stake in the business, like the Nationwide Football League clubs (see Real World 4.2). Limited liability is attractive to shareholders because they can, in effect, walk away from the unpaid debts of the company if their contribution has not been sufficient to meet those debts. This is likely to make any individual, or another business, that is considering entering into a contract, wary of dealing with the limited company. This can be a real problem for smaller, less established companies. Suppliers may insist on cash payment before delivery of goods or the rendering of a service. Alternatively, they may require a personal guarantee from a major shareholder that the debt will be paid before allowing trade credit. In the latter case, the supplier circumvents the company's limited liability status by demanding the personal liability of an individual. Larger, more established companies, on the other hand, tend to have built up the confidence of suppliers.

Legal safeguards

Various safeguards exist to protect individuals and businesses contemplating dealing with a limited company. These include the requirement to indicate limited liability status in the name of the company. By doing this, an alert is issued to prospective suppliers and lenders.

A further safeguard is the restrictions placed on the ability of shareholders to withdraw their equity from the company. These restrictions are designed to prevent shareholders from protecting their own investment and, as a result, leaving lenders and suppliers in an exposed position. We shall consider this point in more detail later in the chapter.

Finally, limited companies are required to produce annual financial statements (which include the income statement, statement of financial position and statement of cash flows) and to make these publicly available. This means that anyone interested can gain an impression of the financial performance and position of the company. The form and content of these statements are considered in some detail later in this chapter and in Chapter 5, which considers the statement of cash flows.

Public and private companies

When a company is registered with the Registrar of Companies, it must be registered either as a public or as a private company. The main practical difference between these is that a public limited company can offer its shares for sale to the general public, but a private limited company is restricted from doing so. A public limited company must signal its status to all interested parties by having the words 'public limited company', or its abbreviation 'plc', in its name. For a private limited company, the word 'limited' or 'Ltd' must appear as part of its name.

Private limited companies tend to be smaller businesses where the ownership is divided among relatively few shareholders who are usually fairly close to one another

– for example, a family company. Numerically, there are vastly more private limited companies in the UK than there are public ones. Of the 2.25 million UK limited companies now in existence, only 9,600 (representing 0.4 per cent of the total) are public limited companies.

Since individual public companies tend to be larger, they are often economically more important. In some industry sectors, such as banking, insurance, oil refining and grocery retailing, they are completely dominant. Although some large private limited companies exist, many private limited companies are little more than the vehicle through which one-person businesses operate.

Real World 4.3 shows the extent of market dominance of public limited companies in one particular business sector.

Real World 4.3

A big slice of the market

The grocery sector is dominated by four large players: Tesco, Sainsbury, Morrison and Asda. The first three are public limited companies and the fourth, Asda, is owned by a large US public company, Wal-Mart. Figure 4.1 shows the share of the grocery market enjoyed by each, during the 12-week period which ended on 24 January 2010.

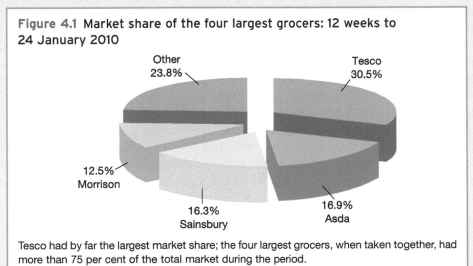

Figure 4.1 Market share of the four largest grocers: 12 weeks to 24 January 2010

Tesco had by far the largest market share; the four largest grocers, when taken together, had more than 75 per cent of the total market during the period.

Source: compiled from information in Mills, E., 'Tesco's grocery market share rises to 30.5% in 12 weeks – Kantar', Dow Jones Newswires, 2 February 2010.

Taxation

Another consequence of the legal separation of the limited company from its owners is that companies must be accountable to the tax authorities for tax on their profits and gains. This leads to the reporting of tax in the financial statements of limited companies. The charge for tax is shown in the income statement. The tax charge for a particular year is based on that year's profit. Since only 50 per cent of a company's tax liability is due for payment during the year concerned, the other 50 per cent will appear on the end-of-year statement of financial position as a short-term liability. This will be illustrated a little later in the chapter. The tax position of companies contrasts with that of sole proprietorships and partnerships, where tax is levied not on the business but on the owner(s). Thus tax does not impact on the financial statements of unincorporated businesses, but is an individual matter between the owner(s) and the tax authorities.

Companies are charged corporation tax on their profits and gains. The percentage rates of tax tend to vary from year to year, but have recently been 28 per cent for larger companies and 21 per cent for smaller companies. These rates of tax are levied on the company's taxable profit, which is not necessarily the same as the profit shown on the income statement. This is because tax law does not, in every respect, follow the normal accounting rules. Generally, however, the taxable profit and the company's accounting profit are pretty close to one another.

Transferring share ownership: the role of the Stock Exchange

We have already seen that shares in a company may be transferred from one owner to another. The desire of some shareholders to sell their shares, coupled with the desire of others to buy those shares, has led to the existence of a formal market in which shares can be bought and sold. The London Stock Exchange and similar organisations around the world provide a marketplace in which shares in public companies may be bought and sold. Share prices are determined by the laws of supply and demand, which are, in turn, determined by investors' perceptions of the future economic prospects of the companies concerned. Only the shares of certain companies (*listed* companies) may be traded on the London Stock Exchange. Less than 1,100 UK companies are listed. This represents only about 1 in 2,000 of all UK companies (public and private) and roughly one in nine public limited companies. However, many of these listed companies are massive. Nearly all of the 'household-name' UK businesses (for example, Tesco, Next, BT, Vodafone, BP and so on) are listed companies.

Activity 4.2

If, as has been pointed out earlier, the change in ownership of shares does not directly affect the particular company, why do many public companies actively seek to have their shares traded in a recognised market?

The main reason is that investors are generally very reluctant to pledge their money unless they can see some way in which they can turn their investment back into cash. In theory, the shares of a particular company may be very valuable because the company has bright prospects. However, unless this value is capable of being turned into cash, the benefit to the shareholders is dubious. After all, we cannot spend shares; we normally need cash.

This means that potential shareholders are much more likely to be prepared to buy new shares from the company (thereby providing the company with new investment finance) where they can see a way of liquidating their investment (turning it into cash) as and when they wish. Stock Exchanges provide the means of liquidation.

Although the buying and selling of 'second-hand' shares does not provide the company with cash, the fact that the buying and selling facility exists will make it easier for the company to raise new share capital when it needs to do so.

Managing a company

A limited company may have legal personality, but it is not a human being capable of making decisions and plans about the business and exercising control over it. People must undertake these management tasks. The most senior level of management of a company is the board of directors.

The shareholders elect directors (by law there must be at least one director for a private limited company and two for a public limited company) to manage the company on a day-to-day basis on behalf of those shareholders. In a small company, the board may be the only level of management and consist of all of the shareholders. In larger companies, the board may consist of ten or so directors out of many thousands of shareholders. Indeed, directors are not even required to be shareholders. Below the board of directors of the typical large company could be several layers of management comprising thousands of people.

In recent years, the issue of corporate governance has generated much debate. The term is used to describe the ways in which companies are directed and controlled. The issue of corporate governance is important because, with larger companies, those who own the company (that is, the shareholders) are usually divorced from the day-to-day control of the business. The shareholders employ the directors to manage the company for them. Given this position, it may seem reasonable to assume that the best interests of shareholders will guide the directors' decisions. However, in practice this does not always seem to be the case. The directors may be more concerned with pursuing their own interests, such as increasing their pay and 'perks' (such as expensive motor cars, overseas visits and so on) and improving their job security and status. As a result, a conflict can occur between the interests of shareholders and the interests of directors.

Where directors pursue their own interests rather than those of shareholders, there is clearly a problem for the shareholders. However, it may also be a problem for society as a whole. Where investors feel that their funds are likely to be mismanaged, they will be reluctant to invest. A shortage of funds will mean that companies can make fewer investments. Furthermore, the costs of finance will increase as companies compete for what funds are available. Thus, a lack of concern for shareholders can have a profound effect on the performance of individual companies and, with this, the health of the economy. To avoid these problems, most competitive market economies have a framework of rules to help monitor and control the behaviour of directors.

These rules are usually based around three guiding principles:

■ *Disclosure*. This lies at the heart of good corporate governance. An OECD report (see reference 1 at the end of chapter for details) summed up the benefits of disclosure as follows:

> Adequate and timely information about corporate performance enables investors to make informed buy-and-sell decisions and thereby helps the market reflect the value of a corporation [company] under present management. If the market determines that present management is not performing, a decrease in stock [share] price will sanction management's failure and open the way to management change.

■ *Accountability*. This involves defining the roles and duties of the directors and establishing an adequate monitoring process. In the UK, company law requires that the directors of a company act in the best interests of the shareholders. This means, among other things, that they must not try to use their position and knowledge to make gains at the expense of the shareholders. The law also requires larger companies to have their annual financial statements independently audited. The purpose of an independent audit is to lend credibility to the financial statements prepared by the directors. We shall consider this point in more detail later in the chapter.

■ *Fairness*. Directors should not be able to benefit from access to 'inside' information that is not available to shareholders. As a result, both the law and the London Stock Exchange place restrictions on the ability of directors to buy and sell the shares of the company. One example of these restrictions is that the directors cannot buy or sell shares immediately before the announcement of the annual trading results of the company or before the announcement of a significant event, such as a planned merger or the loss of the chief executive.

These principles are set out in Figure 4.2.

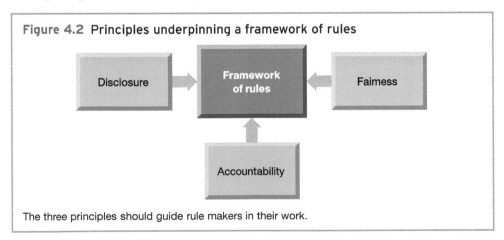

Figure 4.2 Principles underpinning a framework of rules

The three principles should guide rule makers in their work.

Strengthening the framework of rules

The number of rules designed to safeguard shareholders has increased considerably over the years. This has been in response to weaknesses in corporate governance procedures, which have been exposed through well-publicised business failures and frauds, excessive pay increases to directors and evidence that some financial reports were being 'massaged' so as to mislead shareholders. (This last point will be discussed later in the chapter.)

Many believe, however, that the shareholders must shoulder some of the blame for any weaknesses. Not all shareholders in large companies are private individuals owning just a few shares each. In fact, ownership, by market value, of the shares listed on the London Stock Exchange is dominated by investing institutions such as insurance businesses, banks, pension funds and so on. These are often massive operations, owning large quantities of the shares of the companies in which they invest. These institutional investors employ specialist staff to manage their portfolios of shares in various companies. It has been argued that the large institutional shareholders, despite their size and relative expertise, have not been very active in corporate governance matters. Thus, there has been little monitoring of directors. However, things seem to be changing. There is increasing evidence that institutional investors are becoming more proactive in relation to the companies in which they hold shares.

The UK Corporate Governance Code

During the 1990s there was a real effort by the accountancy profession and the London Stock Exchange to address the problems of poor corporate governance mentioned earlier. A Code of Best Practice on Corporate Governance emerged in 1992. This was concerned with accountability and financial reporting. In 1995, a separate code of practice emerged which dealt with directors' pay and conditions. These two codes were revised, 'fine tuned' and amalgamated to produce the Combined Code, which was issued in 1998. Every few years, the impact and effectiveness of the Code has been reviewed and this has resulted in revisions being made. In 2010, the Combined Code changed its name to the 'UK Corporate Governance Code'.

The UK Corporate Governance Code has the backing of the London Stock Exchange. This means that companies listed on the London Stock Exchange must 'comply or explain'. That is, they must comply with the requirements of the UK Code or must give their shareholders good reason why they do not. Failure to do one or other of these can lead to the company's shares being suspended from listing.

Activity 4.3

Why might being suspended from listing be an important sanction against a non-compliant company?

A major advantage of a Stock Exchange listing is that it enables investors to sell their shares whenever they wish. A company that is suspended from listing would find it hard and, therefore, expensive to raise funds from investors because there would be no ready market for the shares.

The UK Code sets out a number of principles relating to such matters as the role of the directors, their relations with shareholders and their accountability. Real World 4.4 outlines some of the more important of these.

Real World 4.4

The UK Corporate Governance Code

The key elements of the UK Code are as follows:

- Every listed company should have a board of directors that is collectively responsible for its success.
- There should be a clear division of responsibilities between the chairman and the chief executive officer of the company to try to ensure that a single person does not have unbridled power.
- There should be an appropriate balance of skills, experience, independence and knowledge to enable the board to carry out its duties effectively.
- The board should receive timely information that is of sufficient quality to enable it to carry out its duties. All board members should refresh their skill regularly and new board members should receive induction.
- Appointments to the board should be the subject of rigorous, formal and transparent procedures and should be drawn from a broad talent pool.
- All directors should submit themselves for re-election at regular intervals, subject to satisfactory performance.
- Remuneration levels should be sufficient to attract, retain and motivate directors of the appropriate quality and should take account of individual and company performance.
- There should be formal and transparent procedures for developing policy on directors' remuneration.
- The board should try to ensure that a satisfactory dialogue with shareholders occurs.
- Boards should use the annual general meeting to communicate with investors and encourage their participation.
- Institutional shareholders should use their votes and enter into a dialogue with the company based on a mutual understanding of objectives.
- The board should publish a balanced and understandable assessment of the company's position and future prospects.
- The board should define the company's risk appetite and tolerance and should maintain a sound risk management system.
- Formal and transparent arrangements for applying financial reporting and internal control principles and for maintaining an appropriate relationship with auditors should be in place.
- The board should undertake a formal and rigorous examination of its own performance each year, which will include its committees and individual directors.

Source: www.fsa.org.uk.

Strengthening the framework of rules in this way has been generally agreed to have improved the quality of information available to shareholders. It has also resulted in better checks on the powers of directors and provided greater transparency in corporate affairs. However, rules can only be a partial answer. A balance must be struck between the need to protect shareholders and the need to encourage the entrepreneurial spirit of directors – which could be stifled under a welter of rules. This implies that rules should not be too tight, and so unscrupulous directors may still find ways around them.

Financing limited companies

Equity (the owners' claim)

The equity of a sole proprietorship is normally encompassed in one figure on the statement of financial position. With companies, this is usually a little more complicated, although in essence the same broad principles apply. With a company, equity is divided between shares (for example, the original investment), on the one hand, and reserves (that is, profits and gains subsequently made), on the other. There is also the possibility that there will be more than one type of shares and of reserves. Thus, within the basic divisions of share capital and reserves, there might well be further subdivisions. This might seem quite complicated, but we shall shortly consider the reasons for these subdivisions and all should become clearer.

The basic division

When a company is first formed, those who take steps to form it (the promoters) will decide how much needs to be raised by the potential shareholders to set the company up with the necessary assets to operate. Example 4.1 acts as a basis for illustration.

Example 4.1

Some friends decide to form a company to operate an office cleaning business. They estimate that the company will need £50,000 to obtain the necessary assets. Between them, they raise the cash, which they use to buy shares in the company, on 31 March 2009, with a nominal value (or par value) of £1 each.

At this point the statement of financial position of the company would be:

Statement of financial position as at 31 March 2009

	£
Net assets (all in cash)	50,000
Equity	
Share capital	
50,000 shares of £1 each	50,000

The company now buys the necessary non-current assets (vacuum cleaners and so on) and inventories (cleaning materials) and starts to trade. During the first year, the company makes a profit of £10,000. This, by definition, means that the equity expands by £10,000. During the year, the shareholders (owners) make no drawings of their equity, so at the end of the year the summarised statement of financial position looks like this:

Statement of financial position as at 31 March 2010

	£
Net assets (various assets less liabilities*)	60,000
Equity	
Share capital	
50,000 shares of £1 each	50,000
Reserves (revenue reserve)	10,000
Total equity	60,000

* We saw in Chapter 2 that Assets = Equity + Liabilities. We also saw that this can be rearranged so that Assets – Liabilities = Equity.

→ The profit is shown in a reserve, known as a revenue reserve, because it arises from generating revenue (making sales). Note that we do not simply merge the profit with the share capital: we must keep the two amounts separate (to satisfy company law). The reason for this is that there is a legal restriction on the maximum drawings of their
→ equity (or payment of a dividend) that the shareholders can make. This is defined by the amount of revenue reserves, and so it is helpful to show these separately. We shall look at why there is this restriction, and how it works, a little later in the chapter.

Share capital

Ordinary shares

Shares represent the basic units of ownership of a business. All companies issue
→ ordinary shares. Ordinary shares are often known as *equities*. The nominal value of such shares is at the discretion of the people who start up the company. For example, if the initial share capital is to be £50,000, this could be two shares of £25,000 each, 5 million shares of one penny each or any other combination that gives a total of £50,000. All shares must have equal value.

Activity 4.4

The initial financial requirement for a new company is £50,000. There are to be two equal shareholders. Would you advise them to issue two shares of £25,000 each? Why?

Such large-denomination shares tend to be unwieldy. Suppose that one of the shareholders wanted to sell her shareholding. She would have to find one buyer. If there were shares of smaller denomination, it would be possible to sell part of the shareholding to various potential buyers. Furthermore, it would be possible to sell just part of the holding and retain a part.

In practice, £1 is the normal maximum nominal value for shares. Shares of 25 pence each and 50 pence each are probably the most common.

Altering the nominal value of shares

As we have already seen, the promoters of a new company may make their own choice of the nominal or par value of the shares. This value need not be permanent. At a later date the shareholders can decide to change it.

Suppose that a company has 1 million ordinary shares of £1 each and a decision is made to change the nominal value of the shares from £1 to £0.50, in other words to halve the value. This would lead the company to issue each shareholder with a new share certificate (the shareholders' evidence of ownership of their shares) for exactly twice as many shares, each with half the nominal value. The result would be that each shareholder retains a holding of the same total nominal value. This process is known, not surprisingly, as splitting the shares. The opposite, reducing the number of shares and increasing their nominal value per share to compensate, is known as consolidating. Since each shareholder would be left, after a split or consolidation, with exactly the same proportion of ownership of the company's assets as before, the process should not increase the value of the total shares held.

Splitting is fairly common. The objective is probably to avoid individual shares becoming too valuable and thus unwieldy, as discussed in the answer to Activity 4.4. If a company trades successfully, the value of each share is likely to rise and, in time, could increase to a level that makes the shares less marketable. Splitting would solve this problem. Consolidating is relatively rare.

Real World 4.5 provides an example of a share split by one business.

Real World 4.5

Doing the splits

A G Barr, the Scottish based maker of soft drinks, including Tizer and Irn Bru, had a share split in September 2009, as announced by the business in its half-yearly report:

> As previously announced, the 2 for 1 share split, which is aimed at improving liquidity and marketability of the company's shares became effective on 21 September.

Source: A G Barr plc Interim Report, August 2009, p. 3.

Preference shares

Some companies not only issue ordinary shares, but also have other classes of shares, preference shares being the most common. Preference shares guarantee that *if a dividend is paid*, the preference shareholders will be entitled to the first part of it up to a maximum value. This maximum is normally defined as a fixed percentage of the nominal value of the preference shares. If, for example, a company issues 10,000 preference shares of £1 each with a dividend rate of 6 per cent, this means that the preference shareholders are entitled to receive the first £600 (that is, 6 per cent of £10,000) of any dividend that is paid by the company for a year. The excess over £600 goes to the ordinary shareholders. Normally, any undistributed profits and gains also accrue to the ordinary shareholders.

The ordinary shareholders are the primary risk takers as they are entitled to share in the profits of the company only after other claims have been satisfied. There are no upper limits, however, on the amount by which they may benefit. The potential rewards available to ordinary shareholders reflect the risks that they are prepared to take. Since ordinary shareholders take most of the risks, power normally resides in their hands. Usually, only the ordinary shareholders are able to vote on issues that affect the company, such as who the directors should be.

It is open to the company to issue shares of various classes – perhaps with some having unusual and exotic conditions – but in practice it is rare to find other than straightforward ordinary and preference shares. Although a company may have different classes of shares whose holders have different rights, within each class all shares must be treated equally. The rights of the various classes of shareholders, as well as other matters relating to a particular company, are contained in that company's set of rules, known as the 'articles and memorandum of association'. A copy of these rules must be lodged with the Registrar of Companies, who makes it available for inspection by the general public.

Reserves

As we have already seen, reserves are profits and gains that a company has made and which still form part of the shareholders' equity. One reason that past profits and gains may not continue to be part of equity is that they have been paid out to shareholders (as dividends and so on). Another reason is that reserves will be reduced by the amount of any losses that the company might suffer. In the same way that profits increase equity, losses reduce it.

Activity 4.5

Are reserves amounts of cash? Can you think of a reason why this is an odd question?

To deal with the second point first, it is an odd question because reserves are a claim, or part of one, on the assets of the company, whereas cash is an asset. So reserves cannot be cash.

Reserves are classified as either revenue reserves or capital reserves. In Example 4.1 we came across one type of reserve, the revenue reserve. We should recall that this reserve represents the company's retained trading profits and gains on the disposal of non-current assets. It is worth mentioning that retained earnings, as they are most often called, represent overwhelmingly the largest source of new finance for UK companies. For most companies they amount to more than share issues and borrowings combined.

Capital reserves arise for two main reasons:

- issuing shares at above their nominal value (for example, issuing £1 shares at £1.50);
- revaluing (upwards) non-current assets.

Where a company issues shares at above their nominal value, UK law requires that the excess of the issue price over the nominal value be shown separately.

Activity 4.6

Can you think why shares might be issued at above their nominal value? (*Hint*: This would not usually happen when a company is first formed and the initial shares are being issued.)

Once a company has traded and has been successful, the shares would normally be worth more than the nominal value at which they were issued. If additional shares are to be issued to new shareholders to raise finance for further expansion, unless they are issued at a value higher than the nominal value, the new shareholders will be gaining at the expense of the original ones.

Example 4.2 shows how this works.

Example 4.2

Based on future prospects, the net assets of a company are worth £1.5 million. There are currently 1 million ordinary shares in the company, each with a face (nominal) value of £1. The company wishes to raise an additional £0.6 million of cash for expansion and has decided to raise it by issuing new shares. If the shares are issued for £1 each (that is 600,000 shares), the total number of shares will be

$$1.0\text{m} + 0.6\text{m} = 1.6\text{m}$$

and their total value will be the value of the existing net assets plus the new injection of cash:

$$£1.5\text{m} + £0.6\text{m} = £2.1\text{m}$$

This means that the value of each share after the new issue will be

$$£2.1\text{m}/1.6\text{m} = £1.3125$$

The current value of each share is

$$£1.5\text{m}/1.0\text{m} = £1.50$$

so the original shareholders will lose

$$£1.50 - £1.3125 = £0.1875 \text{ a share}$$

and the new shareholders will gain

$$£1.3125 - £1.0 = £0.3125 \text{ a share}$$

The new shareholders will, no doubt, be delighted with this outcome; the original ones will not.

Things could be made fair between the two sets of shareholders described in Example 4.2 by issuing the new shares at £1.50 each. In this case it would be necessary to issue 400,000 shares to raise the necessary £0.6 million. £1 a share of the £1.50 is the nominal value and will be included with share capital in the statement of financial position (£400,000 in total). The remaining £0.50 is a share premium, which will be shown as a capital reserve known as the share premium account (£200,000 in total).

It is not clear why UK company law insists on the distinction between nominal share values and the premium. In some other countries (for example, the United States) with similar laws governing the corporate sector, there is not the necessity of distinguishing between share capital and share premium. Instead, the total value at which shares are issued is shown as one comprehensive figure on the company's statement of financial position. Real World 4.6 shows the equity of one well-known business.

Real World 4.6

Funding Thorntons

Thorntons plc, the chocolate maker and retailer, had the following share capital and reserves as at 27 June 2009:

	£m
Share capital (10p ordinary shares)	6,835
Share premium	13,752
Retained earnings	8,151
Total equity	28,738

Note how the nominal share capital figure is only about half as much as the share premium account figure. This implies that Thorntons has issued shares at higher prices than the 10p a share nominal value. This reflects its trading success since the company was first formed. In 2008, retained earnings (profits) had made up over 40 per cent of the total for share capital and reserves. By 2009, this had reduced to around 28 per cent. This reduction was mainly caused by a loss suffered by the company pension fund during the year.

Source: Thorntons plc Annual Report 2009, p. 45.

Bonus shares

It is always open to a company to take reserves of any kind (irrespective of whether they are capital or revenue) and turn them into share capital. This will involve transferring the desired amount from the reserve concerned to share capital and then distributing the appropriate number of new shares to the existing shareholders. New shares arising from such a conversion are known as bonus shares. Issues of bonus shares used to be quite frequently encountered in practice, but more recently they are much less common. Example 4.3 illustrates this aspect of share issues.

Example 4.3

The summary statement of financial position of a company at a particular point in time is as follows:

Statement of financial position

	£
Net assets (various assets less liabilities)	128,000
Equity	
Share capital	
50,000 shares of £1 each	50,000
Reserves	78,000
Total equity	128,000

The company decides that it will issue existing shareholders with one new share for every share currently owned by each shareholder. The statement of financial position immediately following this will appear as follows:

Statement of financial position

	£
Net assets (various assets less liabilities)	128,000
Equity	
Share capital	
100,000 shares of £1 each (50,000 + 50,000)	100,000
Reserves (78,000 − 50,000)	28,000
Total equity	128,000

We can see that the reserves have decreased by £50,000 and share capital has increased by the same amount. Share certificates for the 50,000 ordinary shares of £1 each, which have been created from reserves, will be issued to the existing shareholders to complete the transaction.

A shareholder of the company in Example 4.3 owned 100 shares before the bonus issue. How will things change for this shareholder as regards the number of shares owned and the value of the shareholding?

The answer should be that the number of shares would double, from 100 to 200. Now the shareholder owns one five-hundredth of the company (that is, 200/100,000). Before the bonus issue, the shareholder also owned one five-hundredth of the company (that is, 100/50,000). The company's assets and liabilities have not changed as a result of the bonus issue and so, logically, one five-hundredth of the value of the company should be identical to what it was before. Thus, each share is worth half as much.

A *bonus issue* simply takes one part of the equity (a reserve) and puts it into another part (share capital). The transaction has no effect on the company's assets or liabilities, so there is no effect on shareholders' wealth.

Note that a bonus issue is not the same as a share split. A split does not affect the reserves.

Activity 4.8

Can you think of any reasons why a company might want to make a bonus issue if it has no direct economic consequence?

We think that there are three possible reasons:

■ *Share price*. To lower the value of each share without reducing the shareholders' collective or individual wealth. This has a similar effect to share splitting.
■ *Shareholder confidence*. To provide the shareholders with a 'feel-good factor'. It is believed that shareholders like bonus issues because they seem to make them better off, although in practice they should not affect their wealth.
■ *Lender confidence*. Where reserves arising from operating profits and/or realised gains on the sale of non-current assets are used to make the bonus issue, it has the effect of taking part of that portion of the shareholders' equity that could be drawn by the shareholders, as drawings (or dividends), and locking it up. The amount transferred becomes part of the permanent equity base of the company. (We shall see a little later in this chapter that there are severe restrictions on the extent to which shareholders may make drawings from their equity.) An individual or business contemplating lending money to the company may insist that the dividend payment possibilities are restricted as a condition of making the loan. This point will be explained shortly.

Real World 4.7 cites a recent example of a bonus share issue. Given the discussion above, the rationale provided for the bonus issue is particularly interesting (and perplexing!).

Real World 4.7

It's a bonus?

Medusa Mining is a gold producer that is listed on various international stock markets. In 2010, it announced a one-for-ten bonus issue of shares to all shareholders of the company.

In a statement, the company said it had achieved several significant milestones in the last calendar year and the bonus issue is in recognition of the invaluable support the company has received from its shareholders. The bonus issue was also designed to encourage greater liquidity in Medusa shares.

Geoff Davis, managing director of Medusa, said: 'The board is extremely pleased to be in a position to reward shareholders as a result of the company having rapidly expanded its production over the last twelve months and having met all targets on time.'

Source: adapted from 'Medusa Mining', www.proactiveinvestors.co.uk, 8 March 2010.

Share capital jargon

Before leaving our detailed discussion of share capital, it might be helpful to clarify some of the jargon relating to shares that is used in company financial statements.

Share capital that has been issued to shareholders is known as the issued share capital (or allotted share capital). Sometimes, but not very often, a company may not require shareholders to pay the whole amount that is due to be paid for the shares at the time of issue. This may happen where the company does not need the money all at once. Some money would normally be paid at the time of issue and the company would 'call' for further instalments until the shares were fully paid shares. That part of the total issue price that has been 'called' is known as the called-up share capital. That part that has been called and paid is known as the paid-up share capital.

Raising share capital

Once the company has made its initial share issue to start business (usually soon after the company is first formed) it may decide to make further issues of new shares. These may be:

- *rights issues* – issues made to existing shareholders, in proportion to their existing shareholding;
- *public issues* – issues made to the general investing public; or
- *private placings* – issues made to selected individuals who are usually approached and asked if they would be interested in taking up new shares.

During its lifetime a company may use all three of these approaches to raising funds through issuing new shares (although only public companies can make appeals to the general public).

We shall explore the ways that companies can raise new share capital in more detail in Chapter 11.

Borrowings

Most companies borrow money to supplement that raised from share issues and ploughed-back profits. Company borrowing is often on a long-term basis, perhaps on a ten-year contract. Lenders may be banks and other professional providers of loan finance. Many companies borrow in such a way that small investors, including private individuals, are able to lend small amounts. This is particularly the case with the larger, Stock Exchange listed, companies and involves them making a *loan notes* issue, which, though large in total, can be taken up in small slices by individual investors, both private individuals and investing institutions, such as pension funds and insurance companies. In some cases, these slices of loans can be bought and sold through the Stock Exchange. This means that investors do not have to wait the full term of their loan to obtain repayment, but can sell their slice of it to another would-be lender at intermediate points in the term of the loan. Loan notes are often known as *loan stock* or *debentures*.

Some of the features of loan notes financing, particularly the possibility that the loan notes may be traded on the Stock Exchange, can lead to a misunderstanding that loan notes are shares by another name. We should be clear that this is not the case. It is the shareholders who own the company and, therefore, who share in its losses and profits. Holders of loan notes lend money to the company under a legally binding contract that normally specifies the rate of interest, the interest payment dates and the date of repayment of the loan itself.

Usually, long-term loans are secured on assets of the company. This would give the lender the right to seize the assets concerned, sell them and satisfy the repayment obligation, should the company fail to pay either its interest payments or the repayment of the loan itself, on the dates specified in the contract between the company and the lender. A mortgage granted to a private individual buying a house or a flat is a very common example of a secured loan.

Long-term financing of companies can be depicted as in Figure 4.3.

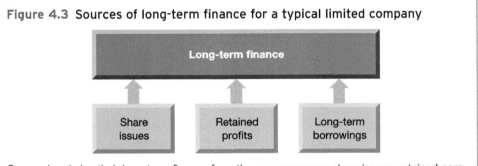

Figure 4.3 Sources of long-term finance for a typical limited company

Companies derive their long-term finance from three sources: new share issues, retained earnings and long-term borrowings. For a typical company, the sum of the first two (jointly known as 'equity finance') exceeds the third. Retained earnings usually exceed each of the other two in terms of the amount of finance raised in most years.

It is important to the prosperity and stability of a company that it strikes a suitable balance between finance provided by the shareholders (equity) and from borrowing. This topic will be explored in Chapter 6. Equity and loan notes are, of course, not the only forms of finance available to a company. In Chapter 11, we consider other sources of finance available to businesses, including companies.

Withdrawing equity

Companies, as we have seen, are legally obliged to distinguish, on the statement of financial position, between that part of the shareholders' equity that may be withdrawn and that part which may not. The withdrawable part consists of profits arising from trading (retained profits or earnings) and from the disposal of non-current assets. It is represented in the statement of financial position by *revenue reserves*.

It is important to appreciate that the total of revenue reserves appearing in the statement of financial position is rarely the total of all trading profits and profits on disposals of non-current assets generated by the company. This total will normally have been reduced by at least one of the following three factors:

- corporation tax paid on those profits
- any dividends paid
- any losses from trading and the disposal of non-current assets.

The non-withdrawable part consists of share capital plus profits arising from shareholders buying shares in the company and from upward revaluations of assets still held. It is represented in the statement of financial position by *share capital* and *capital reserves*.

Figure 4.4 shows the important division between the part of the shareholders' equity that can be withdrawn as a dividend and the part that cannot.

Figure 4.4 Availability for dividends of various parts of the shareholders' equity

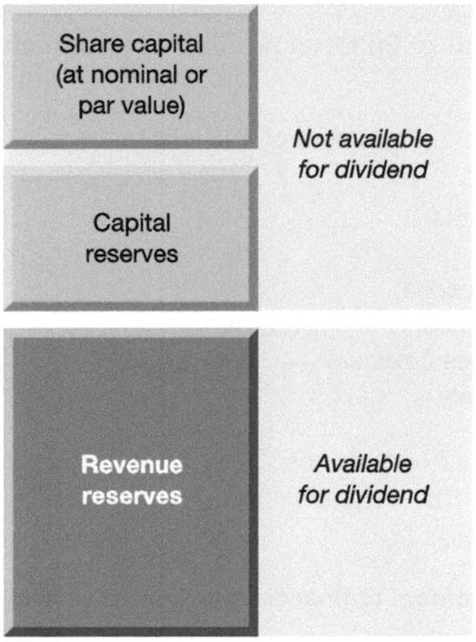

Total equity finance of limited companies consists of share capital, capital reserves and revenue reserves. Only the revenue reserves (which arise from realised profits and gains) can be used to fund a dividend. In other words, the maximum legal dividend is the amount of the revenue reserves.

The law does not specify how large the non-withdrawable part of a particular company's shareholders' equity should be. However, when seeking to impress prospective lenders and credit suppliers, the larger this part, the better. Those considering doing business with the company must be able to see from the company's statement of financial position how large it is.

Why are limited companies required to distinguish different parts of their shareholders' equity, whereas sole proprietorship and partnership businesses are not?

The reason stems from the limited liability that company shareholders enjoy but which owners of unincorporated businesses do not. If a sole proprietor or partner withdraws all of the equity, or even an amount in excess of this, the position of the lenders and credit suppliers of the business is not weakened since they can legally enforce their claims against the sole proprietor or partner as an individual. With a limited company, the business and the owners are legally separated and such a right to enforce claims against individuals does not exist. To protect the company's lenders and credit suppliers, however, the law insists that the shareholders cannot normally withdraw a specific part of their equity.

Let us now look at an example that illustrates how this protection of creditors works.

Example 4.4

The summary statement of financial position of a company at a particular date is as follows:

Statement of financial position

	£
Total assets	43,000
Equity	
Share capital	
20,000 shares of £1 each	20,000
Reserves (revenue)	23,000
Total equity	43,000

A bank has been asked to make a £25,000 long-term loan to the company. If the loan were to be made, the statement of financial position immediately following would appear as follows:

Statement of financial position (after the loan)

	£
Total assets (£43,000 + £25,000)	68,000
Equity	
Share capital	
20,000 shares of £1 each	20,000
Reserves (revenue)	23,000
	43,000
Non-current liability	
Borrowings – loan	25,000
Total equity and liabilities	68,000

As things stand, there are assets with a total carrying amount of £68,000 to meet the bank's claim of £25,000. It would be possible and perfectly legal, however, for the company to pay a dividend (withdraw part of the shareholders' equity) equal to the total revenue reserves (£23,000). The statement of financial position would then appear as follows:

Statement of financial position

	£
Total assets (£68,000 – £23,000)	45,000
Equity	
Share capital	
20,000 shares of £1 each	20,000
Reserves (revenue) (£23,000 – £23,000)	–
	20,000
Non-current liabilities	
Borrowings – bank loan	25,000
Total equity and liabilities	45,000

This leaves the bank in a very much weaker position, in that there are now total assets with a carrying amount of £45,000 to meet a claim of £25,000. Note that the difference between the amount of the borrowings (bank loan) and the total assets equals the equity (share capital and reserves) total. Thus, the equity represents a margin of safety for lenders and suppliers. The larger the amount of the equity withdrawable by the shareholders, the smaller is the potential margin of safety for lenders and suppliers.

As we have already seen, the law says nothing about how large the margin of safety must be. It is up to each company to decide what is appropriate.

As a practical footnote to Example 4.4, it is worth pointing out that long-term lenders would normally seek to secure a loan against an asset of the company, such as land.

Activity 4.10

Would you expect a company to pay all of its revenue reserves as a dividend? What factors might be involved with a dividend decision?

It would be rare for a company to pay all of its revenue reserves as a dividend: the fact that it is legally possible does not necessarily make it a good idea. Most companies see ploughed-back profits as a major – usually *the* major – source of new finance. The factors that tend most to influence the dividend decision are likely to include:

- the availability of cash to pay a dividend; it would not be illegal to borrow to pay a dividend, but it would be unusual and, possibly, imprudent;
- the needs of the business for finance for new investment;
- the expectations of shareholders concerning the amount of dividends to be paid.

You may have thought of others.

If we look back at Real World 4.6 (page 128), we can see that at 27 June 2009, Thorntons plc could legally have paid a dividend totalling £8,151 million. Of course, the company did not do this, presumably because the funds concerned were tied up in property, plant and equipment and other assets, not lying around in the form of unused cash.

The main financial statements

As we might expect, the financial statements of a limited company are, in essence, the same as those of a sole proprietor or partnership. There are, however, some differences of detail. We shall now consider these. Example 4.5 sets out the income statement and statement of financial position of a limited company.

Example 4.5

Da Silva plc
Income statement for the year ended 31 December 2010

	£m
Revenue	840
Cost of sales	(520)
Gross profit	320
Wages and salaries	(98)
Heat and light	(18)
Rent and rates	(24)
Motor vehicle expenses	(20)
Insurance	(4)
Printing and stationery	(12)
Depreciation	(45)
Audit fee	(4)
Operating profit	95
Interest payable	(10)
Profit before taxation	85
Taxation	(24)
Profit for the year	61

Statement of financial position as at 31 December 2010

	£m
ASSETS	
Non-current assets	
Property, plant and equipment	203
Intangible assets	100
	303
Current assets	
Inventories	65
Trade receivables	112
Cash	36
	213
Total assets	516

	£m
EQUITY AND LIABILITIES	
Equity	
Ordinary shares of £0.50 each	200
Share premium account	30
Other reserves	50
Retained earnings	25
	305
Non-current liabilities	
Borrowings	100
Current liabilities	
Trade payables	99
Taxation	12
	111
Total equity and liabilities	516

Let us now go through these statements and pick up those aspects that are unique to limited companies.

The income statement

There are several features in the income statement that need consideration.

Profit

We can see that, following the calculation of operating profit, two further measures of profit are shown.

- The first of these is the profit before taxation. Interest charges are deducted from the operating profit to derive this figure. In the case of a sole proprietor or partnership business, the income statement would end here.
- The second measure of profit is the profit for the year. As the company is a separate legal entity, it is liable to pay tax (known as corporation tax) on the profits generated. (This contrasts with the sole proprietor business where it is the owner rather than the business that is liable for the tax on profits, as we saw earlier in the chapter.) This measure of profit represents the amount that is available for the shareholders.

Audit fee

Companies beyond a certain size are required to have their financial statements audited by an independent firm of accountants, for which a fee is charged. As we shall see later in this chapter, the purpose of the audit is to lend credibility to the financial statements. Although it is also open to sole proprietors and partnerships to have their financial statements audited, relatively few do, so this is an expense that is most often seen in the income statements of companies.

The statement of financial position

The main points for consideration in the statement of financial position are as follows.

Taxation

The amount that appears as part of the current liabilities represents 50 per cent of the tax on the profit for the year 2010. It is, therefore, 50 per cent (£12 million) of the charge that appears in the income statement (£24 million); the other 50 per cent (£12 million) will already have been paid. The unpaid 50 per cent will be paid shortly after the statement of financial position date. These payment dates are set down by law.

Other reserves

This will include any reserves that are not separately identified on the face of the statement of financial position. It may include a *general reserve*, which normally consists of trading profits that have been transferred to this separate reserve for reinvestment ('ploughing back') into the operations of the company. It is not at all necessary to set up a separate reserve for this purpose. The trading profits could remain unallocated and still swell the retained earnings of the company. It is not entirely clear why directors decide to make transfers to general reserves, since the profits concerned remain part of the revenue reserves. As such, they still remain available for dividend. The most plausible explanation seems to be that directors feel that placing profits in a separate reserve indicates an intention to invest the funds, represented by the reserve, permanently in the company and, therefore, not to use them to pay a dividend. Of course, the retained earnings appearing on the statement of financial position are also a reserve, but that fact is not indicated in its title.

Dividends

We have already seen that dividends represent drawings by the shareholders of the company. Dividends are paid out of the revenue reserves and should be deducted from these reserves (usually retained earnings) when preparing the statement of financial position. Shareholders are often paid an annual dividend, perhaps in two parts. An 'interim' dividend may be paid part way through the year and a 'final' dividend shortly after the year end.

Dividends declared by the directors during the year but still unpaid at the year end *may* appear as a liability in the statement of financial position. To be recognised as a liability, however, they must be properly authorised before the year-end date. This normally means that the shareholders must approve the dividend.

Additional financial statements

In the sections below, we turn our attention to two new financial statements that must be provided by those companies that are subject to International Financial

Reporting Standards. We shall consider the nature and role of these standards a little later in the chapter.

Statement of comprehensive income

The statement of comprehensive income extends the conventional income statement to include certain other gains and losses that affect shareholders' equity. It may be presented either in the form of a single statement or as two separate statements, comprising an income statement (like the one shown in Example 4.5) and a statement of comprehensive income.

This new statement attempts to overcome the perceived weaknesses of the conventional income statement. In broad terms, the conventional income statement shows all *realised* gains and losses for the period. It also shows some unrealised losses. However, gains, and some losses, that remain *unrealised* (because the asset is still held) tend not to pass through the income statement, but will go, instead, directly to a reserve. We saw, in an earlier chapter, an example of such an unrealised gain.

Activity 4.11

Can you think of this example?

The example that we met earlier is where a business revalues its land and buildings. The gain arising is not shown in the conventional income statement, but is transferred to a revaluation reserve, which forms part of the equity. (See example in Activity 2.14 on page 59.) Land and buildings are not the only assets to which this rule relates, but revaluations of these types of asset are, in practice, the most common examples of unrealised gains.

An example of an unrealised gain, or loss, that has not been mentioned so far, arises from exchange differences when the results of foreign operations are translated into UK currency. Any gain, or loss, bypasses the income statement and is taken directly to a currency translation reserve.

A weakness of conventional accounting is that there is no robust principle that we can apply to determine precisely what should, and what should not, be included in the income statement. Thus, on the one hand, losses arising from the impairment of non-current assets normally appear in the income statement. On the other hand, losses arising from translating the carrying value of assets expressed in an overseas currency (because they are owned by an overseas branch) do not. This difference in treatment, which is ingrained in conventional accounting, is difficult to justify.

The statement of comprehensive income ensures that all gains and losses, both realised and unrealised, are reported within a single statement. To do this, it extends the conventional income statement by including unrealised gains, as well as any unrealised losses not yet reported, immediately below the measure of profit for the year. An illustration of this statement is shown in Example 4.6.

Example 4.6

Malik plc
Statement of comprehensive income for the year ended 31 July 2010

	£m
Revenue	97.2
Cost of sales	(59.1)
Gross profit	38.1
Other income	3.5
Distribution expenses	(16.5)
Administration expenses	(11.2)
Other expenses	(2.4)
Operating profit	11.5
Finance charges	(1.8)
Profit before tax	9.7
Tax	(2.4)
Profit for the year	7.3
Other comprehensive income	
Revaluation of property, plant and equipment	6.6
Foreign currency translation differences for foreign operations	4.0
Tax on other comprehensive income	(2.6)
Other comprehensive income for the year, net of tax	8.0
Total comprehensive income for the year	15.3

This example adopts a single-statement approach to presenting comprehensive income. The alternative two-statement approach simply divides the information shown above into two separate parts. The income statement, which is the first statement, begins with the revenue for the year and ends with the profit for the year. The statement of comprehensive income, which is the second statement, begins with the profit for the year and ends with the total comprehensive income for the year.

Statement of changes in equity

The statement of changes in equity aims to help users to understand the changes in share capital and reserves that took place during the period. It reconciles the figures for these items at the beginning of the period with those at the end of the period. This is achieved by showing the effect on the share capital and reserves of total comprehensive income as well as the effect of share issues and purchases during the period. The effect of dividends during the period may also be shown in this statement, although dividends can be shown in the notes instead.

To see how a statement of changes in equity may be prepared, let us consider Example 4.7.

Example 4.7

At 1 January 2010 Miro plc had the following equity:

Miro plc

	£m
Share capital (£1 ordinary shares)	100
Revaluation reserve	20
Translation reserve	40
Retained earnings	150
Total equity	**310**

During 2010, the company made a profit for the year from normal business operations of £42 million and reported an upward revaluation of property, plant and equipment of £120 million (net of any tax that would be payable were the unrealised gains to be realised). The company also reported a £10 million loss on exchange differences on translating the results of foreign operations. To strengthen its financial position, the company issued 50 million ordinary shares during the year at a premium of £0.40. Dividends for the year were £27 million.

This information for 2010 can be set out in a statement of changes in equity as follows:

Statement of changes in equity for the year ended 31 December 2010

	Share capital £m	Share premium £m	Revaluation reserve £m	Translation reserve £m	Retained earnings £m	Total £m
Balance as at 1 January 2010	100	–	20	40	150	310
Changes in equity for 2010						
Issue of ordinary shares (Note 1)	50	20	–	–	–	70
Dividends (Note 2)	–	–	–	–	(27)	(27)
Total comprehensive income for the year (Note 3)	–	–	120	(10)	42	152
Balance at 31 December 2010	150	20	140	30	165	505

Notes:

1 The premium on the share price is transferred to a specific reserve.

2 We have chosen to show dividends in the statement of changes in equity rather than in the notes. They represent an appropriation of equity and are deducted from retained earnings.

3 The effect of each component of comprehensive income on the various components of shareholders' equity must be separately disclosed. The revaluation gain and the loss on translating foreign operations are each allocated to a specific reserve. The profit for the year is added to retained earnings.

The directors' duty to account

With most large companies, it is not possible for all shareholders to take part in the management of the company, nor do most of them wish to be involved. Instead, they appoint directors to act on their behalf. This separation of ownership from day-to-day control creates the need for directors to be accountable for their stewardship (management) of the company's assets. Thus, the law requires that directors:

- maintain appropriate accounting records
- prepare annual financial statements and a directors' report and make these available to all shareholders and to the public at large.

The financial statements are made available to the public by submitting a copy to the Registrar of Companies (Department of Trade and Industry), who allows any interested person to inspect them. In addition, listed companies are required to publish their financial statements on their website.

Activity 4.12

Why does the law require directors to account in this way and who benefits from these requirements?

We thought of the following benefits and beneficiaries:

- *To inform and protect shareholders*. If shareholders do not receive information about the performance and position of their investment, they will have problems in appraising their investment. Under these circumstances, they would probably be reluctant to invest and this, in turn, would affect the functioning of the private sector.
- *To inform and protect suppliers of labour, goods, services and finance, particularly those supplying credit (loans) or goods and services on credit*. Individuals and organisations would be reluctant to engage in commercial relationships, such as supplying goods or lending money, where a company does not provide information about its financial health. The fact that a company has limited liability increases the risks involved in dealing with the company. An unwillingness to engage in commercial relationships with limited companies will, once again, affect the functioning of the private sector.
- *To inform and protect society more generally*. Some companies exercise enormous power and influence in society generally, particularly on a geographically local basis. For example, a particular company may be the dominant employer and purchaser of commercial goods and services in a particular town or city. Legislators have tended to take the view that society has the right to information about the company and its activities.

The need for accounting rules

If we accept the need for directors to prepare and publish financial statements, we should also accept the need for a framework of rules concerning how these statements are prepared and presented. Without rules, there is a much greater risk that unscrupulous directors will adopt accounting policies and practices that portray an unrealistic view of financial health. There is also a much greater risk that the financial statements will not be comparable over time or with those of other businesses. Accounting rules can narrow areas of differences and reduce the variety of accounting methods. This should help ensure that businesses treat similar transactions in a similar way.

Accounting rules should help to provide greater confidence in the integrity of financial statements. This, in turn, may help a business to raise funds and to build stronger relationships with customers and suppliers. Users must be realistic, however, about what can be achieved through regulation. Problems of manipulation and of concealment can still occur even within a highly regulated environment and examples of both will be considered later in the chapter. The scale of these problems, however, should be reduced where there is a practical set of rules.

Problems of comparability can also still occur as accounting is not a precise science. Judgements and estimates must be made when preparing financial statements and these may hinder comparisons. Furthermore, no two companies are identical and the accounting policies adopted may vary between companies for entirely valid reasons.

Sources of accounting rules

In recent years there have been increasing trends towards the internationalisation of business and the integration of financial markets. These trends have helped to strengthen the case for the international harmonisation of accounting rules. By adopting a common set of rules, users of financial statements should be better placed to compare the financial health of companies based in different countries. It should also relieve international companies of some of the burden of preparing financial statements as different financial statements would no longer have to be prepared to comply with the rules of different countries in which a particular company operates.

The International Accounting Standards Board (IASB) is an independent body that is at the forefront of the move towards harmonisation. The Board, which is based in the UK, is dedicated to developing a single set of high-quality, global accounting rules. These rules aim to provide transparent and comparable information in financial statements. They are known as International Financial Reporting Standards (IFRSs) or International Accounting Standards (IASs) and deal with key issues such as:

- what information should be disclosed;
- how information should be presented;
- how assets should be valued; and
- how profit should be measured.

Activity 4.13

We have already come across some IASs and IFRSs in earlier chapters. Try to recall at least two topics where International Financial Reporting Standards were mentioned.

We came across financial reporting standards when considering:

- the valuation and impairment of assets (Chapter 2);
- depreciation and impairment of non-current assets (Chapter 3);
- the valuation of inventories (Chapter 3).

In recent years, several important developments have greatly increased the authority of the IASB. The first major development came when the European Commission required nearly all companies listed on the stock exchanges of EU member states to adopt IFRSs for reporting periods commencing on or after 1 January 2005. As a result, nearly 7,000 companies in 25 different countries switched to IFRSs. Further developments have occurred since and there are now more than 100 countries that either require or permit the use of IFRSs. Although non-listed UK companies are not currently required to adopt IFRSs, they have the option to do so. Some informed observers believe, however, that IFRSs will soon become a requirement for all UK companies.

The EU requirement to adopt IFRSs, mentioned earlier, overrides any laws in force in member states that could either hinder or restrict compliance with them. The ultimate aim is to achieve a single framework of accounting rules for companies from all member states. The EU recognises that this will be achieved only if individual governments do not add to the requirements imposed by the various IFRSs. Thus, it seems that accounting rules developed within individual EU member countries will eventually disappear. For the time being, however, the EU accepts that the governments of member states may need to impose additional disclosures for some corporate governance matters and regulatory requirements.

In the UK, company law requires disclosure relating to various corporate governance issues. There is, for example, a requirement to disclose details of directors' remuneration in the published financial statements, which goes beyond anything required by IFRSs. Furthermore, the Financial Services Authority (FSA), in its role as the UK (Stock Exchange) listing authority, imposes rules on Stock Exchange listed companies. These include the requirement to publish a condensed set of interim (half-year) financial statements in addition to the annual financial statements.

Figure 4.5 sets out the main sources of accounting rules for Stock Exchange listed companies discussed above. While company law and the FSA still play an important role, in the longer term IFRSs seem set to become the sole source of company accounting rules.

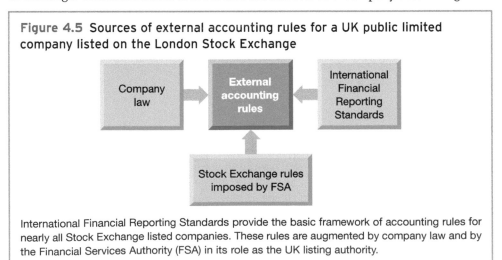

Figure 4.5 Sources of external accounting rules for a UK public limited company listed on the London Stock Exchange

International Financial Reporting Standards provide the basic framework of accounting rules for nearly all Stock Exchange listed companies. These rules are augmented by company law and by the Financial Services Authority (FSA) in its role as the UK listing authority.

The auditors' role

Shareholders are required to elect a qualified and independent person or, more usually, a firm to act as auditors. The auditors' main duty is to report whether, in their opinion, the financial statements do what they are supposed to do, namely to show a true and fair view of the financial performance, position and cash flows of the company. To be able to form such an opinion, auditors must carefully scrutinise the annual financial statements and the underlying evidence upon which they are based. In particular, they will examine the accounting principles followed, the accounting estimates made and the robustness of the company's internal control systems. The auditors' opinion must be included with the financial statements sent to the shareholders and to the Registrar of Companies.

The relationship between the shareholders, the directors and the auditors is illustrated in Figure 4.6. This shows that the shareholders elect the directors to act on their behalf, in the day-to-day running of the company. The directors are then required to 'account' to the shareholders on the performance, position and cash flows of the company, on an annual basis. The shareholders also elect auditors, whose role it is to give the shareholders an independent view of the truth and fairness of the financial statements prepared by the directors.

Figure 4.6 The relationship between the shareholders, the directors and the auditors

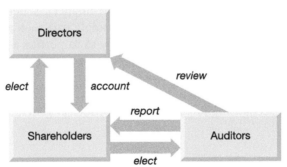

The directors are appointed by the shareholders to manage the company on the shareholders' behalf. The directors are required to report each year to the shareholders, principally by means of financial statements, on the company's performance, position and cash flows. To give greater confidence in the statements, the shareholders also appoint auditors to investigate the reports and to express an opinion on their reliability.

The directors' report

In addition to preparing the financial statements, UK law requires the directors to prepare an annual report to shareholders and other interested parties. The directors' report will contain both financial and non-financial information, which goes beyond that contained in the financial statements. The information to be disclosed is diverse and will include the names of those who were directors during the year, the principal activities of the company and any recommended dividend. The most important element of the report, however, is probably the business review. This is aimed at helping shareholders to assess how well the directors have performed. It should provide an analysis of financial performance and position and should also set out the principal risks and uncertainties facing the business.

In addition to disclosing the above information, the directors' report must contain a declaration that the directors are not aware of any other information that the auditors might need in preparing their audit report. Furthermore, the report must declare that the directors have taken steps to ensure that the auditors are aware of all relevant information. The auditors do not carry out an audit of the directors' report. However, they will check to see that the information in the report is consistent with that contained in the audited financial statements.

For companies listed on the Stock Exchange, the law also requires the publication of an annual directors' remuneration report. This should help shareholders to assess whether the rewards received by directors are appropriate.

Creative accounting

Despite the proliferation of accounting rules and the independent checks that are imposed, concerns over the quality of published financial statements surface from time to time. There are occasions when directors apply particular accounting policies, or structure particular transactions, in such a way as to portray a picture of financial health that is in line with what they want users to see, rather than what is a true and fair view of financial position and performance. Misrepresenting the performance and position of a business in this way is referred to as creative accounting and it poses a major problem for accounting rule makers and for society generally.

Activity 4.14

Why might the directors of a company engage in creative accounting?

There are many reasons including:

- to get around restrictions (for example, to report sufficient profit to pay a dividend);
- to avoid government action (for example, the taxation of excessive profits);
- to hide poor management decisions;
- to achieve sales revenue or profit targets, thereby ensuring that performance bonuses are paid to the directors;
- to attract new share capital or long-term borrowing by showing an apparently healthy financial position; and
- to satisfy the demands of major investors concerning levels of return.

Creative accounting methods

The ways in which unscrupulous directors can manipulate the financial statements are many and varied. However, they usually involve adopting novel or unorthodox practices for reporting key elements of the financial statements such as revenue, expenses, assets and liabilities. They may also involve the use of complicated or obscure transactions in an attempt to hide the underlying economic reality. The manipulation carried out may be designed either to bend the rules or to break them.

Many creative accounting methods are designed to overstate the revenue for a period. These methods often involve the early recognition of sales revenue or the reporting of sales transactions that have no real substance. Real World 4.8 provides examples of both types of revenue manipulation.

Real World 4.8

Overstating revenue

Channel stuffing: A business, usually with considerable market power, may pressurise its distributors to accept more goods than is needed to meet normal sales demand. In this way, the business can record additional sales for a period even though there has effectively been only a transfer of inventories from the business to its distributors. This method of artificially increasing sales is also known as 'trade loading'.

Pre-dispatching: Normally, revenue for credit sales is recognised when goods have been passed to, and accepted by, the customer. To boost sales and profits for a period, however, some businesses have been known to recognise revenue as soon as the order for goods has been received.

Hollow swaps: Telecom businesses may agree to sell unused fibre optic capacity to each other – usually at the same price. Although this will not increase profits, it will increase revenues and give an impression that the business is growing.

Round tripping: Energy businesses may agree to buy and sell energy between each other. Again this is normally for the same price and so no additional profits will be made. It will, however, boost revenues to give a false impression of business growth. This method is also known as 'in and out trading'.

Source: based on information in 'Dirty laundry: how companies fudge the numbers', *The Times*, Business Section, 22/09/2002.

Some years ago there was a wave of creative accounting scandals, particularly in the US but also in Europe; however, it seems that this wave has now subsided. The quality of financial statements is improving and, it is to be hoped, trust among investors and others is being restored. As a result of the actions taken by various regulatory bodies and by accounting rule makers, creative accounting has become a more risky and difficult process for those who attempt it. However, it will never disappear completely and a further wave of creative accounting scandals may occur in the future. The recent wave coincided with a period of strong economic growth and, during good economic times, investors and auditors become less vigilant. Thus, the opportunity to manipulate the figures becomes easier. We must not, therefore, become too complacent. Things may change again when we next experience a period of strong growth.

? Self-assessment question 4.1

This question requires you to correct some figures on a set of company financial statements. It should prove useful practice for the material that you covered in Chapters 2 and 3, as well as helping you to become familiar with the financial statements of a company.

Presented below is a draft set of simplified financial statements for Pear Limited for the year ended 30 September 2010.

Income statement for the year ended 30 September 2010

	£000
Revenue	1,456
Cost of sales	(768)
Gross profit	688
Salaries	(220)
Depreciation	(249)
Other operating costs	(131)
Operating profit	88
Interest payable	(15)
Profit before taxation	73
Taxation at 30%	(22)
Profit for the year	51

Statement of financial position as at 30 September 2010

ASSETS	£000
Non-current assets	
Property, plant and equipment	
Cost	1,570
Depreciation	(690)
	880
Current assets	
Inventories	207
Trade receivables	182
Cash at bank	21
	410
Total assets	1,290
EQUITY AND LIABILITIES	
Equity	
Share capital	300
Share premium account	300
Retained earnings at beginning of year	104
Profit for year	51
	755
Non-current liabilities	
Borrowings (10% loan notes repayable 2014)	300
Current liabilities	
Trade payables	88
Other payables	20
Taxation	22
Borrowings (bank overdraft)	105
	235
Total equity and liabilities	1,290

The following information is available:

1 Depreciation has not been charged on office equipment with a carrying amount of £100,000. This class of assets is depreciated at 12 per cent a year using the reducing-balance method.
2 A new machine was purchased, on credit, for £30,000 and delivered on 29 September 2010 but has not been included in the financial statements. (Ignore depreciation.)
3 A sales invoice to the value of £18,000 for September 2010 has been omitted from the financial statements. (The cost of sales figure is stated correctly.)
4 A dividend of £25,000 had been approved by the shareholders before 30 September 2010, but was unpaid at that date. This is not reflected in the financial statements.
5 The interest payable on the loan notes for the second half-year was not paid until 1 October 2010 and has not been included in the financial statements.
6 An allowance for trade receivables is to be made at the level of 2 per cent of trade receivables.
7 An invoice for electricity to the value of £2,000 for the quarter ended 30 September 2010 arrived on 4 October and has not been included in the financial statements.
8 The charge for taxation will have to be amended to take account of the above information. Make the simplifying assumption that tax is payable shortly after the end of the year, at the rate of 30 per cent of the profit before tax.

Required:
Prepare a revised set of financial statements for the year ended 30 September 2010 incorporating the additional information in 1 to 8 above. (Work to the nearest £1,000.)

Summary

The main points of this chapter may be summarised as follows.

Main features of a limited company

- It is an artificial person that has been created by law.

- It has a separate life to its owners and is granted a perpetual existence.

- It must take responsibility for its own debts and losses but its owners are granted limited liability.

- A public company can offer its shares for sale to the public; a private company cannot.

- It is governed by a board of directors, which is elected by the shareholders.

- Corporate governance is a major issue.

Financing the limited company

- The share capital of a company can be of two main types: ordinary shares and preference shares.

- Holders of ordinary shares (equities) are the main risk takers and are given voting rights; they form the backbone of the company.

- Holders of preference shares are given a right to a fixed dividend before ordinary shareholders receive a dividend.

- Reserves are profits and gains made by the company and form part of the ordinary shareholders' equity.

- Borrowings provide another major source of finance.

Share issues

- Bonus shares are issued to existing shareholders when part of the reserves of the company is converted into share capital. No funds are raised.

- Rights issues give existing shareholders the right to buy new shares in proportion to their existing holding.

- Public issues are made direct to the general investing public.

- Private placings are share issues to particular investors.

- The shares of public companies may be bought and sold on a recognised Stock Exchange.

Reserves

- Reserves are of two types: revenue reserves and capital reserves.

- Revenue reserves arise from trading profits and from realised profits on the sale of non-current assets.

- Capital reserves arise from the issue of shares above their nominal value or from the upward revaluation of non-current assets.

- Revenue reserves can be withdrawn as dividends by the shareholders whereas capital reserves normally cannot.

Financial statements of limited companies

- The financial statements of limited companies are based on the same principles as those of sole proprietorship and partnership businesses. However, there are some differences in detail.

- The income statement has three measures of profit displayed after the gross profit figure: operating profit, profit before taxation and profit for the year.

- The income statement also shows audit fees and tax on profits for the year.

- Any unpaid tax and unpaid, but authorised, dividends will appear in the statement of financial position as current liabilities.

- The statement of comprehensive income extends the income statement to include all gains and losses, both realised and unrealised.

- The statement of changes in equity reconciles the equity figure at the beginning of a reporting period with that at the end.

- The share capital plus the reserves make up 'equity'.

- Limited companies subject to International Financial Reporting Standards must produce a statement of comprehensive income and statement of changes in equity.

Directors' duty

- The directors have a duty to
    - maintain appropriate accounting records;
    - prepare and publish financial statements and a directors' report.

The need for accounting rules

- Accounting rules are necessary to
    - avoid unacceptable accounting practices;
    - improve the comparability of financial statements.

Accounting rules

- The International Accounting Standards Board (IASB) has become an important source of rules.

- Company law and the London Stock Exchange are also sources of rules for UK companies.

Other statutory reports

- The auditors' report provides an opinion by independent auditors concerning whether the financial statements provide a true and fair view of the financial health of a business.

- The directors' report contains information of a financial and a non-financial nature, which goes beyond that contained in the financial statements.

Creative accounting

- Despite the accounting rules in place there have been examples of creative accounting by directors.

- This involves using accounting practices to show what the directors would like users to see rather than what is a fair representation of reality.

→ **Key terms**

limited company
shares
limited liability
public limited company
private limited company
corporation tax
directors
corporate governance
UK Corporate Governance Code
reserves
nominal value
par value
revenue reserve
dividend
ordinary shares
splitting
consolidating
preference shares
capital reserves

share premium account
bonus shares
issued share capital
allotted share capital
fully paid shares
called-up share capital
paid-up share capital
profit before taxation
profit for the year
statement of comprehensive income
statement of changes in equity
International Financial Reporting
   Standards
International Accounting Standards
auditors
directors' report
business review
creative accounting

Reference

1 Business Sector Advisory Group on Corporate Governance, *Corporate Governance: Improving Competitiveness and Access to Capital in Global Markets*, OECD, 1998.

Further reading

If you would like to explore the topics covered in this chapter in more depth, we recommend the following books:

Elliott, B. and Elliott, J., *Financial Accounting and Reporting* (13th edn), Financial Times Prentice Hall, 2010, chapter 10.
IASC Foundation Education, *A Guide through IFRS 2009*, July 2009, IAS 1.
Thomas, A. and Ward, A., *Introduction to Financial Accounting* (6th edn), McGraw-Hill, 2009, chapter 29.

 Review questions

4.1 How does the liability of a limited company differ from the liability of a real person, in respect of amounts owed to others?

4.2 Some people are about to form a company, as a vehicle through which to run a new business. What are the advantages to them of forming a private limited company rather than a public one?

4.3 What is a reserve? Distinguish between a revenue reserve and a capital reserve.

4.4 What is a preference share? Compare the main features of a preference share with those of

(a) an ordinary share; and
(b) loan notes.

✳ Exercises

Exercises 4.4 and 4.5 are more advanced than Exercises 4.1 to 4.3.

> If you wish to try more exercises, visit the website at www.myaccountinglab.com.

4.1 Comment on the following quote:

> Limited companies can set a limit on the amount of debts that they will meet. They tend to have reserves of cash, as well as share capital and they can use these reserves to pay dividends to the shareholders. Many companies have preference as well as ordinary shares. The preference shares give a guaranteed dividend. The shares of many companies can be bought and sold on the Stock Exchange. Shareholders selling their shares can represent a useful source of new finance to the company.

4.2 The following information was extracted from the financial statements of I. Ching (Booksellers) plc for the year to 31 December 2009:

	£m
Finance charges	40
Cost of sales	460
Distribution expenses	110
Revenue	943
Administration expenses	212
Other expenses	25
Gain on revaluation of property, plant and equipment	20
Loss on foreign currency translations on foreign operations	15
Tax on profit for the year	24
Tax on other components of comprehensive income	1

Required:

Prepare a statement of comprehensive income for the year ended 31 December 2009.

4.3 Briefly explain each of the following expressions that you have seen in the financial statements of a limited company:

(a) dividend

(b) audit fee

(c) share premium account.

4.4 Presented below is a draft set of financial statements for Chips Limited.

Chips Limited

Income statement for the year ended 30 June 2010

	£000
Revenue	1,850
Cost of sales	(1,040)
Gross profit	810
Depreciation	(220)
Other operating costs	(375)
Operating profit	215
Interest payable	(35)
Profit before taxation	180
Taxation	(60)
Profit for the year	120

Statement of financial position as at 30 June 2010

	Cost £000	Depreciation £000	£000
ASSETS			
Non-current assets			
Property, plant and equipment			
Buildings	800	(112)	688
Plant and equipment	650	(367)	283
Motor vehicles	102	(53)	49
	1,552	(532)	1,020
Current assets			
Inventories			950
Trade receivables			420
Cash at bank			16
			1,386
Total assets			2,406
EQUITY AND LIABILITIES			
Equity			
Ordinary shares of £1, fully paid			800
Reserves at beginning of the year			248
Profit for the year			120
			1,168
Non-current liabilities			
Borrowings (secured 10% loan notes)			700
Current liabilities			
Trade payables			361
Other payables			117
Taxation			60
			538
Total equity and liabilities			2,406

The following additional information is available:

1. Purchase invoices for goods received on 29 June 2010 amounting to £23,000 have not been included. This means that the cost of sales figure in the income statement has been understated.
2. A motor vehicle costing £8,000 with depreciation amounting to £5,000 was sold on 30 June 2010 for £2,000, paid by cheque. This transaction has not been included in the company's records.
3. No depreciation on motor vehicles has been charged. The annual rate is 20 per cent of cost at the year end.
4. A sale on credit for £16,000 made on 1 July 2010 has been included in the financial statements in error. The cost of sales figure is correct in respect of this item.
5. A half-yearly payment of interest on the secured loan due on 30 June 2010 has not been paid.
6. The tax charge should be 30 per cent of the reported profit before taxation. Assume that it is payable, in full, shortly after the year end.

Required:

Prepare a revised set of financial statements incorporating the additional information in 1 to 6 above. (Work to the nearest £1,000.)

4.5 Rose Limited operates a small chain of retail shops that sell high-quality teas and coffees. Approximately half of sales are on credit. Abbreviated and unaudited financial statements are given below.

Rose Limited
Income statement for the year ended 31 March 2010

	£000
Revenue	12,080
Cost of sales	(6,282)
Gross profit	5,798
Labour costs	(2,658)
Depreciation	(625)
Other operating costs	(1,003)
Operating profit	1,512
Interest payable	(66)
Profit before taxation	1,446
Taxation	(434)
Profit for the year	1,012

Statement of financial position as at 31 March 2010

	£000
ASSETS	
Non-current assets	2,728
Current assets	
Inventories	1,583
Trade receivables	996
Cash	26
	2,605
Total assets	5,333
EQUITY AND LIABILITIES	
Equity	
Share capital (50p shares, fully paid)	750
Share premium	250
Retained earnings	1,468
	2,468
Non-current liabilities	
Borrowings – secured loan notes (2014)	300
Current liabilities	
Trade payables	1,118
Other payables	417
Tax	434
Borrowings – overdraft	596
	2,565
Total equity and liabilities	5,333

Since the unaudited financial statements for Rose Limited were prepared, the following information has become available:

1 An additional £74,000 of depreciation should have been charged on fixtures and fittings.
2 Invoices for credit sales on 31 March 2010 amounting to £34,000 have not been included; cost of sales is not affected.
3 Trade receivables totalling £21,000 are recognised as having gone bad, but they have not yet been written off.
4 Inventories which had been purchased for £2,000 have been damaged and are unsaleable. This is not reflected in the financial statements.
5 Fixtures and fittings to the value of £16,000 were delivered just before 31 March 2010, but these assets were not included in the financial statements and the purchase invoice had not been processed.
6 Wages for Saturday-only staff, amounting to £1,000, have not been paid for the final Saturday of the year. This is not reflected in the financial statements.
7 Tax is payable at 30 per cent of profit after taxation. Assume that it is payable shortly after the year end.

Required:
Prepare revised financial statements for Rose Limited for the year ended 31 March 2010, incorporating the information in 1 to 7 above. (Work to the nearest £1,000.)

E-Business and E-Commerce Management

Dave Chaffey

1

Introduction to e-business and e-commerce

Learning outcomes

After completing this chapter the reader should be able to:

- Define the meaning and scope of e-business and e-commerce and their different elements
- Summarize the main reasons for adoption of e-commerce and e-business and barriers that may restrict adoption
- Outline the ongoing business challenges of managing e-business and e-commerce in an organization

Management issues

The issues for managers raised in this chapter include:

- How do we explain the scope and implications of e-business and e-commerce to staff?
- What is the full range of benefits of introducing e-business and what are the risks?
- How do we evaluate our current e-business capabilities?

Introduction

The Internet

'The Internet' refers to the physical network that links computers across the globe. It consists of the infrastructure of network servers and communication links between them that are used to hold and transport information between the client PCs and web servers.

World Wide Web (WWW)

The most common technique for publishing information on the Internet. It is accessed through web browsers which display web pages of embedded graphics and HTML/XML-encoded text.

Wireless communications

Electronic transactions and communications conducted using mobile devices such as laptops and mobile phones (and fixed access platforms) with different forms of wireless connection.

Organizations have now been applying technologies based on **the Internet**, **World Wide Web** and **wireless communications** to transform their businesses for over 20 years since the creation of the first website (http://info.cern.ch) by Sir Tim Berners-Lee in 1991. Deploying these technologies has offered many opportunities for innovative e-businesses to be created based on new approaches to business. Table 1.1 highlights some of the best-known examples and in Activity 1.1 you can explore some of the reasons for success of these e-businesses.

For the author, e-business and e-commerce is an exciting area to be involved with, since many new opportunities and challenges arise yearly, monthly and even daily. Innovation is a given, with the continuous introduction of new technologies, new business models and new communications approaches. For example, Google innovates relentlessly. Its service has developed a long way since 1998 (Figure 1.1) with billions of pages now indexed and other services such as web mail, pay-per-click adverts, analytics and social networks all part of its offering. Complete Activity 1.1 or view Table 1.1 to see other examples of the rate at which new innovations occur.

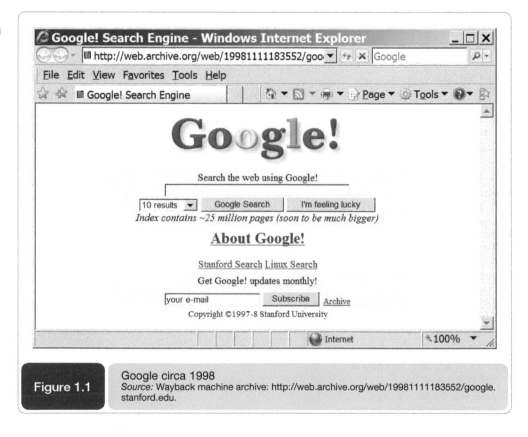

Figure 1.1

Google circa 1998
Source: Wayback machine archive: http://web.archive.org/web/19981111183552/google. stanford.edu.

Table 1.1	Timeline of websites indicating innovation in business model or marketing communications approach

Year founded	Company / site	Category of innovation and business model
1994	Amazon	Retailer
1995 (March)	Yahoo! (yahoo.com)	Directory and portal
1995 (Sept)	eBay	Online auction
1995 (Dec)	AltaVista (altavista.com)	Search engine
1996	Hotmail (hotmail.com)	Web-based e-mail Viral marketing (using e-mail signatures to promote service) Purchased by Microsoft in 1997
1998	GoTo.com (goto.com) Overture (2001)	Pay-per-click search marketing Purchased by Yahoo! in 2003
1998	Google (google.com)	Search engine
1999	Blogger (blogger.com)	Blog publishing platform Purchased by Google in 2003
1999	Alibaba (alibaba.com)	B2B marketplace with $1.7 billion IPO on Hong Kong stock exchange in 2007. See case in Chapter 2
1999	MySpace (myspace.com) Formerly eUniverse	Social network Purchased by News Corp in 2005
2001	Wikipedia (wikipedia.com)	Open encyclopedia
2002	Last.fm	A UK-based Internet radio and music community website, founded in 2002. On 30 May 2007, CBS Interactive acquired Last.fm for £140m (US$280m)
2003	Skype (skype.com)	Peer-to-peer Internet telephony VoIP – Voice over Internet Protocol Purchased by eBay in 2005
2003	Second Life (secondlife.com)	Immersive virtual world
2004	Facebook (facebook.com)	Social network applications and groups
2005	YouTube (youtube.com)	Video sharing and rating
2007	Hulu (hulu.com)	Quality video broadcast service IPTV – Internet Protocol TV
2009	Foursquare (foursquare.com)	A location-based social media website designed for mobile access. Video explanation: http://bit.ly/EBEC-Foursquare
??	The future	??

Activity 1.1	Innovative e-businesses

Purpose

To illustrate innovation in online business models and communications approaches.

Questions

1 Think about the innovation that you have witnessed during the time you have used the Internet and World Wide Web. What would you say are the main sites used in your country that have been created which have changed the way we spend our time or buy online?

> **2** We talk about these businesses being 'successful', but what is success for a new e-business?
>
> **3** What do these sites have in common that you think has made them successful?
>
> *Answers to activities can be found at* www.pearsoned.co.uk/chaffey

The impact of electronic communications on traditional businesses

Social media
A category of media focusing on participation and peer-to-peer communication between individuals with sites providing the capability to develop user-generated content (UGC) and to exchange messages and comments between different users.

Social network
A site that facilitates peer-to-peer communication within a group or between individuals through providing facilities to develop user-generated content (UGC) and to exchange messages and comments between different users.

During the same period managers at established businesses have had to determine how to apply new electronic communications technologies to transform their organizations. As we will see later in this chapter, existing businesses have evolved their approaches to e-business through a series of stages. Innovation in e-business is relentless, with the continuous introduction of new technologies, new business models and new communications approaches. So all organizations have to review new electronic and Internet-based communications approaches for their potential to make their business more competitive and also manage ongoing risks such as security and performance. For example, many businesses are reviewing the benefits, costs and risks of implementing:

- The growth in popularity of **social media** and in particular **social networks** such as Facebook, Twitter and for business-to-business users Linked In, **virtual worlds** such as Habbo Hotel and Second Life, and **blogs** created by many individuals and businesses.
- **Rich media** such as online video and interactive applications into their websites.
- A selection of **mobile commerce** services which exploit the usage of mobile phones and other portable wireless devices such as laptops around the world. The potential of mobile commerce is evident from research by ITU (2010) which estimated that by the end of 2010 there would be 5 billion mobile subscriptions of whom 1 billion would have mobile broadband access. The growth in popularity of **mobile apps** (Chapter 3), from the iPhone store, Google Android store and other handset vendors, is another significant development in mobile communications.
- Location-based tracking of goods and inventory as they are manufactured and transported.

| **Activity 1.2** | The most popular apps today |

Virtual worlds
An electronic environment which simulates interactions between online characters known as avatars. Also known as Massively Multiplayer Online Roleplaying Games (MMORPG).

Blog
Personal online diary, journal or news source compiled by one person, an internal team or external guest authors. Postings are usually in different categories. Typically comments can be added to each blog posting to help create interactivity and feedback.

This can be completed individually or as a group activity comparing popular apps for different mobile handsets. Review the most popular apps today, either using the App Store for your mobile phone or a compilation from an information provider such as Nielsen.

Questions

1 Identify the most popular categories of apps from the top 10 or 20 most popular apps.

2 Discuss the opportunities for companies to promote their brands or services using apps.

At the time of writing the most popular categories of apps catalogued by Nielsen (2010) in order of popularity on Smart Phones were:

1 Games

2 Music

3 Social networking

Rich media
Digital assets such as ads are not static images, but provide animation, audio or interactivity as a game or form to be completed.

Mobile commerce (m-commerce)
Electronic transactions and communications conducted using mobile devices such as laptops, PDAs and mobile phones, and typically with a wireless connection.

Mobile apps
A software application that is designed for use on a mobile phone, typically downloaded from an app store. iPhone Apps are best known, but all Smart Phones support the use of apps which can provide users with information, entertainment or location-based services such as mapping.

4   News/weather

5   Maps/navigation

6   Video/movies

7   Entertainment/food

8   Sports

9   Communication

10 Banking/finance

You can see that an organization's capability to manage technology-enabled change is the essence of successfully managing e-business. The pace of change and the opportunities for new communications approaches make e-business and e-commerce an exciting area of business to be involved in.

In *E-Business and E-Commerce Management* we will explore approaches managers can use to assess the relevance of different e-business opportunities and then devise and implement strategies to exploit these opportunities. We will also study how to manage more practical risks such as delivering a satisfactory service quality, maintaining customer privacy and managing security. We introduce some of the opportunities and risks later in this chapter.

In this chapter we start by introducing the scope of e-business and e-commerce. Then we review the main opportunities and risks of e-business together with the drivers and barriers to adoption of e-business services.

Managing social media

Managing social media is one of the most pressing challenges for many businesses seeking to engage with their prospects and customers online. Some would suggest that managing social media is not possible. But with web users spending an increasing proportion of their time online using social media sites, an approach to determine how to engage users of social networks and communities with brands and monitor and respond to their comments is a priority for many companies today. If you visit the latest list of popular sites worldwide compiled by Google-owned company Doubleclick (www.google.com/adplanner/static/top1000) you will see that Facebook is the most popular site and, of course, within different countries and for different interests each has its own area of interest. Given the importance of social media opportunities, this is a common theme throughout this book.

Real-world E-Business experiences   The Econsultancy interview

Ted Speroni, Director, EMEA (Europe, Middle East and Asia), HP.com

Overview and main concepts covered

Ted Speroni heads the European operations of HP.com, as well as the tech giant's regional preferred online partner programme. This practitioner interview highlights some of the challenges and opportunities for a traditional organization in managing e-commerce. It also introduces some of the important online marketing communications techniques such as search engine marketing, affiliate marketing, social media and widget marketing which are described in Chapter 9.

The interview

Q. Can you briefly summarise your role at HP.com?

Ted Speroni, HP.com: I look after HP.com for the EMEA region. We have around 40 country websites throughout the region in something like 28 languages, so that's my responsibility. I'm also responsible for all of our electronic content management across Europe, which is where we intersect with the online retail community.

At HP, we have a clear strategy of making our products available wherever our customers want to buy them – through high street shops, proximity resellers, online retailers, e-resellers and direct through HP.

We only sell direct through HP.com in five countries in Europe – the UK, France, Germany, Switzerland and Spain. So in most countries, we connect in with the leading etailers. We get daily feeds from all of them on their product availability and pricing, and we display them on HP.com. We then deep link into the shopping basket on each etailer, so we're generating leads for them.

It's just like an affiliate programme [a commission-based sales arrangement covered in Chapter 9], but we don't get a commission because it's for our own products. We track the number and quality of leads we are sending each retailer and their conversion rates. We have all the data on which products sell and which cross-sell.

It's a pretty big programme – we have about 150 partners in Europe that are part of it and we generate quite a considerable amount of leads and traffic for them. You have to qualify to be part of it – there are certain criteria you have to meet.

Q. What are you doing at the moment to drive more traffic to these etailers?

Ted Speroni, HP.com: The first thing is the integrated marketing approach we have. Search engine marketing (SEM) and search engine optimisation (SEO) are probably the two biggest areas we are working on.

The fundamental principle is that we want to drive all that traffic to pages where we give the customer choice. All the marketing traffic drives people to landing pages that give people a choice about where to purchase the product.

Our investment in SEM is probably in line with the growth we see overall in the industry. We're also making quite heavy investments internally in SEO, because a much higher percentage of our traffic comes from natural search and the conversion rate is not that dissimilar to SEM.

Natural search is a big area of focus for us at the moment. With SEM, we always get people to the right page, to specific landing pages. With natural search, we're not as convinced we're always getting people to the correct page.

For that, we're analysing where the traffic is going from natural search results so that we can give the customer choice on those pages, and also looking at how to make sure people go to the pages they want to go to.

Q. How difficult is it to maintain communication with partners across multiple channels?

Ted Speroni, HP.com: We're pretty happy with the multi-channel approach we have taken. Encompassing all the different ways customers want to buy products is the most important thing.

We've struggled with that for a long time and we're just trying to make each channel as efficient as possible. We still have a way to go – I'm still working on a number of projects to optimise the different channels.

One thing is the question of high street retailers and the question of integration of inventory. When a customer wants to buy a specific camera they want to know whether it is in stock today, and I don't want the site to send them to the wrong place.

Q. How are you managing the syndication of your product content to your partners in the programme? How challenging is that?

Ted Speroni, HP.com: My team syndicates out [electronically distributes] all the content to our resellers. What this is all about is we want to control the HP brand in relation to our products. We produce electronic content feeds in 28 languages of all the product information – pictures, marketing messaging, specifications, everything.

Whenever a customer anywhere in Europe is seeing information about an HP product, there's a very high probability that that will be content we have created. The picture is the picture we want people to see. We feel it's been very successful for us – not only in terms of controlling our brand, but also in terms of cutting costs for our partners. They don't need to do content acquisition.

We'll either syndicate the content via XML feeds, or sometimes the resellers are buying the content through content aggregators. And this extends beyond simple product information – we also syndicate out our recommended cross-sell products. If you buy an HP printer, we have a list of recommended accessories.

This is a key thing – similar to what Dell have talked about in terms of increasing the average shopping basket. Our top priority partners are partners that sell complete HP solutions, so this tool helps them sell complete HP solutions. Resellers can't say they don't know which products sell well with others, because we are telling them.

I should also mention another component – we're not just syndicating content, we also syndicate a configurator for configuring PCs.

We feed all the data into the configurator about the different configurations you can build. You as a customer configure the PC and the information goes into the shopping basket of the retailer, as well as coming through to the HP factory so we can build the configuration. We then match up the order when the retailer passes the order through to us, and we ship it.

It goes beyond syndicating content – you're syndicating widgets, real web apps that can be integrated into websites.

Q. How else are you looking to use widgets?

Ted Speroni, HP.com: Another area is product advisors. We have product advisors on HP.com and we would like to syndicate them out. The principle behind this is that we don't want to provide a link on retailers' websites to HP.com, we want to keep the customers on their sites. As we move HP.com to a more modular, Web 2.0-type approach, we'll see which components we can syndicate out. We also have flash demos so there's an opportunity for resellers to have them on their website, although the resellers do have to have some merchandising people that know about the products. Their sites also have to be Web 2.0-enabled.

Q. What are you doing in terms of social media and social shopping?

Ted Speroni, HP.com: We're starting to pilot some social tagging concepts on our product pages, so that people can easily embed our product pages into different sites, like Myspace profiles for example.

It's at a very early stage but it's about the whole concept of exporting our stuff onto the social networking sites, as opposed to trying to get people onto our sites. We haven't implemented it in Europe, but in the US we have started some pilots.

For a while now, we have also had RSS links on promotions from our site – we've had some uptake of that, but it's not a killer app I would say. We're basically looking at how we can help people who want to create content around our products, and facilitate that.

There's a lot of HP content on YouTube – lots of people make videos about how to make the new HP printer, for example. So our approach is 'if people want to do this, let's help them and let's benefit from it'. If we can get user generated linkage to our products, it's incredibly powerful.

Q. Have you looked at user generated reviews?

Ted Speroni, HP.com: We're doing a pilot in the US with user generated reviews. We haven't started that yet in Europe – I'm trying to work out a scaleable model with all the language issues.

We have to have some quality control on the user reviews – we can't depend completely on community policing. We need some proactive moderation – since it's on our website, we can't take risks with legal issues and so on.

You can say our products aren't good but you have to use appropriate language. Also, we don't want you to be able to comment on our competitors' products. You can say what you want about our products but you can't push competitors' products.

We've been runnning this for about six months in the US and there's been good uptake, and we haven't had big issues with appropriateness. In Europe, I am looking to deploy something and looking into the multi-language issues.

Source: www.econsultancy.com/news-blog/newsletter/3200/interview-ted-speroni-director-emea-hp-com. html. Econsultancy.com provides information, training and events on best practice in online marketing and e-commerce management.

What is the difference between e-commerce and e-business?

The rapid advancement of technology and its application to business has been accompanied by a range of new terminology and jargon. The use of the term 'electronic commerce' has been supplemented by additional terms such as e-business and digital marketing, and more specialist terms such as e-CRM, e-tail and e-procurement. Do we need to be concerned about the terminology? The short answer is no; Mougayer (1998) noted that it is understanding the services that can be offered to customers and the business benefits that are obtainable through e-business that are important. However, labels are convenient in defining the *scope* of the changes we are looking to make within an organization through using electronic communications. Managers need to communicate the extent of changes they are proposing through introducing digital technologies to employees, customers and partners. **Social commerce** is an increasingly important part of e-commerce for site owners since incorporating reviews and ratings into a site and linking to social networking sites can help understand customers' needs and increase conversion to sale. It can also involve group buying, using a coupon service like Groupon.

Social commerce
A subset of e-commerce which encourages participation and interaction of customers in rating, selecting and buying products through group buying. This participation can occur on an e-commerce site or on third-party sites.

E-commerce defined

Electronic commerce (e-commerce) is often thought simply to refer to buying and selling using the Internet; people immediately think of consumer retail purchases from companies such as Amazon. But e-commerce involves much more than electronically mediated *financial* transactions between organizations and customers. E-commerce should be considered as *all* electronically mediated transactions between an organization and any third party it deals with. By this definition, non-financial transactions such as customer requests for further information would also be considered to be part of e-commerce. Kalakota and Whinston (1997) refer to a range of different perspectives for e-commerce:

Electronic commerce (e-commerce)
All electronically mediated information exchanges between an organization and its external stakeholders.

1 A *communications perspective* – the delivery of information, products or services or payment by electronic means.
2 A *business process perspective* – the application of technology towards the automation of business transactions and workflows.
3 A *service perspective* – enabling cost cutting at the same time as increasing the speed and quality of service delivery.
4 An *online perspective* – the buying and selling of products and information online.

The UK government also used a broad definition when explaining the scope of e-commerce to industry:

> *E-commerce is the exchange of information across electronic networks, at any stage in the supply chain, whether within an organization, between businesses, between businesses and consumers, or between the public and private sector, whether paid or unpaid.* (Cabinet Office, 1999)

These definitions show that electronic commerce is not solely restricted to the actual buying and selling of products, but also includes pre-sale and post-sale activities across the supply chain.

When evaluating the strategic impact of e-commerce on an organization, it is useful to identify opportunities for buy-side and sell-side e-commerce transactions as depicted in Figure 1.2, since systems with different functionalities will need to be created in an

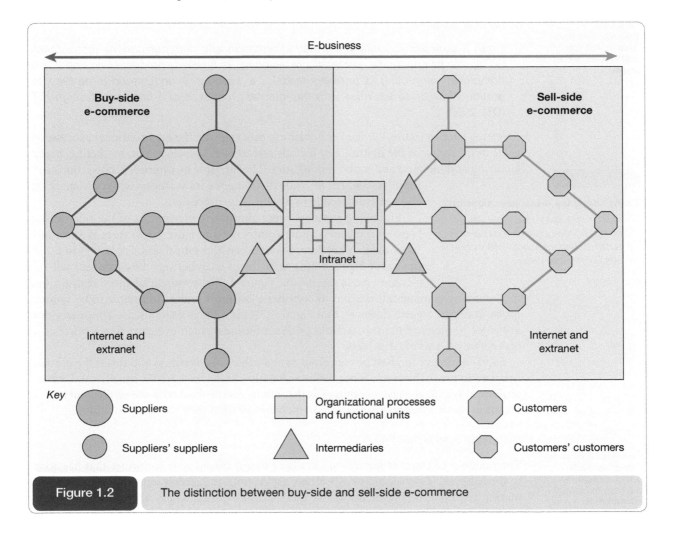

| Figure 1.2 | The distinction between buy-side and sell-side e-commerce |

Buy-side e-commerce

E-commerce transactions between a purchasing organization and its suppliers.

Sell-side e-commerce

E-commerce transactions between a supplier organization and its customers.

Electronic business (e-business)

All electronically mediated information exchanges, both within an organization and with external stakeholders supporting the range of business processes.

Information and communication technology (ICT or IT)

The software applications, computer hardware and networks used to create e-business systems.

organization to accommodate transactions with buyers and with suppliers. **Buy-side e-commerce** refers to transactions to procure resources needed by an organization from its suppliers. In Chapter 6, Case Study 6.1 reviews how Shell has developed an e-business capability that enables buy-side e-commerce for its customers. **Sell-side e-commerce** refers to transactions involved with selling products to an organization's customers. So e-commerce transactions between organizations can be considered from two perspectives: sell-side from the perspective of the selling organization and buy-side from the perspective of the buying organization.

E-business defined

Given that Figure 1.2 depicts different types of e-commerce, what then is **e-business**? Let's start from the definition by IBM (www.ibm.com/e-business), which was one of the first suppliers to use the term in 1997 to promote its services:

e-business (e'biz'nis) – the transformation of key business processes through the use of Internet technologies.

In an international benchmarking study analysing the adoption of e-business in SMEs the Department of Trade and Industry emphasizes the application of technology (**information and communications technologies (ICTs)**) in the full range of business processes, but also emphasizes how it involves innovation. DTI (2000) described the initial applications of e-business as follows:

when a business has fully integrated information and communications technologies (ICTs) into its operations, potentially redesigning its business processes around ICT or completely reinventing its business model... e-business, is understood to be the integration of all these activities with the internal processes of a business through ICT. (DTI, 2000)

Referring back to Figure 1.2, the key e-business processes are the organizational processes or units in the centre of the figure. They include research and development, marketing, manufacturing and inbound and outbound logistics. The buy-side e-commerce transactions with suppliers and the sell-side e-commerce transactions with customers can also be considered to be key business processes.

Debate 1.1

How new is the e-business concept?

'E-business is just a new label – there is no distinction between the role of e-business and traditional information systems management.'

Figure 1.3 presents some alternative viewpoints of the relationship between e-business and e-commerce. In Figure 1.3(a) there is a relatively small overlap between e-commerce and e-business. From Figure 1.2 we can reject Figure 1.3(a) since the overlap between buy-side and sell-side e-commerce is significant. Figure 1.3(b) seems to be more realistic, and indeed many commentators seem to consider e-business and e-commerce to be synonymous. It can be argued, however, that Figure 1.3(c) is most realistic since e-commerce does not refer to many of the transactions *within* a business, such as processing a purchasing order, that are part of e-business.

So, e-commerce can best be conceived of as a subset of e-business and this is the perspective we will use in this book. Since the interpretation in Figure 1.3(b) is equally valid, what is important within any given company is that managers involved with the implementation of e-commerce or e-business are agreed on the scope of what they are trying to achieve!

Intranet

A private network within a single company using Internet standards to enable employees to access and share information using web publishing technology.

Intranets and extranets

The majority of Internet services are available to any business or consumer that has access to the Internet. However, many e-business applications that access sensitive company information require access to be limited to qualified individuals or partners. If information is restricted to employees inside an organization, this is an **intranet,** as is shown in Figure 1.4.

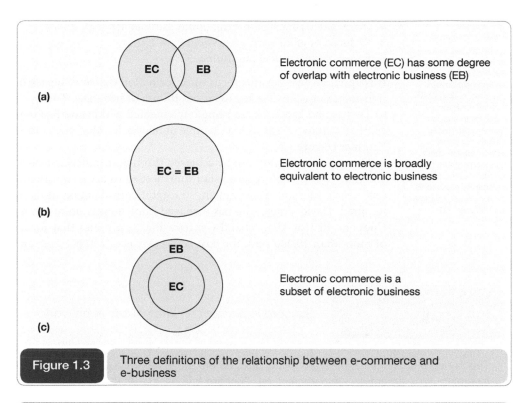

Figure 1.3 Three definitions of the relationship between e-commerce and e-business

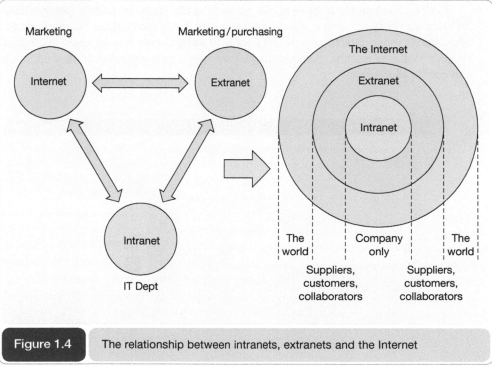

Figure 1.4 The relationship between intranets, extranets and the Internet

In a survey of 275 managers responsible for an intranet featured in *CIO* (2002), the main benefits mentioned by managers were:

1 Improved information sharing (customer service), 97%
2 Enhanced communications and information sharing (communications), 95%
3 Increased consistency of information (customer service), 94%

Enterprise social media software

Systems used inside organizations to enable real-time collaboration between employees and other stakeholders such as customers and suppliers to support business processes such as customer service, supply chain management and new product development. Collectively these tools are sometimes referenced as Enterprise 2.0.

4 Increased accuracy of information (customer service), 93%

5 Reduced or eliminated processing, 93%

6 Easier organizational publishing, 92%

It is apparent that benefits focus on information delivery, suggesting that management of information quality is a key to successful use of intranets. Today, software services similar to Twitter and Facebook are being implemented within companies to achieve similar goals. Mini case study 1.1 shows the example of one such **enterprise social media software** tool, Yammer (Figure 1.5).

Direct cost reduction can be achieved through intranets by the reduced cost of printing and indirectly though reduced staff time needed to access information. However, intranets represent a substantial investment, so careful consideration of the return on investment is required. David Viney, who has managed implementation of intranets at Pricewaterhouse Coopers, British Airways and Centrica PLC, estimates that for a large implementation of more than 10,000 staff, the cost could average £250 per user or seat (Viney, 2003). He

---

Mini Case Study 1.1	Suncorp implement an internal social network

The Suncorp financial services group manages 25 brands in Australia and New Zealand spanning banking, insurance, investment and superannuation. Suncorp has over 219,000 shareholders, over 16,000 employees and around 7 million customers.

Suncorp has used enterprise social networking tool Yammer to help geographically dispersed people and teams to connect, share, discuss and innovate. It has also helped Suncorp create a culture where collaboration is more natural by enabling people to interact online in an open, informal and transparent way. Within a matter of months, Yammer membership grew from a handful of early adopters to over 1,700 users and continues to grow.

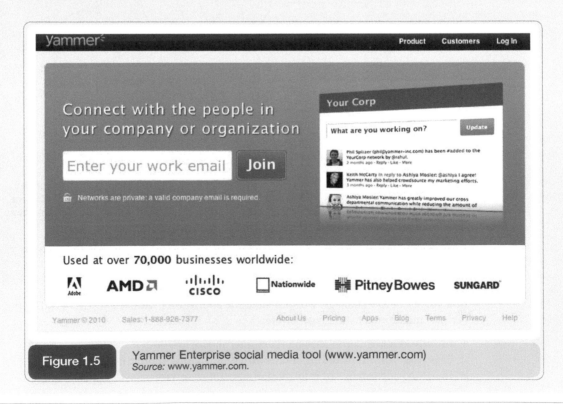

Figure 1.5	Yammer Enterprise social media tool (www.yammer.com) *Source:* www.yammer.com.

Jeff Smith, Suncorp, the Chief Information Office of Yammer explains the benefits as follows:

Yammer has enabled us to harness the wisdom of our people who are spread across multiple teams, geographies and brands to help achieve our purpose of delivering business solutions for competitive advantage.

Brian Robbins, Chief Marketing Office (CMO) added:

We recently signed up for Yammer and are seeing it spread virally among our employees. It is helping us accelerate collaboration and internal communications across our 20,000 employees in 300 offices in 30 countries. We're seeing all kinds of serendipitous connections across projects, cultures and time zones.

The benefits of applying a tool like Yammer to Suncorp can be summarized as:

- Increased informal knowledge flow across the organization through microblogging.
- Overcome barriers to collaboration, providing instant connection for people, teams, informal networks, communities of practice and other shared interest groups.
- Improved alignment between executives and employees by use of broadcast message to communicate messages and quickly crowdsource to get ideas, suggestions and answers to questions.
- Helped stimulate greater sharing and discussion among common role groups e.g. developers, architects and testers.

Source: Adapted from Yammer (2010).

suggests this cost breaks down into four categories: software (content management systems), hardware (servers to store content and applications), integration of information sources and applications, and process change (staff costs and opportunity costs associated within implementation). He also suggests that if the portal project involves integration with ERP systems, this could add £150 per seat.

If access to an organization's web services is extended to some others, but not everyone beyond the organization, this is an **extranet**. Whenever you log on to an Internet service such as that for an e-retailer or online news site, this is effectively an extranet arrangement, although the term is most often used to mean a business-to-business application such as the Shell SIMON capability described in Case Study 6.1 where certain customers or suppliers are given shared access. We look at examples of intranets and extranets in Chapter 3 including the Dell Premier extranet.

Extranet

A service provided through Internet and web technology delivered by extending an intranet beyond a company to customers, suppliers and collaborators.

Different types of sell-side e-commerce

Sell-side e-commerce doesn't only involve selling products such as books and DVDs online, but also involves using Internet technologies to market services using a range of techniques we will explore in Chapters 8 and 9. Not every product is suitable for sale online, so the way in which a website is used to market products will vary. It is useful to consider the five main types of online presence for sell-side e-commerce, which each have different objectives and are appropriate for different markets. These are not clear-cut categories of websites since any company may combine these types, but with a change in emphasis according to the market they serve. As you review websites, note how organizations have different parts of the site focusing on these five functions:

1 **Transactional e-commerce sites**. These enable purchase of products online. The main business contribution of the site is through sale of these products. The sites also support the business by providing information for consumers that prefer to purchase products offline. These include retail sites, travel sites and online banking services.

2 **Services-oriented relationship-building websites**. Provide information to stimulate purchase and build relationships. Products are not typically available for purchase online. Information is provided through the website and e-newsletters to inform purchase

decisions. The main business contribution is through encouraging offline sales and generating enquiries or leads from potential customers. Such sites also add value to existing customers by providing them with information to help support them.

3 **Brand-building sites.** Provide an experience to support the brand. Products are not typically available for online purchase. Their main focus is to support the brand by developing an online experience of the brand. They are typical for low-value, high-volume fast-moving consumer goods (FMCG brands) for consumers.

4 **Portal, publisher or media sites.** Provide information, news or entertainment about a range of topics. 'Portal' refers to a gateway of information. This is information both on the site and through links to other sites. Portals have a diversity of options for generating revenue, including advertising, commission-based sales and sale of customer data (lists).

5 **Social networks.** Social networks could be considered to be in the previous category since they are often advertising-supported, but the influence of social networks such as Facebook, Linked In and Twitter on company and customer communications suggests they form a separate category.

Complete Activity 1.3 to consider examples of these different types of site.

Activity 1.3	Understanding different types of online presence

Purpose

To help you assess how different types of online presence are used for marketing.

Activity

Review the popularity of the different site types in your country or globally. The recommended information sources are:

- The Doubleclick AdPlanner compilation of the 1,000 most-visited sites on the web (www.google.com/adplanner/static/top1000/).
- The Hitwise Data Centers (e.g. www.hitwise.com/us/resources/data-center) available for Australia, Canada, France, Hong Kong, Singapore, New Zealand, UK, and US.

Visit each of the sites below and then indicate which of the five categories of online presence are their primary and secondary focus:

1 Transactional e-commerce site.
2 Services-oriented relationship-building website.
3 Brand-building site.
4 Portal or media site.
5 Social network.

Example sites

- Business site: Silicon (www.silicon.com)
- Bank, e.g. HSBC (www.hsbc.com)
- Lingerie manufacturer, e.g. Gossard (www.gossard.com)
- Management consultants such as PricewaterhouseCoopers (www.pwcglobal.com) and Accenture (www.accenture.com)
- Beverage manufacturers, e.g. Tango (www.tango.com), Guinness (www.guinness.com)
- Travel company, e.g. Thomas Cook (www.thomascook.com)
- An end-product manufacturer such as Vauxhall (www.vauxhall.co.uk)
- Consumer site, e.g. Yahoo! (www.yahoo.com)
- Online retailer such as Amazon (www.amazon.com)

Answers to activities can be found at www.pearsoned.co.uk/chaffey

Digital marketing

Digital marketing, e-marketing or Internet marketing is yet another field that is closely related to e-commerce. 'Digital marketing' is a term increasingly used by specialist e-marketing agencies, in recruitment of specialist staff, and the new media trade publications such as *New Media Age* (www.nma.co.uk) and *Revolution* (www.revolutionmagazine.com) to refer to sell-side e-commerce. We cover digital marketing in more detail in Chapters 8 and 9.

To help explain the scope and approaches used for digital marketing the IDM (www.theidm.com) has developed a more detailed explanation of digital marketing:

> *Digital marketing involves:*
>
> *Applying these technologies which form online channels to market:*
>
> *– Web, e-mail, databases, plus mobile/wireless and digital TV.*
>
> *To achieve these objectives:*
>
> *– Support marketing activities aimed at achieving profitable acquisition and retention of customers … within a multi-channel buying process and customer lifecycle.*
>
> *Through using these marketing tactics:*
>
> *– Recognising the strategic importance of digital technologies and developing a planned approach to reach and migrate customers to online services through e-communications and traditional communications. Retention is achieved through improving our customer knowledge (of their profiles, behaviour, value and loyalty drivers), then delivering integrated, targeted communications and online services that match their individual needs.*

Let's now look at each part of this description in more detail. The first part of the description illustrates the range of access platforms and communications tools that form the online channels which e-marketers use to build and develop relationships with customers including PCs, PDAs, mobile phones, interactive digital TV and radio.

Different access platforms deliver content and enable interaction through a range of different online communication tools or media channels. Some are well-established techniques which will be familiar to you, like websites, search engines, e-mail and text messaging. One of the most exciting things about working in digital media is the introduction of new tools and techniques which have to be assessed for their relevance to a particular marketing campaign.

Recent innovations which we discuss further in Chapters 8 and 9 include blogs, feeds, podcasts and social networks. The growth of social networks has been documented by Boyd and Ellison (2007) who describe social networking sites (SNS) as:

> *Web-based services that allow individuals to (1) construct a public or semi-public profile within a bounded system, (2) articulate a list of other users with whom they share a connection, and (3) view and traverse their list of connections and those made by others within the system.*

The interactive capabilities to post comments or other content and rate content are surprisingly missing from this definition.

The six key types of digital media channels

There are many online communications techniques which marketers must review as part of their e-business communications strategy or as part of planning an online marketing campaign. To assist with planning, Chaffey and Smith (2008) recommend reviewing these six main types of digital media channels for reaching audiences shown in Figure 1.6. Note that offline communications should also be reviewed for their role in driving visitors to a company website or social network presence.

In Chapters 8 and 9, we review these tools in detail, but here is a summary of each digital media channel.

Digital marketing

This has a similar meaning to 'electronic marketing' – both describe the management and execution of marketing using electronic media such as the web, e-mail, interactive TV and wireless media in conjunction with digital data about customers' characterstics and behaviour.

Feed or RSS feed

Blog, news or other content is published by an XML standard and syndicated for other sites or read by users in RSS reader services such as Google Reader, personalized home pages or e-mail systems. RSS stands for 'really simple syndication'.

Podcasts

Individuals and organizations post online media (audio and video) which can be viewed in the appropriate players (including the iPod which first sparked the growth in this technique). The latest podcast updates can be automatically delivered by *really simple syndication*.

Social network

A site that facilitates peer-to-peer communication within a group or between individuals through providing facilities to develop user-generated content (UGC) and to exchange messages and comments between different users.

Digital media channels

Online communications techniques used to achieve goals of brand awareness, familiarity, favourability and to influence purchase intent by encouraging users of digital media to visit a website to engage with the brand or product and ultimately to purchase online or offline through traditional media channels such as by phone or in-store.

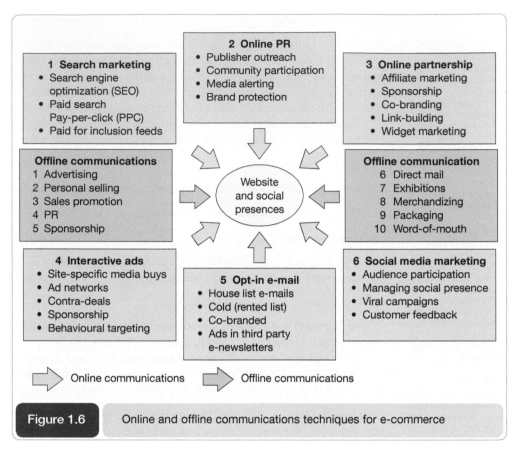

Figure 1.6	Online and offline communications techniques for e-commerce

1 Search engine marketing

Placing messages on a search engine to encourage clickthrough to a website when the user types a specific keyword phrase. Two key search marketing techniques are: paid placements or sponsored links using **pay-per-click**, and placements in the natural or organic listings using **search engine optimization (SEO)**.

2 Online PR

Maximizing favourable mentions and interactions with a company's brands, products or websites using third-party sites such as social networks or blogs that are likely to be visited by your target audience. It also includes responding to negative mentions and conducting public relations via a site through a press centre or blog. It is closely related to social media marketing.

3 Online partnerships

Creating and managing long-term arrangements to promote your online services on third-party websites or through e-mail communications. Different forms of partnership include link building, affiliate marketing, aggregators such as price comparison sites like Money supermarket (www.moneysupermarket.com), online sponsorship and co-branding.

4 Interactive advertising

Use of online ads such as banners and rich media ads to achieve brand awareness and encourage clickthrough to a target site.

5 Opt-in e-mail marketing

Renting e-mail lists or placing ads in third-party e-newsletters or the use of an in-house list for customer activation and retention.

6 Social media marketing

Social media marketing
Monitoring and facilitating customer–customer interaction and participation throughout the web to encourage positive engagement with a company and its brands. Interactions may occur on a company site, social networks and other third-party sites.

Social media marketing is an important category of digital marketing which invovles encouraging customer communications on a company's own site, or a social presence such as Facebook or Twitter, or in specialist publisher sites, blogs and forums. It can be applied as a traditional broadcast medium, for example companies can use Facebook or Twitter to send messages to customers or partners who have opted in. However, to take advantage of the benefits of social media it is important to participate in customer conversations. These can be related to products, promotions or customer service and are aimed at learning more about customers and providing support, so improving the way a company is perceived. In Chapter 9 we identify six main applications of social media.

Facebook is an example of an e-business that is now vital to companies seeking to reach and engage their audience online. Read the case study to understand the drivers behind the growth of the company and the challenges of managing an e-business.

Case Study 1.1 | **A short history of Facebook**

Context

This case is about the social network Facebook. According to its owners,

Facebook is a social utility that helps people communicate more efficiently with their friends, family and coworkers. The company develops technologies that facilitate the sharing of information through the social graph, the digital mapping of people's real-world social connections. Anyone can sign up for Facebook and interact with the people they know in a trusted environment.

In many countries Facebook is one of the most popular sites and in February 2010 exceeded 400 million active worldwide users for the first time. The case illustrates some of the challenges for an owner of a social network managing growth in usage, providing new features, advertising and managing user privacy. It also highlights the challenges for partners and advertisers considering working with a social network.

The case is presented through key events during the development of Facebook.

Facebook launched and extended – 4 February 2004

Facebook was founded while Mark Zuckerberg was a student at Harvard University. Initially membership was limited to Harvard students. The initial viral effect of the software was indicated since more than half of the undergraduate population at Harvard registered on the service within the first month!

Zuckerberg used open-source software PHP and the MySQL database to create the original 'TheFacebook.com' site and these technologies are still in use today.

When Facebook first launched in February 2004, there were just three things that users could do on the site which are still core to the functionality of the site. Users could create a profile with their picture and information, view other people's profiles, and add people as friends.

Since 2004, Facebook has introduced other functionality to create the Facebook experience. Some of the most significant of these include:

- A wall for posting messages
- News feeds
- Messages
- Posting of multiple photos and videos
- Groups
- Applications
- Facebook or engagement ads
- Access by mobile phones

Intellectual property dispute – September 2004 and ongoing

There has been an ongoing dispute on ownership of Facebook since another Harvard-originated social networking site 'HarvardConnection', which later changed its name to ConnectU, alleged in September 2004 that Zuckerberg had used their source code to develop Facebook when they originally contracted him to help in building their site.

It is also alleged that another system predated Facebook. Aaron J. Greenspan, a Harvard student, in 2003 created a simple web service that he called house-SYSTEM. It was used by several thousand Harvard students for a variety of online college-related tasks – six months before Facebook started and eight months before ConnectU went online. Mark Zuckerberg was briefly an early participant. No suit has been filed by Greenspan, but he has published a book about his experience.

Brand identify established – 23 August 2005

In August, Facebook bought the domain name face-book.com from the Aboutface Corporation for $200,000 and dropped 'the' from its name.

International expansion – 11 December 2005

Throughout 2005, Facebook extended its reach into different types of colleges and by the end of 2005 included most small universities and junior colleges in the United States, Canada and Mexico. It was also made available in many universities in the UK and Ireland and by December, Australia and New Zealand were added to the Facebook network, bringing its size to more than 2,000 colleges and over 25,000 high schools.

Initial concerns about privacy of member data – 14 December 2005

Two MIT students downloaded over 70,000 Facebook profiles from four schools (MIT, NYU, the University of Oklahoma, and Harvard) using an automated script, as part of a research project on Facebook privacy.

Facebook receives $25 million in funding – April 2006; Microsoft invests October 2007

In May 2005 Facebook received a $13 million cash infusion from venture firm Accel Partners, followed in April 2006 by a further $25 million from a range of partners including Greylock Partners, Meritech Capital Partners, and investor Peter Thiel, the co-founder of PayPal.

Facebook spokesman Chris R. Hughes explained the rationale for the investment when he said:

This investment supports our goal to build an industry-leading company that will continue to grow and evolve with our users. We're committed to building the best utility to enable people to share information with each other in a secure and trusted environment.

Paul S. Madera, Meritech's managing director, said his firm was impressed by Facebook's rapid growth and its potential for further expansion in the coveted college-age market. 'They've been designated by their community as the chosen community portal,' Madera said. 'This is a company that the entire venture community would love to be a part of.'

In October 2007 Microsoft took a $240 million equity stake in Facebook based on a $15 billion valuation of Facebook. Under the terms of this strategic alliance, Microsoft would be the exclusive third-party advertising platform partner for Facebook, and begin to sell advertising for Facebook internationally in addition to the United States.

New feed functionality launched – September 2006

New information feeds were launched in mid-2006 which show the challenges of balancing the benefit of new functionality against disrupting existing user habits.

Writing in the Facebook blog in September 2006 Mark Zuckerberg said:

We've been getting a lot of feedback about Mini-Feed and News Feed. We think they are great products, but we know that many of you are not immediate fans, and have found them overwhelming and cluttered.

Other people are concerned that non-friends can see too much about them. We are listening to all your suggestions about how to improve the product; it's brand new and still evolving.

Later, in an open letter on the blog dated 8 September 2006, Zuckerberg said:

We really messed this one up. When we launched News Feed and Mini-Feed we were trying to provide you with a stream of information about your social world. Instead, we did a bad job of explaining what the new features were and an even worse job of giving you control of them. I'd like to try to correct those errors now.

Categorizing friends into different types (Friends Lists – December 2007) is one approach that has helped to manage this.

Facebook Platform for applications launched – 24 May 2007

The Facebook Platform provides an API (Application Programming Interface) which enables software developers to create applications that interact with core Facebook features. This was a significant move since the openness enabled applications to grow in popularity and other sites to embed Facebook Fan page and follower information.

By January 2008, over 18,000 applications had been built on Facebook Platform with 140 new applications added per day. More than 95% of Facebook members have used at least one application built on Facebook Platform.

Facebook Platform for mobile applications was launched in October 2007, although many Facebook users already interacted with their friends through mobile phones.

Facebook passes 30 million active users – July 2007

Facebook active users passed 30 million according to the Facebook blog in July 2007. Mashable (http://

mashable.com/2007/07/10/facebook-users-2) reported that this represented a doubling in the first half of 2007.

Data produced by querying the Facebook ad targeting tool (www.facebook.com/ads) completed in November 2007 by blogger P.K. Francis suggests that the majority of Facebook users in many countries are female: http://midnightexcess.wordpress.com/2007/11/ 23/facebook-member-stats-an-update.

In terms of user engagement metrics, Facebook (www.facebook.com/press/info.php?statistics) shows there are:

- 68 million active users
- An average of 250,000 new registrations per day since January 2007
- Sixth most trafficked site in the United States (comScore)
- More than 65 billion page views per month
- More than half of active users return daily
- People spend an average of 20 minutes on the site daily (comScore)

Advertisers assess reputational damage – Summer 2007

In August 2007, the BBC announced that six major mainly financial services firms (First Direct, Vodafone, Virgin Media, the AA, Halifax and the Prudential) had withdrawn advertisements from Facebook, after they appeared on a British National Party page.

At a similar time, bank HSBC was forced to respond to groups set up on Facebook criticizing them for introduction of new student banking charges (although not until the case had been featured in the national media).

Facebook Ads launched – 7 November 2007

Some of the features of Facebook Ads (www.facebook.com/ads) include:

- Targeting by age, gender, location, interests, and more.
- Alternative payment models: cost per click (CPC) or impression-based (CPM).
- 'Trusted Referrals' or 'Social Ads' – ads can also be shown to users whose friends have recently engaged with a company's Facebook page or engaged with the company website through Facebook Beacon.

At the time of the launch the Facebook blog made these comments, which indicates the delicate balance between advertising revenue and user experience. They said, first of all, what's not changing:

- *'Facebook will always stay clutter-free and clean.*
- *Facebook will never sell any of your information.*

- *You will always have control over your information and your Facebook experience.*
- *You will not see any more ads than you did before this.'*

And what is changing:

- *'You now have a way to connect with products, businesses, bands, celebrities and more on Facebook.*
- *Ads should be getting more relevant and more meaningful to you.*
- *You now have the option to share actions you take on other sites with your friends on Facebook.'*

Commercial companies or more commonly not-for-profit organizations (e.g. www.facebook.com/joinred) can also create their own Facebook pages (currently free). Facebook users can then express their support by adding themselves as a fan, writing on the company Wall, uploading photos, and joining other fans in discussion groups. When users become fans, they can optionally agree to be kept up to date about developments which then appear in their news feeds.

Privacy concerns sparked by 'Beacon technology' – November 2007

Facebook received a lot of negative publicity on its new advertising format related to the 'Beacon' tracking system. Mark Zuckerberg was forced to respond to on the Facebook blog (5 December 2007). He said:

About a month ago, we released a new feature called Beacon to try to help people share information with their friends about things they do on the web. We've made a lot of mistakes building this feature, but we've made even more with how we've handled them. We simply did a bad job with this release, and I apologize for it. While I am disappointed with our mistakes, we appreciate all the feedback we have received from our users. I'd like to discuss what we have learned and how we have improved Beacon.

When we first thought of Beacon, our goal was to build a simple product to let people share information across sites with their friends. It had to be lightweight so it wouldn't get in people's way as they browsed the web, but also clear enough so people would be able to easily control what they shared. We were excited about Beacon because we believe a lot of information people want to share isn't on Facebook, and if we found the right balance, Beacon would give people an easy and controlled way to share more of that information with their friends.

But we missed the right balance. At first we tried to make it very lightweight so people wouldn't have to touch it for it to work. The problem with our initial approach of making it an opt-out system instead of opt-in was that if someone forgot to decline to share something, Beacon still went ahead and shared it with their friends. It took us too long after people started contacting us to change the product so that users had to explicitly approve what they wanted to share. Instead of acting quickly, we took too long to decide on the right solution. I'm not proud of the way we've handled this situation and I know we can do better.

New friends list functionality launched – December 2007

A criticism levelled at Facebook has been the difficulty in separating out personal friends and business acquaintants.

In December 2007, Facebook launched a significant new functionality called Friend Lists to enhance the user experience. Friend Lists enables users to create named groups of friends in particular categories, e.g. business or personal and these private lists can be used to message people, send group or event invitations, and to filter updates from certain groups of friends.

December 2007/January 2008 – first drop in numbers using Facebook and new data centres to manage growth in users

Application spam has been considered one of the possible causes to the drop in visitors to Facebook at the beginning of 2008. The fall in visitors between December 2007 and January 2008 was its first drop since the website first launched.

To put this in context, the Facebook blog reported at the end of 2007 that nearly 2 million new users from around the world sign up for Facebook each week.

Facebook expands internationally – February 2008

Despite the hype generated amongst English speakers, Facebook only announced the launch of a Spanish site in February 2008 with local language versions planned for Germany and France. It seems that Facebook will inevitably follow the path taken by other social networks such as MySpace in launching many local language versions.

Privacy setting concerns – Autumn to 2009 to Spring 2010

In December 2009, Facebook implemented new privacy settings. This meant some information, including 'lists of friends', was 'publicly available', when it was previously possible to restrict access to this information. Photos and some personal information were also public unless users were sufficiently knowledgeable and active to limit access. Privacy campaigners including the Electronic Frontier Foundation and American Civil Liberties Union criticized the changes. In May 2010 further changes were made to give users greater control and simplify the settings.

Source: Facebook (www.facebook.com), Facebook press room (www.facebook.com/press.php), Facebook Statistics (www.facebook.com/press/info.php?statistics, Facebook blog (http://blog.facebook.com), Wikipedia (2010) Wikipedia Pages for Facebook (http://en.wikipedia.org/wiki/Facebook), Criticism of Facebook (http://en.wikipedia.org/wiki/Criticism_of_Facebook) and Mark Zuckerberg (http://en.wikipedia.org/wiki/Mark_Zuckerberg)

Questions

1 As an investor in a social network such as Facebook, which financial and customer-related metrics would you use to assess and benchmark the current business success and future growth potential of the company?

2 Complete a situation analysis for Facebook focusing on an assessment of the main business risks which could damage the future growth potential of the social network.

3 For the main business risks to Facebook identified in Question 2, suggest approaches the company could use to minimize these risks.

Video explanation: http://bit.ly/EBEC-Facebook-Video.

Mobile services adoption is increasing rapidly as users purchase the latest models. Table 1.2 shows how more advanced 'Smartphone' devices with improved functionality and download speed encourage adoption of services.

An example of the popularity of location-based mobile services is Qype (www.qype.com). Founded in 2006, Qype is Europe's largest site for user-generated reviews and recommendations of places, events and experiences. Qype allows users to search for and read reviews about a restaurant, shop, service or experience and, with the Qype App, users can read and add reviews on their phone and use the application as a personal satnav to find

Table 1.2	Internet usage habits among mobile phone subscribers, EU-5 3-month average ending March 2010, age 13+					
	Reach (%) of Mobile Subscribers					
	EU5	**UK**	**France**	**Germany**	**Italy**	**Spain**
Sent text message to another phone	82.2%	90.1%	80.4%	80.9%	77.5%	82.0%
Used application (including games)	35.0%	39.2%	25.9%	33.8%	39.4%	37.4%
Used browser	25.0%	33.6%	24.0%	20.3%	23.6%	22.9%
Listened to music on mobile phone	23.8%	22.6%	21.1%	25.8%	21.1%	30.0%
Accessed Social Networking Site or Blog	13.7%	20.7%	12.6%	8.8%	14.2%	12.1%
Accessed news	11.1%	15.5%	10.3%	9.2%	12.0%	7.9%
Smartphone	24.5%	25.0%	17.1%	18.6%	33.3%	30.5%
3G Subscribers	44.0%	43.3%	38.6%	40.4%	45.6%	55.0%

Source: MobiLens (2010).

places nearby. Available in seven different languages, Qype is a pan-European local review site with 2.2 million reviews covering more than 166,000 cities worldwide. (See Figure 1.7)

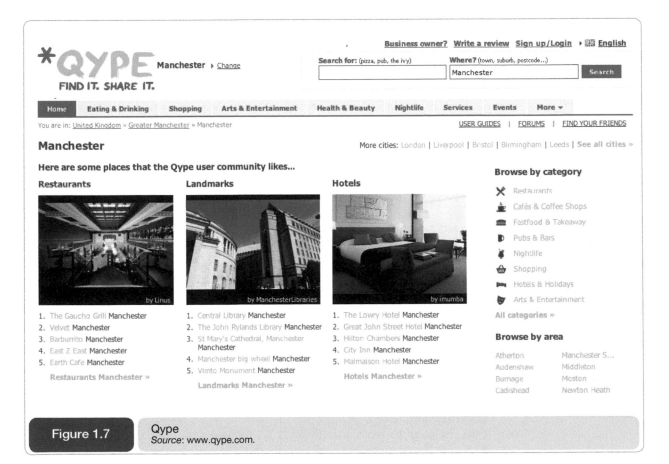

| Figure 1.7 | Qype
Source: www.qype.com. |

Multi-channel marketing
Customer communications and product distribution are supported by a combination of digital and traditional channels at different points in the buying cycle

Multi-channel marketing strategy
Defines how different marketing channels should integrate and support each other in terms of their proposition development and communications based on their relative merits for the customer and the company.

Customer journey
A description of modern multi-channel buyer behaviour as consumers use different media to select suppliers, make purchases and gain customer support.

Customer-centric marketing
An approach to marketing based on detailed knowledge of customer behaviour within the target audience which seeks to fulfil the individual needs and wants of customers.

Customer insight
Knowledge about customers' needs, characteristics, preferences and behaviours based on analysis of qualitative and quantitative data. Specific insights can be used to inform marketing tactics directed at groups of customers with shared characteristics.

Web 2.0 concept
A collection of web services that facilitate interaction of web users with sites to create user-generated content and encourage behaviours such as community or social network participation, **mashups**, content rating, use of **widgets** and tagging.

The second part of the definition of digital marketing shows that it should not be the technology that drives digital marketing, but the business returns from gaining new customers and maintaining relationships with existing customers. It also emphasizes how digital marketing does not occur in isolation, but is most effective when it is integrated with other communications channels such as phone, direct mail or face-to-face. The role of the Internet in supporting multi-channel marketing and multi-channel marketing strategy is another recurring theme in this book and Chapters 2 and 5 in particular explain its role in supporting different customer communications channels and distribution channels. Online channels should also be used to support the whole buying process or customer journey from pre-sale to sale to post-sale and further development of customer relationships. This clarifies how different marketing channels should integrate and support each other in terms of their proposition development and communications based on their relative merits for the customer and the company.

The final part of the description summarizes approaches to customer-centric marketing. It shows how success online requires a planned approach to migrate existing customers to online channels and acquire new customers by selecting the appropriate mix of e-communications and traditional communications. Gaining and keeping online customers needs to be based on developing customer insight by researching their characteristics and behaviour, what they value and what keeps them loyal, and then delivering tailored, relevant web and e-mail communications.

Web 2.0

Since 2004, the Web 2.0 concept has increased in prominence among website owners and developers. The main technologies and principles of Web 2.0 have been explained in an influential article by Tim O'Reilly (O'Reilly, 2005). Behind the label 'Web 2.0' lies a bewildering range of interactive tools and social communications techniques such as blogs, podcasts and social networks. These are aimed at increasing user participation and interaction on the web. With the widespread adoption of high-speed broadband in many countries, rich media experiences are increasingly used to engage customers with the hope they will have a viral effect, i.e. they will be discussed online or offline and more people will become aware of or interact with the brand campaign. Mini case study 1.2 gives an example of a viral campaign which helped sell products.

Web 2.0 also references methods of exchanging data between sites in standardized formats, such as the feeds merchants use to supply shopping comparison sites with data about products offered and their prices. We include examples of Web 2.0 e-business applications throughout the book and discuss them in more detail in Chapter 3.

The main characteristics of Web 2.0 are that it typically involves:

(i) Web services or interactive applications hosted on the web such as Flickr (www.flickr.com), Google Maps™ (http://maps.google.com) or blogging services such as Blogger.com or Typepad (www.typepad.com).

(ii) Supporting participation – many of the applications are based on altruistic principles of community participation best represented by the most popular social networks such as Bebo, MySpace and Facebook.

(iii) Encouraging creation of user-generated content – blogs are the best example of this. Another example is the collaborative encyclopedia Wikipedia (www.wikipedia.com).

(iv) Enabling rating of content and online services – services such as Delicious (www.delicious.com) and traceback comments on blogs support this.

(v) Ad funding of neutral sites – web services such as Google Mail/GMail™ and many blogs are based on contextual advertising such as Google Adsense™ or Overture/Yahoo! Content Match.

(vi) Data exchange between sites through XML-based data standards. RSS is based on XML, but has relatively little semantic mark-up to describe the content. An attempt by Google to facilitate exchange and searching is Google Base™ (http://base.google.com).

| Mini Case Study 1.2 | BlendTec uses rich media and viral marketing to grow awareness and sales |

This example shows how an engaging idea can be discussed initially online and then in traditional media to help increase the awareness of a brand. On the WillItBlend campaign micro-site (www.willitblend.com, Figure 1.8) a blender designed for making smoothies has blended an iPhone, an iPod, golf balls, glow sticks, a video camera and more. It's only meant to make smoothies and milk shakes! As well as the micro-site for the viral campaign, there is also a brand channel on YouTube (www.youtube.com/user/blendtec) where different ads received several million views. There is also a blog (http://blog.blendtec.com) for new announcements and providing information for journalists. The blender has also been extensively featured on traditional media such as TV, newspapers, magazines and radio, showing that traditional media are important in increasing awareness further after the initial impact.

The viral idea was developed by Blendtec employee George Wright who came up with the viral idea and announced that in 2007 sales increased tremendously: '*because we're a smaller company, we were able to put out something edgy and fun. In terms of the product you see on YouTube, our sales have gone up by 500 per cent.*'

| Figure 1.8 | Blendtec viral campaign micro-site
Source: www.willitblend.com. |

Micro-formats
A simple set of formats based on XHTML for describing and exchanging information about objects including product and travel reviews, recipes and event information.

Mashups
Websites, pages or widgets that combine the content or functionality of one website or data source with another to create something offering a different type of value to web users from the separate types of content or functionallity.

This allows users to upload data about particular services in a standardized format based on XML. Data can also be exchanged through standard **micro-formats** such as hCalendar and hReview which are used to incorporate data from other sites into the Google listings (see www.microformats.org for details). New classes of content can also be defined and **mashups** created.

(vii) Use of rich media or creation of rich Internet applications (RIA) which provide for a more immersive, interactive experience. These may be integrated into web browsers or may be separate applications like that downloaded for Second Life (www.secondlife.com).

(viii) Rapid application development using interactive technology approaches known as 'Ajax' (Asynchronous JavaScript and XML). The best-known Ajax implementation is Google Maps which is responsive since it does not require refreshes to display maps.

Figure 1.9 summarizes the evolution of digital and web-related technologies. Box 1.1 discusses the emerging concept of Web 3.0.

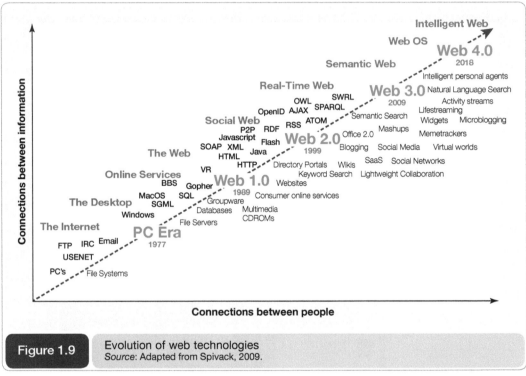

Figure 1.9	Evolution of web technologies
	Source: Adapted from Spivack, 2009.

| **Box 1.1** | Whither Web 3.0? |

Web 3.0 concept
Next-generation web incorporating high-speed connectivity, complex cross-community interactions, full range of digital media (text, voice, video) and an intelligent or semantic web where automated applications can access data from different online services to assist searchers to perform complex tasks of supplier selection.

Since the Web 2.0 concept has been widely applied, it is natural that commentators would try to evolve the concept to Web 3.0, although the term hasn't been widely applied to date. We can suggest that as web functionality evolves, these approaches will become more important:

- *Web applications*. Usage of web-based applications and services (like Google word processor and spreadsheets). This is sometimes termed '*cloud computing*' where all that is really needed for many activities is a computer with a web browser, with local software applications used less widely.

- *Syndication*. Increased incorporation of syndicated content and services from other sites or a network into a site (using tools such as Yahoo! Pipes and XML exchange between **widgets**). We refer to this concept as 'atomization' in Chapter 9.

Widget

A badge or button incorporated into a site or social network space by its owner, with content or services typically served from another site making widgets effectively a mini-software application or web service. Content can be updated in real time since the widget interacts with the server each time it loads.

- *Streamed video or IPTV*. Increased use of streamed video from existing TV providers and user-generated content (as suggested by use of YouTube and IPTV services such as Hulu).
- *Virtual worlds*. Increased use of immersive virtual environments such as Second Life.
- *Personal data integration*. Increased exchange of data between social networks fulfilling different needs (as indicated by the recent Google development of OpenSocial).
- *The semantic web*. Increased use of semantic mark-up leading to the semantic web envisioned by Tim Berners-Lee over 10 years ago. Semantic mark-up will be needed to develop artificial intelligence applications which recommend content and services to web users without their actively having to seek them and apply their own judgement as to the best products and brands.

Video explanation: Kate Ray interviews semantic web commentator Nova Spivack: http://bit.ly/EBEC-Semantic-Web-Video.

Supply chain management (SCM)

The coordination of all supply activities of an organization from its suppliers and partners to its customers.

Value chain

A model for analysis of how supply chain activities can add value to products and services delivered to the customer.

Value network

The links between an organization and its strategic and non-strategic partners that form its external value chain.

Business-to-consumer (B2C)

Commercial transactions between an organization and consumers.

Business-to-business (B2B)

Commercial transactions between an organization and other organizations (interorganizational marketing).

Consumer-to-consumer (C2C)

Informational or financial transactions between consumers, but usually mediated through a business site.

Consumer-to-business (C2B)

Consumers approach the business with an offer.

Supply chain management

When distinguishing between buy-side and sell-side e-commerce we are looking at different aspects of managing an organization's supply chain. **Supply chain management (SCM)** is the coordination of all supply activities of an organization from its suppliers and delivery of products to its customers. The opportunities for using e-commerce to streamline and restructure the supply chain are described in more detail in Chapter 6. The **value chain** is a related concept that describes the different value-adding activities that connect a company's supply side with its demand side. We can identify an *internal* value chain within the boundaries of an organization and an *external* value chain where these activities are performed by partners. Note that in the era of e-business a company will manage many interrelated value chains, so in Chapter 6 we also consider the concept of a **value network**.

Business or consumer models of e-commerce transactions

It is now commonplace to describe e-commerce transactions between an organization and its stakeholders according to whether they are primarily with consumers (**business-to-consumer – B2C**) or other businesses (**business-to-business – B2B**).

Figure 1.10 gives examples of different companies operating in the business-to-consumer (B2C) and business-to-business (B2B) spheres. Often companies such as BP or Dell Computer will have products that appeal to both consumers and businesses, so will have different parts of their site to appeal to these audiences.

Referring to the well-known online companies in Table 1.1 initially suggests these companies are mainly focused on B2C markets. However, B2B communications are still important for many of these companies since business transactions can drive revenue, as for example eBay Business (http://business.ebay.com/), or the B2C service may need to be sustained through advertising provided through B2B transactions; for example, Google's revenue is largely based on its B2B AdWords (http://adwords.google.com/) and advertising service and advertising-based revenue is also important to sites such as YouTube, MySpace and Facebook.

Figure 1.10 also presents two additional types of transaction, those where consumers transact directly with other consumers (**C2C**) and where they initiate trading with companies (**C2B**). These monikers are less widely used (e.g. *Economist*, 2000), but they do highlight significant differences between Internet-based commerce and earlier forms of commerce. Consumer-to-consumer interactions (also known as peer-to-peer or person-to-

	From: Supplier of content/service		
	Consumer or citizen	**Business (organization)**	**Government**
To: Consumer of content/service — Consumer or citizen	**Consumer-to-Consumer (C2C)** • eBay • Peer-to-Peer (Skype) • Blogs and communities • Product recommendations • Social networks: MySpace, Bebo	**Business-to-Consumer (B2C)** • Transactional: Amazon • Relationship-building: BP • Brand-building: Unilever • Media owner – News Corp • Comparison intermediary: Kelkoo, Pricerunner	**Government-to-Consumer (G2C)** • National government transactional: Tax – inland revenue • National government information • Local government services
Business (organization)	**Consumer-to-Business (C2B)** • Priceline • Consumer-feedback, communities or campaigns	**Business-to-Business (B2B)** • Transactional: Euroffice • Relationship-building: BP • Media Owned: Emap business publications • B2B marketplaces: EC21	**Government-to-Business (G2B)** • Government services and transactions: tax • Legal regulations
Government	**Consumer-to-Government (C2G)** • Feedback to government through pressure group or individual sites	**Business-to-Government (B2G)** • Feedback to government businesses and non-governmental organizations	**Government-to-Government (G2G)** • Inter-government services • Exchange of information

Figure 1.10	Summary and examples of transaction alternatives between businesses, consumers and governmental organizations

person, P2P) were relatively rare, but are now very common in the form of social networks. Hoffman and Novak (1996) suggested that C2C interactions are a key characteristic of the Internet that is important for companies to take into account, but it is only in recent years with the growth of always-on broadband connections and mobile access to the web that these have become so popular. P2P transactions are also the main basis for some online business models for e-businesses such as Betfair (see Mini case study 1.3) and eBay (www.ebay.com, see Case study 1.2) which are still run on a business basis, and some blogs which are not run by companies but by individuals.

Finally, the diagram also includes government and public services organizations which deliver online or e-government services. As well as the models shown in Figure 1.10, it has also been suggested that employees should be considered as a separate type of consumer through the use of intranets which are referred to as employee-to-employee or E2E.

Mini Case Study 1.3	Betfair profits with C2C online gambling service

Betfair provides a great example of the creation of an ebusiness with an innovative business model. It holds licences to operate in the UK, USA, Australia, Austria, Germany, Italy and Malta with over 50% of all new registrations coming from outside the UK and Ireland. It has grown rapidly over the last five years with revenue rising from £107m in 2005 to £303m for 2009, while adjusted EBITDA has more than doubled from £30m in 2005 to £72m for 2009.

Betfair is the world's biggest online sports betting company and pioneered the first successful betting exchange in 2000. Driven by cutting-edge technology, Betfair enables customers to choose their own odds and bet even after the event has started. The company now processes over 6 million transactions a day from its 3 million registered customers around the world (the 3 million mark was passed in 2010).

Betfair introduced a novel form of betting which replaces the typical role of the bookmaker such as Ladbrokes or William Hill who provided fixed odds and take their own risk on the outcome. With Betfair, all bets placed are with other Betfair customers rather than with Betfair which has no risks on the outcome. As with all forms of gambling, there is a risk of corruption 'throwing the bet'; to reduce this risk Betfair has a transparent approach where evidence of corruption may be shared with the governing body of a sport.

Through providing an online service, there are additional aspects of its proposition:

- You can either place bets conventionally or request your own odds.
- You can choose the odds you want to play at.
- You can bet whilst the game is in play.

Betfair's revenue model

Betfair charges a commission (typically 5%) on each player's net winnings on a market. If a player loses, there is no commission. There is a discount on commission; when you place more bets this rewards regular punters.

Betfair's growth

This outline history of Betfair shows how it has extended its product range and partnerships to support its growth:

1. 2000 – The Sporting Exchange Ltd launches Betfair.com from Russell Square, London. At launch funds were limited, so the company used 'guerrilla marketing' to promote it, such as a procession through the City of London with coffins with banners 'death of the bookmaker' and fake demonstrations with 'Betfair – unfair' banners.
2. 2001 – Betfair matches £1 million in seven days for the first time.
3. 2002 – Betfair announces a merger with competitor Flutter and sponsorship of Fulham Football Club.
4. 2003 – Betfair launches sites in German, Danish, Greek, Italian, Swedish, Norwegian, Finnish and Chinese.
5. 2004 – Betfair launches Betfair poker, which today has 60,000 registered players. Betfair signs joint venture with Australia's Publishing and Broadcasting Limited.
6. 2005 – Betfair sponsors the Channel 4 Ashes Cricket coverage and records the highest-ever single market turnover, matching £36 million on the Fifth Ashes Test Match alone! Betfair signs exclusive deal with Yahoo! UK and Ireland to launch a simplified betting exchange as well as a co-branded betting exchange.
7. Betfair's key performance indicators are suggested by an annual report for year ending 30 April 2007 when it had an annual turnover in excess of £180 million with operating profit of £35 million based on 18 million 'active player days' which is a key performance measure derived from the 433,000 active customers and an average 9 player-days per month per active customer. International revenues grew most rapidly and contributed 23 per cent of exchange revenues compared with 18 per cent in the previous year.
8. By 2010 Betfair employed over 1,700 people globally. Its headquarters are in Hammersmith in West London, while its international business is based in Malta. It also has large operational bases in the UK in Stevenage, Australia in Tasmania and Melbourne, a software development hub in Romania, as well as offices in Los Angeles and San Francisco.
9. Technology challenges are indicated by the 6 million transactions a day processed, equating to 360 bets a second. Using Oracle database technology, Betfair processes 99.9 per cent of bets in less than one second.
10. In April 2010 an iTunes App was released with Betfair noting that their registered mobile users increased 40% in 2009 with a a 50% increase in year on year mobile revenues.

Source: Corporate site (www.betfaircorporate.com).

E-government defined

E-government
The application of
e-commerce technologies
to government and public
services for citizens and
businesses.

E-government refers to the application of e-commerce technologies to government and public services. In the same way that e-business can be understood as transactions with customers (citizens), suppliers and internal communications, e-government covers a similar range of applications:

- *Citizens* – facilities for dissemination of information and use of online services at local and national levels. For example, at a local level you can find out when refuse is collected and at national level it is possible to fill in tax returns.
- *Suppliers* – government departments have a vast network of suppliers. The potential benefits (and pitfalls) of electronic supply chain management and e-procurement described in Chapters 6 and 7 are equally valid for government.
- *Internal communications* – this includes information collection and dissemination and e-mail and workflow systems for improving efficiency within government departments.

E-government is now viewed as important within government in many countries. The European Union set up 'i2010' (*European Information Society in 2010*) whose aims included

> *providing an integrated approach to information society and audio-visual policies in the EU, covering regulation, research, and deployment and promoting cultural diversity.*
> (eEurope, 2005)

E-business opportunities

E-business has introduced new opportunities for small and large organizations to compete in the global marketplace. Many commentators have noted that one of the biggest changes introduced by electronic communications is how approaches to transmitting and transforming information can be used for competitive advantage. A significant commentary on the disruptive, transformational nature of electronic communications is provided in Box 1.2.

Box 1.2   Evans and Wurster on the impact of disruptive Internet technologies

**Disruptive Internet
technologies**
New Internet-based
communications
approaches which
change the way in
which information about
products is exchanged,
which impact the basis
for competition in a
marketplace.

Evans and Wurster of Harvard argue in their classic 1997 paper 'Strategy and the new economics of information' that there are three characteristics of information which, when combined with disruptive Internet technologies, can have a major impact on a marketplace. These characteristics of information are reach, richness and affiliation:

1 *Reach*. Conventionally, 'reach' refers to the potential number of customers a business can interact with. The Internet enables reach to be increased nationally and internationally at low cost through making content available via search engines. 'Reach' also refers to the number of different categories and products a consumer interface (e.g. store, catalogue or website) can cover: witness the large range of products available through e-businesses such as Amazon, eBay and Kelkoo.com and existing companies such as easyJet.com and Tesco.com which have used the web to extend their product range.

2 *Richness*. This is a characteristic of the information itself. The Internet enables more detailed information about products, prices and availability to be made available. It also enables more interactivity and customization to engage customers and to provide more up-to-date information. But, Evans and Wurster also note that richness is limited by bandwidth (the volume of information that can be

transmitted using a communications link in a given time), the accuracy or reliability of information and its security.

3 *Affiliation*. This refers to the effectiveness of links with partners. In an online context, an organization which has the most and richest links with other compatible organizations will be able to gain a larger reach and influence. Consider how e-businesses such as eBay, Google and Yahoo! have successfully formed partnerships or acquired other companies to provide new diverse information services such as social networking, mapping, voice communications and online photography, to name just a few.

In markets such as car sales which have been transformed by the Internet, understanding how to improve reach, richness and affiliation is crucial. This is not because a large proportion of people buy cars online, but rather the majority research online their preferred make, model and supplier.

The Internet also provides significant opportunities for many businesses to build closer relationships with their existing customers and suppliers online to help achieve customer retention. Encouraging use of online, e-business services by customers and suppliers can significantly reduce costs while providing a new, convenient channel for purchase and customer service. Through providing high-quality online services, organizations can build lasting relationships with their stakeholders. While it is sometimes said that '*online, your customers are only a mouse click away from your competitors*', this is a simplification, and encouraging use of online services can help achieve '**soft lock-in**'. This means that a customer or supplier continues to use a service since they find the service valuable, they have invested time in learning the service or integrating it with their systems and there are some costs in switching. Think of online services you use for different purposes. How often do you switch between them? Of course, the ideal is that the service meets the needs of its users so well and delivers value such that they are satisfied and do not consider switching.

Soft lock-in
Customers or suppliers continue to use online services because of the switching costs.

Business adoption of digital technologies for e-commerce and e-business

As managers, we need to assess the impact of e-commerce and e-business on our marketplace and organizations. What are the drivers of changed consumer and business behaviour? How should we respond? How much do we need to invest? What are our priorities and how quickly do we need to act? Answering these questions is an essential part of formulating an e-business and e-marketing strategy and is considered in more detail in Part 2. To answer these questions marketing research will need to be conducted as described in Chapters 2 to 4 to determine the current levels of adoption of the Internet for different activities among customers and competitors in our market sector and in other sectors.

Drivers of business Internet adoption

Business adoption of e-commerce and e-business is driven by benefits to different parts of the organization. First and foremost, businesses are concerned about how the benefits of e-business will impact on profitability or generating value to an organization. The two main ways in which this can be achieved are:

- Potential for increased revenue arising from increased reach to a larger customer base and encouraging loyalty and repeat purchases among existing customers.
- Cost reduction achieved through delivering services electronically. Reductions include staff costs, transport costs and costs of materials such as paper.

At a relatively early point in e-business adoption, a government report (DTI, 2000) identified two main categories of drivers which remain relevant today:

Cost/efficiency drivers

1 Increasing speed with which supplies can be obtained
2 Increasing speed with which goods can be despatched
3 Reduced sales and purchasing costs
4 Reduced operating costs

Competitiveness drivers

5 Customer demand
6 Improving the range and quality of services offered
7 Avoiding losing market share to businesses already using e-commerce

More recently, in interviews with Australian businesses, Perrott (2005) identifies four key areas driving performance which are cost–benefit, competitive pressures, market advantage and value adding, i.e. improving customer satisfaction while building strong relationships.

When reviewing potential benefits, it is useful to identify both tangible benefits (for which monetary savings or revenues can be identified) and intangible benefits (for which it is more difficult to calculate cost savings). The types of potential benefits are summarized in Table 1.3.

Brochureware
Brochureware describes a web site in which a company has migrated its existing paper-based promotional literature on to the Internet without recognizing the differences required by this medium.

In Chapter 5 (Figure 5.12), an alternative information-based model of value creation is discussed in relation to financial services organization Capital One. This reviews new opportunities for adding value, reducing costs, managing risks and creating a new reality (transformation).

Doherty *et al.* (2003) researched the drivers and barriers to retailers' adoption of Internet technologies to determine the most important factors. Table 1.4 summarizes the ranking in importance for different degrees of Internet adoption from static brochureware (A), through an active website containing product information (B) to a transactional site where items can be purchased (C). You can see that the two most important factors which correlate with adoption are 'Internet target segment', i.e. customers in their market are typically

Table 1.3	Tangible and intangible benefits from e-commerce and e-business

Tangible benefits	Intangible benefits

• Increased sales from new sales leads giving rise to increased revenue from:
  – new customers, new markets
  – existing customers (cross-selling)
• Marketing cost reductions from:
  – reduced time in customer service
  – online sales
  – reduced printing and distribution costs of marketing communications
• Supply-chain cost reductions from:
  – reduced levels of inventory
  – shorter cycle time in ordering
• Administrative cost reductions from more efficient routine business processes such as recruitment, invoice payment and holiday authorization.
	• Corporate image communication
	• Enhancement of brand
	• More rapid, more responsive marketing communications including PR
	• Faster product development lifecycle enabling faster response to market needs
	• Improved customer service
	• Learning for the future
	• Meeting customer expectations to have a website
	• Identifying new partners, supporting existing partners better
	• Better management of marketing information and customer information
	• Feedback from customers on products

Table 1.4	Summary of factors most important in encouraging Internet adoption amongst e-retailers		

Factor influencing adoption		A	B	C
1	Internet target segment	3	2	1
2	Internet strategy	1	1	6
3	Internet marketplace	4	5	2
4	Infrastructure and development capability	2	3	5
5	Internet communications	5	6	4
6	Cost of Internet trading	8	9	10
7	Internet cost opportunity	6	8	7
8	Market development opportunity	7	4	3
9	Concerns	9	10	9
10	Consumer preferences	10	7	8

A = Internet adoption (static website), B = active website, C = online sales (transactional site)
Based on a compilation from separate tables in Doherty *et al.* (2003).

adopters of the Internet, and 'Internet strategy', i.e. a defined Internet strategy is in place. This suggests, as would be expected, that companies that do not have a coherent Internet or e-business strategy are less likely to use higher levels of Internet services. Many larger organizations that have responded to the challenge of e-business have created a separate e-commerce plan and separate resources to implement it. This book covers what needs to go into such a plan and the issues to consider when implementing it.

More recently, in Europe, research completed for the i2010 initiative monitored usage of the Internet by business (European Commission, 2010) and found that around 95% of businesses in the majority of countries surveyed have Internet access, although this figure masks lower levels of access for SMEs (small and medium-sized enterprises) and particularly micro-businesses (Figure 1.11).

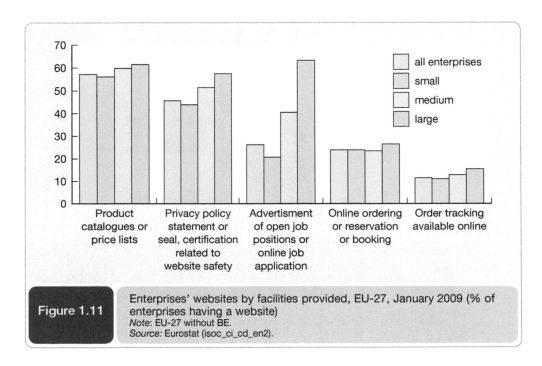

| Figure 1.11 | Enterprises' websites by facilities provided, EU-27, January 2009 (% of enterprises having a website)
Note: EU-27 without BE.
Source: Eurostat (isoc_ci_cd_en2). |

Case Study 1.2 illustrates the benefits of setting up an online operation for a small or medium enterprise (SME). It also highlights some of the challenges of managing an online business and highlights the need for continued investment to refine online services and the marketing needed to attract visitors to the website.

Case Study 1.2 — North West Supplies extends its reach online

North West Supplies (Figure 1.12) was launched as a business in March 1999 when Andrew Camwell, a member of the RAF Volunteer Reserve at the time, spotted a gap in the UK market for mail order supplies of military garments to people active in the Volunteer Reserve and the Air Cadet Force. Andrew, his wife Carys, and her sister Elaine Hughes started running a mail order business out of shop premises in the village of Cemaes Bay.

The web store at www.northwestsupplies.co.uk has been online since November 2002. As it can take several months for a website to be indexed by search engines, NWS used pay-per-click advertising (PPC – see Chapter 9) as a method of very quickly increasing the website's presence in the major search engines. This marketing method proved successful. The directors were pleasantly surprised as they had previously been somewhat dubious about the prospect of the Internet generating sales in their sector. Within six months of running the website, the company had increased turnover by £20,000, but further advances would incur a high advertising cost. Following an eCommerce Review by Opportunity Wales, the company decided to tackle the issues by implementing search engine optimization (SEO – see Chapter 9) and a site redesign which included:

Figure 1.12 North West Supplies Ltd
Source: www.northwestsupplies.co.uk; Opportunity Wales.

- *Improved graphic design* – this was to be changed to a more professional and up-to-date look.
- *Best, featured and latest products* – the introduction of a dynamic front page to entice customers to revisit the site on a regular basis. The contents of this page would feature the best sellers, and latest or featured products.
- *Reviews and ratings* – to provide confidence to consumers and allow some kind of interaction with them, this would allow users to review products they have purchased and give them a star rating.
- *Cross-selling* – when customers view a product other products or categories that may be of interest or complementary would be displayed.
- *Segmentation* – the site would be split into two sections emphasizing the segmentation of product lines into military wear and outdoor wear sectors, thus being less confusing, and easier to use.
- *Navigation by sub-categories* – as the product range had expanded, the additional pages created in each category made it harder for customers to find specific items. The introduction of sub-categories would provide a clear link to the areas of interest and contain fewer pages to browse, thus helping the customer to make a choice more easily and more quickly. A new search tool and order tracking were also seen as important parts of the online customer experience (Chapter 8).

Benefits

The owners describe the benefits of the improvements to the site as follows:

- *Increased direct sales* – '*The new launch increased sales and appealed to a broader audience – young and old.*' The annual turnover of the business has increased from £250,000 to £350,000 and this is mainly attributable to the new website. The high-profile launch aimed at existing customers, the greater visibility in search engines, and the greater usability of the site have all contributed to this.
- *Improved promotion of the whole range of stock* – '*We started selling stuff that we hadn't sold before.*' The changes in navigation, particularly division into two market segments (military and outdoors) and greater use of sub-categories, meant that products were easier to find and hence easier to buy, leading to increased sales of products that had previously been slow sellers.
- *New customers* – '*We now send more items abroad.*' The better performance of the site in search engines has led to an increase in orders from new customers and from abroad. The company now has regular sales to Canada, Australia, New Zealand and various European states. Sixty per cent of orders are from new customers – not bad for a business that was initially set up on the premise of a niche market for UK-based cadet forces.
- *Adding value to the brand* – '*New corporate clients could look at our website and see we weren't fly-by-night and that we meant business.*' Improvements to the design have raised confidence levels in visitors and this has led to increased sales. But perhaps more significantly, the professional image of the site was a good boost to confidence for potential business partners in the emerging business-to-business division that started to trade as North Star Contracts.

> **Question**
> Discuss the new opportunities and risks that need to be managed by North West Supplies with the increased importance of its online channel to market.

E-business risks and barriers to business adoption

Opportunities have to be balanced against the risks of introducing e-business services which include strategic and practical risks. One of the main strategic risks is making the wrong decision about e-business investments. In every business sector, some companies have taken advantage of e-business and gained a competitive advantage. But others have invested in e-business without achieving the hoped-for returns, either because the execution of the plan was flawed, or simply because the approaches were inappropriate. The impact of the Internet and technology varies by industry. Andy Grove, Chairman of Intel, one of the early adopters of e-business, noted that every organization needs to ask whether, for them:

> *The Internet is a typhoon force, a ten times force, or is it a bit of wind? Or is it a force that fundamentally alters our business?* (Grove, 1996)

This statement still seems to encapsulate how managers must respond to different digital technologies; the impact will vary through time from minor for some companies to significant for others, and an appropriate response is required.

There are also many practical risks to manage which, if ignored, can lead to bad customer experiences and bad news stories which damage the reputation of the company. In the section on e-business opportunities, we reviewed the concept of soft lock-in; however, if the customer experience of a service is very bad, they will stop using it, and switch to other online options. Examples of poor online customer experience include:

- Websites that fail because of a spike in visitor traffic after a peak-hour TV advertising campaign.
- Hackers penetrating the security of the system and stealing credit card details.
- A company e-mails customers without receiving their permission, so annoying customers and potentially breaking privacy and data protection laws.
- Problems with fulfilment of goods ordered online, meaning customer orders go missing or are delayed.
- E-mail customer-service enquiries from the website don't reach the right person and are ignored.

Debate 1.2

Limited SME adoption of e-business

'Adoption of e-business by established SMEs is generally less than that in larger businesses. This is principally a consequence of the negative attitude of managing directors and CEOs to the business benefits of information and communication technology.'

The perception of these risks may result in limited adoption of e-business in many organizations, which is suggested by the data in Figure 1.11. This is particularly the case for small and medium enterprises (SMEs). We study adoption levels and drivers in this type of business further in Chapter 4.

A DTI (2002) study evaluated some of the barriers to B2B e-commerce (Figure 1.13) which remain valid today. You can see that reasons of cost were the most important factors. This suggests the importance of managers

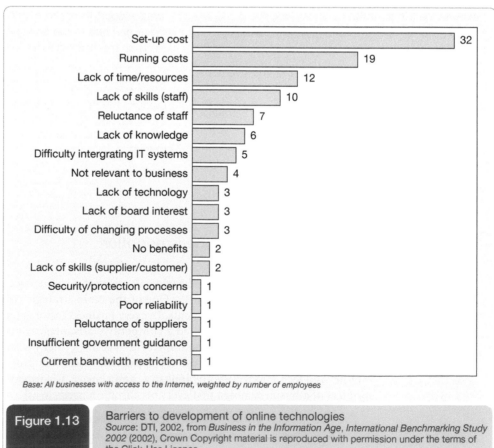

Base: All businesses with access to the Internet, weighted by number of employees

Figure 1.13   Barriers to development of online technologies
Source: DTI, 2002, from Business in the Information Age, International Benchmarking Study 2002 (2002), Crown Copyright material is reproduced with permission under the terms of the Click-Use Licence.

assessing e-business to develop a cost–benefit analysis that considers both the initial investment costs and the ongoing costs that form the **total cost of ownership (TCO)** against the value created from the tangible and intangible benefits. The difficulties in implementation which we will review later in this book, such as the lack of the right resources or difficulty in integrating systems, are also indicated.

Another approach to reviewing the strategy issues involved with implementing e-business is the classic McKinsey 7S strategy instrument (Waterman *et al.*, 1980) which is summarized in Table 10.1.

Evaluating an organization's e-business capabilities

Assessment of an organization's existing e-business capabilities is a starting point for the future development of their e-business strategy. We will see in Chapter 5 how different forms of **stage models** can be used to assess e-business capability. An example of a basic stage model reviewing capabilities for sell-side and buy-side e-commerce is shown in Figure 1.14. This shows how companies will introduce more complex technologies and extend the range of processes which are e-business-enabled. Stage 5 includes social commerce.

Drivers of consumer Internet adoption

To determine investment in sell-side e-commerce, managers need to assess how to adopt new services such as web, mobile and interactive TV and specific services such as blogs, social networks and feeds. In Chapter 4, we see how such demand analysis is conducted in a structured way. One example of demand analysis is popularity or adoption rates for different online services. The range of different ways in which consumers use the Internet to research or transact is shown in Figure 1.15. You can see that male and female usage of the Internet for different activities is now very similar, but with downloading of digital content generally more popular among males.

Total cost of ownership (TCO)

TCO refers to the total cost for a company operating a computer system or other investment. This includes not only the purchase or leasing cost, but also the cost of all the services needed to maintain the system and support the end-user.

Stage models

Used to review how advanced a company is in its use of information and communications technology (ICT) to support different processes.

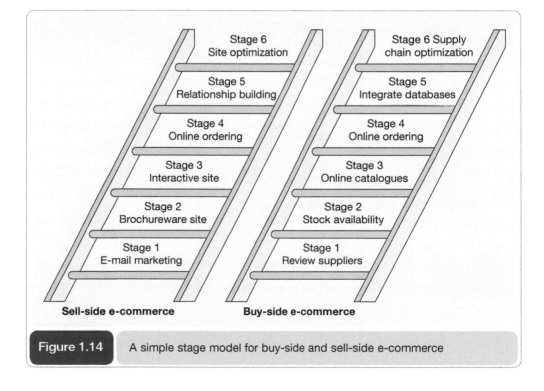

Figure 1.14   A simple stage model for buy-side and sell-side e-commerce

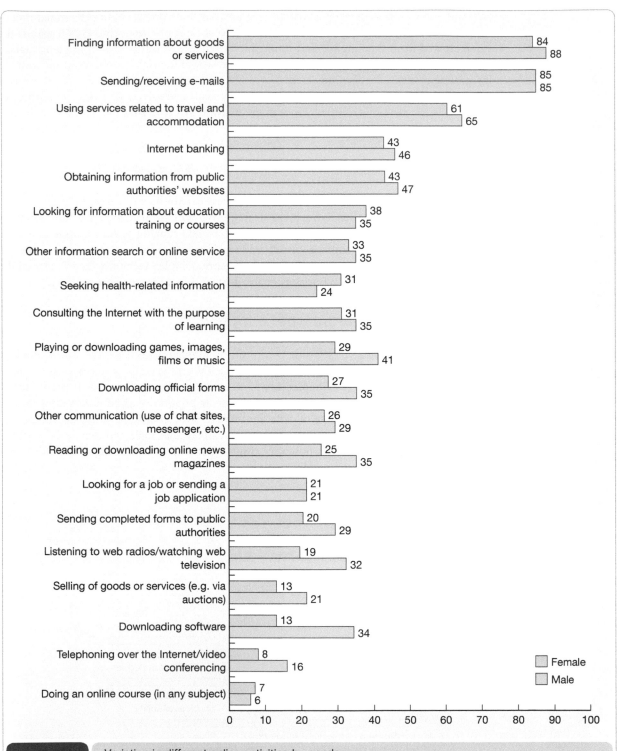

Figure 1.15   Variation in different online activities by gender
Source: UK National Statistics (2009) *Individuals accessing the Internet – Report from the UK National Statistics Omnibus Survey.* Published online at www.ststistics.gov.uk/StatBase/Product.asp?vlnk=5672.

We will see in Chapter 4 on strategy development for e-business how it is important that companies offering e-commerce services create a clear online value proposition (OVP) to encourage customers to use their specific online services. Typical benefits of online services are summarized by the 'Six Cs', a simple mnemonic to show different types of customer value:

Online value proposition (OVP)
A statement of the benefits of online services reinforces the core proposition and differentiates from an organization's offline offering and those of competitors.

1 *Content* – In the mid-1990s it was often said that 'content is king'. Well, relevant rich content is still king. This means more detailed, in-depth information to support the buying process for transactional or relationship-building sites or branded experiences to encourage product usage for FMCG brands.

2 *Customization* – In this case mass customization of content, whether received as website pages such as '*Amazon recommends*' or e-mail alerts, and commonly known as 'personalization'.

3 *Community* – The Internet liberates consumers to discuss anything they wish through forums, chat-rooms and blog comments. We will explore these techniques more in Chapters 2 and 3.

4 *Convenience* – This is the ability to select, purchase and in some cases use products from your desktop at any time: the classic $24 \times 7 \times 365$ availability of a service. Online usage of products is, of course, restricted to digital products such as music or other data services. Amazon has advertised offline using creative ads showing a Christmas shopper battling against a gale-swept street clutching several bags to reinforce the convenience message.

5 *Choice* – The web gives a wider choice of products and suppliers than via conventional distribution channels. The success of online intermediaries such as Kelkoo (www.kelkoo.com) and Screentrade (www.screentrade.com) is evidence of this. Similarly, Tesco.com provides Tesco with a platform to give consumers a wider choice of products (financial, travel, white goods) with more detailed information than are physically available in-store.

6 *Cost reduction* – The Internet is widely perceived as a relatively low-cost place of purchase. Often customers expect to get a good deal online as they realize that online traders have a lower cost-base as they have lower staff and distribution costs than a retailer that runs a network of high-street stores. A simple price differential is a key approach to encouraging usage of online services. In the late 1990s, low-cost airline easyJet encouraged the limited change behaviour required from phone booking to online booking by offering a £2.50 discount on online flight bookings.

Note that the 7Cs of Rayport and Jaworski (2003) provide a similar framework of Context, Content, Community, Customization, Communication, Connection and Commerce.

Barriers to consumer Internet adoption

An indication of some of the barriers to using the Internet, in particular for consumer purchases, is clear from a survey (Booz Allen Hamilton, 2002) of perceptions in different countries. It noted that consumer barriers to adoption of the Internet included:

- No perceived benefit
- Lack of trust
- Security problems
- Lack of skills
- Cost

This lack of demand for Internet services from this group needs to be taken into account when forecasting future demand.

To complete this chapter, read Case study 1.3 for the background on the success factors which have helped build one of the world's biggest e-businesses.

This case summarizes the strategic approach used by eBay to take advantage of increased consumer adoption of the Internet. It summarizes its objectives, strategy and proposition and some of the risks that need management.

Context

It's hard to believe that one of the most celebrated dot-coms has now been established over 15 years. Pierre Omidyar, a 28-year-old French-born software engineer living in California coded the site while working for another company, eventually launching the site for business on Monday, 4 September 1995 with the more direct name 'Auction Web'. Legend reports that the site attracted no visitors in its first 24 hours. The site became eBay in 1997. In 2009, eBay had 90 million active users globally, with the total worth of goods sold on eBay $60 billion, which is equivalent to $2,000 every second. Total revenue was $8.7 billion.

Mission

eBay describes its purpose as to 'pioneer new communities around the world built on commerce, sustained by trust, and inspired by opportunity'.

At the time of writing eBay comprises two major businesses:

1 *The eBay marketplaces (approximately 66% of net revenues in Quarter 4 2009).* These include other sites like comparison site Shopping.com and StubHub. The mission for the core eBay business is to 'create the world's online marketplace'. The marketplace platforms include an average of 100 million products for sale on each day! In 2007, eBay's SEC filing notes some of the success factors for this business for which eBay seeks to manage the functionality, safety, ease-of-use and reliability of the trading platform. In 2010 the strategic priorities had changed to trust, value, selection and convenience.
2 *PayPal (approximately 34% of net revenues in 2009).* The mission is to 'create the new global standard for online payments'. This company was acquired in 2003 and is now a significant contributor to eBay revenue with the service incorporated in many other e-commerce sites.

A third part of the business, *Skype Internet telephony,* was acquired in 2005 by eBay and sold to an investor group in November 2009 with a 30% share retained by eBay.

Advertising and other net revenues represented 4% of total net revenues during 2007. This case focuses on the best-known eBay business, the eBay marketplace.

Revenue model

The vast majority of eBay's revenue is for the listing and commission on completed sales. For PayPal purchases an additional commission fee is charged. Margin on each transaction is phenomenal since once the infrastructure is built, incremental costs on each transaction are tiny – all eBay is doing is transmitting bits and bytes between buyers and sellers.

Advertising and other non-transaction net revenues represent a relatively small proportion of total net revenues and the strategy is that this should remain the case. Advertising and other net revenues totalled $94.3 million in 2004 (just 3% of net revenue).

Proposition

The eBay marketplace is well known for its core service which enables sellers to list items for sale on an auction or fixed-price basis giving buyers the opportunity to bid for and purchase items of interest. At the end of 2007, there were over 532,000 online storefronts established by users in locations around the world.

Software tools are provided, particularly for frequent traders, including Turbo Lister, Seller's Assistant, Selling Manager and Selling Manager Pro, which help automate the selling process, plus the Shipping Calculator, Reporting tools, etc. Today over 60% of listings are facilitated by software, showing the value of automating posting for frequent trading.

Fraud is a significant risk factor for eBay. BBC (2005) reported that around 1 in 10,000 transactions within the UK were fraudulent; 0.0001% is a small percentage, but scaling this up across the number of transactions, this is a significant volume.

eBay has developed 'Trust and Safety Programs' which are particularly important to reassure customers since online services are prone to fraud. For example, the eBay feedback forum can help establish credentials of sellers and buyers. Every registered user has a feedback profile that may contain compliments, criticisms and/or other comments by users who have conducted business with that user. The Feedback Forum requires feedback to be related to specific transactions and Top Seller status was introduced in 2010 to increase trust in the service. There is also a Safe Harbor data protection method and a standard purchase protection system.

According to the SEC filing, eBay summarizes the core messages to define its proposition as follows:

For buyers:

- Trust
- Value
- Selection
- Convenience

In 2007, eBay introduced Neighbourhoods (http://neighborhoods.ebay.com) where groups can discuss brands and products they have a high involvement with.

For sellers:

- Access to broad global markets
- Efficient marketing and distribution
- Opportunity to increase sales

In January 2008, eBay announced significant changes to its marketplaces business in three major areas: fee structure, seller incentives and standards, and feedback. These changes have been controversial with some sellers, but are aimed at improving the quality of experience. Detailed Seller Ratings (DSRs) enable sellers to be reviewed in four areas: (1) item as described, (2) communication, (3) delivery time and (4) postage and packaging charges. This is part of a move to help increase conversion rate by increasing positive shopping experiences, for example by including more accurate descriptions with better pictures and avoiding excessive shipping charges. Power sellers with positive DSRs will be featured more favourably in the search results pages and will gain additional discounts.

eBay obtained increased use of mobile e-commerce in 2009 and into 2010. The eBay mobile app for iPhone was downloaded 7 million times by January 2010. Consumers are shopping more and more via their mobile phones with more than $600 million worth of sales transacted through mobile applications in 2009.

Competition

Although there are now few direct competitors of online auction services in many countries, there are many indirect competitors. SEC (2008) describes competing channels as including online and offline retailers, distributors, liquidators, import and export companies, auctioneers, catalogue and mail order companies, classifieds, directories, search engines, products of search engines, virtually all online and offline commerce participants and online and offline shopping channels and networks.

BBC (2005) reports that eBay is not complacent about competition. It has pulled out of Japan due to competition from Yahoo! and within Asia and China is also facing tough competition by Yahoo! which has a

portal with a broader range of services more likely to attract subscribers.

Before the advent of online auctions, competitors in the collectables space included antique shops, car boot sales and charity shops. Anecdotal evidence suggests that all of these are now suffering. Some have taken the attitude of 'if you can't beat 'em, join 'em'. Many smaller traders who have previously run antique or car boot sales are now eBayers. Even charities such as Oxfam now have an eBay service where they sell high-value items contributed by donors. Other retailers such as Vodafone have used eBay as a means to distribute certain products within their range.

Objectives and strategy

The overall eBay aims are to increase the gross merchandise volume and net revenues from the eBay marketplace. More detailed objectives are defined to achieve these aims, with strategies focusing on:

1 *Acquisition* – increasing the number of newly registered users on the eBay marketplace.
2 *Activation* – increasing the number of registered users that become active bidders, buyers or sellers on the eBay marketplace.
3 *Activity* – increasing the volume and value of transactions that are conducted by each active user on the eBay marketplace. eBay had approximately 83 million active users at the end of 2007, compared to approximately 82 million at the end of 2006. An active user is defined as any user who bid on, bought, or listed an item during the most recent 12-month period.

The focus on each of these three areas will vary according to strategic priorities in particular local markets.

eBay marketplace growth is also driven by defining approaches to improve performance in these areas. First, category growth is achieved by increasing the number and size of categories within the marketplace, for example Antiques, Art, Books, and Business and Industrial. Second, formats for interaction. The traditional format is auction listings, but it has been refined now to include the 'Buy-It-Now' fixed-price format. This fixed-price listing now accounts for 53% of all transactions, suggesting adaptability into the eBay offering. Another format is the 'Dutch Auction' format, where a seller can sell multiple identical items to the highest bidders. eBay Stores was developed to enable sellers with a wider range of products to showcase their products in a more traditional retail format. eBay says it is constantly exploring new formats, often through acquisition of other comapnies, for example through the acquisition in 2004 of mobile.de in Germany and ▶

Marktplaats.nl in the Netherlands, as well as investment in craigslist, the US-based classified ad format. Another acquisition is Rent.com, which enables expansion into the online housing and apartment rental category. In 2007, eBay acquired StubHub, an online ticket marketplace, and it also owns comparison marketplace Shopping.com. Finally, marketplace growth is achieved through delivering specific sites localized for different geographies as follows. You can see there is still potential for greater localization, for example in parts of Scandinavia, Eastern Europe and Asia.

Localized eBay marketplaces:

- Australia
- Austria
- Belgium
- Canada
- China
- Singapore
- South Korea
- Spain
- France
- Germany
- Hong Kong
- India
- Ireland
- Sweden
- Switzerland
- Taiwan
- Italy
- Malaysia
- Netherlands
- New Zealand
- Philippines
- United Kingdom
- United States

eBay's growth strategy

In its SEC filing, success factors eBay believes are important to enable it to compete in its market include:

- ability to attract buyers and sellers;
- volume of transactions and price and selection of goods;
- customer service; and
- brand recognition.

According to its 2010 SEC filing:

Our growth strategy is focused on reinvesting in our customers by improving the buyer experience and seller economics by enhancing our products and services, improving trust and safety and customer support, extending our product offerings into new formats, categories and geographies, and implementing innovative pricing and buyer retention strategies.

Over the course of 2009, we continued to make significant changes that were designed to improve the user experience on all of our sites, including changes to pricing and shipping policies. In 2009, we also made significant steps to create a faster and more streamlined search experience with a greater focus on relevance when sorting search results. Pricing changes reduced the upfront cost of listing fixed price items on eBay so that fees are now based more on the successful sale of items, for both smaller and larger sellers. We encourage sellers to offer free or inexpensive shipping to our buyers by promoting their listings through our 'Best Match' search algorithm.

It also notes that in the context of its competitors, other factors it believes are important are:

- community cohesion, interaction and size;
- system reliability;
- reliability of delivery and payment;
- website convenience and accessibility;
- level of service fees; and
- quality of search tools.

This implies that eBay believes it has optimized these factors, but its competitors still have opportunities for improving performance in these areas which will make the market more competitive.

Risk management

The SEC filing lists the risks and challenges of conducting business internationally as follows:

- regulatory requirements, including regulation of auctioneering, professional selling, distance selling, banking, and money transmitting;
- legal uncertainty regarding liability for the listings and other content provided by users, including uncertainty as a result of less Internet-friendly legal systems, unique local laws, and lack of clear precedent or applicable law;
- difficulties in integrating with local payment providers, including banks, credit and debit card associations, and electronic fund transfer systems;
- differing levels of retail distribution, shipping, and communications infrastructures;
- different employee–employer relationships and the existence of workers' councils and labour unions;
- difficulties in staffing and managing foreign operations;
- longer payment cycles, different accounting practices, and greater problems in collecting accounts receivable;
- potentially adverse tax consequences, including local taxation of fees or of transactions on websites;
- higher telecommunications and Internet service provider costs;
- strong local competitors;
- different and more stringent consumer protection, data protection and other laws;
- cultural ambivalence towards, or non-acceptance of, online trading;
- seasonal reductions in business activity;
- expenses associated with localizing products, including offering customers the ability to transact business in the local currency;
- laws and business practices that favour local competitors or prohibit foreign ownership of certain businesses;

- profit repatriation restrictions, foreign currency exchange restrictions, and exchange rate fluctuations;
- volatility in a specific country's or region's political or economic conditions; and
- differing intellectual property laws and taxation laws.

Results

Financial results are presented in the table below. The growth and profitability figures show that eBay is no longer growting at its original rates. It is useful to identify active users who contribute revenue to the business as a buyer or seller. eBay had 56 million active users at the end of 2004 who are defined as any user who has bid, bought or listed an item during a prior 12-month period. This had increased to 90 million by 2009.

Video explanations: http://bit.ly/EBEC-Ebay-Video; eBay interactive timeline: http://www.ebayinc.com/list/milestones.

> ### Question
> Assess how the characteristics of the digital media and the Internet together with strategic decisions taken by its management team have supported eBay's continued growth.

	Year ended December 31 2007	Year ended December 31 2008	Year ended December 31 2009	Percent change from 2007 to 2008	Percent change from 2008 to 2009
	(In thousands, except percentage changes)				
Net Revenues by Type:					
Net transaction revenues					
Marketplaces	$ 4,680,835	$ 4,711,057	$ 4,461,845	1%	(5)%
Payments	1,838,539	2,320,495	2,641,194	26%	14%
Communications	364,564	525,803	575,096	44%	9%
Total net transaction revenues	6,883,938	7,557,355	7,678,135	10%	2%
Marketing services and other revenues					
Marketplaces	683,056	875,694	849,169	28%	(3)%
Payments	88,077	83,174	154,751	(6)%	86%
Communications	17,258	25,038	45,307	45%	81%
Total marketing services and other revenues	788,391	983,906	1,049,227	25%	7%
Total net revenues	$ 7,672,329	$ 8,541,261	$ 8,727,362	11%	2%

Source: SEC (2010), BBC (2005).

Summary

1 Electronic commerce traditionally refers to electronically mediated buying and selling.

2 Sell-side e-commerce or digital marketing involves all electronic business transactions between an organization and its customers, while buy-side e-commerce involves transactions between an organization and its suppliers. Social commerce encourages customers to interact to support sales goals.

3 'Electronic business' is a broader term, referring to how technology can benefit all internal business processes and interactions with third parties. This includes buy-side and sell-side e-commerce and the internal value chain.

4 Digital marketing involves the application of 6 key digital marketing media channels of search engine marketing, online PR and social media, partnerships, display advertising, email marketing and viral marketing.

5   Web 2.0 is used to referred to web services that facilitate interaction of web users with sites to create user-generated content and encourage behaviours such as community or social network participation, mashups, content rating, use of widgets and tagging.

5   The main business drivers for introducing e-commerce and e-business are opportunities for increased revenues and reducing costs, but many other benefits can be identified that improve customer service and corporate image.

6   Consumer adoption of the Internet is limited by lack of imperative, cost of access and security fears. Business adoption tends to be restricted by perceptions of cost, making return on investment difficult to quantify.

7   Introducing new technology is not all that is required for success in introducing e-commerce and business. Clearly defined objectives, creating the right culture for change, mix of skills, partnerships and organizational structure are arguably more important.

Exercises

Answers to these exercises are available online at www.pearsoned.co.uk/chaffey

Self-assessment questions

1   Distinguish between e-commerce and e-business.

2   Explain what is meant by buy-side and sell-side e-commerce.

3   Explain the scope and benefits of social media and social commerce to an organization of your choice.

4   Summarize the consumer and business adoption levels in your country. What seem to be the main barriers to adoption?

5   Outline the reasons why a business may wish to adopt e-commerce.

6   What are the main differences between business-to-business and business-to-consumer e-commerce?

7   Summarize the impact of the introduction of e-business on different aspects of an organization.

8   What is the relevance of intermediary sites such as Kelkoo (www.kelkoo.com) to the B2C company?

Essay and discussion questions

1   Suggest how an organization can evaluate the impact of digital technology on its business. Is it a passing fad or does it have a significant impact?

2   Explain the concepts of social media and social commerce and how they can assist organizations in reaching their objectives.

3   Similar benefits and barriers exist for the adoption of sell-side e-commerce for both B2B and B2C organizations. Discuss.

4   Evaluate how social media marketing techniques can be applied within an organization and with its stakeholders.

5   The web presence of a company has similar aims regardless of the sector in which the company operates.

Examination questions

1 Explain the relationship between the concepts of e-commerce and e-business.

2 Distinguish between buy-side and sell-side e-commerce and give an example of the application of each.

3 Summarize three reasons why a company may wish to introduce e-commerce.

4 Describe three of the main barriers to adoption of e-commerce by consumers and suggest how a company could counter these.

5 Outline the internal changes a company may need to make when introducing e-business.

6 Summarize the benefits of applying social media marketing approaches to an organization.

7 Name three risks to a company that introduces buy-side e-commerce.

8 Name three risks to a company that introduces sell-side e-commerce.

References

BBC (2005) eBay's 10-year rise to world fame. By Robert Plummer. Story from BBC News, 2 September **http://news.bbc.co.uk/go/pr/fr/-/l/hi/business/42075/10.stm**.

Booz Allen Hamilton (2002) International E-Economy: Benchmarking the World's Most Effective Policies for the E-Economy. Report published 19 November 2002, London.

Boyd, D. and Ellison, N. (2007) Social network sites: definition, history, and scholarship, *Journal of Computer-Mediated Communication*, 13 (1), 210–30.

Cabinet Office (1999) E-commerce@its.best.uk. A Performance and Innovation Unit report – September. UK Cabinet Office. Available online at: **www.cabinet-office.gov.uk/innovation/1999/ecommerce/ec.body.pdf**.

CIO (2002) Measuring the ROIs of Intranets – Mission Possible? By Toby Ward. *CIO Magazine*, October. Available online at: **www.cio.com/research/intranet/study_2002.html**.

comScore (2010) comScore Media Metrix Ranks Top-Growing Properties and Site Categories for April 2010. Press release, 10 May: **http://www.comscore.com/Press_Events/Press_Releases/2010/5/comScore_Media_Metrix_Ranks_Top-Growing_Properties_and_Site_Categories_for_April_2010**.

Doherty, N., Ellis-Chadwick, F. and Hart, C. (2003) An analysis of the factors affecting the adoption of the Internet in the UK retail sectors. *Journal of Business Research*, 56, 887–97.

DTI (2000) *Business in the Information Age – International Benchmarking Study 2000*. UK Department of Trade and Industry.

DTI (2002) *Business in the Information Age – International Benchmarking Study 2002*. UK Department of Trade and Industry.

Economist (2000) E-commerce survey. Define and sell. *Supplement*, 26 February, 6–12.

eEurope (2005) Information Society Benchmarking Report. From eEurope (2005) initiative. Published at: **http://europa.eu.int/information_society/eeurope/i2010/docs/benchmarking/ 051222%20Final%20Benchmarking%20Report.pdf**.

eSuperbrands (2005) *eSuperbrands 2006: Your Guide to Some of the Best Brands on the Web*. Superbrands Ltd, London.

European Commission (2010) i2010 Annual Information Society Report ICT usage in enterprises, 2009. Issue number 1/2010. Published at: **http://epp.eurostat.ec.europa.eu/portal/page/portal/product_details/publication?p_product_code=KS-QA-10-001**.

Evans, P. and Wurster, T.S. (1997) Strategy and the new economics of information. *Harvard Business Review*, September–October, 70–82.

Grove, A. (1996) *Only the Paranoid Survive*. Doubleday, New York.

Hoffman, D.L. and Novak, T.P. (1996) Marketing in hypermedia computer-mediated environments: conceptual foundations, *Journal of Marketing*, 60 (July), 50–68.

ITU (2010) ITU sees 5 billion mobile subscriptions globally in 2010. News release, 15 February 2010: **http://www.itu.int/net/pressoffice/press_releases/2010/06.aspx**.

Kalakota, R. and Whinston, A. (1997) *Electronic Commerce: A Manager's Guide*. Addison-Wesley, Reading, MA.

Mougayer, M. (1998) E-commerce? E-business? Who e-cares? *Computer World* website (**www.computerworld.com**), 2 November.

Nielsen (2010) The State of Mobile Apps, June 2010: **http://blog.nielsen.com/nielsenwire/online_mobile/the-state-of-mobile-apps/**.

ONS (2005) *Social Trends* 35, 2005 edition: **www.statistics.gov.uk/pdfdir/inta0807.pdf**.

O'Reilly, T. (2005) What Is Web 2? Design Patterns and Business Models for the Next Generation of Software. Web article, 30 September. O'Reilly Publishing, Sebastopol, CA.

Perrott, B. (2005) Towards a manager's model of e-business strategy decisions. *Journal of General Management*, 30 (4), Summer.

Rayport, J. and Jaworski, B. (2003) *Introduction to E-Commerce*, 2nd edn. McGraw-Hill, New York.

SEC (2010) United States Securities and Exchange Commission submission Form 10-K. eBay submission for the fiscal year ended 31 December 2009: **http://yahoo.brand.edgar-online.com/displayfilinginfo.aspx?FilingID=7062869-11669-66791&type=sect&dcn=0001193125-10-033324**.

Spivack (2009) Nova Spivack blog posting. How the WebOS Evolves? 9 February: **http://novaspivack.typepad.com/nova_spivacks_weblog/2007/02/steps_towards_a.html**.

Viney, D. (2003) Intranet portal guide (online article: **www.viney.com/DFV**).

Waterman, R.H., Peters, T.J. and Phillips, J.R. (1980) Structure is not organization. *McKinsey Quarterly* in-house journal. McKinsey & Co., New York.

Welch, J. (2001) CEO of GE speech to Annual Shareowners Meeting, Atlanta, GA, 25 April.

Yammer (2010) Suncorp case study accessed May 2010, Yammer website: **https://www.yammer.com/about/case_studies**.

Further reading

Chaffey, D., Ellis-Chadwick, F., Mayer, R. and Johnston, K. (2009) *Internet Marketing: Strategy, Implementation and Practice*, 4th edn. Financial Times Prentice Hall, Harlow. Chapters 10 and 11 highlight the differences between B2C and B2B e-commerce.

Web links

Sites giving general information on market characteristics of e-business:

ClickZ Experts (**www.clickz.com/experts/**) An excellent collection of articles on online marketing communications. US-focused.

ClickZ Stats (**www.clickz.com/stats/**) The definitive source of news on Internet developments, and reports on company and consumer adoption of the Internet and characteristics in Europe and worldwide. A searchable digest of most analyst reports.

European Commission Information Society Statistics (http://ec.europa.eu/information_society/digital-agenda/index_en.htm) Reports evaluating e-business activity and consumer adoption across the European Union.

Econsultancy.com (www.econsultancy.com) Research, best practice reports and supplier directory for online marketing.

Ofcom (http://stakeholders.ofcom.org.uk/) The Office of Communication has an annual Communications Market report on the adoption of digital media including telecommunications and the Internet (including broadband adoption), digital television and wireless services.

University-sponsored research projects on e-business and e-commerce:

Centre for Digital Business @ MIT (http://ebusiness.mit.edu) Created by MIT Sloan School of Management, contains summaries of over 50 research projects.

Intranet Life (http://www.intranetlife.com) A blog summarizing the work of the intranet benchmarking forum.

NetAcademy on Electronic Markets (www.electronicmarkets.org) Research compiled in *Electronic Markets – The International Journal of Electronic Commerce and Business Media.*

Sloan Center for Internet Retailing (http://ecommerce.vanderbilt.edu) Originally founded in 1994 as Project 2000 by Tom Novak and Donna Hoffman at School of Management, Vanderbilt University, to study marketing implications of the Internet. Useful links/papers.

Smart Insights (www.smartinsights.com) Guidance on digital marketing best practice from Dave Chaffey to help businesses succeed online. It includes alerts on the latest developments in applying digital technology and templates to create marketing plans and budgets.

Trade magazines

E-commerce Times (www.ecommercetimes.com) Has 'daily news e-business news and analysis'.

New Media Age (www.newmediazero.com) A weekly New Media magazine, with partial content online.

International country government sites encouraging e-business adoption

Australian Government Information Management Office (www.agimo.gov.au) Formerly the Australian National Office for the Information Economy.

Business.gov.sg (www.business.gov.sg) Singapore government portal for encouragement of e-business.

New Zealand Government E-Commerce (www.ecommerce.govt.nz) Information on e-commerce policy and initiatives.

UK CIO Council (www.cio.gov.uk) The UK government now has a Chief Information Office tasked with managing e-government for 'ensuring that IT supports the business transformation of government itself so that we can provide better, more efficient, public services'.

US Office of Electronic Government and Technology (www.estrategy.gov) US agency facilitating e-government in the USA.

UK Office of Government Commerce (www.ogc.gov.uk) Information on e-government and e-procurement.